TO THE STUDENT: A Study Guide for this textbook is available throu college bookstore under the title *Study Guide: Computers and Infor Processing* by Sarah Evans. The Study Guide can help you with cours by acting as a tutorial, review, and study aid. If the Study Guide is no ask the bookstore manager to order a copy for you.

KAREN CATTIGAN
23 Clyst Road
CLYST ST GEORGE
EXETER
01392 877574

THIS BOOK IS USER FRIENDLY

The Cairn Terrier puppy on the cover symbolizes our goal of providing students and instructors with a text that is dependable, non-threatening, and user friendly.

Many of the characteristics embodied by the Cairn Terrier in the box on page 298 are found in this book. The author and publisher sincerely hope that after reading this book you will feel comfortable and enthusiastic about the increasingly significant world of computers and information processing.

COMPUTERS AND INFORMATION PROCESSING

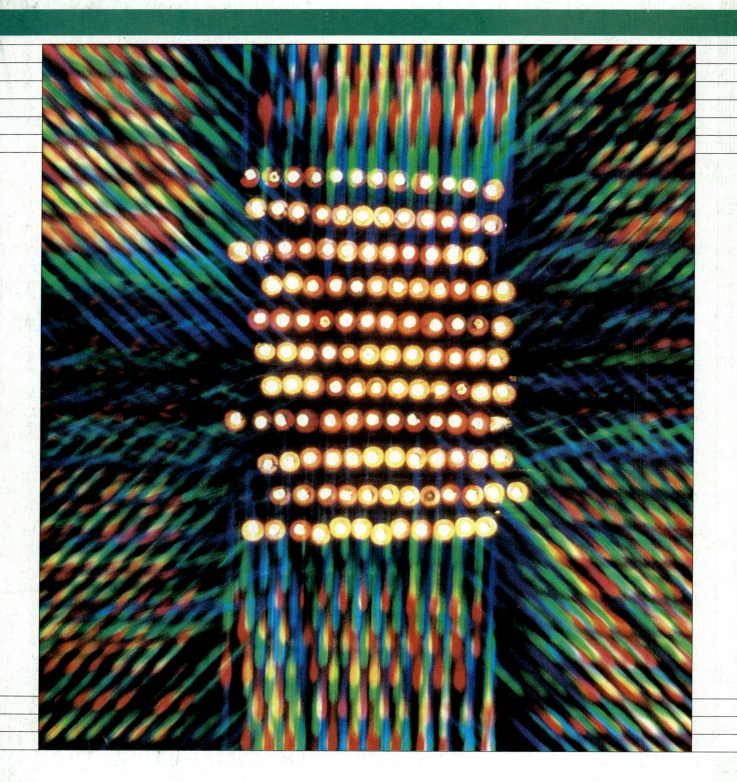

COMPUTERS AND INFORMATION PROCESSING:
AN INTRODUCTION

Robert Behling

BRYANT COLLEGE

KENT PUBLISHING COMPANY
A Division of Wadsworth, Inc.
Boston, Massachusetts

Executive Editor: Richard C. Crews
Production Manager: Tina Samaha
Manufacturing Manager: Linda Siegrist
Art Editing and Interior Design: Carol H. Rose
Cover Design: Nancy Lindgren
Line Art: Boston Graphics, Inc.
Production Editing: Sarah Evans and Margaret Kearney
Developmental Editing and Photo Research: Sarah Evans

Photograph on page ii courtesy of AT&T Bell Laboratories

Part opening photographs courtesy of Computer Sciences Corporation (**Part I**); IBM Corporation (**Part II**); Digital Equipment Corporation (**Part III**); Aetna Life & Casualty (**Part IV**); and Apple Computer, Inc. (**Part V**).

Chapter opening photographs courtesy of Ellis Herwig/Stock, Boston (**Chapter 1**); Cruft Photo Lab, Harvard University, photographed by Paul Donaldson (**Chapter 2**); IBM Corporation (**Chapter 3**); Apple Computer, Inc. (**Chapter 4**); Sperry Corporation (**Chapter 5**); NCR Corporation (**Chapter 6**); Aetna Life & Casualty (**Chapter 7**); Cray Research, Inc. (**Chapter 8**); Aetna Life & Casualty (**Chapter 9**); Commodore Electronics Ltd (**Chapter 10**); Control Data (**Chapter 11**); Hewlitt-Packard (**Chapter 13**); Hewlitt-Packard (**Chapter 14**); Perkin-Elmer Corporation (**Chapter 15**); © John Coletti/Stock, Boston (**Chapter 16**); © Charles Gupton/Stock, Boston (**Chapter 17**); Computer Sciences Corporation (**Chapter 18**); (*clockwise from top left*) Apple Computer, Inc., Sperry Corporation, IBM Corporation, Sperry Corporation (**Chapter 19**); © Bill Gallery/Stock, Boston (**Chapter 20**); AT&T (**Appendix**).

© 1986 by Wadsworth, Inc., 10 Davis Drive, Belmont, California 94002. All rights reserved. No part of this book may be reproduced, stored in a retrieval system, or transcribed, in any form or by any means, electronic, mechanical, photocopying, recording, or otherwise, without the prior written permission of the publisher, Kent Publishing Company, 20 Park Plaza, Boston, Massachusetts 02116.

Printed in the United States of America

1 2 3 4 5 6 7 8 9 — 90 89 87 86

Library of Congress Cataloging in Publication Data

Behling, Robert, 1938–
   Computers and information processing.

   Includes index.
   1. Computers. 2. Electronic data processing.
I. Title.
QA76.B345   1986   004   85-23137

ISBN 0-534-03999-5

PREFACE

STATEMENT OF PURPOSE

This book is designed for beginning students who may have varied academic interests and diverse career goals. While the book draws heavily on examples from the business world, its basic premise is that all students today, regardless of their field of concentration, must become knowledgeable in the use of computers and the handling of information if they are to be successful in their future careers. It is written at a level that requires no previous knowledge of computers and information processing but that will not insult or bore the student who may already be somewhat familiar with these topics. Its purpose is twofold: to give students an understanding of the computer as a tool for processing information, and, by revealing the inherent interest of the subject, to spark the student's curiosity and desire to learn more. Computer jargon and technical detail are kept at a minimum, relevant and realistic examples are at a maximum, and the perspective throughout the book is that of a nontechnical user of information systems.

The book can be used as a core text for introductory computer and data processing courses and is consistent with the course objectives and content of CIS-1 of the DPMA Model Curriculum. It is also suitable for a computer literacy course, as it stresses the ways that organizations use computers to perform business functions.

ORGANIZATION AND CONTENT

The book is organized in a modular fashion, with Part I serving as the basic building block that allows the other four parts of the book to be taught in whatever sequence the instructor chooses. The four chapters in Part I introduce the key concepts related to the areas covered in the rest of the text: hardware, software, systems development and use, and the social issues associated with computer applications. These concepts are covered in sufficient detail that once students have completed Part I, the instructor can move on to any other part or chapter of the book with assurance that the students will be able to handle the material. Chapter 1 introduces the basic concepts of computers and data processing, focusing on the roles of data, hardware, software, and people in a computer system. Chapter 2 reinforces these concepts by chronicling how the computer evolved into today's complex types of computer systems. Chapter 3 introduces the development and use of computer systems from a business perspective. Finally, Chapter 4 gives the student an awareness of today's uses of computers and their social implications.

The chief focus of Part II, "Technology Today," is on the hardware of the computer system. Chapter 5 explores the central processing unit and the data processing concepts associated with it. The perspective of a nontechnical user of a computer system is particularly evident in the treatment of input and output in Chapters 6 and 7. Chapter 8 covers the variety of auxiliary storage devices and techniques used to expand the memory capabilities of the computer system. Chapter 9 presents the concepts of data communications systems and distributed data processing networks in such a way that even the nontechnical, beginning student can easily understand them. The final chapter in Part II is devoted to a discussion of the microcomputer and makes clear the reasons for the meteoric rise in the popularity of these machines. Each chapter in this part of the book ends with a section on selection criteria for the hardware discussed within the chapter.

The first two chapters in Part III, "Software," cover the steps of program development in detail and include discussions of structured programming and design and programming languages. The topic of programming is comprehensively supplemented by the appendix to the text, "Programming in BASIC." Because Chapter 13 views systems software from a functional perspective and concentrates on the role it plays in the computer system, this subject, which can be a difficult one, is easily comprehended. Chapter 14 discusses the state of software today, focusing on two important and timely issues: the problems of and alternatives to in-house software development, and the techniques and applications of artificial intelligence.

Part IV takes an unusual approach to the topic of information systems. Rather than presenting a theoretical, step-by-step approach to systems development, it focuses on the actual issues and problems that students are likely to encounter in their future careers, and it goes beyond systems development to discuss systems use and management. The rationale here is that familiarity with the organizational issues involved in information systems can only make for more effective systems users. Chapter 15 highlights the reasons for introducing systems change and the factors involved in evaluating systems proposals, in planning for systems development, and in managing systems development projects. Chapter 16 examines some design considerations related to output, input, and processing, including output formats, schedules, distribution lists, and file organization. Chapter 17 focuses on the use of computer information systems in business; topics include management information systems, data base management systems, decision support systems, and office automation. Chapter 18, which profiles the information systems manager, delves into the problems of managing hardware, software, organizational change, and technical personnel.

Part V takes a balanced look at the ways that computers affect our lives. Chapter 19 summarizes the positive social effects and the negative social costs of computerization. Chapter 20 ends the text with a discussion of how the social costs of computers can be controlled; it focuses on the topics of personal ethics, computer law, and computer security and control.

PEDAGOGICAL DEVICES

The book contains a number of learning aids that make the material more meaningful and more readily comprehensible. Each chapter begins with a **topical outline,** which gives the student a preview of the material to be covered; an **overview,** which is designed to spark the student's interest and curiosity to proceed; and a list of **learning objectives,** which highlight the most important points covered within the chapter.

All **key terms** are boldfaced and defined at their first mention; additional definitions appear in the **glossary** at the end of the book. Also appearing within the text of each chapter are **boxed inserts,** which are intended to stimulate the student's interest and to provide a focus for class discussion.

Numerous four-color **photographs** and pieces of **line art** accompany the text and graphically depict the concepts under discussion. In addition, a number of concise **tables** enable the student to readily grasp the relationships among complex data.

Each chapter ends with a narrative **summary;** an alphabetical **list of the key terms** that were boldfaced within the chapter, together with the page numbers on which the terms were introduced; and ten **discussion questions,** which not only cause students to think about the material in the chapter but also test their comprehension of what they have just read. The discussion questions can serve as class-discussion starters, quiz questions, or homework assignments.

The **appendix,** "Programming in BASIC," is an easy-to-read tutorial that builds programming skills and understanding while comprehensively covering the syntax of the BASIC language. Review questions at the ends of appendix sections reinforce key points; more detailed questions appear in the "Problems" section at the end of the appendix. The appendix also has its own glossary, which defines key terms that are boldfaced within the appendix text.

SUPPLEMENTAL ITEMS

Study Guide

Sarah Evans, a professional writer and the developmental editor for the book, has produced a comprehensive study guide to supplement the text. The study guide contains material designed to help the student master the subject matter and the vocabulary through self-testing questions and a review of pertinent concepts and terms.

Instructor's Guide

The instructor's guide offers a number of suggestions for preparing classroom presentations. Each chapter begins with chapter objectives, followed by a chapter summary and a feature called "Chapter Blackboards." The blackboards contain key ideas, terms, or points that the instructor can write on a blackboard to focus the attention of the student. The blackboards are boldfaced and isolated to make it easier for the instructor to use them while conducting class, and they provide a comprehensive outline of the material covered in each chapter.

The instructor's guide provides concise answers to each discussion question in the text, as well as a section on teaching tips. It also features two essays for each chapter, which instructors may find useful in enhancing their lectures. One essay presents information about an individual who has been important in the development of computers and information processing; the other focuses on a technological development.

A complete set of transparency masters is available to help instructors graphically present some of the more difficult concepts discussed in the text. While many of the figures are derived from the text diagrams and tables, a number of new graphics are included.

Test Bank

For each chapter of the text, the test bank provides fifty true/false questions, twenty multiple choice questions, ten matching questions, and twenty fill-in questions aimed at testing both concepts and vocabulary. A computerized test bank is also available for the IBM-PC and Apple II families.

Software

A microcomputer-driven tutorial covering the basic concepts of word processing, electronic spreadsheets, and data bases, with practice problems for each, is available to instructors.

A STATEMENT OF GRATITUDE

Before any book is published, many people assist in the design, reviewing, editing, graphics, and production activities. There are several people who deserve special mention because of their dedicated efforts and commitment to the entire project. Key to the success of this book is Sarah Evans, a developmental editor and a tireless worker, who gave much of herself to make sure that the words were put together in a way that made them meaningful and lively. Sarah assisted in numerous revisions of the manuscript, both in organization and content, and made sure that the final product was truly modular. Her creative talents are evident in the layout of the book, the high quality of the artwork and the photographs, and the "user-friendliness" of the final product. Once the manuscript was completed, Sarah focused her talents on preparing a study guide that is meaningful yet easy to read and use, which is no easy task.

Bill O'Hare, Prince George's Community College, wrote the principal manuscript for the BASIC appendix and acted as a valuable resource during the development of the manuscript.

Dick Crews, Executive Editor and project leader, contributed his knowledge of the textbook industry, the market, and encouragement when the going got tough. His foresight and enthusiasm have been greatly appreciated.

I also wish to acknowledge the cooperative spirit of all the education-oriented companies that gave permission to include the many graphics and excerpts that appear in this book.

A FINAL NOTE

It is my sincere hope that we have put together a text that is not only a valid educational tool but also a book that is enjoyable to read. Using computers is a serious and important topic, but it is also a potentially entertaining and interesting one. This book is designed to emphasize the importance and seriousness of the topic while underscoring the interest it contains. I feel we have been successful in our efforts and hope that you agree.

ROBERT BEHLING
Bryant College

A SALUTE TO OUR ADVISERS

This work was reviewed extensively in various stages of manuscript development by a number of highly qualified educators who teach introduction to computers and data processing courses. The suggestions that were made by members of our Review Board greatly aided us in putting together the most effective teaching and learning package possible. In addition, our Focus Group participants and questionnaire respondents provided valuable guidance. We have gained immeasurably through their perceptive insights and helpful comments about how this book could best fill the needs of both students and teachers.

I acknowledge with gratitude the help, advice, and support of the following professionals whose involvement with the project has greatly enhanced the final product.

RICHARD C. CREWS
Executive Editor
Kent Publishing Company

x PREFACE

Editorial Review Board

Randy Albert
Oregon Institute of Technology

Richard Aukerman
Oklahoma State University

Bryan Carney
University of Wisconsin-Eau Claire

Roger Cook
Southern Illinois University

Jane Covillion
Onondaga Community College

James Cox
Lane Community College

Arthur Geis
College of DuPage

Susan Haugen
Drake University

Robin Hill
Metropolitan State College

Joe Kinzer
Central State University

William O'Hare
Prince George's Community College

Robert Pew
Valencia Community College

Larry Seiford
University of Texas

Peter Simis
California State University-Fresno

Focus Group Participants

Roy Kerby
Arizona Western College

Philip Mackey
Delaware Technical and Community College

William O'Hare
Prince George's Community College

Robert Pew
Valencia Community College

Melanie Stopfer
Dakota State College

Questionnaire Respondents

W. James Abbott, Jr.
Broome Community College

James H. D. Allen
Jacksonville State University

Richard Bambery
Brevard Community College

Roger Bickel
St. Louis Community College

Harvey Blessing
Essex Community College

Keith Borders
Whatcom Community College

Thomas Boyer
Lincoln University

John Breshears
Southeastern Community College

Evan Brown
Pasadena City College

J. Brunner
College of the Mainland

Leonard Bunker
Palm Beach Atlantic College

Warren Buxton
Maricopa Technical College

Miroslava Carlson
Northeastern Illinois University

Eric Curtis
Lansing Community College

Kerry Darling
Lansing Community College

Robert Decker
Jefferson Technical College

Raymond Fanselau
American River College

George Fitsos
Truckee Meadows Community College

Kathleen Galway
Wright College

Luther Graves
Tri State University

Douglas Hamilton
Marian College

Carol Jones
Isothermal Community College

Reuven Karni
University of Michigan

Roy Kerby
Arizona Western College

Robert Landrum
Jones County Junior College

Philip Mackey
Delaware Technical and Community College

K. J. Massengill
Piedmont Technical College

Mel McElroy
Bellevue Community College

Priscilla McGill
Dickinson State College

Ruth McQueen
Amarillo College

James Meeks
San Jacinto College

Robert Nash
Central Wesleyan College

Don Nielsen
Golden West College

William Parks
Maricopa Technical College

Jim Phillips
Lexington Community College

Ernst Rilki
Harper College

Jim Schroeder
Dodge City Community College

Linda Shank
Gila Pueblo College

Kenneth Smith
Southwest Missouri State University

Ebrahim Soltani
Donnelly College

Melanie Stopfer
Dakota State College

Frank Thacker
Davidson County Community College

David Thiessen
Lewis Clark State College

William West
Coahoma Junior College

Don Williams
Rockingham Community College

Eileen Wrigley
Community College of Allegheny County

ABOUT THE AUTHOR

Robert Behling is professor and chairman of the Computer Information Systems Department at Bryant College in Smithfield, Rhode Island. A graduate of Colgate University, where he majored in geology, Bob also holds an M.Ed. in psychology from the University of Portland, an M.B.A. from Boise State University, and a Ph.D. from the University of Northern Colorado. He joined the Bryant faculty in 1980 after seven years of teaching at Boise State University and eight years in commercial banking. During his years in the banking industry, Bob participated in several conversions from manual to automated banking systems, conducted an extensive research study to assess and develop automation for law enforcement agencies throughout the state of Idaho, and was an active member of the American Institute of Banking.

The diversity of Bob's own academic background and his experiences in the business community led to his conviction that business education must have a strong practical component that will enable students to solve problems in the real business world. This conviction is a repeated theme in all the classes he teaches and is echoed throughout this text. It is also responsible for Bob's commitment to the Data Processing Management Association, where he was instrumental in developing the DPMA Model Curriculum, serving as the chairperson of the committee that developed the learning objectives and content for the first model course, known as CIS-1.

Bob is also an active member of the Society of Data Educators, where he has served as president and executive director, as well as chairperson of the Certification Council. In recognition of his work on both curriculum and certification, the Society of Data Educators honored Bob in 1984 with the Data Educator of the Year Award.

If it is to meet the needs of a diverse population, an introductory text on the uses of computers requires a well-rounded author with a broad outlook on the business community, technology, and education. Bob Behling's diverse background brings to this book a sense of realism that can have come only from actual experience.

BRIEF TABLE OF CONTENTS

PART I • INTRODUCTION — 1
1. Computers and Data Processing: Some Basic Concepts — 3
2. Computers Past and Present — 33
3. Developing and Using Computer Systems in Business — 65
4. The Social Implications of Using Computers — 95

PART II • TECHNOLOGY TODAY — 121
5. The Central Processing Unit — 123
6. Input — 153
7. Output — 187
8. Auxiliary Storage — 219
9. Data Communications and Distributed Data Processing — 243
10. The Microcomputer Phenomenon — 275

PART III • SOFTWARE — 303
11. Program Development: First Steps — 305
12. Program Development: The Language Connection — 333
13. Systems Software — 367
14. The State of Software Today — 391

PART IV • SYSTEMS DEVELOPMENT, USE, AND MANAGEMENT — 417
15. Systems Development: An Overview — 419
16. Output, Input, and Processing: Some Design Considerations — 447
17. Using Computer Information Systems in Business — 473
18. Managing a Computer Information System — 499

PART V • COMPUTERS AND SOCIETY — 525
19. Computers and Social Issues — 527
20. Controlling the Social Costs of Computers: Solving the Ethical Dilemma — 553

APPENDIX • Programming in BASIC — 577
GLOSSARY — 661
INDEX — 673

CONTENTS

PART I ◆ INTRODUCTION — 1

Chapter 1 — 3
COMPUTERS AND DATA PROCESSING: SOME BASIC CONCEPTS

WHAT IS A COMPUTER?	4
CLASSIFICATIONS OF COMPUTERS	7
DATA AND DATA PROCESSING	10
The Data Cycle	10
Considerations in Computerized Data Processing	13
HARDWARE: TECHNOLOGY AT WORK	15
Input Devices	16
The Central Processing Unit	20
Output Devices	22
Auxiliary Storage Devices	22
SOFTWARE: THE ROAD MAP FOR PROBLEM SOLVING	26
PEOPLE: THE LIFEBLOOD OF COMPUTER SYSTEMS	28
SUMMARY	28
KEY TERMS	30
DISCUSSION QUESTIONS	31
BOXES: The World Goes Digital: Ones and Zeros Are Changing Our Lives	9
On Computer Literacy	27

Chapter 2 — 33
COMPUTERS PAST AND PRESENT

THE EVOLUTION OF THE COMPUTER	34
Ancient Ancestry	34
Contributions of the Scientific Revolution	35
The Nineteenth Century	35
The Great Depression	40
The War Years	42
First-Generation Computers: 1951–1958	46
Second-Generation Computers: 1959–1964	48
Third-Generation Computers: 1965–1970	50
Fourth-Generation Computers: 1971–?	52
TODAY'S COMPUTERS AND HOW WE USE THEM	55
Supercomputers	56
Mainframes	59
Minicomputers	59
Microcomputers	60
SUMMARY	62

KEY TERMS	63
DISCUSSION QUESTIONS	63
BOXES: Human Reactions to Human Inventions	41
From Hobby Kits to Apples: The Impact of the Microprocessor Chip	54

Chapter 3 — 65
DEVELOPING AND USING COMPUTER SYSTEMS IN BUSINESS

THE IMPACT OF THE INFORMATION REVOLUTION	66
COMPUTERIZED INFORMATION: USES AND SOURCES	68
THE SYSTEMS DEVELOPMENT CYCLE	71
Identifying the Need	72
Analyzing the System	74
Developing Design Alternatives	79
Developing the System	80
Implementing and Maintaining the System	80
USING COMPUTER INFORMATION SYSTEMS IN BUSINESS	82
Office Automation	84
The Computer System as a Managerial Tool	89
SUMMARY	92
KEY TERMS	92
DISCUSSION QUESTIONS	93
BOXES: Systems Development in Action: Prototyping	79
Hollywood's 2010: An On-Line Odyssey	88

Chapter 4 — 95
THE SOCIAL IMPLICATIONS OF USING COMPUTERS

PRODUCTIVITY AND THE PROBLEMS OF OFFICE AUTOMATION	96
COMPUTERS IN THE FACTORY: COMPUTER-AIDED DESIGN AND MANUFACTURING OR COMPUTER-AIDED UNEMPLOYMENT?	102
COMPUTERS IN GOVERNMENT: THE POTENTIAL HUMAN COSTS	106
Social Services	107
Elections	107
Local Tax Districts	109
Federal Tax Authority	110
Law Enforcement	110
Military Applications	112
EDUCATIONAL USES AND ABUSES OF COMPUTERS	113
COMPUTERS IN MEDICINE: PROS AND CONS	115
SUMMARY	117

KEY TERMS	119
DISCUSSION QUESTIONS	119
BOXES: The Side Effects of Electronic Mail	99
Adobe-School Computers	114

PART II ♦ TECHNOLOGY TODAY 121

Chapter 5   123
THE CENTRAL PROCESSING UNIT

THE STORED-PROGRAM CONCEPT AND THE CPU: A BRIEF REVIEW	124
PROGRAM INSTRUCTIONS AND STORAGE AREAS	125
Addresses	126
Registers	128
HOW THE CPU EXECUTES PROGRAM INSTRUCTIONS	130
STORAGE CAPACITY AND TERMINOLOGY	132
THE CODING OF DATA	136
The Binary Numbering System	137
Coding Schemes	138
The Parity Bit	140
PRIMARY STORAGE COMPONENTS	141
RAM, ROM, PROM, AND EPROM	146
SELECTION CRITERIA	147
SUMMARY	149
KEY TERMS	150
DISCUSSION QUESTIONS	151
BOXES: Parallel Processing, or Will Microcomputers Develop Split Personalities?	133
The Making of a Chip	144

Chapter 6   153
INPUT

SOURCES OF BUSINESS DATA	154
THE CONVERSION STEP: PROBLEMS AND SOLUTIONS	154
Data Collection Procedures	155
Other Controls on Data	157

METHODS OF DATA COLLECTION AND ENTRY	159
OFFLINE DATA COLLECTION	163
Punched Cards	163
Magnetic Media	166
SOURCE-DATA AUTOMATION	170
Magnetic-Ink Character Recognition	170
Optical Recognition	172
Remote Terminals	176
SELECTION CRITERIA	182
SUMMARY	183
KEY TERMS	184
DISCUSSION QUESTIONS	185
BOXES: Input Methods for the Handicapped	161
Talking to Typewriters	180

Chapter 7   187
OUTPUT

WHY BUSINESSES NEED COMPUTER OUTPUT	188
HOW BUSINESSES USE COMPUTER OUTPUT	189
Traditional Output	190
Output for Management Science	192
Output as Input	193
GENERATING COMPUTER OUTPUT	194
HARD-COPY OUTPUT	196
Printed Output	196
Computer Output Microform	202
Output from Graphic Plotters	205
SOFT-COPY OUTPUT	207
Display Output	207
Audio Output	209
OUTPUT BY ROBOTS	210
SELECTION CRITERIA	213
SUMMARY	215
KEY TERMS	216
DISCUSSION QUESTIONS	217
BOXES: Paper, Paper Everywhere — or Why COM	204
Robots — The Next Generation	212

Chapter 8 — 219
AUXILIARY STORAGE

TYPES OF COMPUTER STORAGE	220
SEQUENTIAL ACCESS AUXILIARY STORAGE	223
Punched Cards and Paper Tape	224
Magnetic Tape	225
DIRECT ACCESS AUXILIARY STORAGE	228
Magnetic Disks	228
Optical Disks	234
Mass Storage	236
Bubble Memory	237
SELECTION CRITERIA	238
SUMMARY	239
KEY TERMS	240
DISCUSSION QUESTIONS	240
BOXES: It All Comes Down to Magnetism	233
Gigabytes and Terabytes: The Quest for the "Ultimate" Storage System	235

Chapter 9 — 243
DATA COMMUNICATIONS AND DISTRIBUTED DATA PROCESSING

COMPUTERS AND COMMUNICATIONS: SOME BACKGROUND	244
DATA TRANSMISSION	246
Transmission Channels	246
Signal Transmission	253
DATA COMMUNICATIONS HARDWARE	255
Modems	256
Multiplexors and Concentrators	257
Front-End Processors	260
DATA COMMUNICATIONS SOFTWARE	261
Transmission Management	262
Function Management	262
Access Management	262
Error Management	263
DISTRIBUTED DATA PROCESSING NETWORKS	263
Star Network	265
Ring Network	266
Complex, or Distributed, Network	266
Local Area Network	267
SELECTION CRITERIA	269

SUMMARY	271
KEY TERMS	272
DISCUSSION QUESTIONS	273
BOXES: Computer Commuting	258
The University of the Future	268

Chapter 10 — 275
THE MICROCOMPUTER PHENOMENON

PERSONAL COMPUTERS: THE NEW WAVE	276
MICROCOMPUTER HARDWARE	278
The Microprocessor and Other Chips	278
Auxiliary Storage Equipment	282
Input and Output Equipment	282
MICROCOMPUTER SOFTWARE	286
Systems Software	286
Applications Software	288
MERGING MICROS AND MAINFRAMES: BRIDGING THE GAP	294
SELECTION CRITERIA	296
SUMMARY	300
KEY TERMS	301
DISCUSSION QUESTIONS	301
BOXES: The Man Who Keeps the Bloom on Lotus	293
Man, Bytes, Dog	298

PART III ♦ SOFTWARE — 303

Chapter 11 — 305
PROGRAM DEVELOPMENT: FIRST STEPS

PROGRAM DEVELOPMENT IN PERSPECTIVE	306
ANALYZING THE PROBLEM	308
DESIGNING A SOLUTION	310
BASIC LOGIC PATTERNS AND THE CONCEPT OF STRUCTURED PROGRAMMING AND DESIGN	312

PROGRAM FLOWCHARTS AND DECISION TABLES AS DESIGN TOOLS	314
Program Flowcharts	314
Decision Tables	319
STRUCTURED DESIGN TOOLS AND PROGRAMMING METHODS	322
Pseudocode	322
Top-Down Design	323
HIPO Charts	325
Modular Programming	326
SUMMARY	328
KEY TERMS	330
DISCUSSION QUESTIONS	330
BOXES: Computer Programming and the Fortunes of Doug Flutie	320
Sage of Software	324

Chapter 12 — 333
PROGRAM DEVELOPMENT: THE LANGUAGE CONNECTION

CODING: COMMUNICATING WITH THE COMPUTER	334
Machine Language	336
Assembly Language	337
High-Level Languages	338
The Translation Process	339
THE CHOICE OF A LANGUAGE	341
BASIC	342
COBOL	345
FORTRAN	348
RPG	350
Pascal	350
Ada	353
C Language	355
APL	356
PL/1	357
DEBUGGING AND TESTING THE PROGRAM	357
DOCUMENTING THE PROGRAM	362
SUMMARY	363
KEY TERMS	364
DISCUSSION QUESTIONS	365
BOXES: Program Development and End-User Programming Aids: Fourth-Generation Languages	354
The Grand Old Lady of Software	360

Chapter 13 — 367
SYSTEMS SOFTWARE

THE DEVELOPMENT OF SYSTEMS SOFTWARE	368
RESOURCE MANAGEMENT	369
CONTROL FUNCTIONS	372
Scheduling and Job Management	372
Input/Output Control and Data Management	374
Systems Monitoring	376
SERVICE FUNCTIONS	377
Language Translators	377
Utility Programs	378
Library Programs	379
SHARED RESOURCES	380
Multiprogramming	381
Timesharing	382
Multiprocessing	383
VIRTUAL STORAGE	385
SUMMARY	387
KEY TERMS	388
DISCUSSION QUESTIONS	389
BOXES: Human Interfaces and the Operating System Approach	373
A Short History of Unix	384

Chapter 14 — 391
THE STATE OF SOFTWARE TODAY

IN-HOUSE SOFTWARE DEVELOPMENT: COSTS, CONSTRAINTS, AND THE NEED FOR PRODUCTIVITY	392
The Economic Issues	392
Constraints on In-House Software Development	393
Techniques for Improving Programming Productivity	396
ALTERNATIVES TO IN-HOUSE SOFTWARE DEVELOPMENT	400
Purchased or Leased Software	400
Contract Programming	403
User-Group Program Sharing	404
ARTIFICIAL INTELLIGENCE	406
AI Techniques	407
AI Applications	411
SUMMARY	413
KEY TERMS	414
DISCUSSION QUESTIONS	415

| BOXES: | Corsairs of the Twentieth Century | 405 |
| | Making Knowledge Useful | 411 |

PART IV • SYSTEMS DEVELOPMENT, USE, AND MANAGEMENT — 417

Chapter 15 — 419
SYSTEMS DEVELOPMENT: AN OVERVIEW

INTRODUCING SYSTEMS CHANGE	420
Volume of Data	420
Internal and External Information Needs	421
Cost Savings	421
CONSIDERATIONS IN THE SYSTEMS DEVELOPMENT CYCLE	423
Evaluating Systems Proposals	424
Planning for Systems Development	431
PROJECT MANAGEMENT	441
SUMMARY	444
KEY TERMS	445
DISCUSSION QUESTIONS	445
BOXES: The Politics of Systems	426
Case Study: Ritchco Auto Parts, Part I	443

Chapter 16 — 447
OUTPUT, INPUT, AND PROCESSING: SOME DESIGN CONSIDERATIONS

OUTPUT	448
Organizational Factors	448
Output Formats, Schedules, and Distribution Lists	452
INPUT	458
Kinds of Information	458
Data Complexity	460
Information Use	461
PROCESSING	462
Sequential File Organization	464
Direct File Organization	465
Indexed-Sequential File Organization	466
SUMMARY	469
KEY TERMS	470

DISCUSSION QUESTIONS	470
BOXES: Graphically Speaking with Dr. Edward R. Tufte	455
Case Study: Ritchco Auto Parts, Part II	468

Chapter 17 — 473
USING COMPUTER INFORMATION SYSTEMS IN BUSINESS

USING THE COMPUTER AS A MANAGERIAL TOOL	474
Managerial Functions and Information Needs	474
Management Information Systems	478
Data Base Management Systems	483
Decision Support Systems	489
USING THE COMPUTER TO IMPROVE PRODUCTIVITY: OFFICE AUTOMATION	490
Word Processing	491
Electronic Messages	492
Electronic Filing	495
SUMMARY	495
KEY TERMS	497
DISCUSSION QUESTIONS	497
BOXES: Database to the Rock Stars	484
Case Study: Ritchco Auto Parts, Part III	493

Chapter 18 — 499
MANAGING A COMPUTER INFORMATION SYSTEM

THE INFORMATION SYSTEMS MANAGER	500
MANAGING HARDWARE	502
Developing Requests for Hardware Proposals	503
Evaluating Hardware Proposals	506
MANAGING SOFTWARE	510
The "Make or Buy" Decision	510
Evaluating Software	514
MANAGING ORGANIZATIONAL ISSUES	516
Organizational Changes	516
Managing Technical Personnel	518
SUMMARY	521
KEY TERMS	523
DISCUSSION QUESTIONS	523
BOXES: Decision Support Systems: Integration or Chaos?	513
Case Study: Ritchco Auto Parts, Part IV	519

PART V ♦ COMPUTERS AND SOCIETY — 525

Chapter 19 — 527
COMPUTERS AND SOCIAL ISSUES

IMPROVED SERVICES AND PRODUCTS	528
PRIVACY	534
EMPLOYMENT	537
COMPUTER DEPENDENCE	542
COMPUTER CRIME	544
SUMMARY	549
KEY TERMS	550
DISCUSSION QUESTIONS	550
BOXES: Fiscal Awareness for Farm Survival	531
The Revenge of the Hackers	546

Chapter 20 — 553
CONTROLLING THE SOCIAL COSTS OF COMPUTERS: SOLVING THE ETHICAL DILEMMA

COMPUTERS AND THE ETHICAL DILEMMA	554
LEGISLATION	557
COMPUTER SECURITY AND CONTROL	560
Threats to Computer Security	560
Computer Controls	564
Computer Auditing	571
SUMMARY	574
KEY TERMS	575
DISCUSSION QUESTIONS	575
BOXES: Fighting Common Sense	556
Computer Law	558
Computer Security and the Vulnerability of Data	563

Appendix ♦ PROGRAMMING IN BASIC — 577

Glossary — 661

Index — 673

PART · I

Chapter 1   COMPUTERS AND DATA PROCESSING: SOME BASIC CONCEPTS
Chapter 2   COMPUTERS PAST AND PRESENT
Chapter 3   DEVELOPING AND USING COMPUTER SYSTEMS IN BUSINESS
Chapter 4   THE SOCIAL IMPLICATIONS OF USING COMPUTERS

INTRODUCTION

Peter McWilliams, author of *The Personal Computer in Business Book,* has made the point that the business person doesn't need to know any more about the technical ins and outs of computers than is necessary and useful for the business. As he puts it, you don't have to know French to travel to Paris, nor do you need to know where or what the differential is in order to drive a car. We wholeheartedly agree with this logic; but to it we would add that the trip can be more fun if you *do* know the language, and to prevent a breakdown, or if you are faced with a breakdown, it helps to know where and what the differential is. That, in a nutshell, is the philosophy of this book — not to delve into the computing intricacies of Boolean algebra and circuit theory, but to provide you with enough information to make your sojourn into the business world more enjoyable and less liable to breakdown. To accomplish that, you need to be familiar with three broad areas: the basic concepts of computers and data processing; the development, use, and management of computer information systems; and the social and ethical dilemmas that computers can pose for business people — and for the rest of the world. When you finish this book, you won't be a computer expert, but you should have a good grasp of these important topics.

The chapters in Part I set the stage for the rest of the book. After you have finished this part, you will have enough background to be able to use any other parts of the book in whatever sequence you choose. Chapter 1 outlines some of the basic concepts of computers and data processing. Chapter 2 adds to an understanding of those concepts by exploring how the computer evolved into today's complex computer systems. Chapter 3 introduces a few of the fundamentals involved in developing and using a computer information system in business, and Chapter 4 highlights some of the social issues that the uses of computers raise.

OUTLINE

WHAT IS A COMPUTER?

CLASSIFICATIONS OF COMPUTERS

DATA AND DATA PROCESSING
- The Data Cycle
- Considerations in Computerized Data Processing

HARDWARE: TECHNOLOGY AT WORK
- Input Devices
- The Central Processing Unit
  - Primary Storage Unit
  - Arithmetic/Logic Unit
  - Control Unit
- Output Devices
- Auxiliary Storage Devices

SOFTWARE: THE ROAD MAP FOR PROBLEM SOLVING

PEOPLE: THE LIFEBLOOD OF COMPUTER SYSTEMS

SUMMARY

KEY TERMS

DISCUSSION QUESTIONS

OVERVIEW

As recently as 1955, computers were little more than laboratory curiosities. Since then, they have evolved into such an accepted fact of life that we tend to lose sight of the many ways in which we depend on them. But, if you stop to think about it, to avoid contact with computers, you'd have to radically change your way of life — assuming, that is, that you don't already live on a desert island. To get away from the reach of the computer, you'd have to avoid contact with most tax agencies (a promising idea, generally considered illegal), police departments, hospitals, gas stations, department stores, utility companies, supermarkets, book clubs, libraries, banks, newspapers, airlines, city transit systems, and so on — and on.

The computer is definitely here to stay. And whether you react to the thought of a computer with a groan, grimace, yawn, or a gleam in your eye — and whether you ultimately embark on a career in forestry, medicine, or business — a knowledge of how this thing called a computer works is bound to make your lot an easier one. This chapter begins with a basic definition of the computer, and it goes on to introduce each of the components that make up a computer system. Its objectives are to

- ◆ describe what a computer is and explain the ways in which computers are classified.
- ◆ define data and information and outline the stages of the data cycle.
- ◆ briefly describe how data are organized for computerized processing.
- ◆ identify the various pieces of hardware equipment and explain their functions.
- ◆ give a brief overview of computer software.
- ◆ explain the roles that people play in a computer system.

CHAPTER 1

COMPUTERS AND DATA PROCESSING: SOME BASIC CONCEPTS

WHAT IS A COMPUTER?

A modern computer is a bit more than a precocious adding machine and a bit less than a magical, electronic Aladdin's lamp. The most complete and concise definition that we can think of is that a **computer** is a programmable electronic device that can accept input data; process, store, and retrieve those data; and produce output. We will elaborate on this definition in the rest of this chapter and throughout Parts II and III of the book; but, to lay the groundwork, let's try breaking the definition down into its elemental parts:

1. *Programmable* refers to the step-by-step instructions the computer must have in order to perform any task. Such a set of instructions is called a **program.** The various programs available to operate and run the computer, together with instructions and procedures that people might need to get the computer to solve specific data processing problems, make up the computer **software.**

2. *Electronic device* refers to the actual machinery of the computer — the chips, electronic circuitry, and keyboards that we usually associate with the word *computer.* In reality, most computers use separate machines for input, processing, and output, as well as for additional storage of data. Collectively, this machinery is known as the computer **hardware.**

3. *Input* **data** are the unevaluated facts and figures that are fed to the computer. They form the raw materials for the processing activities.

4. *Processing, storage,* and *retrieval* are what the computer does as it transforms the data into useful information.

5. *Output,* the reporting of the processing results to people or to other computers, is why the computer exists — its reason for being.

A number of other characteristics help to define the computer. First, the computer is a **system;** that is, it is a group of interrelated elements working to accomplish a specific goal — in the case of the computer, the processing of data to produce output. If any of a system's elements is missing, that system simply won't work. We have already mentioned three of the computer system's elements: hardware, software, and data. But there is a fourth element, and it is the crux of the computer system: Without competent and knowledgeable *people* to design and assemble the system, to prepare the programs, to collect the data, to run the machinery, and to use the output, the computer would be like an empty bus. With no driver, no one to prepare the route and road map or to collect the tickets, no mechanic, and no passengers, it would go absolutely nowhere. Figure 1.1 gives you an idea of how a computer system works.

Two other distinguishing characteristics of the computer are its great speed and accuracy. It is, in fact, because of these characteristics that the computer is as indispensable in today's world as it is. Two hundred years ago, the compilation of a table of calculations needed for scientific and engineering purposes might have taken one person an entire lifetime of

WHAT IS A COMPUTER? **5**

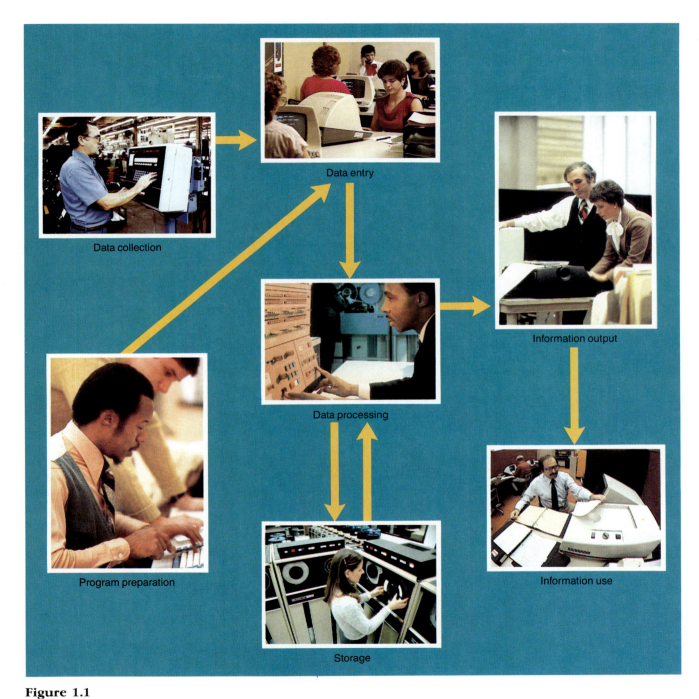

Figure 1.1
A computer system.
Data processing photo, courtesy of Shell Oil Company; storage photo, courtesy of Control Data; data collection photo, courtesy of NCR Corporation; data entry photo, copyright Peter Arnold, Inc.; other photos, courtesy of Aetna Life & Casualty.

Figure 1.2
A computer chip on the petals of a daisy.
Courtesy of Intel Corporation.

work. Just forty years ago, in 1946, even with the aid of a computer (though a primitive one by today's standards), twenty people at the Los Alamos National Laboratory, where the first atomic bomb was developed, had to work around the clock for three weeks to solve one complex differential equation. John G. Kemeny, former president of Dartmouth College and a co-developer of the BASIC programming language, was at Los Alamos at that time. In 1972, he observed, "All the calculations that we did ... at Los Alamos in a full year, a generation ago, can today be carried out by a [college] undergraduate in one afternoon, while a hundred other people are also using the same computer."[1] The reduction in the size of computer components that has taken place since 1972 — the result of new materials, improved manufacturing techniques, and advances in circuit design and computer engineering — means that today's computers operate at even higher speeds (see Figure 1.2).

While some of today's computers are faster than others, all are, by any standards, fast. Table 1.1 shows the units of time in which computer speeds are measured. You may get a better idea of these speeds if you stop to consider that it takes about a hundred milliseconds for you to blink your eye and about a million nanoseconds for the bulb in a camera to flash. The grinding ordeal of building a machine that operates in millionths or billionths of a second is jokingly reflected in this plaintive note that one worn-out computer engineer left in his office: "I'm going to a commune in Vermont [where I] will deal with no unit of time smaller than a season."[2]

[1] John G. Kemeny, *Man and the Computer* (New York: Scribner's, 1972), p. 9.
[2] Tracy Kidder, *The Soul of a New Machine* (Boston: Little, Brown, 1981), p. 220.

Table 1.1 Units of Time for Measuring Computer Speeds

Time Unit	Equivalent Measure (in seconds)	Speed of Today's Computers
Millisecond (ms)	1/1000 (one-thousandth)	Slowest process 1 instruction (e.g., add) in much less than 1 ms.
Microsecond (μs)	1/1,000,000 (one-millionth)	Most process 1 instruction in 1μs or less.
Nanosecond (ns)	1/1,000,000,000 (one-billionth)	Fastest process 1 instruction in 12.5 ns, or 80 million instructions every second; most process 1 instruction in 250 ns.
Picosecond (ps)	1/1,000,000,000,000 (one-trillionth)	None can yet process an instruction in a ps.

Commenting on the accuracy of computers in 1972, John Kemeny noted that "perhaps the most remarkable feature of all is that the typical modern computer can carry out several billion calculations a day without making a single mistake." And, today, the computer is as accurate as ever — which is to say that its output is as correct and meaningful as the input and the processing instructions it has received. Computer people use the acronym **GIGO,** which stands for *garbage in, garbage out,* to describe what happens when the computer receives bad data or faulty instructions. The accuracy of the computer derives from the inherent reliability of its electronic circuitry: The same electric current passing through the same circuit invariably produces the same result.

CLASSIFICATIONS OF COMPUTERS

We speak of "the computer" as if there were only one kind. But, in fact, computers are classified in two ways: A computer is (1) either a general-purpose computer or a special-purpose computer, and (2) either a digital computer or an analog computer. A **general-purpose computer** is just what its name implies: It can perform a variety of tasks. To switch from one task to another, all that is required is that the program be changed. The various programs are stored within the computer only for as long as they are needed. Thus, it is not unusual to find a general-purpose computer processing payroll, monthly budgets, inventory data, and engineering test results, all in the same day. In contrast, a **special-purpose computer** (also called a **dedicated computer**) is designed to perform one task only. Processing instructions are built into its circuitry, and usually they cannot be changed. These computers are used for such special purposes as monitoring

Figure 1.3
Analog and digital computers. A gas station pump uses an analog computer to measure, in approximate terms, the amount of gas pumped (to the nearest tenth of a gallon) and price (to the nearest hundredth of a dollar); a self-service terminal uses a digital computer to count discrete data.
Courtesy of NCR Corporation.

the operation of automobile engines and microwave ovens and controlling the navigation of commercial aircraft.

Basically, the difference between a digital computer and an analog computer is that a digital computer counts, whereas an analog computer measures. A **digital computer** is used when the data to be processed are *discrete*—that is, each item is individually distinct and separate. Examples of discrete data are the Arabic numbers 0 through 9 and the twenty-six letters of the English alphabet. Because these items are distinct and separate, they can be precisely counted as digits (hence the name *digital computer*).

An **analog computer** is used when the data to be processed cannot be precisely or directly counted—that is, the data are variable and ever changing. Examples of such continuously varying data are body temperatures, the fuel consumption of a jet plane or a truck, and the speed of a car as it moves down the road. Because these data are continuously changing, measurement has to be on a continuum: It cannot precisely describe; it can only approximate (i.e., make an *analogy*). For example, measurement of body temperature is to the nearest tenth of a degree, and measurement of fuel consumption is to the nearest tenth of a gallon. Figure 1.3 illustrates the difference between an analog and a digital computer.

The type of computer used for most business applications is the general-purpose, digital computer, and it is on that type that we will be focusing throughout most of the book. Now let's take a look at the interrelated parts of the computer system: data, hardware, software, and people.

THE WORLD GOES DIGITAL
Ones and Zeros Are Changing Our Lives

To our senses, the real world is a continuum. Day smoothly shades into night. The seasons blend, one into the next. Storms come and go, not all at once, but over a period of minutes, hours, or days. In almost every way, nature seems to operate steadily, without pause.

Traditionally, we've built our machines to mimic nature's ways. The cyclical rounds of the hands of clocks, for example, are analogous to the smooth turning of the earth and the steady progression of the sun through the sky. In fact, we refer to timepieces with hands as "analog" clocks and watches....

For all its power, analog machinery has certain limitations; the most notable is an inherent imprecision. For example, an analog timepiece, such as an old mantel clock, might mark the hours passably well but make it hard to note the passing of individual seconds. Of course microseconds, nanoseconds, and even finer divisions of time used in laboratory work are wholly beyond its measure.

The way around the imprecision of analogy is to deal with things in direct, discrete steps: on or off, start or stop, yes or no, one or zero. This kind of step-by-step, or "digital" measurement is inherently accurate. Digital watches, for example, slice time into tiny, discrete components; even the cheapest plastic watch can be vastly more precise than an expensive analog clock. Most modern computers also are digital; they shuffle numbers and letters as groups of discrete ones and zeros to produce incredibly precise results....

But the world doesn't present itself as a neat array of ones and zeros. To handle information with digital precision, we must first convert it into individual elements. Consider audio. You can digitize sound by sampling its waves (via microphone and computer) at frequent, short intervals, thus breaking it up into discrete elements. For very high fidelity, you might sample the sound extremely often, so as not to miss nuances.... For other purposes, lower sampling rates will suffice. The telephone system, for example, digitizes your voice at [a lower] sampling rate....

The sampling rate [used by the telephone system] is a practical compromise between fidelity and economics. Digitized Mom may sound somewhat robotic on long distance, but you still recognize her voice. And because her voice is digitized, rather than continuous, it can share the line with many others. The "bits" of conversation are neatly interwoven by computer, and the end result is more conversations on fewer circuits. That's why telephone companies are switching from analog to digital....

As chips for digital signal processing become smaller and more economical, virtually all our communication—from audio to still photography to video—will be digitized. "Applications will be limited only by our imaginations," says John Scarisbrick, digital signal-processing marketing manager for Texas Instruments. In addition to communication, Scarisbrick sees a variety of applications in text-to-speech processing and voice recognition. No matter if you lose your keys—your car will recognize your voice and unlock for you. But if you have a drunken slur, it might just refuse to let you drive. It's not unreasonable to expect such imaginative refinements as hardware and software improve....

You can like computers or hate them. Regardless, discrete little ones and zeros will inexorably change your environment. With digital-signal processing, scientists and engineers build binary dreams as we move toward speech recognition, computerized vision, and even mimicking the thinking process itself. At this point, we begin to wonder about the nature of man and his creations. Digital people, perhaps? That's far in the future, of course—but a few low-IQ robots already hang out in our warehouses and factories. No telling what they'll be up to next.

— Robert D. Swearengin, "The World Goes Digital." Reprinted with permission from the March 1985 issue of *Popular Computing* magazine. Copyright © by McGraw-Hill, Inc., New York 10020. All rights reserved.

DATA AND DATA PROCESSING

Before they are processed, data are, quite simply, raw, unevaluated facts and figures. Processing reorders these raw facts and figures and transforms them into meaningful **information,** which people can then use to make informed decisions. For example, a retail store's listing of a day's sales has little meaning until the sales are totaled. With this total in hand, the store manager can compare it with totals from other periods to determine how well the store is doing. When the sales figures are further reordered to reflect the type of merchandise sold, the store manager has information that will help in determining the popularity and profitability of the merchandise lines carried in the store and in deciding which inventory to restock.

Processing data into information is not a new activity, and it does not require a computer. In fact, people have been processing data by hand for thousands of years — certainly since at least 2700 B.C., when the Egyptian pharoahs created their version of the Internal Revenue Service. Whether data processing is computerized or manual, it always follows a logical sequence, or data flow, known as the **data cycle.** The stages of the data cycle are input, processing, and output, as shown in Figure 1.4. As you can see in the figure, storage may also be a part of the data cycle.

The Data Cycle

The *input* stage of the data cycle involves collecting and checking the data for accuracy. If processing is computerized, the input stage also involves coding the data into a form that the computer can recognize; that is, the data must be "machine-readable" since the computer cannot deal directly with the numbers, letters, and symbols that people use to represent facts and figures.

Once these activities have been performed, the data are ready for *processing.* The type of processing operation that takes place (as well as the type of input data that are collected) depends on the type of output that is desired. As indicated in Figure 1.4, it may take more than one processing operation to produce the desired output. For example, to produce a summarized monthly sales report for a department store, you (or the computer) might first classify the input data (the sales invoices for the month) by grouping them according to the department in which the goods were sold. You could then calculate a total amount for each department. To make the report easier to use and the data more accessible to the information user, you would probably sort the totals into some kind of sequence — for example, according to the ascending order of department numbers or according to the total amounts sold. This report is already summarized in that it shows only the monthly totals for each department, and it would probably be of more interest to the general manager of the

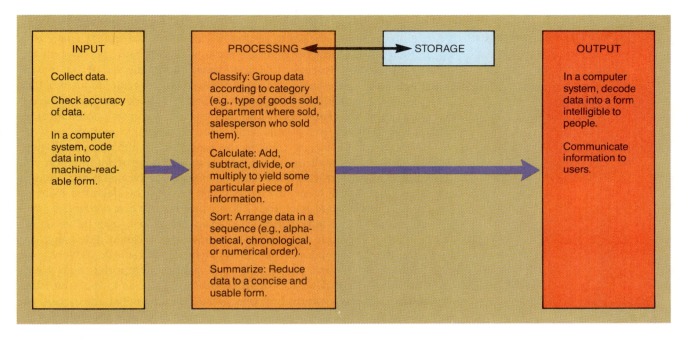

Figure 1.4
The stages of the data cycle.

store than to a department manager. The department manager would no doubt want a more detailed report, including information on such categories as types of goods sold, salesperson who sold them, daily totals, and so on.

Your ability to perform these processing operations stems from that part of your brain that allows you to reason and to make logical deductions. The computer's ability to perform these operations stems from that part of its electronic circuitry that allows it to calculate and to make comparisons as directed by program instructions. The ability to compare is at the basis of much of the computer's power. *Comparing* involves testing data for equality. When X is compared with Y, it can be greater than, equal to, or less than Y. It is this ability of the computer to compare that lets an airline reservation clerk check very quickly to see if there are any seats left on the flight you want to take. Computerized comparing is also usually the activity that precedes a notice from your bank that you have overdrawn your account. In this case, the computer has compared the amount of your check with the balance in your account, and it has found, alas, that the former is greater than the latter.

Once the data have been processed, the information that has been produced can be either stored for future reference or communicated directly to the people who want it. *Storage* of information involves some extra work and cost, especially in a computerized data processing system, where special programs are needed to retrieve the data from the storage equipment. Even in a manual data processing system, someone must go through the often slow-motion process of filing information in a file cabinet or drawer and then later retrieving it. So, a decision must be made about whether keeping the information on file is worth the extra work and cost involved.

Output is the final stage of the data cycle. It involves communicating the information to the people who need it. The information must be communicated at the right time, to the right person, and in an intelligible form; if it isn't, then all the effort it took to produce the information will have been in vain. If the processing has been done by computer, then to be in an intelligible form, the output will have to be decoded from its machine-readable state back into a form that people can recognize.

Communicating information — or even raw data — may be as simple as delivering a spoken message ("Hi. Your husband called. The babysitter quit, the twins have measles, he has to catch the 4:45 shuttle to New York, and your Aunt Lizzie...") or delivering a printed report ("YOU HAVE EXCEEDED THE BUDGET FOR JANUARY BY 20%..."). The term **data communications system,** however, refers to a somewhat more elaborate arrangement. In such a system, computer technology and communications technology combine to form a rapid means of transmitting data in the form of electronic signals from one location to another (see Figure 1.5). The communications technology involved in such a system is often an old and familiar one — that of a telephone system. Data communications systems are becoming an increasingly common means of transmitting data and information at all stages of the data cycle. The information on flight arrivals and departures that you see displayed on screens in airline terminals is conveyed via such a system.

Figure 1.5
A data communications system.
Courtesy of (left) SBS (Satellite Business Systems); (right) AT&T.

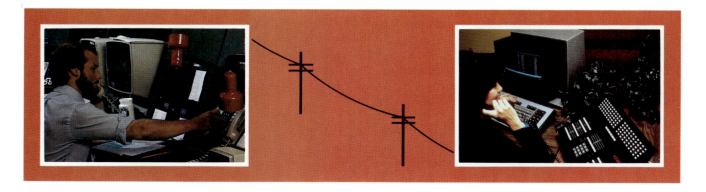

Considerations in Computerized Data Processing

The advantages of processing data by computer are impressive. As we noted earlier, the computer is fast and accurate; in addition, with a computer you can store and have quick access to vast quantities of information. However, computerized data processing does impose certain constraints not found in manual data processing. As we've mentioned, input data must be in a form that the computer can "read," and output data must be decoded from machine-readable form to a form that people can understand. Also, the problem to be solved must be stated as either an arithmetic problem or a logic problem, for, as you will see in the next section, arithmetic and logic operations are the only two kinds of processing operations that the computer can perform.

Another requirement of computerized data processing is that the data be organized in such a way that the computer can locate and process them efficiently. Even when the data processing system is a manual one that does not involve a computer, we still need to organize the data in some way if we are to have any hope of ever finding them again once they've been placed in storage. Labeled manila folders and file cabinets are, of course, the usual means of storing traditional paperwork. Computer systems, too, use the file concept, but without the paper or folders. A computer **file** is a group of data that are stored and processed as a unit. As Figure 1.6 shows, each file is composed of one or more records. A **record** is a collection of data pertaining to a particular person, transaction, or event. Records are made up of fields, and **fields** are collections of related **characters**, such as the digits of a social security number or a student I.D. number. Characters can also be letters or special symbols such as $ or #; blanks, too, are counted as characters.

Figure 1.6
A college's student file.

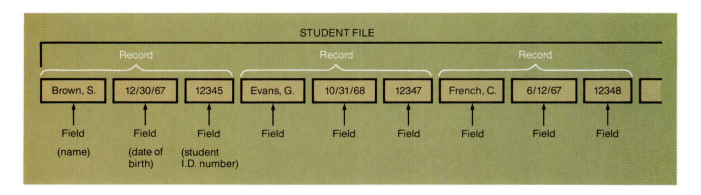

Records may be arranged within the files in different ways to meet the particular processing needs of different applications. Sequential file organization and direct file organization are two common ways of organizing files. In **sequential file organization,** the records are arranged in the file in some kind of sequence. The sequence is usually determined by a particular field of the record. For example, in a college's student file, the records might be arranged according to the ascending order of student I.D. numbers, which would be a field found in all the records in that file. The particular field chosen as the basis for the sequencing of the records is called a **key,** or a **key field.**

When records are organized sequentially, the computer processes each one in turn, one after the other; this is called **sequential processing.** Sequential file organization and processing are quite efficient when all the records in a file have to be processed, as, for example, when student grades are being processed and each student has to be issued a grade. However, since the computer must read each record in the file in turn, sequential file organization and processing are inefficient when individual records need to be processed at random, and you would no doubt soon change banks if your bank used these methods in its automated teller machines (see Figure 1.7).

Direct file organization and **direct processing** provide a more efficient alternative for the random processing of individual records. In direct file organization, a key field is used to indicate the exact location of each record. The computer is thus able to go directly to the needed record without having to read all the preceding records in the file. In other words, it can directly process the record. Because of the way key fields are used

Figure 1.7

Automated teller machines. Direct file organization and the storage of records in a direct access storage device (DASD) allow the computer to process individual records at random.
Courtesy of (left) Burroughs Corporation; (right) IBM Corporation.

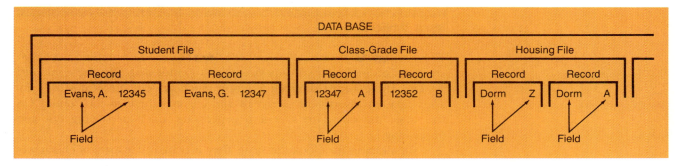

Figure 1.8
A data base.

in direct file organization, each record must have its own unique, identifying key; a student I.D. number would be an appropriate choice, since, of course, each student has a different number. Files organized and processed in this manner are stored in a **direct access storage device (DASD),** a type of storage unit that allows the computer to skip over unwanted data and go directly to the needed data.

A **data base** is another way of organizing data. It is a more complex but often more useful approach than file organization. As you can see in Figure 1.8, a data base may consist of a number of different files, which can be used to satisfy a number of different processing needs. The data fields are maintained independently, but they can be linked when needed for processing. Each data field has a key that associates it with other fields from the original record. This form of organization eliminates data redundancy among files, as each item of data is captured and stored only once. With sequential or direct file organization, personal information for each student would have to be repeated in the housing file, the class-grade file, the admissions file, and so on; with data base organization, each data field is captured and recorded one time only.

Essentially, a computer system performs the same data processing activities as those that could be performed by a manual data processing system: It accepts input data; processes, stores, and retrieves those data; and produces output. The difference, of course, is that the computer can do these things far more quickly and with a greater degree of accuracy than people can. Just as the internal combustion engine shaped the way the world thinks about travel and transportation, the computer has changed our perceptions of data processing. We have come to expect accurate, fast processing, even in complex situations. Let's now take a brief look at the hardware that has brought our expectations to this level.

HARDWARE: TECHNOLOGY AT WORK

Input Devices

The computer hardware that you are most likely to encounter as you go about an ordinary day's business is used to enter data into the computer system. These **input devices** function much as your physical senses do: They take an assortment of signals and channel them to the "brain" (in this case, the computer's central processing unit) for sorting out and processing.

Not all input data look the same; they may be in the form of characters or numbers, unsorted lists of names, customer transactions, inventory codes, and even grade reports. Whatever form they're in, the computer will not recognize them unless they are translated to machine-readable form. Some input devices are capable of performing the needed translation at the exact same time that they enter the data directly into the computer system. To do so, the device must be **online** to the computer — that is, it must be linked to the computer by a plug and cable or a telephone or other communications line. When a device is not online, it is **offline** — that is, it is not in direct communication with the computer. To get anything into or out of the computer system, a device has to be online.

A *video display terminal (VDT)* is a popular type of input device that can simultaneously code the data and enter the data into the system. Such a terminal has a keyboard for entering the data and a screen composed of a *cathode ray tube (CRT)* for viewing both the input and the output. Figure 1.9 shows a VDT as well as some other input devices commonly used in direct data entry.

Figure 1.9
Direct input devices: (*left*) a wand reader; (*center*) a scanner; (*right*) a VDT.
Courtesy of (left) NCR Corporation; (center) National Semiconductor Corporation; (right) Sperry Corporation.

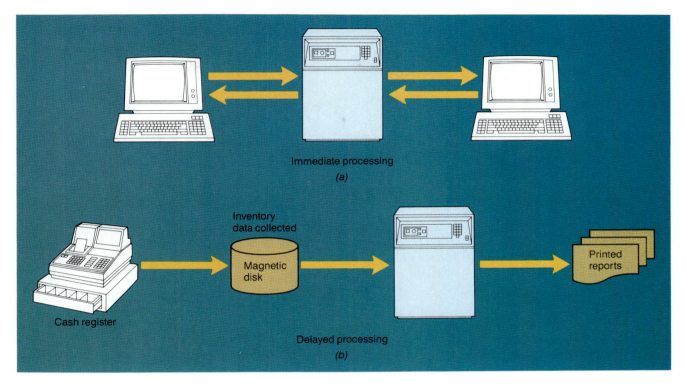

Figure 1.10
Types of processing: (*a*) interactive, or immediate, processing; (*b*) batch, or delayed, processing.

Although direct input devices such as the VDT enter the data directly and immediately into the computer system, the data may or may not be processed immediately. When they are processed immediately, the processing is said to be **interactive.** For example, when you request cash from a bank's automated teller machine, the data are processed at once; you are interacting with the computer while a program is running. But when a clerk in a store enters the data on your transaction directly into the computer system through an online cash register, those data are generally held for processing in one **batch** with all the other sales transactions of the day. Figure 1.10 illustrates the difference between interactive and batch processing.

Another way of handling input data is to record the data in machine-readable form on a **storage medium** — that is, some physical substance capable of storing the data in encoded form. The data are then held in storage on the medium for later entry into the system, where they will be processed in one batch. This type of data collection and preparation

Figure 1.11

Magnetic media. Magnetic tape (*top left*) is made of a plastic material called mylar and is coated with iron oxide, a material that can be easily magnetized. Floppy disks (*bottom left*) and hard disks (*above*) are also coated with iron oxide. The former are made of a flexible plastic, the latter of machined aluminum. The hard disk is shown with the head used to read and write data on it.

Photos courtesy of (top and bottom left) BASF Systems Corporation; (above) 3M.

is referred to as *offline,* since the devices used to encode data on the medium are not connected to the computer.

Today, the media most often used in offline data collection and preparation are *magnetic tapes* and *magnetic disks* (see Figure 1.11). You can't tell by looking at either of these media that anything is recorded on it. On both, the data are encoded as magnetized spots, but the recording leaves no visible change on the surface. Offline *keyboard devices* are used to encode the data on both magnetic tapes and disks. *Tape drives* and *disk drives,* which are online to the computer, then enter the data into the system (see Figure 1.12).

Punched cards, a century-old data recording medium, are still in use in offline data collection, though they are far less popular than they once were. Data are encoded on punched cards as patterns of holes punched into the cards. An offline *keypunch machine* is used for the punching (see Figure 1.13), and an online *card reader* scans the patterns and transmits them into the computer as electronic impulses.

HARDWARE: TECHNOLOGY AT WORK 19

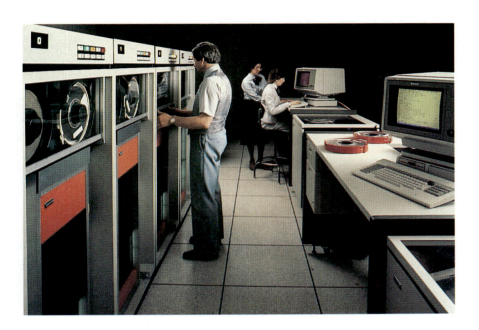

Figure 1.12
Online drive units. Magnetic-tape drives (*top*) and magnetic-disk drives (*bottom*) are used to enter the coded data into the computer.
Courtesy of (top) Sperry Corporation; (bottom) Cray Research, Inc.

Figure 1.13
An offline keypunch machine.
D. Brody/Stock, Boston.

The Central Processing Unit

The **central processing unit (CPU),** also called the **processor** and sometimes simply referred to as the *computer,* is the heart of the computer system. So central is its role that the other types of hardware used for input, output, and storage are often referred to as **peripheral devices.** The CPU has three functional components: the primary storage unit, the arithmetic/logic unit, and the control unit (see Figure 1.14). A distinction is often made between the primary storage unit and the other two units: Because the primary storage unit does not actually process any data but instead stores data so that they can be processed, some people prefer to use the term *processor* or *CPU* to refer to the arithmetic/logic and control units only. However, since the computer's ability to process data relies on the functioning of all three units, and since these units are generally located within the same physical "box" (known as the **processor unit**), we will refer to all three collectively as the CPU.

Primary Storage Unit. The **primary storage unit** is also called **internal storage** or **main memory.** When an input device is activated, it sends electronic signals representing programs and data into the CPU, where they are held in primary storage until they are processed. While the data are being processed, intermediate answers or partial results are also temporarily stored here. Final processing results remain in primary storage

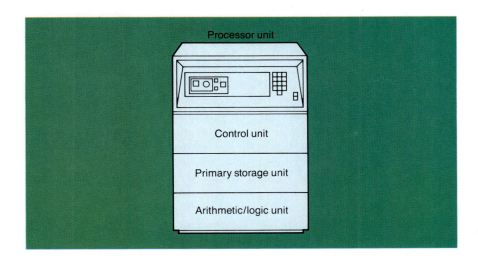

Figure 1.14
The central processing unit.

until the control unit directs them to an output device or to an online auxiliary storage unit. The primary storage unit operates at great speeds: It can access and transfer millions of characters per second. However, primary storage is expensive. To store a few million characters in this unit costs about the same as storing several hundred million characters in auxiliary storage devices. For this reason, the capacity of primary storage is by comparison limited, and the less expensive auxiliary storage units generally handle the bulk of the stored data.

Arithmetic/Logic Unit. As its name implies, the **arithmetic/logic unit** is capable of two processing operations only: It can do *arithmetic* calculations, and it can perform *logic* operations by testing items — both numerical and alphabetical — for such things as equality or inequality. All the data processing activities shown earlier in Figure 1.4 — classifying, sorting, calculating, and summarizing — depend on one or the other of these operations. For example, if you wanted to extract your transcript from the school computer, you would enter your name or student number, instructing the computer to search for the same name or number in the student records. When you look for an exact match, you are using the logic operation of comparing items for equality. If you also wanted a current grade-point average, you would have to instruct the computer to activate the arithmetic circuits to perform the necessary calculations. Any problem that can be stated in mathematical terms or described as a logical procedure is a good candidate for computerized processing.

Control Unit. In response to program instructions, the **control unit** directs the sequence of all input and output activities, as well as the arithmetic/logic operations and the transfer of program instructions and data to and from primary storage. When a program is being run, a number of things take place within the computer. First, when the program instructions and data enter the CPU, they go into primary storage. The control unit is responsible both for storing them and retrieving them in their proper order during program execution. As the program runs and the data records enter primary storage, the control unit interprets each program instruction and activates signals that trigger the appropriate logic or arithmetic circuits. After the arithmetic/logic unit has completed its computations, the control unit routes the results to the proper location in primary storage, and when it is time to display or to permanently record the results of the processing operation, the control unit sends a signal to the terminal, printer, or other output or auxiliary storage device. If you have ever seen a switchboard operator in a busy office sorting out calls, routing them to the proper people, and keeping tabs on everything that's going on, you have some idea of the control unit's activities.

Output Devices

Output is, of course, the computer's reason for being. To be intelligible to people, the output must be decoded from machine-readable form to a form that people can understand. *Printers* and video display terminals, which perform this kind of translation and produce printed matter on paper or on a screen, are the most common **output devices.** However, computers can also produce output in the form of *graphics* (charts, graphs, drawings, etc.), *audio outputs* (spoken messages), special visual effects such as might be found in movies and cartoons, and *microfilm* (miniature photographic copy of the output). Each of these outputs requires special equipment, although at times several output functions can be combined in a single unit, such as a video display terminal that also has printing capabilities. If the output is not to be immediately communicated to a user but is to be stored for later use, it is usually transferred to a magnetic-tape or magnetic-disk drive, which records the data in machine-readable form. Figure 1.15 shows some commonly used output devices.

Auxiliary Storage Devices

Auxiliary storage is also called **secondary storage** or **external storage.** As its name implies, it is used to supplement the computer's primary storage unit, which, as we noted earlier, has a limited capacity and a higher cost. The most common media used for auxiliary storage are magnetic tape and disks, but punched cards are also sometimes used. *Optical disks*, a relatively new medium on which data are recorded as machine-readable bumps or holes rather than as magnetized spots, are becoming increasingly popular (see Figure 1.16).

Figure 1.15

Some commonly used output devices: (*top*) a printer and video display terminal; (*center*) a graphic plotter; (*bottom*) a microimage terminal, which uses the computer to provide very fast access to stored images.

Courtesy of (top) Hewlitt-Packard; (center) IBM Corporation; (bottom) Eastman Kodak Company.

Figure 1.16

Optical disks. Because of the precision of the optical technology used in recording data on these disks, each disk can store hundreds of millions of characters.
Courtesy of 3M.

When the data stored on these media need to be changed or updated, the media have to be placed in a device that is online to the CPU so that electronic signals can be passed back and forth and the control unit can direct the processing operations. These two elements — the medium and the device — make up an auxiliary storage system. Once a device is online, the CPU can access the data without any assistance from human beings.

The devices used to get storage media online to the CPU include the card readers, the tape drives, and the disk drives used for input. As noted in the last section, tape drives and disk drives are also used as output devices when the output is to be stored in machine-readable form. In other words, tape drives and disk drives serve a dual purpose: They act as input devices by transmitting the data to be processed into the CPU, and as output devices by recording the newly processed data in machine-readable form. Card readers, however, serve as input devices only. Figure 1.17 shows the functions of the various pieces of hardware you would be likely to encounter in a large computer system.

In many applications, the media are removed from the drives and are stored offline in a library or vault (see Figure 1.18). When data stored in this manner are needed, computer personnel must retrieve the storage medium and place it in the output device. When processing requirements are infrequent — as, for example, in the periodic processing of student grades — this kind of storage is a very cost-effective way to manage data. For some applications, however, the CPU needs almost continuous and immediate access to the data. In these cases, the data are kept continuously

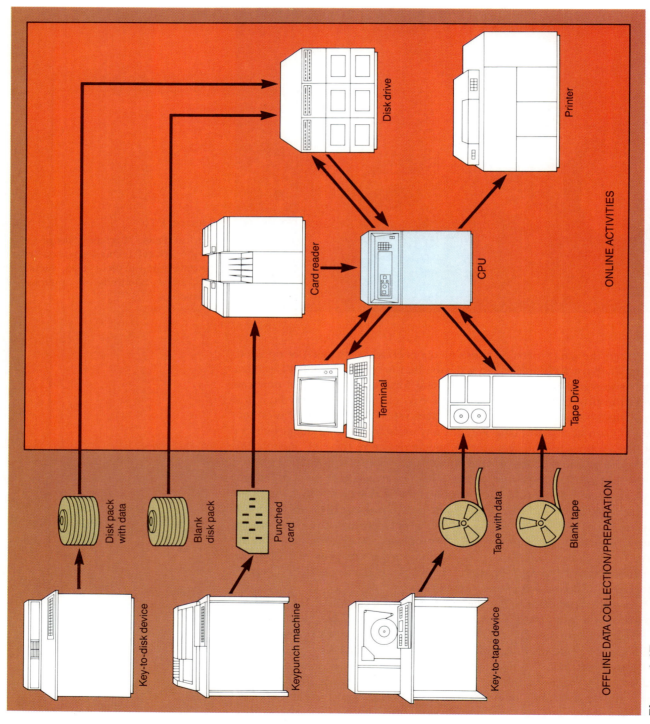

Figure 1.17 Functions of various pieces of hardware found in a large computer system.

Figure 1.18
Offline storage of magnetic tape in a tape library.
Donald Dietz/Stock, Boston.

online in a direct access storage device (DASD), which allows the CPU to go directly to the needed data. The disk drive shown in Figure 1.17 is an example of a DASD. Continuous online storage is generally used when processing must be done frequently and speed is an important factor, as in the processing performed by a bank's automated teller machines.

Think for a minute about what is involved in the seemingly simple transaction that occurs when you request cash from an automated teller machine. Thousands of people have accounts with the bank, and if the computer had to search sequentially through each record in the file until it finally came to yours, it could take a while, unless, of course, you were lucky enough to have your record located at the beginning of the file. By keeping account data on a disk in a DASD that is available to all the teller machines in the system, the computer can skip over unwanted data and go directly to your account, process your request, and update your account record, usually without your being aware of any delay.

The computer's ability to directly access stored data in this manner depends on two factors: the file organization and the storage medium used. **Direct access** requires that the files be organized and the records identified in such a way that the computer can go immediately to the needed data. It also requires a storage medium that allows direct access. Magnetic tape cannot be used for this purpose as it provides **sequential access** only. In this respect, magnetic tape is much like the tape used in an ordinary tape recorder. Just as you have to run through all the songs on a tape before you get to the one you want to hear, so too must the computer run in sequence through all the records stored on a magnetic tape; it cannot skip over any part of the tape to get to a particular record. A magnetic disk, on the other hand, is like a phonograph record in that it can provide either sequential or direct access to the stored data. You can listen to all the songs on a phonograph record in sequence, or you can lift the phonograph arm and place it directly on the exact song you want to hear. In much the same way, a magnetic disk offers a choice of access methods. Whether direct access is superior to sequential access depends entirely on the application. If the files are to be processed in some logical order — as, for example, in the processing of student grades — then sequential file organization and a sequential access medium may be the better choice.

SOFTWARE: THE ROAD MAP FOR PROBLEM SOLVING

Without software, the best computer hardware in the world would be useless. Software provides the road map for problem solving, and it includes not just the programs that the computer needs but also any instructions or procedures that people might need to get the computer to produce the output they want. Instructions and procedures for people might include manuals on how to operate the computer, forms for collecting data, schedules indicating when programs are to be run, and other documentation relating to the use of input data and output information. Although software includes such instructions and procedures for people, the term itself is often used to refer strictly to the programs that the computer needs. These programs are of two types: applications programs and systems software.

Whereas a special-purpose computer has its processing instructions, or program, built into the electronic circuitry, a general-purpose computer must be fed a program for each data processing application it is to perform. Programs instructing the computer to perform such specific tasks are classified as **applications programs.** Applications programs may be prepared by a firm's own **programmers** (i.e., specialists who design, write, and test programs), or they may be purchased from software companies, computer stores, and computer companies.

Computers also need software to direct the operation of the hardware, regardless of the application requirements. **Systems software,** a series of specially designed programs, performs this task. Usually supplied by the manufacturer of the computer hardware, systems software is not concerned with any particular data processing application; rather, its job is to see that the computer performs a variety of functions that improve the overall efficiency of the system. A major component of systems software is the **operating system,** which, among other things, acts as the computer's traffic director. It is the operating system's scheduling of input and output devices that allows a computer to accept input data from a customer transaction at the same time that it prints out a tax report. Other components of systems software are programs that perform frequently needed operations (such as sorting records into a sequence so a file can be updated) and programs that translate instructions into machine language, the only language that the computer can "understand."

SOFTWARE: THE ROAD MAP FOR PROBLEM SOLVING   27

ON COMPUTER LITERACY

Computer literacy has become an important buzzword. Educators describe it as one of the major challenges facing modern society. Textbooks often cite it as the reason for their existence. The term has even been bandied about on the floor of the U.S. Senate; in his first speech before that body, newly elected Senator Frank Lautenberg of New Jersey described computer literacy as a potentially divisive social force. His point was that because computers are proliferating rapidly in the homes and schools of the wealthy, the poor are being saddled with yet another disadvantage: illiteracy in this new technology.

One interesting thing about computer literacy, however, is that despite the heavy workout the term gets, there's no very clear definition of what it actually means. It has yet to find its way into standard dictionaries. If we were to use the accepted definition of literacy as our starting point, we might come up with a definition that read "the ability to read and write about computers." But if that is the meaning of computer literacy, why all the fuss? Such an abstract knowledge wouldn't seem much more useful to most of us than literacy in ancient Sanskrit.

Joseph Weizenbaum, professor of computer science at the Massachusetts Institute of Technology, has defined computer literacy as "basically a disease that was invented when it became necessary to market the cure" — computers. While Weizenbaum may have a point, he's no doubt in the minority. Most people would probably define computer literacy as "the ability to use computers to solve problems."

Thinking about computer literacy in this light, the reason for the buzz in the buzzword becomes clearer: The ability to use computers effectively is already an acknowledged key to successful participation in today's world, and it is sure to become only more so in the future.

Fortunately, despite all the fanfare surrounding the concept, the prerequisites to computer literacy itself are minimal — not much more than access to a computer and a desire to learn. An ability to type helps but is certainly not essential; typing games available for use on microcomputers make learning to type fun. Although a basic ability to read, write, and count is helpful, even that is not a prerequisite to computer literacy; kindergartners all over the world are using computers to learn the "three R's," thus simultaneously becoming literate in both the old and the new senses of the word.

◆

Basically, all a computer can "understand" or respond to are electronic impulses that switch its circuits on or off. Early programmers wrote their program instructions in a way that directly corresponded to this on-off state. To do so, they used the **binary numbering system,** which, because it has only two digits (0 and 1), lends itself to on-off instructions. These early programs thus consisted of long lists of 0's and 1's (see Figure 1.19), and writing them was a very tedious process. This type of code is known as **machine language,** and even with today's advanced systems, it is still the only language that a computer can recognize and understand (hence the need for the translation programs that are part of the systems software). However, tedium as well as necessity is often the mother of invention, and, as you will see in Chapter 2, since those early days, programmers have developed a number of shortcuts that make it easier to communicate with the computer.

Figure 1.19

Program instructions written in machine language.

PEOPLE: THE LIFEBLOOD OF COMPUTER SYSTEMS

As we said earlier, people are crucial to the whole computer system. They are quite literally its "lifeblood." Programmers, of course, play a very important role in a computer system, as do **systems analysts,** who are responsible for designing the system. Other people who are essential to a computer system are **data collection personnel,** who collect the input data; **data entry personnel,** who prepare and enter the data into the system; **computer operators,** who control and coordinate the hardware when it is running; **control clerks** and **librarians,** who catalog, monitor, record, and control the flow of data and programs to the computer; and, last but not least, the system's **users,** those of us whose needs for information are the computer's reason for being.

The performance of the system depends on how well all these people do their jobs; each is important to the successful operation of the system. Error can creep in as the data entry clerk translates the raw data with finger strokes on a keyboard: Missed strokes mean that inaccurate data enter the system. A more serious error can result when a problem is improperly defined or analyzed; this kind of error leads to incorrect system design, which, in turn, leads to incorrect programming. When these things happen, the computer solves the wrong problem or attempts to solve the problem with incorrect logic. In either event, the system appears to be functioning properly, and the user of the output assumes the output is correct, when, in fact, it is incorrect. Users of computer output frequently compound this kind of problem by reacting to anything printed on green-striped computer paper as if it had some magical quality ensuring its accuracy. Nothing could be further from the truth, for, as we've just pointed out, both bad data and bad design can lead to inaccurate computer output. Simply because information is computer-generated is no reason to ignore common sense in evaluating its usefulness. While not much can be done about a lack of common sense, careful checking of data and programs before they enter the system and thorough training of personnel can counteract problems of bad data and design. When all its elements are working in synchronization, a modern computer system can process data with a high degree of accuracy and at phenomenal speed.

SUMMARY

A computer is a programmable electronic device that can accept input data; process, store, and retrieve those data; and produce output. Computers operate as a system — a group of interrelated parts working to accomplish a specific goal. The parts of the computer system are data, hardware, software, and people. Computers are also characterized by great speed and accuracy. They can be classified as general-purpose or special-purpose computers and as digital or analog computers. Most business applications utilize general-purpose, digital computers.

Processing transforms data, which are raw, unevaluated facts and figures, into information. The computer's ability to perform processing operations stems from that part of its electronic circuitry that allows it to calculate and to make comparisons. All data processing, whether computerized or manual, follows a logical sequence known as the data cycle. The stages of the data cycle are input, processing, output, and, often, storage. The output stage of the data cycle involves communicating the results of processing to the information users. Such communication may be as simple as a spoken sentence, or it may involve a data communications system, in which data are transmitted as electronic signals from one location to another.

To be processed by a computer, data must be in machine-readable form and must be organized in files. Files consist of records, records are made up of fields, and fields are collections of related characters. Records in sequentially organized files are arranged in a sequence, usually according to a key field, and they are processed in sequence. Records in directly organized files are located by using a unique, identifying key, and they can be processed randomly. A data base, which may consist of a number of different files, is another way of organizing data; it allows data fields from different records to be linked when needed for processing.

Computerized data processing requires specific equipment to perform the input, processing, output, and storage functions. The types of equipment used depend on the nature of the data being processed and the use of the information that is generated. Data may be entered directly into the computer in machine-readable form by a direct input device, or they may be collected and coded in machine-readable form on some type of medium before being entered into the system. Data entered directly into the system may be held for processing in a batch, or they may be processed interactively. Depending on the file organization and the storage medium used, auxiliary storage may offer either sequential or direct access to the stored data.

The computer can function only under the direction of software. Software includes applications programs, which are the step-by-step instructions the computer must have to perform specific tasks, and systems software, a series of specialized programs that coordinate the computer hardware so that the system functions as efficiently as possible. The major components of systems software are the operating system, programs that perform frequently needed operations, and translation programs. Translation programs are needed because the computer can respond only to machine language.

The lifeblood of the computer system is people, both the technical specialists and the information users. Clearly defining the problem to be solved, correctly entering the data into the system, and properly coding program instructions are just a few of the things that people must do in a smoothly functioning computer system.

KEY TERMS

In each "Key Terms" section throughout the book, the numbers in parentheses following the terms indicate the pages on which the terms are introduced.

analog computer (8)
applications programs (26)
arithmetic/logic unit (21)
auxiliary storage (secondary storage, external storage) (22)
batch (17)
binary numbering system (27)
central processing unit (CPU, processor) (20)
characters (13)
computer (4)
computer operators (28)
control clerks (28)
control unit (21)
data (4)
data base (15)
data collection personnel (28)
data communications system (12)
data cycle (10)
data entry personnel (28)
digital computer (8)
direct access (25)
direct access storage device (DASD) (15)
direct file organization (14)
direct processing (14)
fields (13)
file (13)
GIGO (7)
general-purpose computer (7)
hardware (4)
information (10)
input devices (16)
interactive (17)
key (key field) (14)
librarians (28)

machine language (27)
offline (16)
online (16)
operating system (26)
output devices (22)
peripheral devices (20)
primary storage unit (internal storage, main memory) (20)
processor unit (20)
program (4)
programmers (26)
record (13)
sequential access (25)
sequential file organization (14)
sequential processing (14)
software (4)
special-purpose computer (dedicated computer) (7)
storage medium (17)
system (4)
systems analysts (28)
systems software (26)
users (28)

DISCUSSION QUESTIONS

1. In your own words, explain what a computer is. Describe several characteristics common to all computers.

2. What advantages does a general-purpose computer have over a special-purpose computer?

3. Explain the difference between an analog and a digital computer. What kind of computer is most often used in business applications? Why?

4. Describe the difference between data and information. Give examples of five different kinds of data that a computer might process.

5. What is the data cycle? Describe the activities that take place in each of the stages of this cycle, including the special things that must be done if the data are being processed by a computer. How might a data communications system fit into the data cycle?

6. Explain why computerized comparing is an important concept.

7. Explain how data are organized for computerized processing. Why is it necessary to organize the data in this way?

8. Visit a local business that uses a computer system to process its data. Describe the hardware that the system uses for input, processing, storage, and output. Does it use both direct input devices and offline data collection methods? What media are used in the offline data collection and preparation? How does the system store processed data? What kind of access to the stored data does the CPU have?

9. Define computer software. Describe the difference between systems software and applications programs. What are some of the components of systems software? Why are translation programs needed?

10. What roles do people play in a computer system? How can people cause computer error?

OUTLINE

THE EVOLUTION OF THE COMPUTER

- Ancient Ancestry
- Contributions of the Scientific Revolution
- The Nineteenth Century
- The Great Depression
- The War Years
- First-Generation Computers: 1951–1958
- Second-Generation Computers: 1959–1964
- Third-Generation Computers: 1965–1970
- Fourth-Generation Computers: 1971–?

TODAY'S COMPUTERS AND HOW WE USE THEM

- Supercomputers
- Mainframes
- Minicomputers
- Microcomputers

SUMMARY
KEY TERMS
DISCUSSION QUESTIONS

OVERVIEW

In many ways, life in 1750 A.D. did not differ greatly from life in 1750 B.C. But by the early 1900s, the face of the world had changed, so much so that anyone living in 1750 who had been somehow transported into the world of the 1900s would have had a hard time recognizing it. A new-fangled invention called the telephone was creating a bit of an uproar. Noisy items called horseless carriages were creating the first traffic jams. Businesses were using things called typewriters and cash registers. A bustling city called New York, which in 1750 had been a village of mud tracks, glowed by night by electric light and hummed by day to the tune of subways and electric streetcars. A person could send a message overseas via a trans-Atlantic cable. And two brothers named Wright were tinkering with a flying machine! The years that spawned all these dramatic changes are known, of course, as the Industrial Revolution.

Some modern-day "prophets" have predicted that before this century is out, another technological revolution will have changed our ways of life just as dramatically as the Industrial Revolution changed those of the nineteenth century. But, they point out, this revolution — often called the Computer Revolution but increasingly referred to as the Information Revolution — will have accomplished all this in a much shorter span of time — less than fifty years. Computers and their many applications have become so much a fact of life in the 1980s that we may tend to be skeptical about such predictions. But if we stop to consider the technological advances of recent years, we may be a lot less skeptical. Forty years ago, the electronic components of a computer, if laid side by side two inches apart, would have covered a football field; today, the entire electronic circuitry of a powerful computer can be placed on your fingertip. And, according to what is almost an old saying in the computer world these days, if the automobile industry had kept pace with the computer industry over the past forty years, cars today would cost $2.50 and would run two million miles on one gallon of gas. The story of these forty years of computer development is an interesting one. Like most stories, it is more interesting still if you know something of what preceded it. So, before we look at the computer as we know it today, let's take a look at how it evolved.

Our objectives in this chapter are to

- trace the significant events in history that led to the introduction of the modern computer.

- describe the contributions of key individuals to the development of computers.

CHAPTER 2

- ◆ describe the different computer generations and explain the factors that are used to differentiate between them.
- ◆ discuss computers today and identify some applications in which supercomputers, mainframes, minicomputers, and microcomputers are used.
- ◆ explain why microcomputers have made such an impact on society.

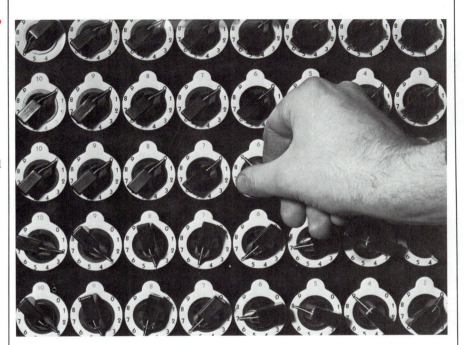

COMPUTERS PAST AND PRESENT

THE EVOLUTION OF THE COMPUTER

Ancient Ancestry

The history of data processing seems to be largely the story of an unending search for labor-saving devices. One very old such device, dating back to at least 450 B.C., is the abacus (see Figure 2.1). To understand why the abacus was invented, just imagine having to multiply MDLIX by CCCXXVIII or having to multiply the same number in Chinese notation. The Arabic decimal system was not introduced in Europe until the twelfth century, and while it is simpler to multiply 1,559 by 328 than in their Roman numeral equivalents, it is still, for most of us, a time-consuming chore. The introduction of the abacus must have been particularly welcomed by merchants in Rome, who until the appearance of this device had relied on small stones or pebbles for keeping track of their accounts. (Interestingly, but not coincidentally, the Latin word for pebbles is *calculi,* from which the English word *calculate* is derived.) Because a skilled abacus operator can calculate sums very rapidly, the abacus continued to flourish even after the introduction of the Arabic numbering system. It is, in fact, still in use in some parts of the world and has only recently disappeared in the highly industrialized nation of Japan.

During the 1400s, the Incas of South America were using a device called the *quipu* to keep their accounts and records (see Figure 2.2). The

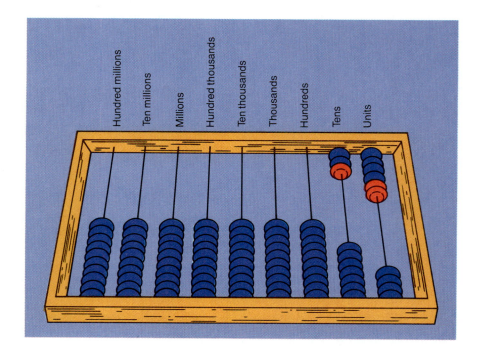

Figure 2.1

An abacus. The wires running across the rectangular wooden frame stand for "places." In a decimal numbering system, these places would be units, tens, hundreds, thousands, and so on. The beads strung along the wires represent digits. To operate the abacus, you move the beads from one side of the frame to the other. Thus, the number represented here is 36. To subtract 12, you would slide two beads down on the units wire and one bead down on the tens wire.

quipu consisted of a series of knotted strings of various colors. The knots, tied at places corresponding to the places of a decimal system, enabled the *quipucamayus* — the keepers of the knots — to accurately record very large numbers. This device seems to be a more sophisticated version of a much older data processing device — the knotted strings that ancient shepherds used to keep track of their flocks.

Contributions of the Scientific Revolution

The 1600s saw the invention of several data processing devices, including the first mechanical one (see Figures 2.3–2.6). It seems to have been no accident that the phrase "necessity is the mother of invention" was also coined during the 1600s. However, the "necessity" of this century was essentially the same necessity that gave rise to the abacus: to relieve the tedium of doing routine computations and to increase the accuracy of the computations. There was one striking difference, though: Such considerations were becoming increasingly important in a world experiencing what is today called the Scientific Revolution. During this era, science, engineering, and medicine flourished, but, in one of history's interesting paradoxes, most people were illiterate. Even well-educated people were often quite ignorant of the multiplication tables — knowledge that most of us today take for granted. Samuel Pepys, a British civil servant during the 1660s, had attended Cambridge University and was, by the standards of his times, a well-educated man. But when he had to buy timber for the king, he could not do the simple calculations required; Pepys was thus forced to get up at four o'clock in the morning to study the multiplication tables by candlelight. Small wonder, then, that machines capable of accurate computation were having something of a vogue.

Figure 2.2
A *quipu*.

The Nineteenth Century

By the early 1800s, the world had grown even more complex, and a great many people were making a living by doing calculations and compiling numerical data of various kinds. Then, as now, such transcriptions were prone to error, and Charles Babbage, a brilliant and fascinating English mathematician, was forever spotting errors in them. One evening in 1812, while a student at Cambridge University, Babbage was sitting in a reading room with a table of logarithms spread before him. As he pondered the routine drudgery that went into doing log calculations, it occurred to him that a machine could do this sort of thing more easily and more accurately than a human being. The result of that idea was Babbage's *Difference Engine*

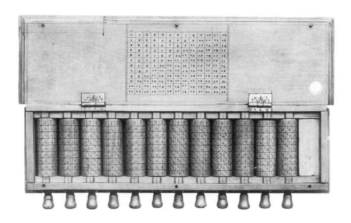

Figure 2.3
Napier's bones. When manipulated, the "bones" perform routine multiplication and division. They were invented by John Napier, a Scottish mathematician, who around 1600 discovered the concept of logarithms — tables of numbers that greatly simplify the processes of multiplication and division.
Courtesy of Trustees of the Science Museum (London).

Figure 2.4
A slide rule of the seventeenth century. Designed in 1621 by English mathematician William Oughtred, the slide rule was a refinement of Napier's ideas. It has two sliding pieces and is marked with graduated scales that represent logarithms. Because it gives an approximation based on the position of the sliding rule over the numbers of the scale, the slide rule functions as an analog computer rather than a digital one.
Courtesy of Trustees of the Science Museum (London).

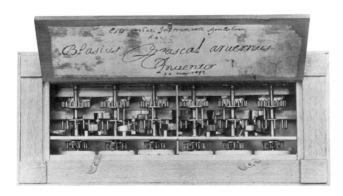

Figure 2.5
The Pascaline. The first mechanical device to aid in data processing, the Pascaline was invented in 1642 by an eighteen-year-old Frenchman named Blaise Pascal. Capable of addition and subtraction, the Pascaline resembles the odometer in a car: Cogs and gears are used to turn the next column of numbers, the principle of carrying numbers in addition.
Courtesy of Trustees of the Science Museum (London).

Figure 2.6
The Leibniz calculator. In 1671, Gottfried Wilhelm von Leibniz, a German mathematician, designed a machine that could multiply as well as subtract and add. The machine was built in 1694, but its functioning proved unreliable.
Courtesy of Trustees of the Science Museum (London).

(see Figure 2.7). In 1822, Babbage displayed a small working model of this machine to the Royal Astronomical Society. So big a hit did the Difference Engine make that the British government undertook to fund work on Babbage's full-scale model. Once work began, it became obvious that the engineering technology of the day lagged well behind Babbage's imagination; the cogs and gearwheels just couldn't be made with the degree of precision required. In 1833, the government, having invested some £17,000 in the unfinished engine, withdrew its support, and Babbage's workmen picked up their tools and left.

Even before work on the Difference Engine had ground to a halt, Babbage had recognized that machine's limitations. It could perform only one function — the solving of polynomial equations — and so would be what today we'd call a special-purpose, or dedicated, computer. Undeterred, Babbage conceived of the *Analytical Engine,* a general-purpose computer that would not only perform any type of arithmetic operation but would also string the operations together to solve any type of arithmetic problem. Sadly, the Analytical Engine, like the Difference Engine, was never built, even though Babbage devoted the rest of his life to this project. The model of the Analytical Engine shown in Figure 2.7 was constructed after Babbage's death.

Babbage planned to power the Analytical Engine with a steam engine. You may be tempted to laugh at the thought of such a strange-looking contraption hooked up to a huffing-puffing steam engine, but before you do, consider this one rather astounding fact: The Analytical Engine was to have had all the essential components found in computers today — an input device; a memory (or "store," as Babbage called it) to hold the numerical data involved in the calculations; a "mill," a series of gears and wheels to perform the arithmetic operations; a control device for transferring numbers back and forth between the store and the mill and for ordering the sequence of operations; and an output device.

For the input device and for instructing, or "programming," the control device, Babbage borrowed from the ideas of the French inventor Joseph Jacquard. In 1801, Jacquard had devised a system of punched cards to automate the workings of a weaving loom. The patterns of the holes punched into the cards determined which threads the loom wove into the pattern of the fabric (see Figure 2.8). The patterns of the holes in Babbage's cards were to represent mathematical symbols. In the words of Ada, Countess of Lovelace, "The Analytical Engine *weaves algebraic patterns* just as the Jacquard-loom weaves flowers and leaves." That was by no means all that this remarkable woman had to say about the Analytical Engine. It is, in fact, because of her that we know as much about Babbage's invention as we do.

Ada, portrayed in Figure 2.9, was the only legitimate daughter of the English poet Lord Byron. She and Babbage first met in 1833, when she was eighteen years old and he forty-one. Ada, ever a strong-minded sort, was determined to become a mathematician, and she saw in Babbage her ideal teacher. Her working relationship with Babbage began nine years

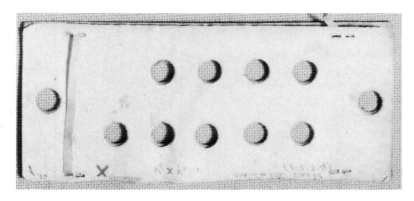

Figure 2.7
Charles Babbage and his inventions: (*top left*) the Analytical Engine, a general-purpose computer; (*bottom right*) the Difference Engine, a special-purpose computer; (*above*) the punched card used for input.
Courtesy of Trustees of the Science Museum (London).

**Figure 2.8
Jacquard's loom.**
Courtesy of Trustees of the Science Museum (London).

after their first meeting, when she translated a French article that summarized a series of lectures that Babbage had given in 1840. Babbage was so impressed with her insights that he encouraged her to add some notes to the translation. The "notes" ultimately became three times as long as the translation. The perceptions that they recorded — that the Analytical Engine could not originate or anticipate anything but could only do what people instructed it to do — have earned Ada the title of the world's first computer programmer.

Despite Ada's competent assistance and her dedication to the project until her death in 1852, Babbage was never able to raise the money to finish constructing the machine. He died in 1871, a man born a few generations too early. Ironically, in the same year, his son finished constructing the model of the Analytical Engine shown in Figure 2.7. The model was housed in the Science Museum in London. Consigned to a museum, Babbage's ideas quickly lapsed into obscurity. And there they remained for almost seventy years, until a new generation of scientists, working under a compelling new kind of impetus and with a new kind of technology, discovered that Babbage, with all his clanking mechanical parts, had been there before them.

Before we leap into the twentieth century, one further data processing development of the nineteenth century deserves comment. In 1887, the U.S. Census Bureau realized it was facing a problem of enormous proportions. In that year, it had finally finished tabulating the results of the 1880 census.

**Figure 2.9
Ada, Countess of Lovelace.**
Courtesy of Trustees of the Science Museum (London).

Figure 2.10

Hollerith's tabulating machine. Data are recorded on cards as punched holes. To "read" the data, Hollerith's machine used a system of sensing pins. When the pins made contact with an electrically charged mercury bath, the electrical charges were recorded as movements on counting dials connected to the sensing pins.
Courtesy of Trustees of the Science Museum (London).

With the waves of immigration to the United States not receding and the population continuing to grow at a rapid rate, it seemed likely that tabulation of the 1890 census would not be completed before the 1900 census was due to begin. The bureau's solution was to hold a contest in which entrants submitted methods of speeding the counting process. The winner was one Herman Hollerith, who was later to form the company that ultimately became IBM. Hollerith's machine, like Jacquard's and Babbage's, used a system of punched cards (see Figure 2.10). The important difference was that it made use of a new technology: electricity. So effective was this machine that an unofficial count of the population was announced just six weeks after the 1890 census ended. A new era in data processing had begun.

The Great Depression

Dismayed by government politics and seeing the commercial possibilities of his data processing equipment, Hollerith left the Census Bureau to establish his own company shortly after the official results of the 1890 census were announced. Known as the Tabulating Machine Company, Hollerith's firm produced equipment used in computing and monitoring the schedules of railroad boxcars. In 1924, after a series of mergers, the Tabulating

HUMAN REACTIONS TO HUMAN INVENTIONS

It is about as reasonable to blame computers for causing the world's social ills as it is to blame a hammer for hitting your thumb or a car for running out of gas; it is nonetheless a fairly common practice. And it's not a new one either. People have been reacting to new technologies in curious ways—from sabotage to scapegoating—for centuries.

SABOTAGE

In early nineteenth-century Europe, the introduction of Jacquard's automated loom created a furor among textile workers. Fearing that they would lose their jobs, the textile workers expressed their anger by throwing their wooden shoes, known as *sabots*, into the loom. From actions such as these, the French verb *saboter*, meaning to clatter one's wooden shoes, took on another meaning: to work clumsily, to bungle, or to botch. And it is from that meaning that the English word *sabotage* is derived.

Recent history abounds with tales of sabotage against computers. Disgruntled former employees, persons convinced that the computer will create a depersonalized world in which human rights are a thing of the past, and protesters of various stripes and convictions have bombed, knifed, and shot at computer systems.

FROM SUPERLATIVES TO SKEPTICISM

In the middle years of the nineteenth century, Ada, Countess of Lovelace, commented on some other curious human reactions to human inventions:

It is desirable to guard against... exaggerated ideas that might arise as to the powers of the Analytical Engine. In considering any new subject, there is... a tendency, first to overrate *what we find... interesting or remarkable; and, secondly, by a sort of natural reaction, to* undervalue *the true... case, when we... discover that our notions have surpassed those that were really tenable.*

The tendency to overrate the powers of the modern Analytical Engine has been a matter of great concern to computer scientist Joseph Weizenbaum. His concern began in the mid-1960s when he wrote an experimental program in which the computer plays the role of psychotherapist. For example, you might key into the computer terminal the phrase, "I am feeling sad today." The computer would respond, "Why are you feeling sad today?" Or you might comment about your older sister. The computer would reply, "Tell me more about your family."

When some psychiatrists suggested to Weizenbaum that he develop the program and make it available so that people could have access to inexpensive "automated psychotherapy," he was very much disturbed. When he came into his office one day to find his secretary having a "conversation" with the computer, so intense that she asked him to leave the room, his alarm grew. It seemed to him that these people could not distinguish between a machine and a human being, or, as he put it in the title of one of his books, between "computer power and human reason."

SCAPEGOATING

Herman Hollerith's experience with the U.S. Census Bureau at the end of the nineteenth century illustrates yet another strange way in which people may react to new technologies. Using Hollerith's tabulating machine, the bureau was able to process the 1890 census data and to make an official announcement of the results in less than one-third the time it had taken to complete the 1880 census. Yet despite the success of his machine, Herman Hollerith did not leave the Census Bureau entirely of his own volition.

The trouble began when the results of the census disagreed with the claims of politicians that the population of the United States in 1890 was 65 million; the census put the figure at some 2 million less. The tabulating machine that made use of that mysterious new technology—electricity—was an easy and obvious scapegoat for the discrepancy. A loud public outcry claiming that the tabulations were inaccurate ensued, and Hollerith, together with his machines, departed from the Census Bureau shortly thereafter. The data for the next census were tabulated on mechanical devices that made no use whatsoever of that strange new demon, electricity.

◆

Machine Company emerged in conglomerate form as the International Business Machines Corporation — IBM. Just a few years later, in 1929, the world, reverberating from the devastating echoes of the stock market crash, entered the gloom of the Great Depression.

Ironically, the Great Depression was to become the force that would give companies like IBM, which were devoted to the manufacture of tabulating machines, their greatest boost. One of the first major pieces of legislation that Franklin Delano Roosevelt sponsored after his election to the presidency in 1933 created the Social Security Administration — and with it the need to process millions of records. This ready-made market was a critical component in the success of companies like IBM. It also established a "need" that was, in effect, to finance much of the experimentation on computers that took place some twenty years later. In the meantime, however, another force was at work.

The War Years

In the late 1930s, the clouds of World War II were looming ever closer, and with them the need for a new kind of data processing. It is an interesting footnote to history that by 1940, two young Germans — Konrad Zuse and Helmut Schreyer — had worked out all the ideas necessary for constructing a fully electronic computer. In that year, they suggested to the German authorities the usefulness of a high-speed computer in cracking enemy codes. Because Hitler believed the war already won, projects of a long-term nature were not being approved; so Zuse and Schreyer were turned down. And Hitler might have been right about the outcome of the war, had the British not at that moment been devoting an enormous effort to developing special-purpose computers to crack the German codes. The result of the British effort was the *Colossus,* the first electronic, special-purpose digital computer. Ten of these machines were built, and they are credited with having played an indispensable role in the victory of the Allied Forces.

In the meantime, across the Atlantic, a young man by the name of Howard Aiken had begun in 1937 to work toward a Ph.D. in physics at Harvard. Like Babbage, Aiken was spurred by the drudgery of solving lengthy equations to invent a machine that could compute them. But it wasn't until after he had spent about three years working to develop a computer that Aiken came across Babbage's work. When he did, he is reported to have felt that Babbage was addressing him personally with these words:

> If unwarned by my example, any man shall succeed in constructing an engine embodying in itself the whole of the executive department of mathematical analysis . . . I have no fear of leaving my reputation in his charge, for he alone will be able fully to appreciate the nature of my efforts and the value of their results.

Aiken, in fact, used this quotation to begin the operating manual for the *Mark I,* the general-purpose computer that was the outcome of his work. The Mark I was an electromechanical device — that is, it had mechanical arithmetic counters that were electronically controlled.

The Mark I was remarkable for several reasons. For one thing, it marked the entry of IBM into the computer field. Aiken had approached Thomas J. Watson, Sr., the "old man" of IBM, with a carefully worked-out proposal, and Watson, in one of the instant, autocratic decisions for which he was famous, granted him more than half a million dollars. With the outbreak of war, Aiken became a naval lieutenant, but the Navy, recognizing the potential usefulness of the Mark I, assigned him to the task of completing the computer's construction.

Another remarkable feature of the Mark I was its appearance (see Figure 2.11). Fifty-five feet long, eight feet high, and containing almost a million components, it was encased in gleaming stainless steel and glass and staffed by uniformed servicemen who appeared to be running it while standing at attention. Because of all its mechanical parts, it was also rather remarkable to listen to. According to Jeremy Bernstein, a physicist and writer who was then a student at Harvard, "The gentle clicking . . . sounded like a roomful of ladies knitting."

By the time the Mark I was put into operation at Harvard in 1944, it was virtually obsolete, for, in the meantime, the war effort had spurred

Figure 2.11
The Mark I.
Courtesy of Cruft Photo Lab, Harvard University. Photographed by Paul Donaldson.

the development of a fully electronic computer (see Figure 2.12). The Electronic Numerical Integrator and Calculator, or *ENIAC*, as the new computer was called, was developed to speed up the computations needed to compile firing tables for guns and other artillery. It was the result of the feverish work of teams from the Moore School of Engineering at the University of Pennsylvania and from the U.S. Army weapons-proving grounds at Aberdeen, Maryland. The ENIAC was the brainchild of John Mauchly and J. Presper Eckert of the Moore School. These men were in turn indebted to the ideas of John Atanasoff, a professor of physics at Iowa State University, who, with the assistance of his student, Clifford Berry, had in 1937 begun developing an electronic, special-purpose computer to solve complex equations. Work on the ENIAC began in 1943, but despite a twenty-four-hour-a-day effort for thirty months, it was not put into operation until February 1946 — too late to help the war effort.

Figure 2.12
The ENIAC.
Courtesy of Sperry Corporation.

The ENIAC was an even more massive affair than the Mark I. Operating on some 18,000 vacuum tubes, it was fully electronic, as was the British Colossus. Both machines were thus much faster than the electromechanical Mark I, and the ENIAC was the fastest of the three. It could compute in three-thousandths of a second what it took the Mark I three seconds to do. While the Colossus was a special-purpose computer, the ENIAC was a general-purpose, programmable computer — in theory, at least. One of its chief problems was that to switch from one program to another, part of the machine had to be disassembled and completely rewired — a slow and tedious process. The solution to this problem was a key to the development of computers as we know them today, and it seems to have come about — or at least been hastened — by a chance meeting.

One day in the summer of 1944, First Lieutenant Herman Goldstine, in prewar days an assistant professor of mathematics at the University of Michigan and now heading the Moore School's ENIAC team, was waiting for a train near the Aberdeen proving grounds. Also waiting was one John von Neumann, a Hungarian-born scientist whose genius seems to have inspired an affectionate awe among his colleagues (see Figure 2.13). (In describing von Neumann's phenomenal intellectual powers, one colleague is reported to have said, "You see, Johnny wasn't human. But after living with humans for so long, he learned to do a remarkable imitation of one.") Since von Neumann was a consultant at Aberdeen, in addition to being involved in the top-secret design of nuclear weapons at Los Alamos, he and Goldstine knew each other slightly. To while away the time, they struck up a conversation. When von Neumann heard about the computer underway, he immediately saw its potential, and Goldstine described him as jumping "into electronic computers with both feet."[1]

Figure 2.13
John von Neumann. Von Neumann's concept of the stored program was the conceptual leap needed to propel computers into the world of commerce.
UPI/Bettmann Newsphotos.

The result of this conversation was that von Neumann came up with two ideas that were to transform the future development of computers. One was the concept of the **stored program** — the idea that rather than having to rewire the machine each time you wanted to change a program, you could simply store the program in the computer, encoding it the same way the stored data were encoded and keeping it in the computer for as long as it was needed. The computer itself, with its great speed, could then be instructed to switch the programs, and the programs themselves could even call for interaction with other programs. Von Neumann's other idea was to use the *binary numbering system* in the design of computers. As we noted in Chapter 1, the binary numbering system has only two digits — 0 and 1; the decimal system, of course, has ten — those from 0 to 9. Basic electronic components have something in common with the binary system: They have only two positions, or modes of operation (e.g., a vacuum tube can be only on or off). Because these two positions correspond to the binary digits 0 and 1, using the binary system in place of the decimal system greatly simplified the process of designing computers.

---

[1]Jeremy Bernstein, *The Analytical Engine: Computers — Past, Present, and Future* (New York: Random House, 1967), p. 59.

Figure 2.14
The EDSAC. Completed by British scientists in 1949, the EDSAC was the first stored-program computer.
Courtesy of Trustees of the Science Museum (London).

By the time von Neumann had fully developed these ideas, it was too late to incorporate them in the ENIAC, which was well on its way to completion. The first computer to use von Neumann's ideas was the British-built *EDSAC* (Electronic Delay Storage Automatic Computer), which was completed in 1949 (see Figure 2.14). It was followed a few months later by the *EDVAC* (Electronic Discrete Variable Automatic Computer), the Moore School's version of a stored-program computer.

First-Generation Computers: 1951–1958

From von Neumann's contributions, it was a fairly easy leap to the so-called first generation of computers. Believing that the computer had great commercial promise, Mauchly and Eckert, the developers of the ENIAC, left the University of Pennsylvania and founded a firm to build and market this electronic marvel. They called their computer *UNIVAC* (Universal Automatic Computer). The installation of the first UNIVAC at the U.S. Census Bureau in 1951 marked the advent of the first generation of computers—and of the Computer Age. The UNIVAC was not only the first commercially built computer; it was also the first computer developed for business data processing rather than military or scientific use (see Figure 2.15).

Although most first-generation computers were oriented to scientific applications, the UNIVAC was otherwise fairly typical of these early computers, all of which had certain drawbacks in common. First, they were expensive to buy and to maintain, and only large firms and research organizations

Figure 2.15
The UNIVAC.
Courtesy of Sperry Corporation.

could afford them. Maintenance was expensive because they ran on vacuum tubes, often as many as 20,000 of them. This meant that they consumed prodigious amounts of energy; it also meant that a staff of people had to be employed to change the tubes when they burned out. The problem was not so much changing the tubes as it was locating which ones were malfunctioning. Because thousands of possibilities had to be investigated, the early computers were *down* more often than they were *up;* that is, more time was spent diagnosing and correcting malfunctions than was spent processing data and producing reports. The vacuum tubes also produced considerable heat, which, in turn, meant the added expense of air-conditioning equipment. Moreover, input and output on punched cards were slow.

Two further drawbacks of first-generation computers were their huge size (owing to the number of vacuum tubes and the wires and switches they used) and the tediousness and complexity of the programming process. All these early machines were programmed in machine language — that is, instructions were coded in the binary digits 0 and 1, which correspond directly to the on and off machine states. To write just one instruction out of the thousands a program could require, a programmer might have to write a string of forty-eight 0's and 1's. The programming process was simplified by the development of **assembly language,** which began in the early 1950s. Assembly language uses letter codes (also called **mneumonics**) to communicate with the computer (see Figure 2.16). However, since the computer itself can't recognize or respond to anything but machine language, some means had to be devised to translate assembly language into machine language. In 1952 at the University of Pennsylvania, Grace Hopper, a pioneer in the programming of computers, came up with the

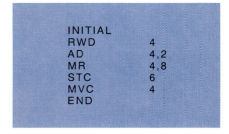

Figure 2.16
Assembly language.

solution: an **assembler** program, which, operating as part of the systems software, uses the computer itself to do the translation.

Despite all the drawbacks of the early computers, business was fairly quick to recognize the advantages of the stored-program computer — its flexibility, speed, and accuracy. Under that commercial impetus, the computer industry has since mushroomed into a giant whose sales exceed $100 billion a year. Research in the industry has proceeded nonstop, and technological change has been the rule rather than the exception. Technological advances in the engineering of the processing hardware and increasing sophistication in the design of the software are, in fact, the usual guidelines for distinguishing between each of the succeeding generations of computers.

Second-Generation Computers: 1959–1964

The research breakthrough that heralded the coming of the second generation of computers was the development of the **transistor** (an acronym for *transfer resistor*) at the Bell Telephone Laboratories. The transistor affected not just the development of the computer; it revolutionized the entire field of electronics. John Bardeen, William Shockley, and Walter H. Brattain, the men who developed the transistor, received the 1956 Nobel Prize in physics for their work.

You're no doubt familiar with the transistor radio. You turn it on, and it responds immediately. But maybe you don't remember the old vacuum-tube radio. You turned it on and waited in suspense while the room crackled with the sound of static as the vacuum tubes warmed up — and the electric meter ticked on. Whereas a vacuum tube relies on the flow of electrons through a vacuum to transmit the electronic signals, a transistor relies on **silicon,** an element abundant in the earth's surface that can act as a semiconductor of electricity. A **semiconductor** conducts electricity (i.e., allows the electricity to pass through it) only when the voltage exceeds a certain level. Because the transistor is made of semiconducting silicon, it can act as a switch that controls the flow of the electrons.

A transistor serves the same function as a vacuum tube — that is, when certain conditions are met, it allows the electronic signal to pass through it. The transistor's great advantages over a vacuum tube are that it takes up much less space and consumes considerably less energy. Because of these characteristics, many transistors can be assembled closely together and connected by flat wires on a *circuit board* (see Figure 2.17). The reduction in the size of the hardware made possible by the transistor meant that the electronic signals had a shorter distance to travel; as a result, computers were able to operate at faster speeds. But even more important than speed was the increase in *reliability* that the transistor brought to computing: Reduced energy requirements and the generation of less heat meant that transistors lasted much longer than vacuum tubes; so, computer performance improved appreciably.

Figure 2.17
The manufacture of a circuit board.
Courtesy of Perkin-Elmer Corporation.

Another major advance during this period was the development of **high-level languages.** The first of these programming languages was FORTRAN (FORmula TRANslator), which was designed for writing scientific programs. COBOL (COmmon Business-Oriented Language), designed for business data processing applications, followed shortly thereafter. Grace Hopper, the developer of the first assembler program, was instrumental in the development of COBOL as well.

Because high-level languages are more like everyday human language than the abbreviated assembly language, they are even easier for people to learn and use (see Figure 2.18). They thus represented yet another shortcut in ways of communicating with the computer. Once again, of course, there had to be a means of translating into machine language. This task fell to groups of programming experts, who wrote long series of instructions telling the computer how to translate each of these high-level languages into machine language. These instructions are called **compiler** programs, and, like an assembler, they are part of the systems software. Once the computer has been fed a specific compiler program, it can "speak" the language without ever making a mistake.

Before the development of high-level languages, each computer manufacturer relied on a unique language for the programming of each series of its computer equipment. Thus, to program different makes of computers, a programmer had to know each of the different languages. At the same time, hardware was developing rapidly, and firms were changing equipment rather frequently. Each time the equipment changed, and each time a programmer changed jobs, the programmer usually had to learn a new language. Because almost all computer manufacturers adopted the high-

```
PROCEDURE DIVISION
    OPEN INPUT  INVENTORY-INPUT-FILE
         OUTPUT INVENTORY-OUTPUT-FILE
    READ INVENTORY-INPUT-FILE
        AT END
            MOVE "NO" TO ARE-THERE-RECORDS
                    (a)
```

```
      READ (4,10) INVENTORY
 10 FORMAT (I8)
      CURINV = INVENTORY – TRANS
      WRITE (2,20) CURINV
 20 FORMAT (10X, "THE CURRENT INVENTORY IS", I8)
                    (b)
```

Figure 2.18
High-level languages: (*a*) COBOL; (*b*) FORTRAN.

level languages as they appeared, programmers were now able to program different makes of equipment using the same language. In short, programming languages had become *standardized*. The skills of the programmer were transportable from job to job, and individual businesses were spared the expense of having to train programmers in the language of their computer systems. Also, firms could use the software developed in a **standardized programming language** with a variety of computer equipment.

Third-Generation Computers: 1965–1970

During the 1960s, interest in the U.S. space program provided an impetus for continued research aimed at creating smaller and more compact computer systems. Out of this research came the **integrated circuit,** which ushered in the third generation of computers. An integrated circuit is created by etching the design of the electronic circuits on a small silicon chip (see Figure 2.19). Because the circuits are etched and the components on the chip are fused as the chip is produced, no wires or soldered connections are needed as they are for a transistor. Thus, with precise manufacturing procedures, the chips can be very small and yet contain hundreds or even thousands of circuits. Figure 2.20 shows the decrease in the size of hardware components between the first and third generations of computers.

The reduced size of integrated circuits meant an increase in speed, and the absence of wires and soldered connections meant that energy consumption and heat generation were further reduced. These factors led to increased reliability and more compact physical units. Moreover, because integrated circuits were manufactured as total units rather than as parts and pieces assembled at a later stage, they were, in effect, mass-produced. For this reason, the price of computers fell.

Figure 2.19

The design of an integrated circuit. Before a chip is etched, its design is laid out; the device being used here to aid in the design is known as a "digitizer."
Courtesy of Sperry Corporation.

Because of the decrease in cost, many medium-sized and small businesses could now afford to buy computers, and the market was thus fast becoming a "mass" one. Partially in response to the decrease in cost, a new force entered the market during this time: a special-purpose computer known as a **minicomputer.** The traditional large-scale computers (known as

Figure 2.20

The decreasing size of hardware components between the first and third generations of computers: vacuum tube compared with chip.
Courtesy of National Semiconductor Corporation.

mainframes) were very expensive, costing hundreds of thousands of dollars and requiring highly trained specialists to run them. There was a need for a more modest system, especially one that could control production equipment. Minicomputers were introduced to meet this need and quickly found a place in monitoring microfilm equipment, the energy and heating systems of large buildings, and many machine tools used in manufacturing. It was only natural that minicomputers would eventually find their way into the more traditional data processing applications of business.

A key difference between minicomputers and mainframes is that minicomputers are commonly interactive-processing rather than batch-processing devices. *Interactive,* as you may remember from Chapter 1, means that the data are processed as the transaction takes place. For example, a sensor monitors heat in a section of a building, and the minicomputer constantly compares the actual temperature with the desired temperature. When a significant deviation occurs, the minicomputer causes the heating system to channel warm or cool air to the area. In contrast, the large-scale computers have traditionally operated in a batch mode; that is, they process the data as a group after the transactions occur. Batch processing is very efficient, but interactive processing offers significant advantages when immediacy of results is important.

Fourth-Generation Computers: 1971–?

No dramatic change in technology, such as the development of the transistor or the integrated circuit, heralded the arrival of the fourth generation of computers. The choice of the year 1971 to mark the beginning of this generation is therefore somewhat arbitrary. The technology of these computers is the same as that of the third generation — the integrated circuit. What does set this generation apart from preceding ones is the continuing and highly successful trend toward miniaturization, which has led to a startling increase in computer use. By the early 1970s, techniques of **large-scale integration (LSI)** had made it possible to cram as many as 64,000 electronic circuits onto a single silicon chip. LSI soon moved on to **VLSI (very large scale integration),** which ultimately produced the rather amazing chip shown in Figure 2.21.

The miniaturization of hardware components was the factor that led to yet another important technological development, this one concerned not with the density of the circuits on a chip but with the architecture of the chip. In 1969, Ted Hoff, a young engineer at Intel Corporation, began working on the idea of placing all the processing circuits of a computer on one chip. Until that time, separate chips had been needed for each function. The result of Hoff's idea was the **microprocessor,** a single silicon chip, smaller than a postage stamp, which contains the circuitry for the arithmetic/logic unit, the control unit, and very often the primary storage

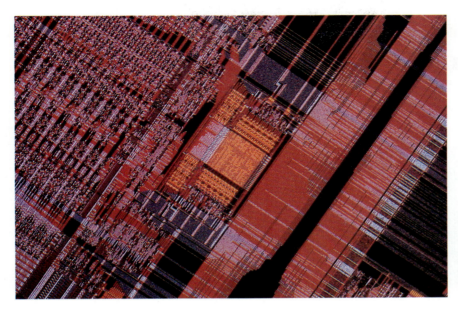

Figure 2.21
A chip made with VLSI techniques. This microprocessor chip has more computing power than a minicomputer.
Courtesy of AT&T Bell Laboratories.

unit as well. It was this development that ensured that the market for computers would become truly a mass one. When Intel began selling the microprocessor chip in 1971, it aptly described the versatile new product as the "computer on a chip." Microprocessors were soon in evidence everywhere, from wristwatches and microwave ovens to jetliners and spacecraft.

The microprocessor chip may be supported by additional memory chips, communications control chips, and input/output control chips. All these chips can be packaged as a single unit called a **microcomputer,** and if it were not necessary to see the output or to use your fingers to enter the input, the whole system could be contained in a unit the size of your thumbnail. Although many of these microcomputers are as powerful as the large computers of a generation ago, they sell for thousands rather than millions of dollars.

With about two hundred brands of microcomputers currently in existence, less than a dozen different microprocessor chips are used in all microcomputers. Many of these systems seem to be almost clones of the more popular brands, using not only the same microprocessor chip but also the same input/output control chips. The differences among microcomputer systems are not in how they process data but in how the electronics are packaged. The appearance of the microprocessor chip meant that for the first time it was easy to move into the computer business: No research and development expenditures were necessary; manufacturing computers became a matter of designing a cabinet and assembling standard parts.

FROM HOBBY KITS TO APPLES:
The Impact of the Microprocessor Chip

Although Ted Hoff's microprocessor chip was the spark that set the microcomputer phenomenon in motion, it was a few years before that spark really caught fire. The first microcomputers that were built around the microprocessor chips were sold not as assembled units but as kits. You could buy the basic kit for about $400 but had to spend another couple of thousand dollars on peripheral equipment to make the unit workable. Because of the lack of software to make the microcomputer useful and the necessity of assembling the parts yourself, micros remained pretty much a hobbyist's toy for several years after the kits first appeared. By the mid-1970s, however, several young entrepreneurs, operating on shoestring budgets, were providing the fuel needed to ignite the spark.

The birth of the Apple computer in a Los Altos, California, garage typifies the way the microcomputer explosion was launched. In 1976, Steve Jobs and Steve Wozniak, then both in their twenties and eager to buy a microcomputer kit but unable to afford one, managed to get hold of a number of microprocessors for the sum of $20. With the microprocessors in hand and with the "loan" of some electronic parts from the computer companies where they worked, Jobs and Wozniak set about building their own computer in Jobs's parents' garage. The actual construction took about sixty hours.

When Jobs and Wozniak showed their Apple I to a computer club meeting on the Stanford University campus, several of their friends decided they had to have one. As a result, Jobs and Wozniak found themselves spending all their nights and weekends helping their friends build computers. To reduce construction time, they needed money to pay someone to design a printed circuit board for the computer. Together, they raised $1,300, Jobs by selling his Volkswagen and Wozniak by selling his calculator. With the printed circuit board, they were able to build a computer in just six hours.

Although Jobs and Wozniak's expectation was that by building 100 computers and selling them for $50 each, they'd make just about enough money to buy back the VW and the calculator, they had in fact launched the microcomputer explosion. In June 1976, they sold fifty fully assembled Apple computers to a local retail computer store; by 1983, Apple Computer had made the Fortune 500 list.

Source of data: Everett M. Rogers and Judith K. Larsen, *Silicon Valley Fever* (New York: Basic Books, 1984), pp. 4–11.

Table 2.1 summarizes some of the remarkable changes that have taken place in computers over the past thirty-five years. More remarkable changes are no doubt yet to come. Although the fifth generation of computers has not yet arrived, intense research into the hardware and software requirements of this future generation is currently underway; the research is particularly intense in Japan, where it has received a good deal of government support. The development of a machine capable of responding with humanlike judgment and of solving problems that appear to require human intelligence — a phenomenon known as **artificial intelligence (AI)** — will signal the arrival of the fifth-generation computer. The obstacles to be overcome in developing such a machine are many. For the computer to respond with apparent common sense to a variety of changing situations, it will have to be programmed to program itself. It will also need quick access to a vast

Table 2.1 Characteristics of Four Generations of Computers

Characteristics	First Generation	Second Generation	Third Generation	Fourth Generation
Hardware characteristics	Vacuum tubes Punched-card-oriented	Transistors Magnetic-tape-oriented	Integrated circuits Disk-oriented	Very large scale integrated circuits Microprocessor chips Terminal-oriented
Size (circuits per cubic foot)	Thousands	Hundreds of thousands	Millions	Billions
Reliability (average operating time between failures)	Minutes or hours	Hours to tens of hours	Tens of hours to hundreds of hours	Hundreds of hours to thousands of hours
Primary storage capacity	Thousands of characters	Tens of thousands of characters	Hundreds of thousands of characters	Millions of characters
Programming (languages and software)	Machine language Assembly language	FORTRAN COBOL	Report-generating languages	Consumer-oriented software (word processing and financial analysis)
Cost (to process 1 million instructions)	$30.00	$1.00	$.10	$.001
Speed (time to process 1 million instructions)	Hundreds of seconds	Tens of seconds	About 1 second	A fraction of a second

amount of information. Organizing and storing this huge quantity of information, as well as providing a fast and efficient means of access to it, will require dramatic increases in memory capacity and processing speed. Once such a machine has been developed, the ways in which it might be used would seem almost limitless. Progress in AI research is already evident in the use of computer systems to aid in medical diagnosis, chemical analysis, and circuit design.

TODAY'S COMPUTERS AND HOW WE USE THEM

Today's computers come in a variety that most people in 1951 could not have imagined. The consensus at that time was that the future of computers was limited. Because of their large size and expense, even such an astute observer as IBM's Thomas J. Watson, Sr., doubted there would ever be a mass market for them. Of course, in 1951, it was all but impossible to foresee that technological advances would continually improve the hardware and that with improved reliability would come broadened market opportunities.

Today, computers range in price from under a hundred dollars to several million dollars. They may occupy a portion of a briefcase or a room

Table 2.2 Characteristics of the Main Types of Computer Systems

Computer Type	Approximate Size	Cost	Processing Speed	Primary Storage Capacity
Supercomputer	Volkswagen bus	$5,000,000–$20,000,000	20–100+ MIPS*	5–40M†
Mainframe	Refrigerator	$250,000–$5,000,000	1–15 MIPS	4–20M
Minicomputer	Washing machine	$10,000–$250,000	$\frac{1}{2}$–2 MIPS	1–8M
Microcomputer	Typewriter	$100–$10,000	Under $\frac{1}{2}$ MIPS	64k‡–1M

* MIPS = million instructions per second.
† M = millions of characters.
‡ k = thousands of characters.

the size of a basketball court. They are used for everything from playing games to assisting in brain surgery. It is harder to think of one area in which they are not used than of twenty-five in which they are. Even Charles Babbage, who in his visionary way noted that "once an Analytical Engine exists, it will necessarily guide the future course of science," might have been startled at just how far-reaching the effects of the twentieth-century Analytical Engine are. Many people today feel that the limit of applying computers is the limit of the human mind.

Today's computers are generally divided into four categories according to processing speed, storage capacity, physical size, and cost. These categories are the **supercomputers,** developed during the 1960s and 1970s as outsized spin-offs of the traditional, large-scale mainframes; the mainframes; the minicomputers; and the increasingly ubiquitous microcomputers. The divisions between these categories are somewhat arbitrary, as there can be considerable overlap between them. For example, the most powerful minicomputer may have more storage capacity and may cost as much as the least powerful mainframe. Generally, however, the larger the computer, the more processing capabilities it has and the more expensive it is. Table 2.2 summarizes the four categories of computers in terms of their size, cost, speed, and storage capacity.

Supercomputers

At the top of the computer hierarchy is the supercomputer, the biggest, fastest, and most expensive of them all. The Cray-1 is perhaps the best known of the supercomputers; over forty of these machines are currently in operation throughout the world. A more recent addition to the Cray line is the Cray X-MP, which is shown in Figure 2.22. Capable of performing

Figure 2.22
A Cray X-MP. Technicians check out the machine during installation. It can process an estimated 400 million mathematical calculations per second.
Courtesy of Boeing Computer Services.

100 million or more operations per second and with a price tag often exceeding $5 million, supercomputers are not for everyone. In fact, only a few organizations need or can support such powerful computing — for example, scientific laboratories such as the Los Alamos National Laboratory; the National Aeronautics and Space Administration (NASA); the Defense Department; commercial airlines that sell tickets and book seats on thousands of flights throughout the country and the world every day; firms that do

engineering research, especially in geologic and petroleum exploration; and companies that produce high-quality, computer-generated graphics such as cartoon movies and cinematic special effects. Figure 2.23 shows a few of the outputs and uses of supercomputers.

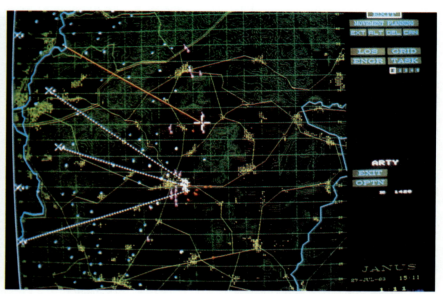
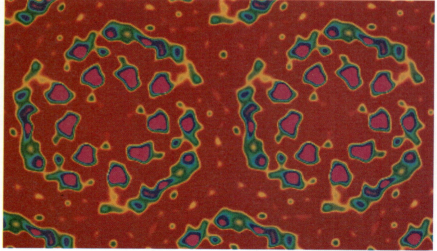

Figure 2.23
Supercomputer applications: (*left*) satellite launching; (*top right*) military command control; (*bottom right*) computer-generated image of DNA structure.
Photos provided courtesy of (left) SBS (Satellite Business Systems); (top right) Ramtek Corporation; (bottom right) Lawrence Berkeley Laboratory, University of California.

Mainframes

When processing requirements include the need for large memory capacities, complex processing capabilities, and high speed, today's mainframe computers are very functional and cost-effective. Smaller than supercomputers but still very powerful — capable of processing up to 15 million instructions per second — these computer systems are applied to a wide range of processing activities. Mainframes are used for scientific research at universities and hospitals, for high-volume data processing at commercial banks, and for the very complex data processing that large business and government organizations require (see Figure 2.24). Because they are capable of processing a number of jobs simultaneously, mainframes can service several hundred terminals, all operating at the same time.

Minicomputers

As we noted earlier, minicomputers were initially designed in the mid-1960s as special-purpose computers for use in such applications as monitoring the machine tools used in factories. Since then, they have evolved into very useful general-purpose computers. Their significant processing power, coupled with a lower cost and smaller physical size than the mainframe, makes them affordable, cost-effective investments for small businesses and public agencies.

Figure 2.24
Mainframe applications: (*left*) terminals in a financial market; (*right*) air traffic control.
Courtesy of (left) Perkin-Elmer Corporation; (right) Sperry Corporation.

Figure 2.25
Minicomputers at work in the factory: (*above*) controlling the manufacturing system from the office; (*right*) controlling the machines.
Courtesy of (above) The Foxboro Company; (right) Digital Equipment Corporation.

Today, minicomputers are found in a wide variety of settings. As Figure 2.25 shows, they continue to be useful in the manufacturing setting. They are also used to process accounting records for small businesses, to handle workstations for word processing and data entry in both business and government offices, and to manage the heating, cooling, lighting, and energy requirements of large office buildings and hospitals.

Microcomputers

To describe the impact of the microcomputer as explosive is perhaps to understate the case. Microcomputers are everywhere — in homes, schools, libraries, large businesses, small businesses, dentists' offices, auto parts stores, stockbrokers' offices, and insurance companies. As personal computers, they are used for playing games, balancing checkbooks, writing letters, linking into stock market reports and other data and educational services, recording tax-deductible items, and storing kitchen recipes. The last might be done more efficiently and economically with a pencil and some 3-by-5-inch index cards — but novelty does have its charms. Novelty also wears off, which may be one of the factors that caused the sales of microcomputers to fall off in 1985. Despite that decline, there is no question that microcomputers have been meeting, and will continue to meet, a very real business need.

Small businesses in which the amount of input data is limited and processing speed is not a critical factor have found microcomputer systems extremely valuable tools, especially in the realm of finance. With an **electronic spreadsheet** (a microcomputer program for manipulating accounting data), managers can evaluate how possible business decisions would affect a company's financial performance. Given a "what-if" approach and the appropriate data on projected expenses, revenues, and so on, the microcomputer is capable of generating probable financial outcomes. Among the many other uses to which small businesses put the microcomputer are preparation of mailing lists, standard letters, customer documents, and tax records. Figure 2.26 shows just two of the many ways in which microcomputers are used.

Amazingly, all this computing power comes from a single silicon microprocessor chip smaller than a postage stamp. But perhaps the most amazing thing of all is that we may have just scratched the surface of the possible uses of micros. It is quite possible that in the not-too-distant future many thousands of people will use microcomputer systems to do much of their banking and shopping and that an increasing number of people will "telecommute" to work — that is, rather than physically getting into their cars and driving to an office, they will do their jobs at home, using a microcomputer and a communications link to their company's mainframe. Never in history has a new machine made so great an impact in so short a time. We will discuss the microcomputer phenomenon in more detail in Chapter 10.

Figure 2.26
Microcomputer applications.
Courtesy of Apple Computer, Inc.

SUMMARY

Processing data is not a new concept: People have been keeping accounts for thousands of years, and they have used a variety of labor-saving devices to help them do so. Two very old such devices are the abacus and the quipu. The first mechanical data processing device — the Pascaline — was invented during the Scientific Revolution of the 1600s, which saw the invention of several other data processing devices as well. During the nineteenth century, Charles Babbage and Herman Hollerith greatly advanced the concept of using machines to assist in the processing of data.

The evolution of the computer accelerated during the twentieth century as a result of efforts to meet the processing needs created by the Great Depression and World War II. Perhaps the most significant computing developments during the 1940s were the concept of the stored program advanced by John von Neumann and the building of the electronic computer ENIAC by Mauchly and Eckert. These efforts ultimately led to the development of the first commercial general-purpose computer, the UNIVAC, which was installed at the U.S. Census Bureau in 1951. This event ushered in the first generation of computers, which ran on vacuum tubes. Assembly language and the first assembler program were developed during this era.

The second generation of computers, introduced in the late 1950s, owed its existence to the development of the transistor. The transistor significantly improved computer performance and reliability. This era also witnessed the creation of the first standardized, high-level programming languages and the first compiler programs.

The third generation of computers, relying on integrated circuits, began about 1965, and it saw the mass production of computers to meet the increased demands of business and government. This was also the time that minicomputers, bringing with them the idea of interactive processing, began to influence the way data were processed. Until then, computing had centered on the batch processing of data.

The fourth generation of computers, dating from the early 1970s, claims the microprocessor, the computer on a chip. Miniaturization of circuits made possible by techniques of large-scale integration allowed an entire arithmetic/logic unit and control unit to be manufactured on a single silicon chip smaller than a postage stamp. Research on the fifth generation of computers, centering on the development of artificial intelligence in a machine, is currently underway. A computer capable of artificial intelligence will require enormous memory and processing capabilities.

Today's computers include supercomputers, the giants of the industry; mainframe computers, the large-scale business systems; minicomputers; and microcomputers. Of these, the microcomputer is having the most dramatic impact on society, bringing computing within a price range that many people can afford while providing the processing capabilities of the mainframes of only a few years ago.

KEY TERMS

artificial intelligence (AI) (54)
assembler (48)
assembly language (47)
compiler (49)
electronic spreadsheet (61)
high-level languages (49)
integrated circuit (50)
large-scale integration (LSI) (52)
mainframes (52)
microcomputer (53)
microprocessor (52)
minicomputer (51)
mneumonics (47)
semiconductor (48)
silicon (48)
standardized programming language (50)
stored program (45)
supercomputers (56)
transistor (48)
very large scale integration (VLSI) (52)

DISCUSSION QUESTIONS

1. Discuss the ways in which three historical events contributed to the development of computers as we know them today.

2. Discuss the contributions of three individuals of the nineteenth century to the evolution of the computer.

3. Identify three individuals who contributed to the development of computers during the twentieth century. What were their ideas?

4. What does the term *computer generations* mean? Describe the characteristics that distinguish each of the computer generations.

5. What was a motivating force behind the early evolution of computers? Is this still a motivating force in the development of computers? Discuss in terms of the possible uses of fifth-generation computers.

6. Why was the development of standardized programming languages important? What might the world be like if there were no standardized human languages?

7. Why would computer reliability be a major concern for businesses that use computers to process their data?

8. Describe some of today's applications for supercomputers, mainframes, minicomputers, and microcomputers.

9. Why have microcomputers made such an impact on society?

10. Do you think the effects of the technological revolution brought about by computers will be as far-reaching as the effects of the Industrial Revolution? Why or why not?

OUTLINE

THE IMPACT OF THE INFORMATION REVOLUTION

COMPUTERIZED INFORMATION: USES AND SOURCES

THE SYSTEMS DEVELOPMENT CYCLE

- Identifying the Need
- Analyzing the System
- Developing Design Alternatives
- Developing the System
- Implementing and Maintaining the System

USING COMPUTER INFORMATION SYSTEMS IN BUSINESS

- Office Automation
- The Computer System as a Managerial Tool
  - Managerial Functions
  - Management Information Systems
  - Data Base Management Systems and Decision Support Systems

SUMMARY

KEY TERMS

DISCUSSION QUESTIONS

OVERVIEW

As you know from Chapter 1, the computer system's whole reason for being is to produce output; and the output that it produces is information. So successful has the computer system been in producing its output that as a society, we've become dependent on computerized information. It has become as vital a force in the decision-making environment as oxygen is in the physical world. Most businesses, for example, have come to rely heavily on computerized information to help them stay alive — figuratively speaking — in a highly competitive and constantly changing world. In other instances, the information the computer produces is quite literally a matter of life or death. When computers are used to aid in navigation of aircraft, planning of military strategies, or medical diagnosis, there's no room for error. This is a sobering thought when you stop to consider the many tales of computer foul-ups that are reported in daily newspapers and weekly magazines. It casts a new and somewhat macabre light on a rather old joke: "To err is human; to really foul up requires a computer."

The ways in which a computer system is developed and used can spell the difference between success and disaster in its operation; management, too, can be a factor. In this chapter, we'll introduce the steps that systems analysts follow in developing a computer information system and explore the ways that businesses use information and computer information systems. Our objectives are to

- explore the impact of the Information Revolution on today's world.

- describe the uses and sources of computerized information.

- discuss the steps involved in the systems development cycle.

- outline the situations in which computer information systems are particularly useful to business and explain why office automation is an increasingly popular phenomenon.

- describe the use of the computer information system as a managerial tool.

CHAPTER 3

DEVELOPING AND USING COMPUTER SYSTEMS IN BUSINESS

THE IMPACT OF THE INFORMATION REVOLUTION

We live in a complex society in which there is continual pressure for more and better information. A number of factors have combined to create this pressure, but probably the most important factors are today's highly efficient communications systems, which can transmit information the moment it is available to most places in the world (and some places out of it), and the computer system itself. In the nineteenth century, the steam engine, feeding on the momentum of its own results, powered the Industrial Revolution and created a demand for more and better machines. With marked similarity, the computer, by virtue of the usefulness of the information it produces, has powered what today is being called an **Information Revolution** and has created a demand for more and better information systems.

What makes computer systems so useful that they have become a revolutionary force? In considering this question, some other interesting parallels between the steam engine and the computer become apparent. Both machines relieved people of a great deal of drudgery—physical drudgery in the nineteenth century and mental drudgery in the twentieth. Computer systems, however, not only relieve a negative aspect of work but also add a positive one: They can be used for the routine, repetitive tasks involved in processing data and as an aid in creative decision making and planning. Their value in providing information for decision making and planning is indicated by an increasing tendency to use the term *computer information system* instead of *data processing system*. Although these two terms are used interchangeably, there is a difference: A computer information system requires hardware, whereas a data processing system processes data into information with or without hardware. In other words, a data processing system may be a computer information system, or it may be a manual information system. (The terms *computer system* and *computer information system* are, of course, also used interchangeably, but they do mean exactly the same thing. The term *system* alone, however, may refer to a program—that is, a functional system; to a series of programs, such as the series of programs that would make up an automated accounting system; or to the computer system.)

Another parallel between the steam engine and the computer is that both proved capable of production on a scale not possible with earlier methods of production—production of goods in the case of the steam engine and production of information in the case of the computer. As people grew accustomed to the results of these new methods, their expectations for more and better products grew; and as these increased expectations were realized, society itself grew ever more complex.

The changes that computer systems have brought about are evident both in the business world and in our personal lives. As individuals, we have come to expect that all the information we receive—from the news in the morning paper to our monthly bank statements—will be accurate, complete, up-to-date if not up-to-the-minute, and delivered on time. For example, we not only expect our electric bills to be prompt and to accurately reflect the consumption of power and the computations that make up the charges; we also expect the electric company to be able to instantly retrieve records of our past bills so that we can check any suspected discrepancy. We rarely stop to consider what a monumental information-handling task this is for a power company that may bill more than half a million customers every month and that may work on a limited budget.

Business today is no longer just a matter of making a deal and delivering the goods. As Figure 3.1 indicates, a number of factors and influences combine to put pressure on businesses to produce information. Not only must a company meet the increased expectations of its customers for more and better information; it must also cope with an unprecedented number of legal requirements, since the government, too, has become accustomed to a new and higher standard of information delivery. These legal requirements include the recordkeeping needed to satisfy regulatory, tax, and human-service agencies. In addition, businesses must observe the many laws pertaining to currency transactions, import and export of goods, tariffs, and sales restrictions on certain types of goods such as high-technology equipment.

Internally, a business must meet the information needs of the four basic organizational components found in any business: administration, production, marketing, and finance. Like legal requirements for information, the information needs of these functional areas of business are not new, but in today's business world, with its rapid communications and computer systems, they are likely to be far more numerous and complex than in the past.

The function of **administration** is to coordinate all the activities of the business to meet a common objective. The information needs of ad-

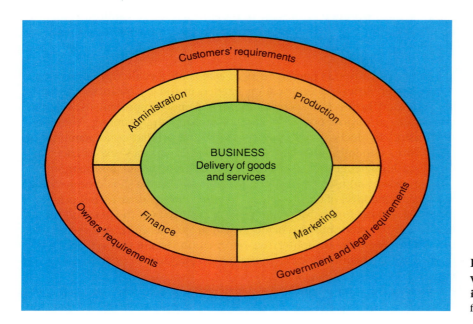

Figure 3.1

Why businesses need to produce information: various factors and influences.

ministration are thus very diverse and include everything from current inventory to the general economic climate in which the business operates. The function of **production** is to manufacture and deliver the company's products. Information needs of production include data on the people, machines, and supplies needed to produce and deliver the goods, as well as details of the work in process and the quality of the finished product. The function of **marketing** is to distribute the products. Information needs here are not so clear, since much of the data must come from observations or evaluations of the competition, as well as from internal operations. For example, in pricing a product, the marketing manager needs information not just on the costs of production, delivery, overhead, administration, and so on, but also on the price charged by the competition. The function of **finance** is to manage the company's funds and to report on how those funds have been applied. In finance as in production, information needs are concise, and the supporting data are derived from the internal operations of the business.

In addition to dealing with complex delivery and production schedules, special orders, pricing competition, and so on, a business must also meet the reporting requirements of its owners, who are often "absentee owners" in the form of corporate stockholders. Such absentee owners rely on information as a substitute for active participation in the firm, much as we, as citizens, rely on the information given us by our elected representatives as a substitute for active participation in government. Businesses must often maintain elaborate and costly reporting systems to meet the needs of absentee owners for information on profits, sales, production, and other operations. Obviously, the volume of information that a large and complex business must produce in this age of the Information Revolution could not be produced by the traditional manual data processing systems of the past.

COMPUTERIZED INFORMATION: USES AND SOURCES

For many companies, a computer system is the only feasible way of producing the complex variety of information needed in today's business world. As we indicated in the last section, one of the most important uses of this computerized information is in decision making and planning. The effectiveness of any decision, whether related to the present or to planning for the future, depends not only on the decision maker's experience and technical knowledge but also on appropriate and useful information. To be appropriate and useful in decision making, information should be *relevant,* at a meaningful level of detail — that is, *complete* yet *concise* — and *accurate.* It should also be *timely,* since if it's not in the hands of the decision maker before the decision must be made, it will go to waste. To gather the data needed to produce computerized information, businesses rely on three main sources: historical data, operational data, and projected data (see Figure 3.2).

Historical data are records of past transactions. They are kept permanently in a company's **archives** to meet long-term recordkeeping re-

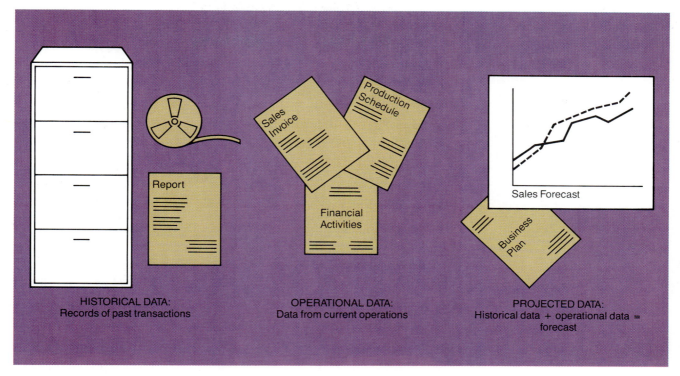

Figure 3.2
Sources of business data: grist for the mill.

quirements, such as customer requests for access to information on past transactions and the recordkeeping requirements of tax agencies and insurance companies. In a manual data processing system, the archives would consist of file cabinets; in a computer system, the archives would be some form of auxiliary storage. Historical data are also useful in business decision making and planning, since to decide a course of action for the future, it's necessary to know what the company has done in the past.

Data from current operations are a business's second main source of information. Such **operational data** are very useful in analyzing a company's present situation. They serve as a basis in making decisions about whether any adjustments in the company's present status are necessary. **Projected data** are the third source of information. They are arrived at mathematically by using historical data as a base and combining those data with current operational data. The resulting projected data are used to forecast the future performance of the firm.

In any data processing operation, there is bound to be some filtering of the data made available to the processing system. **Filtering** means that a part of certain data is not reported or captured, usually for economic reasons. The least amount of filtering takes place with operational data, since they are easily accessible to the organization and are usually quite accurate. Because historical data may be difficult — and therefore costly — to locate and retrieve, they are often filtered. Projected data are the most unreliable kind of data, and they are therefore practically always filtered before being entered into the information system.

Another kind of filtering takes place in the computerized reports used by various levels of management. This kind of filtering is perhaps more accurately described as *summarizing* (see Figure 3.3). At the lowest level of management is the shop supervisor, who is responsible for supervising day-to-day operations and for ordering materials, assigning work teams, and hiring replacement personnel. The shop supervisor needs to know what orders the firm has, which products need to be manufactured first, how many employees will not be available to work so that work schedules can be adjusted accordingly, and a variety of other detailed information. Using operational data, the computer system can produce concise reports of this detailed information. Thus, low-level management's information needs are very efficiently met by the computer system.

Middle-level managers need data consolidated from a number of operations, and the computer system can be a useful tool in assembling and summarizing this information. At times, however, the middle-level manager

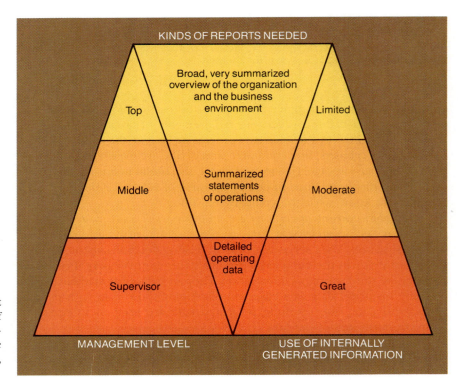

Figure 3.3

The information needs of different levels of managers. The amount of detail needed in a managerial report varies according to managerial level; the farther up the managerial ladder you go, the smaller the need for detail.

needs more than operational or historical data to make a decision and must call upon outside resources. For instance, as we noted earlier, in deciding how to price a product, a marketing manager needs information not only about the cost of manufacturing the product but also about the price charged by the competition; and this latter information cannot be supplied by the firm's computer system. Middle-level managers, then, find their needs for information on which to base decisions less completely met by the computer system than do lower-level managers.

Top-level managers, such as the president and vice-presidents of a company, need even more summarized reports of operating conditions than do middle-level managers, and their needs for decision-related information are usually even more incompletely met by the computer system. Since these managers address decisions about the introduction of new products, creative sources of financing, and new manufacturing technology, they need a broader perspective than can be gleaned from operational or historical data alone. Top-level managers are the firm's planners, and as such, they assemble data from a wide range of sources, most of which are not easily transformed into computerized information. This is one reason that daily and weekly business publications have such a wide circulation among executives. The information provided by such publications gives executives a sense of what is going on around the country and the world.

THE SYSTEMS DEVELOPMENT CYCLE

The preceding sections should have been enough to convince you that the development of a computer information system that can meet the diverse needs of customers, governments, owners, and a company's own information users is not a task to be undertaken lightheadedly or haphazardly. But just in case you remain unconvinced, consider the following anecdotes of errors in systems development:

> A large midwestern university collected over 100,000 documents containing data on patient treatments. A systems analyst was hired to recommend how these data should be converted for producing statistical reports. The systems analyst decided that the best way to handle the data was to enter two fields — type of service and date of service — on punched cards, since punching just these two fields minimized the cost of data entry. After the data cards were punched, the data were virtually useless. Without the patient's I.D. number, there was no way of knowing how many services were for the same person; and without patient type, there was no way of knowing how many of the services were for students, employees, or the public. In short, without additional data, the only information that could be produced was the number and type of services performed each day, each semester, and each year. The money saved in the keying of the data was a foolish savings.
>
> A computer operator was carefully following instructions as he marked the contents of magnetic-tape reels on the reels' labels. The last reel

that he marked contained the company's payroll data. A subsequent deluge of water in the computer room washed off the the water-soluble ink he had used, no instructions existing to tell him to do otherwise. It took about two months to re-create the payroll data, and in the meantime no one in the company got paid.

An upstanding citizen — one of the reviewers of this book, in fact — was denied credit by one of her local department stores because "the computer said" there was a judgment against her. Two weeks and many phone calls later, the store issued her a credit card, apologizing for the "computer's" error. Although no harm was done in this instance —other than the inconvenience that our reviewer suffered — much might have been done in terms of her credit rating.[1]

If we could delve behind the scenes in these situations, tracking down clues as to what went wrong, we would probably find that at least one of the steps that systems analysts customarily follow in developing a computer information system was either omitted or incompletely done. There are five of these steps, and they are collectively known as the **systems development cycle.** They include identifying the need, analyzing the system, developing design alternatives, developing the system, and implementing and maintaining the system. An effective computer information system is not developed by chance; it is the product of careful planning, and the steps of the systems development cycle provide a framework for this planning (see Figure 3.4).

Identifying the Need

Most systems development is initiated by a request from an information user. Changes in legal requirements, the introduction of new company policies or a new product, the acquisition of another company or new hardware, or simply the conviction that there is a better way of producing information for a particular department within the company are just a few of the reasons that an information user might request the development of a new system or a change in an existing one.

The usual response to such a request is for the company's data processing department (also called information systems department) to do a study aimed at identifying and defining the information need and determining whether it's possible for the company to meet this need. This study constitutes the first stage of the systems development cycle.

Conducting this initial study involves preparing a budget, schedule, and plan for the study and getting management approval of these items

---

[1] Our thanks for these anecdotes go to Roger Cook, Southern Illinois University, Carbondale, Illinois; James W. Cox, Lane Community College, Eugene, Oregon; and Jane D. Covillion, Onondaga Community College, Syracuse, New York.

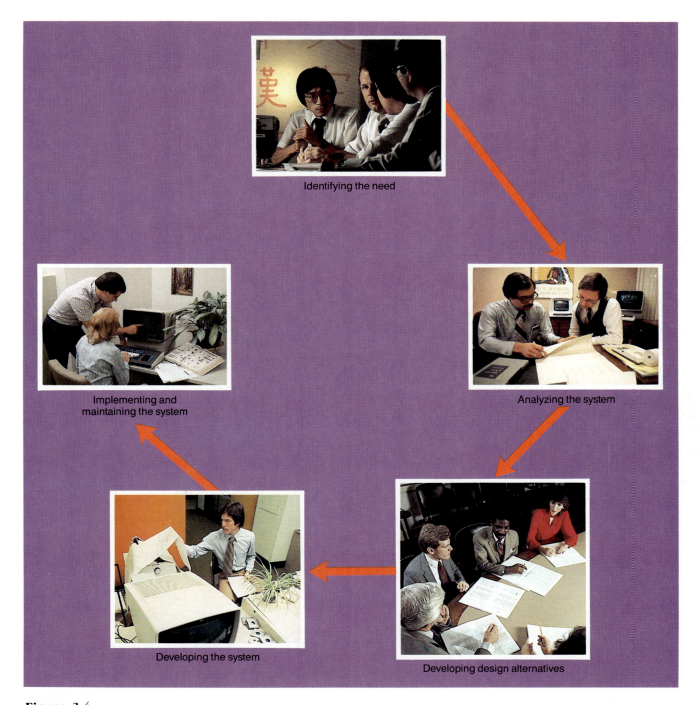

Figure 3.4
The systems development cycle.
Photos (clockwise from top center) courtesy of IBM Corporation; Aetna Life & Casualty; Stacy Pick/Stock, Boston; Aetna Life & Casualty; Perkin-Elmer Corporation.

from the systems users; gathering data to help define the problem and the possibility of solving it; and, after evaluating these data, preparing a **feasibility study,** a document that spells out the findings of the evaluation (see Figure 3.5). The feasibility study does not go into detail about the solution of the problem; it is a "stage-setting" document that describes the initial findings in nontechnical terms that systems users can understand. On the basis of the feasibility study, management (i.e., the systems users) will decide whether to abandon the proposal, gather more data, or proceed to the next step in the systems development cycle.

The requests for systems development and change that a company receives almost always exceed the resources available to implement them. A company must therefore devise a way of evaluating and ranking the usefulness of the proposed systems and systems changes, as well as determining the possibility of implementing them with the resources at hand. The questions addressed in the feasibility study indicate the criteria used:

1. What is the nature of the problem that gave rise to this study, and can a computer be used to solve the problem?
2. Does the company have the technical resources — the hardware and programming skills — needed to solve the problem?
3. Does the proposed system fit into the company's organizational scheme, and does it contribute to the achievement of the company's goals?
4. What are the anticipated costs involved in solving the problem, and what are the benefits of doing so?
5. How much risk does the proposed system entail — that is, what is its potential for success or failure?

Analyzing the System

If management decides to proceed with the project, the systems development cycle enters its second phase. A systems study team (also called a project team) is assembled, and the roles and responsibilities of each team member are defined. Team members usually include systems analysts, programmers, personnel from the auditing department, and information users. The involvement of information users is very important throughout the first three phases of systems development. Since they are the ones who will ultimately use the information that the system generates, their contributions to identifying the need for the system, analyzing the system, and developing design alternatives can be invaluable.

The study team's overall objective in this phase is to develop a rough plan of the new system's output, input, and processing requirements. Like the feasibility study, this plan is described in nontechnical terms so that the information user can understand it. To develop this plan, the study team first gathers data on the ways that information needs are currently

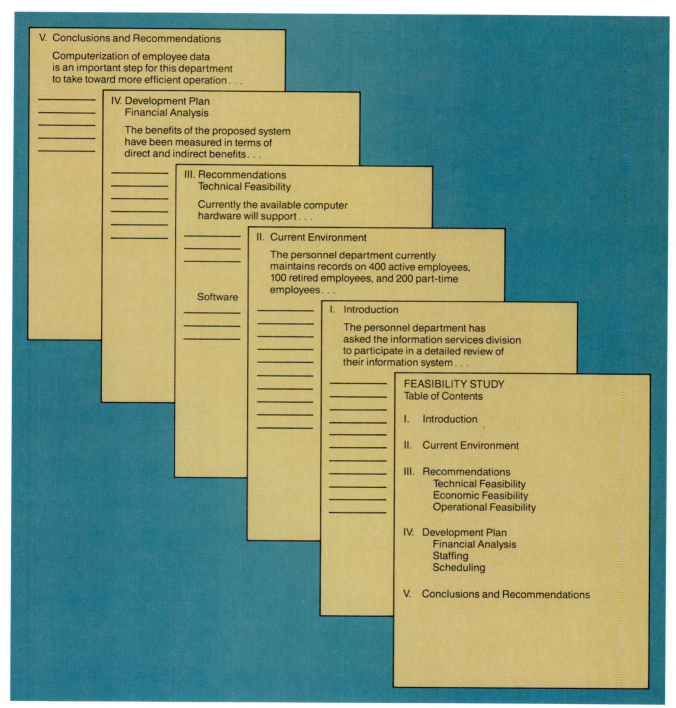

Figure 3.5
A feasibility study.

being met. Data may be gathered by reviewing any documentation available on the existing system (if there is one) and through research (e.g., reviewing relevant publications), observations, questionnaires, and interviews.

Questionnaires can be very useful tools. If the questions to be asked are carefully planned, they are sure to generate relevant data. Questionnaires can also give the team a good feel for the needs of a large number of information users. Questionnaires can be tightly structured, allowing for only yes or no answers, or they can be more open, allowing the respondent to offer opinions or ideas (see Figure 3.6). Interviews, too, can be structured

Figure 3.6
Questionnaires: (*a*) unstructured, or open; (*b*) structured, or closed.

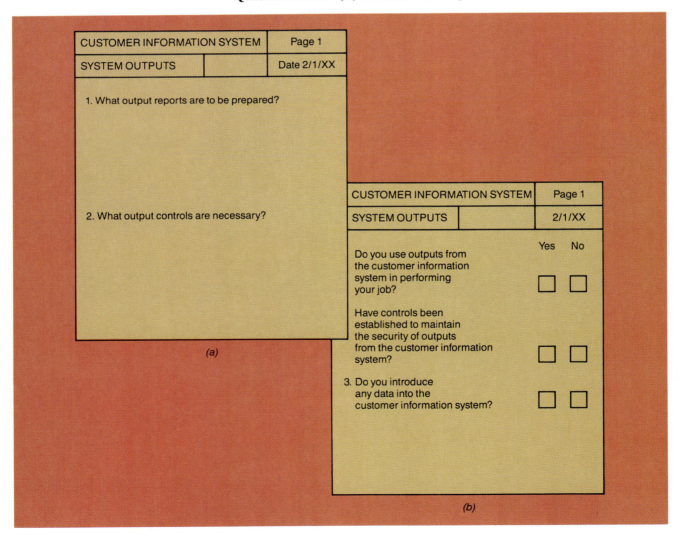

or unstructured. For certain purposes, such as determining sources of data for the information system, structured interviews are inappropriate since the interviewer needs to let the person being interviewed generate ideas and concepts. Interviews are much more time-consuming than questionnaires, and they require well-trained people to conduct them, but they do add a personal touch. They also allow the interviewer to change questions if it seems appropriate. Such flexibility is often very useful.

Systems flowcharts, which provide a broad graphic overview of the processing activities of a computer system, and **information-oriented flowcharts,** which show the flow of information within a system or an organization, are useful tools in communicating analytical findings to nontechnical information users. They are useful as conceptual tools even for technical specialists. Figures 3.7 and 3.8 show how these flowcharts are used.

Once the study team has gathered all possible data on the ways information needs are currently being met, it analyzes these data, paying particular attention to the strengths and weaknesses of the current system.

Figure 3.7
A systems flowchart. A systems flowchart graphically describes the basic activities involved in converting inputs into outputs. The meaning of the flowchart symbols is explained on the right.

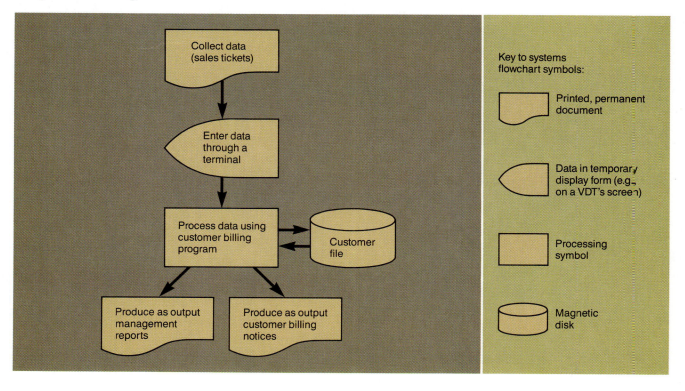

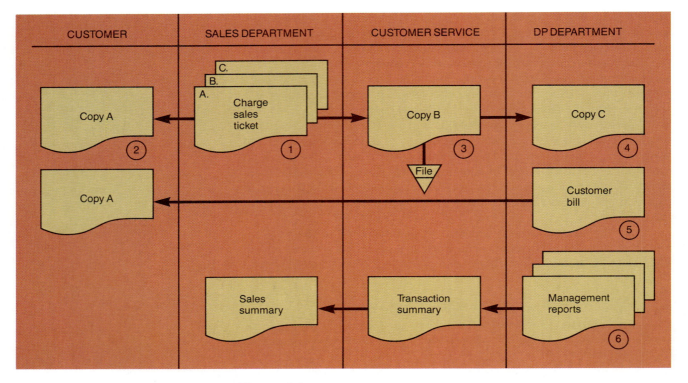

Figure 3.8

An information-oriented flowchart. The circled numbers indicate the flow of data and information. The clerk first records the sales transaction on a three-copy sales ticket and gives the first copy to the customer. The second copy goes to the customer service file, and the third copy becomes the vehicle for data entry by the data processing (DP) department. The output produced includes a customer bill as well as various management reports, which are distributed within the organization.

The findings that result from this analysis provide answers to the following questions:

1. How does the system currently work?
2. Why does it work as it does?
3. How could it be changed or improved to meet the needs of the new system?

These findings will serve as a blueprint in the design work that takes place during the next two stages of the systems development cycle.

SYSTEMS DEVELOPMENT IN ACTION:
Prototyping

Developing a computer information system presents a high-pressure challenge not unlike the one that Larry Bird of the Boston Celtics faces every time he plays a professional basketball game. Bird has proven time and again that he's capable of scoring forty points a game, but on some nights the shots just don't fall. Systems development efforts often begin with the same superstar expectations, and at times the designers, like Bird, are just not able to score the points.

Developing a successful computer information system is a complicated process. It may take a year or more to complete, and in the meantime the user's needs and computing technology may have changed radically. In fact, the ultimate user of the system may not even be the same user who requested the development of the system. This combination of circumstances is enough to frustrate the superstar ambitions and expectations of the most careful of systems planners.

The definition of a successful computer information system is one that satisfies users' needs, and a key to developing such a system is to involve users in the developmental process. A new tool called prototyping is helping systems designers do just that. The basic assumption underlying prototyping is that it is not possible to design and build a perfect system on the first try; any design effort will have to be modified to meet users' needs. Prototyping means that the designer first creates a rough model, or prototype, of the system and then refines it with the user. The prototype gives the user something concrete to react to, and the ensuing collaboration between user and designer ensures that the user becomes involved early in the developmental effort.

The prototype of the system is rather like a stage setting, in which the scenery — stores, trees, castles, and so on — is a false front. The false front of the prototype means that it's easy to make changes as the system evolves; no real pieces of the system are in place. Just as engineers use a model to test various components of an automobile before they build the final product, systems designers can use the prototype to revise, refine, evaluate, and test the system during the design phase. Moreover, because no extensive coding or other developmental effort goes into building the prototype, the designer can make radical changes to the system without causing long delays or wasting previous efforts. It is obviously much easier to change the model than to change the actual system. The "shells" created through prototyping are fully developed only after the user and the systems designer have reached an agreement. ◆

Developing Design Alternatives

The focus of the third phase of the systems development cycle is on specifying the kind of system that will best meet the requirements identified in the preceding phase. The systems analyst prepares a number of logical designs. Usually, each design has both advantages and disadvantages. The study team weighs the positive and negative aspects of each design from both a technician's and a nontechnician's perspective before it selects one alternative. The team's review of the alternative designs is a very thorough one. It includes a close examination of the costs and benefits of each approach, as well as a careful review of the findings resulting from the analysis of the current system.

Once the study team has chosen the alternative it considers best, it draws up detailed specifications for the new system, including its output, input, and processing requirements, as well as the procedures to be used in testing and implementing it. These specifications contain all the technical information necessary to program the system, and they will control the rest of the development activities.

Developing the System

With detailed specifications drawn up, the technical work of programming can begin. The steps involved in program development closely resemble the steps of the systems development cycle. These steps are (1) analyzing the problem, (2) designing a solution, (3) coding the program, (4) testing the program, and (5) documenting the program (see Figure 3.9).

Analyzing the problem requires a clear definition of the problem so a solution can be worked out; this includes a consideration of the desired output and the input and processing requirements. In designing a solution (i.e., developing a program to produce the desired output), programmers have several design tools and programming methods to choose from. These techniques, discussed in detail in Chapter 11, improve programming productivity by simplifying the last three steps of the programming process. They also simplify the maintenance the system will require after it has been installed. The most popular design tool is the **program flowchart,** which graphically describes the logic of a programming solution. **Pseudocode,** a written description of the program logic, is becoming popular also.

Coding and testing the program require a great deal of technical expertise. In coding the program, the programmer translates the steps laid out in the design solution into a language the computer can "understand." The system must then be carefully tested to be sure that it performs properly in all situations. This involves testing not only the elements of the program itself but also its interactions with other systems' programs, data files, and data collection procedures. Coding and testing are the most complicated parts of systems development and, if a major system is being developed, may take the better part of a year to complete. Documenting the program involves compiling any information on the details of the program's development that will be of later use to anyone working with the system.

Implementing and Maintaining the System

After the system has been tested and is considered ready to be installed, the implementation process can begin. Implementation involves a changeover from the existing system or a starting up of operations if no system currently

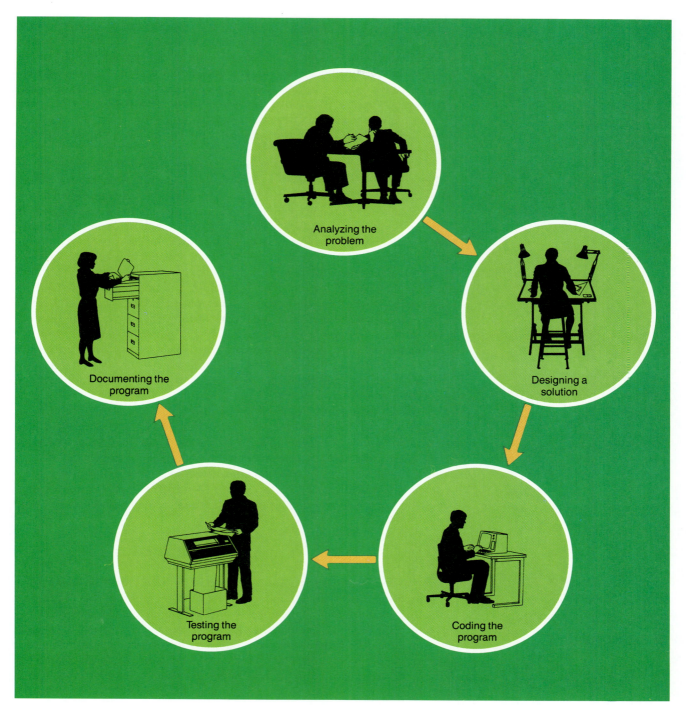

Figure 3.9
Steps involved in program development.

exists. Since it can be risky to install a new system with no backup system in operation, both the old and the new systems are sometimes run together for a short while. This sort of "parallel run" allows the operations of the new system to be checked while providing a backup should the new system fail. Another option is to install only a part of the new system and to delay implementation of the rest of the system until the installed part has been checked. Whatever the conversion process, implementation requires that files be altered to meet the requirements of the new system and that personnel be trained to run it.

In any new system, a few minor errors almost always need to be corrected, or other adjustments have to be made. So, after the system has been in operation for about three months, a **postimplementation review** takes place. This review includes an evaluation of the impact of the system on the organization, of the adequacy of the system in meeting users' needs, and of the costs of the system as compared with the costs projected during development. It also includes a check on the documentation of the system's development. Such documentation would include not only the technical documentation of the program's development but also various reports generated throughout the systems development cycle; budgets and actual cost data; management approvals; data on implementation; materials developed for systems users, such as a users' guide or manual; and the operations manual. All this information is necessary for **audit review**—that is, verification that the system is performing according to specifications—and for guiding future enhancements and modifications of the system.

Once the system is operating, it must be continuously "tuned" to accommodate the various changes that are bound to take place from time to time. Changes, for example, in hardware, users' needs, or company regulations and policies would require modifications of the system. Making such changes is called **systems maintenance,** and it consumes a great deal of technical energy. In fact, more than half of a programmer's time may be spent on maintaining existing systems rather than on developing new ones.

USING COMPUTER INFORMATION SYSTEMS IN BUSINESS

Information is unquestionably as important a resource to business today as labor, raw materials, and money. Without a computer system to produce this information, many businesses would lose their competitive edge and founder. However, as you may have gathered from the last section, developing a computer information system can be a very time-consuming and expensive business, and in certain situations, it would not be worth the effort. For example, developing a system to assess the value of an employee would be a losing proposition; such evaluation requires a good deal of judgment and observation, and these are not areas in which the computer presently excels. Programming the computer to assess skills, motivation, desire, and ability would be extremely difficult, given "state-of-the-art" technology. Situations in which computer systems *are* particularly useful and cost-effective include the following:

1. *When there is a large volume of routine data to be processed.* Large volume can justify the expense of a programming effort. For example, if a program cost $5,000 to prepare, was run for four years, and 5,000 transactions a year were processed, the programming cost of processing each transaction would be $.25. If 50,000 transactions were processed each year, the programming cost would be reduced to $.025 per transaction.

2. *When activities are repetitive.* Tasks done many times and in the same way each time are a good choice for computerized processing since the same program can be used over and over again. Sales transactions, for instance, are generally handled in the same way for all customers, regardless of the size or amount of their purchases. Programming for one-time applications is usually not cost-effective. At times, however, it may be the only alternative, such as when a program is needed for a space flight.

3. *When there is a need to store a large volume of data and to have quick access to those data.* Consider the confusion that would arise if an airline used a manual system to store data on reservations for its flights. Customer service would be impossibly slow, and the disruption would be tremendous. With a computer system, the information can be displayed on a screen while the data remains undisturbed in the computer's memory; the data will never get lost, fall out of a file cabinet onto the floor, or have a staple running through the most important digit.

4. *When there is a need for speedy processing and up-to-the-minute business records.* When a business must process a large volume of transactions, the computer's processing speed is very useful. Also, the computer's ability to continuously update records means that businesses can have the most current information to work with. In some situations, such as in handling airline reservations, this feature is essential.

5. *When there is a need to perform complex calculations.* Mathematical models that simulate the economy, the business environment, or even the situations likely to arise in a professional football game are becoming an increasingly popular tool in decision making. These models rely on complex calculations to manipulate the data and to determine the probable outcomes. Without computers, little simulation would be used in business decision making, since people would find it exceedingly cumbersome to perform the necessary calculations.

The typical business office performs a variety of functions, some of which lend themselves to computerization. Those office functions that do lend themselves to computerization have made **office automation** — that is, the use of computer systems and communications technology to perform office tasks — an increasingly popular phenomenon. Another very important way in which businesses use computer systems is as a managerial tool. In the following pages, we'll take a brief look at both these uses. We'll discuss them in more detail in Chapter 17.

Office Automation

One look at the typical business office is enough to tell you why office automation is becoming so popular. Harry's at the file cabinet, grumbling again because he can't find the record he wants. He slams the drawer shut, and the pile of folders marked "to be filed" falls off the top of the cabinet. Kathy helps him pick them up, and inadvertently sticks a letter from Mr. Zabar into the Abbott and Adams file. The boss has just stormed back into his office after chewing out his secretary for not giving him the message that his stockbroker called with a hot tip yesterday afternoon at two o'clock. He's now sitting behind his closed door, fire in his eyes, reading an article in the *Wall Street Journal* about the rising costs of office labor and the low level of office productivity. Elizabeth is out in the hall, telling Barbara that she's looking for another job because she's so bored retyping Harry's semiannual marketing plan that if he gives her another revision to do she'll scream.

While this picture may be a little exaggerated, it does indicate some common office problems that computing and communications technology can help to solve: **Electronic filing** — that is, computerized filing done with electronic signals rather than paper — can eliminate the problems of lost or misfiled documents and a backlog of records to be filed (see Figure 3.10). **Electronic message systems** (also called **electronic mail**) use telephone lines and the computer to allow you to receive messages from and to leave messages in the computer's memory, to be retrieved when convenient. Thus, delayed or lost telephone messages, busy signals, secretaries telling you the person you want to speak to is unavailable, lost letters, delays in delivery, and misrouted memos are eliminated. Electronic messages are transmitted instantaneously over the telephone lines in the form of electronic signals (see Figure 3.11). They can also be coded for urgency, multiple copies, distribution lists, and file copies.

Word processing — that is, a computer-based system for preparing, editing, storing, and printing text — increases productivity in preparing written documents. A word processor captures the text in memory as it

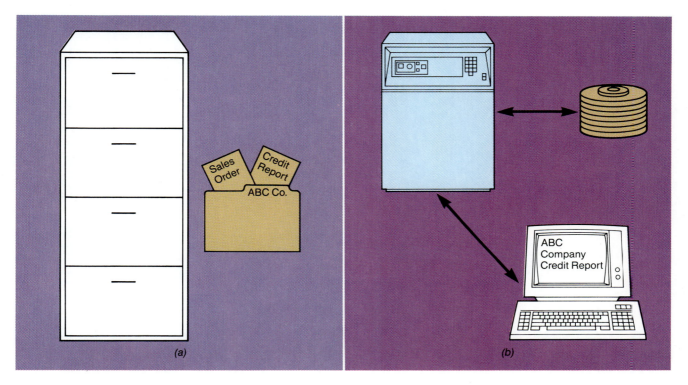

Figure 3.10
Traditional and electronic filing systems. In a traditional filing system (*a*), records are stored in a file cabinet in some logical order, such as by account number or in alphabetical order. Records removed from the file cabinet are not available to other users until they are returned, and misfiled records can be hard to retrieve. In an electronic filing system (*b*), records are placed in computer storage, often on a magnetic disk, and a video display terminal provides ready access to the stored records. A record displayed on a VDT's screen remains in computer storage; thus, multiple users can have simultaneous access to the same information.

is keyboarded. (A word processor may be a "dedicated" word processor, or it could be a microcomputer operating with a word processing program.) The person using the word processor can make changes and revisions where necessary without having to rekey the part of the text that is correct (see Figure 3.12). Word processing thus saves time, and since the correct part of the text doesn't have to be rekeyed, it also improves overall accuracy. In short, office automation offers great promise of improving the productivity of office workers, giving them powerful tools to remove much of the boredom and drudgery from their day-to-day work.

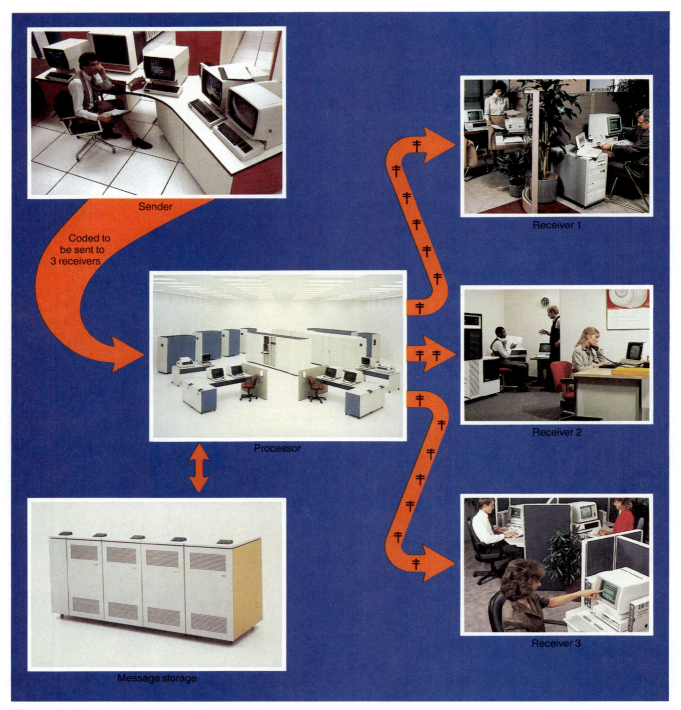

Figure 3.11
An electronic message system.
Photos (clockwise from top left) courtesy of Computer Sciences Corporation; Hewlitt-Packard; Honeywell Inc.; Hewlitt-Packard; IBM Corporation; IBM Corporation.

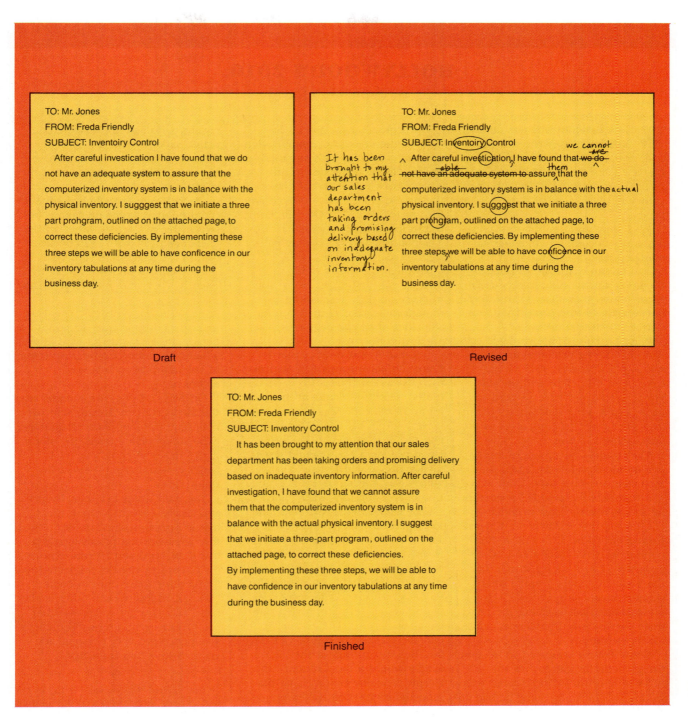

Figure 3.12
Word processing in action.

HOLLYWOOD'S 2010:
An On-Line Odyssey

When Peter Hyams was commissioned to write and produce the movie version of Arthur C. Clarke's latest novel, *2010: Odyssey Two,* Hyams wanted to involve the author in every aspect of the project.

An admirable intention, but one not easily accomplished. A permanent resident of Colombo, on the Indian Ocean island of Sri Lanka, Clarke is not the easiest person to get in touch with. But Hyams would not embark on the project without Clarke's total support....

Practical considerations made conventional forms of communication impossible. "Regular mail would have been ridiculous and the telephone would not have worked because of the time difference," Hyams says. He turned to computers as the only viable solution.

The result — an unprecedented communication link between the filmmaker's Culver City, Calif., office and the author's secluded residence off the southeast coast of India.

Choosing the hardware, a Kaypro, turned out to be a lot easier than coming up with a communications program. "I had a long search for the software before I found Mite (communications protocol)," Hyams says, adding that he chose the program for its "user-friendliness" and for its "versatility."...

While Hyams struggled to become friends with his system, on the other side of the world, Clarke was having less difficulty since he had already done some experimenting with electronic mail.

On September 16, 1983, Clarke opened the lines of communication with a seven-paragraph message that ended, "Do you realize we may have a book here?! (We'd better pay the phone bill.)" The book did, in fact, materialize. *The Odyssey File*, a transcript of their communications, was published in January by Ballantine Books, New York.

Through the magic of electronic mail, Hyams and Clarke were able to carry on daily discussions even though they were virtually on opposite sides of the globe, more than 13 time zones apart.

Because it was much easier for Clarke to get through to California than it was for Hyams to reach Colombo, Clarke initiated all the dialing from his end. Hyams would leave a file in his computer at the end of his work day in California. Upon waking, Clarke would instruct his Kaypro to call Hyams' Kaypro, which was waiting in answer mode. Upon receiving the "ready" message, Clarke would ask Hyams' machine to display all its files. If a new file appeared, Clarke would instruct Hyams' computer to send the file and his computer to receive it. After the entire file had been received in Sri Lanka, Hyams could sever the phone connection and review the file at his leisure. The author would edit the message and make a printout. Before retiring for the night, Clarke would leave a message in Hyams' machine by reversing the send-and-receive instructions.

"It was a perfect example of what electronic mail can do," enthuses Hyams, who had not a single complaint, save his inability to contact Clarke — and that was a shortcoming of the phone system, not of the computers.

Clarke's role as technical advisor required daily communications between the two artists. Much of the exchange dealt with the construction of the spaceship, Leonov.

"The correspondences were frequently a series of questions I had that needed more than short answers," Hyams explains. "This gave Arthur the opportunity to go into detail and it provided a hard copy, which was important because some of the information was very technical."

On Feb. 7, 1984, five months after the initial contact, Hyams sent his colleague the long-awaited message: "The screenplay arrived this morning ... It's a splendid job.... I laughed — and cried — in all the right places."

The daily chats between Hyams and Clarke ceased ... when the movie began production. But a bond that went beyond professionalism had developed and Hyams expects his Kaypro to remain connected to Clarke's for some time to come. "We got to know each other in the same way you get to know a pen pal," Hyams reminisces. "The correspondence got very personal and I grew to love him from that."

— Kim Norris, "Hollywood's 2010: An On-Line Odyssey." Reprinted with permission from *Personal Computing*, April 1985, p. 37. Copyright 1985, Hayden Publishing Company.

The Computer System as a Managerial Tool

Earlier in the chapter, we discussed the uses of computerized information in business decision making. Let's now look briefly at the bigger picture — at how the whole computer system fits into the business organization and at how management uses this system as a decision-making tool.

As you know from Chapter 1, a system is a group of interrelated elements working to accomplish a specific goal. In a business organization, the computer system is a *subsystem;* that is, it is part of a larger system known as the **management information system (MIS).** Any company, no matter how large or how small and whether it has a computer system or not, has a management information system. Such a system is the means by which managers get the information they need to make decisions. In some cases, the business is so small that the manager does not even think about a formal information system; collecting and processing data are part of the daily routine.

You may have been in a small shop where the salesperson has asked you how you liked a certain product, if you had purchased it before, and whether you would purchase it again. That person is gathering data on which to make judgments about customer acceptance, whether the shop should continue to carry the product, and whether the product is something it should promote to its other customers. A large business needs the same kind of information, but it would try to gather the data in a more formal way and would assemble the results in the form of a report. The information requirements of small and large businesses are often the same; the difference is just a matter of the magnitude of the data collection activities and the formality of the information reporting.

Managerial Functions. The reason for the similarity in the information needs of large and small businesses is that regardless of the size of the firm, managers perform many of the same functions. These include planning, organizing, controlling, and communicating, and they are the functions of managers whether they are in administration, production, marketing, or finance. In **planning,** managers formulate goals and develop policies and programs to achieve those goals. **Organizing** involves grouping activities and establishing procedures to implement them. **Controlling** means measuring actual performance against the established goals. **Communicating** involves transferring information both inside and outside the organization. In performing these tasks, managers become involved in decision making, which relies on accurate, complete, relevant, concise, and timely information. The primary job of management is to convert information into action by making decisions that will effectively and efficiently allocate the firm's resources and personnel. Information is used to reduce uncertainty in decision making, and computer systems have provided management with a tool for rapidly and accurately collecting and processing data into useful decision-making information.

Management Information Systems. A management information system is designed to perform a dual role: processing the routine operational data that the firm generates and providing management with reports and decision-making information. The firm's day-by-day transactions form the bulk of the data that an MIS collects and processes, but it was not until computers offered high-speed processing that managers saw such operational data as a resource for decision making. A computer-based MIS is composed of software, hardware, and procedures that allow it to retrieve appropriate data and to process those data to produce meaningful results for the information user. An MIS may also be manually based, but in this case, the company will be limited in the volume and complexity of the data that it can process.

An MIS can help to overcome the redundancy that occurs when there is little coordination between the functional components of a business in meeting information needs. Such a lack of coordination is certainly not uncommon. Duplicate data are often kept to support the processing needs of administration, production, marketing, and finance. All four of these functional areas contribute to and use information from the firm's information system, although they may use it in different ways. For example, if a company has ten delivery trucks, finance needs to know how many miles they have traveled so it can meet the state's requirements for information pertaining to road-use taxes. Production needs to know about the availability of the trucks so it can deliver the products. Administration needs to know the condition and utility of the trucks so it can determine whether it needs to replace them in the near future. All these functional areas are talking about the same thing — trucks — but everyone needs different information about them. An MIS can pull together the data that these different functional areas provide and integrate the data in a common data pool available for use by all.

Data Base Management Systems and Decision Support Systems. Supporting a computer-based MIS are two important software tools: data base management systems and decision support systems. The former have received a great deal of attention as the capacities and processing speeds of computers have increased, and they have become an important component of most large management information systems. A **data base management system (DBMS)** is a collection of programs used to manage and maintain a data base. It is concerned with the location, access, and retrieval of the data rather than the data's meaning. The decision-oriented MIS, which *is* concerned with the meaning of the data, uses the DBMS to assemble and process the data; the DBMS thus becomes part of the management information system. In addition to helping users and programmers find and access records in a data base, the programs included in a DBMS can also make additions or changes to the stored data.

Managers may at times be uncertain of their information needs and may want to explore a number of alternative strategies. A **decision support system (DSS)** includes software that can be used to test ideas and decisions. Such software uses mathematical techniques to model the environment and manipulate the data; the electronic spreadsheets that we mentioned in Chapter 2 are often an important part of this software. The focus of a DSS is on problem solving. Using a terminal and the DSS software, the manager has direct access to the data base and can pose a number of questions to the computer (see Figure 3.13). The replies will decrease the uncertainty related to the outcomes of potential decisions.

The DSS has decided advantages over the traditional static, or fixed, information-reporting system. For example, a manager might be trying to decide whether to continue a product line or to have a close-out sale and delete the product. By posing a number of questions through the DSS, the manager could quickly find the year's sales activity, the product's profit margin, the inventory carrying costs, and the number of units in stock. With the data assembled, the DSS could model consumer acceptance and test pricing strategies that would help the manager make the product decision. The traditional paper reports might contain some, or even all, of the information provided by the DSS, but the information would not be assembled in a way that would make it easily accessible. The manager would have to review a number of reports, and, even then, the information would not be completely up to date.

Figure 3.13
Using a DSS. Decision support system software draws upon the computer's extensive memory and computational processing powers to allow users to try a number of different combinations until a decision question is satisfied.
Courtesy of Apple Computer, Inc.

SUMMARY

Coupled with improvements in communications technology, computer systems have become a revolutionary force. The Information Revolution they have spawned is evidenced by the expectations of individuals for more and better information and by the demands on businesses from individual customers, and from many other quarters as well, to meet such expectations. Businesses gather data to meet these demands, as well as to produce information that will aid them in decision making and planning, from three main sources: historical data, operational data, and projected data.

Effective computer information systems that can meet today's many demands for information are not developed by chance; they are the product of careful planning. The steps of the systems development cycle provide a framework for such planning. They include (1) identifying the need, (2) analyzing the system, (3) developing design alternatives, (4) developing the system, and (5) implementing and maintaining the system.

Computer information systems are time-consuming and expensive to develop, and they are not useful and cost-effective in every situation. The typical business office performs several functions that lend themselves to computerization. Office automation uses computer systems and communications technology to provide electronic filing, electronic message systems, and word processing. Using electronic signals rather than paper documents, workers in automated offices are able to increase their productivity.

Any business, no matter how large or small, has a need for information to support managerial decision making. A management information system (MIS) is designed to provide this information as well as to process routine operational data. In a computer-based MIS, these data serve as a resource for decision making. A computer-based MIS also provides a common data pool that helps to reduce data redundancy. Data base management systems (DBMS) and decision support systems (DSS) are two important software tools used in the MIS. A DBMS is concerned with the location, access, and retrieval of data. A DSS can be used to test ideas and decisions; it provides mathematical models that allow managers to explore the potential impact of various decisions.

KEY TERMS

administration (67)
archives (68)
audit review (82)
communicating (89)
controlling (89)

data base management system (DBMS) (90)
decision support system (DSS) (90)
electronic filing (84)

electronic message systems
  (electronic mail) (84)
feasibility study (74)
filtering (69)
finance (68)
historical data (68)
information-oriented flowcharts
  (77)
Information Revolution (66)
management information system
  (MIS) (89)
marketing (68)
office automation (84)
operational data (69)
organizing (89)
planning (89)
postimplementation review
  (82)
production (68)
program flowchart (80)
projected data (69)
pseudocode (80)
systems development cycle (72)
systems flowcharts (77)
systems maintenance (82)
word processing (84)

DISCUSSION QUESTIONS

1. Why are there pressures for more and better information today? How do these pressures affect businesses?

2. What are a business's sources of information? How is each used in decision making? If you were making a personal decision about buying a car, how would you gather pertinent data and process those data into decision-making information?

3. Explain how various levels of managers use computerized information. Why are the information requirements of shop supervisors easier to meet than those of middle-level and top-level managers?

4. Why is planning for computer information systems necessary? How does the systems development cycle aid in this process?

5. Describe the contents and objectives of a feasibility study.

6. Describe the role of an information user in systems development.

7. Describe how a systems study team analyzes the current information system. What are the objectives of this analysis? What tools can aid in this process?

8. What are the objectives of a postimplementation review? What does *systems maintenance* mean?

9. Describe three situations in which computer systems are particularly useful and cost-effective. Why does the typical business office lend itself to automation? What functions can office automation serve?

10. Interview the manager of a large local business and the manager of a small specialty shop. Describe the managerial functions and information needs of each. How are they similar or dissimilar? Explain how the MIS of each of these businesses operates.

OUTLINE

PRODUCTIVITY AND THE PROBLEMS OF OFFICE AUTOMATION

COMPUTERS IN THE FACTORY: COMPUTER-AIDED DESIGN AND MANUFACTURING OR COMPUTER-AIDED UNEMPLOYMENT?

COMPUTERS IN GOVERNMENT: THE POTENTIAL HUMAN COSTS

    Social Services
    Elections
    Local Tax Districts
    Federal Tax Authority
    Law Enforcement
    Military Applications

EDUCATIONAL USES AND ABUSES OF COMPUTERS

COMPUTERS IN MEDICINE: PROS AND CONS

SUMMARY

KEY TERMS

DISCUSSION QUESTIONS

OVERVIEW

As you've no doubt gathered from the preceding chapters, computers today are used in just about everything from anthropology to zoology. The reason for their widespread use is their ability to process, store, and retrieve vast quantities of data with enormous speed and accuracy. However, with computers, as with most things in life, there's no such thing as a "free lunch"; computers, too, have their costs. The very qualities that make them so attractive in such a wide variety of applications also magnify the potential for their misuse. Their ability to process massive amounts of data in a short time not only compounds the effects of data errors and makes the correction of errors much more difficult and costly; it also increases the chances for deliberate manipulation of the information system. Whether errors in computer systems are accidental or deliberate, they are going to affect someone, somewhere, to one extent or another. At the least, such errors will cause minor inconveniences; at the worst, they will infringe on personal rights and represent invasions of personal privacy. The installation of computer systems can also spell job elimination.

People who take a dim view of the power of the computer feel that in addition to robbing us of our jobs and privacy, computers can distort democratic principles and processes and create a more stressful, depersonalized world. The opposing point of view is that computers create new jobs, new opportunities for creativity and job satisfaction, greater productivity and a higher standard of living, and increased opportunities to participate effectively in the democratic process. Obviously, which of these points of view becomes the social reality of the future won't depend on the computer itself but rather on those of us who use it. If the more optimistic view is to prevail, it will require us to have a knowledge of the workings and capabilities of computer systems and a willingness to do something about computer abuses and misuses.

In this chapter, we'll take a look at just a few of the ways in which our society uses computers. Our objectives are to

◆ discuss the issue of productivity in the business office and the problems involved in office automation.

◆ describe the positive and negative social effects of using computers in the factory.

◆ discuss some of the important government uses of computers and the potential social consequences of these applications.

◆ identify the pros and cons of using computers in the classroom.

◆ explain the uses of computers in medicine and the social implications of these uses.

CHAPTER 4

THE SOCIAL IMPLICATIONS OF USING COMPUTERS

PRODUCTIVITY AND THE PROBLEMS OF OFFICE AUTOMATION

In the last chapter, we described how computers are used in office automation, and we alluded to their potential for improving the productivity of office workers. **Productivity** (i.e., the rate at which workers produce goods) has become a matter of considerable concern in U.S. business in recent years. The reason for this concern, as you can see in Figure 4.1, is that productivity gains in this country have been slackening. This current trend is a reversal of the increasing productivity gains that have characterized American business since 1800. These gains in productivity — the result of workers' being able to produce more goods with the same amount of effort — have usually been linked to the application of technology and machines. The recent flattening of productivity gains is not the result of any single cause; it is a sign of a major shift in the kind of work being done in America.

For the first time in history, white-collar workers (also sometimes called **knowledge workers** or **information workers**) outnumber blue-collar workers. Generally, white-collar workers have had less opportunity than their blue-collar counterparts to apply technology and machines to improving their work performance. A look at Figure 4.2, which shows ten-year productivity gains for three broad segments of the workforce, will help to bring this observation into focus. Productivity increases over the last ten years in agriculture, where machinery plays a significant role in

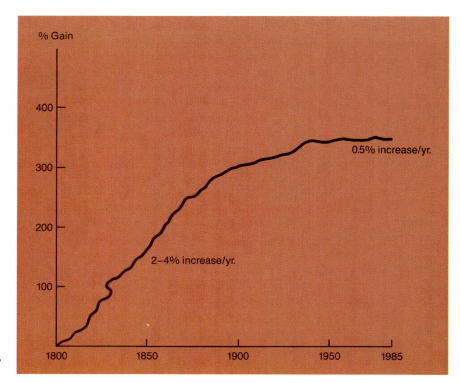

Figure 4.1
Productivity gains in U.S. business, 1800–1985.

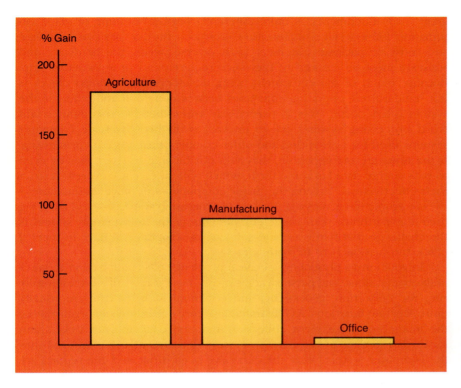

Figure 4.2
Productivity gains in different segments of the U.S. workforce, 1975–1985.

the way work is done, have exceeded 180 percent. In manufacturing, with investments in plants and equipment of over $30,000 for each employee, the productivity increases have approached 90 percent. But in the business office, where the investment is just slightly over $3,000 for each employee, the increased productivity over the past ten years has been only 4 percent. Many business people believe that one challenge for the remainder of the century will be to apply modern communications and computer technology to improving the productivity of office workers.

Fully automating the business office is not going to be an easy task, and it will not be without technical and organizational problems or social costs. Certainly, many clearly defined business tasks, such as preparing payrolls, keeping records of transactions, and controlling inventory, have been very successfully computerized over the past two or three decades. However, the activities that have yet to be computerized in most offices are those that don't fit easily into a pattern — nonrepetitive tasks such as one-time reports, data analysis, and other matters requiring some judgment. As you know, such activities don't lend themselves easily to computerization.

Another technical problem in automating "the" business office is that there are many kinds of business offices, and each has different objectives. The meaning of office automation for a law firm, which must produce a great many documents, is quite different from the meaning of office automation for a service organization such as a theater. No one hardware and software package can meet such diverse needs; the hardware and software must be tailored to the office requirements of a particular firm. Because much of the equipment being developed for business offices is not standardized, operating difficulties between one unit and others in the system often occur. This is particularly true when microcomputer and word processing systems try to interact with the large-scale computer systems used for accounting and other complex business data processing. If the units are incompatible, they will not be able to share files or even to pass simple data back and forth, which will, of course, severely restrict their effectiveness. Linking the major components of office automation — the electronic filing, message, and word processing systems — and ensuring their compatibility with other components of the information system is the challenge that hardware and software developers will have to meet if office automation is to be truly effective.

In addition to presenting technical problems, office automation requires both organizational and personal adjustments. In a business that is traditionally run, the collection, processing, and communication of data are usually quite separate functions. As illustrated in Figure 4.3, in such an organization, the marketing department collects transaction data on sales tickets and forwards the data to the data processing department to be entered into the computer system. After the data have been processed, the reports are distributed through the mail to managers in individual departments. The organizational boundaries are usually clearly defined, and each department has its own system for collecting and maintaining its own data. In an automated environment, these functions can be integrated and coordinated so that the data the firm collects are available for a variety of processing and reporting needs (see Figure 4.4). Such integration requires that standards for the collection of data be more carefully structured and enforced and that access to the now centralized data be monitored and controlled. In consequence, authority and responsibility have to shift from the system's users to the data center's management, and this adjustment can cause unrest.

Personal adjustments to an automated office system mean that individuals have to adapt to changes in the ways data are collected and processed and information is communicated. Whereas traditional communications have been verbal or have been conveyed via printed matter, communication in an automated office is via electronic signals. For a person accustomed to reading reports printed on paper, viewing information displayed on a terminal's screen may cause anxiety or distrust. Long hours at a screen may even pose a health hazard. A study conducted by the National Institute for Occupational Safety and Health during the early 1980s found that a large majority of employees who worked at such screens all day complained of health problems — most often headaches, back pain, and visual disturbances. Some states, Rhode Island among them, have become so alarmed at the possible effects of video display screens on health that they have

THE SIDE EFFECTS OF ELECTRONIC MAIL

Electronic mail affects organizations in ways they may not expect or be prepared for. When electronic mail opens up new channels of communication and increases the flow of information, structural boundaries in the organization become fuzzier and its culture becomes looser, less formal. Decisions reached electronically tend to be more extreme, riskier. And the electronic messages themselves are much looser — frequently using profanity and emotional outbursts.

This side of electronic mail and computer decision making has been documented, and is being studied by researchers at Carnegie-Mellon University, both in experimental situations and in real corporate settings. "The reasons for these effects are not yet clear, because we don't have enough examples," says Dr. Sara Kiesler, a social psychologist at the Pittsburgh, Penn., campus of Carnegie-Mellon. "But it seems we have found some very interesting behavior when computers are used for communication."

Dr. Kiesler began studying the social and organizational impact of computers "almost by accident." Four years ago she stumbled across literature that claimed people using computers made "cleaner" decisions. She couldn't believe this, so she set up a test. It included two groups of three people. One group was to make a decision face to face, the other group through the computer. The problem the groups were given, involving risk, had been used in other tests so Kiesler knew what to expect.

The results, however, were totally surprising. The group making the decision through the computer stayed from 9 o'clock in the evening to 2 o'clock in the morning. "They got so involved in the process that they began swearing at each other and making incredible remarks," Kiesler says. "I couldn't believe it. None of this happened in the face to face group." Thinking the test may have been poorly run, Kiesler did it over twice more — both times coming up with similar results....

Perhaps [Keisler's] most dramatic finding concerns the excessive language frequently found in electronic messages. "It's amazing," says Kiesler, "we've seen messages from managers, with language in them that would normally be heard only in the locker room." The reasons for this extreme language, known by people in the communications industry as "flaming," can be linked to the reduced social clues in electronic messages, Kiesler hypothesizes. "It (electronic mail) makes communication more depersonalized and reduces social regulation," she comments. "There are none of the social context clues that come with written mail — such as the letterhead, or formalized style — nor are there the facial clues that are part of face to face meetings or the verbal clues one hears over the telephone." Keisler adds, "Electronic mail is so absorbing the user's attention gets focused on the message rather than the people who are receiving it."

Another observation ... is that decisions made through electronic communication tend to be extreme — either more risky or more conservative, but not in-between. And the people who make decisions in this way don't realize they are extreme, expressing more confidence in the decisions. The reason or reasons for this are unclear. But points out Kiesler, riskier decisions need not be damaging, they can be innovative and positive for an organization. To avoid trouble, companies using electronic mail in place of other avenues of decision making should keep this phenomenon in mind.

... The use of electronic mail ... breaks down the social barriers of gender and hierarchy in an organization. "Electronic mail makes it easier to communicate with anybody and takes away the normal social constraints," says Kiesler....

While the work being done at Carnegie-Mellon is still filled with guesses and hunches, it is evident that electronic mail has some rather definite side effects that can be both positive and negative. But, every tool is neutral: the way it is used makes the difference. Electronic mail can either support and augment the culture of an organization or it can hinder it. Learning how is what the study by Kiesler and others is all about. "If you know something of what the technology does," says Kiesler, "then you can be more informed about choices in using it."

— Henry Fersko-Weiss, "The Side Effects of Electronic Mail." Reprinted with permission from *Personal Computing,* January 1985, p. 72. Copyright 1985, Hayden Publishing Company.

Figure 4.3
Flow of data and information in a nonautomated office. A nonautomated office may use computers to process some data, but it relies heavily on methods and machines — typewriters, file cabinets, and telephones — that date from the early 1900s. There is generally no coordinated system whereby different departments can easily and efficiently share the same data.

begun legislative hearings on the matter. Other sources of stress in an automated office include the lack of a physical file to store documents and the substitution of computer-generated messages for telephone conversations. For some people, the replacement of a helpful co-worker with an electronic message system can create a feeling of depersonalization.

To overcome these problems, which center to a large extent on ways of collecting data and communicating information, the automated office system will have to be flexible and easy to access and use — or, to put it in the technical jargon, it will have to be "user-friendly." In other words, the user will have to be comfortable with the technology. Developing this comfort will be a large job for both business and the computer industry. It will require careful design of the physical equipment, such as the keyboards and screens, as well as of the software. Programs will have to be very clear and easy to access and implement if the system is to be effective.

As hardware and software developers meet these challenges, more

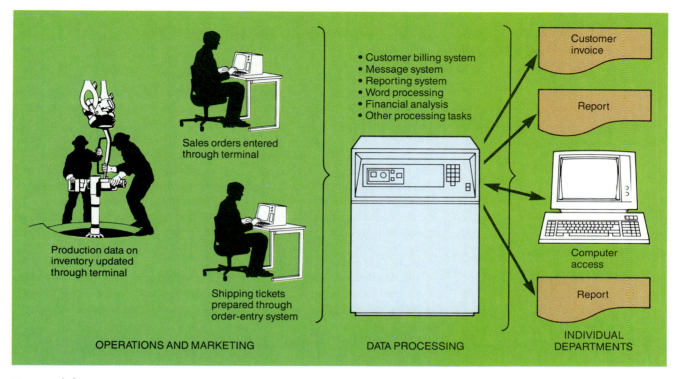

Figure 4.4
Flow of data and information in an automated office. An automated office captures much of the data as they are generated, and it uses a computer to process and store them. Terminals offer easy access to the stored data, which can be used for a variety of processing needs. Regularly scheduled reports add to the wide range of outputs.

equipment will be made available to support office workers, and, as a result, their productivity will improve. However, improved productivity means that some office jobs will undoubtedly be eliminated. A change in employment brought about by technological change is referred to as **job displacement.** Workers displaced by office automation may be retrained to perform other jobs, or they may be laid off, in which case they could join the ranks of the unemployed. Either way, another form of stress will be created, as workers worry about job security. For those who cannot be retrained — because there are no jobs available, because they have difficulty in adapting to the new technology, or because they have so much time and effort invested in their present positions that they are unwilling to start at the bottom again — the human costs of automation can be very high, with unemployment, depression, and even despair the end result. We should note, however, that while automation eliminates jobs, it also creates new jobs. Trained people are needed to design and prepare the office system, to assemble and manufacture the equipment, and to operate the new equipment once it is installed in the office.

When office automation is applied to improving the efficiency of collecting data and reporting information on individuals — in such matters as credit ratings — it raises another serious social issue. In a sense, manual systems, which cannot handle a large volume of data, protect the privacy of the individual. When automation is applied, a comprehensive personal record from birth to death becomes a reality, and there seems to be little chance of escaping the dossier that monitors and tracks you and your activities throughout your lifetime. Moreover, the possibility that data errors — whether accidental or deliberate — will occur is magnified, and such errors, particularly when they relate to things like credit ratings, can have serious consequences. When the person who enters the data into the system also collects the data at the site of the transaction, the chances for data error are reduced. Such a person has a frame of reference for making a judgment about the data; a data entry clerk with no first-hand knowledge of the transaction does not. Modern technology places a great deal of power in the hands of those few individuals who manage the information system, and it also gives them a great responsibility, as they must oversee both the collection and entry of the data and the dissemination of the information.

COMPUTERS IN THE FACTORY: COMPUTER-AIDED DESIGN AND MANUFACTURING OR COMPUTER-AIDED UNEMPLOYMENT?

Computer-aided design and computer-aided manufacturing (abbreviated as **CAD/CAM**) have been revolutionizing the way work is done in the factory. Before a product can be manufactured, careful engineering studies must be conducted, and designs and manufacturing procedures must be tested. The specifications that result from these studies are eventually translated into manufacturing operations and machine-tool settings. In the past, these tests and design activities were done manually, and they were time-consuming and prone to error. The introduction of computer-aided design has assisted engineers in a number of ways. CAD techniques are used in everything from the development of electronic circuits to the design of automobiles and airplanes (see Figure 4.5).

To understand the value of computer-aided design, try to visualize the specifications, blueprints, materials lists, and other engineering documentation required to build a modern automobile or a large airplane such as a DC-10. Thousands, often tens of thousands, of highly technical drawings and charts are required, and they must be very accurate. If the engineers should decide that several structural components need to be modified, all the plans and drawings will have to be changed. If computer-aided design has been used, the computer can mathematically evaluate the modification by calculating such things as stress, weight, and flexibility. Programming the computer to analyze such variables is very complex, but once the program has been prepared, the variables can be changed any number of times.

When the engineers are satisfied with the results of the computerized

**Figure 4.5
Computer-aided design.**
Courtesy of Chrysler Corporation.

evaluations, blueprints and materials lists can be drawn up. The computer can serve as a tool in preparing these documents as well. Given the data for the new components and the required modifications, the computer can adjust the lists and redraw the plans (see Figure 4.6). Using the computer thus saves weeks or even months of drafting time and gets the updated documents to the manufacturing facility in a finished and accurate form rather than in some temporary form that might be used if they were being hand-drawn.

The computer is also useful to engineers when they must design and build structures and products unlike any that have been seen before. In this case, the computer can provide the engineer with the means to test ideas and designs by developing a mathematical model, or simulation, of the anticipated environment. The value of this capability has been particularly evident in the space program, where engineers must deal with a great many unknowns. The trial-and-error method would be to design and build a space vehicle and to test and modify it until it was satisfactory. With this approach, much time would be lost in testing and modification. Moreover, testing would be quite difficult without actually sending the unit into space. Under these conditions, in-space testing would be exceptionally risky, since without pretesting in a simulated environment, a serious engineering error could very well result in the destruction of the space vehicle and, far worse, in loss of life.

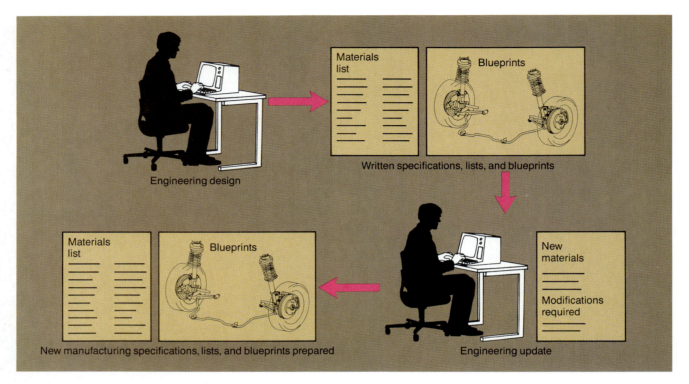

Figure 4.6
Saving time and effort with CAD.

The simulation of the anticipated environment developed by the computer can include the forces of gravity, friction of the atmosphere, stresses from thrust and speed, heat from the sun, and any other concerns the engineers might have. The design is entered into the computer's memory and tested in the simulated environment for weaknesses and flaws. In this way, most design problems can be discovered and corrected before a prototype is built. The prototype can then be used for wind-tunnel or stress testing before the final unit is actually constructed. **Engineering simulation** thus saves a great deal of time and money, and it may even save lives.

Because many of the tasks performed in manufacturing plants are repetitive, they lend themselves very well to CAM techniques. Computer-controlled machines, or **robots,** which are connected to and programmed by a computer, can package products, assemble components, weld and paint car bodies, load and unload inventory, and precisely cut and shape metal and other materials (see Figure 4.7). These industrial robots have been making such significant contributions to streamlining manufacturing and assembly operations that they have ushered in what has been referred to as the "steel-collar" age. Tens of thousands of these robots are currently in operation in manufacturing plants throughout the world. Although some robots that can walk and talk have been designed, at their present state of development, these "humanoid" forms are more appropriate for press releases and newspaper stories than for useful functions.

Because robots work twenty-four hours a day and don't get headaches, take sick leave, complain about poor working conditions, get tired, or lose interest in the job, they can manufacture products that meet closer tolerances

Figure 4.7
Computer-aided manufacturing.
Robots in this factory consistently weld all components of the automobiles' body structures.
Courtesy of Chrysler Corporation.

and stricter standards of quality control than those produced by people. In other words, in some manufacturing situations, robots do a better job than people. With the wages for factory workers in some industries approaching $20 an hour, robots can present a very attractive alternative to human labor. This is especially true in an industry like automobile manufacturing, where there is stiff competition from several other nations and both price and quality of the product are important considerations to buyers.

Robots were first developed in the United States, but they met such opposition from organized labor and workers who feared they would lose their jobs that they failed to develop as quickly as they might have. The leader in applying this new technology has been Japan, where job security is much greater than it is in the United States. However, pressures for more effective manufacturing and more cost-effective products have caused many U.S. manufacturing firms to address employees' concerns about job security and to begin to incorporate robots into the workplace. Nowhere is this more evident than in automobile plants, where robots weld and paint cars as they are assembled.

The social benefit of CAD/CAM is that better, less expensive products are produced. The social cost is that people stand to lose their livelihood. Every time a factory installs a computer-controlled robot, someone is out of a job; and when CAD techniques are used, fewer engineers and draftsmen are needed. At the same time, those engineers who do not lose their jobs have much more stimulating work to do, as the computer takes over the routine tasks and they can devote themselves to testing ideas and refining designs. Thus, one group loses, while another gains, as do all of us who are consumers. This dilemma is likely to increase in intensity as CAD/CAM and robots become ever more sophisticated, and its solution isn't going to be easy. Some kind of balance needs to be struck to serve the interests of both the worker and the consumer.

COMPUTERS IN GOVERNMENT: THE POTENTIAL HUMAN COSTS

The federal government of the United States is the single largest owner of computers. It is estimated to have over 20,000 systems throughout the world. As you might expect, much of the data that the government processes are very similar to the data processed by businesses. The Internal Revenue Service, the Social Security Administration, and numerous other government agencies accept payments, process transactions, and keep detailed financial records. At the state and local levels, much the same kind of data processing takes place, the only difference being that the volume of data processed is smaller. No reliable estimate of the number of computer systems owned by state and local governments exists, but there is little doubt that it exceeds the number of federally owned systems. Governments also have processing needs that differ from those traditionally found in business. Let's take a brief look at some of these unique applications and their social implications.

Social Services

A key to providing effective social services is a knowledge of the characteristics of the population to be served. With computers, the Census Bureau is able to maintain information about more than 230 million people in the United States. Through an elaborate data collection procedure, approximately 80 million households complete questionnaires to supply data to the census computers. Once the data are in machine-readable form, they can be tabulated and processed to produce information that will be useful in planning for the delivery of social services. For example, in preparing their social service budgets, states have access to census data describing family income within geographic districts, number of children per household, housing characteristics, and a wealth of other information that is useful in determining the services needed. Planning in advance means there is a better chance of delivering social services where and when they are needed, and computer information systems are of great value in this planning process.

When data collection expands under the umbrella of providing better social services, the question of "snooping" and personal privacy arises. Many people believe that the government has no business gathering data from various sources and assembling individual files to "check out" or "check up" on people. Since the early 1960s, when large-scale computers began to markedly increase the efficiency of government data collection, there has been a continual search for a reasonable balance between providing effective planning data and invading the privacy of individuals.

Elections

Computers play a large role in elections to public offices. More and more communities are using computerized voting cards and special voting machines. Many communities also maintain computerized voter registration lists. Candidates and political parties frequently use computers to reach one step beyond these activities, conducting opinion polls, projecting voting outcomes, and evaluating candidates and their platforms. Although in most, if not all, of these latter applications the computers used are not government-owned, the results of the processing may very well influence the course of government.

During any election campaign, you will hear about how candidates are doing in the polls, how voters feel about issues, and what the strong and weak geographic areas for a particular candidate appear to be. These projections would not be possible without access to the speed and power of modern computers. In the course of a campaign, you are also likely to receive letters from candidates, addressed to you personally, asking for your vote or for a campaign contribution and giving you information on the candidate's political views. The personalized touch to these letters is

Figure 4.8
The first exit poll. Gathered around a UNIVAC during the 1952 election are J. Presper Eckert, co-developer of the UNIVAC, and a younger but familiar Walter Cronkite. With only 5 percent of the vote counted, UNIVAC startled CBS management by predicting Eisenhower's victory. No announcement was made until the vote was complete. In 1984, the TV networks projected Reagan as the winner shortly after 8:00 P.M., EST — well before the polls closed in about half the states. Democrats complained that the early projection cost them congressional seats as, with the presidential winner declared, many voters felt there was no reason to go to the polls.
Courtesy of Sperry Corporation.

the result of the text editing and word processing capabilities of the computer. These capabilities also allow candidates to adjust or update their speeches without having to rewrite the entire text.

Computers are also used in conducting exit polls. Such a poll involves collecting data from voters after they have voted but before the polls close, processing the data through a computer, and projecting the outcome of the race on the basis of the sample data. As indicated in Figure 4.8, exit polls are not a new practice.

Not everyone agrees that these uses of computers are always for the good of society. In fact, exit polls have fallen into disfavor in the past several years because they tend to lead people into believing that casting a late vote won't matter if the exit poll already shows a clear winner. In 1985, in response to such criticism, the three major television networks — CBS, NBC, and ABC — agreed not to use exit polls to project the probable winner in a presidential election in any state until after the polls in that state close. However, such an agreement has yet to become law.

Using word processing to fool voters into believing they are receiving personalized letters is probably not so large an issue as exit polls, as we have become accustomed to a wide range of direct-mail marketing techniques. This practice can, however, have the effect of creating a certain amount of cynicism among voters. A very large issue related to these computer applications is the potential for manipulation of the voting system. It has, of course, always been possible to rig an election, but computers make it possible to easily manipulate a very large volume of data. Using a computer to alter the outcome of an election by rigging the voting machines could conceivably affect not just a community or a state but even the entire nation. The opposite side of the coin, of course, is that computers can count votes accurately, quickly, and without bias. They can also provide voters with an abundance of valuable information on which to base their decisions, thus increasing the overall effectiveness of the democratic process.

Local Tax Districts

Municipal and local governments often use computers in the appraisal of real estate and the maintenance of tax records. As the fair market values of properties change, the computer can be programmed to adjust property appraisals to keep them in line with changes in inflation, the cost of living, and other economic conditions such as unemployment; fluctuations in the desirability of an area; the average amount of sales of like properties in the past year; and changes in the features and style of the residence or building. By coding specifics about individual properties (lot size, square footage of the structure, construction features, and other useful data), the tax agency develops a base of data for each property in the tax district. The data on economic conditions, sales in the area, and so forth are entered into the system to represent current conditions. A model is then developed that takes the base of data about a property and relates it to the data on current conditions to arrive at an appraisal (see Figure 4.9).

Figure 4.9
Computerized assessment of real estate.

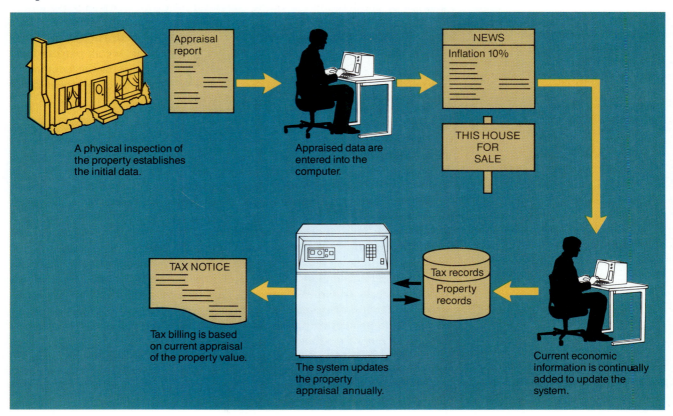

Computerized appraisal of real estate is no substitute for a thorough physical assessment of the property by an on-site inspector. It does, however, give tax agencies a current estimate of the fair market value of taxed properties between physical appraisals. One danger in substituting a computer's assessment for routine human observation is that some relevant facts may be overlooked. Another criticism of this particular computer application is that giving "technocrats" and computers the responsibility for appraising property allows them an inordinate amount of power that could be difficult to retrieve should their performance prove unsatisfactory.

Federal Tax Authority

The Internal Revenue Service uses computers to scan data from tax returns, to check computations, and to search out extraordinary income or deductions. By checking the data against normal ranges developed over time, the IRS computers single out for examination tax returns that exceed reasonable or normal values. Once identified, such returns are referred to a revenue agent for further action.

For the person who files a tax return hoping that it will be overlooked and not be audited, this use of the computer probably seems an imposition, since the computer makes it much more difficult to get away with declaring a questionable deduction or one that's not easily verified. The social value of this computer application is that it helps ensure that we all pay our fair share of taxes. One major concern arising from this use of the computer is the question of who has access to the vast amount of personal data stored in IRS files and how those data will be used.

Law Enforcement

Law enforcement is one area of government that has been slow to take advantage of the capabilities of the computer, largely because of funding restrictions and the lack of commercially available software. However, several large law enforcement agencies, in particular the FBI's National Crime Information Center (NCIC) and police departments in major metropolitan centers such as Los Angeles, have been using computers for some years to meet challenging and difficult information needs. Law enforcement requires access to large volumes of data quickly and at any time of day or night. Computer systems are proving very useful in meeting this need, as well as in protecting police officers from undue danger and in managing law enforcement personnel and resources.

You've probably seen dramatizations of an officer checking a license plate number or a driver's license through a "want and warrant" computer search. Computer systems can quickly search out an individual's record and report it to a radio operator to be relayed to the field officers, thus giving the officers a better understanding of the person with whom they are dealing. Computers are also used to identify stolen property; to determine crime frequencies and locations for increased patrol assignments; to manage traffic-light systems from sensors located throughout a city; and to identify suspects through habits, techniques, personal characteristics, or fingerprints.

A **police intelligence system** enables law enforcement officials to more effectively utilize their personnel. The heart of such a system is a computer that maintains information derived from a number of sources, such as officers' field reports, surveillance, traffic violations, bookings and arrests, and court actions (see Figure 4.10). By combining information from such a variety of sources, it is possible to develop a fuller picture of criminal activity, as well as to follow the movements of an individual or a group of individuals. This kind of monitoring would be impossible without a computer; sorting, combining, and relating the many pieces of information is physically beyond human ability.

Should the police have such a powerful capability to monitor the activities of individuals? How can the average citizen be protected from abuse if the system falls into the wrong hands? Is it really necessary to gather and process all this information, some of which may border on

Figure 4.10
A police intelligence system.

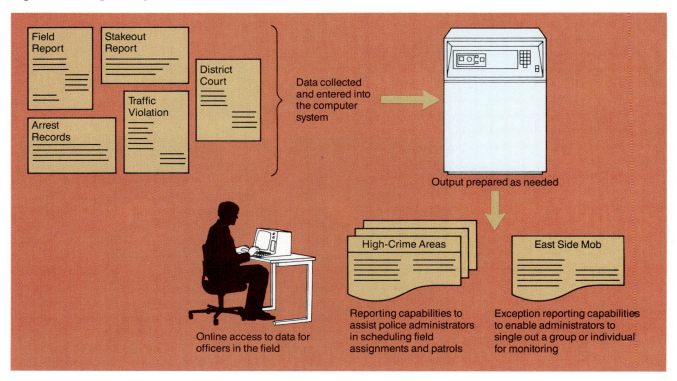

invasions of privacy for the individuals involved, to effectively enforce the law? These are only a few of the questions being asked by advocates of citizens' rights. The position taken by most law enforcement agencies is that more and better information makes for better services.

Military Applications

The military has computing requirements quite unlike any others in society, among them the evaluation of early warning radar signals. A network of radar sites located along the northern boundary of Canada feeds signals from radar sightings to a large computer installation at Malmstrom Air Force Base in Montana, where the computer system evaluates them. If there is a sighting of unfriendly or unknown aircraft, the system activates communications links to command centers, notifies various operations and defense locations, and continues to track the object until it is identified, evaluated, and accounted for.

Information on most of the military uses of computers is classified. Among the uses that are public knowledge are simulations of battles, the control of weaponry, and complex command communications systems. The "Star Wars" defense system proposed in the early 1980s would also rely heavily on computing technology (see Figure 4.11).

Computers undoubtedly increase the efficiency of military planning and the chances of achieving military objectives. However, in these computer applications, as in all others that presently exist, computers operate only under the control of human beings. To launch and target a missile requires a human finger to press the button. The solutions to the problems of military buildup and the threat of nuclear war won't be found in banning computer technology, as the technology doesn't create the problems. These solutions will be found only in the human, political arena.

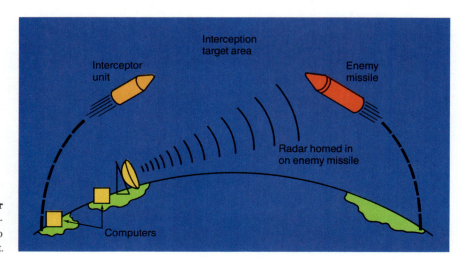

Figure 4.11
Computer technology and "Star Wars." Computers translate radar signals homed in on the enemy missile into flight corrections for the interceptor unit.

EDUCATIONAL USES AND ABUSES OF COMPUTERS

When computers were introduced, many educators believed they would revolutionize education by providing self-paced, individualized, teacherless learning. Computers have not lived up to these early expectations for several reasons, including the difficulty of developing effective learning routines as well as reservations on the part of both instructors and students. Numerous applications are, however, contributing to the educational process, particularly for special groups such as handicapped learners. In performing drill and routine practice exercises, such as would be done for students with learning disabilities, the computer offers great promise. Instead of having to work individually on both learning and drill with each student, the teacher can focus on the learning activities and let students use the computer for the drill work. Because the computer never gets tired, bored, or upset with the student, it is a perfect drill medium. With special peripheral equipment, such as a voice-activated input device or a braille printer, a computer can be configured to meet almost any special educational requirement.

Such **computer-assisted instruction (CAI)** is not limited to use with handicapped students; it can be used with gifted and average students as well. A danger is that it can be overused, but that, of course, depends on the teacher. Teachers can also use the computer to tailor educational programs to meet the specific needs of individual students (see Figure 4.12). This use of the computer is sometimes referred to as **computer-managed instruction (CMI).**

One major problem that educators face in regard to CAI, whether the instruction is for special or average students, is the variety of procedures, languages, programs, and routines found in different computer systems.

Figure 4.12
Computer-managed instruction.
Programs can be tailored to meet the educational needs of individual students.
Courtesy of Apple Computer, Inc.

ADOBE-SCHOOL COMPUTERS

Eagles soar majestically in the clean mountain air, gliding through the clear and crystalline light that for generations has attracted world-class artists to Taos, a small mountain town in northern New Mexico. Little has changed there in over a thousand years, including the ancient Tiwa Indian village of Taos Pueblo, a rambling collection of earth-red adobes at the northern edge of the town....

Taos Pueblo is a community committed to tradition: It has no running water, no electrical lighting, no central heating and no plumbing—little, in fact, that would identify it as a member of the modern community of Man.

Except for a computer-assisted education program that is changing the way Tiwa Indian children learn, think, and even the way they play.

"For the first time in the history of this school we have 50 percent of the student body reading at or above grade level," says Taos Day School superintendent Roy French. "I can't tie that directly to computers, but putting them in is the only change we've made in the past year. The connection is clear—and it validates our original thinking that computers were necessary to make our kids competitive in today's world."

French is a Bureau of Indian Affairs employee responsible for day-to-day administration of the 120-student school. The facility is modern only by comparison: It, too, is adobe, with a roof held up by the massive wood beams called vigas that characterize architecture in the region. The school, which is adjacent to but separate from the Pueblo, has electric lights, modern heating—and 13 Apple IIc's networked and linked with an Echo II voice synthesizer....

More than 100 separate software packages are available, each chosen to suit the needs of individual grade levels. They range from the popular Bank Street Writer, which offers students a chance to improve their word processing skills, to much more sophisticated math and technology teachers like Rocky's Boots—an introduction via an imaginary world to principles of circuit design and logic....

The school emphasizes programs that supplement the Three R's....

Not-so-basic topics like music, sociology and information on physical education are also offered. But the favorite—at least by student standards—is probably Talking Typewriter, a program with voice capability.

Taos Pueblo starts exposing its children to computers early — in kindergarten. But what possible benefit can a 5-year-old who's barely mastered his own Tiwa language draw from a computer that speaks English? "Everyone wonders about that," French says. "Well, no problem. It took [Pueblo Board of Education member] Gil Suazo just about half an hour to get them (the computers) speaking Tiwa."

The five-year-olds, in fact, have two talking programs available — Typewriter and another called Talking Screen Textwriter. A huge A appears on the screen when a child strikes a key, and the computer then pronounces the letter. Watching the children use the system is a lesson in the joys of learning: Each keystrike is followed by an explosion of giggles and hot jostling to see who's next.

"The biggest advantage for preschoolers is instant reinforcement," French says. They type in a letter and bang — the machine prints it and says it aloud."

French says that the machines can — and do — halve the time required to teach a youngster English.

"It's instant enlightenment when they hit a button and the machine says the letter," French says with a laugh.

Students aren't the only ones who benefit, either. Computers in the classroom make life significantly easier for the instructors, too — if they're willing to try them.

"Some instructors do seem to see them as a threat," French says. "They're not. We use them purely to supplement traditional instruction — we're not here to train programmers. And in fact, I think that when they're fully accepted they'll make teaching a much more attractive profession — they'll take over the boring part, the drills and the exercises that don't permit a creative involvement by the instructor."...

Running water or no running water, Taos Pueblo is in the computer age and it intends to stay there.

◆

— Kim Anderson, "Adobe-School Computers." Reprinted with permission from *Personal Computing*, May 1985, pp. 25, 29. Copyright 1985, Hayden Publishing Company.

Efforts are underway to overcome this problem. At the University of Waterloo in Ontario, Canada, researchers are developing software that will run identically on a wide range of equipment and that will give students and instructors a consistent set of operating instructions and a "friendly" computer environment. When such a standardized system is developed, students will be able to use the same computer procedures for carrying out assignments in a computer class, for evaluating the results of an experiment in a chemistry class, and for sharpening their foreign language skills in a language laboratory. Instead of having to learn three distinct systems, students will have to learn only one.

Critics of CAI believe that individuality and interpersonal relationships suffer when a computer is used in an educational setting; some feel that curiosity, imagination, and creativity are also stifled. Proponents of CAI, on the other hand, believe that the computer can enhance a student's natural tendency to explore, to learn, and to create. Probably the most reasonable perspective is that in the hands of a competent teacher, the computer is a useful educational tool, much like a textbook or a chalkboard. If the teacher uses it properly, the computer can contribute to the learning process; improperly used, it will certainly fulfill all the critics' expectations. Whatever way it is used, a computer system probably will never substitute for the human model that a teacher can provide.

COMPUTERS IN MEDICINE: PROS AND CONS

The most frequent use of computers in a medical setting is for business purposes, such as maintaining patient records and billing individuals and insurance companies. In addition, computers are used in medical research, physical diagnosis, medical training, x-ray analysis, and patient monitoring (see Figure 4.13).

A rapidly evolving use of computers can be found in the medical laboratory, especially in the areas of hematology (the study of blood cells) and biochemistry (the study of chemical changes in the body). Computers control the laboratory equipment that processes the patient samples, monitor the testing procedures, and tabulate the test results. Because computer-controlled testing equipment reduces human handling of specimens and equipment, the chances of human error are reduced. Processing is quicker, and overall accuracy is improved. It is, of course, still up to the physician to interpret test results, although software systems are being designed to assist in this diagnostic activity as well.

The prototypes of the systems being developed to aid in diagnosis look very promising. Unless physicians have seen a certain disease, they may have difficulty in recognizing its symptoms and making the proper diagnosis. For example, if a physician has never seen rabies, a somewhat uncommon disease, the first diagnosis of a patient suffering from rabies might be incorrect. With this new software, the computer can calculate probabilities based on the test data and observations that the physician enters into the system. The computer then tells the physician of the probability

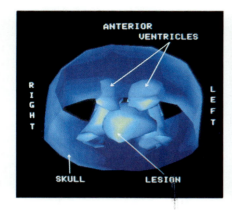
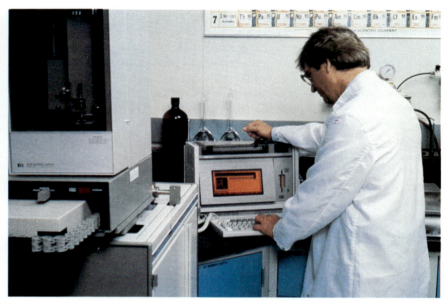
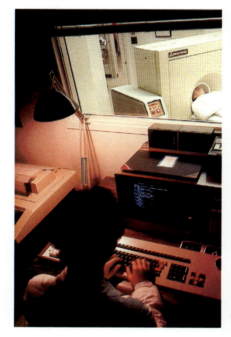
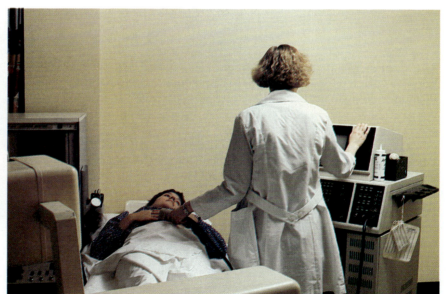

Figure 4.13
Medical uses of computers: (*top left*) x-ray analysis; (*top right*) laboratory analysis; (*bottom left*) physical diagnosis; (*bottom right*) patient monitoring.
Photos provided courtesy of (top left) Ramtek Corporation; (top right) Hewlitt-Packard; (bottom left) Nubar Alexanian/Stock, Boston; (bottom right) Herb Snitzer/Stock, Boston.

that with a certain set of circumstances, a number of diseases might be indicated, including rabies. These software systems don't substitute for observation, medical training, and common sense, but they do provide one more tool for the physician to use to be sure that nothing has been overlooked in the diagnosis and treatment of disease.

Medical training is an area that lends itself to the computer's ability to simulate a real-world environment. For example, one medical school in New England has computerized its patient records for a five-year period. The records include test results, medications prescribed, patients' vital signs and progress, and other pertinent data. When medical students go to the lab to sharpen their diagnostic skills, the computer can provide them with a "patient" (in this case a patient record and simulation program rather than an actual person), present the vital information, and let them proceed with the diagnosis and therapy. When the students order tests, the computer will present the test results it has on file; and when they prescribe medication, the system will cause the simulated patient to respond to the drugs. The simulation program will take over whenever the file doesn't have the necessary data for the students to proceed, but it will present actual data when available. This setting is not a contrived one, as it is in most computerized simulations; rather, it allows the students to work from data on actual patients with real illnesses. The benefit, of course, is that if students make a mistake, they can review the circumstances leading to the mistake and can learn from it without harming anyone.

As in office automation and in CAI, computers in medicine raise the issue of depersonalization. The practice of medicine has traditionally been a person-to-person activity. When technology is brought to bear, the direct, personal relationship between physician and patient may suffer. On the other hand, computers may enhance the medical care that patients receive. Another problem related to the use of computers in medicine is the protection of confidential information — such as patient records and test results stored in computer files — against unauthorized access.

SUMMARY

In this chapter, we have touched on just a few of the ways in which our society uses computers. Clearly, computers can be very useful tools, but they can also have their social costs. However, it is not the computers that create the social problems associated with computer applications; rather, it is the ways in which people use these tools.

Automation can improve the productivity of office workers, but implementing it presents certain technical and organizational problems. In addition, office automation raises questions about stress, health problems, depersonalization, job loss or displacement, and increased chances of data errors that can infringe on personal rights.

Computer-aided design and computer-aided manufacturing (CAD/CAM) have brought computing technology into the factory, with the result that operations have become more efficient and more economical. Computer-controlled machines, or robots, have been making such significant contributions to manufacturing that this era has been dubbed the "steel-collar" age. The savings made possible by CAD techniques and robots have been translated into better and less expensive products for consumers. A social cost of these techniques is job elimination. However, for those engineers who don't lose their jobs when CAD techniques are introduced, the result can be more stimulating and creative work.

Federal, state, and local governments use computers not only to process business-related data but also to plan the delivery of social services, to tabulate the results of elections, to assess and verify property and income taxes, and to support law enforcement and military operations. Generally, computers improve the delivery of government services, but they raise some serious social concerns, among them invasions of privacy and the possibility of manipulations and errors that could affect large segments of society. The uses to which computers are sometimes put by candidates, political parties, and the news media have caused concern that computers can erode democratic processes by creating voter cynicism or apathy. On the other hand, these same uses can give voters an abundance of information on which to base their decisions.

Computer-assisted instruction (CAI) can be especially useful in meeting the educational needs of handicapped learners, and computer-managed instruction (CMI) can be used to tailor educational programs to meet the needs of any student. The development of standardized software for educational purposes should greatly enhance the uses of both CAI and CMI. Criticisms of using the computer in education are that it contributes to a loss of individuality and to depersonalization and that it can stifle curiosity, imagination, and creativity. Probably the most reasonable view is that in competent hands, the computer can be a useful educational tool but that it cannot substitute for a teacher.

Among the unique ways that computers serve in a medical setting are in the automation of laboratory procedures, in assisting in the diagnosis of disease, and in training medical students. Like computer applications in other fields, the application of computers to medicine raises the issue of depersonalization, as well as the possibility of unauthorized access to confidential information stored in computer files.

KEY TERMS

computer-aided design and
  computer-aided manufacturing
  (CAD/CAM) (102)
computer-assisted instruction
  (CAI) (113)
computer-managed instruction
  (CMI) (113)

engineering simulation (104)
job displacement (101)
knowledge workers (information
  workers) (96)
police intelligence system (111)
productivity (96)
robots (104)

DISCUSSION QUESTIONS

1. How can computers help improve office productivity? What technical and organizational problems does office automation present?

2. Identify the social problems posed by office automation and explain what you, as president of a business, would do to alleviate these problems. What do you think is the most important of these social issues? Explain your reasoning.

3. Explain how CAD/CAM techniques improve productivity in the manufacturing plant. How do these uses of computers benefit society?

4. Why would CAD/CAM be a concern to union leaders? To factory workers? To draftsmen and engineers?

5. Discuss the effects of using computers in elections.

6. Describe the debate that might take place between an advocate of citizens' rights and a law enforcement official on the subject of using computers in law enforcement.

7. How have computers been used in education? Can you think of any new ways in which they might help you in your studies?

8. Discuss your views on the pros and cons of CAI.

9. Describe three ways in which computers serve the medical profession. How would you feel about these uses if you were a patient in a hospital?

10. Why are invasions of privacy and depersonalization such large issues in the application of computing technology?

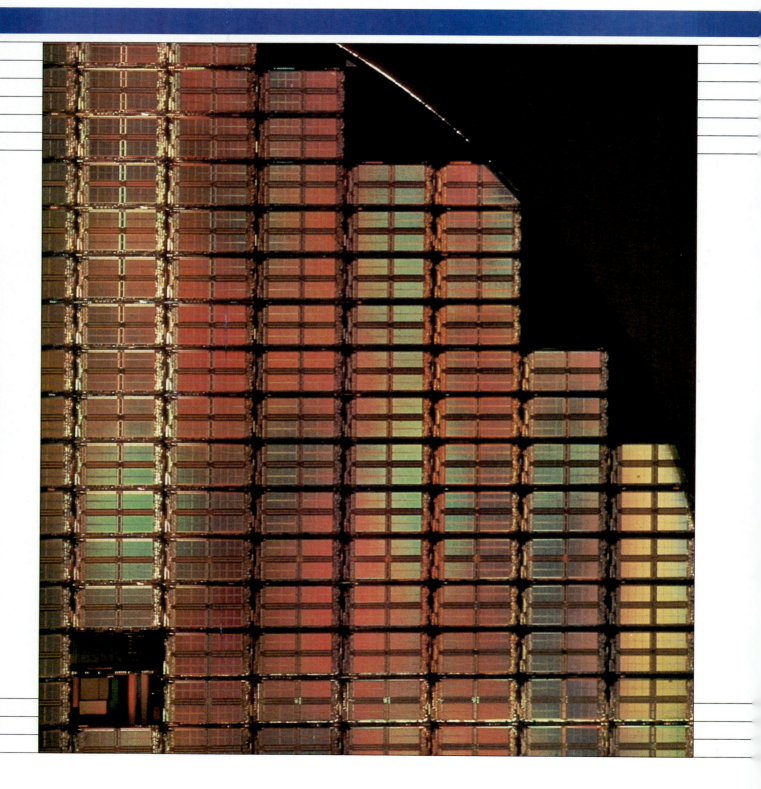

PART·II

Chapter 5 THE CENTRAL PROCESSING UNIT
Chapter 6 INPUT
Chapter 7 OUTPUT
Chapter 8 AUXILIARY STORAGE
Chapter 9 DATA COMMUNICATIONS AND DISTRIBUTED DATA PROCESSING
Chapter 10 THE MICROCOMPUTER PHENOMENON

TECHNOLOGY TODAY

It has been said that if all technological development of computers stopped today, it would take us at least fifty years to fully utilize the computer resources that we presently have at our disposal. In Part I, you got some feel for the technological developments that have brought us to this rather amazing state of affairs — the progression from vacuum tubes to large-scale circuit integration and the microprocessor chip. Despite the current abundance of resources, computing technology is in a state of rapid and dynamic change, with no end in sight. The distribution of computing to branch offices and from country to country has created a need for both improved communications technology and faster and more powerful computers. The marvel of optical scanning as an input technique has led to other remarkable innovations in this area. When powerful processing capabilities are tied to scanning and other sensory input techniques, robots and the automated factory emerge.

In Part II, we'll look at the "state of the art" of all this computer hardware: Chapter 5 focuses on that "black box" that is the heart of the computer system. Chapters 6 and 7 look at today's array of input and output devices. Chapter 8 concentrates on the various types of auxiliary storage devices, those extra "brain cells" the computer needs for its long-term memory. Chapter 9 explores the hardware appendages that make distributed data processing possible. Finally, Chapter 10 examines the computing phenomenon that has beset us all: the microcomputer.

OUTLINE

THE STORED-PROGRAM CONCEPT AND THE CPU: A BRIEF REVIEW

PROGRAM INSTRUCTIONS AND STORAGE AREAS

    Addresses
    Registers

HOW THE CPU EXECUTES PROGRAM INSTRUCTIONS

STORAGE CAPACITY AND TERMINOLOGY

THE CODING OF DATA

    The Binary Numbering System
    Coding Schemes
    The Parity Bit

PRIMARY STORAGE COMPONENTS

RAM, ROM, PROM, AND EPROM

SELECTION CRITERIA

SUMMARY

KEY TERMS

DISCUSSION QUESTIONS

OVERVIEW

You are running through an airport, late for a plane, when you discover that you forgot to bring your plane ticket with you. In despair, you confront the airline agent with your problem. As you watch in amazement, the agent enters a few keystrokes at a terminal; a slight pause; the agent enters a few more keystrokes — and suddenly the sound of printing. In a minute, the agent processes your charge card and hands you your replacement ticket, and you are able to make your flight. While the keystroking and the printing are obviously an important part of your ticketing, the real heart of the matter is the ability of the computer reservation system to process ticket inquiries and requests quickly and efficiently.

As you settle into your airplane seat, still out of breath, the question of how the computer handled your request so efficiently might cross your mind. The answer: a program that is stored in the computer's central processing unit. But how can the computer respond so quickly, you might wonder. The answer to that is that the program instructions and necessary data are stored in such a way that they can be accessed and processed as a stream of electronic signals without human intervention. Because electricity travels at the speed of light, substituting electronic signals for human activities is bound to speed the process of searching for information.

In this chapter, we'll take a look at what goes on inside the "black box" known as the CPU. You may be surprised at how uncomplicated the CPU's activities really are. And you may also be surprised at how unmysterious computer acronyms can be. Our objectives in this chapter are to

◆ explain the functions of the CPU's storage addresses and registers.

◆ describe how the CPU works in a coordinated effort to execute a program and to process data.

◆ discuss primary storage capacity and the terminology used in that context.

◆ explain how data are coded for the computer.

◆ identify types of storage components.

◆ explain the meaning of RAM, ROM, PROM, and EPROM.

◆ discuss the criteria used in the selection of a central processing unit.

CHAPTER 5

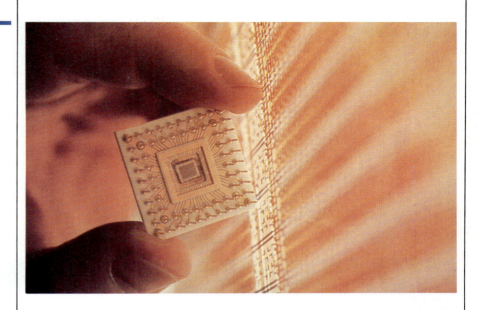

THE CENTRAL PROCESSING UNIT

THE STORED-PROGRAM CONCEPT AND THE CPU: A BRIEF REVIEW

As you know from Part I, today's general-purpose computer operates on the *stored-program* principle — that is, different programs and data are stored in the CPU's *primary storage unit* for as long as they are needed. The *control unit* of the CPU oversees the input and initial storage of both the program instructions and the data to be processed, as well as their orderly retrieval from storage during program execution. As it interprets each program instruction, the control unit sends signals to activate the proper electronic circuits in the arithmetic/logic unit. The *arithmetic/logic unit* then carries out the required operations on the stored data, and the control unit sees that the results of the processing are stored and delivered to the proper output device when needed. Working in synchronization, these three functional units of the CPU — primary storage, control, and arithmetic/logic — are at the heart of any computer system (see Figure 5.1). Before we look at exactly how the CPU goes about executing program

Figure 5.1
The role of the CPU in the computer system.

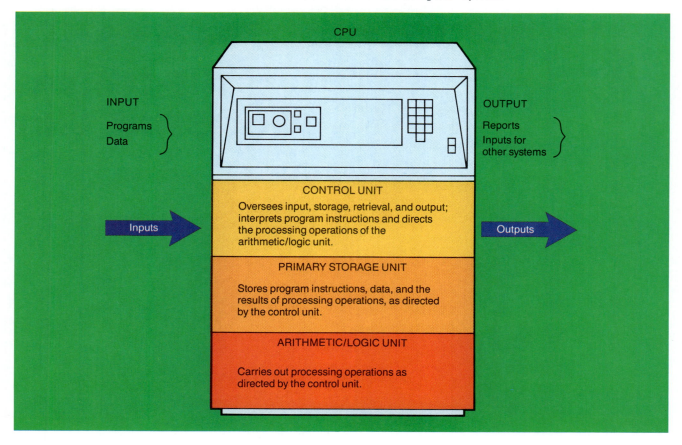

instructions, a closer look at some of the features of these instructions and of storage areas is in order.

PROGRAM INSTRUCTIONS AND STORAGE AREAS

In Chapter 1, we described a program as the set of step-by-step instructions that the computer must have in order to perform any kind of operation. What we didn't mention in Chapter 1, however, is that each of these program instructions has two parts: an **operation code (op code),** which specifies the type of operation to be performed, and an **operand,** which specifies the storage location of the item of data to be processed. For instance, a program instruction written in a high-level programming language might read "ADD A,B." ADD is the op code (other examples of op codes are SUBTRACT, COMPARE, READ DATA); and A,B are the operands, indicating in code the places in primary storage where the data to be added are located. To be executed by a computer, a program instruction must contain both an op code and an operand. To be understood by the computer, of course, the high-level code would have to be translated into machine language (see Figure 5.2).

When the program instructions, each containing an op code and an operand, are loaded into the CPU's primary storage unit, they are entered in the order required for execution so that they can be easily retrieved. Because the computer processes only one instruction at a time, and it processes all instructions in sequential order unless the program tells it to do otherwise, the program instructions are placed in sequential locations within the storage unit. To keep input data, programming instructions, and the results of processing separate, the programmer designates separate areas within primary storage for these purposes. Figure 5.3 shows how primary storage is divided. As you can see in the figure, an additional area

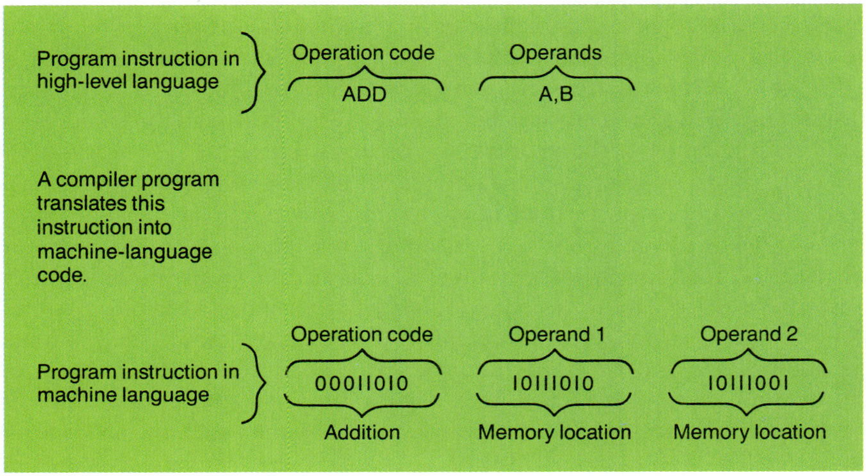

Figure 5.2
A program instruction's operation code and operands translated from a high-level programming language into machine language.

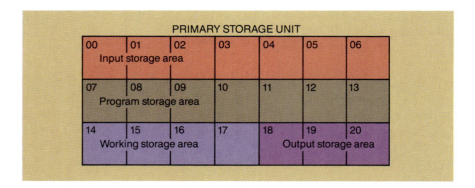

Figure 5.3
Divisions of primary storage.

called the working storage area is used to hold the results of intermediate processing. These divisions are not set physical areas; the programmer may use the same area for input storage in one application as for output storage in the next.

Addresses

How does the control unit keep track of the data and instructions that are placed in primary storage, and how does it let the arithmetic/logic unit know where to find the data that are to be processed? The answer is, by **address.** The primary storage unit has a number of small storage areas, each with enough capacity to hold a few characters or numbers — often four, in a mainframe computer. Each of these storage areas is given a unique address, designated by an address number. For example, a computer with a primary storage capacity for 512,000 characters would have 128,000 addressable memory locations, numbered from 000000 to 127999, if it was designed to hold four characters per address. If the data to be stored have more than four characters, as, for example, in a five-character name like Jones, several addressable storage areas can be linked. The computer can do this linking automatically as needed. It is to these numbered addresses that the operands of the program instructions refer.

Each address, or storage location, holds either a processing instruction (i.e., an op code) or an item of data to be processed (i.e., an operand). (Thus, *operand* really has two meanings: It is the part of the program instruction that specifies the address of the data in primary storage; it is also the item of data to be operated on.) For example, in Figure 5.4, the storage space at address 08 contains the instruction "read [the contents of address] 01 into A/L unit," and the space at address 01 holds the data to be processed. (The figure shows the program instructions in human language; in reality, of course, they would be stored in machine language —

that is, as a series of 0's and 1's, following the coding system of the specific machine being used.)

It's convenient to think of these primary storage spaces as a group of post-office mailboxes, each with its own identifying number, in that the contents of a mailbox may change, but its identifying number will stay the same. Similarly, in the program shown in Figure 5.4, once the data on

Figure 5.4

Storage areas for a payroll program. Once the data and instructions have entered primary storage, processing proceeds from one instruction to the next. This simplified payroll program shows, in an abbreviated form, how gross and net pay are calculated in the arithmetic/logic unit. To keep the illustration as simple as possible, the leading zeros in the storage addresses have been omitted.

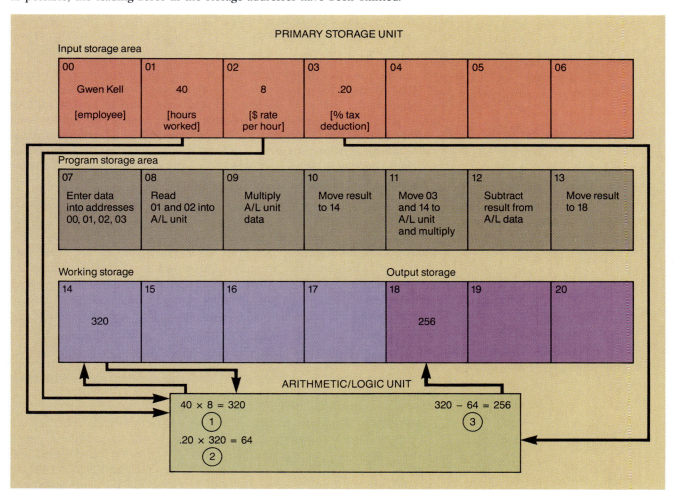

employee Gwen Kell have been processed, a program instruction will call for new data on another employee to be entered at addresses 00, 01, 02, and 03; so, the contents of the addresses will change, but the addresses will be the same. However, there are some important differences between primary storage spaces and post-office mailboxes:

1. A mailbox can hold several items; a primary storage space can hold only one item at a time.

2. When you place an item in a mailbox that already contains other items, those items do not disappear. But when the CPU enters a new item into a primary storage space (i.e., *writes* a new instruction or a new piece of data), the item that was in that space is destroyed and disappears. In this way, primary storage is like a tape recorder: When you record on a tape, you erase the old contents. This feature of primary storage is known as **destructive write.** Thus, in Figure 5.4, when new data are written into addresses 00, 01, 02, and 03, the old data on Gwen Kell are destroyed.

3. When you take the contents out of a mailbox, the mailbox is empty. That doesn't happen in the CPU's mailboxes. When the control unit goes to the indicated address and *reads* the contents at that address, it leaves the data there undisturbed while it goes on to transfer what it's read to the arithmetic/logic unit. This feature of primary storage is known as **nondestructive read,** and it means that the same instructions and data can be processed again and again until the program calls for them to be changed.

With the large capacities of modern computers, it would be a tremendous job for a programmer to keep track of what is being stored at each address. Fortunately for programmers, computer manufacturers have developed **indexing systems** that do this job for them. These systems are rather like library card catalogs: They provide a quick means of locating data. When the control unit calls for an instruction, the indexing system determines the address to be read. It is then a simple matter for the control unit to search out the data or instruction and send it to the arithmetic/logic section.

Registers

Registers are temporary storage places for instructions and data. They are not part of primary storage, but they are part of the CPU. And like everything else in the CPU, they operate under the direction of the control unit. Registers are used because they improve the efficiency of the CPU by speeding up the transfer of instructions and data and the performance of arithmetic and logic operations. Because registers provide much faster access to stored items than the primary storage unit does, instructions and data are usually moved out of primary storage into the registers just before processing begins.

As shown in Figure 5.5, the CPU may contain various kinds of special-purpose registers. The **instruction register** and the **address register** are generally located in the control unit. Just before a program instruction is due for processing, the control unit breaks it down into the operation code and the operand, and it puts the op code in the instruction register and the operand in the address register. The **storage register** temporarily stores data to be used in processing, and the **accumulator** stores the accumulated results of computations; these registers are located in the arithmetic/logic unit. Computers vary in the number and types of registers that they have. Some computers have no special-purpose registers but instead use a **general-purpose register** for both addressing and computation.

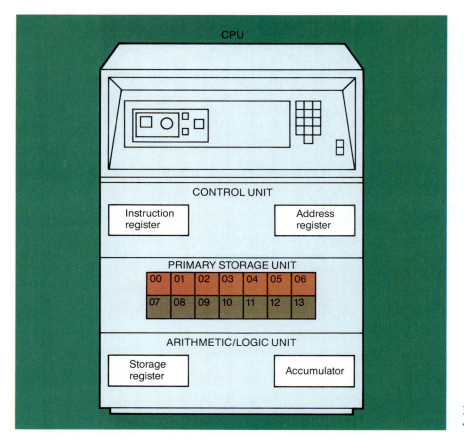

Figure 5.5
The location of registers in the CPU.

HOW THE CPU EXECUTES PROGRAM INSTRUCTIONS

Each program instruction goes through two cycles as it is executed. First is **instruction time,** or **I-time,** the time during which the control unit fetches an instruction from primary storage, decodes it, and puts it in the registers. The second cycle, called **execution time,** or **E-time,** is the time during which the data are retrieved from primary storage and the arithmetic/logic unit performs the specific operation called for in the instruction. Taken together, these two cycles are called the **machine cycle.**

Figure 5.6(a)
I-time activities.

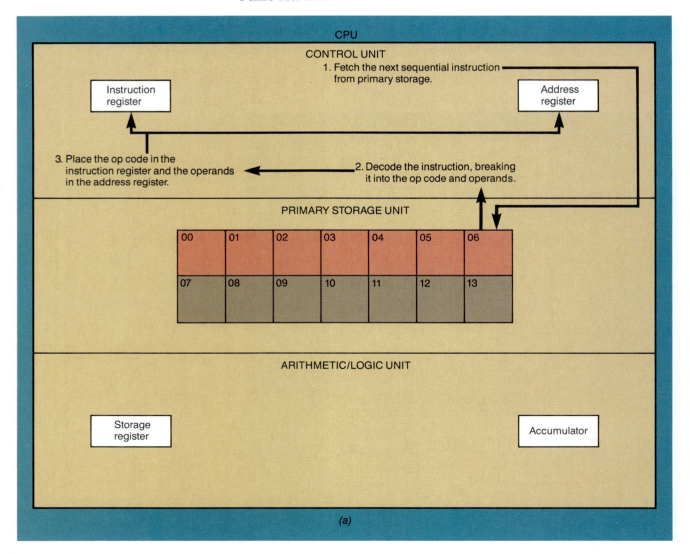

Figure 5.6 shows what goes on inside the CPU as it executes a single instruction in a payroll program. Although the figure isolates a single program instruction, a typical payroll program would contain thousands of instructions. Once the data from the payroll time cards have entered the system, an operator sets the computer to the first program instruction. At that point, human intervention ends and the control unit takes over. I-time activities are as follows:

Figure 5.6(b)
E-time activities.

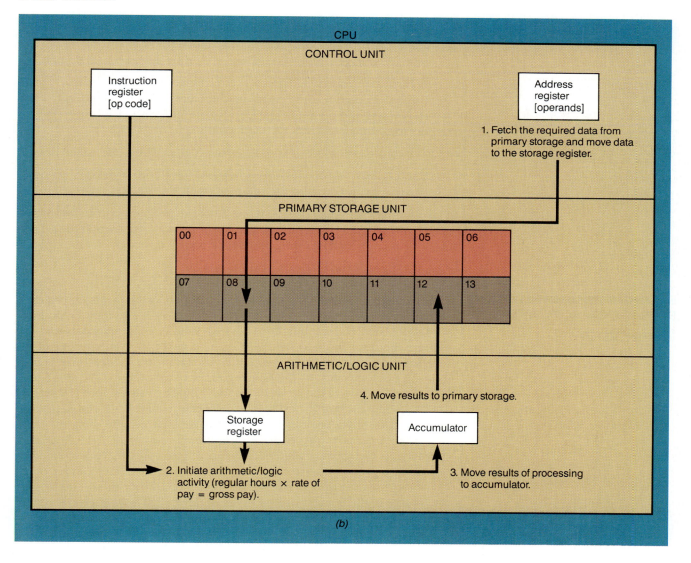

1. The control unit fetches the instruction for computation of gross pay from primary storage.

2. The control unit decodes the instruction so that the computer can execute it. We would think of the instruction as being REGULAR HOURS × RATE OF PAY = GROSS PAY.

3. The control unit loads the decoded processing instruction (op code) into the instruction register in preparation for processing, and it loads the operands into the address register to show where the data to be processed are stored and where the results of processing are to be placed in storage.

E-time activities to complete the processing operation include the following:

1. Using the operands, the control unit moves the time-card data out of primary storage to the storage register in the arithmetic/logic unit to make the data accessible for processing.

2. Using the op code, the control unit instructs the arithmetic/logic unit to perform the computation to calculate gross pay, and the arithmetic/logic unit performs the computation.

3. The control unit moves the results of the computation to the accumulator.

4. The control unit moves the processing results to a primary storage location as directed by the information in the address register.

A new I-time cycle then begins. When all of the program instructions have been executed, the control unit instructs the primary storage unit to release the processing results to the appropriate output device.

STORAGE CAPACITY AND TERMINOLOGY

When computer designers assemble the electronic components for primary storage, they use particular terms to represent the concepts they are dealing with. Let's step back a minute to review some of these concepts and to explore the terms used to represent them. If we relate computer memory to what we know about the properties of matter, these ideas may come into sharper focus. Just as the building block of all matter is the atom, the **bit** (short for *bi*nary digi*t*) is the building block of all computer storage. The bit is represented by a 0 or a 1, either electronically or magnetically, and it can be thought of as a switch that is off or on. The concept that the bit represents is the two-state, or *binary,* nature of the electronic components of digital computers. As Figure 5.7 indicates, these components can be in only one of two states at any one time: A circuit can be only closed or open, a magnetized spot is either there or not there, and so on. The binary digits 0 and 1 are therefore a convenient way of representing data and programs within the computer system.

A combination of atoms produces a molecule, which has distinctive features; similarly, when bits are put together, they form a byte. A **byte**

PARALLEL PROCESSING, OR WILL MICROCOMPUTERS DEVELOP SPLIT PERSONALITIES?

Back in the 1950s, when the public was first becoming aware of the power of computers, the machines were often described as "electronic brains." Some people felt threatened by the implied comparison, but the truth is that brains are still more powerful than computers. Yet the metaphor may have been prophetic, for parallel processing, a new approach to developing faster, more capable computers, makes the old brain-computer analogy more apt.

The human brain is nature's parallel processor: countless neuron networks communicate simultaneously, and we quickly store the tremendous amounts of data that enable us to see, hear, and think.... Traditional electronic brains are not so sophisticated. They operate serially, reading sequential bits and bytes with a single processor.

This time-honored approach dates back to the nineteenth century and Charles Babbage's mechanical "Analytical Engine," which worked on much the same principle, with one gear activating the next....

Near the end of World War II, Hungarian-American John von Neumann and colleagues developed the traditional serial architecture that underlies virtually all of today's computers, from massive mainframes to the micro in your home. It's true that on larger computers certain advanced techniques provide a degree of parallel operation. But basically, serial computers do one thing at a time, one after another.

Parallel processing, in several versions of "Non-von" architecture, may change all that. It's based on a simple principle: two microprocessors are better than one, four are better than two, and so on — up to perhaps 10,000 or more in the future. Instead of relying on one processor to solve a lengthy calculation, a computer with parallel architecture assigns portions of the problem to multiple processors operating simultaneously....

Parallel processing is beginning to answer the need for faster, smarter computers to perform complex tasks such as three-dimensional simulations of real-world events, seismic exploration, aerodynamic design, computer speech and vision, and problem solving with artificial intelligence. The technique, whose primary benefit is speed, shows great potential for tackling very large problems with multiple variables. It's not that you couldn't get the same answer with a serial machine; you just might not have the time to wait for it. If you're a fighter pilot, to use a graphic example, your interactive expert system had better talk fast.

Historically, we've increased computer speed and capacity by cramming more and faster devices onto smaller and smaller chips. But this approach does have limits. The sophisticated Cray-2, with a price tag of several million dollars, is a good example. Its components are so densely packed that they must be submerged in an inert liquid fluorocarbon coolant to reduce heat.

The Cray and almost all other "supercomputers" represent one parallel-processing design philosophy: linking a small number of expensive, state-of-the-art processors....

Most academic research has embraced a second philosophy: designing computers with a much larger number of relatively inexpensive, off-the-shelf microprocessors....

It will be quite a few years before microcomputers take on the characteristics of the human brain. But parallel processing seems a tentative step in that direction. Researchers at Carnegie-Mellon University envision a brainlike computer with memory distributed throughout a parallel network. Such a machine might be able to deal with concepts and generalizations. It also would, like the human brain, have built-in redundancy — if one processor (cell) were damaged, another would take over.

John von Neumann was himself quite familiar with parallel processing; he often related his "automata," or thinking machines, to nature's computers. But parallel processing just wasn't feasible with the large, power-hungry relays and vacuum tubes of the 1940s. The 1990s will be another story. Your new micro just might develop a split personality.

— Robert Swearengin, "Parallel Processing." Reprinted with permission from the May 1985 issue of *Popular Computing* magazine. Copyright © by McGraw-Hill, Inc., New York 10020. All rights reserved.

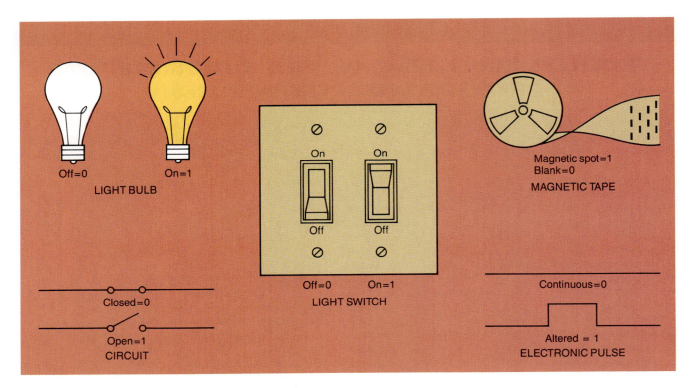

Figure 5.7
The binary state of electronic components.

is a number of bits, often 8, that form a storage unit capable of holding one *character* of data—that is, one number, letter, symbol, or blank (see Figure 5.8).

Most data processed today consist of more than one character (or byte); so a number of bytes are combined to form a **word,** which can be given a uniquely numbered address and placed in one storage location (see Figure 5.9). Some computers are designed to hold **fixed word-lengths** in each numbered address. The number of characters in these fixed word-

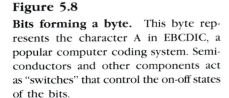

Figure 5.8
Bits forming a byte. This byte represents the character A in EBCDIC, a popular computer coding system. Semiconductors and other components act as "switches" that control the on-off states of the bits.

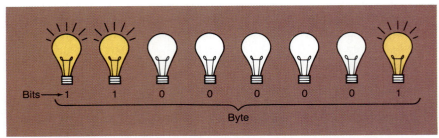

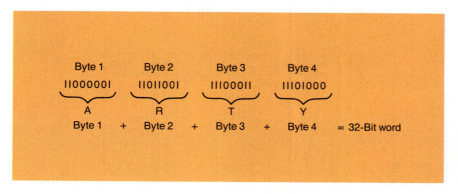

Figure 5.9

Bytes assembled to form a word. In this configuration, each 32-bit word is addressable.

lengths depends on the computer. For example, as we noted earlier, primary storage in many mainframes has a fixed word-length of 4 bytes (or 32 bits); in a supercomputer, the fixed word-length might be 8 bytes (or 64 bits). Table 5.1 shows the word sizes used in some modern computers.

Machines with fixed word-lengths move the data a word at a time. Other computers are designed with **variable word-lengths;** each numbered address holds one character of data, and the data are moved a character at a time. Figure 5.10 illustrates the differences between these two types of design. The fixed word-length offers faster computational speed, especially in numerical calculations, since it moves the data a word at a time; but it can result in wasted space if the entire word capacity isn't used. Variable word-length makes better use of storage space, as a character can be stored at each address; but it is slower because more small addressable units are used to store the data and the data are moved a character at a time.

Table 5.1   Word Sizes in Modern Fixed Word-Length Computers

	Bytes per Word	Bits per Word
Microcomputers		
Apple II	1	8
TRS-80 III	1	8
IBM-PC	2	16
Mainframes		
Data General	4	32
IBM	4	32
Supercomputers		
Cray-1	8	64
Cyber 205	8	64

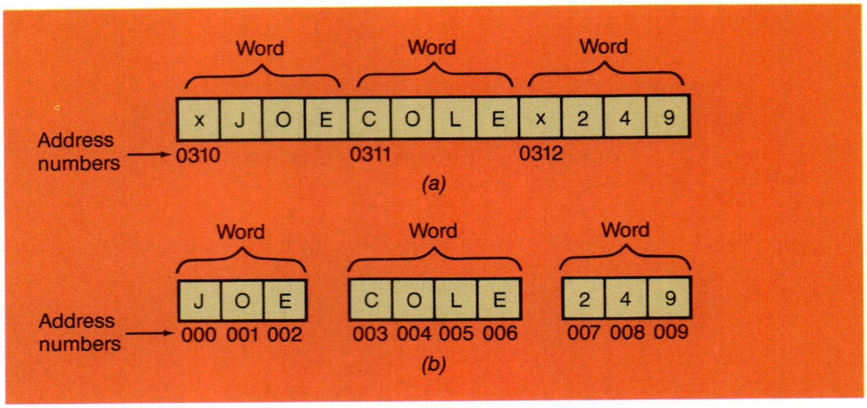

Figure 5.10

Primary storage design: (*a*) fixed word-lengths; (*b*) variable word-lengths. A computer having the fixed word-length shown here could hold four characters in each storage address.

If you lined up hundreds or thousands of coffee cups, each capable of storing a small amount of liquid and each accessible on a grid or map, you'd have something resembling the layout of the primary storage unit of the CPU. To make it easy to organize and find data, storage is usually set up in units of 1,024 (2^{10}) bytes each. Each such unit is called a **kilobyte**, or **K**. When you hear that a computer has 512K, you know that its primary storage unit has the capacity to store 512 × 1,024 bytes, or 524,288 characters. Occasionally, storage is also described in terms of **megabytes (M's)**, which are approximately 1 million bytes each.

THE CODING OF DATA

People communicate by using numbers, letters, and special symbols. Some of these symbols can convey rather complex ideas. For example, the parking space nearest the door of your local supermarket probably has the outline of a wheelchair painted on it. This symbol tells you that the space is reserved for someone with a physical handicap and that if you don't have a handicap, you shouldn't park there. From a single symbol, you are able to understand a rather complex concept. The computer, of course, can't understand any such thing. Nor can it really understand numbers or letters. In fact, all it can "understand" or respond to are electronic signals that activate its switches. How, then, is it possible to represent data so that the computer can store and process them?

For the earliest computers, data were coded according to the familiar decimal numbering system. The electronic circuitry, consisting of vacuum tubes, was designed in a way that corresponded to the decimal system's ten digits—0 through 9—and getting the precise gradations in the voltages to represent the digit was no easy job for the computer engineers. When there was even a small fluctuation in the power supply or a weakness in a vacuum tube, data could be misrepresented and could produce inaccurate results.

When computer designers abandoned the decimal system and used the binary numbering system in its stead, the process of designing the electronic circuitry was greatly simplified: Because the binary system has only two digits, 0 and 1, the circuits had eight fewer digits to handle. Also, as noted earlier, these binary digits, or bits, correspond nicely to the on-off machine states. With the 0 representing "off" and the 1 representing "on," coded procedures can be set up within the computer system to control the various electronic switches. Dealing with simple on-off states is much easier than attempting to represent data by controlling the voltages of vacuum tubes. Moreover, these two digits can be combined to represent any of the numbers, letters, and characters that can be represented by the ten digits of the decimal system. In the next section, we'll look at exactly how this can be done. Although our discussion will focus exclusively on the use of the binary system in coding data, you should be aware that most computer systems convert binary to an octal (base 8) or a hexadecimal (base 16) coding system to improve readability. Both the octal and hexadecimal coding systems provide a more compact method of expressing values than the often lengthy strings of 0's and 1's required by the binary system; each group of three binary digits can be expressed as one octal digit, and each group of four binary digits can be expressed as one hexadecimal digit.

The Binary Numbering System

The **binary numbering system** has a base of 2, whereas the decimal numbering system has a base of 10. Other than that difference, however, the two systems work in a similar fashion. The placement of digits in both systems is a critical factor. As you know, in the decimal system, the digits to the left of the decimal point represent units, tens, hundreds, thousands, tens of thousands, hundreds of thousands, and so on. Each of these places represents a specific power of the base 10 (remember that any number raised to the 0 power equals 1):

Power of the base	10^5	10^4	10^3	10^2	10^1	10^0
Decimal equivalent	100,000	10,000	1,000	100	10	1

When we write the decimal number 6,532, we are really employing four specific powers of the base 10:

$$(6 \times 10^3 = 6{,}000) + (5 \times 10^2 = 500) + (3 \times 10^1 = 30) + (2 \times 10^0 = 2) = 6{,}532.$$

If we were to change the placement of any of these digits, we would completely change the value of the number.

The same is true in the binary system. And the significance of the placement of the digits in the binary system is like that in the decimal system — that is, digits farther to the left represent larger powers of the base. In this case, however, the base is 2:

Power of the base	2^{10}	2^9	2^8	2^7	2^6	2^5	2^4	2^3	2^2	2^1	2^0
Decimal equivalent	1,024	512	256	128	64	32	16	8	4	2	1

How do you write a number in binary, where there are only the digits 0 and 1 to work with? You use a 0 to indicate the absence of a specific power of 2, and a 1 to indicate its presence. For example, if you wanted to write a 9, you would use a 1 to indicate that you want a 2^3 (i.e., an 8) and another 1 to indicate that you want a 2^0 (i.e., a 1); thus, you get your 9:

$$
\begin{array}{cccc}
1 & 0 & 0 & 1 \\
\downarrow & \downarrow & \downarrow & \downarrow \\
(2^3 = 8) & (2^2 = 4) & (2^1 = 2) & (2^0 = 1) \\
(8) \ + & (0) \ + & (0) \ + & (1) \ = 9.
\end{array}
$$

Another way of expressing this same concept is

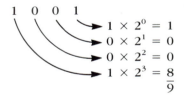

$$
\begin{array}{l}
1 \times 2^0 = 1 \\
0 \times 2^1 = 0 \\
0 \times 2^2 = 0 \\
1 \times 2^3 = 8 \\
\overline{9}
\end{array}
$$

To code the decimal number 326 in binary, you would write

$$
\begin{array}{ccccccccc}
1 & 0 & 1 & 0 & 0 & 0 & 1 & 1 & 0 \\
\downarrow & \downarrow & \downarrow & \downarrow & \downarrow & \downarrow & \downarrow & \downarrow & \downarrow \\
(2^8) & (2^7) & (2^6) & (2^5) & (2^4) & (2^3) & (2^2) & (2^1) & (2^0) \\
(256) + & (0) + & (64) + & (0) + & (0) + & (0) + & (4) + & (2) + & (0) = 326.
\end{array}
$$

Coding Schemes

As you can imagine, representing large decimal numbers as strings of 0's and 1's can get very complicated. In addition, a large number of letters and special symbols must be represented, and they require additional coding arrangements to differentiate them from decimal numbers. To simplify matters, various kinds of coding schemes have been developed. The two most popular of these coding schemes are the *Extended Binary-Coded Decimal Interchange Code* (**EBCDIC,** pronounced EBB see dik) and the *American Standard Code for Information Interchange* (**ASCII,** pronounced AS key).

EBCDIC was developed as an 8-bit code by IBM, and it is the standard on most of their equipment. ASCII, a 7-bit code, was the result of a joint effort by several computer manufacturers to create a standard code that could be used on any computer, regardless of make. (Another version of ASCII, known as ASCII-8, is used on machines that accept 8-bit code patterns.) Because computers differ in design and electronics according to their make, a standard code is necessary if communication among computers is to be possible. The Morse code set the same kind of standard for the transmission of radio signals. Table 5.2 shows the EBCDIC codes and the ASCII codes for digits, letters, and a few of the many special symbols that can be represented.

Table 5.2 EBCDIC and ASCII Codes

Character	EBCDIC Bit Representation	ASCII Bit Representation	Character	EBCDIC Bit Representation	ASCII Bit Representation
0	11110000	0110000	K	11010010	1001011
1	11110001	0110001	L	11010011	1001100
2	11110010	0110010	M	11010100	1001101
3	11110011	0110011	N	11010101	1001110
4	11110100	0110100	O	11010110	1001111
5	11110101	0110101	P	11010111	1010000
6	11110110	0110110	Q	11011000	1010001
7	11110111	0110111	R	11011001	1010010
8	11111000	0111000	S	11100010	1010011
9	11111001	0111001	T	11100011	1010100
A	11000001	1000001	U	11100100	1010101
B	11000010	1000010	V	11100101	1010110
C	11000011	1000011	W	11100110	1010111
D	11000100	1000100	X	11100111	1011000
E	11000101	1000101	Y	11101000	1011001
F	11000110	1000110	Z	11101001	1011010
G	11000111	1000111	#	01111011	0100011
H	11001000	1001000	$	01011011	0100100
I	11001001	1001001	%	01101100	0100101
J	11010001	1001010	>	01101110	0111110

The Parity Bit

Sending coded signals from one machine to another may sound easy, as simple as picking up the telephone and making a long-distance call, but it presents numerous opportunities for errors to occur. What happens to the data if an electrical storm interferes with the transmission or if a car slams into a telephone pole, damaging the lines? When we make a telephone call, we know when too much static on the line is interfering with our understanding of what the other person is saying, and we can easily ask the person to repeat what was said. Computers, however, have no ability to judge whether they've missed anything; they don't know what to expect, and therefore they can't determine if what they've received is correct or not. Problems in telephoned transmissions are not the only source of data error: Equipment failure, dust on storage media, and too much moisture near the computer are just a few of the other causes of data loss or distortion.

The addition of a **parity bit** to each byte, or character, is a method of checking that the data the computer receives are the same as the data that were sent — that is, that no bits were lost or altered in the course of transmission. Figure 5.11 shows the addition of a ninth bit, as the parity bit, to each 8-bit EBCDIC character. Depending on the computer, parity may be odd or even. With **odd parity,** the number of 1 (or "on") bits in each character must add up to an odd number; conversely, with **even parity,** they must add up to an even number. As you can see, the parity shown in Figure 5.11 is odd; the addition of a 1 bit as the parity bit for the character K, for example, makes the total number of 1 bits in that character come out to the odd number 5. The sending terminal or machine adds the parity bits to each byte; the receiving machine automatically checks the number of 1 bits in each byte, and if they do not come out to the required odd or even number, the machine sends an error message. Figure 5.12 shows an example of even parity, using the ASCII code, in which an error has occurred.

Figure 5.11
Odd parity.

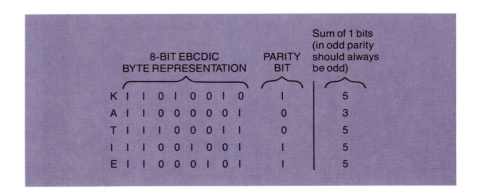

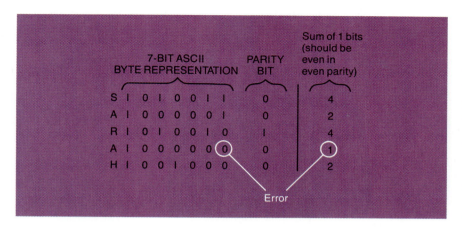

Figure 5.12

Even parity with an error. The signal that was sent included a 1 bit in the second A, but it was lost during transmission because of interference or some other signal problem. When the signal was received, the sum of the ASCII 1 bits and the parity bit was an odd number, indicating that some part of the bit configuration was inaccurate. The usual procedure would be to send the signal a second time.

Parity checking helps to detect single-bit errors, the most common kind, but it is not a guarantee that the data are correct, as 2-bit errors may go undetected. For example, in the odd parity shown in Figure 5.11, if two 0 bits were to become 1 bits, the total number of 1 bits would still come out to be an odd number, and so the computer would not be able to detect the error. Although parity checking can detect errors in coding, it cannot detect inaccuracies in the data themselves.

PRIMARY STORAGE COMPONENTS

Over the years, computer manufacturers have used various kinds of components in their primary storage units. The vacuum tubes of the earliest computers gave way to magnetic drums (see Figure 5.13). Magnetic drums, in turn, were replaced by magnetic cores, which remained a popular storage medium for many years. Semiconductor storage, consisting of tiny integrated circuits etched on silicon chips, is today's most common type of internal memory.

Regardless of the components used, all primary storage units in digital computers operate on essentially the same principle: Data are represented as binary signals, which work much like a series of electric switches. The switch can be only on or off. An "on" state is designated by the binary digit 1, or the 1 bit; an "off" state by the 0 bit. And, as you saw in the last section, these two digits can be combined and coded to represent any number, letter, or special symbol. The binary code operates in the computer in much the same way the Morse code does in the transmission of radio signals. With the Morse code, data are represented by long (dash) or short (dot) tone signals. With the binary code, data may be represented in several ways, among them the presence or absence of a magnetic spot or the open or closed state of an electronic circuit.

The "electric switch" that signals "on" or "off" in primary storage might be a magnetic core or, in semiconductor storage, a miniaturized

Figure 5.13

A magnetic drum. The magnetic drum is a metal cylinder coated with a magnetic recording material. It rotates at a fixed speed, and stationary heads positioned over it read and write data on its surface.

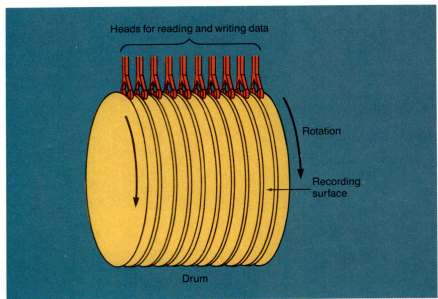

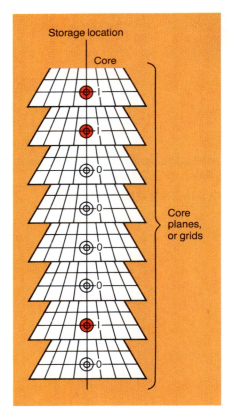

Figure 5.14

Core plane representation of the character B in EBCDIC (11000010).

transistor on an integrated circuit. Magnetic cores were the most common primary storage components during the 1960s and early 1970s; since then, they have all but disappeared in the wake of semiconductor storage. A **magnetic core** is a small, donutlike metallic core strung on a wire **grid** (also called a **core plane**). Each grid contains 1,024 cores, and the grids are stacked vertically to represent the data. As you can see in Figure 5.14, eight grids are required to represent the eight bits of an EBCDIC-coded character.

When an electric current flows through a magnetic core, it causes the core to be magnetized in the direction of the electric flow. Thus, as Figure 5.15 shows, when magnetized in one direction, the core represents an "on" state; when magnetized in the opposite direction, it represents an "off" state. The core can be *sensed,* or read, by sending a small electrical pulse down the wire — not enough of a pulse to alter the magnetic properties; just enough to allow the sensing, or reading, to take place. Since the grids are assembled in a vertical stack, all the bits in the byte can be sensed at the same time. Because the core remains magnetized even after the flow of current stops, magnetic-core storage is said to be **nonvolatile** — that is, its retention of the data is not dependent on a constant source of electrical power.

In contrast, **semiconductor storage** is **volatile** — that is, if the power fails, semiconductor storage forgets everything it ever knew. This is because semiconductor storage depends on a constant supply of electric current to maintain an "on" state in the semiconductor material. The miniaturized transistor, composed of a semiconductor material, acts much like an electric light switch. It allows electricity to flow through it when voltage is applied, and it will stay activated as long as there is a continuous supply of power. You might think of semiconductor memory as trapping an electron for a 1 bit and letting it pass for a 0 bit. To keep the door closed on the trapped electron, semiconductor storage needs a constant supply of electric energy. Also, to stay alive, the electron must be fed small doses of power. To ensure that the supply of power is uninterrupted and to compensate for the signal problems that result from variations in the power supply, large computer systems often have backup generators and batteries.

Despite the volatile nature of semiconductor storage, it has several advantages: Because silicon chips can be mass produced, semiconductor storage is cheaper than magnetic-core storage. The materials of a magnetic-core grid might cost several dollars, and it might take one or more hours to assemble such a grid. In contrast, a single, mass-produced silicon chip containing many thousands of integrated circuits has a total manufacturing cost of only a dollar. Because so many circuits can be packed onto a single chip, semiconductor storage has improved both the speed and the capacity of primary storage units. Very large scale integration (VLSI) techniques continue to improve, and it is now possible to produce half a million circuits on one chip by using as many as ten layers of coatings and very precise etching techniques (see Figure 5.16). Circuit paths only a few molecules wide, with similarly narrow insulating barriers, allow for such high densities on each chip.

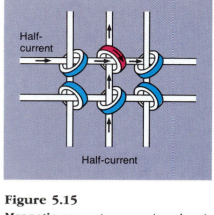

Figure 5.15

Magnetic-core storage. An electric current is passed through the core to alter its magnetic properties. Because a single core is selected, the current is passed through the two wires on the grid with half the amount of current necessary to alter the core's magnetic state. When the two charges meet, the core at that intersection is altered by the combined charges.

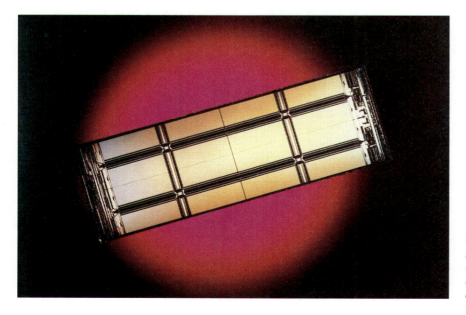

Figure 5.16

A VLSI chip. This megabit memory chip can store over 1 million digital bits of information.
Courtesy of AT&T Bell Laboratories.

THE MAKING OF A CHIP

As a designer of integrated circuits in the 1970s, you would have found long arms a handy feature; the circuit designs often sprawled over eight feet of blueprintlike diagrams. Good eyesight, too, would have been useful: The fine circuit lines didn't just sit accommodatingly in front of you; they ran all over the entire width of the diagram. You would also have needed a goodly supply of pencils, erasers, and patience, as the drafting of the design was intricate and tedious work. After you had drafted the design, you would have had to translate its lines, figures, and symbols into machine-readable digital signals by moving a "digitizing" device over the surface of the design. Computer-controlled machines then took over the rest of the chip-manufacturing processes.

While this work may sound tedious, it was something of a picnic compared with stringing beads on a wire, which was essentially what was done in constructing magnetic-core storage devices. Moreover, integrated circuits dramatically increased computer reliability and storage capacity (the latter by tenfold); they also dramatically reduced power consumption. With the size and weight of computers decreased by a factor of ten, they could be mounted in airplanes and spacecraft.

Remarkable as these achievements of the 1970s were, they were only the beginning of the "small is beautiful" saga. Very soon, circuit designers were using techniques of very large scale integration (VLSI) to pack as many as half a million circuits onto a single silicon chip the size of a pencil eraser. And, today, people are talking about ultra large scale integration (ULSI), or "giga-scale" integration; this technology would allow a billion components to be assembled on one chip. It's predicted that this technology will be in common use before the end of the century. But given the accelerated pace of computer history, who knows?

Today, circuit designers approach their task with a tool box full of the technology their predecessors created. They draw the blueprint of the chip on a CRT screen. A CAD (computer-aided design) system provides useful color graphics and a means not only of testing the circuits but also of translating the tested product into manufacturing requirements. The manufacturing model that results is then used to make a photomask—a greatly reduced film version of the circuit design. The photomask, which can be as small as 1/2000 of a square inch, becomes the controlling plan for an intricate photoetching process that translates the design onto a silicon chip.

Chips are generally manufactured on a relatively large wafer of silicon, which will eventually contain several hundred chips. Because the manufacturing is so precise and the chip will be so small, there is no room for error. After the wafer is loaded into the etching machine, virtually all the manufacturing is done under computer control; people have little to do with the actual manufacturing activities. With the photomask in place and the wafer properly aligned in the etching machine, ultraviolet light does the actual etching. The exposure of the wafer to controlled amounts of light stabilizes, or fixes, the circuit paths. An acid bath then precisely erodes away the surface layer of the chip, leaving the pathways surrounded by empty space. The process is normally done a number of times, with the ultraviolet light exposure of the photomask followed by a controlled acid bath until the chip is completed.

Once the circuits have been etched, the next step is to cut the wafer and separate it into individual chips; this is done with a precisely controlled laser-cutting tool. The individual chips are then mounted on carriers, which provide the necessary connections to the electronic signal sources of the computer system. The final step is extensive testing to be sure the chip has no flaws; something as small as a human hair can ruin more than fifty chips if it gets in the way during the photoetching process. In fact, manufacturers find about 25 percent of the chips they make defective because of flaws in the wafer, coating materials, or etching process. Once the chip has passed the last inspection, it is packaged for sale and installation in a computer system.

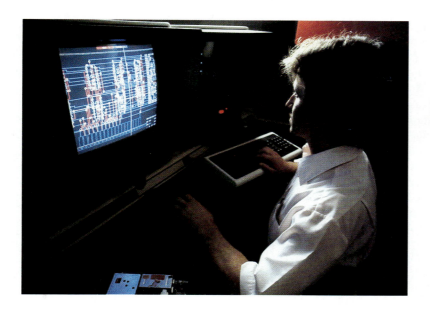

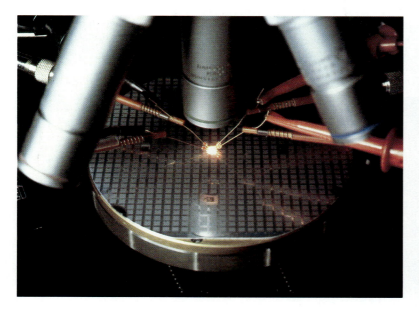
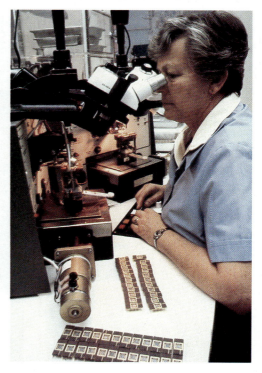

Top left: Designing the chip on a CRT screen. *Top right:* Loading the wafers into the etching machine. *Bottom left:* Cutting the wafer into individual chips. *Bottom right:* Testing the chips.
Photos courtesy of Commodore Electronics Ltd.

RAM, ROM, PROM, AND EPROM

RAM, ROM, PROM, and EPROM all have one thing in common: Each is a memory chip used in computers. The first, shown in Figure 5.17, is the type of memory found in the primary storage unit, and the rest provide storage for frequently used programs.

RAM stands for random access memory. It is called random access because the computer can go directly to any address in RAM (i.e., primary memory) without passing through or disturbing any other address; in other words, it can write (i.e., store) and read (i.e., retrieve) data at random. The advantages of RAM include very fast retrieval and the ability to write and alter data in one address without interfering with the data or program instructions in other addresses.

ROM stands for read-only memory—that is, the CPU can read the contents of ROM, but it cannot write new data or instructions over them and thus destroy them. This read-only feature of ROM chips means that they cannot be used to store variable data or variable program instructions, as RAM chips can. The advantages of ROM, other than its preventing the user from accidentally destroying its contents by writing over them, are that it will not be erased by a power failure, it frees up storage space in RAM, and it provides very fast access to the program that it stores. The program itself is etched into the ROM chip, and it cannot be changed by the user. Software built into the circuitry of a chip in this way is called **firmware.** ROM, the most common type of firmware, is often part of a microcomputer system (see Figure 5.18). For example, many microcomputers have their systems software for language translation on a ROM chip. Electronic spreadsheets, which, as you may remember from Chapter 2, are applications

Figure 5.17
A RAM chip.
Courtesy of Commodore Electronics Ltd.

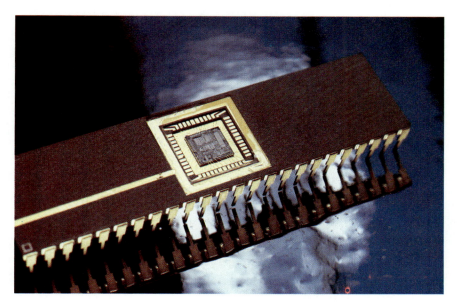

Figure 5.18

A microprocessor chip containing ROM. The chip rests on top of its carrier, which has a number of pins that connect to the electronic signal sources of the computer.
Courtesy of Commodore Electronics Ltd.

programs for analyzing financial data, are also good candidates for ROM firmware.

PROM (programmable read-only memory) chips are just like ROM chips, except that, using special equipment, the user writes the program on a blank chip. Once the program is written, it cannot be altered. PROM chips are often used to display standardized, unchanging forms or data collection instructions on the screens of terminals.

EPROM (erasable programmable read-only memory) is PROM that is erasable. The erasure, which is done by exposing the chips to a strong ultraviolet light, requires special equipment. Being able to erase the contents of the chip and replace them with something else gives the user added flexibility, and it is a particularly valuable feature when programs need to be altered on a fairly regular basis. For example, because the financing rate for car payments changes once or twice a month, an automobile dealership that finances such payments might use EPROM chips in its computer system; with EPROM, it could continually erase the previous financing program and substitute an updated version.

SELECTION CRITERIA

The selection of a CPU depends on the different processing needs posed by particular computer applications. For instance, the processing needs of a large organization that uses the CPU to manipulate a large volume of complex data are quite different from the needs of someone who uses the CPU to balance a personal checkbook and to write letters or term papers.

If you were choosing a CPU for the latter purposes, you would no doubt want a microcomputer, and your choices would be dictated by the microprocessors available with those systems. If, on the other hand, you were choosing a CPU for the large organization, your choices and concerns would not be so limited. Among other things, you would have to be sure that the CPU's processing speed was fast enough to guarantee satisfactory data processing performance; at the same time, to ensure that your choice was cost-effective, you would have to bear in mind the direct relationship that generally exists between speed and cost. The largest, most powerful, and most expensive CPU may process several million instructions per second, but a less expensive CPU that processes half a million instructions per second might be quite adequate for your organization's needs. Other criteria to be considered in the selection process are the CPU's capacity, the ease with which it can be upgraded, and its compatibility with other components of the system.

One measure of capacity is the number of bits that the CPU can address at one time. As you saw in Table 5.1, this can range from 8 to 64 bits. You might think of the 8-bit system as moving data over a one-lane country road, whereas the 64-bit system uses a superhighway. For a casual afternoon drive, the country road is perfectly acceptable; but for a long trip built around a tight and busy schedule, the superhighway offers numerous advantages. Similarly, for personal computing applications, 8- and 16-bit systems are very satisfactory; but for large organizations with complex processing needs, the 32-bit system is the standard. Another measure of capacity is the amount of primary storage available in the CPU. Microcomputers measure primary memory in kilobytes, and the range is from 64K to 512K for the most popular systems. Larger systems contain megabytes of primary memory — 2M to 16M in the commonly used systems. The larger the primary storage unit is, the more data it can accommodate at any one time and the more efficiently the CPU can carry out the processing. As with speed and cost, a direct relationship between capacity and cost exists; so it is wise to carefully study both current and anticipated capacity needs, as well as anticipated changes in technology that might affect capacity during the economic life of the CPU.

Because business is dynamic and ever changing, and because computing technology is constantly improving, organizations often quickly outgrow their current systems. When that happens, they must look for efficient and economical ways of upgrading their processing capabilities. Hardware designers, aware of this critical need, have developed a modular approach to CPU development. With this approach, an organization can upgrade its CPU or replace it with a more powerful one without reconfiguring the rest of the system. The modular approach saves the firm from having to make major changes in its data files, applications programs, and systems software.

The CPU's compatibility with other components of the system is another important selection criterion. As you know, computers always work as a system, and all the components must work together effectively if the system is to perform at peak level. Thus, when selecting a CPU, you should be sure that it is compatible with existing systems components; you should also be sure that it will be compatible with any input, output, or auxiliary storage devices that you might want to add to the system in the future. Ensuring compatibility therefore requires a knowledge of the current inventory of equipment and an awareness of possible future applications.

By spending more, you can improve the CPU's speed, capacity, access to stored data, and, in general, the performance of the system. However, the most expensive CPU is not always the best possible choice for a particular setting; intelligent selection depends on an understanding of the kind of processing needed in specific situations.

SUMMARY

Today's computers operate on the stored-program principle, with program instructions and data stored in the primary storage unit of the CPU for as long as they are needed. Other components of the CPU are the control unit, which — among other things — oversees retrieval of data and instructions from storage, and the arithmetic/logic unit, which carries out the processing instructions. The processing instructions are embedded in the program instructions as operation codes; program instructions also contain operands, which specify the storage locations of the data to be processed. The primary storage unit contains a number of small storage areas, each of which has a unique address that is referred to by the operand. Each storage area can hold only one item at a time — either a processing instruction (an op code) or an item of data to be processed (an operand). The primary storage unit is characterized by destructive write and nondestructive read. Registers are another kind of temporary storage place located within the CPU; they improve the CPU's efficiency by speeding up the transfer of instructions and data and the performance of arithmetic and logic operations. All these elements of the CPU — its functional units and its registers — work together in a concerted effort to execute program instructions. As they are executed, all program instructions go through two cycles — I-time and E-time; together, these cycles form the machine cycle.

A bit is a binary digit — either a 0 or a 1 — and it is the basic building block of all computer storage. A number of bits, often eight, make a byte, which is a storage unit capable of holding one character of data. A number of bytes form a word. Computers are designed to hold fixed word-lengths or variable word-lengths. A kilobyte is 1,024 bytes; a megabyte is approximately 1 million bytes.

Digital computers operate in a binary mode — that is, the signals consist of 0's and 1's. The binary numbering system has a base of 2, whereas the decimal numbering system has a base of 10; otherwise, however, the two systems follow similar rules of digit placement and computation. Since representing data as 0's and 1's can get quite complicated, several coding systems have been established to represent numbers as well as letters and symbols. The most popular of these codes are the Extended Binary-Coded Decimal Interchange Code (EBCDIC) and the American Standard Code for Information Interchange (ASCII). To help validate the correctness of transmitted data, an additional bit, called a parity bit, is added to each byte. Parity is either odd or even and represents the total of the 1 bits in each byte.

The components of primary storage have evolved from vacuum tubes and magnetic drums and cores to semiconductor storage. Despite its volatile nature, semiconductor storage has important advantages, among them lower cost and tightly packed integrated circuits, which have improved both the speed and the capacity of primary storage. The type of memory found in primary storage is called random access memory (RAM). It can be supported by firmware, such as read-only memory (ROM), programmable read-only memory (PROM), and erasable programmable read-only memory (EPROM). ROM, PROM, and EPROM can store frequently used programs, thus freeing up storage space in RAM. They also allow rapid access to the stored programs.

CPU selection depends on the nature of the processing required by particular computer applications. Selection criteria include the CPU's processing speed, its capacity, the ease with which it can be upgraded, and its compatibility with present and future components of the system. In general, the greater the cost of the CPU, the better the system's performance. However, the most expensive CPU is not always the best CPU; what's best depends on the processing needs found in specific settings.

KEY TERMS

accumulator (129)	EPROM (147)
address (126)	even parity (140)
address register (129)	execution time (E-time) (130)
ASCII (139)	firmware (146)
binary numbering system (137)	fixed word-lengths (134)
bit (132)	general-purpose register (129)
byte (132)	grid (core plane) (142)
destructive write (128)	indexing systems (128)
EBCDIC (139)	instruction register (129)

instruction time (I-time) (130)
kilobyte (K) (136)
machine cycle (130)
magnetic core (142)
megabytes (M's) (136)
nondestructive read (128)
nonvolatile (142)
odd parity (140)
operand (125)
operation code (op code) (125)
parity bit (140)
PROM (147)
RAM (146)
registers (128)
ROM (146)
semiconductor storage (142)
storage register (129)
variable word-lengths (135)
volatile (142)
word (134)

DISCUSSION QUESTIONS

1. Describe how a computer uses primary storage to hold data and program instructions. Include in your discussion definitions of the following terms: *operation code, operand, address, destructive write, nondestructive read.*

2. What are registers? How and why are registers used?

3. Describe the functions of the control unit, the arithmetic/logic unit, and the primary storage unit. Why is coordination of these functions necessary for effective data processing? Explain the activities that take place during I-time and E-time.

4. If you were told that a computer system had 256K RAM, what would this mean to you? What is the difference between that system and a 2M system?

5. Explain how binary arithmetic differs from decimal arithmetic. What is the decimal equivalent of 10011? What is the binary equivalent of 7?

6. Why is a coding system necessary for computers? What are the most popular coding systems being used today?

7. What is the purpose of a parity bit in data transmission? How is it used?

8. Explain what volatile and nonvolatile memory mean. Why would anyone use volatile memory for computerized processing?

9. Explain the difference between RAM and ROM. What are the features of PROM and EPROM? What is firmware?

10. Discuss the criteria to be considered in the selection of a CPU. What is the relationship between cost and overall system performance?

OUTLINE

SOURCES OF BUSINESS DATA

THE CONVERSION STEP: PROBLEMS AND SOLUTIONS

Data Collection Procedures
Other Controls on Data

METHODS OF DATA COLLECTION AND ENTRY

OFFLINE DATA COLLECTION

Punched Cards
Magnetic Media

SOURCE-DATA AUTOMATION

Magnetic-Ink Character Recognition
Optical Recognition
Remote Terminals
- Dumb, Smart, and User-Programmable Terminals
- Point-of-Sale Terminals
- Audio-Input Devices
- Touch-Sensitive and Light-Sensitive Devices

SELECTION CRITERIA

SUMMARY

KEY TERMS

DISCUSSION QUESTIONS

OVERVIEW

How would you like to receive a hospital bill for 111 intravenous injections you never received? Or a bill for $1,500 for inpatient services when you were not a patient in the hospital at the indicated time? Or a bill for $600 for an ambulance ride you never took? "Computer" errors of this kind have become so common and have contributed so much to soaring health costs that firms specializing in the auditing of hospital bills have become a booming industry. Commenting on computer keyboarding errors, the president of one such firm said, "You'd be amazed how many times the decimal point is put in the wrong place.... The remarkable thing is that it is always too far to the right."

Hospitals, of course, are not the only institutions plagued with such problems, and the costs are not always merely monetary. An error in the computerized records of the FBI's National Crime Information Center resulted in one man's spending five months in a Marine Corps brig. He had been stopped by local police for making an illegal left-hand turn into the parking lot of a supermarket, where he was going to buy groceries for his dinner. The computer check that ensued went from the patrol car that had stopped him to the local police headquarters to the state capitol to the NCIC in Washington, all in a matter of minutes. The message that came back said that he had gone AWOL from the Marine Corps eleven years before. In fact, he had eleven years before been given a special discharge. The result: After five months, he was set free to go about picking up the broken pieces of his life.

To call these "computer" errors is to miss the point. The information that a computer system produces is as good or as bad as the data that people feed it. The quality of that data depends on three factors: data collection and data entry personnel, procedures, and equipment. Properly integrated, these factors contribute to the smooth running of the system and to the production of accurate, meaningful information. Improperly integrated, they can be the Achilles' heel of the entire system, spelling out in living — and sometimes lurid — color the truth of the acronym GIGO: garbage in, garbage out. In this chapter, we'll look at some of the considerations involved in data collection, at the reasons people are so important in this process, and at the hardware used for data entry. Our objectives are to

- identify and describe the sources of business data.

- describe how errors in data collection can arise, why it is important that these errors be controlled, and some methods for controlling them.

- discuss the media, hardware, and procedures used in offline data collection.

CHAPTER 6

- ◆ define source-data automation and describe the procedures and equipment used in this form of data collection and entry.
- ◆ discuss the criteria used in selecting input devices and procedures.

INPUT

SOURCES OF BUSINESS DATA

Where do the data that businesses feed into their computer systems come from? Most data are internally generated by the companies themselves, a by-product of doing business. They include the historical, operational, and projected data that we described in Chapter 3. Sales tickets and invoices accumulated in the course of a business day are obvious examples of internally generated operational data. This type of transaction record, which provides an internal source of data, is called a **source document.** Other internal sources of data include the accounting department's evaluations of the company's assets, expenditures, losses, and general financial condition. The numerical data provided by source documents and accounting records are the easiest kind of data to deal with in a computerized data processing system. But other, less quantifiable data can also be very useful. Employees can be a valuable source of both kinds of data. Reporting customers' reactions to new products, describing their impressions from sales calls, and sharing their observations of a segment of the business are a few of the ways employees can provide data for the computer system. At times, such data may be very subjective (i.e., nonnumerical), as in the reporting of customers' reactions. At other times, the data may be more quantifiable, as in recommendations concerning credit limits or shipment delays.

Other data may come from people and organizations that are not part of the company. Such external sources of data include customers and prospective customers, who may provide data in response to questionnaires or in the form of sales orders; the general business literature, which includes specialized trade publications and business newspapers, journals, and magazines; competing firms, whose products, prices, and quality control may provide valuable comparative data; trade associations and government agencies that furnish statistics pertinent to the business or information on changes in legal requirements; and the company's own suppliers.

As you can see, there is no shortage of data to feed to the computer system. In fact, many managers these days are worried about an information overload and a lack of concern for the quality and usability of the information that their computer systems generate. The problem is not where to find more data, but how to collect only data that will produce usable and useful output.

THE CONVERSION STEP: PROBLEMS AND SOLUTIONS

Most of the data that businesses generate cannot be fed directly into the computer system because they are not in machine-readable form. Some type of keyboarding is required to convert the data from the form that people recognize to one that the machine can deal with. Errors in the form of inaccuracies or omissions may occur as data are recorded on the original source document; they are also very likely to occur as a keyboard operator transcribes the data into machine-readable code. Regardless of the stage at which they occur, if they go undetected, such errors can be very costly to a business — and, as we noted in the Overview, to individuals as well. For example, if you, as a customer, were depending on the timely delivery of a shipment of particular goods, and the shipment arrived two days late and contained the wrong goods, you might very well think of taking your business elsewhere.

Errors on source documents and in keyboard transcriptions can also be a matter of inconvenience for employees. For instance, if you had a part-time job and worked four hours a day for two weeks, your time card for the pay period should show forty hours. If your supervisor miscalculated and entered thirty-six hours on the time card, this figure would be entered into the system, and the paycheck issued to you would be for less money than you expected, no doubt causing you some consternation. This is a source document error created in the process of data collection. Since neither the keyboard operator nor the computer may be able to recognize a source document error, mistakes of this kind can be very difficult to detect until after processing is completed. A more common error is the miskeying of the data by a keyboard operator, who might enter a 3 instead of a 4. The result would be thirty hours worked and paid instead of the forty listed on your time card. With thousands of entries keyboarded each day, some keystroke errors are bound to occur. Keyboard errors are generally easier to detect than source document errors since the keyboard operator can check the keyboarded data against the source document.

Obviously, in these situations it is people who create the incomplete or inaccurate data—not the machines. And this is why people are so important in the input process. By organizing the data for collection in a certain way, and by instituting carefully worked-out procedures and controls, it is possible to help people reduce the number of data errors and to promote accuracy and completeness in the data.

Data Collection Procedures

The more logically organized data are, the greater the chance they will be accurate and complete. Forms designed to record data on specific business transactions are a convenient way of promoting both completeness and accuracy. Such a form provides spaces for the particular data to be recorded and indicates where to record each item (see Figure 6.1). Obviously, a form is far more likely than a blank piece of paper or a notebook to produce all the data needed—unless, of course, the person collecting the data has a thorough understanding of the business and the data requirements. When that is not the case, training people in the proper use of a data collection form is a good way of fostering accuracy and completeness.

A well-designed form also makes it easier for data entry operators to scan the data as they do the keyboarding. A data collection form can thus also reduce the number of keyboard errors.

Sloan Wine Company
Duxfield, Mass. 02999
Sold to: Date
Address
City

Sold by	Cash	COD	On Acct.	

Quantity	Description of Purchase	Price	Amount

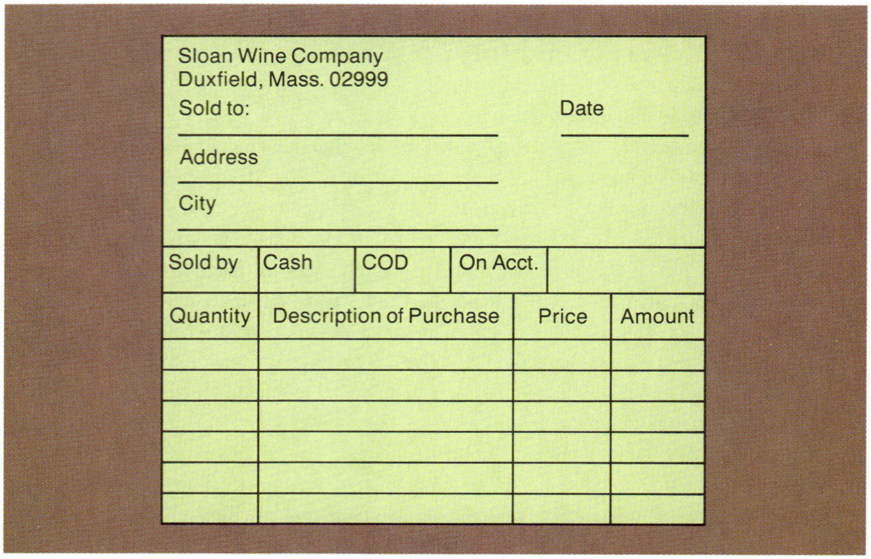

Figure 6.1
A printed data collection form.

Data collection forms do not necessarily have to be on paper; graphics on the screens of **video display terminals (VDTs)** can function in the same way. As we noted in Chapter 1, a VDT has a keyboard for data entry and a **cathode ray tube (CRT)** screen for viewing both the input and the output. Like a paper form, a form on a screen can lead the person who is collecting the data through a series of questions and can provide places for the entry of specific data. Tax assessors and airline reservation clerks often use this sort of graphic data collection form (see Figure 6.2).

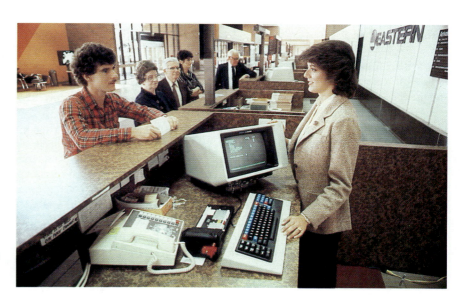

Figure 6.2
A data collection form displayed on a CRT screen.
Courtesy of Sperry Corporation.

Another procedure aimed at promoting the accuracy and completeness of data is to have the same employee who handles the transaction also enter the data into the computer system. The originator of the transaction has a better understanding of the data generated, is better able to make an adjustment if there is an error that the computer will not accept, and usually has more interest in the correct processing of the transaction than a data entry clerk who is unfamiliar with the transaction. In many retail establishments, sales clerks now enter transactions directly into the computer system rather than making up a sales invoice to be entered by a keyboard operator at a later time. An erroneous stock number that generates an unexpected item price can be easily corrected by a sales clerk before the transaction is completed.

Other Controls on Data

Other controls designed to ensure data accuracy and completeness include verification, batch controls, and editing (see Figure 6.3). Parity checking, as you may recall from Chapter 5, is also a way of controlling the accuracy of data. It differs from these other controls in that it is not a check on errors created by people, but rather on errors occurring in the physical transmission of data.

Verification is the process of repeating the keyboarding operation in an attempt to catch inaccuracies in the transcription. The results of the first and second keyboardings are compared; if any items don't match, they are checked against the source document, and the correct data are rekeyed. Verification is most often done with punched cards, but it is sometimes done with other methods of data collection as well. Although such rekeying of data may be time-consuming, it is not a waste of time — or of money. As we've pointed out, data errors can be very costly, and finding and correcting them before processing takes place is easier and more economical than doing so later. If an error is not found until after processing, the whole program may have to be rerun to correct it; if found before processing, it can be eliminated with a few corrective keystrokes.

As you can see in Figure 6.3, a **batch control** involves a manual tally of the transactions going into the computer system and a comparison of that total with the total produced by the computer. If these two figures don't match, then some data have been lost or altered sometime between the completion of the transaction and the execution of the computer program. Like verification, batch controls may be time-consuming, but they can be a cost-effective security measure, particularly when source documents must be transported from one location to another and are handled by several people.

As Figure 6.3 also shows, **editing** occurs as the data are prepared for processing. It includes checking the reasonableness and range of the data. **Reasonableness of the data** refers to data expectations based on what

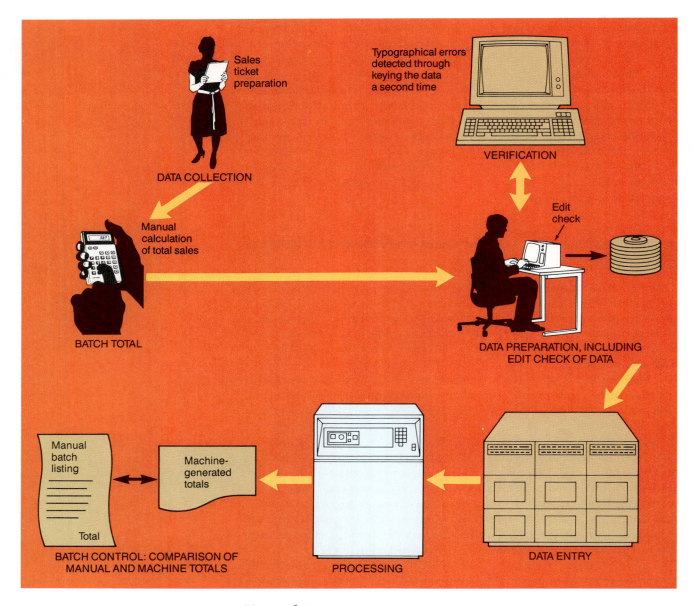

Figure 6.3
Data controls: verification, batch control, and editing in a system for processing sales invoices.

is possible. A check might be made of all sales transactions; any having a date later than the current date would be considered unreasonable and would be listed by the computer as an edit message for further checking. **Range of the data** is based on an expected bracket into which the data

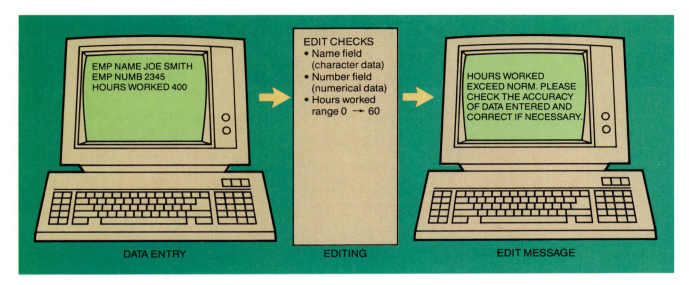

Figure 6.4
Editing check on the range of data entered for a weekly payroll.

should fall. With a two-week payroll, for example, the range of hours worked might be from zero to a hundred. Anything more than ten hours a week overtime would be very unusual and would fall outside the range, again causing the computer to generate an edit message for further checking (see Figure 6.4).

Editing might also consist of a simple test of the fields' alphabetical or numerical characters. For example, if the fields consisted of all numerical characters like social security numbers, and an alphanumerical item like 125 5A 066 appeared, the computer could pick out the inconsistency caused by the appearance of the alphabetical character and send a message identifying the error.

Programmers may write as many edit checks as they wish into the program instructions for the computer to carry out. Such procedures help to maintain a high level of accuracy as the input data enter the system. Editing checks may also be built into the hardware (i.e., they may be part of the firmware).

METHODS OF DATA COLLECTION AND ENTRY

The data conversion problems that we discussed in the last section are most characteristic of **offline data collection methods,** in which data from source documents are keyboarded into machine-readable form using offline devices. The data are then held for later entry into the system, where they are processed in a batch. The media onto which the data are keyboarded include punched cards and magnetic tapes and disks. The steps involved in this kind of data collection and processing can be summed up as follows:

1. Preparing the original source documents and beginning a batch control by manually tallying the transactions.
2. Transferring the source documents to the keyboarding area.
3. Reading the source documents and keyboarding them into machine-readable form on some storage medium.
4. Verifying the coded data by repeating the keyboarding.
5. Running an edit check on the data.
6. Rejecting or fixing any incomplete or inaccurate data.
7. Transferring the storage medium to the processing area and putting it in an online input device (i.e., one that is directly linked to the computer).
8. Processing the data in a batch.
9. Completing the batch control by comparing the hand-generated total with the machine-generated total.

As you can imagine, all this transferring, checking, and double-checking of data can add up to be a very time-consuming and expensive business. In fact, data entry can account for 30 to 50 percent of a company's data processing budget. However, without the checking and double-checking safeguards, the blunders that could result might be an even more expensive proposition.

Other methods of data collection, which overcome some of the problems inherent in offline data collection, are an increasingly evident part of our daily lives. Collectively, these other methods are known as source-data automation. **Source-data automation** means that the data are collected in machine-readable form at the source of the data—that is, at the time and place the data are generated. A variety of direct input devices are used in source-data automation, among them online video display terminals and the scanners that you see at supermarket checkout counters. **Scanners** use a reflected light beam to scan the machine code on a product's label. They then convert the image into an electronic signal and transmit it directly into the CPU. Because source-data automation captures the data in machine-readable form, it eliminates the second-party keyboarding required in offline data collection. It thus not only eliminates one cause of data error but also does away with some of the duplication of effort involved in offline data collection.

Data collected through source-data automation may be entered directly into the CPU and processed interactively, as they are with supermarket scanners. Another possibility with direct input devices is to enter either part or all of the data into the system but not directly into the CPU—that is, to hold the data in an online auxiliary storage unit until such time as a batch processing run is needed. For example, while the sales data that the supermarket scanner enters into the system are processed interactively,

INPUT METHODS FOR THE HANDICAPPED

In Dalton Trumbo's 1970 film "Johnny Got His Gun," a seriously injured World War I vet, paralyzed, blind, and dumb, spends his life shut up in a room so the world can't see him. All attempts to communicate fail.... The film is tragic, not because of his wounds, but because he is both frozen in his plight and deeply frustrated.

If Johnny were real and living today, he could probably communicate [through a] personal computer.

"If you can twitch a muscle," says Dr. Howard Shane of Children's Hospital in Boston, "you can probably use a computer." New developments in software, hardware, and access devices make it possible for even pre-school age handicapped children to use computers faster, easier, and yes, cheaper than ever....

A person who can do little more than breathe can operate a computer with a "sip and puff" switch. Blowing activates one function, like scanning a menu; sucking enlists another, like increasing the scanning rate. [Other input devices for the handicapped] include a "lever switch" for head motion; a flat "leaf switch" to use inside the elbow, under the chin, or in the mouth; and a "brow-wrinkle" switch attached to the head via a sweat band. According to Dr. Bruce Gans of Tufts New England Medical Center, an electromagnetic switch can detect electrical activity in a twitched muscle and transform it into a switching signal....

The key to most computer operations for the disabled is row/column scanning, invented in 1972 by a young Tufts University engineer named Rick Foulds. Called the Tufts Interactive Communicator (TIC), the device uses a double line LED [light-emitting diode] display that scans the alphabet in groups of five letters. When it passes by the group containing the desired letter, the user presses the switch. The scanning mode then shifts to individual letters within the group. With another touch of the switch the user selects the letter, which then appears on the top line. In this way words are constructed ... like a puzzle, one piece at a time....

Rehab engineer Patrick Demasco at Tufts New England Medical Center ... is [today] working on the line-of-gaze method, the most exciting development yet in handicapped access. Aided by a head motion tracker developed by McDonnell Douglas Electronic Corporation (and popularized in the film "Blue Thunder"), a miniature video camera mounted on a pair of special glasses "looks" at the operator's eye making a selection on the video display screen. By tracking its location relative to the head position, the camera sends the information back to the computer which presents the selection.

This technology is attractive because it does away with the slower row/column scanning — the eye scans instead. It does, however, require those special glasses. Demasco is currently working on the "corneal reflection pupil center" technique that tracks eye motion without glasses....

Today [more federal funding is] available for motorized wheelchairs than for special computers. "This is very short-sighted," says Patrick Demasco. "If I were disabled and had a choice, I would prefer communication to mobility." But that choice should not have to be made.

◆

— Peter Bates, "New Developments in Handicapped Access." Reprinted from *Creative Computing*, March 1985. Copyright © 1985 AHL COMPUTING, INC.

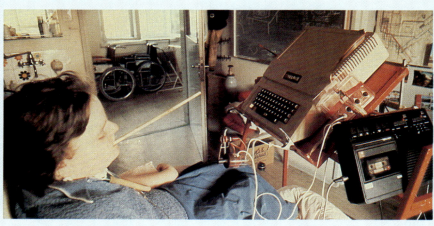

Courtesy of Apple Computer, Inc.

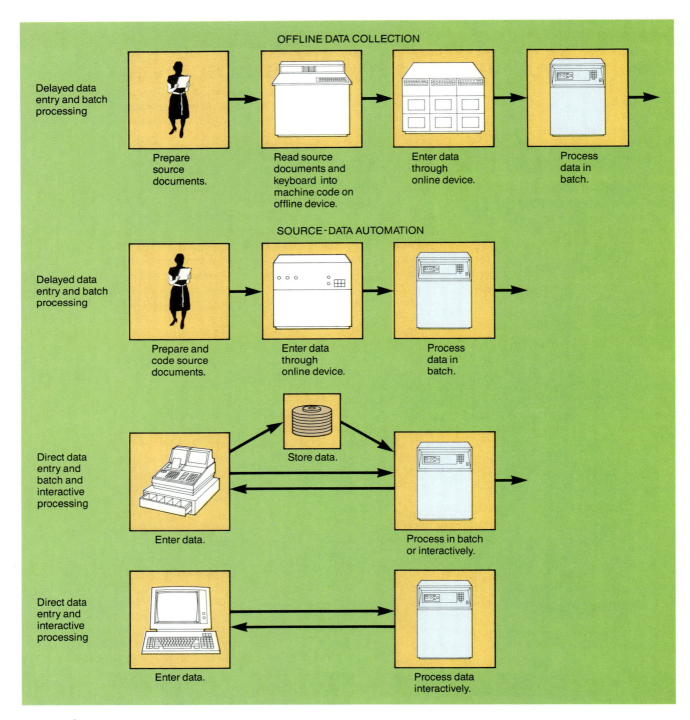

Figure 6.5
Steps involved in offline data collection and source-data automation.

data pertaining to changes in inventory could be held in online storage for later batch processing.

Although direct data entry is a very visible method of source-data automation — one that we see every day — it is not the only method. Data collected in machine-readable form at their source do not have to be entered directly into the system; they can instead be stored offline. For example, when you fill in the boxes on a standardized test form, you are in effect generating the data at the same time that you are preparing them in machine-readable form. However, those data do not go directly into the system; they are held offline for later entry into the system, where they will be processed in one batch together with all the other test data. The chief difference between this particular method of source-data automation and offline data collection methods is that the latter require an extra step: A keyboard operator must transcribe the data from a source document into machine-readable form. In the former method, the user simultaneously creates and codes the source document. Figure 6.5 illustrates the steps involved in offline data collection and in some of the various methods of source-data automation.

Many businesses find it useful to incorporate multiple methods of data collection and entry into their computer systems. Let's now take a look at the array of equipment available to them.

OFFLINE DATA COLLECTION

Punched Cards

Punched cards have been used to record data since before the turn of the century, long before the existence of computers as we know them today. Although they are rapidly being phased out by magnetic media, punched cards are still used in many business applications. Regardless of their continuing usefulness, their historical importance alone makes them worth discussing.

To represent data, the standard punched card uses a coding scheme developed by Herman Hollerith in the 1880s. Figure 6.6 shows how this scheme works. As you can see in the figure, the card can hold 80 characters, or data units; and it is called a **fixed record.** In this **80-column punched card** (also sometimes called a **Hollerith card**), each character is represented by a hole or holes punched in one of the 80 columns. When one card can hold all the data pertaining to a particular transaction, it is said to be a **unit record** — that is, a complete record. When it cannot hold all the data, the spillover data must go on a second card. This makes processing somewhat more cumbersome, since any merging of decks of cards must account for the two-card record. It is particularly troublesome when some records require two cards and others require only one. For example, if customer purchases are recorded on punched cards, small orders will require only a single card, while large orders may require multiple cards. The computer must determine whether a card is a new record or a con-

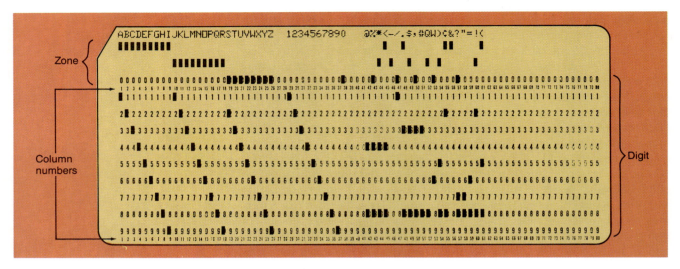

Figure 6.6
The 80-column punched card and the Hollerith code. Notice that numbers are represented with a single punch while letters require a combination of zone and digit punches. Special characters also require both zone and digit punches and often have three punches in the column.

tinuation of an earlier record, which necessitates several additional steps in each processing cycle. Also, unless all of a card is punched, part of it is going to be wasted because of the fixed-record format.

A more recent kind of punched card is the **96-column punched card,** introduced by IBM especially for use with their minicomputer systems in the late 1960s (see Figure 6.7). The 96-column card is less than half the size of the 80-column card; it is also more fragile because its holes are much smaller and closer together. The 96-column card can hold more data in a smaller space than the 80-column card, but the small size of its holes and the wear and tear on the card when it is processed can create problems of incorrect data pickup. The 80-column card is by far the most popular punched card in use today.

The steps in preparing data for punched-card entry are as follows:

1. A data entry operator, using the keyboard of an offline **keypunch machine,** transfers the data from source documents onto the punched cards (see Figure 6.8). The keypunch machine records the data by punching patterns of holes into the cards.

2. The punched cards are transferred to a **verifier,** a machine used to rekey the data from the source document. To avoid repetition of errors, the person who does the rekeying on the verifier is usually not the person who did the original keypunching. Instead of punching holes, the verifier compares the keystrokes with the holes already in the cards. When it finds a discrepancy, it notifies the operator, who checks

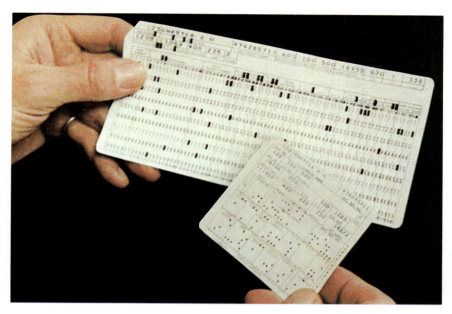

Figure 6.7
A 96-column punched card compared with an 80-column card.
Courtesy of IBM Corporation.

the source document for the correct data and compares it with the data on the punched card. To correct a keypunch error, the operator duplicates the card to the point of the error, keystrokes the correction, and duplicates the remainder of the original card.

3. When corrected and ready for processing, the cards are entered into an online **card reader,** which translates the patterns of holes into electronic signals and transmits them into the CPU.

Figure 6.8
Punched-card equipment: (*foreground*) operators at keypunch machines; (*background*) a card reader.
D. Brody/Stock, Boston.

Punched cards offer a permanent record of the data, and, if handled carefully, they can be processed a number of times before they are affected by wear. However, once the data are recorded on punched cards, they cannot be erased or removed. Since the keypunch machine makes a hole, the correction of an entry means that a new card must be punched. Also, because punched cards can hold only 80 or 96 units of data, many thousands of cards are needed to store the data found in a business information system, and, of course, storing so many cards takes up a lot of space. Moreover, punched-card processing is slow because each card must be physically moved across a surface during the reading process. With only 80 characters per card and reading speeds of a thousand cards a minute, a maximum of 80,000 characters per minute can be entered into the computer system. Magnetic-media drives, which can transfer over a million characters per second, are hundreds of times faster.

Even with these limitations, punched cards do have important applications, especially when the computer system is used to process payments. A prepunched card can be mailed along with a statement or bill, and when the card is returned, it can serve as a data entry vehicle with no further modification. All the clerk needs to do is see that the amount paid corresponds to the amount due, as indicated on the bill or card.

Cards also have the advantage of being easy to manipulate. If a record needs only one modification or correction, it is easy to prepare a new card and physically substitute it for the old one. Another, often overlooked advantage of punched cards is that if you understand the punching code, you can read the data directly from the card—something you cannot do with magnetic media.

Magnetic Media

As we mentioned in Chapter 1, magnetic media may be either **magnetic tape** or **magnetic disk.** Magnetic tape looks much like sound-recording tape. It is generally a half-inch wide and is made of a plastic material called mylar. The mylar is coated with a thin film of iron oxide, a material that can be easily magnetized. Magnetic disks are either flexible or rigid and look much like phonograph records. The flexible disks, called **floppy disks** (also called **floppies** or **diskettes**), range in diameter from 3½ to 8 inches and are made of plastic. The rigid disks, called **hard disks,** are made of machined aluminum, and they may have a diameter as wide as 14 inches. Both kinds of disks are coated with iron oxide.

Data on magnetic tapes and disks are represented as magnetized spots arranged in predetermined locations (see Figure 6.9). The process of recording data on both these media is not unlike the process of recording data on punched cards: In both instances, a data entry operator, using a keyboard, transfers data from source documents, and the machine on which the keyboarding is done translates the data into machine-readable form.

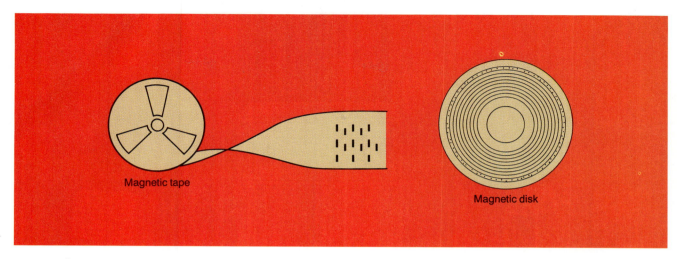

Figure 6.9
Data representation on magnetic tape and disk.

Magnetic tape may be on a **cassette,** much like the tape cassettes used for recording music, or on a **reel.** The cassette is normally used in conjunction with a keyboarding device in a small system; because it is much larger, the reel is used for recording data generated by mainframe systems during processing. A cassette usually stores about 200 bytes, or characters, per inch, giving it the storage capacity of thousands of punched cards in a much smaller space.

To transfer the data from a source document onto magnetic tape, the data entry operator uses a **key-to-tape device.** The data are held in temporary storage and are displayed on the screen of the device, where the operator can review them and check their accuracy. Once that is done, they are written onto the tape, and the screen is cleared for the next record entry. When the program is to be executed, the tape containing the coded data is mounted on a **magnetic-tape drive,** which senses the magnetic spots and generates electronic signals, sending them into the CPU (see Figure 6.10).

A **key-to-disk device** is used to record data on magnetic disks. Usually, several key-to-disk devices are linked to a minicomputer, so that the key-to-disk device is really part of a system (see Figure 6.11). Devices used in this way are often called *workstations* (see Figure 6.12), and they function somewhat like a microcomputer with logic and memory circuits. The minicomputer, responding to stored-program instructions, edits the data for reasonableness and range, and the operator reviews the data on the screen of the key-to-disk device to verify correct entry. When the data on a disk are to be processed, the disk is placed in a **magnetic-disk drive,** which feeds the data into the CPU.

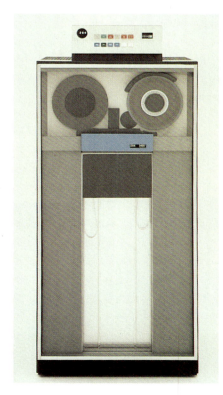

Figure 6.10
A magnetic-tape drive.
Courtesy of IBM Corporation.

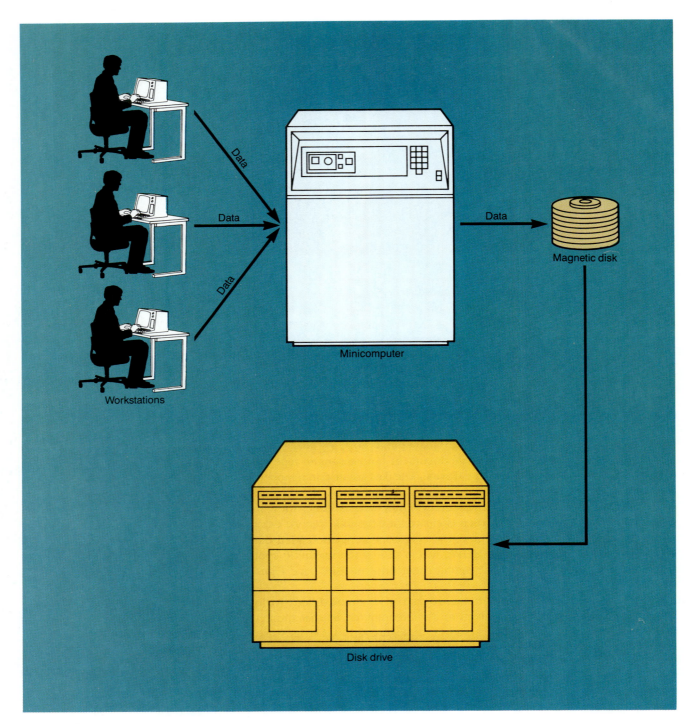

Figure 6.11
Key-to-disk devices and a minicomputer forming a system.

OFFLINE DATA COLLECTION **169**

**Figure 6.12
Workstations.**
Courtesy of Honeywell Inc.

Floppy disks have become a popular data collection medium with stand-alone microcomputers. *Stand-alone* means that a device is not dependent on another computer; it can function on its own as a self-contained unit. The floppy disk is the primary source of data input and storage for a stand-alone micro, and data can be easily edited when displayed on the micro's screen.

Magnetic tapes and disks have several advantages over punched cards:

1. Holes punched into cards are permanent; once the cards are punched, the data cannot be erased. In contrast, magnetic media are erasable and reusable.

2. Magnetic media can hold more data in a more compact form than punched cards. One inch of magnetic tape can hold up to 6,400 characters, and one inch of a floppy disk can hold as many as 100,000 characters; one inch on a standard punched card can hold about 12 characters. Thus, magnetic media take up far less storage space, and transferring these media to the input equipment is a faster and less cumbersome matter.

3. Record length is not limited to 80 or 96 characters. Given the continuous nature of magnetic tape, the record can be as long or as short as is necessary to capture the data. Tape thus may have either a variable or a fixed record length. Like punched cards, magnetic disks always have fixed record lengths, but each record can hold several hundred characters or more.

4. Correction of errors spotted during keyboarding is, in a way, easier

on magnetic media; the keyboard operator can make the correction simply by backspacing and rekeying. However, if the error is not spotted during keyboarding, detecting and correcting it may be more difficult than on punched cards. Magnetic media cannot be read without special devices, and errors must be corrected on the original medium in the available recording space. In contrast, you can read data directly from a punched card, and corrections involve simple removal and replacement of the card.

5. Because they operate electronically, key-to-tape and key-to-disk devices are much quieter than the mechanically operated keypunch machines, which can make a rather deafening racket.

6. Magnetic devices can transfer data at far greater speeds — from 250,000 to over a million characters per second. As we noted earlier, the speed of a card reader is less than a 100,000 characters per *minute*.

SOURCE-DATA AUTOMATION

Magnetic-Ink Character Recognition

Certain industries have unique data entry requirements, which can be met only by unique data entry systems. The banking industry is a case in point; the system that it uses to meet its data entry needs is known as **magnetic-ink character recognition (MICR).** With this system, checks, deposit slips, and other banking documents are preprinted with stylized symbols that represent various kinds of data. Figure 6.13 explains the meaning of the symbols that appear on the lower part of bank checks. The printing of these symbols is done with a special, high-carbon magnetic ink that produces a sharp image when run through a machine scanner. The preprinted symbols contain all the information the bank needs about sorting and routing (i.e., the information needed to identify the bank on which the check was drawn and the individual account to be charged). The only information generally not included in the preprinting is the amount of the transaction. When the amount of the transaction is predetermined, as is the case with a traveler's check, even that information is included.

When the check or other source document is processed, the bank's first step is to enter the amount of the transaction on the document. This is done with a device known as a **MICR inscriber** (see Figure 6.14). The MICR inscriber reproduces the amount of the transaction in magnetic-ink characters, as shown in the lower right-hand corner of the check in Figure 6.13. The amount appearing in this space should always correspond exactly to the amount written on the check. The operation of the MICR inscriber is similar to the keypunch operation described earlier: An operator reads the amount and keys it into the machine, and the machine prints the symbols. The MICR process differs from offline data collection in that the MICR operator is simultaneously preparing and coding the source document; MICR is therefore considered source-data automation.

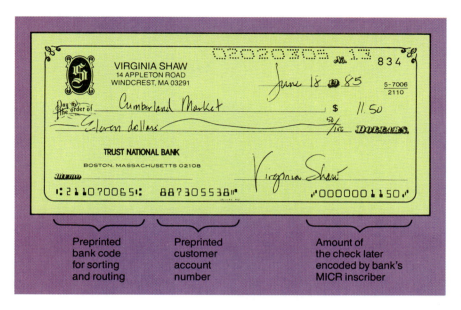

Figure 6.13
A bank check's symbols.

Once the MICR inscriber has done its work, the document can be entered into a **MICR reader/sorter** (see Figure 6.15). The MICR reader/sorter sorts and scans the data, translates the magnetic-ink characters into electronic signals, and records them on tape or enters them into the CPU. With the amount of the transaction encoded on the document, the document

Figure 6.14
A MICR inscriber.
Courtesy of Burroughs Corporation.

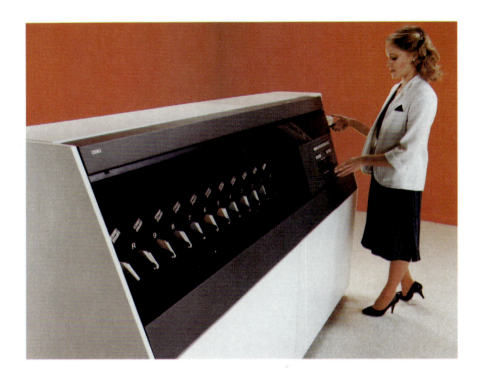

Figure 6.15
A MICR reader/sorter.
Courtesy of NCR Corporation.

can be machine-scanned and processed any number of times with no further handling by people, except the handling required to place the documents in a MICR reader. The amount of handling involved in check processing is an important consideration: Because a check may have to be routed through several clearinghouses before you finally get it back in your monthly statement, processing checks would be much more expensive than it now is if people had to do all the handling. Because the bank's routing codes are prerecorded and the amount of the transaction is encoded at the bank that accepts the check, the MICR system also removes most of the opportunity for error from check processing.

Optical Recognition

Optical-recognition devices include the supermarket scanners that we described earlier. Such devices use a reflected light beam to scan data on various source documents and to translate these data into electronic signals. The signals may be transferred to magnetic media for later entry into the system, or they may be transmitted directly into the CPU. The data to be scanned may be coded in various ways: as marks, as characters, as series of lines known as bar codes, or even as carefully handwritten numbers and letters.

If you've ever taken a standardized test, you've no doubt coded the test form with a mark to be scanned by an optical-recognition device. This kind of optical recognition is known as **optical-mark recognition (OMR)**, and it uses a device called a **mark-sense reader** to do the scanning. The mark-sense reader recognizes the presence or absence of a mark within a specific boundary. The process is thus quite similar to the way punched cards are processed, except that the mark-sense document contains marks instead of holes. Figure 6.16 shows a typical mark-sense form. OMR is also used in questionnaires and surveys, with the mark representing the option selected on a preference question.

In **optical-character recognition (OCR)**, the data are coded not as marks but as special characters consisting of numbers, letters, and symbols.

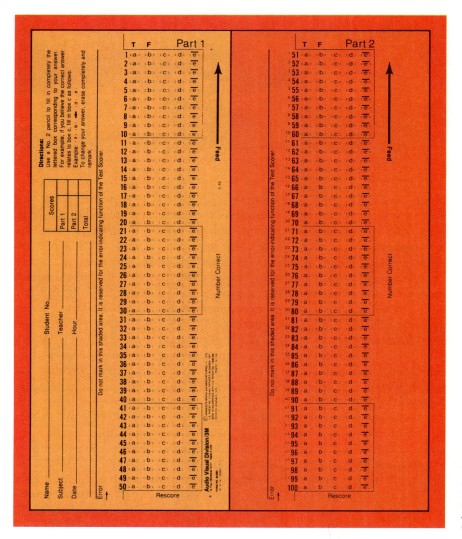

Figure 6.16
A mark-sense form.

Test Form No. 50SB2 is reproduced by permission of and copyrighted 1979 by Minnesota Mining and Manufacturing Company (3M). The form is covered by U.S. Patent No. 3,808,406.

Figure 6.17
A wand reader.
Courtesy of NCR Corporation.

These codes are often in a form that people can read, which improves their usefulness. For example, sales clerks and customers can read department store sales tags, which contain information helpful to them in selecting the appropriate product. These same tags can be optically scanned to provide the computer with data on inventory, price, and size.

A popular device for scanning optical characters is the hand-held **wand reader** that you see in many department stores (see Figure 6.17). It operates on the same principle as all other scanners, bouncing a light beam off the data and collecting the reflected image on a photosensitive cell or plate. The image is then converted to electronic signals. Other OCR devices are able to scan pages of typewritten or printed material and to convert the characters to electronic signals. Thus, a typewritten manuscript can be typeset without being rekeyed, a feature particularly useful in the publishing business.

There are various types of **bar codes,** but probably the most familiar one consists of those strange-looking, unevenly spaced stripes that you see on the labels of supermarket products. The particular bar-code system that most supermarkets use is called the **Universal Product Code (UPC).** As shown in Figure 6.18, the UPC's stripes represent the name of the product's manufacturer and the product's contents and size. Nothing in the code

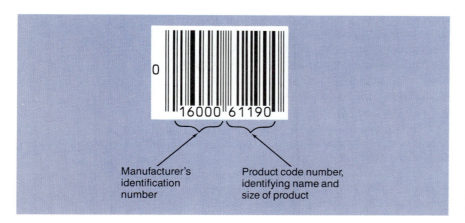

Manufacturer's identification number

Product code number, identifying name and size of product

Figure 6.18
The Universal Product Code.

represents the price; that is determined by the retailer at the time of sale. The UPC is similar to a social security number in that a unique UPC is issued for each product sold. Even different sizes of identical products have separate UPCs. Bar codes are also used to identify library books, library patrons, and charge card transactions.

The bar-coded data may be entered into the computer either through a wand reader or through a **bar-code reader,** a fixed scanner mounted in a convenient area for checking purchases (see Figure 6.19). Both the wand and bar-code readers translate the presence of bar-code marks, which are indicated by reflected light, into electronic signals that can be routed directly into the CPU for processing. The CPU searches for the unique number indicated by the bar code and sends a return signal with a price and other information about the purchase back to a cash-register terminal located in the checkout area. The checkout clerk has only to be sure that the package is positioned so that the light beams of the machine reflect on the bar code. If the signal is properly picked up, the process of data collection and entry is completed automatically. If for some reason the code can't be scanned, or if an item isn't coded, the clerk can override the automatic system. In addition to displaying purchase data, totaling purchases, calculating sales tax, and printing a sales tape, the computer can store the transaction data for later use in inventory reporting, sales forecasting, and even analysis of product placement within the store.

For a number of years, researchers have been trying to develop a device for scanning handwritten characters. Such a device could be used to scan everything from time cards to sales slips, and it would be particularly useful in the postal system, where it could be used in scanning zip codes. Efforts to date have not been very successful, one reason being that there are so many ways to form letters and numbers. A data entry operator is able to make a judgment after looking at the data; a computer is not. A

Figure 6.19
A bar-code reader.
Courtesy of IBM Corporation.

growing component of artificial intelligence (AI) — that is, the use of computers to solve problems that appear to require intelligence or imagination — is pattern recognition, and it deals with the same logic concerns involved in scanning handwritten documents. As we noted in Chapter 2, AI research is currently receiving a good deal of attention; so we may see some progress in this area in the near future.

Remote Terminals

Remote terminals are input (and output) devices located at the source of the data. Since they can use a **telecommunications link** (such as a telephone line or a satellite-transmission system) to send and receive signals, remote terminals may be located anywhere in the world that data are being generated. They may be in the same building as the computer facility or in another country thousands of miles away. This single fact has transformed the way that business data processing is organized. Before the introduction of remote terminals, all transaction documents had to be collected from the site of the transactions and transferred to a central site where the data from the documents could be keyed onto punched cards or magnetic media. The media then had to be transferred to the site of the CPU for processing. Today, with remote terminals located at the sources of the data, all the transaction data collected in the course of a business day can be accumulated on a floppy disk, ready for processing at the end of the day, or they can be processed as they are generated. Remote terminals also reduce the chances for error in data entry, not only because the data do not have to be rekeyed onto some type of media, but also because the people entering the data are those most familiar with the transactions that generated the data.

Remote terminals can be classified as dumb, smart, or user-programmable. They can also be classified according to type. The types that we will discuss are point-of-sale terminals, audio-input devices, and touch-sensitive and light-sensitive devices.

Dumb, Smart, and User-Programmable Terminals. A **dumb terminal** is one that can perform only as an input and output device for the computer to which it is connected. It has no storage capacity, and it cannot perform any processing functions. In contrast, a **smart terminal** can serve as more than an input/output device. For instance, a smart terminal might be able to do some editing checks on the reasonableness of the data, or it might produce graphic forms on its screen to aid in data collection. Smart terminals operate with preprogrammed plug-in circuits, or firmware, and they offer greater flexibility in operations than dumb terminals.

A **user-programmable terminal** has all the features of a true computer, including arithmetic/logic circuits, primary storage, systems software, and often auxiliary storage. Such a device may, in fact, be a microcomputer. A user-programmable terminal is therefore able to serve a dual purpose: It can perform stand-alone processing, and it can also function as an input/output device for a central computer. Because of these characteristics, user-programmable terminals are frequently referred to as **intelligent terminals.**

Let's consider the way in which a business might use user-programmable terminals to process orders. Each day, the business accepts telephoned sales orders for inventory stored in warehouses throughout the country. The telephone operators who take the orders are located in sales offices at each warehouse site. They have at their workstations terminals linked to the central computer (see Figure 6.20). Each terminal is programmed to display on its screen a graphic that looks like a printed order form, a standard design that is easy to complete.

When the operator keyboards the order data into the terminal, an editing program is activated to check the data. These checks may be as

Figure 6.20
Order processing using remote user-programmable terminals.

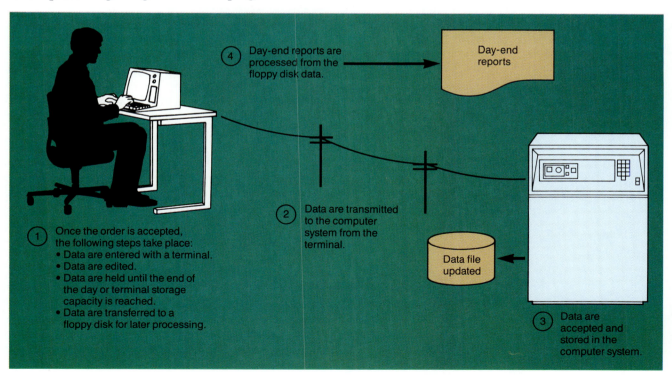

simple as testing for numerical or alphabetical data for each entry, or they may be more complex and involve such things as data ranges and reasonableness. For example, if the average customer order is for twenty units, a simple editing check can alert the operator when an order for a hundred or more units is entered. The large order may be correct, in which case the operator has a procedure to override the edit control. It may be, however, that the operator keyed in an extra digit by mistake, and it is, of course, easier to correct the order as it is keyed into the system than to make the adjustment after delivery to the customer. At the same time that the editing check is being done, an inventory-search program accesses the inventory file to determine whether enough inventory is on hand to fill the order. Notation of the order is made for the inventory file, and the sale is closed.

The terminal holds the data from each order in its memory until its storage capacity is exhausted. At that point, a telecommunications link is made to the computer system, and the data stored in the terminal's memory are transmitted to the computer. Sending the data in a burst reduces communications charges since the communications link to the central processing unit doesn't need to be continuously maintained. The terminal then begins functioning as a stand-alone computer, generating a number of end-of-day reports, using tabulation and accounting programs developed for this purpose.

Remote, user-programmable terminals allow businesses to capture data with fewer errors than the offline methods that have been the usual means of collecting data in the past. Visual inspection of data, editing checks, and corrections can all be done while the transaction is being processed and while both the data entry clerk and the customer are available. With the accuracy and performance of the system so dependent on the quality of the data, user-programmable terminals are becoming a very popular way of processing business data.

Point-of-Sale Terminals. **Point-of-sale (POS) terminals** function both as cash registers and as a means of collecting data at their source and transmitting them as electronic signals directly into the computer system. Sometimes the equipment used in POS data entry looks much like the manual equipment that it replaced. For example, the POS terminals used at supermarket checkout counters and in department stores don't look too much different from the cash registers that used to be there. However, they may have as part of their equipment the bar-code reader or the wand reader that we described earlier. Figure 6.21 shows the components of a POS terminal: the keyboard for data entry, the screen for displaying the amount of the transaction, the cash drawer, and the printer for producing a receipt. These devices have been the greatest innovation in consumer sales and transactions since the introduction of the cash register at the end of the nineteenth century.

**Figure 6.21
Components of a point-of-sale terminal.**
Courtesy of NCR Corporation.

Audio-Input Devices. An **audio-input,** or **voice-recognition, device** can accept spoken words as input data and enter them into the CPU as electronic signals. This form of input is about as direct as data entry can get; and, as most of our communications are in the form of spoken rather than written messages, it is also very compatible with our usual way of doing business. To enable the computer to understand the voice characteristics of the user, a tape of the user's voice is entered into the computer's memory; the computer then compares the data on the stored tape with the audio-input data. At present, computers can be programmed to understand only a limited vocabulary (usually under 500 words). Audio-input devices may be connected to the computer system through a plug and cable or through a telephone link. In either case, the user speaks into a microphone, which picks up the audio signal and transmits it to the computer (see Figure 6.22). Problems arise in voice-recognition systems when there are variations in the user's speech patterns (e.g., a head cold will confuse the computer) and when static, echoes, and background noises alter the audio characteristics of the input data. Present applications include the control of certain manufacturing equipment requiring the operator's hands to be free. Audio-input devices are also useful to physically handicapped people who cannot effectively operate a keyboard.

TALKING TO TYPEWRITERS

The voice-activated typewriter — a machine able to transcribe human speech — has been sought after since the 1940s. For more than 10 years, corporate heavyweight IBM has funded a research project aimed at developing a 5,000-word voice-activated typewriter. Other commercial giants pursuing the development of a machine with the ultimate man-machine interface include Nippon Electric Corp. and Bell Labs. Nor has there been a dearth of academic research. The defense department has contributed $15 million to programs researching voice-activated systems at MIT, Stanford, and Carnegie-Mellon. But an English language voice-activated system ready for the market still does not exist, and many experts believe such a machine is a decade or more away.

Ray Kurzweil — inventor, artificial intelligence expert, 36-year-old president of Kurzweil Applied Intelligence of Waltham, Mass. — says his company will be selling a voice-activated word processor capable of transcribing speech drawn from a 10,000-word vocabulary by early 1986. The machine, designed to work with many existing personal computers, must be taught to recognize the individual characteristics of a speaker's voice, typically a two-hour session.

Xerox and Wang Labs are now major backers of the project, and Kurzweil claims to have demonstrated a machine that can understand a 10,000-word vocabulary with an accuracy rate as high as 95 to 98 percent.... Kurzweil, unlike researchers at IBM and Bell Labs, is using artificial intelligence... in the development of his product.

A group of eminent scientists has been assembled to work with Kurzweil on a project some skeptics believe cannot succeed.... Says Michael Tomasic, chief operating officer of Kurzweil Applied Intelligence: "Ray's technical and intellectual leadership and the ambitious nature of our project have attracted the very best scientific talent."

Top scientific talent may not be enough to develop a cost-effective product that will wind up on the desks of executives and managers in mass. The machine's expected $10,000 to $20,000 price is a far cry from the previously predicted price of $5,000. Nor will the first field units scheduled for delivery in late 1985 deliver real-time performance, says Tomasic. David E. Gold, a consultant specializing in the commercial potential of new technologies, notes that a voice-activated system with a large vocabulary would require enormous computational power. Kurzweil's answer: Computers employing many chips that perform computations simultaneously will eventually solve the power problem. "When integrating a number of subprocessors — each dedicated to specific tasks — onto a single computer chip, the chip can perform 10 to 20 different computations simultaneously. Put 100 of these dedicated, inexpensive chips in a product and you have the power of several thousand microprocessors," he notes.

If past accomplishments are an indicator of future success, Kurzweil just might deliver a breakthrough product. In 1974, four years after graduating from MIT, he began work on a reading machine for the blind that could translate any printed material into understandable speech. Released two years later, it was hailed as the greatest achievement for the blind since Braille. It also attracted the attention of musician Stevie Wonder, who became an enthusiastic user. Wonder later expressed interest in a keyboard synthesizer that could reproduce the sounds and tone of acoustical instruments. In 1983, one year after Wonder's request, Kurzweil began selling a digital synthesizer that accurately reproduces the sound of a piano, a trumpet blast, a drum set, and more than 100 other instruments.

Short, reserved, and bearing a physical resemblance to tennis star John McEnroe, Kurzweil considers himself a business man as well as an inventor. He sold his first company, Kurzweil Computer Products, to Xerox Corp. for $6 million, and he still acts as its chairman. "Part of the inventing process is properly targeting a product toward a market need," he says. Soon, Kurzweil forecasts, business people and secretaries will be talking to their word processors. "And I am confident we'll capture half of a predicted $3.5 billion market."

— "Talking to Typewriters," *Business Computer Systems* (March 1985), p. 82. Reprinted by permission of *Business Computer Systems*.

SOURCE-DATA AUTOMATION **181**

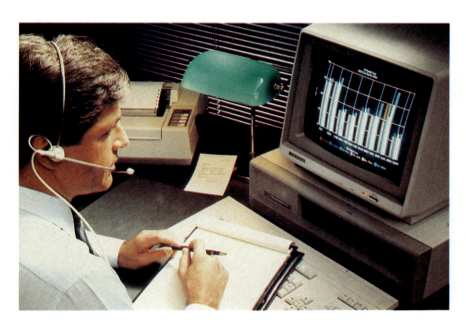

Figure 6.22
An audio-input device.
Courtesy of Texas Instruments.

Touch-Sensitive and Light-Sensitive Devices. For special applications, particularly those involving graphics, engineering design, and aids to the handicapped, **touch-sensitive and light-sensitive devices** can be a very useful way of simultaneously generating and entering data into the computer. Touch-sensitive **digitizing tablets,** for example, are often used in preparing maps for military activities and geological exploration. *Digitizing* refers to the process whereby a graphic image is translated into digital data acceptable to the computer. In effect, a digitizing tablet consists of a matrix of thousands of small dots; each dot is represented in the computer's primary storage unit. The user places a document on the tablet and enters data by touching the document with a stylus or other instrument (see Figure 6.23). In the same way, the user can also alter the data. Each touch creates a signal that causes a change in the data stored in the computer's memory. The computer can then display an image of the altered document on a CRT screen. With overlays, some CRT screens are themselves touch-sensitive, so that the user can enter data into the computer merely by touching the screen with a finger (see Figure 6.24).

Similarly, a **light pen** can be used to enter data on a light-sensitive CRT screen. A light pen contains a light-emitting photocell, which, when touched against the screen, creates signals that are picked up by the computer. Simply by moving the pen, the user can also alter the data. The data may consist of words or graphics. For example, the screen may display a **menu** (a set of possible activities); by touching the light pen to the spot on the screen that displays the desired activity, the user enters the input data. Figure 6.25 shows a light pen being used to alter data in a graphic display.

Figure 6.23
A touch-sensitive digitizing tablet.
Courtesy of IBM Corporation.

Figure 6.24
CRT screen with touch-sensitive overlay.
Courtesy of Hewlitt-Packard.

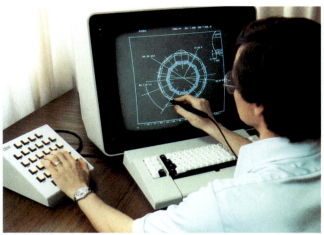

Figure 6.25
A light pen.
Courtesy of IBM Corporation.

SELECTION CRITERIA

The kind of input that you enter into a computer system depends on the output you want to produce and the processing activities needed to produce that output. In other words, the application will in large measure determine the choice of input devices and procedures. In making the selection, it's desirable to achieve a cost-effective balance between the needs of the application and input hardware, personnel, and data collection and control procedures. For example, because costs rise when data are collected at the time of the transaction, especially when communications charges are involved, it would normally not be cost-effective to collect sales data from a shoe store each time a pair of shoes is sold. In this case, it would be adequate to collect the data and process them at the end of the day, balancing the cash receipts with sales and producing an inventory report.

The more complex the hardware, the more costly it is. A simple keypunch machine is easier to build and maintain than a complex light-beam scanner. If punched cards will do the job, then they might be a more cost-effective solution than scanning. Complex equipment can also require training of personnel. However, in many cases the complex equipment performs the difficult tasks and the personnel perform rather simple ones; using a scanner to pass a coded product over a light beam is easy work for most people. Thus, if you add in the costs of labor and of the card readers involved in punched-card data collection, scanners *could* be a more cost-effective alternative. At times, it's not possible to substitute one automated method for another (e.g., there is presently no computerized substitute for supermarket scanning equipment); so it then becomes a choice of either implementing that particular method or relying on non-computerized data collection.

Input control procedures such as data verification, editing, and batch controls, which are designed to ensure that the data are captured completely and accurately, add to the costs of the system. The more complex these control procedures, the more costs involved. Again, the application will determine how complex and costly the procedures have to be. In some instances, such as bank deposits, complex, strict controls are critical to ensure that the transaction is handled properly, whereas in other data collection activities, such as the processing of subscription lists, these controls may be less important. If a name is misspelled on a magazine label, the magazine will probably still be delivered to the correct person; so controls on entering subscriber data can be more relaxed than controls on entering bank-account data. A miskeyed deposit amount could expose the bank to a loss or cause a customer to overdraw an account — both serious enough consequences to justify stricter procedures.

SUMMARY

Business data come from internal sources, such as employees, source documents representing transactions, and accounting records. They also come from external sources, such as customers and business publications. The problem in business computer systems today is not a shortage of input data; it is how to collect only data that will produce usable and useful output.

Data errors, which may occur as a source document is prepared or as it is keyboarded into machine-readable form, can be very costly. Collection procedures and controls play an important role in ensuring that the data will be as complete, accurate, and error-free as possible. These procedures and controls include using forms as data collection tools, having the originator of the transaction also enter the data into the system, verifying the correctness of the keyboarded data by keyboarding them a second time, using batch controls, and editing the data before processing.

When data are collected offline, they are keyboarded from source documents into machine-readable form and are held for later entry into the system, where they are processed in a batch. The media onto which the data are keyboarded include punched cards, magnetic tape, and magnetic disks. Offline devices — keypunch machines and key-to-tape and key-to-disk devices — are used to key the data into machine-readable form on these media. The data are then later entered into the CPU through online card readers and magnetic-tape and magnetic-disk drives. The magnetic media have several advantages over punched cards, among them reusability of the media, more compact storage, and faster data transfer speeds.

Source-data automation means that the data are collected in machine-readable form at the time and place they are generated. This method of data collection helps to overcome some of the keyboarding errors and duplication of effort associated with offline methods. Data collected through source-data automation may be entered directly into the system through such devices as video display terminals and scanners, or they may be held offline for later entry and batch processing. Depending on the application, the data entered directly may be processed interactively, or they may be held in an online auxiliary storage unit for later batch processing.

Source-data automation includes the magnetic-ink character recognition (MICR) system used in banking; the optical scanning of marks, characters, and bar codes used in automated test scoring and department store and supermarket sales; and the use of remote terminals to capture the transaction data at their source in machine-readable form. Remote terminals may be dumb, smart, or user-programmable. They include point-of-sale terminals, audio-input devices, and touch-sensitive and light-sensitive devices.

The choice of input devices and procedures depends on the application in which they will be used. In making the selection, it's desirable to achieve a cost-effective balance between the needs of the application and input hardware, personnel, and data collection and control procedures.

KEY TERMS

audio-input (voice-recognition) device (179)
bar-code reader (175)
bar codes (174)
batch control (157)
card reader (165)
cassette (167)
cathode ray tube (CRT) (156)
digitizing tablets (181)
dumb terminal (176)
editing (157)
80-column punched card (Hollerith card) (163)
fixed record (163)
floppy disks (floppies, diskettes) (166)
hard disks (166)
intelligent terminals (177)
keypunch machine (164)
key-to-disk device (167)

key-to-tape device (167)
light pen (181)
magnetic disk (166)
magnetic-disk drive (167)
magnetic-ink character recognition (MICR) (170)
magnetic tape (166)
magnetic-tape drive (167)
mark-sense reader (173)
menu (181)
MICR inscriber (170)
MICR reader/sorter (171)
96-column punched card (164)
offline data collection methods (159)
optical-character recognition (OCR) (173)
optical-mark recognition (OMR) (173)
point-of-sale (POS) terminals (178)

range of the data (158)
reasonableness of the data (157)
reel (167)
remote terminals (176)
scanners (160)
smart terminal (176)
source-data automation (160)
source document (154)
telecommunications link (176)
touch-sensitive and light-sensitive devices (181)
unit record (163)
Universal Product Code (UPC) (174)
user-programmable terminal (176)
verification (157)
verifier (164)
video display terminals (VDTs) (156)
wand reader (174)

DISCUSSION QUESTIONS

1. Identify internal and external sources of business data. Describe how these data might be used in a computer information system and how easy or difficult it would be to use them.
2. Describe how errors in offline data collection commonly arise. What can their effects be? How might errors arise in source-data automation?
3. What do verification and batch controls have in common? When would these procedures be used? How are editing checks implemented and what might they include?
4. What two procedures used in an airline reservation system help to prevent data errors? Would this system be an example of offline data collection or source-data automation? Why?
5. Describe the steps involved in offline data collection. What advantages does source-data automation have over offline data collection? Do you think source-data automation will ever completely replace offline data collection? Why or why not?
6. Discuss the advantages that magnetic media have over punched cards.
7. Describe how optical-recognition devices work. What kind of data can they scan? What unique problems might occur in this kind of scanning?
8. Visit your local bank and investigate how its MICR system works and how it uses remote terminals to transmit data to and from its central computer. What is the usefulness of the MICR system? Are the remote terminals dumb, smart, or user-programmable? How could these terminals be used in other businesses?
9. Identify some applications in which point-of-sale terminals, audio-input devices, and touch-sensitive devices would be particularly useful.
10. What selection criteria would the registrar of your school be particularly concerned with when developing an online student registration system?

OUTLINE

WHY BUSINESSES NEED COMPUTER OUTPUT

HOW BUSINESSES USE COMPUTER OUTPUT

- Traditional Output
- Output for Management Science
- Output as Input

GENERATING COMPUTER OUTPUT

HARD-COPY OUTPUT

- Printed Output
  - Character-at-a-Time Impact Printers
  - Character-at-a-Time Nonimpact Printers
  - Line-at-a-Time Impact Printers
  - Page-at-a-Time Nonimpact Printers
- Computer Output Microform
- Output from Graphic Plotters

SOFT-COPY OUTPUT

- Display Output
- Audio Output

OUTPUT BY ROBOTS

SELECTION CRITERIA

SUMMARY

KEY TERMS

DISCUSSION QUESTIONS

OVERVIEW

Useful output is, of course, what the whole computer system is about. It's the first thing a company — or an individual — must consider when acquiring or designing a computer system. And it's the first thing that must be considered at each succeeding step along the way. The perennial question is, what kind of output do we need? The answer to this question will determine the kinds of input data collected and the manner in which they are processed and stored. By choosing the appropriate output devices, a company can get the most from the system, both for itself and for its customers.

While choosing an appropriate output device may sound like a simple matter, many companies have found to their sorrow that it can be a bit more complicated than it sounds. When selection of output devices is based on a whim or a fancy rather than on solid technical analysis, you can end up with as simple a problem as a dot matrix printer that you can't connect to your microcomputer because its cable pins are in the wrong places, or as disastrous a situation as a costly laser printer that won't accept signals from your CPU and that has a speed and production capability far greater than you need. A knowledge of the characteristics of output devices, as well as of why the output is needed and how it will be used, will go a long way toward preventing such problems.

Our objectives in this chapter are to

- explain why businesses need computer output.
- identify the types of computer output that businesses use.
- describe the various types of hardware used to produce hard-copy output.
- describe the hardware used in producing soft-copy output.
- discuss the output produced by robots.
- define the criteria used in selecting output devices.

CHAPTER 7

OUTPUT

WHY BUSINESSES NEED COMPUTER OUTPUT

From time immemorial, people have been processing business data and keeping records of the processing results in order to have reliable information for later use. Today, the need is much the same, but the methods of output — not to mention those of input and processing — differ mightily. From the clay tablets of the ancient Egyptians, we have progressed to green-striped computer printouts and a variety of other outputs that the ancients would no doubt have found unimaginable. There are six essential reasons for businesses to produce computer outputs today, and it is likely that they, too, have existed from time immemorial, although perhaps not in the exact form that we know them today:

1. *To fulfill legal requirements.* In 2700 B.C., Egyptians were reporting their annual earnings to the pharoah's version of the Internal Revenue Service. Today, we pay similar homage not only to the IRS in Washington but to state and local tax agencies as well. Publicly owned companies must meet several additional requirements: They must report their annual earnings to stockholders in a very precise way specified by the Securities and Exchange Commission. And, whether publicly owned or privately held, companies must furnish information on their employees and operations to insurance companies and to agencies designed to protect workers, consumers, the environment, and the community. Such agencies might include trade unions, the Environmental Protection Agency, and citizens' groups.

2. *To report the results of operations to interested parties.* Owners of businesses are particularly interested in the results of business operations, most particularly in the company's profits and losses. An owner might be the individual owner of a store, a franchisor, or a corporate stockholder. Other interested parties are banks, lending institutions, suppliers, and wholesalers, all of which must have information about business operations in order to make informed decisions about providing funds and materials to the business.

3. *To plan effectively.* Planning for a business's future requires information about past operations, current and projected market conditions, and numerous other variables. Good planning based on this kind of information can result in a smooth operation. Poor planning based on inadequate information produces one crisis after another — everything from a lack of raw materials to an overdrawn bank account.

4. *To make effective use of the company's resources.* The better the information that management has on the resources of the business, the more effectively it can put these resources to work to achieve desired goals. Resources include both capital resources — money, materials, and machines — and human resources — the company's employees.

5. *To compete effectively.* To make the most of business opportunities, management needs information on the competition, the business climate, and the market forces at work. Such data can be gleaned by sales staff, who can ask their clients about the competition, pricing, consumer requirements, and demand. By assembling the data from numerous sales calls, it is possible to gain information and insights that will make for better decisions.

6. *To provide market responsiveness.* Business success is often predicated on understanding the marketplace. Because markets are dynamic and ever changing, information must be reported in a timely fashion. The longer the data collection and processing take, the less responsive the business will be and the greater the chance it will miss meeting the needs of the market.

As you can see, even if a business had no interest in collecting and processing data, it would have little choice but to do so in today's business environment. Because information requests come from all components of a business enterprise, coordination in developing the outputs is often lacking. It is not uncommon for the information system to generate almost the same report for two different users, neither of whom is aware that the other has similar information needs. A little advance planning can make the information system both more effective and more efficient.

HOW BUSINESSES USE COMPUTER OUTPUT

For all the reasons we've just discussed, businesses collect and process vast amounts of data every day. Certainly, the recent explosion of microcomputers, which has affected even the smallest businesses, has done nothing to diminish the quantity of data being processed. If the information generated by all this processing is to support effective decision making and lead to the attainment of a company's goals, it must be accurate, complete, relevant, concise, and timely. These characteristics have always been important considerations in business output, but in view of the amount of information that business managers must deal with today, they are more important than ever. As we mentioned in Chapter 6, managers are faced with an information overload, and unless a report is relevant and timely, and in as concise and readable a form as possible, it is very likely to go unused.

The specific kinds of outputs that businesses need vary from firm to firm. They depend in large measure on the company's size, management style, goals, and the nature of its business. But, in general, business data processing produces three categories of outputs: traditional outputs in the form of reports, outputs used in management science techniques, and outputs used as input data in other processing activities.

Traditional Output

Traditional output consists of various types of reports (see Figure 7.1). **Scheduled reports** are generated at regular intervals and are most often used in the supervision of business operations. The subject of a scheduled report might be the current inventory of raw materials, the tabulation of a day's transactions, or the latest payroll listing. Depending on its subject, a scheduled report may be issued as often as every day or as seldom as once a year. A calendar can be set up to establish the dates on which data for scheduled reports are to be processed. Once the programs are prepared, the production of these reports becomes an almost completely automatic activity.

Exception reports contain information only on significant deviations from the norm — that is, on results that differ substantially from those that were planned or projected. These reports do not contain information on anything that falls within the accepted or normal ranges. Exception reports thus save managers from having to plow through page after page telling them that everything is just as planned. Equally as important, they alert managers when there is a need to take action or to make a decision, as, for example, when a deviation from a budget occurs. When expenditures exceed the planned, or budgeted, amount, an exception report is triggered. Depending on the level of management concern, exception reports may be issued periodically, as scheduled reports, or at the time the exception occurs. For instance, an exception report showing inventory items that fall below a specified quantity might be issued on a weekly or monthly basis to the person in charge of reordering inventory, but a report on an overdraft in a checking account would no doubt be issued at once.

Inquiry reports are used when the timing of the request for the information cannot be predicted in advance, but the information itself must be supplied at the time the inquiry is made. Since it's impossible to predict when the information will be requested, no reporting routine can be established. For example, you probably don't cash a check at your bank every day; but when you do cash a check, the teller must be able to find out immediately whether there are sufficient funds in your account to cover the check. Since the bank has no way of knowing when you are going to cash a check, it would be foolish to establish a regular reporting routine on your daily bank balance. Inquiry reports have become important in the last few years because managers must make decisions very quickly, and they need information that is as current and relevant as possible.

Detailed reports, which we mentioned in Chapter 3, contain information on day-to-day business activities and are used in making operating decisions. For example, to schedule work assignments, a shop supervisor needs to know the number of employees available in the workforce on a day-to-day basis, as well as the availability of raw materials and machines. Detailed reports, which contain this kind of information, are generally not of much interest to managers at higher levels in the organization. In fact, the higher

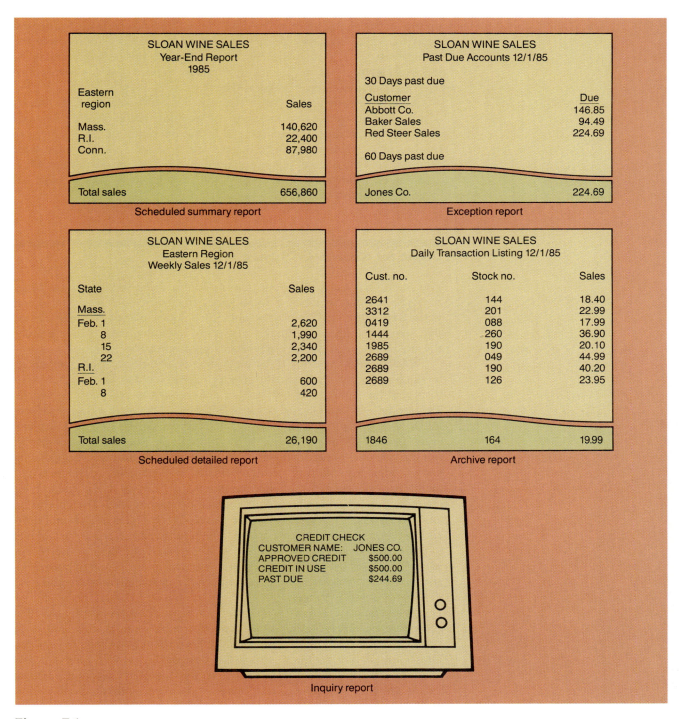

Figure 7.1
Traditional business reports.

up the manager, the more condensed the report is likely to be. **Summary reports,** which contain a great deal of condensed information, allow the manager to get a look at the "big picture" of the business operations. At the highest levels of management, summary reports are generally more like briefings than actual decision data.

Archive reports are files of detailed historical data, such as listings of account and transaction balances and documentation of other financial activities. These reports are not used in the operation or management of the business, but they must be maintained as support data to meet legal requirements for tax and revenue reporting. They are also necessary when a transaction file must be reconstructed, which would be the case, for example, if a customer disputed a bill.

Output for Management Science

The traditional kinds of output that we've just discussed are fine as far as they go, but managers must think about tomorrow as well as today and yesterday. Using management science techniques, managers today can go one step beyond the traditional analysis of operating data as they ponder the unknowns of the future while making business decisions.

Management science is the application of mathematical, or quantitative, techniques to business decision making. These techniques are often used to model, or simulate, a situation or activity in the real business world. The model is a mathematical representation of the data being analyzed, much as a model airplane is a physical representation of a real airplane (see Figure 7.2). The purpose of the model is to enable the manager to test the potential impact of different decisions by mathematically manipulating known data derived from previous events. For example, a farm manager might use management science techniques to arrive at the most cost-effective but still nutritive mix of grains for livestock feed. The data to be analyzed would include the current price of such grains as oats and corn and the protein content of each. The computer would execute the formula found in the model (which might be prepared by the farm manager but would more probably be part of a purchased farm-management program); and it would generate outputs describing the characteristics of each feed mix.

Management science techniques can be used without the aid of a computer, but because they often require complex calculations and large volumes of data, they are ideally suited to a computerized business system. The outputs they produce, which are designed to reflect how the real world would react to various decisions, are very useful in long-range planning and in allowing managers to test "what-if" decisions without actually committing company resources or taking business risks. These techniques are also very useful in training business decision makers. Using simulation

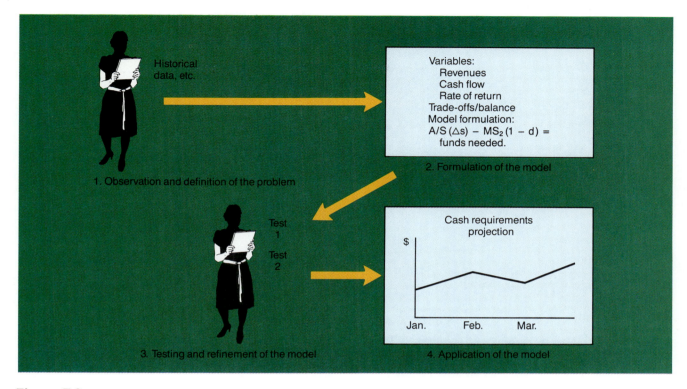

Figure 7.2
Management science: developing and using a financial model.

techniques, managers can practice making decisions in a compressed time frame and at a low cost to the firm. Management science techniques are a main component of most decision support systems (DSSs), which we described briefly in Chapter 3.

Output as Input

The final category of computer output used by businesses is information that can be used as input data in other processing activities. For example, the primary output of payroll processing consists of paychecks and associated records. However, a by-product of that processing is the data needed to fulfill the reporting and payment requirements of the Social Security Administration and the Internal Revenue Service. The paychecks would be generated in a form usable by people, but the other data would most likely be generated in machine-readable form — probably as magnetic impressions on tapes or disks — and would be held in auxiliary storage until needed

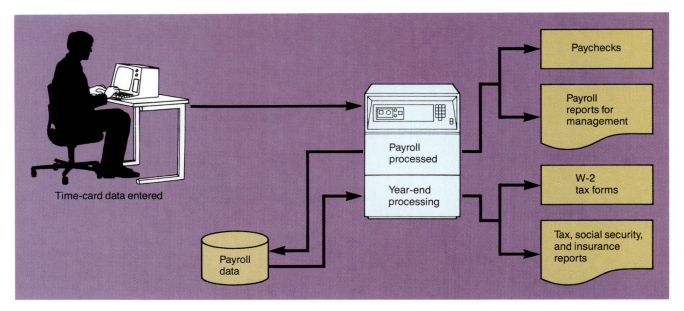

Figure 7.3
Using output as input. The time-card data are entered into the CPU and are processed to produce paychecks and reports. Selected data (e.g., withholds for taxes, social security, and insurance) are stored for later processing. When year-end reports for W-2 tax forms and other purposes are due, these data become input for other processing activities.

for processing (see Figure 7.3). When it comes time to prepare the year-end W-2 tax form for each employee, the data collected during payroll processing become input for the W-2 preparation program.

GENERATING COMPUTER OUTPUT

The outputs that computers generate as machine-readable magnetized spots are, as we've just noted, very useful as input to the computer for other processing activities. To be useful to people, however, outputs must be produced as something other than magnetized spots or electronic signals. Computer outputs destined for immediate use by people are produced as **hard copy,** which provides a permanent record of the output, or as **soft copy,** which is output in a temporary form. Another kind of computer output, which cannot be classified as either hard copy or soft copy, is the work done by robots.

Most hard copy is printed on paper by a variety of printers, but computer output microforms, which are outputs recorded on film, can also provide permanent records. Graphic plotters, which produce maps, charts, and engineering drawings, are another source of hard-copy output. Because they are specially designed for graphic output, graphic plotters offer the advantages of color and very precise graphic reproduction. However, some of today's printers are also capable of color output and graphics. The output produced by printers and plotters comes in a variety of sizes; the choice depends on how the output is to be used. The use of preprinted forms can further enhance the readability and usability of printed outputs. A nice feature of all hard copy is that once it is prepared, you don't have to communicate with the computer to have access to the information; so you are not dependent on the system's being operational.

An example of soft copy would be a temporary message on the CRT screen of a video display terminal. Screens are particularly useful in inquiry reports, in which computer files must be searched for specific data. For example, information in response to inquiries on credit ratings, bank account balances, and the availability of seats on airline flights is often relayed in soft-copy form on a terminal's screen. Another, more recent type of soft copy is audio output, in which the computer system synthesizes speech and responds to an inquiry verbally. This type of output has obvious advantages for anyone unable to read or for anyone with impaired vision. It also means that even without a terminal, you can have access to computer files. For instance, when you telephone for directory assistance and the operator has entered the correct spelling of the name of the person whose phone number you want, the computer searches the file and generates the number as audio output, which frees the operator to respond to the next inquiry.

Most modern computer systems can generate both soft-copy and hard-copy output by using a combination of devices—for example, a terminal with a screen for displaying the soft copy and a printer for producing the hard copy (see Figure 7.4). In the following sections we'll take a look at

Figure 7.4
A combination output device.
Courtesy of Hewlitt-Packard.

HARD-COPY OUTPUT

the kinds of equipment used to generate both hard-copy and soft-copy outputs; we'll also take a brief look at the use of robots in generating output.

Printed Output

A number of different types of printers are used to generate printed hard-copy output. As Table 7.1 shows, printers vary in the speed with which they print, in the quality of the print they produce, and in their cost. These three factors are important considerations in selecting the most appropriate printing equipment for any computer system.

As Table 7.1 also shows, printers can be classified in two ways: according to whether they print a character, a line, or a page at a time, and according to whether they are impact or nonimpact printers. An **impact printer** involves a mechanical motion that creates a physical contact between character, ribbon, and paper; these devices form characters in much the same way a typewriter does. In **nonimpact printers,** there is neither mechanical motion nor actual physical contact between printer and paper; characters are formed by ink spray, heat on chemically treated paper, laser beams, and electrostatic processes similar to photocopying processes.

Nonimpact printers have the advantage of being quieter than impact printers since they create no physical impact; they also have no difficulty in aligning letters and numbers, which can be a minor problem in line-at-a-time impact printers. Another advantage of nonimpact printers is that because they have fewer moving parts, they are less apt to break down than impact printers. One of their disadvantages is that since they make no impact, they can't make carbon copies.

Character-at-a-Time Impact Printers. Character-at-a-time printers are also called **serial printers.** Because they print only one character at a time, they are the slowest of all printers; the fastest of them prints at speeds of just over 200 characters per second. They are therefore best suited to low-volume printing jobs. Character-at-a-time impact printers fall into two categories: formed character and dot matrix.

Because the print heads used in **formed-character printers** can be easily detached and type styles and sizes can be quickly changed, these devices provide a great deal of flexibility. The characters are embossed on a ball, a cylinder, a thimble, a ribbon, or a rotating device called a **daisy wheel.** The characters are either struck by a hammer or are part of the hammer mechanism itself. Figure 7.5 shows the action of a daisy wheel printer. Because each character is controlled during the printing process, the quality of the print produced by formed-character printers can be very good, or **letter quality,** which means quality acceptable for business correspondence.

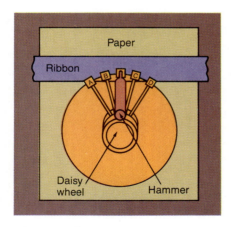

Figure 7.5

A daisy wheel printer. A daisy wheel is a rimless plastic or metal wheel with a character embossed on the end of each of its spokes. When the hammer strikes the character against the ribbon, the character is printed out on the paper.

Table 7.1 Characteristics of Computer Printers

	Maximum Speed (in lines per minute[1])	Print Quality	Cost[2]
Character-at-a-Time			
Impact Printers			
Formed character	30	Excellent	Low to medium low
Dot matrix	100	Fair to good	Low
Nonimpact Printers			
Inkjet	100	Good to excellent	Medium
Electrothermal	60	Good to very good	Low
Line-at-a-Time			
Impact Printers			
Chain	3,000	Good	High
Drum	2,000	Good	High
Page-at-a-Time			
Nonimpact Printers			
Electrostatic	18,000	Excellent	High to very high
Laser	21,000	Excellent	Very high

[1] 132 characters per line.

[2] Low cost = under $2,000; medium cost = $2,000–$5,000; high cost = $5,000–$50,000; very high cost = over $50,000.

In a **dot matrix printer,** the print head consists of a rectangular grid, or matrix, of wire pins. Combinations of these pins representing particular characters are electronically activated to press against a ribbon and paper, thus forming the desired character as a series of small dots. The print head then moves on to the next printing position, and the process is repeated. Because the pins are in a grid, the character can be enlarged by printing it on two or more lines, the top half on the first line(s) and the bottom half on the next line(s). Pins can also be activated in combinations to produce graphics and charts, which makes these devices quite versatile.

The grid is usually arranged so that there are seven vertical columns and five horizontal rows of pins (see Figure 7.6), but grids of seven by nine rows are also used. The closer together the pins are, the better the quality of the print. Because a grid of seven by nine rows of pins has more overlap than a grid of seven by five, it produces a better quality of output. Typically, however, the print quality produced by dot matrix printers is not as good as that produced by a daisy wheel mechanism, but they are relatively inexpensive and, like the daisy wheel printer, are often used as output devices for microcomputer systems.

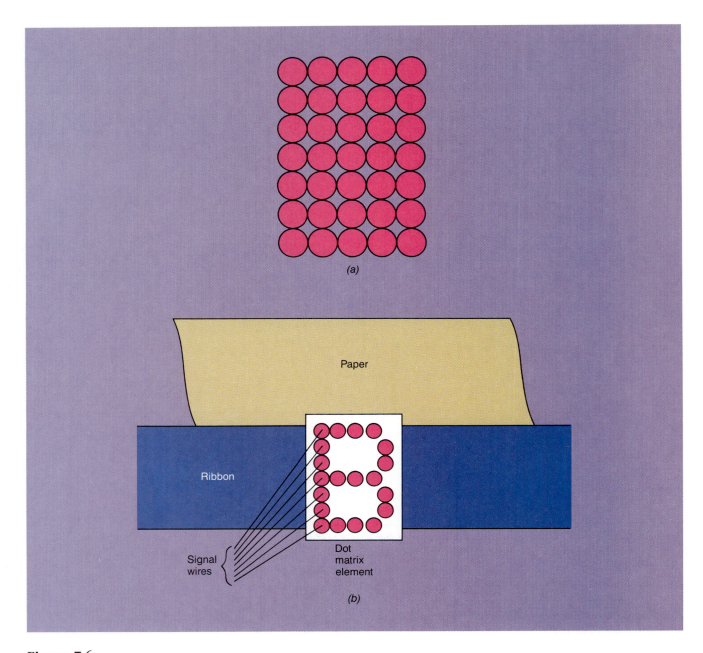

Figure 7.6
Dot matrix printing: (*a*) the grid; (*b*) the printing action. As shown in (*b*), to print the letter B, the dot matrix printer selects the appropriate pins to form the character, strikes them on the ribbon, and impresses the character on the paper behind the ribbon.

Character-at-a-Time Nonimpact Printers. Character-at-a-time nonimpact printers include inkjet and electrothermal printers. An **inkjet printer** (Figure 7.7) uses a nozzle to spray a stream of electrically charged ink particles onto a surface. This surface is usually paper, but it could be any material that can be fed through a machine, including packages and other materials with uneven contours. The charged ink particles pass through an electromagnetic field and are aligned in a configuration similar to that produced by the dot matrix printer. Inkjet printers are among the fastest of the character-at-a-time printers, printing about 200 characters per second. The print quality is quite good if a high-quality paper is used. If the paper is not of good quality, the ink may run through the fibers, creating a somewhat fuzzy image. Inkjet printers have the advantages of being able to use several colors and to produce good graphics. They are particularly useful in producing output that combines text and graphics on the same page.

Electrothermal printers use specially treated, heat-sensitive paper and a print head containing elements that can be electrically heated. As the print head moves down the paper, its elements are individually activated and heated, producing a pattern much like the dot matrix configuration. Although relatively slow (about 120 characters per second or less), electrothermal printers are popular because they have few moving parts and are easy to service. They are also less expensive than the nonimpact inkjet printers, although their print quality may not be as good. However, the special paper they require represents an added cost, and the paper itself has a tendency to fade over time. Also, because of the special paper required, electrothermal printers can't produce color.

Figure 7.7
An inkjet printer: (*left*) the printer; (*right*) the printhead.
Courtesy of Hewlitt-Packard.

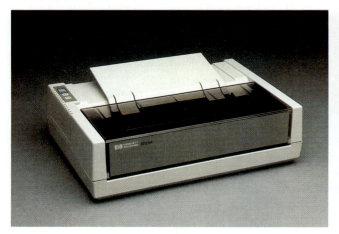

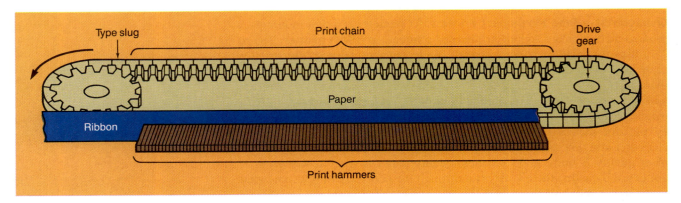

Figure 7.8
A chain printer.

Line-at-a-Time Impact Printers. **Chain printers** are the most popular **line-at-a-time printers.** In a chain printer, a character set, or in some cases multiple character sets, is assembled on a chain that revolves past all the printing positions in each line of output (see Figure 7.8). Each printing column has a print hammer, and when the appropriate character is in place, the hammer strikes. This action presses the paper and ribbon against the character slug on the chain, causing an impression to be made on the paper. Chain printers are classified as high-speed printers; they can produce printed output up to the rate of 3,000 lines per minute.

A **drum printer** (Figure 7.9) operates much like a chain printer, except that its character set is embossed on a drum. As the drum turns and the desired letters move to the appropriate print position, a hammer strikes the paper, pushing it against the ribbon and the character.

As we noted earlier, line-at-a-time impact printers can have trouble in aligning letters and numbers; this problem occurs when the chain or drum becomes worn. These output devices are relatively costly, but they are also relatively fast and produce a good-quality print. They are therefore often used to produce routine reports in large organizations.

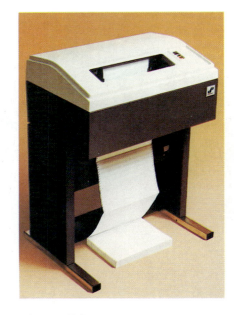

Figure 7.9
A drum printer.
Courtesy of Dataproducts Corporation.

Page-at-a-Time Nonimpact Printers. All **page-at-a-time printers** use nonimpact technology to produce the output. These devices include laser and electrostatic printers. **Laser printers** use a light beam to project an image onto a photosensitive surface, thus producing an entire page of output at a time (see Figure 7.10). Similarly, an **electrostatic printer** creates output for an entire page as a charged field, which passes through charged ink attracted to the charged field. This image is then transferred to paper while the next page image is being prepared. The electrostatic process is thus similar to photocopying.

Page printers, such as the one shown in Figure 7.11, can operate under

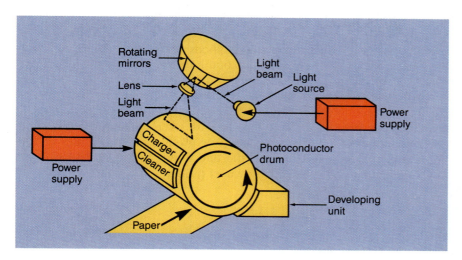

Figure 7.10
A laser printer. The light beam generates an image on the photoconductor drum, and the drum transfers the image to the paper.

program control and can store digital signals that represent various business forms; so, when it is time to print, they can produce both the data and the form at the same time. This feature saves time in changing paper in the printer, reduces the cost of forms, and produces consistency in the quality of output, which is usually excellent. Because page printers are nonimpact printers, they can't use carbon paper or other methods normally used to produce duplicate copies; multiple-copy outputs therefore require

Figure 7.11
A high-speed page printer.
Courtesy of Sperry Corporation.

additional runs. However, because these printers can produce over 20,000 lines a minute, running the extra copies is often faster and more cost-effective than the other duplicating methods would be. A speed of 20,000 lines a minute is very fast indeed; 20,000 lines are perhaps as many as are contained in this text. Page-at-a-time printers are expensive, but they can be cost-effective when the volume of printed output is very high.

Recent technological breakthroughs have enabled manufacturers to produce laser printers suitable for use with microcomputers. Obviously, these printers do not have the speed or production capabilities of the printers just described. However, the one shown in Figure 7.12 is eight times faster than the typical daisy wheel printer.

Figure 7.12
A laser printer for use with a microcomputer.
Courtesy of Hewlitt-Packard

Computer Output Microform

The bulk of printed output sometimes makes it difficult, if not impossible, to use the output effectively. In such cases, modern filming technology provides an alternative: **Computer output microform (COM)** is computer output that has been greatly reduced and placed on film. COM makes it possible to store a large volume of information in a very small space, and it comes in two varieties: microfilm and microfiche (see Figure 7.13). Hundreds of pages of computer printouts of sales transactions can be reduced to a single roll of microfilm or a sheet of microfiche, which you can easily (and cheaply) mail, store in a desk drawer, or even carry around in your pocket. When you consider that one small fiche of microfilm can hold the equivalent of 600 pages of printed matter, you can see that the film used in COM can be much less costly than the paper used in printing. However, COM does require special reading equipment to enlarge the film so that it is legible to the human eye.

As Figure 7.13 shows, **microfilm** is a continuous strip, or roll, of film. When it is used to photograph printed output, the image is usually taken from a CRT screen. Page-size reduction by a factor of 200 or 300 is not unusual. The microfilming process is faster than impact printing because its only moving parts are a film carrier and a photographic shutter. The image is created on the screen, the shutter is tripped, the film is advanced, and the system is ready to photograph the next page. In effect, since it reproduces a whole page at a time, the filming process operates in a manner similar to that of page-at-a-time printers, which, as we noted, are the fastest hard-copy printing devices.

Microfiche, also shown in Figure 7.13, consists of a rectangular piece of film approximately 4 by 6 inches. Each microfiche has as many as 300 frames, each capable of storing a page of output. The microfiche filming process is similar to the microfilming process. In some applications, the fiche is easier to handle than a roll of film. For example, a catalog can be stored on one or two fiche, with an index as the first few frames of

Figure 7.13
Microfilm and microfiche. Microfilm comes in a roll; microfiche, in a sheet.
Courtesy of Eastman Kodak Company.

information. By placing the fiche over the index in the microfiche reader, you can quickly determine the coordinates for the desired information, move the reader to them, and scan the information (see Figure 7.14).

Originally, all COM was prepared offline using magnetic tapes containing the output information. For high-volume operations, a number of firms now produce equipment that will generate COM online; the output is thus produced as the programs are run, and the delays associated with offline

Figure 7.14
Using a microfiche reader.
Courtesy of Eastman Kodak Company.

PAPER, PAPER EVERYWHERE — OR WHY COM

At first glance, the ability to produce more and better information seems like a blessing for most businesses. For some, however, it has turned out to be a bit less than that. The phenomenon known as "information overload" has threatened to bury many a business in mountains of paper reports.

One high-technology company in Colorado found itself producing over 50 million pages of reports each month, thus ranking as one of the state's most prolific paper consumers. Each report was needed by someone, and each had to be produced, distributed, filed, and duplicated. Even more problematic than handling the huge volume of paper, however, was finding the space to store it.

The solution the Colorado firm hit upon has been around longer than computers. Using microfiche — a sheet of film smaller than a single printed page yet able to hold the equivalent of more than 200 printed pages — the firm was able to reduce both the handling and the storage expenses of the information system. The use of microfiche resulted in savings in four areas: paper and supplies, printing, storage, and mailing. For the printed paper report, costs in the first two areas were about $.20 per page; for the microfiche sheet, which contains as many as 200 pages of output, the equivalent costs were $.25 per sheet. The office space required for storage was reduced by 90 percent; a file cabinet can store in microfiche what a 9-by-12-foot room can hold in paper. Mailing costs went from tens of thousands of dollars to hundreds of dollars per month.

Another benefit of using microfiche is easy access to the stored information. Because the top of each fiche contains an index of its contents, it's a fairly easy matter to flip through the microfiche sheets to find the information you want. Taking advantage of this feature, one police department in a Western state has installed microfiche readers in its patrol cars. Without having to search through a trunk full of paper, police officers have quick access to information on stolen property and current or pending criminal investigations — all contained in a small box of fiche.

Conservationists, too, approve of microfiche use. No one has ever bothered to calculate the number of trees it takes to keep up with the world's paper consumption, but it would surely take all the timber harvested in New England each year — and no doubt large portions of the timber harvested in other portions of the country and the rest of the world as well. Whatever the amount, one way to make more economical use of the trees that are cut is to record data on film rather than on paper, saving the wood fibers for more important uses.

processing are avoided. Figure 7.15 shows both methods of preparing COM. The offline method is still popular because the cost of the COM equipment may be difficult to justify if the equipment is used only a few hours a day; companies using offline methods can keep costs down by using a COM service. With microfilming speeds as high as 30,000 lines per minute, microfilming is often more cost-effective than high-speed printing. However, special reading devices necessary to use the film do create an expense not found with traditional hard-copy output.

The "bottom line" for microforms, then, is to determine the application and the uses of the information. Since hard-copy printouts don't require special reading equipment, they are often more convenient for people to use. But if mailing or transporting large volumes of information is involved,

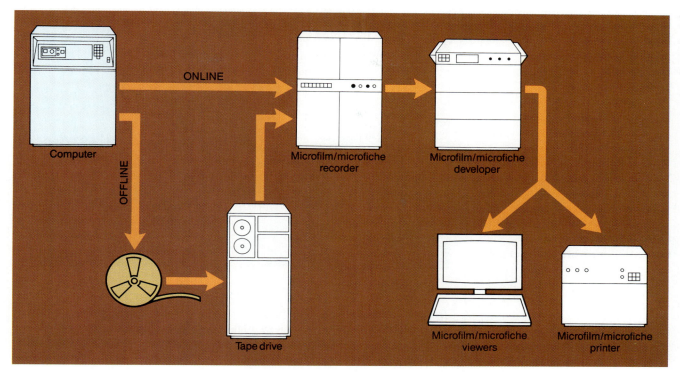

Figure 7.15
Offline and online preparation of COM. When the output is first written on magnetic tape and later recorded on microfilm or microfiche, the process is called an offline operation.

film has a size and weight advantage over bulky printouts. Film also saves storage space, and the cost of the paper needed for the printed outputs may offset the additional expense of film readers. In most large firms, there is a place for both printed and microform output.

Output from Graphic Plotters

Although a CRT screen can generate graphic outputs, it cannot produce them in hard-copy form without using special filming devices. A **graphic plotter** is a device specially designed for producing hard-copy graphics, and it may use either a single sheet or a continuous roll of paper. In a **drum plotter,** a continuous roll of paper moves forward and backward over a drum; computer-controlled pens suspended over the paper move

Figure 7.16
Computer-controlled plotter pens.
Courtesy of Gerber Scientific, Inc.

from side to side (see Figure 7.16). The pens also have an up-and-down motion, which allows them to make or break contact with the paper. Because the paper is continuous, the drum plotter can be used to prepare very large and complicated drawings, such as are required in the design of complex electronic circuits.

A **flatbed plotter** functions like a drafting table: A single sheet of paper is held stationary while the pens, which are in a pen frame attached to a control frame, move forward and backward and from side to side over it (see Figure 7.17). The pens can also be moved up and down to make or break contact with the paper. Flatbed plotters are restricted in the size of

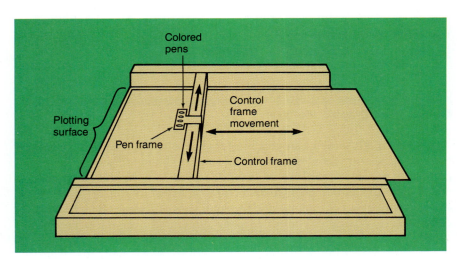

Figure 7.17

The mechanism of a flatbed plotter. The pen frame moves up and down while the control frame moves from side to side. Each pen is electronically controlled so it can be lowered to draw or raised when its action is not wanted.

Figure 7.18
Plotter-produced business outputs.
Photo provided courtesy of Ramtek Corporation.

paper they can accommodate, but they are much less expensive than drum plotters.

Plotters can have a number of pens, each of a different color. They can thus produce a variety of colored outputs, and they are particularly useful in preparing business charts and graphs, maps, and engineering diagrams. Plotters are often the output device used in computer-aided design (CAD). For example, in developing the specifications and blueprints for a modern airplane, thousands of different drawings and materials lists, all very precise and all necessary, might be required. If, during testing, the engineers find a design flaw, the plans and blueprints have to be adjusted, and the drawings then need to be redone to reflect the changes. With a plotter, it is possible to enter the data for the changes, adjust the materials list if necessary, and have the drawings redone on the plotter, with no hand-drafting involved. Figure 7.18 shows some of the kinds of business outputs produced by graphic plotters.

Display Output

The most commonly used display output device for computer systems is the VDT's cathode ray tube (CRT) screen. The soft-copy output produced on a CRT screen can be easily changed or erased. However, the terminal has no printing capability; so if hard copy is needed, it must be generated by another unit.

The CRT screen is designed in a gridlike fashion, with thousands of

SOFT-COPY OUTPUT

pixels (picture elements) formed by the intersections of the grid. Each of these pixels can be stimulated electronically to create an image. When activated as a group, the pixels form patterns somewhat like those produced by a dot matrix printer. However, because many more pixels than matrix rods are available to create the image, the image formed on a CRT screen is of a much higher quality than that produced by a dot matrix printer.

We've already mentioned the usefulness of display screens in inquiry reports. They are also a great aid in **text editing**—that is, in making revisions to a written document. Lawyers, for example, spend a great deal of time making sure that the contracts they prepare for clients are correct and cover all the conditions the clients have requested. Negotiation with other parties to the contract is often necessary, as all sides seek to protect their own interests and to make the contract favorable to them. Thus, the contract might have to be drafted several times before it is acceptable to everyone involved. If the contract is prepared on a typewriter, both the acceptable and the unacceptable parts must be retyped each time a change is made, and errors may be introduced in the course of the retyping. If the contract (or any other document) is prepared on a computer equipped with text-editing or word processing software, an initial copy can be printed out for review. Changes can then be made on the screen as necessary, while the unchanged parts stay as they are on the storage medium; they will be reproduced accurately no matter how many times other parts of the document are modified and no matter how many times the document is printed. When all parties concerned are satisfied with the document, it is an easy matter to print an accurate final copy.

With specialized software, it is possible to display complex graphics on a CRT screen. Data and information that have traditionally been reported in numerical form are now being displayed in this way. Numbers representing various budget expenditures become slices of a pie chart shown on a CRT screen. The addition of color can create a striking effect and can be used to differentiate information, to enhance images, and even to create computer "art" (see Figure 7.19).

Despite the old saying that "one picture is worth a thousand words," businesses have been slow to recognize the value of this graphic capability, but they are rapidly making up for the oversight, and in an interesting variety of ways. For example, a recent breakthrough in computer graphics has led to the creation of a process called *color spectography*. Color spectography can convert a black-and-white film to color in good enough detail that if you saw it on television you probably wouldn't know it had been converted. In fact, you may already have seen such a film. The company that holds the patent to the process, which involves programming the computer to read the gray tones and to assign color values to them (i.e., to digitize them), has begun converting black-and-white film classics such as *Yankee Doodle Dandy* and is marketing them to television and videocassette audiences.

Touch-sensitive and light-sensitive devices are also a fairly recent in-

Figure 7.19
The use of color in CRT graphics.
Photos provided courtesy of Ramtek Corporation.

novation. As you may remember from Chapter 6, instead of entering data or instructions through a keyboard, the user can both enter and alter data directly on a touch-sensitive digitizing tablet or a touch-sensitive or light-sensitive CRT screen by touching it with a stylus, a finger, or a light pen. The ability to alter the data while entering the input means that the user receives immediate output, or feedback. These devices thus make for "friendly" computer systems. They are also of great value to engineers who are designing complex circuits and to anyone unable to operate a keyboard.

Audio Output

Historically, businesses have used computers to process accounting and statistical data. The numerical information that comes out of such processing is best studied, analyzed, and reviewed when it is in a printed form or when it can be read from a display screen. Today, however, businesses are processing much more than just accounting and statistical data, and some of the information produced as output can more easily and more appropriately be communicated through spoken messages. **Audio-output devices** are becoming an increasingly common way of transmitting such messages (see Figure 7.20). These devices are best suited to applications in which a brief reply can answer a telephoned inquiry. All the sounds likely to be used in the inquiry are recorded and stored in the computer system. When an inquiry is made, the computer accesses these "data,"

Figure 7.20
An audio-output device. Used in conjunction with software and telephone lines, this device gives businesses 24-hour-a-day access to the data stored in their computer systems.
Courtesy of Digital Equipment Corporation.

converts them to signals that contain the reply, and sends them to the audio-output device. The audio-output device then assembles the signals in the proper order and activates a voice synthesizer to deliver the message. You've no doubt heard the "voice" of the computer when you've telephoned a number that is out of order or when you've called for information on time and weather, although in these instances, you don't need to make any sounds. The first part of the message—"At the tone, the time will be..."—is on tape; the last part—"sixty-three Fahrenheit, seventeen Celsius"—is the computer speaking.

A great deal of business is transacted over the telephone each day. By using audio-output devices to link the computer to the telephone, businesses can give their customers a much wider range of services than they could with systems that produce only visual outputs. For example, some businesses have automated their inventory systems with audio-output devices so that customers can phone in to see whether a product is in stock, what its current cost is, and how long it will take to get delivery. Audio-output devices are also used to respond to telephoned inquiries about stock market prices and airline departure times and to store and forward office messages and communications. These are but a few of the rapidly growing number of ways in which audio-output devices are used. Another feature of audio outputs worth noting is their value to people with visual handicaps, reading difficulties, and problems with attention span.

OUTPUT BY ROBOTS

One of the most exciting technologies of the century is **robotics,** the study of the construction, maintenance, and use of robots. The term *robot,* which was coined by a Czechoslovakian writer during the 1920s, is derived from a Czech word meaning compulsory service. It has since come to mean a programmable machine whose output is some type of work.

Robots were first used only for dangerous or health-threatening jobs or for jobs that people could not perform—for example, handling hazardous materials such as radioactive elements, working in high temperatures or among toxic fumes, and controlling equipment on unmanned space vehicles. Today, as you may recall from Chapter 4, robots are used in a wide range of repetitive manufacturing activities. They can be found assembling parts in automobile and electronics plants and monitoring complex activities in oil refineries. The industrial robot functions as a production-line worker: It paints, welds, drills, turns valves, and moves materials. Seldom do these robots look like R2D2 of *Star Wars* or the humanoid form we associate with science fiction. Rather, they usually look like other factory machines; most of them have two parts—the arm, or manipulator, and the control system (see Figure 7.21).

One of the great things about robots, aside from the perennial fascination they hold for the human imagination, is the flexibility they provide in a manufacturing facility. Unlike the standard assembly-line fixture, which is designed to perform one function, robots are designed to perform multiple functions. They have at their "heart" a microprocessor, and they can be

Figure 7.21
The parts of a robot. Shown on the right is the control system.
Courtesy of Chrysler Corporation.

ROBOTS — THE NEXT GENERATION

I met Dewey and the Imp on a cold afternoon in Pittsburgh on the campus of Carnegie-Mellon University. They weren't much alike. Dewey stood about six feet tall, rolled on six rubber wheels, and at the moment had its innards scattered around the room. The Imp — Intelligent Mobile Platform — was a disembodied representation on a cathode-ray screen, reaching out with simulated sonar to find pathways through an imaginary apartment.

Beyond their differences, Dewey and the Imp have an important feature in common. They are previews of coming attractions in the world of robotics — ancestors of robots that will see, feel, roam, and even think in ways impossible for today's automatons.

When I saw it, Dewey was being prepared for a reconnaissance trip into the crippled nuclear reactor at Three Mile Island. Dewey and comrades Huey and Louie will make a number of visits to the radiation-drenched reactor interior, initially to carry cameras that will give the first clear view of the damage, and later to take samples of material and cut away debris.

The Imp is destined for more-domestic service. It will memorize a floor plan and follow spoken orders to go to specific places in a house. The Imp is scheduled to be marketed by the end of this year for less than $1,000. It's also scheduled to be the first generation of a robot family that will vacuum, wash windows, and fetch drinks....

The Imp will be three feet high and 18 inches around. When it arrives in a household, ... the owner will first put it in a "world-model learning mode" and walk it around the place. During that tour, the robot will memorize a number of specific locations. You'll say, "Go to the kitchen," and it will go there....

[James L. Crowley, the computer scientist who developed the Imp at Carnegie-Mellon] punched up a simulation on a computer screen to show how the Imp will perform. I could see the sonar beam, whose range will be 20 feet, probing, allowing the robot to create pictures of walls, alcoves, and doors. I watched it go around a corner, through a door to a specified spot, and then avoid an obstacle that Crowley put in its way.

The Imp's performance wasn't perfect. Now and then a wall would vanish from its schema or it would hesitate — because of bugs in the program, Crowley said. And of course I wasn't watching a real robot, just a picture on a screen. That wasn't important, Crowley said, because I was getting a look at the computer program that will make the real thing go.

The first Imps to be marketed will be no more than playthings, Crowley conceded. The next models might perform such chores as vacuuming or sweeping floors in homes and hotels. "After that," he said, "we can have whole generations of specialized robots for such tasks as window washing. I see this as a 25- to-30-year evolution."

Dewey is something of a blue-collar first cousin of the Imp. It was built by a group of engineers led by William L. Whittaker and Dwight Sangrey, the head of Carnegie-Mellon's civil-engineering department. Like Crowley, Sangrey has a timetable for the evolution of his department's robots. Dewey and Louie will be tele-operated when they go into the Three Mile Island reactor — that is, a human operator will send instructions through a cable. Huey, a more advanced model, will be programmed ... to take samples from the reactor ... for analysis. Future models will ... use cutting tools to widen some of the openings that hinder work inside the reactor.

— Edward Edelson, "Robots — The Next Generation." Reprinted from *Popular Science* (February 1985, pp. 42–46) with permission, © 1984, Times Mirror Magazines, Inc.

---

quickly reprogrammed to carry out new tasks. These features make it an easy matter to enter data for a new manufacturing process and to change the control instructions governing the robots' motions and activities. The flexibility that robots thus provide can save a business a great deal of money. For instance, if a shipment of materials needed in a manufacturing process doesn't arrive on schedule, or if demand for a particular product is low, the robots can be quickly reprogrammed to perform another task, and "downtime" is thus avoided. At General Electric, when demand for locomotive motor frames fell, the company took advantage of this flexibility: Within a few hours, its robots had been reprogrammed to produce subway motor frames, a smaller but similar product.

As we noted in Chapter 4, Japan has been the leader in applying robotics technology. At the Nissan assembly plant near Tokyo, where Datsun cars are manufactured, fifty robots handle more than 90 percent of the welding done on hoods, fenders, roofs, and doors. At Fujitsu Fanac, Ltd, robots are used to make other robots, the company's main product. During the day, the production line looks much like any other production line, with about 100 workers tending machines and doing other jobs around the factory floor. During the night shift, however, the factory operates with only a control room supervisor and a security guard; the machines run themselves, continuing production according to the planned schedule. And in Yokahama, a grocery store is staffed almost entirely by robots: They automatically stock the shelves and slice, weigh, wrap, and price meat purchases. Other robots that synthesize speech welcome customers to the store and introduce them to special sale items and new products. A piano-playing robot entertains children as their parents shop. The possible uses of these labor-saving devices seem limited only by human imagination.

SELECTION CRITERIA

Selecting a computer output device is somewhat like buying a car: There are many models, sizes, prices, and styles, as well as special equipment and options, to be considered. Faced with so many choices, it is important to know what the uses of the output will be and to match the output equipment to those uses. Once these applications requirements have been established, the other selection criteria to be considered are speed, quality of output, cost, and maintenance. The flexibility of the system — its ability to deliver output when and where it is needed — depends on a balanced approach to output-device selection. Large computer systems generally have multiple output devices to ensure flexibility; microcomputer systems usually have only one or two.

Speed usually refers to printers' speeds; and the greater the speed, the greater the cost of the equipment. In computing environments in which there is a large volume of outputs, as in the banking industry, speed may be the primary selection criterion. In scientific applications, in which a large amount of processing takes place and a small volume of output is the norm, print speed is not usually a concern.

Quality of output is becoming more important as computers take over more office functions. If the output is for internal use only, as is the output used in making management decisions, print quality is not usually a great concern; type that is slightly misaligned or fuzzy is acceptable. However, when output is for external as well as internal use (e.g., letters to customers, catalogs, and publicly distributed reports of business activities), print quality becomes more of an issue. And as with speed, the better the quality, the higher the cost of the equipment.

The maintenance associated with output devices is an important concern. Of all the computer equipment, printing units are the most subject to breakdown and malfunction. Almost all printers have some moving parts: Paper passes over surfaces and through feed devices, print heads move or strike, and motors operate paper feeds and other components. Very few of the components in printers are electronic; most of them are very mechanical. Whenever you have mechanical devices, you have the opportunity for breakdown: Motors burn out, paper feeds jam, and print chains break.

The key to success in any information system is the ability to generate output and to deliver it to the user when and where it is needed. If a computer system is tied to one output device and that device malfunctions, the information system may be unusable. As a safeguard against such an occurrence, a business may maintain several output devices, or it may contract for quick-response repair and maintenance of its output equipment. In any case, a business must evaluate the impact of the malfunction in terms of the interruption of business activities. While there is no simple answer, a well-managed computer center will have a contingency plan for operation if the output device isn't functioning or is unable to produce the desired outputs. This plan should be in writing, and it should be tested periodically and modified as necessary to ensure that it is relevant to current conditions.

Because most large systems have multiple output devices, they have output alternatives, even though the print quality of the alternatives may not be the best or the printing may be slow. But when the one and only output device of a small business's computer system fails, it can cause a serious problem in continuing operations. Contingency plans are just as important in small systems as in large systems. Perhaps the addition of a low-cost electrothermal printer or a spare terminal might provide the backup needed to ensure access to the stored information and the opportunity to continue operations without interruption.

By now, you can see that the selection of an output device is not a simple matter. The selection criteria of speed, quality, cost, and maintenance are locked into a balanced relationship. A more complex output device will produce a wider range of outputs, will cost more, and will require more maintenance. A simple dot matrix printer will serve you well for most printed outputs, but it doesn't produce the quality a customer would expect in a business letter. Whenever one of the criteria is modified, one or more of the others will need to be adjusted as well. By spending more, you can improve quality, speed, or both. By spending less, you must compromise on speed, quality, or reliability. Understanding the applications that generate the output and the needs of the users of the output is the key to selecting the appropriate device.

SUMMARY

Businesses collect data and generate information to fulfill legal requirements, to report the results of operations to interested parties, to plan effectively, to make effective use of the company's resources, to compete effectively, and to provide market responsiveness. If the output generated is to support effective decision making, it must be accurate, complete, relevant, concise, and timely.

Traditional output consists of various types of reports. Scheduled and exception reports have served businesses well, and inquiry reporting provides flexibility. Detailed reports are crucial to a business's operations, and summary reports give managers a broad view of those operations. Archive reports — files of historical data — must be maintained to meet legal requirements and to provide a means of reconstructing a transaction. Another kind of output used in business includes outputs produced by management science techniques; they reflect how the real world would react to various decisions. Output recorded in machine-readable form that can be used as input to the computer for other processing activities is a third kind of output used in business.

Computer outputs not stored in machine-readable form but destined for immediate use by people are generated as hard copy and soft copy. The devices used to generate hard copy include various types of printers, microform equipment, and graphic plotters. Printers can be classified according to whether they are impact or nonimpact printers and according to whether they print a character, a line, or a page at a time. Character-at-a-time printers include formed-character and dot matrix printers, which are impact printers, and inkjet and electrothermal printers, which are nonimpact printers. Chain and drum printers are line-at-a-time impact printers. All page-at-a-time printers use nonimpact technology; these include the laser and electrostatic printers. Printers vary in speed, print quality, and cost. Generally, nonimpact printers are less subject to breakdown than impact printers. They are also quieter. However, they cannot make carbon copies.

Microform equipment is used to photograph computer output and to produce it on film in a greatly reduced form. Computer output microform comes in two varieties: microfilm and microfiche. This type of output can save both storage space and mailing costs. Graphic plotters produce hard-copy outputs in a variety of colors. They may be either drum or flatbed plotters.

Most soft copy is displayed on CRT screens, which can produce a high-quality image. With specialized software, a CRT screen can also display complex graphics in color. Touch-sensitive and light-sensitive devices are another means of producing soft-copy output, as are audio-output devices. Touch-sensitive and light-sensitive devices make for "friendly" computer systems; they are also very useful to engineers and to handicapped people. Audio-output devices are becoming an increasingly popular way of transmitting business information.

The output produced by robots is work. These labor-saving machines are designed to perform multiple functions and can be quickly reprogrammed to carry out new tasks. Because of the flexibility they provide, they are being used in an increasing number of applications in modern manufacturing plants.

The anticipated computer applications are the first thing to be considered when selecting an output device. Other selection criteria to be considered include speed, quality, cost, and maintenance. The flexibility of the system depends on a balanced approach to output-device selection. To ensure flexibility, any business with a computer system should have a contingency plan for operation if an output device fails.

KEY TERMS

archive reports (192)
audio-output devices (209)
chain printers (200)
character-at-a-time printers (serial printers) (196)
computer output microform (COM) (202)
daisy wheel (196)
detailed reports (190)
dot matrix printer (197)
drum plotter (205)
drum printers (200)
electrostatic printer (200)
electrothermal printers (199)
exception reports (190)
flatbed plotter (206)
formed-character printers (196)
graphic plotter (205)
hard copy (194)
impact printer (196)
inkjet printer (199)

inquiry reports (190)
laser printers (200)
letter quality (196)
line-at-a-time printers (200)
management science (192)
microfiche (202)
microfilm (202)
nonimpact printers (196)
page-at-a-time printers (200)
pixels (208)
robotics (210)
scheduled reports (190)
soft copy (194)
summary reports (192)
text editing (208)

DISCUSSION QUESTIONS

1. Explain why businesses need computer output.

2. What types of computer outputs do businesses use? Differentiate between detailed and summary reports, and explain how each is used. Briefly describe the value of an exception report and an inquiry report.

3. What is management science? How does the computer help in implementing management science techniques? Describe how you, as president of a college, might use management science techniques.

4. Why do you think so many different kinds of printers have been developed? Explain the differences between impact printers and non-impact printers.

5. Identify five different business applications in which a CRT screen would be a more suitable device than a printer for delivering computer outputs.

6. Prepare a chart that lists the advantages and disadvantages of COM.

7. How are graphics used on terminals? What are the advantages of using computer graphics in business and engineering? What other advantages might computer graphics have?

8. Visit your local computer store and ask for a demonstration of audio output. What are the limitations of this technology?

9. Explain how a robot works and the kind of work it does. What is one of its chief advantages in a manufacturing facility?

10. Prepare a brief plan outlining how you would select output devices. In what order of importance would you rank your selection criteria?

OUTLINE

TYPES OF COMPUTER STORAGE

SEQUENTIAL ACCESS AUXILIARY STORAGE

    Punched Cards and Paper Tape
    Magnetic Tape

DIRECT ACCESS AUXILIARY STORAGE

    Magnetic Disks
      • Hard Disks
      • Winchester Disks
      • Floppy Disks
    Optical Disks
    Mass Storage
    Bubble Memory

SELECTION CRITERIA

SUMMARY

KEY TERMS

DISCUSSION QUESTIONS

OVERVIEW

The CPU's memory and human memory have several things in common: Both store data in a random fashion, and both can instantly recall data for everyday use. Both can also suffer from amnesia—the computer as the result of a power failure, and the human mind as the result of injury or illness. Finally, computers have a limit to the amount that they can store at any one time, as do most people. To handle the information overload, computer systems—and most people—rely on some kind of auxiliary storage. For people, this may mean taking notes and filing them away for future reference. For computers, it may mean having access to data that are stored both online and offline.

While there are some similarities between the CPU's memory and human memory, there are also some important differences. People have the option of not relying on auxiliary storage; they may be able to keep all the data they need stored in their heads. But for computers, auxiliary storage is really a necessity. Each line of program and each piece of data that you feed into a computer take up a certain amount of the computer's limited primary memory. If the program and data exceed the computer's memory, the computer won't be able to process the data—hence the need for auxiliary storage. Moreover, amnesia in people is a rarity; in computer systems, it's a commonplace. Every time you shut down the computer, it forgets everything it ever knew. Auxiliary storage provides a safeguard against the computer's amnesia: Data recorded on auxiliary storage media will stay recorded until erased, regardless of the power supply.

In this chapter, we'll look at the various types of auxiliary storage found in computer systems. Our objectives are to

♦ explain the differences between primary and auxiliary storage, and describe how both types of storage are used.

♦ differentiate between sequential access and direct access auxiliary storage, and describe the methods of processing and file organization associated with each.

♦ identify the media and devices used in sequential access storage.

♦ describe how data on magnetic disks can be organized for direct access and the devices used to read and write data on these media.

♦ explain the advantages of optical disks, mass storage, and bubble memory for direct access storage.

♦ define the criteria used in selecting auxiliary storage devices.

CHAPTER 8

AUXILIARY STORAGE

TYPES OF COMPUTER STORAGE

Auxiliary storage, also called secondary storage or external storage, supplements the primary storage unit of the CPU. It serves as the file cabinet of the computer system, storing data and programs in vast quantities. Primary storage, on the other hand, holds only data and program instructions used during processing, and it provides instant recall of those items. Figure 8.1 shows the roles of both types of storage in the computer system. The main differences between primary and auxiliary storage are in access speed, storage capacity, cost per stored byte, and storage volatility. **Access speed** is the time it takes to retrieve stored data, including the time needed for an auxiliary storage unit to activate a motor or to move a sensing device.

As you know from Chapter 5, primary storage is composed of electronic circuits, which operate at almost the speed of light. In contrast, storing and retrieving data on auxiliary storage media involves mechanical motion, which is always slower than movement controlled by electronics. Although slower than primary storage, the access speed of auxiliary storage devices is by most other standards fast. These devices can also hold much larger

Figure 8.1
Computer storage. Primary storage temporarily stores the intermediate results of processing, the program instructions being executed, and the data being used during processing. Auxiliary storage provides long-term storage for applications programs and systems software, for all data to be processed, and for the results of processing.

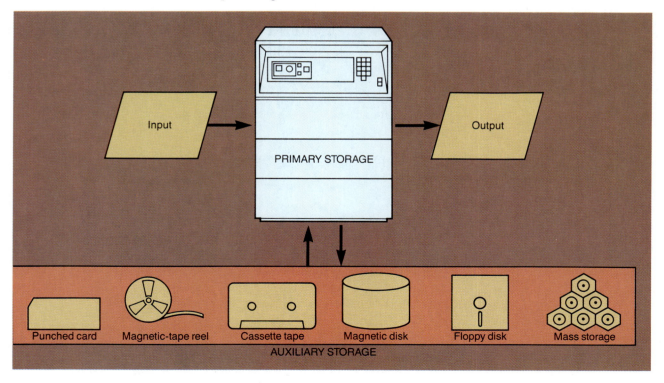

volumes of data at a much lower cost than primary storage. Because of the expense of the electronic circuitry, the capacity of primary storage is limited to a few million bytes, whereas auxiliary storage devices can store hundreds of millions or even billions of bytes on low-cost media. The cost of storage on tape or disk can be as low as one dollar per million bytes, while the cost of primary storage can be thousands of dollars per million bytes. As we noted earlier, data recorded on auxiliary storage media will remain recorded until erased, regardless of machine shutdown or power interruption. In contrast, because primary storage in most modern computer systems is volatile, a power interruption will result in the erasure of all the stored data. In short, then, auxiliary storage is slower, more spacious, cheaper, and safer than primary storage.

When compared with traditional kinds of paper-oriented storage, the computer's auxiliary storage has some decided advantages. Because magnetic media allow much greater densities than the printed matter necessary for human interpretation, storing data on these media greatly reduces the bulk of the stored data. A hundred spools of magnetic tape, for example, can hold the equivalent of a 9-by-12-foot room full of file cabinets. Auxiliary storage may also be cheaper than paper storage, particularly if the file cabinets take up expensive office space, if the clerical costs of filing and retrieving the data are high, and if filing accuracy is given economic consideration.

Auxiliary storage can be classified according to whether it provides sequential or direct access to the stored data. The type of access to stored data and the kind of processing possible depend on the way files are organized and on the storage medium used. These factors always go hand in hand.

Sequential access means that records are entered in the file in some kind of sequence. The sequence is usually determined by a particular field of the record, or key field. Files organized in a sequential fashion are often stored offline and are made available to the computer only when the program is to be run. When files are organized this way, the computer processes each record in turn, one after the other. In other words, sequential file organization requires sequential processing, and vice versa. Sequential access storage media include punched cards, punched paper tape, magnetic tape, and magnetic disks. Sequential access storage is most efficient when many records are processed in one batch at periodic intervals, as in the processing of a payroll.

When files are organized for *direct access,* a key field is used to indicate the exact physical location of the record on the storage medium. The media used in direct access storage include magnetic disks and optical disks, which allow the computer to skip over unwanted data and go directly to the desired data — in other words, to directly process the records. For directly organized files to be processed, they must be online in a direct access storage device (DASD). Since there is no need to read all the preceding records to retrieve the desired record, the computer can search out the data in fractions of a second rather than in the minutes that sequential access storage would require. Direct access storage is used when the computer processes individual records at random and at the time the transaction takes place — for example, when it processes airline reservations.

Because the equipment must operate continuously to keep the data available to the CPU at all times, the operating costs of direct access storage are higher than those of sequential access storage. In some applications, such as automatic banking transactions, immediate and direct access to the data is essential; in others, such as the periodic processing of customer billings, the less expensive sequential access storage methods are more appropriate. The type of application will determine the method of auxiliary storage needed. Auxiliary storage methods vary not just in the operating cost of the equipment. They also vary in the capacity, cost, and erasability of the storage media; the cost of the devices; and the data transfer rate they provide. **Data transfer rate** is the speed at which data can be read from a storage medium to the CPU. Table 8.1 summarizes some of these factors as they apply to the types of auxiliary storage that we will discuss in the rest of the chapter. Most large computer systems have both direct access and sequential access storage to ensure flexibility and economy.

Table 8.1   Characteristics of Different Methods of Auxiliary Storage

Storage Medium	Method of Recording Data	Capacity of Medium (in characters)	Cost and Erasability of Medium[1]	Cost of Device[2]	Data Transfer Rate (in characters per second)
Punched cards	Punched holes	Less than 100 per card	High, not erasable	Low	Several thousand
Punched paper tape	Punched holes	Several thousand per roll	Medium high, not erasable	Low	Several thousand
Magnetic tape	Magnetized spots	5–120 million per cartridge, cassette, or reel	Very low, erasable	Medium low	Up to a million
Hard disks and Winchester disks	Magnetized spots	20–500 million per disk unit	Medium, erasable	Medium	A million or more
Floppy disks	Magnetized spots	$\frac{1}{4}$–2 million per disk	Low, erasable	Low	Tens of thousands
Optical disks	Holes or bumps on surface	Hundreds of millions per disk	Medium, generally not erasable	Medium	More than a million
Mass storage	Magnetized spots	Up to 472 billion per unit	Medium, erasable	High	Some access delay before data transfer, then up to a million
Magnetic bubble chips	Magnetized spots	$\frac{1}{4}$–$\frac{1}{2}$ million per chip	Medium, erasable	Medium	Hundreds of thousands

[1] Low cost = under $1 per million characters; medium cost = $1–$2 per million characters; high cost = over $2 per million characters.

[2] Low cost = under $3,000; medium cost = under $25,000; high cost = over $25,000.

SEQUENTIAL ACCESS AUXILIARY STORAGE

As we've noted, records that are organized for sequential access can be retrieved only in the order in which they were entered in the file; that is, the computer must process each record in turn. Figure 8.2 shows a typical sequential processing application in which a customer master file is updated. A **master file** contains relatively permanent information such as customer name and account number. In our illustration, the master file is organized sequentially, with the records arranged according to the ascending order of customer account numbers. The **transaction file** (a file of data on

Figure 8.2
A sequential processing application.

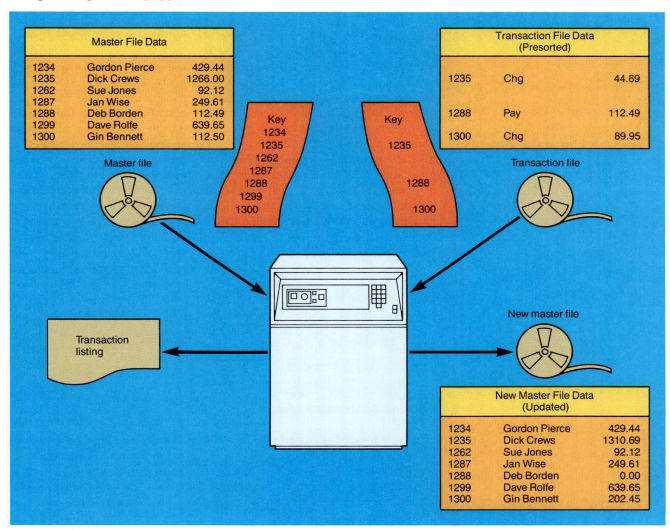

current activities) contains the data to be used in updating the master file. Before processing begins, the computer sorts the transaction file in the same sequence (in this case, ascending numerical order) and with the same key fields (account numbers) as the master file. The computer then reads each record from both files in sequence, comparing the key field on the master record with the key field on the transaction record. When the keys match, the computer makes the change to the master record and writes the record to the new master file. If there's no matching key on the transaction record, the computer goes to the next master record, making no change to the master record at the point in the file where no matching transaction-record key occurs. The output of the processing is a new, updated master file and a printed transaction listing; the old master file and the transaction file are stored as backup in the event that the system malfunctions or the data are lost or destroyed. As an additional precautionary measure, a copy of the updated master file is made (usually on magnetic tape, though it could be on a disk) and is placed in separate storage; copies made for this purpose are referred to as **backup files.**

To find a particular record on a sequentially organized master file, the computer must start at the beginning of the file and search through all the records until it finds the proper one, much as you have to run through all the other songs on a tape until you come to the song you want to hear. The computer has no fast-forward speed, as your tape recorder does, so it's a tedious processing job to search for a specific record. However, when processing follows a logical, sequential order, as it does in the updating of customer master files, having the records in sequence actually speeds up the processing because the computer doesn't have to search for each individual record as it is needed; the next record needed is available as the next physical record in the file. The limitations of sequential record formats, then, become advantages in some processing situations.

The two most commonly used sequential access storage media are punched cards and magnetic tape. **Paper tape** (tape punched with holes similar to those on punched cards) is used in limited applications. Magnetic disks can also be used in sequential access applications, but as they owe their popularity largely to their usefulness in direct access processing, we will discuss them in that context only.

Punched Cards and Paper Tape

The same kind of punched card used for data entry can be used for offline auxiliary storage of data as well. As we noted in Chapter 6, the Hollerith code, developed at the turn of the century, is still the most popular method of coding punched cards. Data density of cards is low, with each card containing a maximum of 80 bytes of data. Once punched, the cards can be stored until needed and can even be sent to customers as a part of

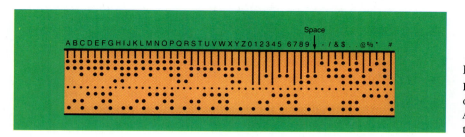

Figure 8.3
Punched paper tape. The tape works on the same principle as punched cards: A brush or a light-sensitive device senses the presence of a hole.

their billing statements. Correcting an error on a card requires, however, that an entirely new card be punched, and the cards take up considerable storage room. Because they must physically move across a reading surface, processing speeds are slow: 1,000 cards, or a maximum of 80,000 bytes of data, a minute. Because of these drawbacks, magnetic media have replaced punched cards in most auxiliary storage operations.

Figure 8.3 shows an example of punched paper tape. A **paper-tape reader** is used to enter the data recorded on paper tape into the computer. Like punched cards, punched paper tape can be used for both data entry and auxiliary storage. It has the same limitations as punched cards, but it is even more fragile. One advantage that tape has over cards is an unlimited record size due to its being on a continuous roll of paper. Although the communications industry has used paper tape for quite some time to record long-distance telephone charges for billing purposes, it is not widely used in other segments of computing.

Magnetic Tape

As soon as magnetic tape was introduced in the 1940s, it became a popular auxiliary storage medium. It was the first of the new generation of magnetic media to move computing away from punched cards into high-speed auxiliary storage. Today, magnetic tape is the most commonly used medium for computer backup files. Magnetic tape may be stored on reels that hold up to 2,400 feet of tape. As we noted in Chapter 6, it is also produced in cassettes for use with smaller computer systems. Cassettes hold less tape than the standard tape reel, usually about 200 feet. It's interesting to note that when magnetic tape manufactured for the computer industry doesn't meet strict quality standards, it is often trimmed and used in the music-recording industry. The latest cassette of popular music you purchased for your stereo may very well be recorded on tape that was originally destined to contain your income tax records or bank balances.

The equipment used to read from and write on tape is the tape drive that we described in Chapter 6, and it is connected to the computer by a cable so that electronic signals can be transmitted back and forth. As

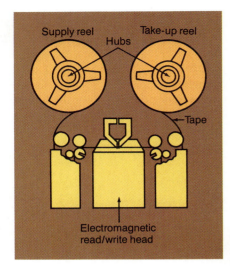

Figure 8.4

Schematic of a tape drive. Electric motors rotate the tape reels so that the tape can pass across the surface of the read/write head.

Figure 8.4 shows, a tape drive consists of hubs to mount the tape, an electromagnetic read/write head, a supply reel, and a take-up reel. When *writing* on tape, the **read/write head** magnetizes small spots that represent a code system for data, much as a keypunch makes holes in cards to represent data (see Figure 8.5a). Data on tape are organized in **tracks,** and the tape reads as a column (see Figure 8.5b). As the tape moves across the read/write head during the *reading* operation, the head senses the magnetic spots on the tape, converts them to electronic signals, and transmits them to the CPU.

The capacity of storage media is known as **data density.** The data densities of tape reel range from 1,600 to 6,400 bytes per inch, while cassettes store data at about 200 bytes per inch. At a density of 3,200 bytes per inch, a reel of tape 10½ inches in diameter can store as much

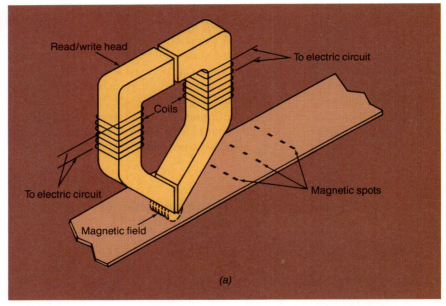

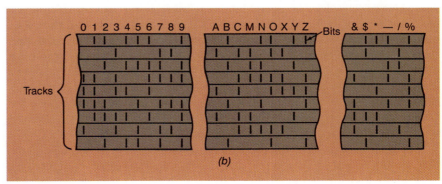

Figure 8.5

Reading and writing with magnetic tape: (*a*) close-up of a tape drive's read/write head; (*b*) data representation on magnetic tape.

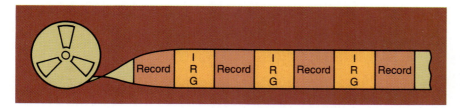

Figure 8.6

Interrecord gaps (IRGs) on magnetic tape. Each IRG is approximately 0.6 inch.

data as 400,000 punched cards in the space taken up by two or three medium-sized pizzas.

Because tape has a high density, data from tape can be transferred very rapidly to or from a storage location, often at speeds of a million bytes a second. The data transfer rate is important in the overall performance of a computer system, and it is a function of both the data density of the medium and the speed at which the medium passes over the read/write head of the drive unit. Because of reduced data densities and slower tape-drive speeds, the data transfer rates of cassettes are much slower than those of tape reels.

Tape data density depends not only on the number of bytes stored per inch of tape but also on the blank space between the individual records encoded on the tape. This space is known as the **interrecord gap (IRG)** (see Figure 8.6). It is not unusual to find IRGs taking up more tape than the records themselves; however, they are necessary in order to give the tape drive room to start and stop, much as a gap between moving cars on a freeway is necessary.

To improve performance, the space taken up by the IRGs can be reduced by blocking the records: Individual records, called **logical records,** are grouped together to be read as a single unit, a physical record called a **block,** and each block is separated by an **interblock gap (IBG).** As shown in Figure 8.7, with a blocking factor of five, each block contains five logical records, and five IRGs are thus reduced to an IBG of one. Because either an IRG or an IBG generally takes up about a half-inch of tape, more than two inches of tape can be saved by grouping five logical records in a single block. The speed of the tape passing over the read/write

Figure 8.7

Blocked records on magnetic tape. Blocking makes more economical use of the tape. The blocking factor shown here is 5.

head is the same whether data are being read or not; so blocking records can dramatically improve tape performance.

DIRECT ACCESS AUXILIARY STORAGE

In direct access storage, each record in the storage unit is identified by using a key, and the computer can retrieve a record in any order, without having first to read through all the preceding data in the file. Figure 8.8 shows a direct processing application in which a file organized for direct access is updated. As you can see, a customer has placed an order for a sailboat. The salesperson, using an online terminal, keys the data into the CPU, and a search of the inventory file is made. Because the file is organized for direct access and because it is stored in a DASD, the CPU can go directly to the inventory record for the desired sailboat, skipping records for all other boats in the inventory file. Since the sailboat is available, the order is confirmed, and the inventory file is then updated to show that the sailboat is no longer available. A copy of the order is printed, and a report of changes to the master file is prepared.

The retrieval process in direct access storage is similar to the routing of a phone call in that the telephone-switching equipment avoids all other phones and routes the signal directly to the specific phone that was dialed. The computer's ability to go directly to an individual record provides much faster data retrieval than sequential access storage methods — an important consideration in online systems. Magnetic disk is the most widely used direct access storage medium, but optical disks, mass storage units, and bubble memory are also used.

Magnetic Disks

The most popular types of magnetic disks in use today are hard disks, Winchester disks, and floppy disks. All disks operate in the same general way but differ in size and in the materials of which they are made. All are covered with iron oxide, the same material that coats the mylar strip used for magnetic tape. As we noted earlier, data on magnetic tape are organized in *tracks*. Similarly, tracks are used to store records on magnetic disks; however, these disk tracks form rings around the disk. The pattern that they make is like that found on a phonograph record, except that no grooves are cut into the coating and the tracks are concentric instead of spiral — that is, each forms a closed circle. Each track can be separated into addressable segments, or **sectors** (see Figure 8.9). Each sector of each track is given a numerical **address,** which corresponds either directly or indirectly to the record key. This address, provided by a computer program,

DIRECT ACCESS AUXILIARY STORAGE   **229**

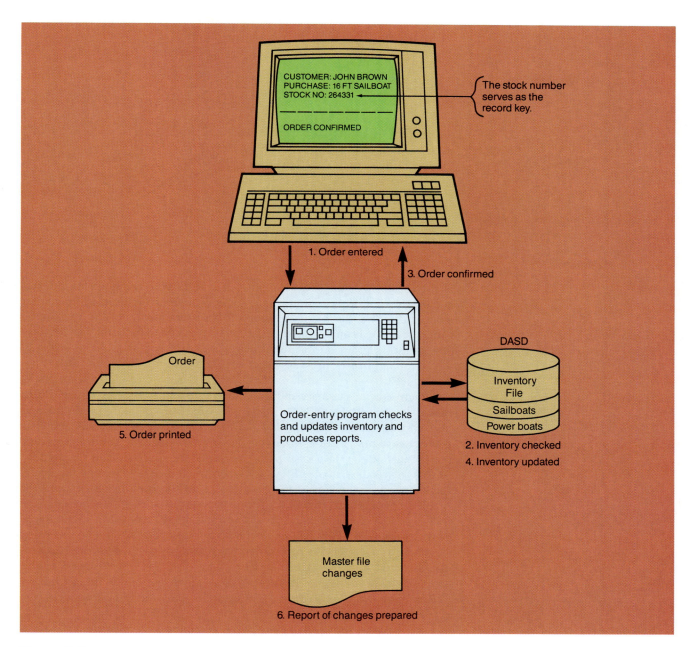

Figure 8.8
A direct processing application. In this particular illustration, the stock number serves as the record key; the number identifies the specific record within the inventory file.

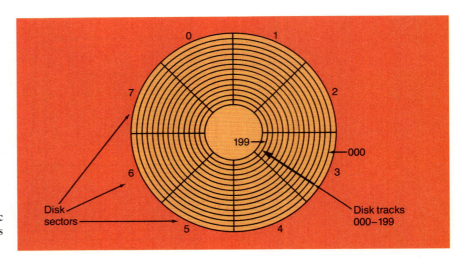

Figure 8.9

Sector organization on a magnetic disk. Each sector of each track is addressable.

is the means by which the computer is able to go directly to the desired record. The address includes the surface number (indicating on which side of the disk the record is stored), the track number, and the sector number. Records on magnetic disks can be blocked to increase data density, just as they can be on magnetic tape.

The disk drives used to process data stored on magnetic disks may accommodate a single disk, or they may be designed to hold a **disk pack**, in which several disks are mounted on a hub and spindle. A motor in the disk drive keeps the disk (or disks, if a disk pack is being used) turning at a constant rate of speed, and one or more read/write heads attached to **access arms** read or write the data on the tracks of the rotating disk (see Figure 8.10). In a disk pack, the disks are spaced along the spindle so that the read/write heads can move between them. No read/write heads are assigned to the top of the first disk or to the bottom of the last disk in a disk pack; these exposed surfaces are not used to store data because they are often damaged while the disk pack is being mounted or dismounted. Thus, as Figure 8.11 shows, an eleven-platter disk pack has ten access arms, all attached to one access mechanism. Each arm has two read/write heads — one assigned to the bottom surface of one disk, and one assigned to the top surface of another. The access arms move the heads in and out in unison over the tracks while the disk drive spins the disk at about 3,000 revolutions per minute.

The sectors shown in Figure 8.9 may be used to organize and locate data on both single disks and the multiple disks of a disk pack. When data from disk packs are being processed, all the read/write heads must move in unison to a position over the same track on which the data are to be read or written, since all the heads are controlled by the same access mechanism. Thus, when the sector method of data organization is used, the heads have to move back and forth repeatedly as they seek sectors located on different tracks.

Figure 8.10
Disk equipment: (*left*) a magnetic-disk pack being inserted in a disk drive; (*right*) close-up of a read/write head.
Courtesy of (left) BASF Systems Corporation; (right) Sperry Corporation.

Another method of organizing data stored in disk packs is called the **cylinder** method. The advantage of this method is that records from a number of disk surfaces can be read or written with only one movement of the access arms, thus substantially increasing access speed. This is accomplished by organizing the disk tracks in "cylinders" in a vertical fashion; that is, all like-numbered tracks on each surface of the disk pack are lined

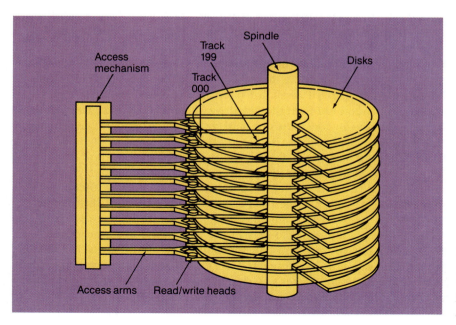

Figure 8.11
Interior of a disk pack. As the disks rotate, the access mechanism moves the heads in and out between the disks to read or write data on the disk tracks.

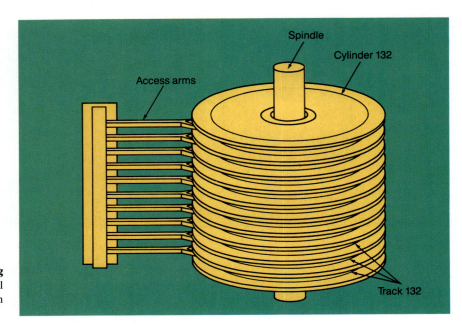

Figure 8.12
The cylinder method of organizing data on a magnetic-disk pack. All tracks numbered as 132 collectively form cylinder 132.

up in vertical rows to form one cylinder (see Figure 8.12). Thus, with one movement of the access arms, the read/write heads can read or write a number of records, all stored on like-numbered tracks on each disk surface. The addresses assigned to records organized in this way include the surface, cylinder, and record numbers.

Hard Disks. As you know from Chapter 6, hard disks are rigid platters of machined aluminum with diameters as wide as 14 inches. They are often used in high-volume processing, such as is done by a bank's automated teller machines. Both the upper and lower surfaces of the hard disk are used to record data, and as many as 800 tracks may be located on each hard-disk surface. Hard disks are often grouped together in a disk pack, which can be removed from the disk drive. In most disk packs, the read/write heads never actually touch the disk surface: The space between the read/write head and the disk surface is measured in millionths of an inch, and a combination of very light, flexible head materials and a jet of air flowing between the head and the disk surface allows the head to "fly" less than 20 millionths of an inch over the surface. With such small tolerances, any contamination — even something as small as a particle of dust or smoke or a human hair — will result in damage to the head, the disk, and the data. When such an obstacle gets in the way of the flying head, the head bounces in the air and lands on the other side of the obstacle, creating what is known as a **head crash** (see Figure 8.13). However, the close tolerances also create better signals between the disk surface and the head, resulting in less distortion and greater data densities.

IT ALL COMES DOWN TO MAGNETISM

Floppy disk, hard disk and tape storage are all based on the same scientific technique—magnetizing particles of an oxide material on the surface of the disk or tape. The differences in the data capacity of each medium depend only on the relative stability and flatness of the surface and the degree to which it is handled.

To store information on any of these media, the surface is passed within millionths of inches from a write head in the drive mechanism. This write head is made from a ferromagnetic material with a coil wrapped around it. The circuit of the coil is interrupted in one spot by a non-magnetic material and it is at this gap that a magnetic "flux" bulges outward around the gap as an electric current flows through the coil. The flux produces a magnetic field that touches the surface of the disk or tape, penetrating the oxide coating. The contact magnetizes the oxide particle. In the case of a hard disk, the write head is capable of emitting flux lines at the rate of about 5 million per second.

"Think of it as putting down tiny bar magnets on the surface of the storage medium," explains Gary Foulger, the director of research and development for Tallgrass Technologies in Boulder, Colorado. "Put simply, a disk is divided up into concentric tracks that are divided into arc sectors. The magnets are put down on these tracks so that the north/south polarity runs along the arc of the track and the width of the magnet is the width of the track."

The information stored on the disk or tape is really in the form of changes from magnetized to unmagnetized areas, or "flux transitions." The medium starts off unmagnetized and the first flux transition changes the binary 0, or 1, depending on the format being used, to its opposite, and only changes again when there is another flux transition. This is how 1s and 0s build up in 8-bit groups to form bytes of information. On a hard disk, which squeezes the bar magnets and unmagnetized gaps into much smaller spaces on the surface than floppy disks, there are about 10,000 bits stored to the inch.

The read head is a separate coil. As the disk or tape passes under this coil, the magnetized particles induce a voltage. The transitions from magnetized to unmagnetized areas —or voltage to no voltage areas— are translated into binary code. As with the recording of information, the drive mechanism reads the medium in units of time that are the equivalent of bit cells.

A disk or tape must be formatted to be used. There is a raft of formatting schemes which determine the pattern of flux transitions and how they are translated into binary code. Track and sector addresses for the medium are also stored on the disk in an area called the ID sector. Once a disk is formatted, it has less space available, and this is why some companies will quote two storage capacity figures when they talk about their disks or tapes.

—"It All Comes Down to Magnetism." Reprinted with permission from *Personal Computing*, June 1985, p. 69. Copyright 1985, Hayden Publishing Company.

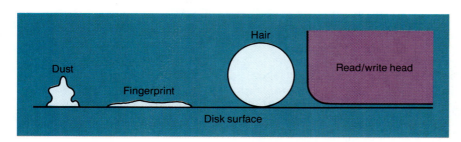

Figure 8.13

A head crash. With such close tolerances between the read/write head and the disk surface, even a single hair or a fingerprint can cause the head to crash.

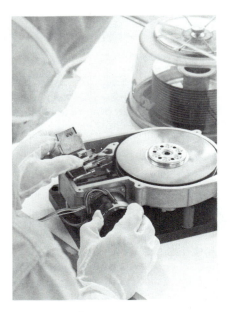

Figure 8.14
A Winchester disk drive. A sealed module protects the disks from environmental contamination.
Courtesy of BASF Systems Corporation.

Winchester Disks. The chief difference between **Winchester disks** and hard disks is that to protect against head crashes caused by contamination, the Winchester disks and read/write heads are packaged in a sealed module (see Figure 8.14). The access arms are calibrated for each individual disk, so the "fudge factor" needed for slight alignment changes when different disks are inserted isn't necessary. This feature, as well as the precise control of the environment, allows data to be packed much more densely on Winchester disks than on removable disks, and the read/write operations can therefore be completed much more quickly. Moreover, failure rates are lower than with removable-disk systems; with its control of the environment, Winchester technology goes a long way toward eliminating head crashes.

Scaled-down versions of the Winchester disk have been introduced for use in microcomputer systems and include self-contained air-filtration systems to prevent contamination. Winchester disk systems are more expensive than conventional auxiliary storage systems, but when figured on the cost per byte stored or the cost per processing transaction, they are often the least expensive system for both mainframes and microcomputers.

Floppy Disks. Floppy disks are made of flexible plastic and are permanently enclosed in a paper cover. Because of their paper covers, they can be inserted and removed from a disk drive without suffering handling damage (see Figure 8.15). The read/write heads, which ride directly on the surface of the disk, do not require the precise alignment of the hard disk or the Winchester disk. However, this feature results in reduced data density. Also, the disk drive accommodates only a single disk at a time, and disk rotation speeds are slower, which increases data retrieval time. Floppies are less expensive than hard disks and are generally used for input and auxiliary storage in microcomputer systems.

Figure 8.15
Floppy disk being inserted in a microcomputer's disk drive.
Courtesy of Texas Instruments.

Optical Disks

A single 12-inch **optical disk** can store more data than an entire pack of eleven magnetic disks. An optical disk is sometimes called a **laser disk** because a laser (*l*ight *a*mplification by *s*timulated *e*mission of *r*adiation) is used to record the data. A laser is a tightly packed light beam that can be precisely controlled. When directed at the surface of an optical disk, the laser burns holes into the surface to record the bit pattern of the data. The precision of lasers makes it possible to achieve densities as high as 14,000 tracks per inch. Reading is done with a less intense beam that reflects light from the surface, causing different reflections when a hole is present. Another method used to record data on optical disks is to insert on the disk a film of material that can be decomposed with a laser beam. The decomposition creates a bump on the surface, which reflects with a different intensity than the flat surface.

GIGABYTES AND TERABYTES:
The Quest for the "Ultimate" Storage System

The "ultimate" storage system has been eluding computer designers for over thirty years, and it will no doubt continue to do so. Just as it appears that technology has reached the saturation point and no further advances are possible, a breakthrough occurs, and the engineers are off and running again. The latest such breakthrough is the optical disk.

Today, one square inch of an optical disk holds more than ten square feet of the storage media of twenty years ago. A goal of one gigabyte (billion bytes) per square inch seems attainable in the next few years. Optical disks with capacities of one terabyte (trillion bytes) per square inch could easily be a reality by the end of the century.

Most optical disks currently in existence are not erasable. A new technology known as EDRAW (erasable-direct-read-after-write), which combines magnetic and laser techniques, is overcoming this deficiency. Because of their enormous storage capacities, both the erasable and the nonerasable disks have important commercial applications. One side of a nonerasable disk can hold a hundred times more than a high-capacity magnetic disk, and a single 5-inch EDRAW disk can hold the same amount as 500 5¼-inch floppy disks.

An EDRAW optical disk.
Courtesy of 3M.

The ability to record so much data on a single disk frees organizations that have enormous needs for information from reliance on warehouses full of magnetic-tape reels. Oil companies engaged in geological exploration, for example, may have hundreds of thousands or even millions of reels in storage, and they may generate several thousand new reels each month. Using a single 14-inch optical disk, they can store 4 gigabytes of data. Another advantage of the optical disk is that, unlike magnetic tape, it does not have to be refreshed every seven years. In addition, with special recording techniques, it is even possible to store analog data on an optical disk.

As costs come down and the technology evolves, the applications of optical disks will broaden. At present, there is concern that moisture on the disks will cause data errors to occur over time, but manufacturers are already predicting triumph over that problem. Like other computing technologies, optical disks are probably not the ultimate answer, but they do seem to be a very important step along the way. ◆

Until recently, a drawback of all optical-disk technology has been the permanent, unerasable nature of the recording done by laser beams. The permanence of the recording has limited the use of optical disks to applications in which the data are unlikely to change—for example, in recording backup files, commercially available computer programs, and historical information such as census data. However, a promising new method of preparing optical disks combines laser and magnetic technology to make the disks erasable. Erasable optical disks are made of a different material than the glass substrate used to make standard optical disks. The new material allows for a thin magnetic coating. Working together, an electromagnetic coil and a laser make the disk erasable. One 5-inch disk prepared in this manner can store 550 megabytes, the equivalent of the data that can be stored on 500 5¼-inch floppies.

Erasable or not, with no flying head to cause crashes and with large storage capacities, optical disks offer a very promising auxiliary storage medium. They are sure to soon become a major form of direct access storage.

Mass Storage

Disk technology does not meet the needs of all organizations for direct access to large amounts of stored data. For example, to be able to answer customers' inquiries about bills and other matters, a major public utility company must keep a very large volume of data online to the computer at all times. Using disk drives to do so would be a very expensive proposition, since, with only a few billion characters of storage per disk unit, hundreds or even thousands of disk drives would be required. Because magnetic tape must be read sequentially, it, too, is a poor storage medium when quick response to inquiries is needed. An alternative to using magnetic tape or disk is the **mass storage unit.** Combining the best features of both tape and disk, such a unit has the capacity to store and retrieve more than 400 billion bytes of data without operator assistance.

The IBM 3850 mass storage system is capable of storing 472 billion bytes of data in 9,440 data cells. As you can see in Figure 8.16, the cells

Figure 8.16
A mass storage system: the IBM 3850.
Courtesy of IBM Corporation.

resemble a honeycomb. Each cell contains a small spool of magnetic tape that is 770 feet long and that can store 50 million bytes. A mechanical arm retrieves the required tape and mounts it on a read/write device, which transfers the data from the tape onto a disk. The disk then becomes a direct access storage device, and the appropriate data are retrieved. Because the movement of the tapes is mechanical, and because the contents of the tape spool must be transferred onto a disk before they can be used, up to fifteen seconds may elapse between the time information is requested and the time it becomes available. This retrieval time is much faster than it would be if a tape had to be retrieved from a tape library and mounted by hand, but it is not as fast as disk access. In applications that can sacrifice immediate data access for tremendous online storage volume and economy, the mass storage unit serves as a useful alternative to tape and disk.

Bubble Memory

Magnetic **bubble memory** avoids the mechanical motion that is necessary in the read/write operations of tape and disk. Data are represented by the presence or absence of tiny bubbles in a thin film of magnetic material that coats an electronic chip (see Figure 8.17). The bubbles, which are a few thousandths of an inch in diameter, are produced by applying a controlled magnetic field to the film. Because the film already has magnetic properties, the application of the controlled magnetic field makes the bubbles stand out with magnetic polarity that is the opposite of the film's polarity.

Two important features of bubble memory are that it is nonvolatile and that it has no moving parts. Data flow is controlled by applying small

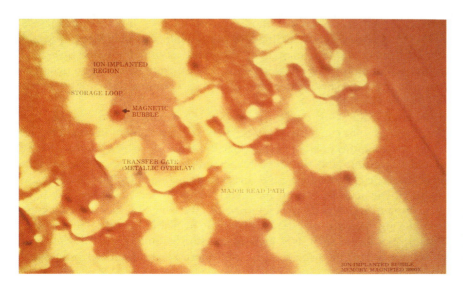

Figure 8.17
Magnetic bubble memory. The chip shown here has been magnified 3,000 times.
Courtesy of AT&T Bell Laboratories.

magnetic fields, and the reading operation does not destroy the data. Reliability is very good, and maintenance is minimal. However, the cost of producing these units is still quite high, and, largely for this reason, bubble memory has not yet become widely used as an alternative to tape and disk.

SELECTION CRITERIA

As in selecting other components of a computer system, the first thing to be considered in selecting auxiliary storage devices is the kind of processing applications in which the system will be used. Most microcomputer users find one or two storage devices — usually disk drives — adequate for their processing purposes, but businesses that process large volumes of data generally need multiple devices with both online and offline capabilities. The needs of the application also dictate the capacity, type of access, and speed that the auxiliary storage devices should provide. While these selection criteria will vary according to the needs of the application, a constant factor to be considered is the compatibility of the auxiliary storage equipment with the rest of the system. If the system is to function smoothly, there can be no mismatch among the technical specifications of its hardware components.

The greater the capacity of the auxiliary storage device, the more expensive it will be. The drives used to process data on cassette tapes and floppy disks are among the least expensive storage devices, but these media also have less capacity than the other magnetic media. While they are very satisfactory for most personal computing applications, for storing large amounts of data, hard disks and tape reel are more appropriate; of course, the devices used to process data on these media are also more expensive.

A need for continuous, online, direct access to stored data will also increase the cost of the equipment, but regardless of the expense, in certain applications, a direct access storage device is the only possible option. For instance, when you ask a telephone operator for the number of a friend in Chicago, you are not inclined to wait while the computer searches through a magnetic tape containing thousands of telephone numbers. You might be willing to wait a few seconds but probably would become angry if you had to wait several minutes. In this case, online disk storage is the only reasonable choice.

A large volume of data to be processed usually dictates a need for speed, and as with capacity and cost, there is a direct relationship between the speed and the cost of an auxiliary storage device. A factor closely related to volume and the need for speed is the amount of backup that must be done. For safety's sake, every system must include a duplicate record of the data stored on magnetic media. When many records have to be copied, the backup procedures can take several hours of processing time, during which the system will not be available for other processing. Certain conditions such as a high transaction volume, large data files, or an extraordinary need for security will increase the hours of processing time needed for backup. Backup is therefore an important, if often overlooked, factor to be considered when selecting auxiliary storage devices. By choosing equipment with capacities and speeds greater than are required for normal processing, it is possible to reduce the time consumed by backup. In short, as in choosing other components of a computer system, the key to choosing appropriate auxiliary storage devices is a thorough understanding of the processing applications.

SUMMARY

Computer storage consists of both primary storage and auxiliary storage. Primary storage has a very fast access speed, and, in most modern computers, it is volatile. In comparison with primary storage, auxiliary storage provides a slower, safer means of storing data. Auxiliary storage also greatly expands the storage capacity of the computer system, and at a relatively low cost.

Access to data kept in auxiliary storage can be either sequential or direct. The type of access and the kind of processing possible depend on the way files are organized and on the storage medium used. The application will determine the type of access needed.

Sequential access storage media include punched cards, often used in billing applications; punched paper tape, used chiefly in the communications industry; and magnetic tape, the most popular medium for computer backup files. Magnetic disks may also be used. The data density of magnetic tape, as well as of magnetic disk, can be increased by blocking the records to reduce the space taken up by interrecord gaps. Because tape has a high data density, it allows for the rapid transfer of data to and from a storage location. The data transfer rate depends not only on the tape data density but also on the speed at which the tape passes over the read/write head of the tape drive. The read/write head records the data on tape in a track arrangement.

Magnetic disks are a popular direct access storage medium. They include hard disks, which are used in high-volume operations; Winchester disks, which improve performance and reliability by reducing the possibility of head crashes; and floppy disks, which are generally used for input and auxiliary storage with microcomputers. Magnetic-disk drives may accommodate a single disk, or they may hold a disk pack. In a disk pack, access arms move the read/write heads in and out in unison over the disk tracks while a motor in the disk drive keeps the disks rotating at a constant speed. Data stored in disk packs may be organized in cylinders, with the record address including surface, cylinder, and record numbers. Data stored on single disks are organized in addressable sectors.

Optical disks, mass storage units, and bubble memory also provide direct access to stored data. Optical disks offer very high data density, and a new technology that combines lasers and electromagnetic coils makes the disks erasable. Mass storage technology combines features of tape and disk to provide hundreds of billions of bytes of online storage. Bubble memory is an emerging technology that uses a controlled magnetic field to create charged bubbles, representing data, on a magnetic film. Two advantages of bubble memory are that it is nonvolatile and has no moving parts.

The selection of appropriate auxiliary storage devices depends on a thorough understanding of the processing applications. Other selection criteria to be considered include the compatibility of the devices with other components of the system, capacity, type of access, and speed. Backup requirements are another important, if often overlooked, factor to be considered when selecting auxiliary storage devices.

KEY TERMS

access arms (230)
access speed (220)
address (228)
backup files (224)
block (227)
bubble memory (237)
cylinder (231)
data density (226)
data transfer rate (222)
disk pack (230)
head crash (232)
interblock gap (IBG) (227)

interrecord gap (IRG) (227)
logical records (227)
mass storage unit (236)
master file (223)
optical disk (laser disk) (234)
paper tape (224)
paper-tape reader (225)
read/write head (226)
sectors (228)
tracks (226)
transaction file (223)
Winchester disks (234)

DISCUSSION QUESTIONS

1. Discuss the differences between primary storage and auxiliary storage.
2. Give examples of two business data processing applications in which sequential access to stored data would be desirable. Explain the method of processing that takes place and identify the storage media that might be used.

3. Explain what the following terms mean: *data density, data transfer rate, blocking.* How do these factors affect the performance of a computer system?

4. Give examples of two business data processing applications in which direct access to stored data would be desirable. Explain the method of processing that takes place and identify the storage media that might be used.

5. Describe the devices used to read and write data on magnetic tape and magnetic disks.

6. What is a disk track? What is an address? Identify two methods of organizing data on magnetic disks.

7. What is a head crash? How can it be prevented?

8. What is a mass storage unit? When would it be used?

9. Describe the advantages and disadvantages of optical disks and bubble memory.

10. Discuss the selection criteria you would use in choosing auxiliary storage devices for a large utility company.

OUTLINE

COMPUTERS AND COMMUNICATIONS: SOME BACKGROUND

DATA TRANSMISSION

Transmission Channels
- Telephone Lines
- Coaxial Cables
- Microwaves
- Communications Satellites
- Fiber Optics
- Lasers
- Waveguides

Signal Transmission

DATA COMMUNICATIONS HARDWARE

Modems
Multiplexors and Concentrators
Front-End Processors

DATA COMMUNICATIONS SOFTWARE

Transmission Management
Function Management
Access Management
Error Management

DISTRIBUTED DATA PROCESSING NETWORKS

Star Network
Ring Network
Complex, or Distributed, Network
Local Area Network

SELECTION CRITERIA

SUMMARY

KEY TERMS

DISCUSSION QUESTIONS

OVERVIEW

Data communications systems have been the late bloomer of the Computer Age. But in recent years, they have been making up for lost time — and in rather dramatic ways. We're already seeing signs of the "wired world" of "electronic cottages" that some people predict will be the dominant lifestyle of the 1990s. Using communications links from their home computers to their place of work, many people are now "telecommuters," working from their homes through a computer. It may not be too long before you see sprouting from your own rooftop a "dishlike" sending/receiving antenna that will link your personal computer to a variety of shopping, banking, educational, and entertainment services. With microcomputers becoming almost as common an office fixture as a pencil sharpener (which they may one day soon make obsolete), *networking* has become the buzzword of the day. For small businesses, networking means connecting several small computer systems so that they can process independently and yet "talk" to each other to share data, programs, and processing capabilities. For large businesses, it means the ability to simultaneously process data at computer sites distributed throughout the world and to have immediate access to the most current information.

Data communications systems are still in the formative stages; their evolution is nowhere near complete. Current research shows great promise for new transmission materials and techniques, such as fiber optics and transmissions by satellite. In this chapter, we'll look at some of these newer materials and methods, as well as at some of the proven ones. We'll also explore the hardware and software used in data communications and the various networking configurations. Our objectives are to

- define a data communications system and explain how today's distributed data processing networks evolved.

- describe the channels used to transmit data and explain the characteristics of that transmission.

- identify the hardware components of data communications systems.

- describe the software requirements of data communications systems.

- explain the features of the major networking configurations currently in use.

- define the criteria used in selecting data communications equipment.

CHAPTER 9

DATA COMMUNICATIONS AND DISTRIBUTED DATA PROCESSING

COMPUTERS AND COMMUNICATIONS: SOME BACKGROUND

In the earliest computer systems, all data processing was done in a batch environment; that is, data were collected offline and physically transported to a central site for processing. At that central site were located all the system's software and hardware for input, processing, storage, and output. The computer itself was most often a single, powerful mainframe. With a growing trend toward the decentralization of business resulting in multiple business locations, elaborate data collection procedures for "feeding" the computer were often necessary, and courier firms and the postal service were widely used to transport raw data and processed information within an organization. It wasn't long before the limitations of such a *centralized* data processing environment became obvious. The transporting of data to and from the computer system began creating severe bottlenecks, causing delays in the processing and distribution of information. The need to find a more efficient means of communicating data became imperative.

The solution lay in combining computer technology with communications technology to form a **data communications system** — that is, a means of electronically transmitting data from one location to another. The first data communications systems, introduced in the 1960s, relied almost exclusively on the telephone system: These were **timesharing systems,** in which a number of terminals were connected to a central computer by a telephone link (see Figure 9.1). In that the central computer did all the processing, this "teleprocessing" environment was still a centralized one; but it was a great improvement over the batch environment, as it gave a number of users access to the computer at the same time and reduced the number of processing bottlenecks.

The interactive nature of timesharing processing, controlled by terminals located away from the processor site, was a major challenge for hardware designers. As they began addressing the architecture and design requirements

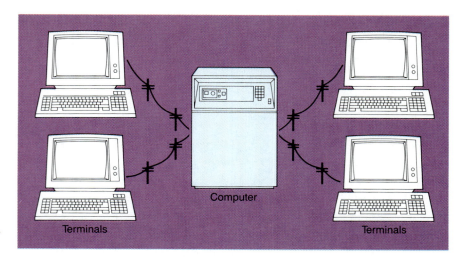

Figure 9.1
A timesharing system in a teleprocessing environment.

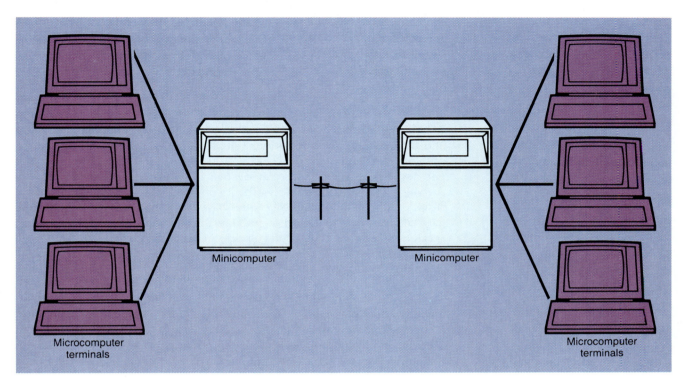

Figure 9.2
A distributed data processing network.

of timesharing systems, the minicomputer evolved. A number of computer companies devoted to the manufacture of minicomputers emerged during this time, including Digital Equipment Corporation, now the second largest computer firm in the world.

With the increasing use of minicomputers in the early 1970s, **distributed data processing (DDP)** came into being, and with it a *decentralized* data processing environment. Distributed data processing means that processing can be done either by a **host computer** (i.e., a main computer at a central site) to which the minicomputers are linked or by the minicomputers themselves at sites remote from the host computer. In some DDP network configurations, no host computer is involved; instead, a number of minicomputers are linked to process data independently or in concert with each other. Today, microcomputers are becoming an increasingly common part of the DDP network (see Figure 9.2). Such a **network** is, in effect, a system of computers and terminals connected by a communications link that allows the rapid transfer of data from terminal to computer, computer to computer, or computer to terminal.

Compared with other aspects of computer systems, data communications systems have been slow to develop. The primary reason for this delayed development is that before 1968, all data communications had by law to pass through the communications channels of *common carriers* — that is, firms licensed by the local, state, and federal governments to provide communications services to the public. These firms are highly regulated, and both their services and charges (called "tariffs") are subject to approval by the regulating agencies, which include the state public utilities commissions and the Federal Communications Commission (FCC). With only a limited number of common carriers and with competition thus lacking, research and development efforts were modest. In 1968, a ruling by the FCC enabled *private carriers* to compete for data communications business, and, as a result, data communications services have since expanded rapidly. Private carriers are firms that do not provide the full range of communications services of a public telephone company. They usually concentrate on high-traffic routes, such as New York to Los Angeles and Chicago to Boston, and they often carry only digital signals, ignoring voice communications altogether.

At present, over 300 billion transactions are processed each day through a wide variety of data communications networks. The companies involved in providing these services include the Bell Telephone System and its subsidiaries, MCI Communications Corporation, McDonnell Douglas Automation, Control Data Corporation, and many others. You should keep in mind that data communications systems are just a facilitator; the processing of data is the ultimate objective of any data communications system.

DATA TRANSMISSION

Transmission Channels

Data communications systems use a variety of **channels,** or communications lines, to transmit signals to and from the computer system. These transmission channels include the traditional voice channels maintained by telephone companies; coaxial cables, similar to those used for cable television; microwaves; communications satellites; fiber optics; lasers; and waveguides.

The range of frequencies that any of these channels can transmit depends on the widths of their **bands,** or bandwidths — that is, the range of signals they are able to transmit and carry. When you move a radio tuner from one station to another, you are changing frequencies within a band whose width is limited by the top and bottom of the tuner range. Human hearing is between 100 **hertz (Hz)** and 20,000 Hz, which is also the range of frequencies of most radios. (A hertz is a unit of frequency equal to one cycle per second.) A telephone system has a more limited bandwidth; it usually transmits signals from 300 Hz to 3,300 Hz. The narrower the bandwidth, the fewer individual signals that can be sent simultaneously, by either radio or telephone. The number of signals transmitted simultaneously is called **transmission density.** Think of a country road and an eight-lane superhighway; which can carry more traffic? The telephone system is comparable to the country lane, while the radio is more like the freeway.

The width of a transmission channel's band also determines the *speed* at which it can transmit data. The speed of data communications is measured in **bits per second (bps),** and the wider a transmission channel's band, the more bits per second it can transmit. There are three bandwidths: A telegraph line has a **very narrow bandwidth;** it transmits data at the relatively slow rate of 45 to 150 bps, for which reason it is not very commonly used in today's data communications systems. Telephone lines have a **narrow bandwidth;** they can transmit data at 1,800 to 9,600 bps. Coaxial cables, microwaves, and communications satellites have a **broad bandwidth;** they transmit data at speeds up to 500,000 bps and are used for the rapid transmission of large volumes of data.

A **baud** is another unit for measuring the speed of data transmission. It describes signaling speed, which is the number of times per second that a line is able to change condition and alter the signal. In the formative years of data communications technology, only one bit of data could be sent each time the line condition changed; so bits per second and baud rate were the same. Today's systems can send several bits with each change in line condition, increasing transmission speeds by two or three times over earlier performance. Because data processing is concerned with the units of data being sent, not with changes in the transmission line, bps is a more useful measure of speed for our purposes.

Today's telephone system provides service to every corner of the world. It is therefore a convenient system to use in the transmission of computer data, even though it has inherent limitations because it was designed for voice communication only. As we've just noted, microwaves have a much broader band than telephone lines, are able to carry many more simultaneous signals, and can transmit many more bits per second. However, they do not have the universal coverage of the telephone system. Table 9.1 summarizes some of the characteristics of these two transmission channels as well as of others that we will describe in the pages that follow.

Telephone Lines. Standard telephone lines are widely used as data communications channels, and, of course, a vast and complex network of such lines has been established for some time. Because the telephone was designed to transmit voice signals rather than data signals, using it for data communications has presented problems in the speed and quality of transmission. Interference, static, and signal echo are just a few of the problems encountered in telephone lines. New transmission technologies such as microwave and satellite systems are constantly being developed and are contributing to a

Table 9.1 Characteristics of Transmission Channels

Transmission Channel	Bandwidth	Transmission Speed (in bps)	Transmission Density	Transmission Quality	Limitations/Advantages
Telephone lines	Narrow	1,800–9,600	Under 100	Poor	System is already installed, but was intended for voice transmission when designed.
Coaxial cables	Broad	Up to 500,000	Less than 10,000	Good	Better speed and quality than telephone lines, but installation and maintenance over long distances are difficult.
Microwaves	Broad	Up to 500,000	Up to 50,000	Good	Good transmission density, but towers for sending and receiving signals must be installed every 25–30 miles.
Communications satellites	Broad	Up to 500,000	Up to 100,000	Good	No need for towers to send and receive signals, but equipment is very expensive.
Fiber optics	Broad	Millions	50,000	Very good	Signal distortion is very low; not subject to interference from external factors.
Lasers	Broad	Millions	100,000	Very good	High transmission density, but technology of sending/receiving signals is still evolving, and equipment is quite expensive.
Waveguides	Broad	Up to 100,000	More than 100,000	Good	Excellent transmission density, but transmission is limited to short distances (several thousand feet).

higher level of performance by the telephone systems. Even with limitations in speed and quality, telephone lines carry the bulk of data transmitted today.

As shown in Figure 9.3, **telephone lines** consist of pairs of insulated copper wires. The wires are bundled into a cable and are joined at terminal or junction blocks, forming a network of interconnected lines that operate at a voice frequency. Routing of signals is done by switching equipment, for the most part computer-controlled and very fast. The switching is much like the switching in your home electrical system: When you want to activate a circuit to turn on a light, you throw a switch, and energy passes through the selected line. The telephone company does the same thing, except that the switches are much smaller and are automatically controlled.

Coaxial Cables. Whereas the standard telephone line consists of a pair of insulated copper wires, **coaxial cable** consists of a conductive cylinder of copper and an inner wire insulated from the conductive cylinder. As you can see in Figure 9.4, the coaxial cable resembles a copper garden hose with a wire down the middle, and with insulation between the hose and the wire and covering the outside as well. These cables can be bundled together, covered with an insulation sheath, and used both on land and under the sea. In fact, coaxial cables have provided an important means of intercontinental communications for many years.

Coaxial cables are a better communications channel than telephone lines. They can transmit signals at a much higher speed. Because they are insulated, there is less signal loss than with telephone lines. Also, their broad bandwidths enable them to operate at higher frequencies and to transmit many signals simultaneously. The combination of better signals and simultaneous transmission makes coaxial cable very useful when large volumes of data are being transmitted.

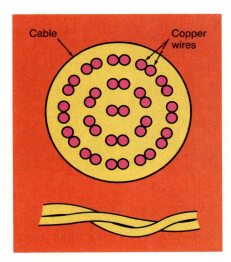

Figure 9.3
A telephone line: (*top*) a cutaway view of the cable; (*bottom*) a pair of the copper wires.

Figure 9.4
A coaxial cable: (*left*) a side view; (*right*) a cutaway view.
Photo courtesy of AT&T Bell Laboratories.

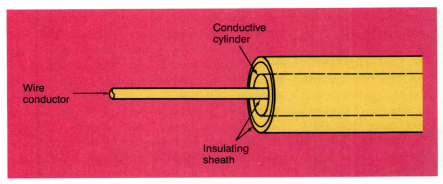
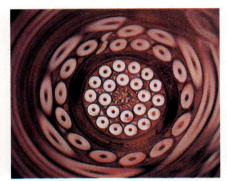

Figure 9.5
Microwave transmission: (*left*) a sending/receiving unit on top of a building in Minneapolis; (*right*) the line-of-sight signal path.
Photo courtesy of SBS (Satellite Business Systems).

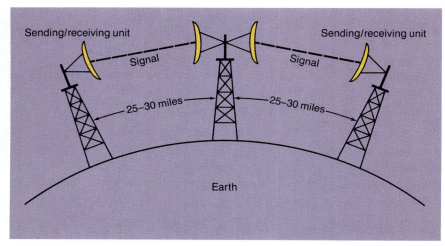

Microwaves. **Microwaves** are super-high-frequency radio waves that can transmit data signals through open space, much as television and radio signals are transmitted. These signals are carried in a straight line through the atmosphere and reach approximately thirty miles if the sending and receiving units are at the same elevation and there is no intervening obstruction. In other words, the signal is **line of sight** — that is, it does not bend with the curvature of the earth but goes in a straight line from the sending unit to the receiving unit. The sending and receiving units are mounted on "towers" or are located on the tops of buildings (see Figure 9.5). To maintain the strength of the signal, these units generally amplify or boost the signal before retransmitting it. Since the signal is transmitted through the atmosphere, the cost of installing and maintaining cables is avoided. Also, because microwaves can simultaneously transmit thousands of narrow band channels within the broad band, transmission density is much greater than with coaxial cable.

Communications Satellites. When a **communications satellite** is placed in permanent orbit at a speed that matches the rotation of the earth, it can be used as a relay station for the transmission of signals. The communications satellite is designed to accept, store, and transmit signals sent from one earth station and directed to another earth station (see Figure 9.6). The disk antennae that you see sprouting up everywhere may be used to capture signals from such a satellite.

Whereas a land-based microwave system must retransmit a signal every thirty miles, a satellite system receives, boosts, and transmits the signal only once. Also, most signal interference is created by atmospheric conditions; with a satellite system, all but a small portion of the transmission path is outside the atmosphere. Thus, a high-quality signal is possible even during electrical storms and unsettled weather conditions.

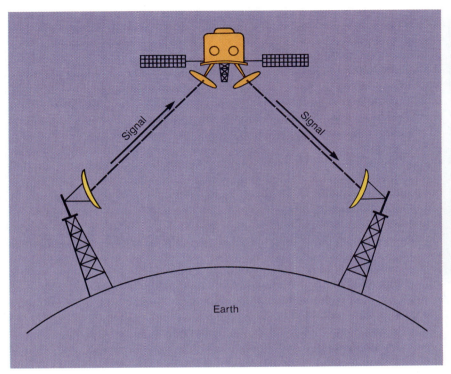

Figure 9.6

A communications satellite: (*left*) the signal transmission; (*right*) photo of an artist's rendition of a communications satellite.

Photo courtesy of RCA American Communications, Inc.

Fiber Optics. **Fiber optics** are very thin, light-conducting threads of glass or plastic that are used to transmit data signals at the speed of light (see Figure 9.7). High-frequency light sources, such as a light-emitting diode (similar to that used in the display screen of many hand-held electronic calculators), put the signal into a light form. The fiber cable then transmits the signal, and on the receiving end, special equipment decodes it back into a conventional electronic signal.

Because the fibers are hair-thin, they can be highly concentrated, which is an important consideration in crowded "utility tunnels" in major cities and in other applications in which space is an important factor. Fiber optics are also much lighter than copper wires, and they have certain advantages in preventing wiretapping and in maintaining distortion-free signals during nuclear-test detonations and electrical disturbances. One pound of fiber optics can replace twenty pounds of copper wire, and a single fiber-optic cable is capable of carrying 50,000 individual signals simultaneously; in contrast, coaxial cable carries less than 10,000 signals at one time. The signal quality is very good, and future applications of fiber optics as transmission channels look very promising.

Lasers. A **laser,** as we noted in Chapter 8, is a tightly packed light beam that can be precisely controlled. Such light beams are of a very high

Figure 9.7

Fiber optics. A single high-capacity lightguide directs a test signal toward the camera. A lightwave route using cables of fiber optics stretches 776 miles from Massachusetts to Virginia. One pair of fiber optics can transmit 1,344 voice conversations.

Courtesy of AT&T Bell Laboratories.

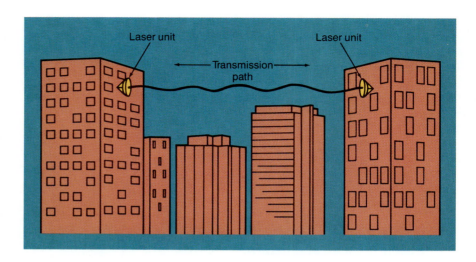

Figure 9.8
Laser transmission.

frequency and can carry thousands of times as much information as microwaves. But, like microwaves, lasers require a line-of-sight transmission path (see Figure 9.8). The sending and receiving equipment is quite expensive, and the technology of transmitting data via lasers is still evolving. The most promising applications appear to be building-to-building transmissions in congested areas, rather than long-distance transmissions between multiple stations. Despite very good transmission quality, the future of lasers as a communications technology may not be as bright as that of fiber optics because of the expense of the equipment involved.

Waveguides. Waveguides are round or rectangular metal tubes that act as pathways for very-high-frequency radio waves (see Figure 9.9). They are rather like the pipes in a water delivery system in that they are hollow and serve as conduits. The waves themselves, however, are unlike water in that they will not flow through a pipe with sharp bends or corners, which limits applications of waveguides to short, rather straight runs. Waveguides have the capacity to carry in excess of 100,000 simultaneous transmissions, but they are rarely used for transmission beyond one mile.

Waveguide technology is just now emerging, and its applications for

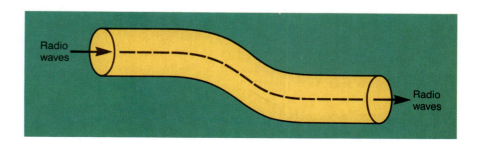

Figure 9.9
A waveguide.

data communications are presently unclear. The very high density of waveguide transmission channels is attractive, but the installation and maintenance of these systems present significant challenges.

Signal Transmission

After choosing the desired transmission channel (or channels) for communicating data, the designer of a data communications system must decide which mode of transmission to use. Channels operate in one of three basic modes (see Figure 9.10):

1. **Simplex:** Transmission takes place in one direction only. For example, a car radio operates in a simplex mode: It can only receive a signal; it cannot transmit. In a data communications system, simplex transmission is used when the computer needs to receive data but does not need to return a signal. For instance, when a computer collects data from a weather-forecasting meter that measures such things as atmospheric conditions, snow pack in the mountains, or temperature, data must be transmitted to the computer, but no signal needs to be returned to the meter.

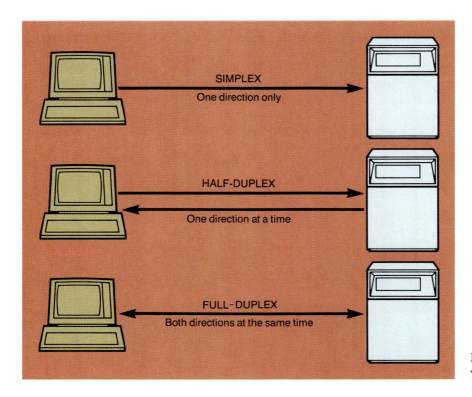

Figure 9.10
Transmission modes.

2. **Half-duplex:** Transmission can go in either direction, but in only one direction at a time. A CB radio operates in the half-duplex mode: It can send *or* receive, but it cannot do both at the same time. Similarly, most computer terminals can send and receive signals, but not simultaneously. While the terminal is receiving a signal from the CPU, it cannot return a signal until the CPU has finished transmitting.

3. **Full-duplex:** Transmission can go both ways at the same time. A telephone, for example, which allows simultaneous two-way communication, operates in the full-duplex mode. In a data communications system, a computer system that is sending critical data may be in the full-duplex mode so that a distorted transmission can be immediately interrupted and restored; if the system is not transmitting in the full-duplex mode, retransmission has to wait until the original transmission is completed.

The mode of transmission chosen will depend on the application and the type of equipment used.

Most data communications systems use **serial transmission,** in which data signals are transmitted one after another. Serial transmission can be either asynchronous or synchronous (see Figure 9.11). In **asynchronous transmission,** each character of data is transmitted as an isolated unit. Special signal bits identify the beginning and end of each character. The "start bit" signals the receiving unit to monitor the incoming transmission at a standardized rate according to a predefined code. The "stop bit" signals that the transmission of the character is completed. Because each character is initiated with a start bit, transmission does not need to follow any special timing; a delay of several seconds or minutes will not cause signal confusion.

Synchronous transmission transmits blocks of characters, rather than a character at a time, by synchronizing the sending and receiving units. The block may contain several thousand data bits, with no individual character separation. This method is more efficient and usually less costly than asynchronous transmission, but there is some loss of control with the transfer of each large block of data. A transmission malfunction may destroy only one character in an asynchronous transmission, whereas hundreds or

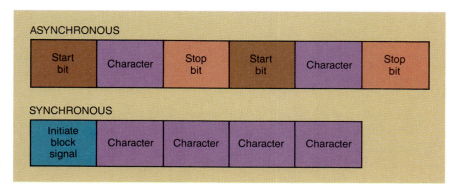

Figure 9.11
Asynchronous and synchronous transmission of data.

thousands of characters may be lost when an error occurs in synchronous transmission. Thus, in deciding whether to use asynchronous or synchronous transmission, the designer of the data communications systems would have to weigh the higher efficiency and lower costs of synchronous transmission against the possibility that it could result in debilitating errors, which asynchronous transmission can prevent.

DATA COMMUNICATIONS HARDWARE

The merging of communications technology and computer technology into a data communications system requires specialized hardware as well as the typical hardware used in both areas — for example, a CPU, a terminal, and a communications device known as a modem. Although it is possible to have a data communications system without terminals (as in a computer-to-computer system), the vast majority of communications systems do involve terminals. The most commonly used type of terminal is the VDT, with its keyboard and CRT screen for entering data into the system and receiving output. Figure 9.12 shows the equipment used in a typical teleprocessing system. The modems, concentrator, and front-end processor shown in the figure are described in the sections that follow.

Figure 9.12
Equipment used in a teleprocessing system.

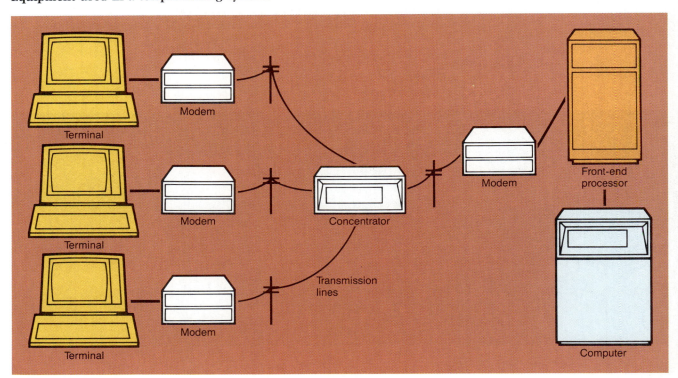

Modems

Transmission channels carry data in either **analog** form (i.e., as variable wave patterns) or in **digital** form (i.e., as binary, or on-off, pulses) (see Figure 9.13). All telephone lines transmit data in analog form, since digital signals don't travel well over these voice-oriented channels. But, of course, the computer operates only in a binary, or digital, mode. Thus, before being transmitted over a telephone line to a computer, data entered at a terminal in digital form must be converted to analog form; after transmission, the data must be converted back into digital form so that they will be intelligible to the computer. The process of converting data from digital form to analog form is known as **modulation;** the opposite process — conversion from analog form to digital form — is called **demodulation.** A device known as a **modem** (*mo*dulator/*dem*odulator) is used for both conversion processes. Modems transfer data at speeds measured in baud rates; these rates range from 300 to 19,000 baud, depending on the line condition. For effective data transmission, the rate of speed of the device supplying the data must be coordinated with the modem's rate.

Modems are often permanently attached to input/output equipment. Such modems are said to be "hard-wired" (see Figure 9.14). To accommodate portable terminals, which are being used in increasing numbers, a device known as an **acoustic coupler** has been developed. An acoustic coupler is a special type of modem that is attached to a portable terminal (see Figure 9.15). It has two suction cups to hold a telephone handset. The

Figure 9.13
Signal conversion: modulation and demodulation.

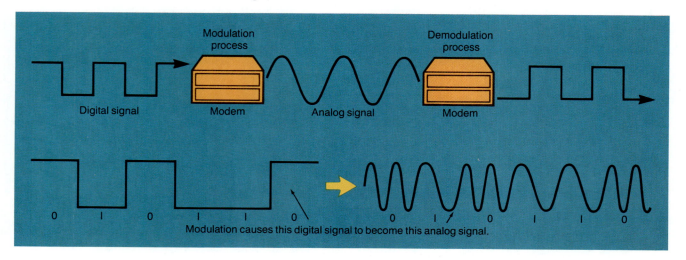

Figure 9.14
A hard-wired modem.
Courtesy of IBM Corporation.

Figure 9.15
An acoustic coupler.
Courtesy of Texas Instruments.

user places the telephone handset on the coupler and dials the telephone number. The coupler then converts the digital signals from the terminal into analog signals, and the analog signals go to a modem that converts them to digital signals for the computer. To demodulate analog signals, the earpiece of the telephone handset is connected to a microphone that picks up the analog wave tones and converts them to digital signals. A common problem with acoustic couplers is that they easily pick up static in the telephone line as well as any background noise, and as a result, the computer may receive garbled signals. The hard-wired modems don't have this problem.

Multiplexors and Concentrators

A transmission channel can transmit data at a much faster speed than a terminal can supply the data. For example, a telephone line transmits data at 300 to 9,600 bps, whereas a terminal transmits data at 300 bps. Thus, a single terminal can't make full use of a channel. Because data communications are quite expensive, it is often advantageous to use special devices to improve transmission efficiency. Devices used for this purpose include multiplexors and concentrators.

A **multiplexor** combines the data signals from a number of terminals into one input flow that can be sent over a single channel. At the receiving end, the data flow is disassembled into its component parts according to

COMPUTER COMMUTING

Wouldn't it be wonderful if you could get to work in less than five minutes, avoid traveling in inclement weather, and kiss long lines at conventions goodbye?

Is it possible? Yes. The technology, in the form of personal computers, modems and phones, is already in place. But actually doing it — telecommuting to work *from* home — is another story. Less than 5 percent of all Americans telecommute to the office. Plenty of people work *at* home, but then their office *is* the same place as their home, and that's not telecommuting.

There are two reasons why we don't telecommute to work from home. First, people simply don't realize that almost every personal computer can be configured to communicate with any other computer in the world. Modems and communications software make this possible. The more important reason, though, has to do with the politics of the workplace.

The way companies are organized has shut most of us out of the electronic commuting ballgame. In the upscale world of managers and executives, few corporate ladders reach as far as the home. Whether aspiring to their boss's job or paranoid about protecting their turf, people perceive a need to be attached to a rung of the ladder. Charismatic or not, office presence means being present in the office. No one wants to commit professional suicide by disappearing into an electronic ether. Working away from the office translates, for insecure souls, into a loss of authority. To them, there is no such thing as remote control.

Let's face it. There is a certain assurance in daily, face-to-face contact with your co-workers. The body language of eye contact and gestures often provides you with more feedback in terms of your standing within the organization than a CRT could ever communicate. Yet, American corporate culture is ripe for change.

Until 1957, most of the work in our economy was manufacturing — moving materials and changing their physical form. Today, 71 percent of what we produce is service or information — changing and moving ideas. Manufacturing and service industries require that employees be at a physical location, but information industries do not. You cannot telecommute to build a house, but you can to design one....

The technology that created the personal computer and telecommuting has implications that society is just beginning to tackle. The concept of going to work came about because people had to be together in one location to accomplish work. To manufacture, you went to the plant. To manage information, you went to the office.

The development of the car allowed us to create suburbs. We could work in one place and live miles away. Telecommuting will allow our ideas to go to work, while we stay at home.

The only reason the office of tomorrow isn't here today is that we have not figured out how to dismantle our current way of organizing work. While a solution is not imminent, it is not likely to be found around the office water cooler either.

— Matthew Puleo, "Computer Commuting." Reprinted with permission from *Personal Computing,* April 1985, p. 145. Copyright 1985, Hayden Publishing Company.

---

a predefined plan (see Figure 9.16). Most multiplexors combine a number of slow data flows into a single, high-speed flow by using a time-slice allocation system or by establishing a number of narrow bandwidths within the communications line. The **time slice** provides a segment of time for each terminal, whether it is active or not: Signals are continually collected, assembled, and transmitted in a predefined order, which makes it easy to disassemble the data stream on the receiving end of the transmission.

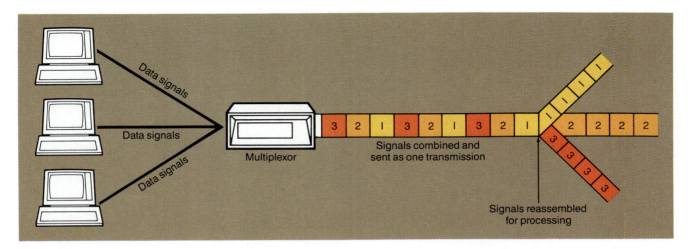

Figure 9.16

A single data flow. Multiplexors combine multiple signals into one flow by allocating time slices to the sending terminals or by simultaneously transmitting over numerous narrow bandwidths.

Simultaneous transmission with narrow bandwidths "tunes the computer" so that it collects and routes the signals as they are received. The increased message density that a multiplexor provides means more efficient use of the receiving equipment and the transmission channels.

A **concentrator** is an "intelligent" multiplexor — usually a programmable minicomputer. In addition to combining data signals into one data flow, it can evaluate signals and route them through specific channels. Concentrators can store messages while waiting for a channel to clear, can change message formats from one coding system to another, and can compress the data (**compression** involves removing blanks and recoding numerical data in a more concise form). The coordinating function that concentrators perform is very important in networks where traffic is heavy or line charges are high, such as in overseas transmissions. Figure 9.17 shows the role of concentrators in a large data communications system typical of today's complex communications/computing networks.

Both multiplexors and concentrators use two techniques to collect messages and send them to the CPU. **Polling** is the process of continuously checking each terminal to see if there is a message to be sent, much as a bus checks at each stop to see if there are passengers to be loaded or unloaded (see Figure 9.18). **Contention** is somewhat like calling a friend on the telephone. If the line is in use, you will get a busy signal and must continue trying until the line is free. The terminal contends for an available line in the same way.

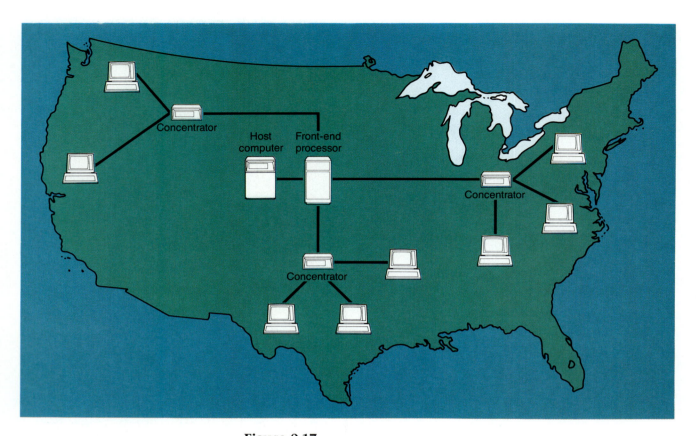

Figure 9.17
The role of concentrators in today's complex communications/computing networks.

Front-End Processors

As you can see in Figure 9.17, **front-end processors** also play an important role in the data communications system. These units are usually either special-purpose or programmable minicomputers, and their primary function is to relieve the host computer of a number of communications-control chores. When the volume of data being transmitted reaches a certain level, a front-end processor is a more economical means of handling data than assigning all chores to a single CPU. In addition to accepting incoming data and sorting and storing them for later processing by the CPU, front-end processors are capable of a number of other activities. Polling input and output devices for current signal activity, checking for signal errors, switching signals, dialing automatically through the telephone system, com-

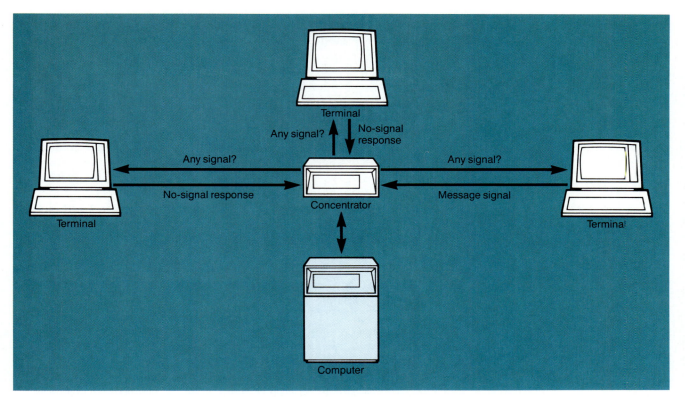

Figure 9.18
Polling. The concentrator or multiplexor polls each terminal to give it the opportunity to send a signal. A "no-signal response" causes the device to poll each additional terminal until it encounters a message signal.

pensating for differing transmission speeds, and assigning message priorities are just a few of the capabilities found in most front-end processors.

DATA COMMUNICATIONS SOFTWARE

Data communications systems require specialized systems software. The main function of this software is to integrate the computing and communications hardware and to coordinate, monitor, and evaluate the communications and computing activities. The four fundamental software requirements of a data communications system are programs for transmission management, function management, access management, and error management. This software can be located in the central computer, or it can be partially incorporated into the various system components. For example, concentrators and front-end processors include complex communications software, and smart terminals have limited software incorporated in their design. However, a modem generally has no software capabilities.

Transmission Management

Coordinating different computing and communications devices, transmission channels, and speeds, and assigning and maintaining the proper communications routes are some of the tasks associated with **transmission management software.** To perform these tasks, the software must establish **protocols** (i.e., procedures that synchronize the activities of network components), poll the channels to see which are active, and activate and deactivate the communications link. It would be very expensive and cumbersome to perform these functions manually.

Function Management

Once a data signal is communicated to the host computer in a data communications system, **function management software** must be available to process the input/output requests, log the communications activity, determine message priority, and manage the temporary storage, compression, and editing of signals. In batch-processing systems, people perform these tasks, but in a data communications system, such an arrangement would be impossibly inefficient.

Access Management

Security and privacy can pose some sticky problems in data communications systems. Terminals have direct links to the computer system and are often accessible to both authorized and unauthorized users. **Access management software** includes programs for limiting system access and controlling the level of access (e.g., the personnel director would be allowed to see data on all employees, but a department manager would be allowed access only to data pertinent to employees in that specific department). Other access management programs protect data through **encryption** (i.e., coding) and provide routines for alerting the computer operator to unauthorized use of the system. Encryption is becoming an increasingly important part of access management. Because banks transmit a tremendous volume of electronic signals in transfers of funds with government agencies, the Treasury Department has ordered all banks engaged in such transfers to use the Data Encryption Standard developed by the National Bureau of Standards.

Error Management

The addition of communications channels to a computer system creates a significant opportunity for the occurrence of errors that have nothing to do with the computer itself or the programs being executed. Typical communications errors include lost and missing data, inaccurate data, signal interruptions, and equipment malfunctions on the sending or receiving end of the signal. In reality, communications errors are a fact of life, and preparing for them is a matter of standard procedure. As you know from Chapter 5, parity checking is one common way to check for signal errors.

Errors most often found in systems that rely on telephone lines result from line noise and signal distortion. For example, the last time you made a long-distance telephone call, you may have heard buzzing, hissing, static, echoes, or perhaps the hint of someone else's conversation. All these factors create problems in data communications, which lead to transmission errors.

All transmission channels, whether telephone lines or channels of a higher quality, can suffer from power surges, power loss, and line failure. In fact, *spikes,* or power surges, are the primary source of errors in data communications. In telephone conversations, such surges would not create a problem, as they usually last only a fraction of a second. In transmitting data, however, even a fraction of a second can affect the transmission of tens or hundreds of bits of data.

Error management software has two types of procedures for controlling errors in data transmission. One type requests retransmission when an error is detected. The other type automatically activates correction procedures and continues the message transmission. Transmission requirements — that is, the time the line is in use — are increased between 25 and 100 percent over those of the original signal whenever error management software is used.

DISTRIBUTED DATA PROCESSING NETWORKS

As we noted earlier, a distributed data processing (DDP) network consists of a number of computers and terminals linked by a communications channel. The link provides the opportunity to share not only processing capabilities but also programs, data files, and storage space. The computers of the network may include minicomputers, microcomputers, and a mainframe or supercomputer host computer. All these computers have processing capability as well as memory capacity; so processing can be performed both by the host computer and by the outlying computers. As you can see in Figure 9.19, the network may be maintained locally, or it may be distributed over a large geographical area.

The overall objective of DDP networking is to provide maximum computing at minimal cost. The network's incorporation of multiple computers means that the system is more reliable than a system composed of

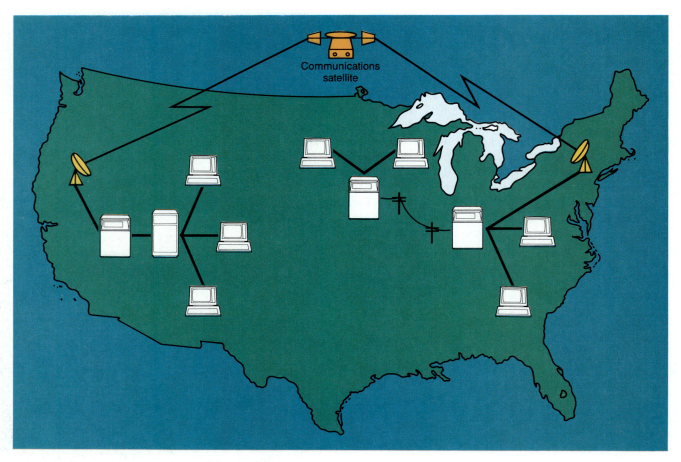

Figure 9.19
Local and long-distance distributed data processing networks (DDPs).

a single computer and multiple terminals, such as is found in timesharing systems. In a timesharing system, the whole system will fail if the central computer fails; the DDP network avoids this possibility. Networking has not only brought computing to users who don't have the resources to support a mainframe system; it has also brought more computing power to the mainframe user.

Because local units can do much of the routine processing, transmission errors and problems of unauthorized system access are reduced. At the same time, data redundancy can also be reduced, as a number of systems can share a central file, calling for data only when needed.

DDP networks have three fundamental configurations: the star network; the ring network; and the complex, or distributed, network. The local area network is a communications network rather than a computer system, and it may use any of these configurations.

Star Network

The identifying characteristic of a **star network** is a central host computer. As you can see in Figure 9.20, several minicomputers are independently connected to the host system, allowing for the sharing of a central source of information and local processing with or without interaction with the central system. In this configuration, failure of the central system does not cause the minicomputers to fail, although it may restrict their ability to process data from the centralized files. A business might use a star network in a point-of-sale system in which each store has a minicomputer to process sales transactions; the sales and inventory data would then be fed to the central computer each night to update company records.

Figure 9.20
A star network.

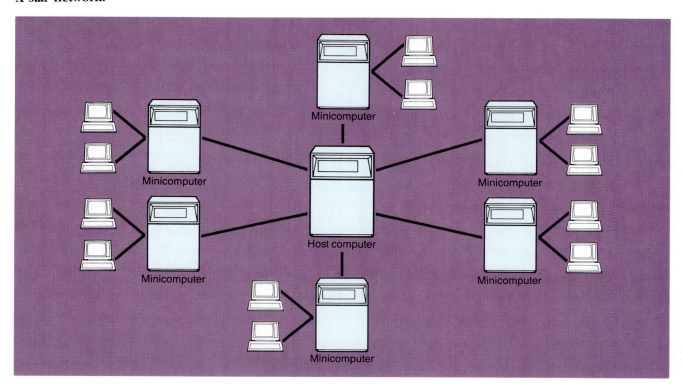

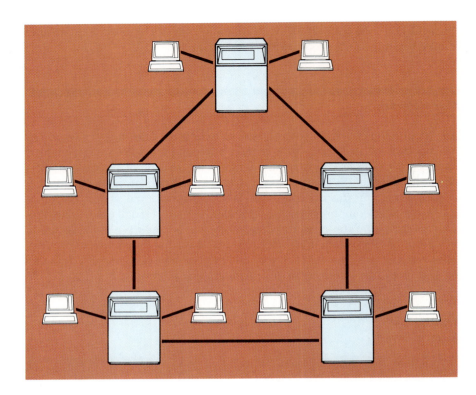

Figure 9.21
A ring network.

Ring Network

In a **ring network,** every computer is connected to two other computers (see Figure 9.21). There is no central host system, and information can flow equally in both directions. This "serial" linking allows adjacent computers to take over operations when a computer failure occurs. A limitation is the linking that must take place to pass requests and data when one computer needs information from another computer not in a direct link with it. A business with widely scattered warehouses, each of which does most of the processing for its own orders, might choose to use a ring network. When an item is out of stock at one warehouse, its computer can communicate through each of the other warehouse computers, searching until it finds the required item.

Complex, or Distributed, Network

The **complex,** or **distributed, network** is a modification of the ring network. As Figure 9.22 shows, it includes cross-communications links

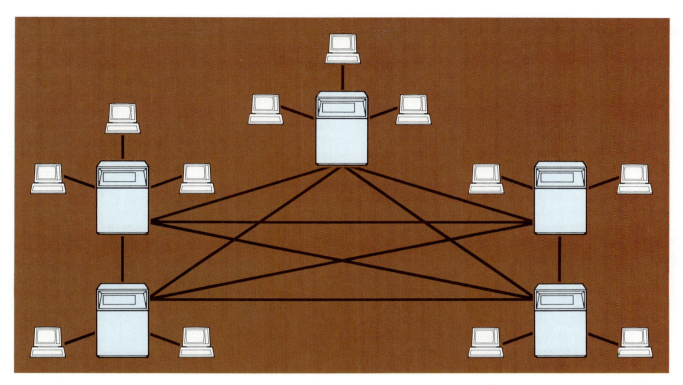

Figure 9.22
A complex, or distributed, network.

between all the computers in the network. Thus, a computer requesting access to a shared file does not have to route the request through a series of other computers in the ring until it reaches the computer with the desired file. Although this type of network configuration saves time, it requires much more elaborate communications control, which increases the complexity of the system. A business that relies on interoffice communications for the sharing of resources and up-to-the-minute information about the activities of any branch location might decide to use a complex network. With each location connected to every other location as well as to headquarters, there is no waiting for a line to the concentrator or rerouting of signals. A direct link can be made quickly and efficiently from one location to another.

Local Area Network

A newly emerging system is the **local area network (LAN),** which is a communications network privately owned by the organization using it.

THE UNIVERSITY OF THE FUTURE

Universities, for centuries centers for experimentation and the development of new ideas, are entering the Information Age. Personal workstations that provide students with significant computing power are cropping up on college campuses throughout the country and the world. Two schools leading the drive to bring integrated computing capabilities to all their students are Carnegie-Mellon University in Pittsburgh, Pennsylvania, and Brown University in Providence, Rhode Island. At both schools, personal workstations provide students not only with stand-alone processing capabilities but also with electronic access to faculty and other students and to a variety of data bases. Local area networks tie the personal workstations into clusters, providing communications links to the large central computer and its data bases, various commercial data bases, and library resources.

As a student at the university of the future, you would no doubt find your personal workstation a very useful tool. Before your feet even touch the floor in the morning, you might use it to check your electronic mail, to dash off a message to your lab partner reminding her of the chemistry experiment you are doing at two o'clock that afternoon, and to review your assignments and class schedule for the day. Before your first class, you might prepare the final draft of a term paper, proofread it, and send it via electronic mail — no paper or printing involved — directly to your instructor's workstation. That done, you might even have time to browse through the electronic catalog of library references looking for material for a history paper and to reserve several articles and books. Later, in physics class, a workstation simulates for you — in color — the physical changes that occur as an electric current flows through semiconductor materials.

After dinner, you might link your workstation to a cable television service and activate whatever accounts you have with videotext services — commercial enterprises that provide immediate access to stored information. On this particular evening, you call for Startext, a Texas-based electronic newspaper that provides continuously updated news about business and world events. Startext combines the features of the traditional newspaper (it even includes local classified ads) with the immediacy and visual impact of television. You also have access to Viewtron, a Knight-Ridder service that not only gives you the news but also allows you to shop and bank electronically. After catching up on current events, you call for the Dow Jones Market Analyzer — a service that provides stock market analyses — to help you complete a class assignment. At this point, having ingested so much information, you might be too tired to contemplate the role your workstation played in your life that day. But if you did, you would probably conclude that it saved a great deal of time you would have otherwise spent waiting in lines or listening to busy signals, and, in general, made your day a more productive one.

Because it is a communications network rather than a computer system, the LAN may be used with the star, ring, or complex network configurations or in timesharing systems. Transmitting signals through coaxial cables or fiber optics with broad bandwidths, the LAN connects terminals and computers within a confined area, generally no more than a few thousand feet between network distribution points. Usually used in a single building, industrial site, or college campus, the LAN is capable of providing high-speed communications. These systems support data, voice, and video transmission, providing potential for voice data terminals, video teleconferencing,

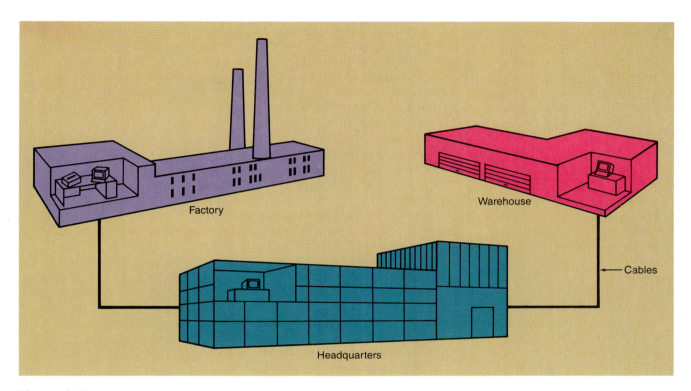

Figure 9.23
A local area network (LAN).

graphics, and office-automation applications (see Figure 9.23). The LAN is generally less expensive than the communications services provided by common carriers, and it is most effective when there are a large number of users at a central location.

Data communications systems can obviously be a boon for businesses that operate in geographically scattered locations, and, in fact, for many firms today, they are a necessity. However, they also represent a significant part of the overall cost of acquiring and operating a computer system, and care must be taken when selecting the necessary equipment. Among the factors to be considered are the nature of the data the system will handle, issues related to the equipment itself, and physical and structural requirements.

The types and length of the messages to be sent and the expected total traffic will determine how fast the data communications system needs to be and how many signals it should be able to send simultaneously. How fast it can be and how many signals it can send simultaneously depend,

SELECTION CRITERIA

of course, on the bandwidth of the transmission channel used. Telephone lines, having a narrow bandwidth, are the most appropriate choice for data that are keyed into the system from a terminal, since such keying is always relatively slow. However, for data that are communicated directly from computer to computer, the broad-band microwave and satellite transmission systems have definite advantages. In deciding on the transmission density that a communications channel should provide, it's wise to note whether the system will support continuous record updating, whether it will include microcomputers, and whether it will provide direct access to a data base, since these factors can increase communications traffic dramatically. The sensitivity of the data is another concern. While data security is important in any computer system, it becomes particularly important when the computer's resources are available to users who cannot be screened or evaluated at the site of the computer system. Data communications systems therefore require additional security measures.

Compatibility of hardware is an obvious equipment-related concern. Problems arise when devices within the same system do not operate in the same way — for example, when synchronous terminals are incorporated into the same network as asynchronous terminals. Another equipment-related issue is whether to use switched lines, such as are used in a telephone system, or hard-wired lines, which usually involve a coaxial cable from the device to the computer. A third choice is a leased line, which is often a part of the telephone system but is continuously connected to the sending and receiving units so that no one else can use it. When switched lines are used, it is not always possible to maintain a clear signal, and incomplete data transfer or erroneous data may be the result. However, switched lines are often cheaper than hard-wired lines. The cost of using communications equipment can mount quickly, and it is therefore a particularly important consideration. Concentrators, which assemble several slow signals into a stream to be sent as one fast signal, can help to reduce communications charges. These devices have proven very cost-effective for geographically widespread organizations that need to maintain continuous signal traffic.

Physical and structural requirements are a frequent headache for planners of data communications systems, who find that they must wire buildings, snake cables through conduits, and add things to buildings and streets that were not considered when the building and streets — or even the city — were designed. Problems can arise from conflicts with local building codes, from construction impediments (such as several feet of concrete barrier, no space to pull a cable, or lack of access to the part of the building where cables must be installed), and from the nature of the building itself (some buildings simply don't lend themselves to the installation of companywide data communications). Firms are finding that it is often cheaper to provide their operating units with stand-alone personal computers than to install communications equipment that allows access to a central computer and a data processing network.

SUMMARY

A data communications system combines communications technology with computing technology to provide a means of electronically transmitting data from one location to another. The first data communications systems were timesharing ones, in which a number of terminals were connected to a central computer by telephone lines. The modern distributed data processing network that evolved from these early systems is a system of computers and terminals connected by a communications link that allows for the rapid transfer of data and information throughout the system; processing may be done by a host computer or by minicomputers and microcomputers at remote sites.

Data are transmitted through a number of routes, called channels, the most important being telephone lines. Additional channels include coaxial cables, microwaves, communications satellites, fiber optics, lasers, and waveguides. The bandwidths of each of these channels determine their transmission density — that is, the number of signals they can send simultaneously — as well as their transmission speed, which is measured in bits per second. There are three bandwidths: very narrow, narrow, and broad.

Data can travel a number of ways through the channel: in one direction only (simplex), in one direction at a time (half-duplex), and in both directions at the same time (full-duplex). The transmission of the signal through the channel is either asynchronous (each character is controlled with a start and a stop signal) or synchronous (blocks of data are sent by synchronizing the sending and receiving units).

Specialized communications hardware includes a modem, which converts the digital signal from the computer to an analog signal that can be used by the communications channel and also does the reverse; and multiplexors and concentrators, which improve transmission efficiency. Procedures used by multiplexors and concentrators include time-slice allocation, polling, contention, and data compression. Front-end processors are used in data communications systems to relieve the host computer of a number of communications-control chores.

Data communications systems require four categories of specialized software: software for transmission management, function management, access management, and error management. Encryption is a rapidly evolving technique used in access management to protect the data from unauthorized use.

Distributed data processing networks allow the sharing of processing capabilities, storage space, programs, and data files. The multiple computers of the network provide some protection against system downtime. DDP networks have three basic configurations: star; ring; and complex, or distributed. A local area network (LAN) is not a computer system but rather a communications network. It may use any of the DDP network configurations. The LAN usually operates within a confined area, providing high-speed communications.

Effective management of complex business organizations requires high-speed data communications. Data communications equipment represents a significant portion of the overall cost of a computer system; so equipment must be selected carefully. Three important factors to be considered in selecting data communications equipment are the nature of the data the system will handle, issues related to the equipment itself, and physical and structural requirements.

KEY TERMS

access management software (262)
acoustic coupler (256)
analog (256)
asynchronous transmission (254)
bands (246)
baud (247)
bits per second (bps) (247)
broad bandwidth (247)
channels (246)
coaxial cable (249)
communications satellite (250)
complex (distributed) network (266)
compression (259)
concentrator (259)
contention (259)
data communications system (244)
demodulation (256)
digital (256)
distributed data processing (DDP) (245)
encryption (262)
error management software (263)
fiber optics (251)
front-end processors (260)
full-duplex (254)
function management software (262)

half-duplex (254)
hertz (Hz) (246)
host computer (245)
laser (251)
line of sight (250)
local area network (LAN) (267)
microwaves (250)
modem (256)
modulation (256)
multiplexor (257)
narrow bandwidth (247)
network (245)
polling (259)
protocols (262)
ring network (266)
serial transmission (254)
simplex (253)
star network (265)
synchronous transmission (254)
telephone lines (249)
timesharing systems (244)
time slice (258)
transmission density (247)
transmission management software (262)
very narrow bandwidth (247)
waveguides (252)

DISCUSSION QUESTIONS

1. What is a data communications system? Explain why these systems evolved. How are they used by businesses? By government?
2. What is distributed data processing? What are some advantages of distributed processing?
3. What is the importance of bandwidth in transmitting data? What transmission channel has the most restricted bandwidth?
4. Why has the telephone system been so important in data communications technology and development? Discuss three alternatives to telephone lines in the transmission of data.
5. Differentiate between simplex, half-duplex, and full-duplex signal transmissions. What is the advantage of using asynchronous transmission?
6. What is a modem? Why is it necessary in some data communications applications?
7. Describe how multiplexors, concentrators, and front-end processors improve data communications.
8. Why is unique software necessary for data communications? Discuss the functions that this software performs.
9. Describe the three basic configurations of a DDP network and identify a business application for each. How does a LAN differ from these three kinds of DDP networks?
10. Discuss the factors that should be considered in selecting data communications equipment.

OUTLINE

PERSONAL COMPUTERS: THE NEW WAVE

MICROCOMPUTER HARDWARE

   The Microprocessor and Other Chips
   Auxiliary Storage Equipment
   Input and Output Equipment
- Keyboards
- Video Display Units
- Printers
- Other Peripheral Devices

MICROCOMPUTER SOFTWARE

   Systems Software
   Applications Software
- Word Processing
- Data Base
- Graphics
- Electronic Spreadsheets
- Integrated Software

MERGING MICROS AND MAINFRAMES: BRIDGING THE GAP

SELECTION CRITERIA

SUMMARY

KEY TERMS

DISCUSSION QUESTIONS

OVERVIEW

Microcomputers, in the form of personal computers and small business systems, have sprung up as though planted from seeds. With over 200 microcomputer manufacturers presently producing almost 700 different models, and literally thousands of software developers working on programs to help micros do more, it is no wonder that these computers are ushering in a new age of computing. No longer the exclusive prerogative of wealthy corporations, electronic computing is now very much a consumer-oriented resource. In fact, even microcomputers designed for business applications are being marketed as personal computing solutions to information problems.

In this chapter, we'll look at the functional components of microcomputers and at the kinds of software available for them. We'll also explore how these systems are used in business and discuss some of the problems they can present. Not since the introduction of the internal combustion engine has a product so revolutionized society. Microcomputers are changing the way that we live, and part of this change is coming about because of the business applications of this technology.

Our objectives in this chapter are to

- identify some of the uses of personal computers.

- describe the hardware components of microcomputer systems.

- describe the kinds of microcomputer software most often used in business applications.

- discuss the problems associated with merging mainframes and microcomputers.

- outline some of the factors to be considered in selecting a microcomputer.

CHAPTER 10

THE MICROCOMPUTER PHENOMENON

PERSONAL COMPUTERS: THE NEW WAVE

A **personal computer** is any computer acquired for individual use. Fifteen years ago, to own a personal computer, you would have had to be in the uppermost stratum of income brackets. Today, the term *personal computer* is synonymous with *microcomputer,* and you can buy your own personal microcomputer from a toy store, variety store, or computer store. Micros are everywhere, and they are making an impact on individuals in all walks of life. Thanks to advances in hardware engineering and design and to improved chip-manufacturing techniques, for as little as a few hundred dollars you can today acquire computing capabilities that ten years ago cost thousands or tens of thousands of dollars. With popular pricing, the scope of users and applications continues to broaden. At present, microcomputers are being produced at the rate of over 5 million units a year. As Figure 10.1 shows, these machines come in a variety of shapes and sizes and are used in a variety of ways. They range all the way from small portable models to a "supermicro," which uses a hard disk capable of storing twenty times as much data as a floppy disk.

To understand the popularity of these machines, consider the opportunity that a personal computer offers a high school student: Microcomputer software for word processing can format and manipulate words, check spelling, and insert and correct letters or whole blocks of text. A term paper no longer means a marathon session at the typewriter. Once the student has researched the information for the paper, the computer becomes a convenient tool for entering, manipulating, and correcting the information and printing the report. With modern communications technology, it is even possible to connect one personal computer to another or to a school computer. References can be shared, resources explored, and assignments reviewed.

The applications of microcomputers are limited only by the availability of software and the imagination of the users. The hardware currently available offers processing capabilities that until the end of the 1970s, only mainframe computers could provide. The software is still catching up, and its developers are placing a heavy emphasis on "user-friendly" systems. The fewer technical skills required to use a **software package** (i.e., mass-marketed software designed to meet a common need), the more likely it will have widespread acceptance. Software for household financial management, self-paced education, entertainment, and energy management is sure to be popular for many years to come.

Personal microcomputers are not limited to uses in the home and at school. Business and industry are also using these systems in increasing numbers. The microcomputer has provided individual managers with a low-cost alternative to manual data collection systems and commercial timesharing systems (and to no systems at all!). It is not unusual for job applicants today to include in the usual discussion of salary and fringe benefits the question of the availability of microcomputers in the office or on their desks.

Microcomputers are used in business in two general ways: as a tool to assist in performing the routine functions of a business office, and as a

Figure 10.1
Microcomputers in use.

Photos (clockwise from top left) courtesy of Hewlitt-Packard; Apple Computer, Inc.; Hewlitt-Packard; Commodore Electronics Ltd; Xerox Corporation; Hewlitt-Packard.

tool to support managerial decision making. The routine office functions in which they are used include accounting, payroll, inventory control, billing, text editing, and filing. For example, with a microcomputer system, the business office of a contractor's supply firm can keep up-to-the-minute records of materials on hand, bills outstanding, and projected deliveries based on jobs in progress. Even your dentist may use a microcomputer for business purposes, such as billing, maintaining patient records, and sending patients reminders when they are due for a checkup. Used with financial modeling and DSS (decision support system) software, microcomputers can be very useful to managers as they plan business strategies. When used in conjunction with a communications link, microcomputers can also give managers access to various commercially available data bases and other specialized information resources that aid in decision making.

MICROCOMPUTER HARDWARE

The microcomputer is the smallest and most portable of computer systems. At the heart of every microcomputer is a *microprocessor,* the microcomputer's CPU. As you may recall from Chapter 2, the microprocessor is a "computer on a chip." Consisting of a single silicon chip the size of a pencil eraser, it contains all the circuitry necessary for carrying out the arithmetic/logic and control functions (see Figure 10.2). It often contains primary storage, or random access memory (RAM), as well. The microcomputer system's peripheral hardware includes equipment for auxiliary storage, input, and output.

The Microprocessor and Other Chips

Microprocessor chips come in two sizes: 8 bits and 16 bits. The number of bits determines how many characters of data the computer can move at a time. The 8-bit chip is rather like a 4-cylinder economy car. The 4-cylinder model is low in cost and useful in meeting the transportation needs of millions of people, but if you need to transport a large family or to pull a boat and trailer up a mountain, it probably won't give you enough horsepower. In that case, you'd no doubt want an 8-cylinder car. Like the 8-cylinder car, the 16-bit microprocessor chip has more power. It can process more data much more quickly than the 8-bit chip; it is generally from four to six times as fast.

The microprocessor chip is mounted on a **main board,** or **mother board,** within the microcomputer. Because the amount of random access memory that may be contained on a microprocessor chip is limited, additional RAM chips are frequently mounted on other boards that are inserted in slots within the microcomputer. These slots can also hold boards containing chips for read-only memory (ROM) and for interfaces to input and output

Figure 10.2
A microprocessor chip.
Courtesy of Motorola Inc.

devices. Such add-on features are very useful in expanding the capabilities of the microcomputer system. Figure 10.3 shows what the interior of a microcomputer looks like.

RAM, as you know, is used as a temporary storage area to hold input data and program instructions, which, of course, vary from program to program. ROM, on the other hand, is used to store systems software and programs that will not have to be changed or altered. For example, if the microcomputer has a built-in word processing program, it would be stored in ROM. Similarly, a built-in language-translation program would also be stored in ROM. Not all microcomputers have such built-in features. The inability to change the contents of ROM limits flexibility, but ROM also frees up space in RAM.

Figure 10.3
A microcomputer's interior.
Courtesy of Apple Computer, Inc.

The function of an **input interface circuit** is to decode the signal created by the depression of a key on the microcomputer's keyboard and route it to the microprocessor unit. As part of its control unit, the microprocessor has a clock that schedules signals so that they don't interrupt and collide with each other. When the arithmetic/logic unit finishes executing the current instruction and is ready for another signal from the keyboard, the control unit activates a routine for accepting the next signal; the waiting signals are stored in a holding area known as a **data bus.** The "bus" is the internal circuit-board path that controls signals and data travel during program execution. Finally, when the program has been executed, an **output interface circuit** coordinates the output signals with the indicated output device (see Figure 10.4). If the output is to be displayed on the microcomputer's CRT screen, the signal has to be continually refreshed to keep the screen image "painted," whereas if a printer is activated, it is necessary to send the signal only once. A single input interface circuit is often part of the microprocessor chip; but because multiple output devices (such as CRT screens, printers, and audio-output devices) are commonly used, the output interface circuits are likely to be contained in chips placed on add-on boards.

The input and output signals are routed through **ports.** Ports are simply outlets in the back of the microcomputer where cables for peripheral devices can be attached (see Figure 10.5). Like the output interface circuits themselves, ports for output are usually part of an add-on board, such as a printer interface board. The routing of input and output signals through the ports can be controlled by both the systems software and the applications programs. For example, when an applications program calls for printed

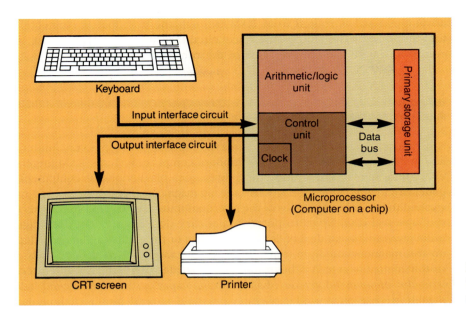

Figure 10.4
The interior workings of a microcomputer.

Figure 10.5

Ports. Located on the back of the microcomputer, these outlets can greatly expand the system's input, storage, and output capabilities.

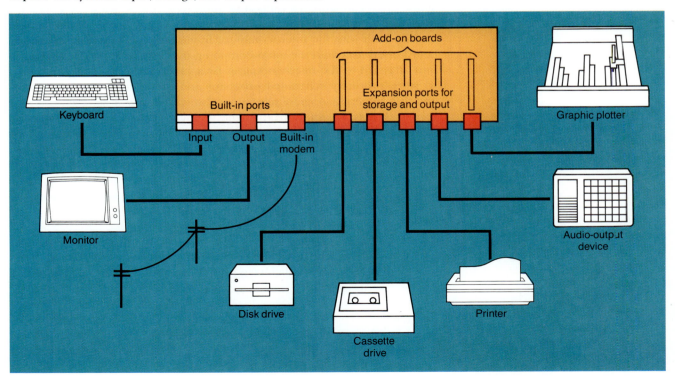

output, a signal is routed from RAM through the port that is connected to the printer. The output interface circuit establishes a signal that is compatible with the requirements of the printer.

Auxiliary Storage Equipment

Any random access memory found on a microprocessor chip is very limited, and in a microcomputer, as in most modern computer systems, RAM forgets everything it ever knew once the power goes off. Peripheral equipment, generally in the form of magnetic-tape or magnetic-disk drives, is used to expand the storage capacities of the microcomputer system. Cables connect the tape and disk drives to ports, just as they do a printer. These storage units provide a great deal of flexibility, as data or programs can be recorded on the magnetic medium, removed, and filed away. When needed, it is a simple matter to retrieve the proper tape cartridge or floppy disk and insert it in the drive. A floppy disk has a storage capacity that can exceed half a million characters, and cassette tapes hold several hundred thousand characters each.

While floppy disks and cassette tapes are adequate for the home computer or for occasional office use, for office applications that require a large amount of data to be available online, hard disks are more appropriate. These disks can store 10 million or more characters. They are contained in sealed drive units from which they cannot be removed. The drive unit may be built into the microcomputer frame or mounted on an expansion board inserted within the microcomputer; the drive may also be a separate unit attached to the microcomputer by a cable. Hard disks are often used to store routinely scheduled programs and the necessary program data, and they generally operate in conjunction with floppy disks. Data from the hard disk may be transferred to the floppy, which can be removed and placed in offline storage. A floppy disk may also be used to enter new programs and purchased software on the hard disk.

Input and Output Equipment

The usual means for getting data and instructions into a microcomputer is a keyboard, and the most common output device is a CRT screen. Many microcomputer systems also have printers as well as additional peripheral equipment designed for specific applications.

Keyboards. The major portion of a microcomputer keyboard looks like a standard typewriter keyboard, with the same key placement and layout; so if you've taken a course in touch typing, you'll find the microcomputer

Figure 10.6
Microcomputer keyboards.
Courtesy of (left) Apple Computer, Inc.; (right) Commodore Electronics Ltd.

keyboard very easy to use. The keyboard usually has additional keys for deleting or correcting data, interrupting a program run, and moving the screen **cursor** right, left, up, or down. (The cursor is a symbol that appears on the CRT screen to show where the next character will appear.) Many microcomputers also have a ten-key pad for quick entry of numerical data. There may be additional keys, called **function keys,** that can be programmed to execute certain routines. Function keys are especially useful in applications in which a number of data collection forms are used. Simply by depressing a single function key, you can call these forms to the CRT screen. The microcomputer's keys may look like those of a typewriter, or they may be **membrane keys** similar to those used on some cash registers. Membrane keys are depicted on a flat plastic surface and have no physical separation between them. Because they don't provide a very good "feel" for touch typing, most people don't find membrane keyboards satisfactory.

Many keyboards are detachable from the microcomputer unit; they maintain their connection through a cord. They can be placed in a convenient location near the equipment and easily moved to suit personal preference. Some keyboards can even send out infrared signals, much as the remote tuner on a television set does; these keyboards have no cable connection to the microcomputer at all. Figure 10.6 shows some of the features of microcomputer keyboards.

Video Display Units. The microcomputer's video display unit, also called a **monitor,** includes a CRT screen. The traditional screen is in black and white tones. For operators who have to look at the screen for hours at a time, monitors come in special tones, such as amber and green, which reduce eyestrain. For displaying graphics, monitors come in full color. Because it is important that a monitor give a clear image, the screen on a standard television set is usually not a good choice for displaying computer outputs. Monitors can be built into the microcomputer, as they are in portable computers and in some desktop units, or they can be acquired as a separate unit. A technology known as "plasma screen technology" is

Figure 10.7
Monitors.
Photos (top left) courtesy of Sperry Corporation; (top right) Hewlitt-Packard; (bottom left and right) Radio Shack, a Division of Tandy Corporation.

used in making the screens for portable, briefcase-style microcomputers. It allows for a flat screen that has none of the protrusion caused by cathode ray tubes. Figure 10.7 shows some of the monitors commonly used with microcomputers. Because the electronic circuits are different for color and for black and white, different interfaces are required for each.

Printers. The printers most often attached to microcomputers are character-at-a-time dot matrix and daisy wheel devices. As we noted in Chapter 7, dot matrix printers often have the ability to produce graphics, and they can change the size and style of the printed letters. Dot matrix printers offer a good-quality output at a low cost and are satisfactory for many applications. However, for letter-quality printing, such as might be required in word processing applications, printers with daisy wheels or thimbles are usually used. In these units, the character set is affixed to a carrier wheel, which rotates until the correct character is in front of the hammer. The hammer strikes one character at a time, creating a well-defined impression on paper.

Other Peripheral Devices. As you know from Chapter 9, in a data communications system that uses voice-oriented channels, a modem is needed for the conversion of digital and analog signals; and this is just as true for

Figure 10.8
Two types of computer mice.
Courtesy of (left) Apple Computer, Inc.; (right) Sperry Corporation.

a microcomputer operating in a data communications system as it is for a mainframe. The modem may be fabricated on a board that can be inserted into the microcomputer, or it may be a separate device.

Another peripheral device, which can be used for input with a microcomputer, is known as a **mouse.** The computer mouse bears little resemblance to an actual member of the species, except that it's small enough to hold in your hand and it has a long cord resembling a tail (see Figure 10.8). By moving the mouse over a flat surface like a desktop or over a special touch pad, you can easily and freely manipulate a cursor over a wide portion of a CRT screen without actually having to touch the screen or keyboard. The mouse is thus a particularly handy device in preparing graphics, since you are not restricted to moving the cursor a line or a position at a time but can instead quickly place it anywhere on the screen that you want it. One type of mouse uses a mechanical ball that rotates as you push the mouse over a flat surface; software then translates this movement into cursor movement. A second, less popular type has an optical grid and is used in conjunction with a touch pad that operates much like a touch-sensitive screen; again, software translates the signals created by the movement of the mouse into movement of the cursor on the screen.

Other peripherals include audio-input and -output devices, which can be used in place of the keyboards and CRT screens traditionally used to enter data and report processing results. The vocabulary of the audio-input units is quite limited, usually not over a few hundred words. The audio synthesizer used for output is quite remarkable: It can play music as well as synthesize speech.

Light pens, which generate a light signal that can be picked up on a screen and entered as input, are useful in computer-aided design and graphics applications in which the microcomputer's CRT screen is used as the working area. Touch-sensitive screens on a microcomputer's video display unit allow you to enter data merely by touching the screen. These screens can be very useful, especially for graphics applications and for handicapped persons who can't use a keyboard. The conquering of *computerphobia,* or the fear of computers and their keyboards, is another reason for using touch-sensitive screens. Monitoring devices such as

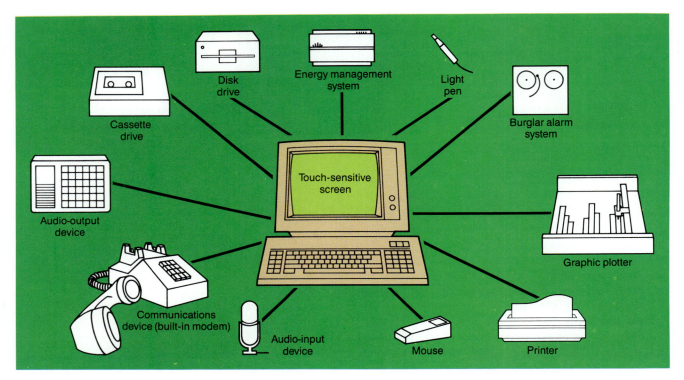

Figure 10.9
Peripheral devices for microcomputers.

temperature-sensitive thermostats and motion-sensitive burglar alarms can also be connected to the microcomputer.

All peripheral devices require a special interface board and connection. Figure 10.9 indicates the variety of peripherals that can be used with a microcomputer system.

MICROCOMPUTER SOFTWARE

Like software for any kind of computer system, software for microcomputers consists of both systems software and applications software. Systems software directs the internal workings of the computer and allows it to run the applications programs that the computer needs to perform specific tasks.

Systems Software

As we noted earlier, systems software for microcomputers may be permanently stored on ROM chips as firmware; it may, however, also be loaded

Table 10.1 Some Microcomputer Utility Programs

Utility Program	Function
DIRECTORY	Displays a listing of the files available on a disk.
FORMAT	Places addresses on the tracks and sectors of a blank disk so it can accept files.
COPY	Duplicates the contents of one disk, writing them on another disk.
HELP[1]	Provides help in using software or functions of the system.

[1] Usually associated with a particular software product.

into RAM from a floppy or a hard disk. Systems software for microcomputers includes language-translation programs; operating systems, which allocate the hardware resources; and **utility programs,** which perform certain routine, or housekeeping, tasks. Utility programs can be very helpful to the user of a microcomputer system. Table 10.1 describes some utility programs commonly used with microcomputers. Most such programs are supplied by the computer manufacturer.

Operating systems, like most systems software, are designed for specific computer hardware. Table 10.2 lists several of the more popular operating systems supplied by commercial vendors, the microprocessor chips for which they are designed, and the hardware with which they are compatible.

Table 10.2 Popular Microcomputer Operating Systems

Operating System and Supplier	Microprocessor Chip	Chip Bit Designation	Compatible Hardware
CP/M[1] (Digital Research, Inc.)	Zilog Z-80	8	North Star PC, Xerox 820, Radio Shack TRS-80 III
MS-DOS[2] (Microsoft, Inc.)	Intel 8088 and 8086	16	IBM-PC, DEC-Rainbow, Wang PC
UNIX (AT&T, Inc.)	Motorola MC68000	16	AT&T PC, Cromenco PC
Vendor-supplied systems (provided by Apple, Commodore, etc.)	MOS Technology 6502	8	ATARI, Apple II, Commodore, etc.

[1] CP/M is an acronym for Control Program for Microcomputers.
[2] DOS is an acronym for Disk Operating System.

Applications Software

Applications software for microcomputers includes programs for word processing, data base, graphics, and electronic spreadsheets. These programs are available from both hardware vendors and independent software suppliers. Another kind of commercially available applications software is called an integrated software package. It allows the different types of applications programs to work together. All these programs have been very successfully used in business applications, contributing to better business decisions and better performance.

Word Processing. Word processing software is designed to format and edit text. It is used mainly to prepare reports and to write letters and memos. In both cases, text is keyed into the microcomputer, a draft copy is prepared, and necessary editing changes are made after the draft is reviewed. As you may recall from our discussion of text editing in Chapter 7, the text that does not require change is stored in the computer's memory, and it will be correctly reproduced as output together with any changes that have been made in the course of editing. Table 10.3 lists a few of the more popular word processing software packages available today.

Most word processing software includes routines for inserting and deleting text, blocking text for movement to another position, formatting the screen with margin and tab controls, numbering the pages and laying them out with headings, and searching out and replacing characters and words. Other desirable features to be considered when selecting word processing software are routines for word wrap, hyphenation, and spelling verification.

Word wrap is used to reformat the text after insertions or deletions have been processed. Reformatting keeps the paragraph where changes have been made neatly composed, with no voids where words have been

Table 10.3   Some Word Processing Software Packages

Word Processing Package	Cost[1]	User Level
Einstein Writer	Moderate	Beginner
Peachtext 5000	High	Intermediate
Perfect Writer	High	Advanced
PFS:Write	Low	Beginner
SuperWriter	Moderate	Intermediate
WordPerfect	High	Advanced
WordStar	High	Advanced

[1] Low cost = under $150; moderate cost = $150–$300; high cost = over $300.

removed or squeezed lines where words have been added. With most word processing software, word wrap is done automatically.

The hyphenation routine uses an electronic dictionary to search out the correct place to break a word that will not fit completely on a line of text. When text is reformatted because of editing, the hyphenation routine is responsible for closing up a word that was previously hyphenated because of its end-of-line position.

The routine for spelling verification uses an electronic dictionary to check spelling. These dictionaries contain 50,000 words or more. All spelling verification routines point out words that do not match up with those in the dictionary, and the more sophisticated routines display possible corrections after a misspelled word has been singled out. Spelling verification routines can also be custom-designed to include special terms such as those used in the fields of law and medicine.

Data Base. **Data base software** is probably most often used in conjunction with lists of customers or prospective customers. A pool of data consisting of names and addresses, with keys to identify attributes of each name, can be accessed and processed in a number of ways. For example, if you want to send a newsletter to all your active customers, you can search the data base for the names of customers who have made a purchase in the last year and then print a mailing label for each of them. And if you want to send a special promotion to customers who have not made a purchase within the last year, you can search the data and identify this group (see Figure 10.10).

If your software allows you to link the data base with word processing, you can write form letters in a personalized way. Suppose you've decided to run for public office and want to ask your business customers to support you. Some of your customers are in your sales territory and know you personally, and some are in other sales districts and only know of you

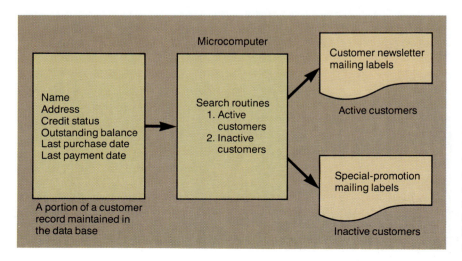

Figure 10.10

Using microcomputer data base software. The data base provides a pool of customer records that can be searched and sorted by last purchase date to generate mailing labels for a newsletter for active customers and mailing labels for a special promotion for inactive customers.

because you also functon as sales manager. Using your microcomputer software, you can send a personalized letter to those customers who know you personally and a more general letter to those who don't. If the file has the date of your last sales call, it would be easy to include a sentence in the personalized letter reminding customers of the last time you called on them. Among the most popular data base packages are dBase II, dBase III, and PFS:File.

Graphics. There are probably few things less interesting than column after column and page after page of numbers or long-winded business reports whose point could be made more effectively with one simple picture. Microcomputer **graphics software** can create just such a picture with bar graphs, pie charts, and line charts that convert numerical data to pictorial form. Used to show relationships, volumes, and proportions, graphics can have a meaningful place in almost any business report. With specialized software, an entire report can be prepared by passing data from other analytical programs through a graphics program into a word processing program. Figure 10.11 shows some of the variety of business and nonbusiness outputs that graphics software can produce.

Figure 10.11
Outputs of microcomputer graphics software.
Photos (clockwise from left) courtesy of Commodore Electronics Ltd; Apple Computer, Inc.; Apple Computer, Inc.; Texas Instruments.

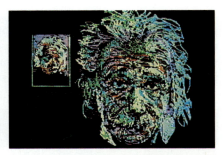

Electronic Spreadsheets. One of the most exciting applications of microcomputers is the use of **electronic spreadsheets** in financial analysis. VisiCalc, the first of the electronic spreadsheets, was introduced by VisiCorp, Inc., in 1979, and it helped to sell thousands of Apple computers. Other well-known spreadsheets include Perfect Calc, a versatile product of Perfect Software, Inc.; MultiPlan, a powerful, modestly priced product of Microsoft, Inc.; and Context MBA, a popular but expensive product of Context Management Systems. The purpose of this kind of software is to show the financial impact of decisions. The spreadsheet starts out with a foundation of financial data, usually relating to income. As decisions are tested, the program calls for computation, and the projected income is adjusted to reflect the changes brought about by the decisions (see Figure 10.12).

Preparing an electronic spreadsheet involves five steps:

1. Formulate the concept: a home budget worksheet for comparing actual expenses with planned expenses

2. Identify available data: expenditures for housing, food, utilities, gasoline, luxuries, miscellaneous, and savings.

3. Identify the data to be processed and develop worksheet headings:
   Home Budget Worksheet
   Item   Budgeted   Actual   Over/Under   % Over/Under   % Total

4. Determine the computations and formulas required: calculations for comparing actual expenses with budgeted expenses and arriving at percentages based on the budgeted amount and the actual total amount.

5. Enter the data and make the calculations. The results are reported on the worksheet:

Home Budget Worksheet

Item	Budgeted	Actual	Over/Under	% Over/Under	% Total
Housing	$700	$830	$130	18.6	39.5
Food	300	250	(50)	−16.7	11.9
Utilities	150	170	20	13.3	8.1
Gasoline	130	140	10	7.7	6.7
Luxuries	100	27	(73)	−73.0	1.3
Miscellaneous	500	600	100	20.0	28.6
Savings	220	83	(137)	−62.3	3.9
Total	$2,100	$2,100			100.0

Figure 10.12

Using an electronic spreadsheet to prepare a home budget.

Figure 10.12 shows how you might use an electronic spreadsheet to prepare a home budget; let's consider also how an electronic spreadsheet might be used in business. Suppose you own a motel and charge $50 per night for a room. Your current occupancy rate is 70 percent, and your net income is $55,000 a year. You must make a decision about advertising expenditures for the coming year; you estimate that if you spend $20,000 for radio advertising spots and billboard signs, you will increase your occupancy rate to 75 percent. Should you do it? The spreadsheet analysis will calculate the increased revenues and the added expenses associated with increased maintenance and cleanup costs and will show the impact on your income. Your next question might be, What will happen to my income if I raise the room charge to $60, spend the money on advertising, and anticipate an occupancy rate of 70 percent? And on and on the questions can go, as you try new combinations and test their impact.

Spreadsheets take the drudgery out of testing ideas and calculating the results. In the past, these calculations were done by hand, and it was usually too cumbersome to try more than a few combinations. With this new tool, many combinations can be tested, and the financial impact of various decisions can be evaluated.

Integrated Software. With the growing popularity of various kinds of microcomputer software, such as graphics software, a feature that is becoming increasingly important is the ability to integrate word processing text with nontextual outputs. **Integrated software** allows you to do just that. It combines a number of the standard microcomputer applications — word processing, graphics, spreadsheets, and data communications — and lets you easily merge data from separate programs. Thus, work performed in one application can be passed to another; the different software products work together. Without having to reenter or rekey data several times, you can produce a report that combines financial analysis, graphics, and word processing.

Suppose, for example, that you've spent several hours using your microcomputer and accounting software to evaluate the financial impact of the introduction of a new product. You now want to prepare a report for the president of your firm. If you were using an integrated software package, you could move your analytical data from the accounting program to the text in the word processing program, thus preventing errors that might occur if the data had to be rekeyed and saving time as well.

One of the first, and still very popular, integrated software packages is Lotus 1-2-3, a product of Lotus Development Corporation. Combining spreadsheet, graphics, and data base programs with some word processing capabilities, it has been very successful as a planning and reporting tool for the busy business manager. Symphony, a more powerful Lotus product, adds data communications software and more word processing capability. Framework, produced by Ashton-Tate, is another popular integrated software package; it is simple to use and combines words, numbers, and graphs to generate finished documents quickly and easily.

THE MAN WHO KEEPS THE BLOOM ON LOTUS

Mitch Kapor, 34, software industry tycoon and founder of Lotus Development Corp., has been much happier since he promoted Jim Manzi, 33, to president and kicked himself upstairs. Kapor, who occasionally wears tennis shoes and Hawaiian shirts to the office, gets to spend more time blue-skying new software programs. Manzi, president since last October, minds the store — a burgeoning business that last year tripled to $157 million in sales. With not an MBA between them, the two are sufficiently self-assured to joke about their unconventional credentials. Says Manzi: "We add up to one competent 67-year-old manager."...

To get Lotus where it is, Kapor has relied on a style that combines showmanship, technical virtuosity, marketing discipline, and flower-child values. "One of the perks of being the founder," he says, "is that you get to build the company in your image." Kapor is a Sixties child who, before emerging as an Eighties entrepreneur, studied psychology and what he refers to as "Eastern spiritual practices," worked as a disk jockey and stand-up comic, and taught transcendental meditation. With Lotus he has achieved a union of opposites, finding a way to make plenty of money and be revered as a guru at the same time....

Lotus owes its enormous profits to Lotus 1-2-3, coauthored by Kapor and the biggest software hit ever. Introduced in 1982 as a multipurpose program for IBM's Personal Computer, 1-2-3 turns the machine into an electronic spreadsheet for financial analysis, and lets users make graphs and file data without stopping to summon up separate programs dedicated to those tasks. Lotus has sold more than 850,000 copies of 1-2-3, which retails for $495. As a result, Lotus has become, at age three, the largest independent software company, outdistancing both Microsoft Corp., which sells the basic operating software for IBM PCs, and Cullinet Software, the largest independent supplier of programs for IBM mainframes.

The problem Kapor faces is that no one has ever built a software house into a major corporation. According to the market research firm InfoCorp, retail sales of personal computer software hit $2.9 billion last year, but 15 companies have divided two-thirds of this fierce, expanding business into fiefdoms. Every time personal computer makers launch a new generation of machines — the industry has seen four in its eight-year history — a few software leaders topple, giving way to newcomers....

Lotus is as paradoxical as its founder: fleecy inside, yet one of the roughest players in the business. The company lavishes attention on its employees — high salaries, comprehensive benefits, unusually large stock option and stock purchase plans, and quarterly outings.... Kapor's lollipop approach seems to work: productivity at Lotus, about $300,000 in annual sales per worker, puts it ahead of other major software houses and in the same league with the oil companies that rank at the top of the FORTUNE 500 productivity lists.

The marketplace sees a rougher side of Lotus. Struggling hardware and software companies that request endorsements or financial support generally get turned away. Nor is Lotus shy about disciplining unscrupulous dealers and customers. Early last year it stunned the industry by dragging a subsidiary of Schlumberger, the oil services firm, into court for software piracy. Lotus has also made dramatic efforts to choke off the flow of its products to the so-called gray market: unauthorized dealers and mail-order houses that offer 1-2-3 for as much as $215 off the retail price. It terminated two of its five distributors and is the first software house to install bar-coding equipment to help trace how gray marketers get the merchandise.

Kapor doesn't try to explain Lotus in business school terms. Instead he invokes the Zen of management. "Stand or sit, but don't wobble," he says, citing what he insists is a Zen maxim. "You have to separate things into two piles, loose and tight. More than two is confusing. Then you must make sure that you put each part of the business into the right pile."

In fact, loose and tight tell a great deal about Lotus. Employee compensation is loose, pricing and distribution tight. Development of new product lines, loose; extension of existing products, tight. Communication, loose; concern about the Lotus image, tight. The same dichotomy applies to Kapor (loose) and Manzi (tight).

◆

— Excerpted from Peter Petre, "The Man Who Keeps the Bloom on Lotus," *Fortune* (June 10, 1985), pp. 136–146.

An alternative to using integrated applications software is to use integrated systems software. With this software, you can select any combination of commercial applications programs and run them together. Vision, a product of VisiCorp, has been a forerunner in this area. The developers of these integrated systems packages claim that since the integrated operating systems allow the user to select the most appropriate applications programs, they in effect give the user customized software in a commercial package.

MERGING MICROS AND MAINFRAMES: BRIDGING THE GAP

Many of the numerous microcomputers purchased in recent years are used by managers in firms that have larger and more powerful mainframe computers. The microcomputer often gives faster and more consistent response than the mainframe system because it is entirely in the control of the user. It is also much less expensive, usually costing little more than a high-quality mainframe terminal. For the most part, microcomputer users in these environments have operated independently of the larger systems, collecting their own data, developing their own programs or using purchased software, and generally operating outside the firm's data processing department.

For the first-time computer user, the experience of being in complete control of a wide range of computing power, coupled with the excitement of a technology previously reserved for only a select few in the data processing department, has been exhilarating. One of the interesting side effects of the introduction of microcomputers into the business community has been the infatuation of executives with the machine: A $55,000-per-year accounting supervisor may spend a large part of every day acting like a $25,000-per-year programmer! Of course, the supervisor could also take on the computer-related assignments of a $15,000-per-year secretary and spend time preparing memos, reports, and documents; but since this kind of work is generally less exciting, it does not pose as large a time-management problem.

Data processing managers see the proliferation of microcomputers as a mixed blessing. Because the user becomes more involved, both in controlling the data and in developing and using the software, data processing responsibility is distributed to the department in which the information requirements and processing problems are best understood. Once the initial infatuation is over, however, dissatisfaction with the coordination and interface of the microcomputer and the mainframe system often surfaces. Why should a manager or secretary have to obtain a listing of last month's sales data from the mainframe and rekey it into the microcomputer? Why not just connect the microcomputer to the mainframe and let it "talk" to the data base, extracting whatever data are needed for the sales analysis? When such an interface is possible, the microcomputer, with its spreadsheet tools and capabilities for financial analysis, can relieve the mainframe of most of the processing related to analysis and planning. The merging of mainframes and micros can have other advantages as well: Not only does it give the microcomputer user access to data already collected and stored in the mainframe system; it also allows interaction with the mainframe's programs and other microcomputers linked to the system.

However, the interfacing, or merging, of micros and a mainframe within a company can present a difficult technical challenge. Despite the advantages of merging, there is very often little compatibility between the hardware found in various departments: Machines of different makes, with different operating systems, different formats for data, and different keyboards turn up throughout the firm. Even when the micro and mainframe have been produced by the same manufacturer, incompatibilities may still exist. A micro is designed to operate as an interactive, stand-alone unit, whereas a mainframe is designed to process large volumes of sequential data, with some interactive capabilities.

Software has been developed to help bridge the gap between micros and mainframe, but it often compromises some of the processing power of the micro, turning it into something resembling a smart terminal. Software/hardware combinations offer more promise, providing the best of both the micro and the mainframe worlds. In these combinations, a circuit board containing built-in logic is inserted into the microcomputer, which allows it to operate in the same mode as the mainframe.

None of the software/hardware combinations is entirely satisfactory from a technical perspective, and any microcomputer interface with the mainframe causes data processing management new concerns. In the controlled environment of mainframe processing, it's a fairly easy matter to establish and maintain standards for the development of systems and programs; when microcomputer users develop their own programs for unique applications, it can be an altogether different matter. These users generally have all their energies concentrated on solving a problem and have little concern for procedures or standards. When they run into a snag and call for support, the data processing manager often finds it difficult, if not impossible, to help them modify their programs or data. Data processing managers are finding that when users develop their own microcomputer programs, it is nearly impossible to impose standards of any kind. The result can be a somewhat chaotic situation characterized by strained relations between users and technical staff.

Passing data from the mainframe to the microcomputer is another area of concern. Corporate data are generally maintained in a mainframe data base, and most microcomputers don't have the power, structure, or tools necessary to access this data base. Files must therefore be restructured before they can be passed from the mainframe to the micro, a difficult task but an important and necessary one if the application is to be successful. Another consideration in passing data from the mainframe to the micro is the matter of unauthorized access to data, but passing data from the micro to the data base is even more worrisome in terms of security and control. It is difficult to prevent data manipulation and the entry of untrue data into the system when microcomputers are scattered throughout the organization and almost anyone can have access to them at any time.

Table 10.4 Organizational Issues Raised by Microcomputers

Issue	Consequences
Loss of central control	Systems and programs may be developed without regard for standards or overall organizational objectives. Purchasing of equipment by different departments may result in incompatibility between systems.
Incompatibility	Most microcomputers are designed to operate as stand-alone devices. Serious technical problems can therefore arise when a microcomputer attempts to use programs from different systems, to share data with other systems, or to operate within a data communications system.
Threats to security	Problems of unauthorized access to data, data manipulation, and insecurity of data files are far greater with small, desktop systems than with traditional mainframe systems.
Problems in the operating environment	Power supplies, static electricity, and ventilation to disperse heat and humidity are some of the operating environment concerns that must be addressed when installing a microcomputer in an office setting.

Table 10.4 summarizes some of the issues that the presence of microcomputers within an organization can raise. To overcome these problems and to make the mainframe/micro system work, the roles of the user and the data processing department must be clearly identified, and definite standards and procedures must be established and observed. This is obviously a bit more difficult than it sounds, but if put into practice, the rewards can be great. By taking advantage of the wide range of software available for the microcomputer, a business can spread much of the data processing load throughout the firm, providing better service to everyone in the organization. The successful merging of micros and a mainframe can give managers easy access to data when they need it, allowing them to base their decisions on accurate and up-to-date information. The implementation of mainframe/micro systems, while presenting a great challenge, offers great promise to the business world.

SELECTION CRITERIA

Buying a microcomputer should be no more difficult than buying a car — except that there are approximately two hundred brands of microcomputers to choose from as opposed to twenty-odd makes of automobiles. What you will quickly find when you begin to search for a microcomputer, however, is that you keep bumping into the same few systems wherever you shop. Most of the two hundred brands of micros on the market today are designed for the business user or the more sophisticated personal computer user, and although available to the novice, they are not widely promoted. If you are buying a computer for the first time, you would probably be wise to buy one designed for the mass market and produced by a vendor with a sound business reputation.

The first and most important thing to consider when buying a microcomputer is what your data processing needs are. These needs will control your software requirements, which are crucial to the successful selection of a computer system. Don't worry about trying to define your needs in computer terms; that's the job of the computer salesperson. Ask yourself how you will use your computer. Will you use it to manage your household budget; to monitor energy use and security in your home; to store addresses, tax documents, or kitchen recipes; to write letters or, perhaps, the Great American Novel? Hundreds of off-the-shelf programs for a wide range of computers are available to meet all these needs, as well as many others that you might define. Your requirements are the most important component of the hardware decision; so give your needs assessment a great deal of thought. To get an idea of the range of possibilities, you might even ask other owners of personal computers how they use their systems.

The second step is to identify the software available to meet your needs. For this step, you need a knowledgeable computer salesperson who can explain the operational features and advantages of individual packages. It is also worthwhile to ask others who have purchased software packages how easy these packages are to learn and use and whether they perform as stated in the promotional literature. You'll be surprised at the number of packages that look great during a demonstration but turn out to be very difficult to use when you apply your own data and inexperience to them. For the first-time user, ease of use is perhaps the most important criterion in choosing any software product. Table 10.5 lists some criteria that would be useful in selecting software for word processing.

The next step is the selection of the hardware itself. You should look

Table 10.5 Criteria for Selecting Word Processing Software

Software Features	User Features	Value
Document creation	Availability of a tutorial	Price as measured
Editing	Ease of startup	against performance
Formatting	Ease of learning; quality	based on software
Error-handling	of documentation	and user features
Printing	and reference	
Integration with other software	materials	
	Ease of use	
	Program versatility	

MAN, BYTES, DOG

By James Gorman

Many people have asked me about the Cairn Terrier. How about memory, they want to know. Is it I.B.M.-compatible? Why didn't I get the I.B.M. itself, or a Kaypro, Compaq, or Macintosh? I think the best way to answer these questions is to look at the Macintosh and the Cairn head on. I almost did buy the Macintosh. It has terrific graphics, good word-processing capabilities, and the mouse. But in the end I decided on the Cairn, and I think I made the right decision.

Let's start out with the basics:

MACINTOSH:
  Weight (without printer): 20 lbs.
  Memory (RAM): 128 K
  Price (with printer): $3,090

CAIRN TERRIER:
  Weight (without printer): 14 lbs.
  Memory (RAM): Some
  Price (without printer): $250

Just on the basis of price and weight, the choice is obvious. Another plus is that the Cairn Terrier comes in one unit. No printer is necessary, or useful. And — this was a big attraction to me — there is no user's manual.

Here are some of the other qualities I found put the Cairn out ahead of the Macintosh:

Portability: To give you a better idea of size, Toto in "The Wizard of Oz" was a Cairn Terrier. So you can see that if the young Judy Garland was able to carry Toto around in that little picnic basket, you will have no trouble at all moving your Cairn from place to place. For short trips it will move under its own power. The Macintosh will not.

Reliability: In five to ten years, I am sure, the Macintosh will be superseded by a new model, like the Delicious or the Granny Smith. The Cairn Terrier, on the other hand, has held its share of the market with only minor modifications for hundreds of years. In the short term, Cairns seldom need servicing, apart from shots and the odd worming, and most function without interruption during electrical storms.

Compatibility: Cairn Terriers get along with everyone. And for communications with any other dog, of any breed, within a radius of three miles, no additional hardware is necessary. All dogs share a common operating system.

Software: The Cairn will run three standard programs, SIT, COME, and NO, and whatever else you create. It is true that, being microcanine, the Cairn is limited here, but it does load the programs instantaneously. No disk drives. No tapes.

Admittedly, these are peripheral advantages. The real comparison has to be on the basis of capabilities. What can the Macintosh and the Cairn do? Let's start on the Macintosh's turf — income-tax preparation, recipe storage, graphics, and astrophysics problems:

	Taxes	Recipes
Macintosh	yes	yes
Cairn	no	no

	Graphics	Astrophysics
Macintosh	yes	yes
Cairn	no	no

At first glance it looks bad for the Cairn. But it's important to look beneath the surface with this kind of chart. If you yourself are leaning toward the Macintosh, ask yourself these questions: Do you want to do your own income taxes? Do you want to type all your recipes into a computer? In your graph, what would you put on the x axis? The y axis? Do you have any astrophysics problems you want solved?

Then consider the Cairn's specialties: playing fetch and tug-of-war, licking your face, and chasing foxes out of rock cairns (eponymously). Note that no software is necessary. All these functions are part of the operating system:

	Fetch	Tug-of-War
Cairn	yes	yes
Macintosh	no	no

	Face	Foxes
Cairn	yes	yes
Macintosh	no	no

Another point to keep in mind is that computers, even the Macintosh, only do what you tell them to do.

Cairns perform their functions all on their own. Here are some of the additional capabilities that I discovered once I got the Cairn home and housebroken:

Word Processing: Remarkably, the Cairn seems to understand every word I say. He has a nice way of pricking up his ears at words like "out" or "ball." He also has highly tuned voice-recognition.

Education: The Cairn provides children with hands-on experience at an early age, contributing to social interaction, crawling ability, and language skills. At age one, my daughter could say "Sit," "Come," and "No."

Cleaning: This function was a pleasant surprise. But of course cleaning up around the cave is one of the reasons dogs were developed in the first place. Users with young (below age two) children will still find this function useful. The Cairn Terrier cleans the floor, spoons, bib, and baby, and has an unerring ability to distinguish strained peas from ears, nose, and fingers.

Psychotherapy: Here the Cairn really shines. And remember, therapy is something that computers have tried. There is a program that makes the computer ask you questions when you tell it your problems. You say, "I'm afraid of foxes." The computer says, "You're afraid of foxes?"

The Cairn won't give you that kind of echo. Like Freudian analysts, Cairns are mercifully silent; unlike Freudians, they are infinitely sympathetic. I've found that the Cairn will share, in a nonjudgmental fashion, disappointments, joys, and frustrations. And you don't have to know BASIC.

This last capability is related to the Cairn's strongest point, which was the final deciding factor in my decision against the Macintosh — user-friendliness. On this criterion, there is simply no comparison. The Cairn Terrier is the essence of user-friendliness. It has fur, it doesn't flicker when you look at it, and it wags its tail.

— © 1984 James Gorman. Originally in *The New Yorker* (July 2, 1984, p. 33).

---

for a system that will run your software at the least cost, not a system that is "state of the art" but doesn't quite do all the things you need. Old technology is not bad if it will meet your needs; in fact, it may even be good in the sense that it is a proven technology.

Once you've selected a system, it is time for the "test drive," which is just as important in buying a computer as in buying a car. Never purchase a computer before trying it out with the software that you've selected and some of your own data. A salesperson telling you it will work is not a guarantee that it will work as you want it to. Once you've paid for the system, you are on your own; so get answers before you write your check. The salesperson is likely to be much more eager to assist you before the sales commission is earned than after the sale is completed.

Maintenance should be a concern, especially if the computer is not one of the popular brands. Do you have to box the computer and ship it to some far-off corner of the country when it malfunctions, or can you drop it off for repairs while on your way to a football game? If your applications are important and time-sensitive, reliable and convenient maintenance should be an important consideration in your hardware decision.

Also, as you find more uses for the computer, you may want to expand the system. Expansion possibilities in some systems are quite limited, and a bargain price is not such a bargain if the system cannot be expanded to meet new needs. If possible, get the names of several people who have purchased systems similar to the one you are looking at and talk to them. You may find them to be the best source of information, especially if they are willing to tell you about their problems with their systems as well as their successes. A personal computer is a wonderful tool if selected with care and thought, but a source of frustration if purchased on impulse with no particular goal in mind.

SUMMARY

Microcomputers are so powerful and easy to use that they are being used just about everywhere — in schools, homes, and businesses, to name but a few locales. Businesses use microcomputers in two general ways: as a tool to assist in performing routine office functions, and as a tool to support managerial decision making.

The microcomputer's CPU consists of a microprocessor chip. Additional RAM chips, ROM chips, and interfaces to input and output devices can be mounted on boards that are inserted in slots within the microcomputer. These add-on features can greatly expand the capability of a microcomputer system. Other pieces of hardware found in microcomputer systems include disk drives and tape drives for auxiliary storage, keyboards for input, and CRT screens for output. Many microcomputers also have printers, modems, audio-input and -output devices, and light pens or touch-sensitive screens for entering data. Another peripheral device for microcomputers is the mouse, which is particularly useful in preparing graphics.

A microcomputer, like any other computer, requires both systems software and applications software. Today's most popular applications software for microcomputers consists of word processing programs, used to format and edit text; data base software, used to manage large files of data; graphics software, used to prepare charts and graphs; electronic spreadsheets, used for financial analysis; and integrated software, which combines a number of the other applications programs and lets them work together. Each of these types of software packages has proven quite useful, both with personal computers and with micros used in a business setting. Integrated systems software offers an alternative to the integrated applications software packages. In the former, integrated operating systems allow various combinations of applications programs to be run together.

Merging microcomputers and mainframes can be very advantageous, but it is very often problem-ridden. Incompatibility of hardware and lack of concern for standards in software development have frustrated microcomputer users who would like an easy-to-use link to a mainframe. Software is being developed to bridge the gap, but, to date, it has not been completely satisfactory.

Important concerns in selecting a microcomputer system are the buyer's data processing needs, the software available to meet those needs, ease of maintenance, and expansion possibilities.

KEY TERMS

cursor (283)
data base software (289)
data bus (280)
electronic spreadsheets (291)
function keys (283)
graphics software (290)
input interface circuit (280)
integrated software (292)
main board (mother board) (278)
membrane keys (283)
monitor (283)
mouse (285)
output interface circuit (280)
personal computer (276)
ports (280)
software package (276)
utility programs (287)
word processing software (288)

DISCUSSION QUESTIONS

1. Why have microcomputers become popular both as personal computers and as business tools? Describe two general ways in which they are used in business.

2. Identify the main hardware components of a microcomputer system and describe their functions.

3. How does ROM differ from RAM? How is each used in a microcomputer? What is the purpose of the expansion slots found within a microcomputer?

4. Discuss the functions of the microcomputer's input and output interface circuits and its ports.

5. Describe the main forms of auxiliary storage, input, and output in a microcomputer, and identify three less common peripheral devices.

6. What is word processing? Describe some features often found in word processing software.

7. What is an electronic spreadsheet? How does it work, and why is it such a popular business tool?

8. What is integrated software? What are its advantages?

9. Discuss some of the problems associated with merging micros and large computer systems. Why would this merging seem desirable?

10. Develop a plan for purchasing a microcomputer. Describe the objectives of your plan.

PART·III

Chapter 11 PROGRAM DEVELOPMENT: FIRST STEPS
Chapter 12 PROGRAM DEVELOPMENT: THE LANGUAGE CONNECTION
Chapter 13 SYSTEMS SOFTWARE
Chapter 14 THE STATE OF SOFTWARE TODAY

SOFTWARE

The Analytical Engine has no pretensions whatever to originate anything. It can do whatever we know how to order it to perform. It can follow analysis; but it has no power of anticipating any analytical relations or truths. Its province is to assist us in making available what we are already acquainted with.

Despite all the technological development of computers that has taken place since Ada, Countess of Lovelace, wrote those words, they are as accurately descriptive of computers today as they were of the nineteenth-century Analytical Engine: The computer can still do only what it is programmed to do. The fact that today's computers can do so much does not reflect a newfound intelligence on the part of computers; it is, instead, a tribute to human ingenuity — not only to the ingenuity of the people responsible for the technological advances in computer hardware, but also to the ingenuity of those individuals who created the successively more sophisticated generations of programming languages. These languages have made communicating with computers today a relatively simple matter.

In Chapter 11, we'll look at the first two steps involved in developing a program for the computer: the analysis of the problem and the design of its solution. In Chapter 12, we'll explore how the programmer goes about translating the steps laid out in the design solution into a programming language; we'll also explore how the programmer debugs, tests, and documents the program. In Chapter 13, we'll examine the role of systems software. Finally, in Chapter 14, we'll look into some important issues pertaining to the state of software today, among them programming productivity and artificial intelligence.

OUTLINE

PROGRAM DEVELOPMENT IN PERSPECTIVE

ANALYZING THE PROBLEM

DESIGNING A SOLUTION

BASIC LOGIC PATTERNS AND THE CONCEPT OF STRUCTURED PROGRAMMING AND DESIGN

PROGRAM FLOWCHARTS AND DECISION TABLES AS DESIGN TOOLS

   Program Flowcharts
- Symbols for Program Flowcharts
- A Flowcharting Example
- Advantages and Disadvantages of Program Flowcharts

   Decision Tables

STRUCTURED DESIGN TOOLS AND PROGRAMMING METHODS

   Pseudocode
   Top-Down Design
   HIPO Charts
   Modular Programming

SUMMARY

KEY TERMS

DISCUSSION QUESTIONS

OVERVIEW

Programming is only one step in the overall development of a computer information system. But it's an exciting step, a chance to solve a puzzle. It's a time when people can apply their creative talents to the notion of getting a machine with an IQ of zero to do what they want it to do. However, too much creativity, like too much of anything, can produce some negative results — in this case, a clever and artistically pleasing but otherwise useless program. In one notable case of extravagant creativity, a programmer spent a day and a half of company time developing a program that would enable the computer to produce payroll checks with the amount written in script rather than printed as numbers. The outcome? The program worked; the programmer did not.

To prevent such unproductive use of programming time, programmers and systems analysts have developed a methodical way of going about their business. The first two steps in this approach — analyzing the problem and designing the solution — are the focus of this chapter; we'll discuss the rest of the program development steps in Chapter 12. In this chapter, we'll also look at the basic logic patterns that can be used to solve any problem and at some of the design tools and methods that programmers use to improve their productivity.

Our objectives in this chapter are to

- give an overview of program development.

- describe how systems analysts and programmers go about analyzing a problem.

- define an algorithm and explain its usefulness.

- discuss the four basic logic patterns used in problem solving.

- explain how flowcharts and decision tables aid in program design.

- identify some of the structured design tools and programming methods used to improve programming productivity.

CHAPTER 11

PROGRAM DEVELOPMENT: FIRST STEPS

PROGRAM DEVELOPMENT IN PERSPECTIVE

In Chapter 3, we talked about the **systems development cycle** — that is, the series of steps involved in developing a computer information system. You may recall from Chapter 3 that program development is the next-to-last step in that cycle. To get some perspective on what goes into the actual preparation of a program, let's just briefly review the steps of the systems development cycle:

1. *Identifying the Need.* In this initial phase, the problem that gave rise to the request for a systems study is spelled out. A feasibility study documents the nature of the problem, the resources available to solve it, and the value to the firm of doing so. If it turns out that the problem can be solved without developing a computer information system, or if there are insufficient resources available to develop such a system, management will no doubt abandon or at least delay the project. If the feasibility study leads management to decide otherwise, the project goes on to phase 2.

2. *Analyzing the System.* A study team composed of users, programmers, systems analysts, and other personnel develops a plan of the new system's requirements. To do this, the team reviews any available documentation on the existing system (if there is one) and gathers data through observations, interviews, questionnaires, and research. The objective of this step is to provide a blueprint of the way information needs are currently being met. This blueprint will be used as a basis for the design work that will take place in phase 3.

3. *Developing Design Alternatives.* The question to be decided during this phase is what kind of system will best meet the requirements that were identified in phase 2. A systems analyst draws up specifications for alternative designs, and the study team reviews the advantages and disadvantages of each alternative from both a technician's and a user's perspective. Once a design is selected, it will control the rest of the development activities.

4. *Developing the System.* Not until all these steps have been taken can program development profitably begin. Program development starts with an analysis of the problem and the design of a logical solution. The actual programming effort involves converting specifications to a code that the computer can understand and debugging and testing the resulting program. Program development also involves continuing documentation of the program. The coding and testing can take the better part of a year, especially if there are **interfaces** — communications or sharing of data and outputs — with other systems.

5. *Implementing and Maintaining the System.* The system is now installed. Personnel are trained to run it, files are converted, and a postimplementation review evaluates the usefulness of the new system. Keeping the system responsive to users' needs, making program adjustments

for new hardware, correcting minor errors that invariably crop up in any system—all this requires a great deal of maintenance work by the programmer. In fact, programmers may spend more than half their time on maintaining existing programs.

As you can see, much work must be done before the programming effort can begin. If you were to start programming without having the detailed specifications of the system, you would no doubt find yourself redoing a lot of that work. This is because **programming** is really the process of converting systems specifications into step-by-step instructions that the computer can understand. Without knowing precisely what the system is meant to accomplish, you'd have little chance of developing a successful program. Moreover, because systems are generally developed by teams rather than by individuals, it's necessary before you begin programming to have an overall plan for coordinating the efforts of individual programmers.

To further ensure a successful outcome, programmers generally follow a structured **program-development approach.** This approach consists of the five steps involved in developing the system: (1) analyzing the problem; (2) designing a solution; (3) coding the program; (4) debugging and testing it; and (5) documenting it. The first two steps focus more on meeting the needs of users than on the computer itself. Communications regarding analysis and design are prepared in human language; so programming languages do not come into play in these early steps. The goal of analyzing the problem and designing a solution is to develop an *effective* means of meeting information needs.

In **coding** the program, the programmer translates the steps laid out in the design solution from human language to programming language. In **debugging and testing** the program, the programmer tries to ensure that it is free of errors. These steps require intensive work with the computer and a great deal of technical expertise, including a knowledge of programming languages. The goal of these two steps is the *efficient* use of the computer resources. As you can see, the first two steps in program development are user-oriented, while the second two are machine-oriented.

Documentation is the ongoing process of compiling information on the program that will be of use to the system's users, programmers, and operations personnel. This step in program development can be a source of controversy, as it is often expensive in terms of both time and resources. Although it should be ongoing, it often comes "after the fact," and it can be slighted or overlooked in the rush to get to the next interesting project. It is, however, a very important step—one that can make maintenance of the system a great deal easier—and we will discuss it in detail in the next chapter, together with coding and testing. In the rest of this chapter, we'll focus on the first two steps in program development—that is, on how the programmer goes about analyzing a problem and designing a program that will solve it.

ANALYZING THE PROBLEM

When the study team begins its analysis and design of the system, it focuses on developing the gross design specifications—that is, the overall logic to be used in solving the problem. **Logic** refers to the organization, sense, and sequence of the problem solution. When it is time to develop the actual program, the gross design specifications have to be refined. The first step in this refinement process is to analyze the problem in more detail. This analysis is often done by a systems analyst or a programmer analyst (someone who performs both functions) rather than a programmer. It requires a clear definition of the problem so that a means to its solution can be worked out.

As a programmer/analyst assigned the task of getting the programming process underway, the first thing you would have to consider is what kind of *output* the users need. To answer this question, you would have to work closely with the system's users; so program development is not necessarily the solitary activity that many people imagine it to be. It can require not only analytical skill and a creative bent but also an ability to communicate well with people. Among the questions you would have to ask at this stage are: What should the contents of the output be? What medium should be used (hard copy in the form of a printed report or soft copy displayed on a screen)? How often should the output be prepared? Are there sensitive data for which security measures need to be taken? What format should be used?

Only after you and the system's users have answered all these questions can you begin to consider what kind of *input* data you need to produce the desired output. In other—and not very original—words, you can't put the cart before the horse. Once you've determined what kind of input data you need, you'll have to ask whether you can get those data from the current system or whether you'll have to collect new data. If new data are needed, how will you collect them? How will you enter those data into the computer? How will you check for the accuracy of the data before they do enter the computer? Will the system have to handle unusually large volumes of data at certain peak periods?

Once you've decided upon the output and input requirements, you can determine the *processing* requirements of the system—that is, the kinds of operations the system will be called upon to perform. Processing would include classifying, calculating, sorting, and summarizing the input data to meet the output requirements. Processing design relies heavily on careful identification and description of appropriate outputs. If these have been thoroughly worked out, it is then just a matter of determining how the inputs can be converted to produce the desired output.

Let's suppose you've been assigned the task of preparing a computer program for processing customer orders and producing invoices. You'd begin this assignment by reviewing the current order-entry system, which, in this case, is a manual one. You might use a systems flowchart, such as the one shown in Figure 11.1, to graphically describe your initial analysis. A systems flowchart, as you may remember from Chapter 3, illustrates the

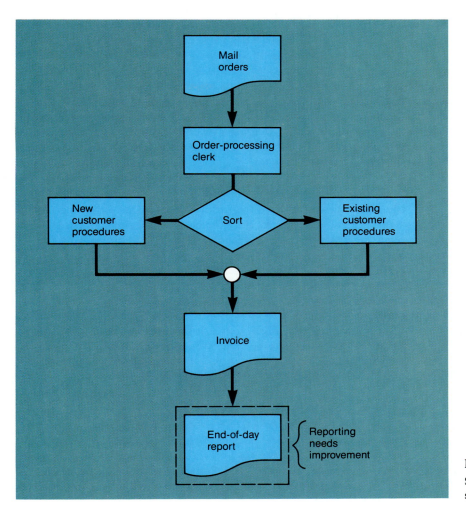

Figure 11.1
Systems flowchart for an order-entry system: analyzing the problem.

general processing activities, giving a brief graphic overview of the system design.

Your first step in approaching this assignment would be to examine the current system's outputs, inputs, and processing activities. You might do this by observation, by reviewing various forms, and by interviewing those involved with the processing operations. After careful analysis, you know that the invoice — the output — should contain a description of the transaction (purchases, prices, and quantity ordered), a total due for purchases, and any tax due. You also know that the order — the input — is received through the mail and is routed to an order clerk for processing and invoice preparation. Computations are done on a calculator when the invoice is prepared. During the observation, you also find that there are procedures for checking and granting credit to existing customers and that different credit procedures are used for processing new customer orders. At the end of the day, a report on all the day's transactions is prepared.

With this information in hand, you can now assess whether any changes should be made to the system. The first question to be asked is whether the system is performing in a satisfactory manner. Are customers and the firm happy with the outputs generated? If not, what would they like improved or enhanced? It is, of course, not always a good idea to automate a manual system as is, without thought to improvements; the power of the computer allows much greater computational ability, as well as the means to generate a wide variety of reports from the available data. In this case, you find that the invoices are being prepared in a satisfactory manner and that the procedures for new and existing customers are adequate. However, the sales department would like some improvements in the reporting system to help them evaluate their performance — specifically, information on orders over credit limits, first-time customers who place orders, and average order amount. Your final step before proceeding to the design phase would be to review your findings with the manager of the order-entry department to be sure nothing has been overlooked.

DESIGNING A SOLUTION

With the problem clearly defined, you can begin developing a solution to the problem — that is, a program that will give you the desired output. The least productive way to do this would be to sit at a terminal with some ideas in mind and key the instructions into the system. Through the process of trial and error, your program would no doubt eventually look pretty good, but whether or not it would satisfy users' needs is another matter. To avoid such haphazard results, programmers generally begin their attack on a problem by developing an **algorithm,** a logical sequence of steps that inevitably lead to the solution of a problem. You would use an algorithm, for example, if you wanted to calculate the average number of words per line on this page: Your first two steps would be to count all the words and all the lines on the page; your next step would be to divide the total number of words by the total number of lines.

You could also think of the cycles of a dishwashing machine as a simple illustration of an algorithm. The steps that the dishwasher goes through in cleaning the dishes occur in a routine pattern. If a break were to occur in the dishwasher's routine (as would happen, for example, if you advanced the timer after the cycle had started), you'd end up with dirty dishes. Thus, in the algorithm for getting clean dishes, the wash cycle needs to come before the rinse cycle, and both need to come before the dry cycle. Programmers use algorithms in much the same way you would use an outline in preparing a term paper — as an aid in organizing their thoughts. It's important to note, however, that there's no predetermined way to develop a program algorithm; in many cases you could solve the same programming problem with a number of different algorithms, just as you might use a number of different approaches to organizing a term paper.

The analysis of the manual order-entry system that we described in the last section showed a lack of reporting for over-credit customers, first-time customers, and average order amounts. A program algorithm developed to meet these reporting needs might include the following steps:

1. Enter the order into the system.
2. Calculate order detail.
3. Compare customer identification with existing customer records.
4. If new customer, add customer data to new customer report.
5. If existing customer, check credit detail and add to over-credit report if appropriate.
6. Accumulate order totals for calculations of average order amounts.
7. Produce customer invoice.
8. Produce sales reports.
9. Produce over-credit, first-time customer, and average order reports.

The steps involved in data entry and calculation would undoubtedly require much greater detail if we were developing an actual algorithm; we've simplified them here for purposes of illustration.

As indicated in our example, a program algorithm is not in a computer language. In fact, it's important that the algorithm be in an easily understandable form: Clear communication between the programmer and the user is essential at this stage, since the user must fully understand the proposed solutions in order to evaluate them. False starts and differences of opinion are certainly not uncommon, and a number of logical solutions are usually evaluated before the user and the programmer agree upon the final program design.

In developing a problem solution, programmers have at their disposal a number of design tools and programming methods. These tools and methods not only make the programmer's design efforts more productive; they also clarify the proposed solutions for the system's users and simplify maintenance of the program once it is operational. We'll discuss some of these design tools and programming methods in the sections that follow. But before we do, it's important to note that no matter which design tool or programming method a programmer uses, the design of the program must conform to the processing capabilities of the computer. As you know, the CPU can perform only two kinds of processing operations: arithmetic and logic. The logic patterns that it can execute are called simple sequence, selection, loop, and branch. The solution to any problem must be based on these patterns. So, before we look at the tools and methods that programmers use in designing solutions, let's look at these basic patterns of logic — that is, the four ways in which program instructions can be organized and sequenced so that the computer can process them.

BASIC LOGIC PATTERNS AND THE CONCEPT OF STRUCTURED PROGRAMMING AND DESIGN

Figure 11.2 shows the four basic patterns that programmers may use in designing computer programs. These logic patterns are also called **control structures,** because they control the sequence in which program instructions are executed.

The **simple-sequence pattern** is a series of steps that follow one after another without opportunity for a decision or transfer. In the simple sequence, all of the steps are in some predefined logical order, and the computer executes them in that order, one after the other. In fact, the computer will always execute instructions in this sequential order unless the program explicitly tells it to do otherwise. An example of a simple sequence would be program instructions to enter a customer purchase, compute the total due, and print an invoice.

The **selection pattern** takes advantage of the computer's ability to make a selection between two processing paths, using the **IF-THEN-ELSE structure.** For example, if you were designing a payroll program for employees who receive an hourly rate, you would structure the program to check for overtime, since the rate of overtime pay would differ from the regular rate. If the hours worked were for regular pay, then processing would follow the regular-pay path; if there were overtime hours, then processing would take the alternate overtime-pay path. After overtime pay was calculated, the paths would converge, and processing would continue.

The **loop pattern** can be a **DO-WHILE structure** or a **DO-UNTIL structure.** With a DO-WHILE structure, the computer will repeat a series of program steps *while* a certain condition is being met; with a DO-UNTIL structure, it will repeat the steps *until* a certain condition occurs. An example of the DO-WHILE structure would be the portion of a payroll program that enters employee data. As long as there are more employee

Figure 11.2
Basic logic patterns.

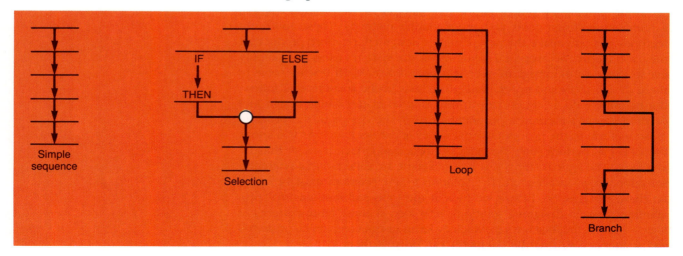

records to process — that is, while a certain condition is being met — the instructions will be repeated. When all employee records have been processed, the program will instruct the computer to proceed to the next segment of the program, and the loop will end. With a DO-UNTIL structure, the computer will continue to process records until it encounters a certain condition; record 299, for example, could be the condition that causes processing to cease and the loop to end. The loop pattern thus saves the programmer from having to repeat the same series of processing instructions for each employee record.

In the **branch pattern,** the computer breaks the normal sequence of instructions by bypassing or skipping a number of instructions. Branching is what enables the computer to skip instructions in both the selection and loop patterns. For example, in the selection pattern, a jump from one program instruction to another is made in response to a test condition. For instance, is the value of the tested data field over 10? If yes, branch to one set of instructions; if no, branch to another set or continue processing in the normal sequence. Branching can also be used without test conditions, with the program instructions causing the branching to take place.

A problem with the branch pattern is that a business program often has several thousand program instructions, and it could contain hundreds of branching statements. With branching, the program logic can very quickly become difficult to follow; and without a clear picture of the processing sequence, maintenance of the program can be something of a nightmare. To modify the program, the programmer must sort through the whole program to be sure that a change in one part of the program will not affect other parts. Unless the programmer who designed and coded the program does the modification, time is lost following all the branches to be sure the logic is understood and the proposed changes will not cause other problems.

For these reasons, more and more programmers today are limiting branching within their programs and are using a conglomeration of design tools and programming methods known as **structured programming and design.** These structured methods rely on the three basic logic patterns of simple sequence, selection, and loop. Because each of these three control structures has only one entry point and one possible exit path, they simplify the flow of the problem solution. This is an important concept, since the smaller the opportunity for misinterpretation, the smaller the chance that there will be serious errors in the program.

The common denominator of all structured design tools and programming methods is the limiting of the branch pattern both to make the processing sequence more straightforward and to improve programming productivity. We'll discuss these structured tools and methods in detail later in the chapter. In the next section, we'll take a look at flowcharts and decision tables. Because these particular design tools may or may not use the branch pattern, they are not considered structured design tools. They are, nonetheless, very valuable and commonly used tools in program design.

PROGRAM FLOWCHARTS AND DECISION TABLES AS DESIGN TOOLS

Program Flowcharts

Flowcharts are the most popular of all the design tools available to the programmer. The type of flowchart used in programming is called a program flowchart, and it evolves from a systems flowchart, as shown in Figure 11.3. The systems flowchart is an especially useful tool in communicating with top management since it addresses the *overall* processing rather than the technical details of the problem solution. In contrast, a **program flowchart** gives a *detailed* illustration of the programmer's algorithm. It maps out in picture form exactly what the program will do and how it will do it. One reason for the program flowchart's popularity is that it helps the programmer break major program segments down into smaller and more manageable parts known as program modules. **Program modules** are self-contained units that can be coded and tested independently of the rest of the program.

Symbols for Program Flowcharts. To make their program flowcharts as easy to read as possible, most programmers use a set of easily recognized, standardized symbols that have been adopted by the American National Standards Institute (ANSI). These symbols, which depict the program operations, are arranged on the flowchart in the same logical order as the order in which the instructions will appear in the program. They are shown next to their descriptions, which follow. If you look again at Figure 11.3, you can see how they appear in a program flowchart.

The **terminal symbol** is used to represent the beginning or end of a **routine** (i.e., a sequence of instructions) or of an entire program.

The **input/output symbol,** an equilateral parallelogram, is used to represent either input or output on all types of media — cards, tapes, disks, printed output, and so on.

The rectangular **processing symbol** is used to represent the processing operations (such as addition, subtraction, division, and multiplication) that are used to transform the data.

The **decision symbol** is used when there is need of a logic operation calling for a comparison. It has one entry point and three possible exit paths. The exit path taken will depend on the answer to the comparison.

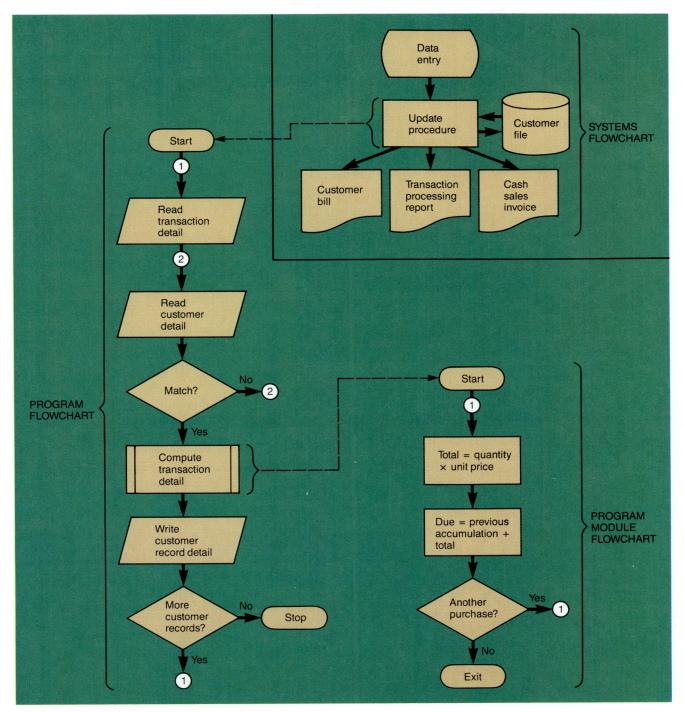

Figure 11.3
Evolution of the program flowchart from the systems flowchart.

Flowlines are used to connect the other symbols of the flowchart. These lines are of variable lengths and have arrowheads that indicate the direction of the program flow from one instruction to the next.

The **connector symbol** is used instead of flowlines when flowlines would make it difficult to follow the chart. Connector symbols are particularly useful when the chart has more than one page of diagrams.

 Operations and procedures that have been specified elsewhere are represented by the **predefined-process symbol.** For example, if the program calls for the same step to be repeated at various places throughout the program, the programmer writes the instructions once and uses the predefined-process symbol to indicate the places at which that process is to be repeated.

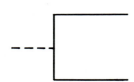 The **annotation symbol** is used for descriptive comments that are written directly on the flowchart.

    Figure 11.4 shows how some of these flowchart symbols are used in representing the basic logic patterns that we discussed earlier. As you can see in the figure, flowlines indicate the top-to-bottom, sequential flow of instructions used in the simple-sequence pattern. In the selection pattern, the decision symbol represents the comparison that must be made. There are three possible exits from the decision symbol, and the exit that is taken depends on the answer to the comparison. Notice that in the loop pattern, the flowline from the last instruction in the block to the first one to be repeated is in the direction opposite the normal flow. In the branch pattern, the connector symbol indicates the jump from one program instruction to another.

A Flowcharting Example. In the order-entry system described earlier in the chapter (see Figure 11.1), the analysis of the problem showed that the invoice-preparation system performed in a satisfactory manner but that the reporting system needed improvements to accommodate the sales department. Automating the system will allow the computer to prepare the new reports that are desired and to continue the invoice-preparation activities in a satisfactory manner. Figure 11.5 shows a program flowchart that maps out the algorithm for automating the order-entry system. It uses three of the basic logic patterns. In the simple-sequence pattern, the computation routine calculates the amounts of all orders based on price and quantity ordered. The next structure is the selection pattern. In this program, because credit is involved, two tests are necessary: the first to determine if a customer has been approved for credit (the new-customer/existing-

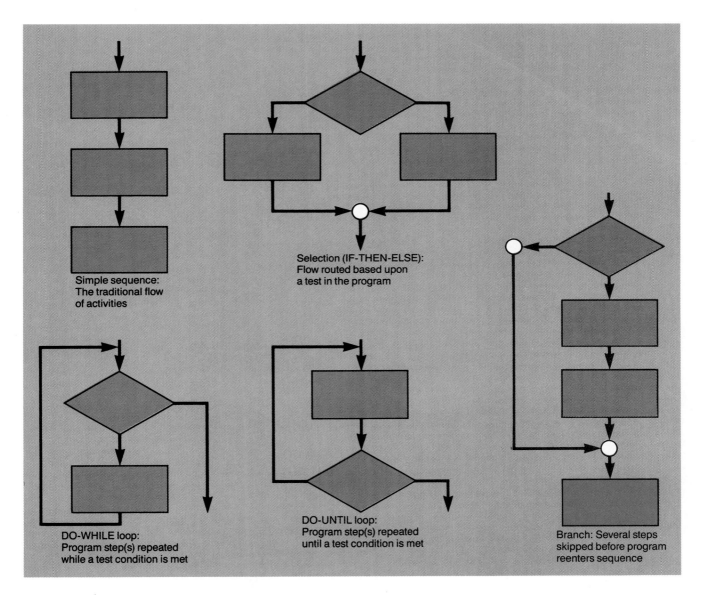

Figure 11.4
Program flowchart symbols used with basic logic patterns.

customer test), and the second to determine if the order is within the credit limits of $500 for each customer. If it is not within the credit limits, the program will print an "OVERCREDIT." For new customers, the order is always sent COD, and it is so printed.

After a customer invoice has been printed, the program looks for

318 11/PROGRAM DEVELOPMENT: FIRST STEPS

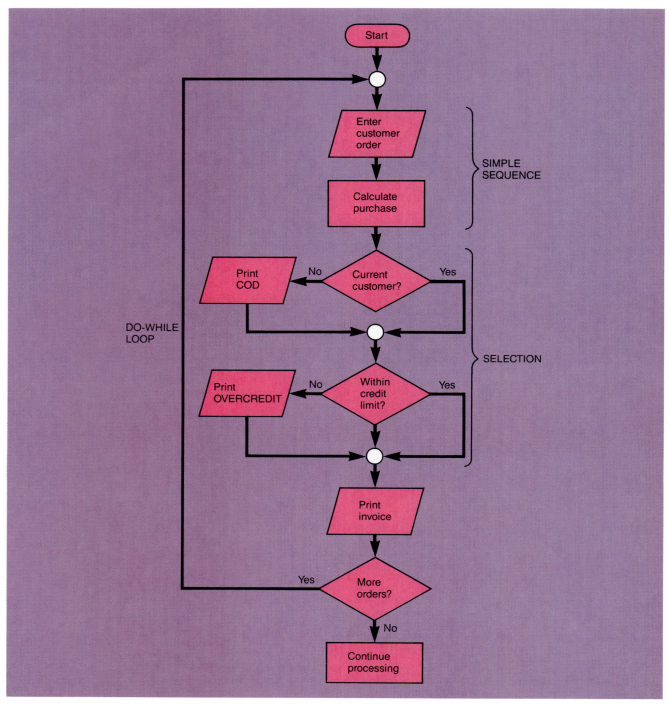

Figure 11.5
Program flowchart for part of an order-entry system: designing the solution.

another order to begin the processing routine once again. Because the program uses a DO-WHILE loop pattern, the computer will leave the loop and move to other processing activities only when all customer orders have been processed. The program then proceeds to the next phase, which would be the preparation of the various reports required by the sales department.

Advantages and Disadvantages of Program Flowcharts. Program flowcharts have several advantages. They can help the programmer/analyst identify and analyze alternative solutions to a processing problem, both by breaking the problem down into its elemental parts and by providing a graphic overview of the whole solution. Because flowcharts are graphic, they can, like the proverbial picture, be worth a thousand words. They tend to describe the flow of the program much more clearly than detailed, written specifications; and they simplify communication of the proposed solution to everyone involved in the project, as even people who have no technical knowledge can easily understand these graphic maps. Once a program flowchart is completed, the programmer can use it as a guide in coding the program in the appropriate programming language and in testing the program for errors. Program flowcharts also provide excellent documentation of the program. They are kept on record after the system is operational, and when program changes are necessary, the programmer has a ready point of reference for locating the instructions that need to be changed. In short, program flowcharts can be a great boon to programming productivity.

However, in certain situations, flowcharts have decided disadvantages. Redrawing and rearranging the various symbols of a flowchart is not an easy job; so if many changes to the system are anticipated, an alternative design tool should be considered. Also, charting creates a "busy" look; so if the program involves many decision paths, another design tool would probably be preferable.

Decision Tables

When flowcharts don't fit the bill, programmers have some alternative design tools to choose from, among them decision tables. A **decision table** is a type of table that shows the actions that should be taken if certain conditions exist. The basic logic of the decision table is, "If this condition is met, then do this." Figure 11.6 shows the format of this kind of table. The condition stub is the space where the various conditions are listed; the action stub is the space for listing the actions to be taken in response to the conditions.

Figure 11.7 shows a decision table that a company might use in hiring a sales representative. The rules governing the hiring process are based on the conditions of ownership of a car, education, and work experience.

COMPUTER PROGRAMMING AND THE FORTUNES OF DOUG FLUTIE

Richard Flutie had a very hot property and a powerful problem to go along with it. The property: his son Doug, the former Boston College quarterback and 1984 Heisman Trophy winner who leapt to national acclaim with a last-second 64-yard touchdown pass to defeat the University of Miami last November. The problem: the 69 agents, lawyers and assorted hawks who rushed forward, waving contracts, to represent the young soon-to-be-a-professional star.

"At the beginning I thought: 'There has got to be a better way than just interviewing all these guys.' I wanted to have some objective data to back up my personal feelings. So I wrote my own computer program," says Flutie Sr., a technician at a microchip company. "The computer and program brought results in mere weeks.

"Basically, what I did was rank each prospective agent in categories from 1 to 10, weighing each category according to its importance. Things like experience in direct negotiations with the National Football League (NFL), tax expertise, entertainment connections, chemistry and 'rough around the edges.' The last one I added because I didn't want a fist-slammer. I wanted a professional with high integrity and experience who wouldn't get anyone angry during negotiations.

"Finally, when I printed all this out, I was able to say to Doug: 'Here is the guy I picked for you.'"

The guy turned out to be Boston attorney Bob Woolf who immediately launched into promising negotiations with the New Jersey Generals of the United States Football League, a team owned by New York real estate mogul Donald Trump. Woolf emerged as point leader on the computer scale, particularly in the category of integrity, which Richard Flutie rated highest of all.

"Woolf had outstanding honesty. He was totally professional and very experienced in negotiating high-figure contracts. The fact that he handles Larry Bird of the Boston Celtics, who earns $2 million a year, didn't hurt him either."

But even Woolf, hardened professional that he is, reeled with astonishment when he heard the Generals' offer: an estimated up-front $1.3 million per year over four years. Such a contract would make Doug Flutie the highest paid rookie in professional football history.

And so began the next phase of the quarterback's computer fortunes. Richard Flutie programmed his DEC 350 to examine the contracts of all the players drafted by the 28 NFL clubs in 1982 and 1983. "I plotted a curve from left to right, based on the total value of the draft contracts. In theory, first pick should have been the highest point on the curve, descending down to number 28 on the right. But there were blips on the curve, and if they were lower, then I knew that the agent had done a bad job or the club drove a tough bargain in negotiations.

"However, it was totally misleading just to evaluate the total value of the contracts. The up-front value is really the vital figure. With the financing available today it is possible that a $6.5-million contract over five years, say, will cost the club only $185,000."

From his array of programs and printouts, the senior Flutie has an exact idea of how his son's contract should be structured to achieve minimum taxation and maximum take-home, and he further insists that any contract must be guaranteed by the team owner, not the club itself.

So far, the junior Flutie — the short one with the arm (he is only 5 ft. 9¾ in.) — has concentrated on throwing footballs, not wading through printouts. He seems remarkably modest for a 22-year-old with good looks, clean-cut marketability, the all-time collegiate offense record and a dad with a computer.

Whatever the final outcome, Doug Flutie's father can bask in the glow of a job well done. And he can measure his achievement by the number of agents, even the unsuccessful ones, who were so impressed by his computer quizzing that they advised him to write a book. If he ever does, he says it will recommend a computer as the best way to save time, organize thoughts and come to a conclusion which is backed by objectivity.

— Sue Mott, "The Computer Fortunes of Doug Flutie." Reprinted with permission from *Personal Computing,* April 1985, p. 35. Copyright 1985, Hayden Publishing Company.

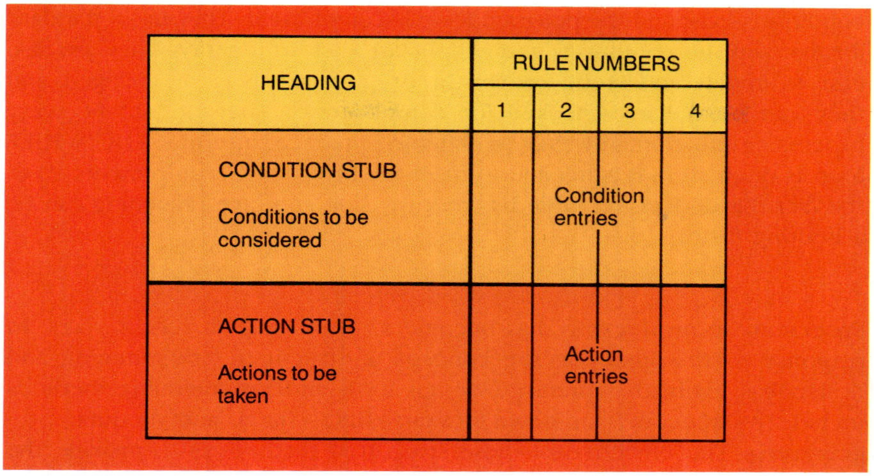

PROGRAM FLOWCHARTS AND DECISION TABLES AS DESIGN TOOLS **321**

HEADING	RULE NUMBERS			
	1	2	3	4
CONDITION STUB Conditions to be considered	Condition entries			
ACTION STUB Actions to be taken	Action entries			

Figure 11.6

Format of a decision table. The condition entries represent the "IF" statements, and the action entries represent the "THEN" activities.

To be considered at all, the applicant must own a car; if the applicant doesn't meet this condition, he or she is automatically rejected. To be interviewed as a possible candidate, the applicant must have two years of college *or* three years of work experience. If the applicant meets neither of these two conditions, no interview is granted, and the applicant is rejected. If an applicant meets all three conditions, he or she is accepted immediately, with no need of an interview. The Y's in the table mean yes, the N's stand for no, and the X's show the actions to be taken.

The nice thing about decision tables is that they can show a number of different conditions and actions in a single uncluttered chart. A flowchart might take several pages to illustrate the same logic and would be more difficult to follow. Decision tables are useful design tools when multiple

	HIRING CRITERIA	RULES				
		1	2	3	4	5
CONDITIONS	Owns a car	N	Y	Y	Y	Y
	<2 years college		Y	N	Y	N
	<3 years work experience		Y	Y	N	N
ACTIONS	Reject	X	X			
	Interview			X	X	
	Accept					X

Figure 11.7

Decision table for hiring a sales representative.

conditions exist and the program logic is complicated. They use a standard format, and the conditions and actions are easy to identify. They are also easy to update and modify when the program needs to be changed, and they can be quickly checked for completeness. They do not fit every processing situation, however, as a simple-sequence pattern or a DO-WHILE loop is often all that is needed to meet the processing requirements. Also, the fact that a decision table has no provision at all for branching can be a limiting factor.

STRUCTURED DESIGN TOOLS AND PROGRAMMING METHODS

Programming productivity has become a major issue in recent years. In response to this concern, the concept of structured programming and design has evolved. Structured design tools and programming methods include pseudocode, top-down design, HIPO charts, and modular programming. The objective of these structured methods is to provide the programmer with a set of clearly defined techniques that have built-in controls to ensure ease of coding, testing, and documenting the program; as noted earlier, they also make the processing sequence more straightforward.

Pseudocode

Pseudocode is a design tool that can be used to develop and illustrate the logical flow of a program. It uses ordinary human language to describe the steps of the problem solution. These written descriptions, which follow the same order as the actual program instructions, have more of the look of a real program than a flowchart does (see Figure 11.8). However, they, like a flowchart, are but an intermediate step for mapping out the logic of the program, and the steps described in pseudocode, just like the steps of a flowchart, will have to be coded into a programming language in order to be executed by the computer.

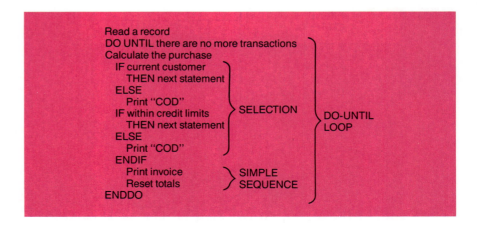

Figure 11.8
Pseudocode for an order-entry system.

The rules for constructing pseudocode are not nearly so rigid as the rules for constructing a formal programming language. The programmer can thus concentrate on the problem at hand without having to worry about the **syntax**—that is, the rules of construction—of a formal programming language. Programmers who are familiar with flowcharts may be reluctant to use pseudocode because it describes the problem solution in a significantly different way. However, pseudocode does simplify the communication of the problem solution by enabling the programmer to describe the solution in terms that everyone can understand, and it is becoming a very popular design tool.

Top-Down Design

Top-down design begins with a broad problem definition and breaks that definition down into successively smaller and more detailed program modules. The alternative to top-down design has been **bottom-up programming,** which, in contrast, tends to concentrate on the detail of the problem solution without regard for the *overall* problem requirements. Figure 11.9 shows the **structure chart** that evolves from top-down design's initial problem definition. As you can see, a structure chart looks very much like an organization chart, with its varying levels of responsibility. The farther

Figure 11.9
Structure chart for an order-entry system.

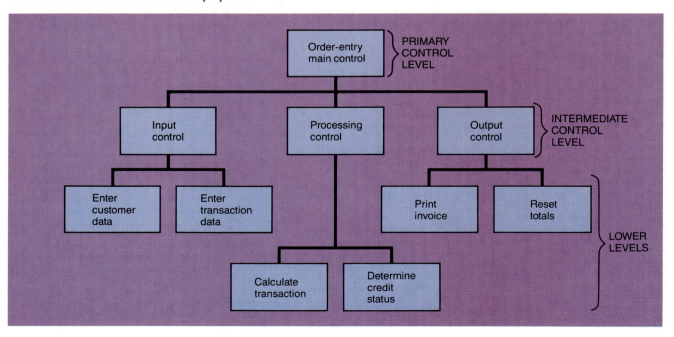

SAGE OF SOFTWARE

The countdown was coming to an end. Lying on their backs in the cockpit of the space shuttle *Columbia* [were] astronauts John Young and Robert Crippen.... Within less than an hour they would be the first people to fly the space shuttle into orbit....

Then, 20 minutes before launch time, warning lights at mission control began to flash. Something was wrong with the computer system. The countdown was halted; the computer analysts went to work. They had three hours before the flight would have to be scrubbed.

It quickly became apparent that nothing was physically wrong with the computers. All of the circuits were working. The communication lines were intact. The problem seemed to lie instead in the programs....

Technicians immediately realized they faced a serious problem. The software on board the space shuttle consists of nearly 500,000 elaborately interwoven instructions. Finding a programming error, a bug, in that web would be like trying to find a single misspelled word in an encyclopedia. Soon the news began to circulate: The maiden flight of the space shuttle would have to be delayed.

"It was precisely the type of error that one would expect," says the Dutch computer scientist Edsger W. Dijkstra.... "You see, most of NASA's software is full of bugs."

His eyebrows arch with pleasure, a sure sign that a story follows. "I saw the first moon shot in 1969, when Armstrong, Aldrin, and Collins went to the moon, and shortly thereafter I met Joel Aldron of IBM's Federal Systems Division, who I knew had been responsible for a large part of the software.... I said, 'Joel, how did you do it?' 'Do what?' he said. I said, 'Get that software to work okay.' 'Okay?' he said. 'It was full of bugs. In one of the trajectory computations, we had the moon's gravity repulsive rather than attractive, and this was discovered by accident five days before count zero.'"

Dijkstra draws back in his chair, the picture of astonished outrage. "When I had regained my composure, I said, 'Those three guys, they have been lucky.' 'Oh yes.' Joel said."

For more than 20 years, Dijkstra has been fighting against the kind of programming that inevitably leads to bugs in computer software. To him, the way organizations like NASA program computers is foolhardy at best, perilous at worst.

He believes there is another way, a better way. It involves structuring how a person thinks about programming so that programs themselves acquire a firm mathematical basis.

down the chart you go, the more detail associated with the program module. Just as the first level of an organization chart represents the president of an organization, who assumes responsibility for overall control, the first level of a structure chart represents the *control level*. There may be one or more *intermediate control levels* as well, and at the *lower levels* are the specific processing modules.

Along with this breaking down of the problem into successively more specific modules, top-down design arranges the modules so that they are independent of each other. Because of the modules' independence, different programmers can work on different parts of the entire program at the same time without having to coordinate their work. Thus, some programmers may be working on the coding and testing of the intermediate-level modules while others are working out the design details of the lowest-level modules. Another advantage of the modules' independence is that errors in one module don't affect the other modules; so, to correct an error, the programmer has to change only the module containing the error.

The discipline his work has spawned, called structured programming, has been one of the most important advances in computer software of the past two decades....

Structured programming is an attempt to deal with what Dijkstra feels is a programmer's most insidious problem — sheer complexity....

The complexity of software comes from the dense interrelationships of the instructions in a program. Very large software systems consist of millions of separate instructions, generally written by hundreds of different people. All these instructions must dovetail with perfect accuracy. If even a single instruction is wrong, the software system can fail.

No one person can completely understand a system of such complexity. A programmer may understand one part of it. A manager may grasp its outlines. But the system as a whole surpasses human understanding. Many computer scientists claim that these large software systems are the most logically complex things that human beings have ever built.

This complexity has two effects: It causes software for large computers to be expensive and to almost invariably contain errors. Some of the software fiascos of the past have become legendary. The *Mariner I* Venus probe, for example, had to be blown up immediately after its launch in 1962 because of a missing word in its control program. But much more [pervasive] and important are the countless small programming errors that afflict our computerized society. "There are," says Dijkstra, "minor annoyances in great multitude — banks erroneously computing your interest, airline reservations getting screwed up, and what we are suffering from now, failures of computer-controlled telephone exchanges to make connections."

These are the problems that Dijkstra's work ultimately addresses....

He studies very small programs, often just a few commands long, demonstrating the snares that complexity can set even in something that seems obvious. He dissects the problems he chooses with a ruthless logic, probing them for insights into the process of programming. When he has found what he wants, he writes up his results in a concise, elegant document....

Elegance is an important word to Dijkstra. For him it describes much more than just a way of writing or presenting oneself to the world. It describes qualities, such as precision and simplicity, that are essential to science. "In programming," Dijkstra says, "elegance is not a dispensable luxury. It is a matter of life and death."

— Steve Olson, "Sage of Software," *Science 84* (January/February 1984), pp. 75–77. © 1984 by the American Association for the Advancement of Science (AAAS).

HIPO Charts

HIPO (hierarchy plus input-processing-output) charts are design tools that depict a problem solution in varying levels of detail, depending on the needs of the programmers and users. There are generally three levels of HIPO charts. At the most general, least detailed level is the *visual table of contents (VTOC)* (see Figure 11.10). VTOC charts illustrate the program modules that comprise the processing activities and the hierarchy, or levels, of each of the modules shown. Each block in the VTOC is given an identifying number; these identifying numbers describe the processing sequence. The chart at the intermediate level depicts an *overview* of the input, processing, and output for each module represented in the VTOC (see Figure 11.11). The explanations at this level are brief and do not attempt to define any program logic or processing operations. At the third level, the *detailed chart* describes each module more completely, illustrating the processing

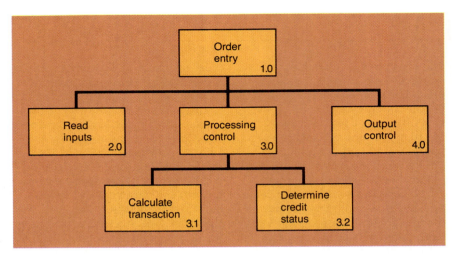

Figure 11.10
Partial visual table of contents (VTOC) for an order-entry system.

activities and data needed to fulfill the module requirements (see Figure 11.12).

The varying degrees of complexity and detail provided by HIPO charts ensure that there is something of interest for everyone — programmers, analysts, and the system's users. Communication of the proposed design solution is tailored to the interests and viewpoints of specific individuals. Because they provide excellent documentation of the program and thus make future maintenance much easier, HIPO charts are also a boon to programming productivity.

Modular Programming

Modular programming is a method of programming that divides the problem solution into work packages, each of which is a self-contained module, or unit, of processing. Each module does one task, and it operates independently of the other modules in the program. For example, if a program to enter orders for merchandise and to produce an invoice for the customer was developed with modular programming, the modules might consist of individual work packages that, respectively, capture the customer data; capture the order data; process the order data; update the customer record; update the inventory record; and produce an invoice. Each of these packages would be programmed as a self-contained unit, and a *master control program* would call for the routines as needed (see Figure 11.13).

The advantage of modular programming is that each package is developed to stand alone; if adjustments or enhancements of the program are necessary,

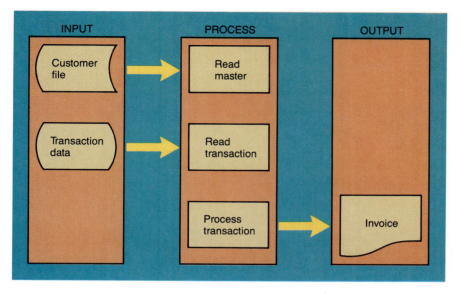

Figure 11.11
HIPO chart for an overview of a module of an order-entry system.

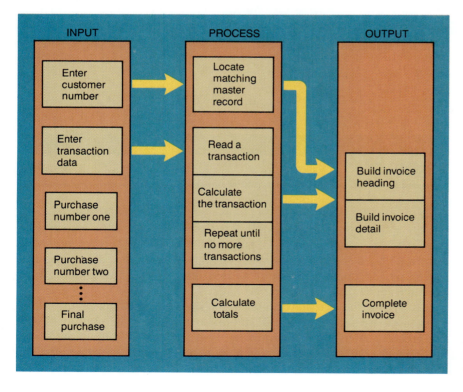

Figure 11.12
Detailed HIPO chart for a module of an order-entry system.

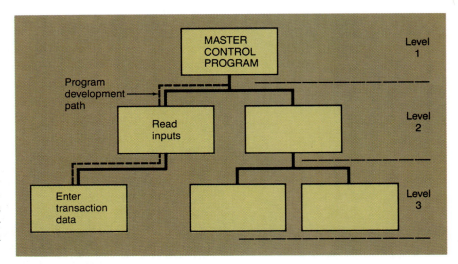

Figure 11.13

Modular programming. A programmer is responsible for one or more modules and may program and test modules at a single level before proceeding or may program and test modules along a path on several levels.

a change in one module will not affect any other module of the program. Program maintenance is thus much easier and much less time-consuming than it would be with bottom-up programming, in which the program operates as a unit. Insofar as each module stands alone, modular programming does exactly the same thing as top-down design. The difference is that the former is a programming method and the latter is a design tool. Modular programming can be used effectively with either top-down or bottom-up design.

SUMMARY

Program development is the next-to-last step in the systems development cycle. It cannot profitably begin until the specifications of the system have been worked out. The steps in program development include analyzing the problem; designing a solution; coding the program; debugging and testing it; and documenting it. The first two steps in this process have been the focus of this chapter.

Analyzing the problem requires a clear understanding of the users' information needs and a clear definition of the logic to be used in solving the problem. It involves determining, first, the desired output and, then, the input data and the processing steps needed to produce the output. It also involves a careful scrutiny of the way the existing system works. This analysis is often done by a systems analyst or a programmer/analyst, and it is frequently aided by use of a systems flowchart, which provides a brief graphic overview of the general processing activities of the system.

Usually, the first step in designing a solution to the problem is to develop an algorithm — that is, a logical sequence of steps that inevitably lead to the solution of a problem. There is no predetermined way to develop a program algorithm; the same problem can often be solved in a number of different ways. However, any problem solution must conform to the basic logic patterns that the computer can execute: simple sequence, selection, loop, and branch. In the simple-sequence pattern, the computer executes the program instructions in a strictly sequential order, one after the other. In the selection pattern, the computer must make a decision about which processing path to follow. In the loop pattern, the computer repeats a series of steps while a certain condition is being met or until a certain condition occurs. In the branch pattern, the computer breaks the normal sequence of instructions by skipping a number of instructions. Branching can make the logic of the program difficult to follow and can complicate the maintenance of the system. For this reason, an increasing number of programmers are limiting the use of the branch pattern in their programs.

A number of design tools and programming methods are available to help the programmer describe the logic of the problem solution — that is, to map out the algorithm — in a way that the system's users can understand. Program flowcharts, which give a detailed graphic illustration of exactly what the program will do and how it will do it, are the most popular of the design tools. However, when multiple conditions exist and the program logic is complicated, decision tables, which show the actions that should be taken if certain conditions exist, may be a more appropriate alternative. Because program flowcharts and decision tables may or may not use the branch pattern, they are not considered structured design tools.

Limiting program branching is basic to the concept of structured programming and design, which is aimed at improving programming productivity and at making the processing sequence more straightforward. Among the design tools and programming methods that fall under the umbrella of structured programming and design are pseudocode, which uses ordinary human language to describe the steps of the problem solution; top-down design, which begins with a broad problem definition and breaks that definition down into successively smaller and more detailed program modules; HIPO charts, which depict the problem solution in varying levels of detail; and modular programming, which divides the problem solution into self-contained modules of processing.

The objective of using any design tool or programming method is to simplify the coding, testing, and documentation of the program, which are the subject of the next chapter. Clear and complete documentation, in turn, simplifies program maintenance. These design tools and programming methods also help to clarify communication of the design solution to everyone involved in the project — programmers and users alike.

KEY TERMS

algorithm (310)
annotation symbol (316)
bottom-up programming (323)
branch pattern (313)
coding (307)
connector symbol (316)
control structures (312)
debugging and testing (307)
decision symbol (314)
decision table (319)
documentation (307)
DO-UNTIL structure (312)
DO-WHILE structure (312)
flowlines (316)
HIPO (hierarchy plus input-output-processing) charts (325)
IF-THEN-ELSE structure (312)
input/output symbol (314)
interfaces (306)
logic (308)
loop pattern (312)
modular programming (326)
predefined-process symbol (316)
processing symbol (314)
program-development approach (307)
program flowchart (314)
programming (307)
program modules (314)
pseudocode (322)
routine (314)
selection pattern (312)
simple-sequence pattern (312)
structure chart (323)
structured programming and design (313)
syntax (323)
systems development cycle (306)
terminal symbol (314)
top-down design (323)

DISCUSSION QUESTIONS

1. Outline the steps taken in program development. Explain why these steps are necessary.

2. In analyzing a problem, what are some of the things a programmer/analyst might do?

3. How is an algorithm helpful in program development? Prepare an algorithm for writing a check and recording it in your checkbook.

4. Describe the four basic logic patterns used in problem solving. Give an illustration of how each is used.

5. How would a programmer use a flowchart? A decision table? Pseudocode? Top-down design? HIPO charts? Modular programming?

6. Suppose your school was converting from a manual grade-reporting system to an automated one. Analyze the problem and design a solution for the new system.

7. Develop a flowchart describing how you would select a meal in a cafeteria. How is this process different from what a programmer would do in solving a business problem?

8. What is structured programming and design? Explain its advantages.

9. Why is communication so important in the development of a problem solution?

10. Why are all the programming design tools and methods independent of any particular programming language?

OUTLINE

CODING: COMMUNICATING WITH THE COMPUTER
- Machine Language
- Assembly Language
- High-Level Languages
- The Translation Process

THE CHOICE OF A LANGUAGE
- BASIC
- COBOL
- FORTRAN
- RPG
- Pascal
- Ada
- C Language
- APL
- PL/1

DEBUGGING AND TESTING THE PROGRAM

DOCUMENTING THE PROGRAM

SUMMARY

KEY TERMS

DISCUSSION QUESTIONS

OVERVIEW

Perhaps of all the creations of man language is the most astonishing.
— Lytton Strachey

Therefore is the name of it called Babel; because the Lord did there confound the language of all the earth.
— Genesis, 11:9

We would not be at the trouble to learn a language, if we could have all that is written in it just as well in a translation.
— Samuel Johnson

A translation is no translation, he said, unless it gives you the music of a poem along with the words of it.
— J. M. Synge

The wasting moth ne'er spoil'd my best array;
The cause was this, I wore it every day.
— Alexander Pope

To err is human;
To debug is necessary.
— Computer folklore

If you have gathered from the foregoing that this chapter has something to do with languages, translations, and bugs, you are right. It also has to do with documentation — that unfortunate Cinderella of the programming process, who always seems to come last but who can emerge as the shining heroine much later in the day. In this chapter, we'll attempt to explain what languages, translations, flying insects, and Cinderella have to do with the computer. Our objectives are to

◆ describe how people communicate with computers and identify the levels of language available for that communication.

◆ explain how languages are translated into a language that the computer can "understand."

◆ give an overview of the most popular programming languages, explaining the distinctive features and applications of each.

◆ discuss the debugging and testing of a program.

◆ Explain why documentation is so important in the programming process and identify some of the things that must be documented.

CHAPTER 12

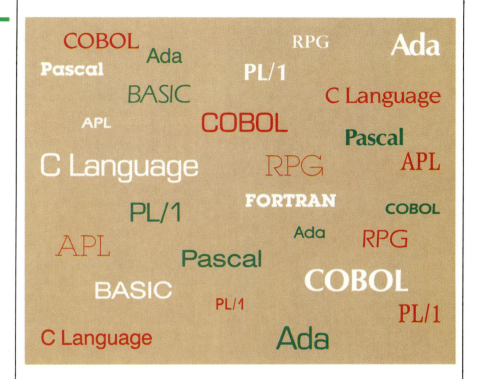

PROGRAM DEVELOPMENT: THE LANGUAGE CONNECTION

CODING: COMMUNICATING WITH THE COMPUTER

As you know from the last chapter, the first two steps in program development don't require any consideration of a **programming language** — that is, a system of communicating with the computer. But once the problem has been analyzed and a program design worked out, the programmer's next task is to *code* the charted steps in a programming language so that the computer can "understand" them. Each instruction is then referred to as a **program statement,** and the statements together make up the program.

Another way of thinking about communicating with the computer is to visualize the entire program as a solution to an information problem and the program statements as steps in the solution. Each statement constitutes a single instruction, which can be to accept input data; to perform calculations; to perform logic operations such as comparisons; to store, retrieve, or transfer data; or to produce output. A program may consist of just a few statements, but most programs contain hundreds or thousands of them.

If you recall the flowcharts described in Chapter 11 and the logical problem solution they represent, you have the starting point for coding a program. In coding, each of the logical steps illustrated by a flowchart symbol is translated into one or more program statements. Figure 12.1 shows how the steps of a simple flowchart would look when translated into the BASIC programming language. Remember that the flowchart communicates the logic of the solution and is independent of any programming language; so the programmer can translate the program steps of the flowchart

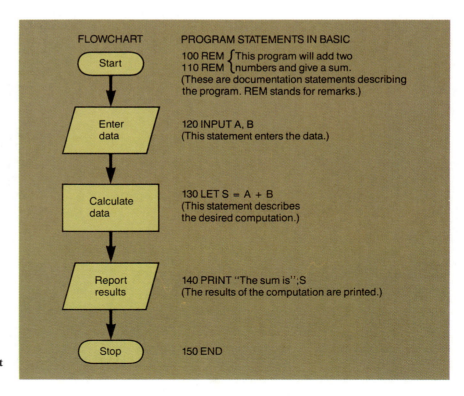

Figure 12.1
The steps of a program flowchart coded in BASIC.

PSEUDOCODE	PROGRAM STATEMENTS IN BASIC
Read a record	120 INPUT A,B
DO WHILE there are data	125 IF A = −1 THEN 150
Calculate a sum	130 LET S = A + B
Print the sum	140 PRINT "The sum is";S
ENDDO	145 GOTO 120
Stop	150 END

Figure 12.2

Programs steps in pseudocode translated to BASIC. This program is the same as that shown in Figure 12.1 except that it has been expanded to allow entry of more than one set of data and processing of more than one sum.

into any programming language he or she chooses. Other design tools, such as decision tables, pseudocode, structure charts, and HIPO charts, can, of course, also be used to describe the logic of the program design. Figure 12.2 shows how program steps plotted out in pseudocode would look when translated into BASIC.

Even though much of today's programming is done online with terminals, programmers still use coding forms (see Figure 12.3). **Coding forms** are

Figure 12.3
A COBOL coding form.

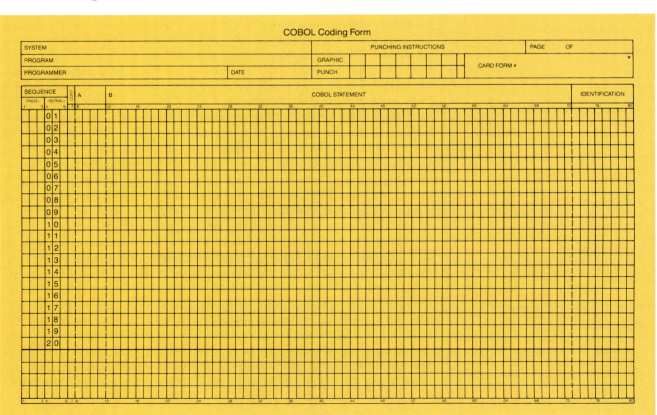

standardized forms for preparing instructions for entry into the system. Each programming language has different requirements for positioning the instructions, sequencing them, and identifying their function; and these forms help the programmer stay within the constraints of the language. Coding forms also help the programmer in reviewing the program instructions before they go into the computer system, thus enabling the programmer to correct errors before valuable machine time is lost.

You may recall from Part I that the only language the computer can "understand" is machine language, and that if a program is coded in any other language, it must be translated into machine language before the computer can process the instructions. Assembler programs perform this translation on assembly language; compilers are used for translating high-level languages. Let's now take a look at the levels of languages in which programs may be coded and at how the computer translates these languages into the language it "understands."

Machine Language

Machine language uses a binary code — that is, a series of 0's and 1's — to deliver instructions to the computer's electronic circuits. The design of the arithmetic and logic circuits, as well as the circuitry for storing and retrieving data from memory, determines the specific machine codes necessary to operate the computer. Because different computer manufacturers design their hardware in different ways, machine language is not standardized: Each make and model of computer has its own unique language, which cannot be used on any other computer system. In other words, machine language is *machine-specific.* Thus, machine language designed for a specific series of IBM equipment will not work on any other system; and a programmer working in machine code on that series of IBM equipment must either know its language or be trained in it. Also, if a company chooses to program in machine language, it is committed to specific hardware. Should it acquire a different computer system, all programs will have to be recoded.

Each machine-language instruction tells the computer what operation is to be performed, as well as where to find the stored data or where to store the processing results. Expressing each of these instructions in a long string of 0's and 1's is a cumbersome, tedious, and time-consuming task. It is also prone to error; if you look at Figure 12.4, which shows a program instruction for a simple arithmetic operation written in three different languages, including machine language, you'll get some idea of why this is so. Of course, in the early days of computing, programmers had little choice but to code their instructions in machine language; assembly language was not developed until the early 1950s, and high-level languages did not come upon the scene until late in that decade. However, in those early days, even having to code a long stored program in machine language

```
BASIC
    100 LET S = A + B

ASSEMBLY LANGUAGE
    Operation
      Code      Operand   Comments
        L          A      Load register with A
        A          B      Add B to the register
        ST         S      Store the sum as S

MACHINE LANGUAGE
    Operation
      Code      Operand   Comments
       10100     11011    Load register with A
       11100     10110    Add B at location 10110 to A in the register
       10111     11001    Store S in the accumulator
```

Figure 12.4

Program statement for a simple addition problem written in BASIC, assembly language, and machine language.

seemed like a significant improvement over having to rewire the computer each time you wanted to change a program. Machine language does have the advantage of not requiring a translation program that takes up storage space and requires extra operating time. But with the greatly increased storage capacity and speed of modern computers, and with the availability of easy-to-use high-level languages, it is more efficient today to put the burden of translation on the computer.

Assembly Language

Assembly language is a "level" above machine language in the sense that it is closer to human language and thus is easier for people to use. Assembly language replaces the 0's and 1's of machine language with abbreviated commands such as "MP" for multiply. However, each assembly-language instruction must be translated into one machine-language instruction, indicating the operation to be performed as well as the storage location of the data. So, coding programs in assembly language is still a time-consuming and tedious process. Like machine language, assembly language also has the disadvantage of being machine-specific. The programmer therefore has to know the specific assembly language of the computer system that is being used, and if the equipment is changed, all the programs have to be recoded.

Assembly language is not normally used for coding applications programs, but it is regularly used to code systems software, which is usually machine-specific. One business application in which assembly language does have an advantage is in the coding of reusable routines for regularly run jobs such as sorting. Because assembly language is close to machine language, programs coded in it take a shorter time to run and require less storage space than similar programs coded in a high-level language. For routine jobs, these factors may outweigh the cost of the extra time involved in coding in assembly language. Because of the need for speedy processing, programs for arcade games are also often written in assembly language.

High-Level Languages

High-level languages use ordinary words such as "ADD HOURS WORKED" or symbols like "+" to code the program instructions. These words and symbols are closer to everyday language than the abbreviations of assembly language and so are even easier for people to use. Because of the structure of high-level languages, systems software can enable the computer to keep track of the storage locations of data, thus sparing the programmer from having to include that information in each program instruction.

High-level languages use **macrocode** — that is, a code in which a single instruction conveys a number of machine-language instructions. As Figure 12.5 shows, one instruction in the macrocode of a high-level language can combine a number of commands, such as commands to retrieve data from storage, to do an arithmetic calculation, and to transfer to storage the data that result from the calculation. In machine language or assembly language, each of these commands would have to be coded as a separate instruction. Because of macrocode, as well as the contribution of the systems software, programs written in a high-level language are shorter and easier to prepare than those written in either assembly or machine language. They do, however, take a longer time to run. On the other hand, because the coding takes less time, the programmer has more time to devote to the overall program development. You may already have noticed the relative briefness of the BASIC-language instruction shown in Figure 12.4.

Programs written in a high-level language are not only easier to prepare; they are also easier to correct and change. Moreover, these languages are not machine-specific; they can be used on different makes of computers. Almost all business programs today are written in a high-level language, with COBOL being the most popular.

Figure 12.5
Macrocode.

COBOL STATEMENT:

COMPUTE GROSS PAY = SALES ∗ COMMISSION RATE

The macrocode instruction for the multiplication to determine commission due (G = S × C) would be translated into three machine-language instructions required for the multiplication:
  1. Load value for sales into a register.
  2. Multiply the value for commission rate by the value in the register.
  3. Save the sum called gross pay in the accumulator.

The Translation Process

Once a program written in assembly language enters the computer system, systems software known as an **assembler** translates it into machine language. Similarly, systems software known as a **compiler** translates a program written in a high-level language into the machine code. The program as it has been written by the programmer is called the **source program.** The compiler or assembler takes the source program and transforms it into an **object program.** The compiler or assembler does not address the logic of the source program; it merely translates the source instructions into machine-language instructions. In other words, the *object program* is the same source program that was used as input except that it is now in machine code.

As you can see from Figure 12.6, compilers (as well as assemblers) do more than just translating from one language to another and producing object programs. They also produce **source listings** (or **assembly listings,** if an assembler program is at work) and **diagnostic messages.** *Source listings* are printed reproductions of the program instructions that were entered into the computer system. Programmers use these listings to double-check their instructions. If the programmer developed the program on a terminal screen, he or she probably had to review it in small segments since terminal screens can display only about twenty lines at a time. The source listing, on the other hand, displays the entire program. Source listings also provide valuable documentation of the program.

The *diagnostic messages* that the compiler or assembler produces describe the **syntax errors** that it has found during the translation process. The misuse or absence of punctuation, a misspelling, and the misuse of a

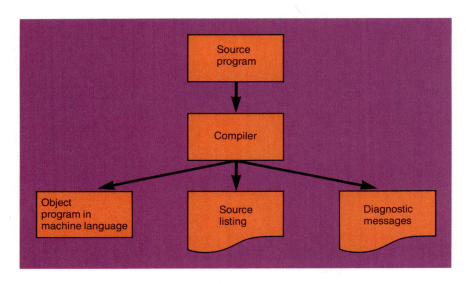

Figure 12.6
A compiler's output.

program command are a few of the syntax errors that might occur. (*Syntax,* as you may remember from the last chapter, refers to the rules of language construction.) If the instructions contain any significant syntax errors, such as those shown in Figure 12.7, the computer will not execute them. The programmer would have to correct these before the computer would compile the source program into an object program ready for execution. However, once all significant syntax errors have been corrected and the source program has been compiled into an object program, the program can be stored in that form for future runs, and the compilation step will not have to be repeated.

Although with the compiler, the computer can detect errors in programming-language construction, it cannot check for errors in the logic of the program solution. The *logic,* which includes the organization, sense, and sequence of the instructions, is the responsibility of the programmer. Because the computer has no way of knowing what the programmer is trying to do, it can only react to errors in the program's logic with generalized error messages such as "OUT OF DATA" or "NUMBER TOO LARGE FOR THE FIELD." Some logic errors, such as a wrong formula, will not interrupt the execution of the program; therefore, they will never be caught by the computer. In other words, the computer — as always — can do only what it is programmed to do.

For each high-level language, there is a specific compiler program: COBOL has a COBOL compiler for translating COBOL to machine language, FORTRAN has a FORTRAN compiler, and so on. In addition, as we noted earlier, each make of computer has its own specific machine language. In other words, compilers are both language-specific and machine-specific. This might be easier to understand if you think of a COBOL-to-machine-language compiler as an English-to-French dictionary that a tourist is using while traveling in Europe. The dictionary is useful in France but not in Germany, just as a compiler for translating COBOL to an IBM machine language would be useless on a Honeywell system.

Figure 12.7
Syntax errors that would prevent program execution.

BASIC STATEMENT	ERROR MESSAGE	PROBLEM
100 WET S = A + B	Illegal statement	Programmer typed "W" for "L".
INPUT A, B	Instruction not recognized	Programmer omitted the statement number.
100 LET S = AB	Illegal variable	Programmer omitted the "+" sign.
100 S = 2A + B	Illegal format	Programmer used an illegal variable—2A instead of A2.
200 PRINT SUM, S	Illegal variable	Programmer omitted quotation marks around "sum"; if a word is a heading, it must be in quotes.
100 LET D = A × B	Illegal format	Programmer used an incorrect symbol; in BASIC, the symbol for multiplication is * (not ×).

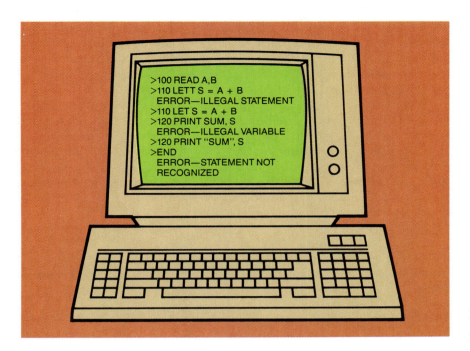

Figure 12.8
An interpreter's output.

An **interpreter** is another kind of translation program, and it is often used with microcomputers to translate high-level programming languages into machine code. The interpreter translates each source-program statement, one at a time, before proceeding to the next one. Errors can therefore be detected immediately after a statement is entered and so can be easily corrected (see Figure 12.8). Because interpreters do not create object programs that can be stored in machine language, a program must be translated each time it is run. As you might expect, because it translates each instruction just before it executes it, an interpreter is much slower than a compiler. Interpreters do have the advantage of reduced storage-space requirements, however, which is one reason they are so often used with microcomputers.

THE CHOICE OF A LANGUAGE

The decision on which programming language to use involves a number of factors, among them the programmer's own knowledge of particular languages and the standards that a company's data processing department may have set. For example, to standardize hiring and training requirements and program maintenance within the company, a data processing department may require that all programs be written in COBOL. Because hardware technology changes so rapidly, the ease with which a language may be adapted to different computer systems is another important consideration when choosing a programming language. The nature of the application will also affect this decision, as different languages are designed for different purposes. COBOL, for instance, has features that make it attractive for business applications; FORTRAN, on the other hand, is more suited to scientific applications.

FORTRAN and COBOL, which were developed in the late 1950s, were the first of the high-level languages. Today, programmers can choose from a very wide variety. Interestingly, however, although several hundred high-level languages are presently available, less than a dozen account for 90 percent of all the programming that is done. In the following pages, we'll take a look at some of the more popular high-level programming languages in use today. Table 12.1 gives you an overview of the features of these languages and the applications in which they are used.

BASIC

BASIC (Beginner's All-purpose Symbolic Instruction Code) was developed at Dartmouth College in 1963 by John Kemeny and Thomas Kurtz, under a grant from the National Science Foundation. The idea behind BASIC was to provide students with a language that was easy to learn and that could be used in conjunction with timesharing systems, which were a new idea in computing at that time. Using BASIC and online terminals, a number of students, all working simultaneously, could use the same computer to solve mathematics problems and other assignments. BASIC is said to be an **interactive language** because it allows the user to communicate directly with the computer while preparing or using programs and to receive an immediate reply.

The primary feature of BASIC is its simplified code structure, which makes it easy to learn and use. In addition, its interactive nature makes BASIC a very "friendly" language; it allows users to communicate with the computer in a conversational manner, interacting in a question-and-answer environment. Because it uses an interpreter for translation to machine language, debugging is easy, and it has become the standard language for microcomputer programming. Its ease of use and quickly learned features have also made BASIC popular as an instructional language. Figure 12.9 shows a sample program written in BASIC.

Because BASIC has been applied to a wide range of hardware and software applications, a number of versions of the language have evolved. Thus, BASIC commands are not always exactly the same for all computer systems, and programs prepared for one computer may require modification before they will run on another system. Also, some versions of BASIC may

Table 12.1 Overview of High-Level Languages

Language	Applications	Features
BASIC	Designed for instructional use in a timesharing environment. A very popular language for microcomputer applications.	Easy to learn and use. Its use of an interpreter for language translation facilitates debugging.
COBOL	The standard language for business data processing.	English-like statements help document the program. Syntax is standardized, so the language is machine-independent.
FORTRAN	Designed for scientific and mathematical applications. Used for modeling and simulation programming in business.	Strong computational capabilities. Library routines for mathematical functions and calculations are easy to assemble and use.
RPG	Designed for preparing reports with a minimum of coding.	Easy to learn and use. Provides file-manipulation capabilities for small business systems.
Pascal	Developed for instructional use. Especially useful in the microcomputer environment.	Compatible with most structured techniques. Also has excellent graphic capabilities.
Ada	Developed by the Department of Defense as their language standard.	Standardized, so the language can be used on many different computers. Modular, so programs can be developed in "packages" that can be assembled into a larger program.
C Language	Especially suitable for use with microcomputers.	Combines characteristics of assembly and high-level languages. Very portable.
APL	Primarily a scientific language, but useful in business analysis as well. Best suited for unstructured problems with limited input and output.	Based on a system of mathematical notations. Powerful interactive features reduce the need for coding.
PL/1	Developed to combine the best of FORTRAN and COBOL in one language.	Operates effectively as a batch or interactive language and handles files and calculations with equal ease.

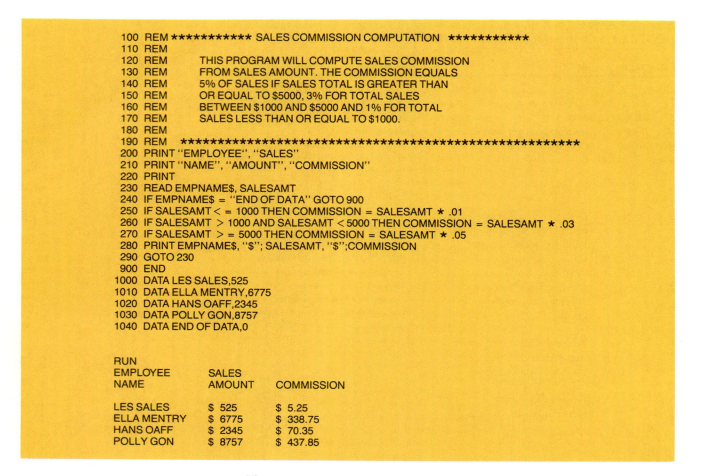

Figure 12.9
Sample program written in BASIC.

not have the features necessary to conform to structured programming standards. Some fundamental features of BASIC are, however, available in almost all versions of the language. These include input and output formatting options designed to relieve the programmer of much of the coding detail — for example, the arrangement of the output in five equal columns on the printed page and the acceptance of input data of varying sizes. Options such as these are often referred to as **default options,** meaning that the computer will execute them unless explicitly instructed to do otherwise, and they are one of the reasons that BASIC is easy to use. If the programmer does not have to be concerned with the layout of the input or output data and can concentrate on just the processing activities, the program becomes much simpler to code and understand. The simplicity of BASIC coding is both a strength and a weakness. BASIC is somewhat like automatic transmission on a car: It does a lot for you, but you outgrow it when you want more control.

COBOL

Development of **COBOL** (COmmon Business-Oriented Language) began in the late 1950s. The effort was sponsored by the Department of Defense, which was interested in creating a standardized high-level language that could be used in business applications. Business systems need the capacity to process a great number of inputs and outputs, but they usually do not need extensive computational features. When COBOL was introduced in 1960 at the Conference on Data Systems Language, it was the first language specifically designed to meet the needs of business, and it was standardized so that it could operate on the equipment of different manufacturers. Because computer manufacturers adapted their equipment to meet the requirements of this new language, a certain amount of *machine-independence* had been achieved. In other words, COBOL could be used on a Honeywell system and, with only slight modification, on an IBM system as well. Programmers were thus no longer tied to the machines whose language they knew; their skills had become transferable.

As you can see in Figure 12.10, COBOL uses English-like instructions. It also separates each program into four divisions, making the program modular and easy to develop and maintain. The first division is the IDENTIFICATION DIVISION, which documents the names of the program and the programmer and any other relevant data. The ENVIRONMENT DIVISION specifies the equipment used and assigns the input and output devices to the files that will be used in the program. The DATA DIVISION defines the input and output data, assigns storage locations, and describes the editing procedures that will be used. The final division is the PROCEDURE DIVISION, which describes the processing activities required to solve the problem.

Although its similarity to plain English may increase the user's comfort in learning and using it, COBOL is complex and can be difficult to work with. This complexity is probably its greatest disadvantage. The program statements are wordy and can be redundant, and they generally take more time to prepare than statements in other languages. Because COBOL is a very powerful language, it requires a complex compiler, which uses a large amount of primary storage. COBOL is thus best suited to large computer systems.

```
IDENTIFICATION DIVISION.
PROGRAM-ID.           COMPUTE COMMISSION.
AUTHOR.               RUDY MENTRY.

*  PROGRAM DESCRIPTION: THE FOLLOWING PROGRAM WILL COMPUTE
*  AN EMPLOYEES COMMISSION WHEN SUPPLIED WITH THE EMPLOYEES
*  TOTAL SALES. THE COMMISSION EQUALS 5% OF SALES IF SALES
*  TOTAL IS GREATER THAN OR EQUAL TO $5000, 3% FOR TOTAL
*  SALES BETWEEN $1000 AND $5000 AND 1% FOR TOTAL SALES
*  LESS THAN OR EQUAL TO $1000.


ENVIRONMENT DIVISION.

CONFIGURATION SECTION.

SOURCE-COMPUTER.         IBM-PC.
OBJECT-COMPUTER.         IBM-PC.

INPUT-OUTPUT SECTION.

FILE-CONTROL.
      SELECT DATA-FILE
            ASSIGN TO "COMMDATA.DAT".
      SELECT PRINT-FILE
            ASSIGN TO "OUTDATA.DAT".


DATA DIVISION.

FILE SECTION.

FD    DATA-FILE
      LABEL RECORDS ARE OMITTED
      DATA RECORD IS INPUT-RECORD.

01    INPUT-RECORD             PIC X(24).

FD    PRINT-FILE
      LABEL RECORDS ARE OMITTED
      DATA RECORD IS PRINT-LINE.

01    PRINT-LINE               PIC X(80).

WORKING-STORAGE SECTION.

01    FLAG-VALUES.
      05   MORE-RECORDS        PIC X(3)       VALUE "YES".
      05   BLANK-LINE          PIC X(80)      VALUE SPACES.

01    COMPUTATION-VALUES.
      05   WS-COMMISSION       PIC 9(5)V99.

01    SALES-RECORD.
      05   EMPLOYEE-NAME       PIC X(20).
      05   SALES-AMOUNT        PIC 9(4).
```

Figure 12.10
Sample program written in COBOL.

```
01  REPORT-LINE.
    05  EMPLOYEE-NAME-OUT      PIC X(20).
    05  SALES-AMOUNT-OUT       PIC $ZZ,ZZ9.99.
    05  FILLER                 PIC X(10)         VALUE SPACES.
    05  COMMISSION-OUT         PIC $ZZ,ZZ9.99.
    05  FILLER                 PIC X(30)         VALUE SPACES.

01  HEADING-ONE.
    05  FILLER                 PIC X(20)         VALUE "EMPLOYEE"
    05  FILLER                 PIC X(10)         VALUE "SALES".
    05  FILLER                 PIC X(50)         VALUE SPACES.

01  HEADING-TWO.
    05  FILLER                 PIC X(20)         VALUE "NAME".
    05  FILLER                 PIC X(10)         VALUE "AMOUNT".
    05  FILLER                 PIC X(10)         VALUE SPACES.
    05  FILLER                 PIC X(10)         VALUE "COMMISSION".
    05  FILLER                 PIC X(30)         VALUE SPACES.

PROCEDURE DIVISION.

0000-MAIN-LOGIC.
    PERFORM 1000-INITIALIZATION.
    PERFORM 2000-PROCESS-RECORDS
        UNTIL MORE-RECORDS = "NO".
    PERFORM 3000-TERMINATION.

1000-INITIALIZATION.
    OPEN INPUT DATA-FILE
         OUTPUT PRINT-FILE.
    WRITE PRINT-LINE      FROM HEADING-ONE
        AFTER ADVANCING 4 LINES.
    WRITE PRINT-LINE      FROM HEADING-TWO
        AFTER ADVANCING 1 LINE.
    WRITE PRINT-LINE      FROM BLANK-LINE
        AFTER ADVANCING 1 LINE.

2000-PROCESS-RECORDS.
    PERFORM 2100-READ-RECORDS.
    IF MORE-RECORDS = "YES"
        PERFORM 2200-COMPUTE-COMMISSION
        PERFORM 2300-BUILD-REPORT
        PERFORM 2400-WRITE-REPORT.

2100-READ-RECORDS.
    READ DATA-FILE    INTO SALES-RECORD
        AT END
            MOVE "NO" TO MORE-RECORDS.

2200-COMPUTE-COMMISSION.
    IF SALES-AMOUNT NOT LESS THAN 5000
        COMPUTE WS-COMMISSION ROUNDED = SALES-AMOUNT * 0.05
    ELSE
        IF SALES-AMOUNT NOT GREATER THAN 1000
            COMPUTE WS-COMMISSION ROUNDED
                = SALES-AMOUNT * 0.01.
```

Figure 12.10 (continued)

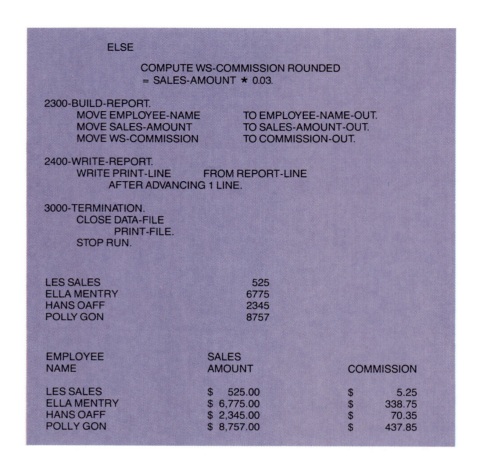

Figure 12.10 (continued)

FORTRAN

FORTRAN is an acronym for FORmula TRANslator. Originally developed at IBM in the 1950s for use by scientists and engineers, it follows a mathematical-notation form, and it is brief, concise, and easy to learn (see Figure 12.11). It handles very large and very small numbers very well, and it can perform complex mathematical computations with ease. It can calculate numbers to a much greater degree of accuracy than other languages, which introduce small errors through rounding procedures. FORTRAN is thus very useful when precise calculations are required, as, for example, when the trajectory of a space vehicle must be determined. Business applications that would take advantage of this capability include the modeling and simulation activities used in management science techniques, in which complex statistics are used to replicate the real environment.

```
$TITLE: 'EMPLOYEE COMMISSION COMPUTATION PROGRAM'
$STORAGE:2
              PROGRAM SALCOM
*
* THIS PROGRAM WILL COMPUTE SALES COMMISSION FROM A GIVEN
* TOTAL SALES AMOUNT FOR EACH EMPLOYEE. THE COMMISSION
* EQUALS 5% OF SALES IF SALES TOTAL IS GREATER THAN OR
* EQUAL TO $5000, 3% FOR TOTAL SALES BETWEEN $1000 AND
* $5000 AND 1% FOR TOTAL SALES LESS THAN OR EQUAL TO $1000.
*
              DIMENSION SALAMT(10), COMMIS(10)
              CHARACTER * 20 EMPNAM(10)
*
              WRITE(*,15)
15            FORMAT('0',15X, 'EMPLOYEE COMMISSIONS')
              WRITE(*,10)
10            FORMAT(16X, '_____  _____')
              WRITE(*,20)
20            FORMAT('0', 'ENTER THE NUMBER OF EMPLOYEES')
              READ(*,25) NEMP
25            FORMAT(I2)
              WRITE(*,30)
30            FORMAT('0', 'EMPLOYEE NAME           ', 'SALES')
              DO 35 I = 1,NEMP
                     READ(*,40) EMPNAM(I), SALAMT(I)
40            FORMAT(A20,F4.0)
35            CONTINUE
              WRITE(*,45)
45            FORMAT('0', 'EMPLOYEE                      SALES')
              WRITE(*,50)
50            FORMAT(1X, 'NAME        AMOUNT        COMMISSION')
              WRITE(*,55)
55            FORMAT(1X)
              DO 60 I = 1,NEMP
                     IF (SALAMT(I) .GE. 5000) THEN
                            COMMIS(I) = SALAMT(I) * 0.05
                     ELSEIF (SALAMT(I) .LE. 1000) THEN
                            COMMIS(I) = SALAMT(I) * 0.01
                     ELSE
                            COMMIS(I) = SALAMT(I) * 0.03
                     ENDIF
                     WRITE(*,65) EMPNAM(I), SALAMT(I), COMMIS(I)
65            FORMAT(1X,A20, '$',F8.2,4X, '$', F7.2)
60            CONTINUE
              END
```

Figure 12.11

Sample program written in FORTRAN. (Figure 12.11 continues next page.)

Notice in Figure 12.11 how each input and output must be described with a format statement, something that BASIC can do for the programmer automatically. Because it was designed as a computational language, FORTRAN does not move large volumes of data easily, and it therefore does not handle file processing well. It also does not lend itself to structured programming, although the latest version, FORTRAN 77, has incorporated a number of structured features.

```
            EMPLOYEE COMMISSIONS

ENTER THE NUMBER OF EMPLOYEES
4


EMPLOYEE NAME                   SALES
LES SALES                        525
ELLA MENTRY                     6775
HANS OAFF                       2345
POLLY GON                       8757


EMPLOYEE              SALES
NAME                  AMOUNT                COMMISSION

LES SALES             $  525.00             $      5.25
ELLA MENTRY           $ 6775.00             $    338.75
HANS OAFF             $ 2345.00             $     70.35
POLLY GON             $ 8757.00             $    437.85
```

Figure 12.11 (continued)

RPG

RPG (Report Program Generator) was developed by IBM in the 1960s as a language for use in the preparation of business reports. The language has very limited computational capabilities, and it is best suited to manipulating files and reporting financial information. RPG is a **nonprocedural language,** which means that programs are designed around the language's *built-in logic.* The programmer describes the inputs and desired outputs, and the RPG compiler generates a program to meet the requirements specified by the programmer. In contrast, all the other languages discussed in this section are **procedural languages**—that is, the programmer develops and codes the computational and logical procedures to produce the sequence of instructions needed to solve the problem. RPG is easy to learn and use, and it is a popular business-reporting language. Using an RPG specifications sheet (see Figure 12.12), a programmer can produce an excellent business report.

Pascal

Pascal, introduced in 1971, was developed by Niklaus Wirth, a Swiss computer scientist. Named in honor of Blaise Pascal, the seventeenth-century French philosopher and mathematician who invented the first mechanical data processing device, the language is designed for structured

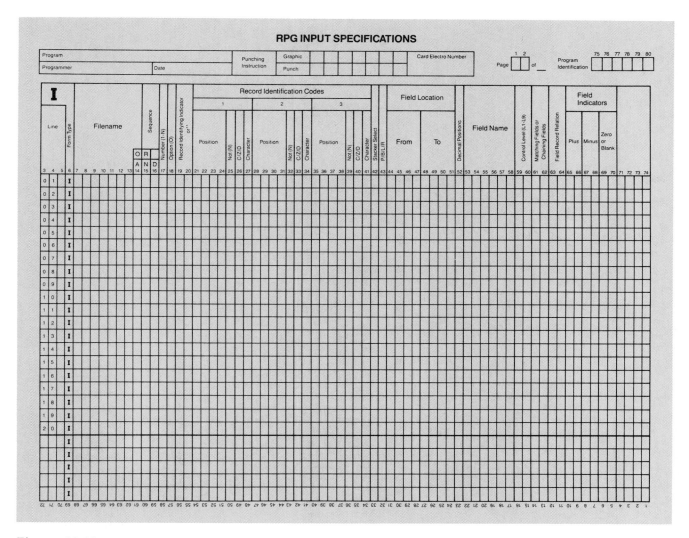

Figure 12.12

An RPG input specifications sheet. Additional coding sheets are used for file description, processing, and output specifications.

programming applications. It has easy-to-use structured statements for the simple-sequence, selection, and loop logic patterns. It is also easy to learn, has excellent graphic capabilities, and is often used with microcomputers. Pascal handles both business and scientific applications well, but it can process only sequential files. It is particularly well suited for someone who is just learning how to program, since it provides good structure and is easy to use. Figure 12.13 shows a sample program written in Pascal.

```
{ * Program Description: This program will ask for the
    employees name and total sales. From that data it
    will then compute the employees commission. The
    commission equals 5% of sales if sales total is
    greater than or equal to $5000. 3% for total sales
    between $1000 and $5000 and 1% for total sales less
    than or equal to $1000.    * }

program ComputeCommission (input, output);

type
  empname = string [25];

var
  EmployeeName : empname;
  SalesAmt, Commission : real;

begin
  writeln ('Please enter the employees name. When finished    ');
  writeln ('enter END.   ');
  readln (EmployeeName);
  writeln;
  while EmployeeName <> 'END' do

    begin
      writeln ('Enter this employees total sales. ');
      readln (SalesAmt);
      writeln;
      if SalesAmt <= 1000 then
         Commission := SalesAmt * 0.01
      else
        if SalesAmt >= 5000 then
           Commission := SalesAmt * 0.05
        else
           Commission := SalesAmt * 0.03;
      writeln (EmployeeName, ' earned $', Commission :8:2, ' commission');
      writeln ('on sales of $', SalesAmt :8:2, '.');
      writeln;
      writeln;
      writeln ('Please enter the employees name. When finished');
      writeln ('enter END.');
      readln (EmployeeName);
      writeln;
    end

end.


Please enter the employees name. When finished
enter END.
LES SALES

Enter this employees total sales.
525
```

Figure 12.13
Sample program written in Pascal.

```
LES SALES earned $      5.25 commission
on sales of $    525.00.


Please enter the employees name. When finished
enter END.
ELLA MENTRY

Enter this employees total sales.
6775

ELLA MENTRY earned $    338.75 commission
on sales of $   6775.00.

Please enter the employees name. When finished
enter END.
HANS OAFF


Enter this employees total sales.
2345

HANS OAFF earned $      70.35 commission
on sales of $   2345.00.


Please enter the employees name. When finished
enter END.
POLLY GON

Enter this employees total sales.
8757

POLLY GON earned $    437.85 commission
on sales of $   8757.00.


Please enter the employees name. When finished
enter END.
END
```

Figure 12.13 (continued)

Ada

Ada, introduced in 1980, was developed by the Department of Defense, a prime user of computer systems, in an effort to establish a single, powerful, standardized language that could be used in both business and scientific applications. Numerous versions of various languages were being used on the department's computer systems, and department officials realized that a single, standardized programming language would have many advantages, among them easier programmer training and program maintenance.

PROGRAM DEVELOPMENT AND END-USER PROGRAMMING AIDS:
Fourth-Generation Languages

End-user programming aids come in all shapes and sizes. Sometimes they are called report writers and are advertised as a substitute for COBOL programming; at other times, they travel under cover as part of a data base management system. Often, they are referred to as fourth-generation languages. Whatever the label, all these programming aids have one thing in common: They allow the user to develop applications programs without the services of a professional programmer.

End-user programming aids are becoming increasingly important as computers proliferate in business offices; according to some estimates, by the end of the decade, there will be one computer for every ten employees. Given this kind of growth, it's unlikely that the supply of programmers will keep up with the demand for programs. The proliferation of data communications systems and the resulting decentralization of computing resources make programming aids all the more important: With end-users increasingly located at diverse geographical sites, the problems professional programmers face in meeting users' needs will mount.

Without end-user programming aids, nontechnical users who want to obtain information from the computer must communicate their information needs to a programmer. Such communication doesn't always produce the desired results — a not surprising fact given the differences between nontechnical personnel and technically oriented programmers. Moreover, because programmers generally have several jobs in process at any given time, there is usually a delay before the programmer can produce the required program. Thus, the time for decision making may be past before users have the information they need.

Fourth-generation languages move the user directly from recognizing a need to designing a solution. Because the user already understands the problem, the problem analysis performed by a professional programmer can be skipped. With a fourth-generation language, the user, following on-screen prompts, actually custom designs a business program, accomplishing in minutes what it might take days for a COBOL programmer to do. False starts are easily overcome, and the constant passing back and forth of memos that accompanies the development of software by a programmer is eliminated. Fourth-generation languages do not, however, lend themselves to the efficient processing of large volumes of data, nor do they allow for the use of subroutines. For processing business data in quantity, COBOL still provides the best solution.

Three popular fourth-generation languages are FOCUS, a product of Information Builders, Inc.; DYL-280, from Dylakor, Inc.; and Express, marketed by Management Decision Systems, Inc. These languages are designed for retrieving and reporting from a data base, and they are nonprocedural — that is, rather than describing the steps needed to produce the information, the user describes the information requirements, and the language selects the most appropriate means of meeting the requirements. This feature means that users do not have to learn the complex rules of structure and grammar typical of earlier generations of languages. Whereas it may take weeks or months to learn a procedural language like COBOL, a fourth-generation language can be learned in a matter of hours or days.

Because fourth-generation languages require more computing resources than earlier languages, they may not be efficient for complex applications. However, with the price of computing power falling rapidly, the efficiency of coding in a fourth-generation language may outweigh the inefficiency of the processing operation; a hundred instructions in a fourth-generation language can substitute for a thousand lines of COBOL-coded instructions. Many people claim that fourth-generation languages also make maintenance much easier, a significant argument when a backlog of program requests extends several years into the future.

You may recall from Chapter 2 that Ada, Countess of Lovelace, has been called the world's first programmer because of her work with Charles Babbage on the Analytical Engine. The language named in her honor resembles Pascal, and it is very powerful. In addition to being standardized, Ada has modular features that allow programs to be developed in packages that can be assembled into a larger program. Supporters claim that Ada will provide processing capabilities not now available with any of the other programming languages, and detractors insist that it is too complex and has features that will seldom be used. The Department of Defense has mandated that all critical systems must be programmed in Ada, but it remains to be seen if this will influence commercial applications to any appreciable degree.

C Language

C language is becoming widely used in the development of commercial word processing and spreadsheet software, and it is for this reason often referred to as a "programmer's language." Originally designed for use with the UNIX operating system (a product of Bell Labs), C language has a great deal of "portability" — that is, it can be used with a number of microprocessors with very little modification. This feature makes C language attractive to software development firms, which design programs for particular computer systems, knowing full well that it won't be long before the introduction of a new computer will create a new market for their products. If the programming code a firm uses is easy to convert to the new microprocessor, it can more quickly modify its software and bring the revised product to the market.

C language is relatively low level — that is, it has many characteristics of an assembly language and deals with characters, numbers, and addresses. It cannot manipulate an entire table, as most high-level languages can, and it must call special routines to enter data and generate output. These apparent weaknesses have provided much of C language's strength. Because it is compact, it can be easily learned, and compilers are easy to write. The reason for C language's portability is that much of the language corresponds to the machine-language codes; in most cases, as much as 80 percent of C-language code is transferable from one microprocessor to another. Thus, C language matches the capabilities of many computers but is independent of any particular machine architecture.

To ensure compatibility among the various software products being written in C, work is currently underway to standardize the language. A standardized version of C language could have a major impact on the development of software during the remainder of the century. Figure 12.14 shows a sample program written in C.

```c
#include <stdio.h>

main ()
{
    FILE *stream;
    float salesAmount, commission;
    char employee[21];

    printf("Employee              Sales\n");         Commission\n\n");
    printf("  name                amount

    /* Open file for input */
    stream = fopen("employee data", "r");

    employee[21] = '\0';

    while (fscanf(stream, "%20c %f\n", employee, &salesAmount) = 2) {
        if (salesAmount <= 1000.00)
            commission = salesAmount * 0.01;
        else if (salesAmount < 5000.0)
            commission = salesAmount * 0.03;
        else
            commission = salesAmount * 0.05;

        printf("%s      %10.2f    %10.2f n", employee, salesAmount, commission);
    }
}
```

```
             Data
Les Sales        525.0
Ella Mentry     6775.0
Hans Oaff        334.30
Polly Gon        437.85

             Output
Employee    Sales
  name      amount         Commission
Les Sales    525.00           5.25
Ella Mentry 6775.00         338.75
Hans Oaff    334.30           3.34
Polly Gon    437.85           4.38
```

Figure 12.14

Sample program written in C language.

APL

APL (A Programming Language) was developed in the early 1960s by Kenneth Iverson and was made available to the public in the late 1960s by IBM, which had found the language well suited to the needs of its scientific staff. The language is designed for use in problem solving where input and output are at a minimum and where calculation and table manipulation (i.e., processing of groups of numbers in a table) are major activities. The language seems best suited to applications that lack structure—

that is, applications in which the programmer/user must continually interact with the program during execution because the nature of the problem being addressed is not completely clear. As information develops, the programmer can adjust the program to better handle the data or to provide more exact processing operations. APL's powerful interactive features reduce the need for extensive coding in complex programs for business simulation, performance analysis, and financial planning.

Limitations include the need for a special keyboard to code the program and the difficulty involved in reading a program coded in APL; these limitations arise from APL's use of special characters, such as Greek letters and mathematical symbols. Because much of the unstructured processing for which APL seems best suited can now be done with commercially available spreadsheets and integrated microcomputer software, it is unlikely that APL will become a widely used programming language.

PL/1

PL/1 (Programming Language 1) operates effectively as a batch or an interactive language. It was developed by IBM in the early 1960s in an effort to combine the best attributes of FORTRAN and COBOL. In addition to having powerful computational features and file-handling capabilities, PL/1 has several built-in functions and default features. These features allow the program to select a course of action that has not been specified by the programmer; the action is based on the processing activities being carried on. In a sense, given certain conditions, PL/1 assumes certain things. For example, if you neglect to specify where you want the output printed, the system will default into zone printing, much as it would with BASIC. Some programmers are wary of this feature, claiming that it could lead to logic errors during program development.

Programmers have generally resisted PL/1, and it has not become the standard business programming language its developers had envisioned. The need for a very large compiler limits the language to larger systems, where COBOL is well established. PL/1 will probably remain a viable language but will not play a major role in the development of business systems.

DEBUGGING AND TESTING THE PROGRAM

"Bugs" are program errors. They can result from simple keyboarding errors that create misspellings, punctuation and spacing mistakes, misused commands, and other types of syntax errors. They also occur when programmers make errors in program logic, such as those shown in Figure 12.15. Bugs are almost impossible to avoid, and rarely does a program compile and properly execute the first time it is run. But bugs of the syntax variety are

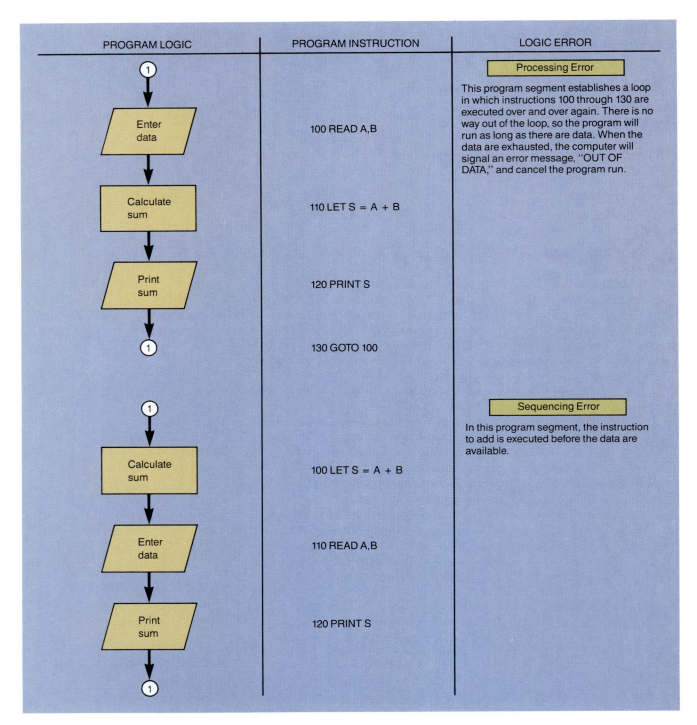

Figure 12.15
Common logic errors.

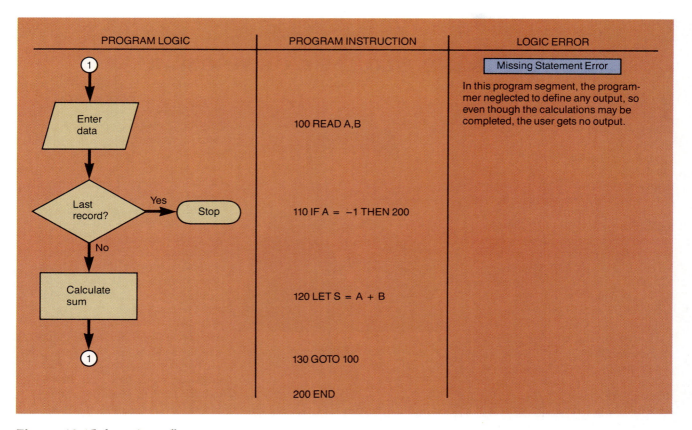

Figure 12.15 (continued)

also fairly easy to get rid of, although the "debugging" process can be a lengthy one. A programmer may spend as much time on debugging and testing a program as on coding it.

As you know, the compiler or assembler program can detect syntax errors, but it cannot check for logic errors. To reduce the chance that either kind of error will occur, the programmer should desk-check the program for both syntax and logic errors before submitting it to the computer for compilation. In **desk-checking** the program, the programmer plays the role of the computer, sifting through each instruction to see if the logic and syntax are correct (see Figure 12.16). When the programmer is satisfied that the program is as correct as it can be, the program goes into the computer for compilation, and the computer issues a report on all the syntax errors it has found. The programmer corrects the errors, and the program goes back into the computer. The process is repeated until an errorless run is made. However, even an errorless run is no guarantee that the program is free of *logic* errors. The program may be grammatically correct, but it may not be doing what the programmer meant it to do. Flowcharts and other design tools help to combat logic errors, but some

Figure 12.16
Desk-checking a program.
Courtesy of Aetna Life & Casualty.

THE GRAND OLD LADY OF SOFTWARE

For years, Capt. Grace Hopper's office at the Naval Data Automation Command had a clock that ran counterclockwise. It was there, she says, to remind people that things don't always have to be done the conventional way. Hopper has demonstrated that repeatedly in her own life. At 76, she is the Navy's oldest officer on active duty ... and has spent her career at the forefront of the computer revolution. Hopper worked with the first large-scale computer, Mark I, invented the first practical compiler and created the now ubiquitous COBOL computer language. Her computer team also coined the term "bug" to refer to a computer glitch in 1945 after someone pulled a two-inch moth from the circuit of a malfunctioning Mark I.

"The grand old lady of software" doesn't spend much time in her Washington office. Instead, she travels around the country and abroad, lecturing to college students and attending computer conventions. Her message: "Get in, start learning, get as much computer time as you can." Future developments in the field will be "even more rapid than they've been so far," Hopper believes. The Mark I, a mammoth ma-

Grace Hopper: a lifetime of creating and debugging.
UPI/Bettmann Newsphoto.

chine that measures 51 feet across, was considered the state of the art in 1944 because it could do three additions a second. "That sounds pitiful today," says Hopper, noting that computers now do the same calculations in 300 nanoseconds — or 1 billion times as fast...

The challenge now, says Hopper, is to improve the way we use computers. For one thing, she says, the information fed into them is often wrong or extraneous or both: "There's not one single article, not one single chapter of a book on the value of information.... We put all our time on the processing and we've spent no time at all on the information." Hopper is also concerned about the difficulty of keeping computer records private. She cites a case three years ago in which students at New York's Dalton School tapped into computer systems belonging to several Canadian companies and universities.

Hopper's one career disappointment occurred when the Navy retired her with the rank of commander in 1966. She says simply: "It was the saddest day of my life." Her sorrow was short-lived, however, since she was called back seven months later to standardize the Navy's computer programs and languages. In 1973, too old for a regular promotion, she was elevated to captain by a special act of Congress.

Eileen Keerdoja, Paul Vercammen, and Mary Lord, "The Grand Old Lady of Software," *Newsweek* (May 9, 1983), p. 13. Copyright 1983, by Newsweek, Inc. All rights reserved. Reprinted by permission.

bugs of this variety are bound to find their way into every major program. Nonetheless, once a program has made an error-free run, it is considered ready for testing.

The purpose of testing the program is to see if the output of the program is correct — that is, if it's doing what the programmer intended it to do. Testing involves feeding the computer certain kinds of data that will produce particular kinds of output in order to see how the program will perform in specific situations. For example:

1. Test data, typical of the kind of data the program will handle, are fed to the computer to see how well the program performs under *routine* conditions. To determine what the results should be, the programmer generally processes the test data by hand before feeding them to the computer. The computer's results are then checked against the manually processed results. Test data for a payroll program would include such items as employee number, name, address, and hours worked. Different combinations of data would be used to test the program's capacity to deal with overtime, sick leave, vacation, and holidays.

2. To test the program's ability to deal with *unexpected* situations (such as an employee number that cannot be matched with a number in the employee file), the programmer includes as many examples of unexpected data as possible and tests the program routines for handling these exceptions. Such routines would include special handling, exception messages, and program interruptions.

3. To test the program's ability to handle *errors,* the programmer feeds the computer erroneous data. The questions to be answered here are: What does the program do when data are incomplete (e.g., no data for number of hours worked are given)? When data are inappropriate (e.g., number of hours worked are expressed not in numerical terms but by such symbols as #)? When data are incorrect (such as happens when a data entry operator makes a keyboard mistake)? All programs must have procedures for dealing with such events, and the purpose of testing the program is to see that those procedures work.

If a program does not pass the test and the programmer cannot figure out why, he or she may call for a program dump (see Figure 12.17). A

Figure 12.17

A segment of a program dump coded in hexadecimal.

```
JCB ASGN45            STEP GO            TIMF 131237   DATE 34160    ID = 000                              PAGE 0020

0EE620   000C47F0 C34A4130 0100D700 10001000    19234740 C3BED7FF 1C001000 41131000   *...0C.....P........ C.P..........*
0EE640   18234720 C3A81222 47D0C3CA 062C4420    C3A207FE 90ECD00C 05801872 50D0704C   *....C.....C.....C...............*
0EE660   41A07048 50AC0008 18DA9601 71FF9110    70C04710 81389108 72024780 BC700700   *................................*
0EE680   4510B060 00360000 C9D2C6F1 F9F3C940    40C5D9D9 D6D940C9 D540C6D3 D6E640D6   *........IKF193I  ERROR IN FLOW O*
0EE6A0   C640C3D6 D5E3D9D6 D3406060 40D1D6C2    40C3C1D5 C3C5D3D3 C5C40A23 47F0B06A   *F CONTROL .. JOB CANCELLED...0..*
0EE6C0   80000DB1 5810B066 0A0D9608 7202D25F    7090B84A 91047203 4710B086 96107204   *..............K.................*
0EE6E0   91107204 4780B094 D20770B8 B9B49280    72144110 721494FC 1000960F 1C0043E1   *.........K..............0.......*
0EE700   00004100 70905001 000042E1 00000A13    911070C0 4710B138 91107204 4710B0CE   *................................*
0EE720   96107204 47F0B08E 4510B126 00508000    C9D2C6F1 F8F0C940 40E4D5C1 C2D3C540   *.....0...........IKF180I  UNABLE *
0EE740   E3D640D6 D7C5D540 E3C8C540 E2E8E2C4    C2D6E4E3 40C4C1E3 C140E2C5 E3406060   *TO OPEN THE SYSDBOUT DATA SET ..*
0EE760   40C4C5C2 E4C7C7C9 D5C740D6 D7E3C9D6    D5E240C3 C1D5C3C5 D3D3C5C4 00004020   * DEBUGGING OPTIONS CANCELLED.. .*
0EE780   0A239604 72025810 72B89630 100147F0    B1721B33 58207108 91FF7108 4740B232   *...............0............. ..*
0EE7A0   433071FE 89300002 47F3B152 47F0B16E    47F0B180 47F0B190 47F0B198 47F0B198   *..........3...0...0...0...0...0..*
0EE7C0   47F0B184 47F0B220 94FE71FF 58D0704C    502D001C 98ECD00C 07FE4540 81E29537   *.0...0..................... .S..*
0EE7E0   72094780 B18447F0 B16E4540 B1E247F0    B16ED21B 202F72EC 4540B1E2 92402000   *........0... .S.0..K...... .S. ..*
0EE800   D2772001 20004540 B1E247F0 B16ED201    7208B9BC 92F1710C 411C7090 4100710C   *K....... .S.0..K......1..........*
0EE820   53F01030 05EF4110 70904100 718558F0    103005EF 92F0723C 47F0B16E 48507208   *.0...............0......0...0......*
0EE840   41505001 95602000 4740B1FE 41505001    4720B1FE 41505001 40507208 41107090   *.......... ............... .......*
0EE860   4100723C 58F01030 05EF4120 723C9240    20000277 20012000 07F492F1 20004140   *......0......... ..K......4.1... *
0EE880   B16ED701 72087208 47F0B1E2 58507108    4100B23E 47F08246 C9D3C2D6 C4C2C5F0   *..P.......0.S..........0..ILBODBE0*
0EE8A0   18110A08 18F005EF 4500B25A C9D3C2D6    C4C2C5F0 0AC99400 71085820 71084140   *......0.......ILBODBE0........... *
0EE8C0   B16E47F0 B1E20501 103EF676 4770F010    D201103E 105207FE 90ECD00C 05C05900   *...0.SN...6...0.K................*
```

program dump is a printout of the entire contents of the computer's memory at any point during program execution. Tracing through the data of the dump searching for the error can be a very time-consuming process, especially with large and complex programs. If modular programming is used, each segment of the program is small and stands alone, so testing and debugging are much easier.

Even after all this debugging and testing, a logic error may still slip through and cause a problem months after the program has been installed. Because some programs are more complicated than others, and because testing must sometimes be done under the pressure of time, it is not always possible to test every program situation and option before the system is installed.

DOCUMENTING THE PROGRAM

Have you ever tried to assemble a new bicycle or to install a complicated part on a car? If so, you know that the first thing you looked for was the instruction manual. Instruction manuals are to bicycle and automobile "do-it-yourselfers" what program documentation is to computer users, maintenance programmers, and operations staff. Poorly written, they are disasters; well written, they allow people to get home on time.

Documentation for users is usually in the form of a manual that explains the input procedures, the language commands, and the processing routines available. A user's manual also generally includes a menu, or listing, of the available programs and a number of sample situations that walk the user through each program. Without good documentation for users, some of a system's strongest features may go unused.

Table 12.2 describes the components of a programmer's documentation file and the purposes that these various components of documentation serve. Such documentation is extremely valuable to the programmer who must maintain the program. That person, who is usually not the same person who wrote the program, has to have some means of understanding what the program does and how it does it before he or she can make the adjustments, modifications, and enhancements that are necessary during the "life" of the program. When you stop to consider that more than half of a programmer's time may be spent on maintaining existing programs—that is, out of every two programmers, only one will be working on the development of new projects—you can see just how important good documentation is. Documentation should begin at the beginning—that is, at the moment the idea of the system is conceived—and it should continue throughout the life of the system.

The computer operations staff needs to know when the program is to be run, where the input data are to come from, how to run the program and what to do if it won't run, where to deliver the reports, how long to save the information and data, and whether there are any special concerns, such as data security. The programmer's documentation file is the source for developing an operations manual that answers these questions in advance, thus preventing mixups and problems once the program is operational.

Table 12.2 Components of a Programmer's Documentation File

Component	Purpose
Problem definition	To describe the reason for developing the system
Systems definition	To describe the system's specifications, its interfaces with other systems, and the required inputs, files, outputs, and controls
Developmental references	To identify the personnel assigned to the project and the time required to complete various program modules
Design tools used (flowcharts, structure charts, HIPO charts, pseudocode)	To describe visually or otherwise the logic of the problem solution
File description	To describe by format (numerical, character, decimal positions) and by size the various data elements to be processed
Input/output specifications	To describe the sources of the input data, the layout of each of the outputs, and the routing of the outputs
Source listings/test data/test results	To show the program instructions in their original form and to describe the data used in testing the program and the results that indicated the program could handle anticipated inputs and errors
Benchmarks	To describe processing and response times for various activities and the impact of the program on the computer system
Security/control	To describe the program's built-in audit and control procedures
Program listing	To show the coded instructions that make up the program
Technical references	To describe hardware and systems software specifications
Maintenance changes	To describe any changes made in the program after implementation

SUMMARY

Program development begins with an analysis of the problem and the design of a solution to the problem. As described in the last chapter, designing the solution involves developing an algorithm and using a flowchart or some other design tool to describe the steps of the algorithm. The next step in program development is to code the program. In coding the program, the programmer translates the steps laid out in the design solution into a programming language. Most applications programming today is done in a high-level language, although assembly language is often used for coding routine jobs. High-level languages are not machine-specific, whereas assembly and machine languages are.

Since machine language is the only language the computer can "understand," a program written in any other language must be translated into machine language before the computer can execute the instructions. Compilers translate programs written in high-level languages; assemblers translate those written in assembly language. Compilers and assemblers transform source programs into object programs, which can be stored in machine code for future use. They also produce listings of the program instructions and diagnostic messages describing the syntax errors found in the program. Interpreters are another kind of translation program, often used on microcomputers. They do not produce object programs.

Programmers today have a wide variety of programming languages to choose from, among them BASIC, COBOL, FORTRAN, RPG, Pascal, Ada, C language, APL, and PL/1. BASIC is commonly used on microcomputers; COBOL is the most popular business language; FORTRAN is the most popular for scientific processing; RPG is used to generate business reports; Pascal is very popular in teaching structured programming; and Ada is becoming the standard programming language of the federal government. A standardized version of C language could have a major impact on future software development. The limitations of both APL and PL/1 make it unlikely that they will become widely used in writing business programs.

Once the program has been coded in a programming language, it must be debugged and tested. Before submitting it to the computer for compilation, the programmer should desk-check the program for both syntax and logic errors. After the program has made an error-free run through the computer, the programmer tests its ability to perform in particular conditions by using various kinds of test data as input.

Documentation of the program is necessary for users, programmers (especially maintenance programmers), and operations staff. The programmer's documentation file should contain all the details of the program's development.

KEY TERMS

Ada (352)
APL (356)
assembler (339)

assembly language (337)
assembly listings (339)
BASIC (342)

C language (355)
COBOL (345)
coding forms (335)
compiler (339)
default options (344)
desk-checking (359)
diagnostic messages (339)
FORTRAN (348)
high-level languages (338)
interactive language (342)
interpreter (341)
machine language (336)
macrocode (338)

nonprocedural language (350)
object program (339)
Pascal (350)
PL/1 (357)
procedural languages (350)
program dump (362)
programming language (334)
program statement (334)
RPG (350)
source listings (339)
source program (339)
syntax errors (339)

DISCUSSION QUESTIONS

1. What does the term *language connection* mean in relation to programming? Why is language such an important consideration in computing? What is the programmer actually doing when coding in a programming language?

2. Describe the differences in these levels of programming languages: machine, assembly, and high level. Explain how each is used.

3. Discuss the translation process by which assembly and high-level languages are translated into machine language. What are some of the outputs of this process? Why are they important?

4. Describe the advantages and disadvantages of COBOL, FORTRAN, BASIC, Pascal, RPG, Ada, C language, APL, and PL/1. Which language would you select for a college student to learn? Why?

5. Explain why most business programs are coded in COBOL.

6. What is the most important feature of a programming language? Explain your reasons.

7. What is program debugging? Why is it important?

8. Describe how programs are tested and why this testing is necessary.

9. How would an operations supervisor use program documentation?

10. "The wasting moth ne'er spoil'd my best array; The cause was this, I wore it every day." What relevance does this quote have for program documentation and maintenance?

OUTLINE

THE DEVELOPMENT OF SYSTEMS SOFTWARE

RESOURCE MANAGEMENT

CONTROL FUNCTIONS

    Scheduling and Job Management
    Input/Output Control and Data Management
    Systems Monitoring

SERVICE FUNCTIONS

    Language Translators
    Utility Programs
    Library Programs

SHARED RESOURCES

    Multiprogramming
    Timesharing
    Multiprocessing

VIRTUAL STORAGE

SUMMARY

KEY TERMS

DISCUSSION QUESTIONS

OVERVIEW

The programs we've been talking about in the last two chapters are applications programs — that is, computer instructions developed to meet particular information needs. But, as you may recall from Chapter 1, there is a second type of software: the systems software, which coordinates all the computer's operations. The operating system, a major component of the systems software, is really the traffic director for the computer: It controls the input, output, and processing activities; allocates parking spaces in primary storage; runs the signal lights to route traffic; decides which jobs will run first, scheduling them according to their priority; and investigates errors as if they were crimes, even to the point of issuing reports on them. Other components of the systems software perform services that make the life of the applications programmer a good deal easier.

The value of systems software becomes evident when you stop to consider that the computer always processes only one instruction at a time, and yet it can process millions of instructions per second. Keeping all the instruction signals straight is something of a Herculean task, and it is very efficiently performed by the operating system. The operating system is what makes it possible for the computer to run different applications programs concurrently and to respond to simultaneous processing requests from numerous online terminals. The services performed by the systems software allow the applications programmer to write programs in a high-level language rather than having to code them in the 0's and 1's of machine language; they also save the programmer from having to write out instructions for frequently repeated routines.

In this chapter, we'll take a look at the ways in which systems software contributes to the overall efficiency of the computer system. Our objectives are to

- explain how and why systems software evolved and what its purpose is.

- describe how systems software is categorized and how it operates.

- identify the main control and service functions performed by the systems software.

- explain multiprogramming, timesharing, and multiprocessing, and describe how they can be used to solve problems in handling business information.

- discuss the value and the problems of virtual storage.

CHAPTER 13

SYSTEMS SOFTWARE

THE DEVELOPMENT OF SYSTEMS SOFTWARE

The key to profitable business is the efficient and effective use of resources. The same applies to the profitable use of a computer system. As computer hardware has become more complex, more powerful, and more available, it has become increasingly important to find ways of more fully utilizing its power and speed. Two areas that have always been prone to inefficiency are the routine input and output operations. In the data processing systems of the early 1950s, the computer had to sit idle while the operations personnel loaded the program and entered data into the input device, cleared primary storage of any data remaining from the last job, and set the electronic switches. After the computer had run this single job, the operators had to unload the program, data, and output results; and the process began all over again for the next job. As computer systems became faster and larger, the problem of inefficiency became even more marked. The computer was operating at lightning speeds, while the pace of the operations personnel remained constant.

Computer manufacturers saw that if they were to improve the performance of their systems, they had to come up with a means of reducing the idle time and making fuller use of the computer's resources. The solution, as it turned out, did not come from further engineering advances. Instead, by the early 1960s, computer manufacturers had developed a set of specialized programs that allow the computer to manage its own resources and operations, at its own speed, and without the need for human intervention. Collectively, these programs are known as the **systems software.** The operating system, which functions as the computer's traffic director, is an important part of this systems software.

Systems software is most efficiently coded in a machine-specific language (i.e., assembly language or machine language). For this reason, and because software must correspond to the design and engineering characteristics of the hardware used, manufacturers develop systems software specifically for their own line of computing equipment. In other words, systems software is usually machine-specific, meaning that these programs will function only on the machine for which they were designed. We say "usually" because the microcomputer explosion has led to the development of *generic* systems software — generic in the sense that it will work with the equipment of a number of different manufacturers. Such standardization has been possible because microcomputer manufacturers use only a few kinds of microprocessor chips. In contrast, manufacturers of large systems use a wide variety of components, most of which are unique to those particular systems.

Developing systems software is a complex and costly process, and businesses very seldom choose to develop their own. The systems software that they acquire from computer manufacturers is naturally designed in as general a way as possible to meet the diverse needs of as many users as possible. Table 13.1 describes some of the operating systems provided by manufacturers for use on different types of computer systems. Although this software is designed in a general way, it can be adjusted to meet a particular company's needs; and, in fact, because every system configuration

Table 13.1 Representative Operating Systems for Different Types of Computer Systems

Operating System	Features	Applications
Mainframes		
DOS/VS OS/VS MVS VM/370 (all products of IBM)	Allocate the computer resources in such a way that simultaneous processing of multiple jobs is possible.	Used in large-scale applications in which extensive online storage is available and a high volume of jobs are processed.
Minicomputers		

UNIX
  (Bell Labs)
XENIX
  (Microsoft, Inc.)
UNOS
  (Charles River
  Data Systems)
	Written in C language, and easy to modify. Provide a set of software tools that can be used individually or sequenced to form a program "shell," which in other systems would require a special-purpose program. Easily adaptable for use with many different computer systems.	Particularly well suited for DEC computer systems used in universities. UNIX allows the user to create new functions by connecting modules; it is a multiuser system designed for timesharing.

Microcomputers		
CP/M CP/M3.0 CP/M-86 (all products of Digital Research, Inc.)	Easy-to-use English commands control a processor, a disk operating system, and a basic input/output system. Very "user-friendly." Portable to many different computer systems.	CP/M and CP/M3.0 are the primary operating systems used on 8-bit microprocessor systems. CP/M-86 is an expanded version for 16-bit micros.

is different, with a different arrangement of input and output devices and with different processing needs to be met, systems software must be "fine-tuned" when installed. Once functioning, the systems programs must be maintained; and when new hardware is added to the computer system, the programs have to be adjusted to meet the requirements of the new equipment. The person who installs and maintains these programs is called a **systems programmer.** A systems programmer does not usually get involved with individual applications but must be thoroughly versed in the computer hardware and the way it operates.

RESOURCE MANAGEMENT

The overall purpose of systems software is to manage the computer's resources as efficiently and effectively as possible. The functions that this software performs include both **control functions,** which are concerned with the operation of the system and the performance of various tasks, and **service functions** (also called **processing functions**), which simplify the preparation of applications programs. As Figure 13.1 shows, both the

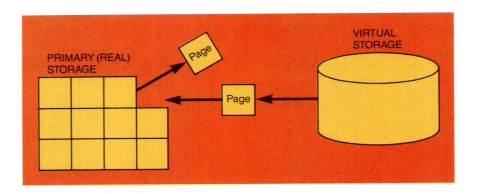

Figure 13.1
Components of systems software.

control functions and the service functions are under the direction of an operating systems program known as the **supervisor** (also called the **executive** or **monitor**). The control functions are carried out by specialized operating systems programs: scheduling and job-management programs, input/output control and data management programs, and systems-monitoring programs. These specialized programs, together with the supervisor, make up the operating system. The service functions are carried out by language translators; utility programs, which perform frequently used routines such as sorting; and library programs, which contain directories of frequently used program segments.

The supervisor program is kept in primary storage; the other programs are available from an online **systems-residence device,** usually a magnetic-disk drive (see Figure 13.2). The supervisor is responsible for overseeing the operation of the entire computer system. It calls the specialized programs into the CPU as needed and gives them temporary control. When the specialized task is finished, the supervisor resumes control.

For some purposes, such as the allocation of primary storage, the systems software is activated automatically. For specific *job* information, however, the supervisor needs specific instructions. (In this case, a **job** can be defined as a unit of work to be performed by the computer, such as the processing of a payroll or the copying of a file.) The specific job instructions that the supervisor needs relate to such matters as which input or output device to activate, which specific program to run, and which compiler program to use to translate applications programs written in a high-level language into machine language. The applications programmer communicates these instructions to the supervisor through a code known as **job-control language (JCL).** The particular form of the JCL is specific to the make and/or model of the hardware being used. JCL bears little resemblance to the applications programming languages; but, like them, it does require translation into machine language. A **job-control program,** similar to a compiler, is used for this translation.

Thus, to get a data processing job done, the applications programmer writes two sets of instructions (see Figure 13.3). The first to enter the

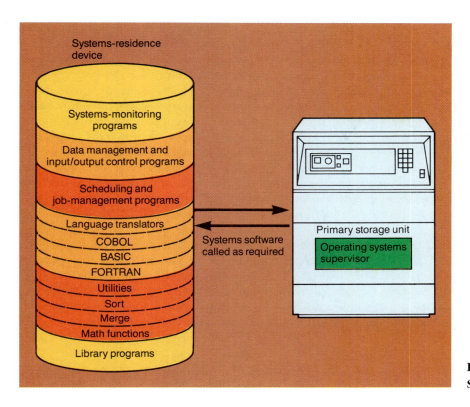

Figure 13.2
Storage locations of systems software.

Figure 13.3
Processing a computer job. Two sets of instructions — job control instructions and an applications program — are needed.

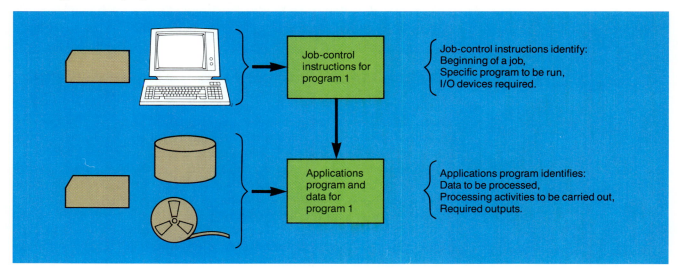

computer is in JCL and has to do with information on the specific job. In the absence of specific JCL instructions, the operating system has a *default option* — that is, it assumes that input, processing, and output activities are to be handled in a standard, predetermined way. For example, a printer may be the standard default option for output; and unless the programmer includes specific JCL instructions to the contrary, the system will produce output on a printer. If printed output is desired, the programmer doesn't need to include any instruction; but if output on a graphics plotter is needed, the programmer must specifically include that in the JCL instructions. The second set of instructions to enter the computer is the applications program, usually written in a high-level language and containing instructions on processing data and producing specific outputs.

Once the JCL instructions and the applications program have entered the computer, the CPU proceeds to execute them at enormous speed, with no further need of human intervention. With procedures mapped out by the systems software, operations can be carried out at the speed of electricity rather than at a human pace. Thus, although people could do all the tasks performed by the systems software, the systems software can do them faster and more efficiently. Let's now look at the two main functions of this software: the control functions and the service functions.

CONTROL FUNCTIONS

The control functions of the operating system include scheduling both the jobs to be run and the computer resources available to run them (scheduling and job management); allocating the computer resources needed to complete the job (input/output control and data management); and keeping track of the processing activities as well as maintaining a record of the system's users and the jobs run (systems monitoring). The level and complexity of the operating system's programs for each of these functions depends on the size and nature of the computer system being used. The objective of all these programs is, of course, to improve the efficiency of the system.

Scheduling and Job Management

Scheduling programs are used to assess priorities and to select jobs for processing as computer resources become available. The order in which jobs are processed may be determined in various ways: on a first-come–first-served basis; on the basis of the priority of the user or the type of job; or on the basis of a priority assigned by the programmer. A request by the president of a firm for a summary of sales to date might be given a high priority, and the job would be processed before a routine budget report scheduled for the end of each period. In this case, the user (the president) establishes the priority. Priorities based on the type of job are often related to legal requirements or business needs — for example, tax reports due by a certain date or payroll and billing jobs that must be

HUMAN INTERFACES AND THE OPERATING SYSTEM APPROACH

As computers became more popular and sophisticated, a profession that once consisted entirely of scientists and engineers began attracting many eager but less knowledgeable people. These new programmers could not be expected to cope with the ever-changing complexities of hardware. Schemes for addressing core memory cells, storing bits on magnetic drums and disk tracks, and decoding holes in the columns of Hollerith cards were always changing and each improvement in hardware design left the new breed of software specialists farther behind.

A buffer of some sort was needed. A buffer for the people writing software and a buffer for the software programs themselves, for whenever the hardware changed the software had to be changed too.

To solve these problems a relatively small group of interdisciplinary specialists began developing such a buffer. First came the Input/Output Control Systems (IOCS) with which an application program could indirectly request a variety of input or output data services. Later, as systems were improved to handle more than one job at a time, an executive or master program was created to schedule jobs and to mediate among jobs contending for scarce systems resources. Upon this base — the operating system — designers built libraries of device control and communication instruction sets (macros) and a host of utility programs and development tools.

This buffering layer of software ... solved two problems. First, it simplified programming by enabling software developers to define tasks without having to know all the details of the hardware system on which the task would run. Second, it encouraged the development of portable software that could be written once, yet run on several different hardware systems.

For obvious economic reasons, true software portability was not enthusiastically endorsed by the major hardware manufacturers. Instead, they concentrated on limited, vendor-specific versions of portability.... This allowed users to purchase ever more powerful machines without having to rewrite all of their programs, and yet it gave them a strong incentive to stay within the vendor's fold. Proprietary operating systems were the order of the day.

Today the industry seems obsessed with two ideas: user friendliness and industry compatibility....

In many respects these two goals — true user friendliness and maximum portability — are mutually exclusive. To be truly user friendly a program must be tailored to the individual likes and dislikes of the users, and most importantly to their preferred methods of working....

Software portability as practiced today, on the other hand, requires adherence to one cardinal rule: you can't write software code for input or output devices that aren't there. Assume for a moment that you are designing an application for two different personal computers. One machine has a keyboard, a touch screen, and a color monitor. The other has a keyboard, a mouse, and a speaker device for simulated voice response. Which of these devices can you use in your application? You guessed it: only the keyboard!

Now some designers would argue that you could devise a clever scheme to allow the users of these two different systems to dynamically tailor generic versions of the application to their own unique environments. But is such an approach viable when an application is to run on 20 to 50 different systems, some of which haven't even been fully specified when the software is being written? Obviously not.

[There are] parallels between this apparent paradox and the problem that led to the development of operating systems years ago. We have [an] interface problem (user friendliness) that nonspecialists cannot hope to master [and] an economic imperative to build systems for the broadest possible market (portable software).... The machine interface system approach (operating system) is [already] beginning to be applied to the human interface problem....

Human factors are no longer viewed as mere cosmetic details; indeed, many analysts hold that the ultimate success [of] personal computer products will [depend on] the user interfaces they provide.

— D. Verne Morland, "The Evolution of Software Architecture," *Datamation* (February 1, 1985), pp. 123–128. Reprinted with Permission of *Datamation*® magazine, © Copyright by Technical Publishing Company, A Dun & Bradstreet Company, 1985. All rights reserved.

processed on time because they involve large sums of money. When the programmer knows that a job has a high priority—such as a special financial report urgently needed by the firm's auditors—he or she can code the JCL to establish the priority. In any busy computer system, jobs are always waiting to be processed. As storage space, input and output devices, and other required hardware become available, the operating system's scheduling program selects the job to be processed next, always trying to balance the use of the hardware to gain the most efficiency from the system.

Job-management programs control the computer resources used during program execution, including the resources needed to load, process, and terminate jobs. These programs are used to initiate jobs, to control errors caused by instructions and equipment, and to deal with interruptions in program execution. Initiating jobs is the most straightforward of these activities. When the scheduling routine indicates that computer resources are available, a job is transferred into the CPU, and execution begins. The job-management program checks that all the necessary job information is in order—information on such things as location of the input data, the availability of any special forms required for the printer, and the need for any special activities, such as the mounting of a magnetic tape.

The errors that job-management programs control include data errors; errors in program instructions, such as an instruction calling for a file from an unavailable source (unavailable because it does not exist, a tape is not mounted, or there is a machine problem); and errors caused by equipment malfunction. Many of these problems would cause an **interrupt;** that is, the program would stop executing, and the job-management program would either abort it or signal the operator of the need for intervention. To illustrate how a job-management program would control an instruction error, let's suppose that an instruction in an applications program asks for data to be executed, but the storage file contains no such data. The program cannot continue, and the computer cannot evaluate whether the error is in the program or in the file. The operating system's job-management program would terminate the program execution and send a message to the computer operator describing the error.

Input/Output Control and Data Management

The CPU is normally much faster than the input and output devices. It can manipulate data at speeds of several million characters per second, whereas the fastest printer operates at speeds of only a few thousand characters per second. Input from a keyboard would be even slower. Even data coming from a magnetic unit such as a disk drive, which is considered a high-speed storage device, is transferred at less than half the internal speed of the CPU. It is up to the operating system's **input/output control**

programs to coordinate all three functions — input, processing, and output — to make the most effective use of the hardware. The goal of this component of the operating system is to balance the workload so that there is a smooth flow of jobs through the system, keeping the CPU active and preventing idle time while the CPU waits for data to be loaded or a report to be printed.

The input/output control program overcomes the speed differences between the input/output equipment and the CPU by making use of small, fast storage devices known as **buffers.** With buffers, the CPU can execute one job, print a second job, and accept input for a third job, all at the same time. Buffers provide temporary storage for input/output data either in a disk drive or in primary storage. When buffer storage is located in a disk drive, operating systems software known as a **spooling** program transfers, or "spools," data from the CPU to the disk, from the input device to the disk, or from the disk to the output device (see Figure 13.4). An *input buffer* can accept input data at the rate of speed of the input device, but it can release those data to the CPU at its own, much faster speed. Similarly, an *output buffer* can accept data from the CPU at a very fast speed, but it can release the data to an output device at the slower speed of the output device. Buffers thus greatly increase the overall efficiency of the system.

Input/output control has taken on a new dimension with the increased use of data communications systems and devices located at places remote from the computer system. In systems that use online terminals or that have remote data collection devices, signal traffic in and out of the computer system is constant. The operating system's **data management programs** provide some procedures for dealing with this traffic. **Polling routines** (software designed to monitor terminals on a continuing basis) are used

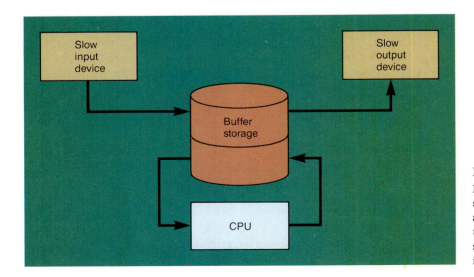

Figure 13.4
Buffering input and output data with spooling software and disk storage. To improve the performance of the system, input and output data are stored in buffers, and spooling software is used to control the data transfer.

to ask each terminal if a signal is being sent. Because many signals come into the system at the same time, some form of waiting line must be established; the software that establishes and manages the waiting line is called a **queuing routine.** Because signals are sent over telephone lines or via microwaves, a number of factors may interrupt the transmission of the signals, among them storms, accidents, and equipment failure. Data management programs can deal with these signal interruptions by requesting retransmission or by aborting the program.

The operating system's control of data communications is very important for two reasons. First, to get the most from the hardware, the polling and queuing must be done instantaneously. This kind of fast response is beyond human capability. Second, in data communications systems, it is also important to control the charges associated with signal transmission. Whether a telephone company, a private carrier, or a data communications firm is involved, efficient signal management can save a great deal of money. The operating system makes such efficiency possible.

In addition to controlling data communications, data management programs keep track of the storage locations of data. They provide data addresses by generating them through mathematical formulas or by maintaining a directory of data addresses, and they also systematically store and retrieve data created during processing. Processing requirements normally dictate the manner in which data are stored. For example, incoming payroll data from a transaction file are normally organized in a sequential fashion. However, to complete the processing of the payroll, the computer will need access to the master personnel file, and this file may be organized in a direct fashion. As you may remember from earlier chapters, when files are organized in a direct fashion, they are stored in a direct access storage device, and records are identified by addresses. These addresses are mathematically derived or are listed in the directory maintained by the data management program. When the input data from the transaction file enter the CPU, the data management program will determine where to place them in primary storage; using the address directory or mathematical formulas, it will also supervise the access and retrieval of master-file data from secondary storage devices. This feature of the operating system thus permits data to be organized and stored in different ways and yet called up and combined for processing in a single program.

Systems Monitoring

Who should be allowed access to sensitive computer programs and data? Should anyone with a terminal be able to scan personnel files, to look at salary data, personal data, and work-record data? Of course not — but how is it possible to control access to programs and data? With terminals scattered literally all over the world, access to the system cannot be controlled simply by locking the door to the computer room. Systems-monitoring programs and passwords offer some protection. **Systems-monitoring programs** discourage unauthorized access to the system by keeping a record of the processing activities and of the users who have had access to the system and by monitoring the system's activities while processing is underway. **Passwords** are codes that users must enter to prove their authorization before they are allowed entry to the system.

As it logs each job run and each user who has had access to the system, a systems-monitoring program provides a clear record of the activities that have taken place. This record, or **log,** is used for billing for computer time. It is also helpful in auditing and evaluating how efficiently the system is being used. In addition, the systems-monitoring program is responsible for keeping track of processing, and it will terminate a job that is using too much processing time or that exceeds available memory. When it terminates a job, the systems-monitoring program sends a message to the computer operator, and a new job is started automatically, thus preventing idle time while the operator evaluates the termination message and corrects the situation.

SERVICE FUNCTIONS

As we noted earlier, the service functions of systems software simplify the preparation of applications programs. Figure 13.5 shows how two of these systems programs — language translators and utility programs — are used in the execution of an applications program.

Language Translators

As we pointed out in Chapter 12, compilers and assemblers translate applications programs from high-level and assembly languages into machine language. What we didn't mention in Chapter 12, however, is that the compiler and assembler programs are stored in a systems-residence device. As a program is being developed, the programmer, using JCL, tells the supervisor which translation program is needed, and the supervisor retrieves that particular compiler (BASIC, COBOL, FORTRAN, or whatever is needed) or assembler from the systems-residence device and brings it into the CPU. The translation program then converts the source program (the high-level language program) into the object program (the program translated into machine language) to make it ready for execution. Once the program is operational, it is stored in object code for future runs.

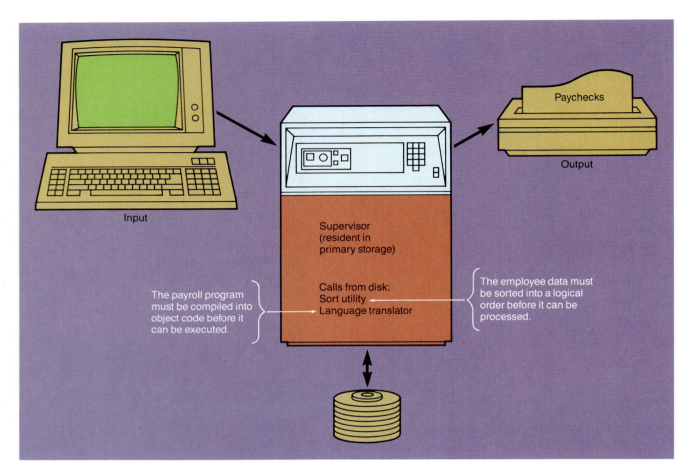

Figure 13.5
Systems software and program execution. The supervisor calls programs from disk storage as needed to complete the payroll processing.

Utility Programs

Almost every applications program calls for some of the same routine activities. It would be a waste of time for the programmer to rewrite these instructions each time they are needed. To avoid such duplication of effort, utility programs, which consist of **subprograms** (i.e., instructions on routine parts of applications programs), are stored in a systems-residence device so that they can be called into the CPU when needed. Figure 13.6 shows some of the routine activities that utility programs perform. These include sorting data into a sequence so that a file can be updated; merging sorted

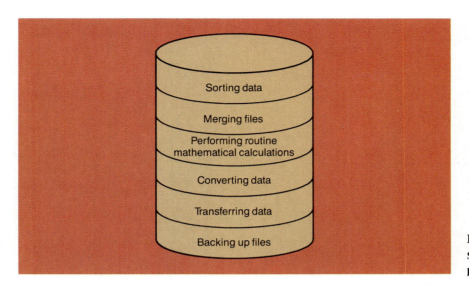

Figure 13.6
Some routine activities commonly performed by utility programs.

transaction files and master files into an updated master file; and performing mathematical calculations of square roots, sines, and cosines. Other utility programs are used to convert data from one medium to another (e.g., from tape to disk) and to transfer data from one input or output device to another — for example, from tape drive to printer — without processing.

One commonly used utility program is **DITTO,** which makes a copy of a file. On microcomputers, this program is usually called **BACKUP,** and it is particularly important because the floppy disks that microcomputers use for auxiliary storage are somewhat fragile. If the primary disk were damaged and no backup were available, programs, data, or information would be lost. Large systems have other, more complex backup utility programs, which they may use as often as once or twice a day to copy transaction data, and every three or four days to copy master files. If the transaction and master files are on disk, the backup copies are usually on the less expensive magnetic tape; the tapes are then removed and stored at places other than the computer center.

Library Programs

Library programs catalog and maintain a directory of the frequently used subprograms available to the system. These programs are stored in machine language in a systems-residence device. When needed, they are linked to an object program by a systems software routine known as **link/edit.** Since the link/edit routine automatically adds the standard subprogram instructions to the object program, the applications programmer is spared

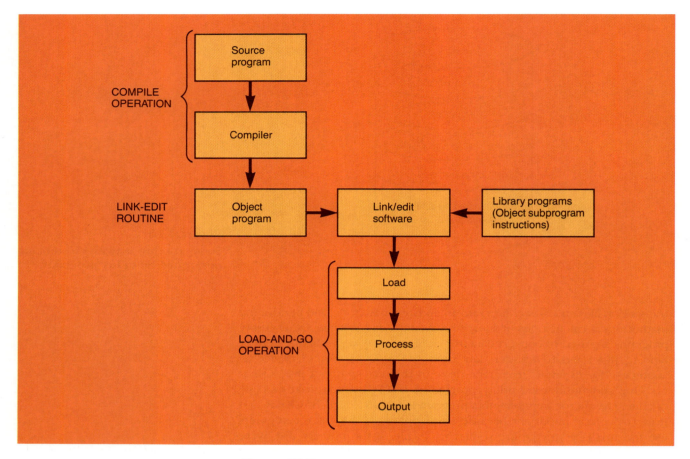

Figure 13.7
The link/edit routine and the load-and-go operation.

the trouble of having to write out the extra instructions. The operating system then proceeds with a **load-and-go** operation that actually executes the program (see Figure 13.7).

SHARED RESOURCES

The benefits of systems software that we have discussed so far are that it reduces idle time in the CPU, makes fuller use of all computer resources, and generally makes the life of the applications programmer a bit easier. But there are some benefits we haven't mentioned yet: The operating system also makes multiprogramming, timesharing, and multiprocessing possible. With these features, the computer's traffic director enables the system's users to share the roadways of the computer in harmony, usually unaware of a traffic jam — a rather remarkable feat when you consider that the computer can process only one instruction at a time.

Multiprogramming

Multiprogramming means that a number of applications programs are in primary storage at the same time and that the CPU gives each of these programs its undivided attention for a short period of time, usually a fraction of a second (see Figure 13.8). Thus, the CPU switches from one job to another, giving each a time slice, even though it may not have finished processing the first job. Because of the speed of the CPU and the control functions of the operating system, the interruptions are usually not apparent to the computer user. The typical program will call for data to be entered from input devices and from secondary storage devices, for data to be written into secondary storage, and for output data to be fed to a printer. All these tasks are performed at speeds much slower than the internal processing speed of the CPU; so rather than standing idly by waiting for the activity to be completed, the CPU will move to another program

Figure 13.8
Multiprogramming. A number of programs are in primary storage at the same time, and each is given a slice of processing time. In time slice 4, job 1 is loading input record 4, while record 2 is being processed; and job 2 is loading input record 4, while processed record 1 is being transmitted to the output device.

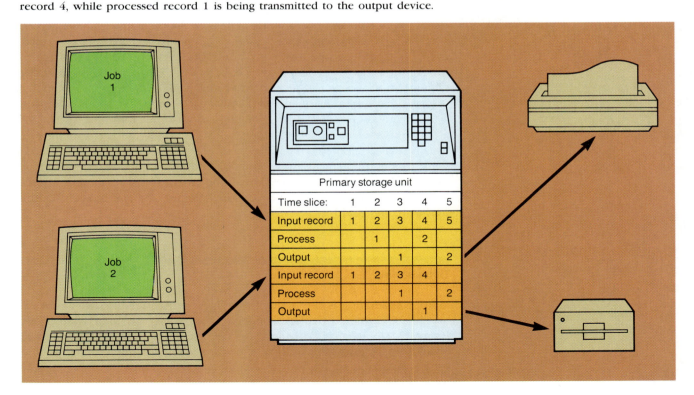

and begin processing. When the "slow" activity is completed on the first program, the CPU will return and finish the processing.

Multiprogramming works in much the same way an automobile repair shop does. A mechanic tests your car and diagnoses its problem. The shop then calls you for authorization to complete the repairs. If you don't answer, the mechanic moves to another job, and the shop will try you again later. Once you have authorized the repairs, the shop may have to order parts; so once again there is a wait, and the mechanic starts a new job. When the parts arrive, the mechanic fixes your car, and the shop calls you to come and pick it up. While waiting for you to come and get your car, the mechanic begins work on another job. The object is to keep the mechanic busy and not standing around while waiting for approval, parts, or payment. The same principle holds true for the computer, with the operating system managing the schedule to keep the system busy.

Multiprogram processing is said to be *concurrent* rather than simultaneous. That is, although the programs are in the computer system at the same time, they are not receiving the same kind of processing at exactly the same time. Instead, they act in *concurrence,* or cooperation, in sharing the system's resources over the same time period. The operating system sees that the way the sharing takes place makes the fullest possible use of the computer resources.

The advantages of multiprogramming are twofold. First, it contributes greatly to the efficient use of the system since all resources are used as much as possible and as efficiently as possible. Because the CPU is so much faster than the input/output devices, if only one job at a time were processed, the CPU would be idle for considerable portions of time. Second, multiprocessing gives users better service. Before the introduction of multiprogramming, processing requests were lined up in a queue. The computer took the first job in the queue, processed it to completion, and then moved on to the next. As a user, you simply had to wait your turn in the queue — a situation that gave rise to many a frayed nerve. A long printing job, usually the slowest function of computing, might mean that you waited while hundeds of pages were printed and the CPU took a nap! Thus, multiprogramming has improved **throughput** — that is, the time that elapses between the placement of a processing request and the delivery of the output to the user.

Timesharing

Multiprogramming is the basis of timesharing. In **timesharing,** unrelated users have terminals that are connected to a single computer system (see Figure 13.9). Each active terminal (i.e., one that is entering data or requesting processing) is given a small time slice for each processing cycle. The time slice is generally a fraction of a second, which is enough for the computer to do a great deal of processing but usually not enough for it to complete

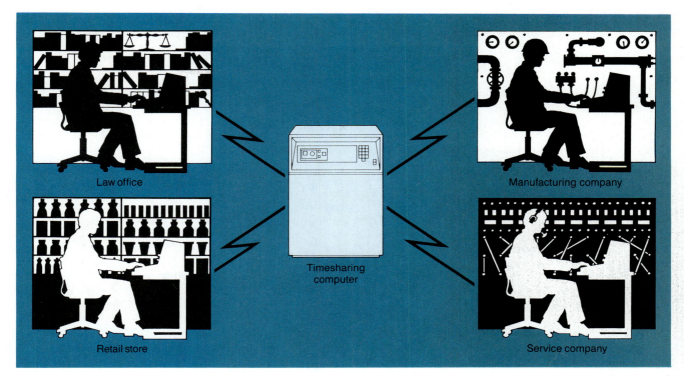

Figure 13.9
Timesharing.

the job. Each terminal is polled, and the active ones are given their segment of time until all terminals have had a turn. Then the cycle starts all over again, with each active terminal given another time slice during each cycle until the job is completed. Timesharing thus gives a number of users access to the system at the same time, and all get their jobs worked on without having to wait in line. This technique is particularly useful when a number of small processing jobs are constantly being requested. Most users would prefer to wait a few seconds for the computer to respond because of the time-slice allocation than to get immediate processing response if immediate response means they have to wait in a queue for twenty jobs to process ahead of theirs.

Multiprocessing

Multiprocessing means that two or more CPUs are linked to form a coordinated system. In such a system, the different CPUs are able to process different instructions from the same program at the same time, or they

A SHORT HISTORY OF UNIX

It all began with Kenneth Thompson's and Dennis Ritchie's frustration with the operating systems available in 1969. The Murray Hill Computer Center for Bell Laboratories was running a General Electric 645 mainframe under the Multics operating system, which was one of the first multiuser interactive systems. Before Multics, however, only batch-oriented operating systems — typically using punched cards and producing printouts — were available. Following in the batch-processing tradition, a major emphasis of Multics was isolating users from one another with several layers of protection to ensure that they did not inadvertently alter each other's disk files. Since sharing files among a well-organized team of programmers was the emerging software project style at Bell Labs, Thompson . . . set out to build a better system. The final result — Unix — was not written all at once, however, but rather evolved in response to more immediate needs.

One of Thompson's ambitious software projects that spurred him on toward Unix was his Space Travel program, which simulated the movement of the major celestial bodies in the solar system. A little-used Digital Equipment Corp. PDP-7 with an excellent display processor was a natural for rewriting Space Travel, especially since it cost $75 to run the program on the GE machine.

The project served as a painful introduction to how difficult program development can be with a computer lacking an adequate operating system. Initially, programs for the PDP-7 were developed on the 645 and carried to the DEC machine on paper tape. But Thompson soon tired of that, first implementing a rudimentary operating system and, finally, an assembler for the PDP-7, both of which were written entirely in assembly language. That adventure set him thinking about the kind of file system that would by its nature encourage cooperative programming projects. As he implemented these ideas, the name Unix was suggested as a play on the name of the soon-to-be-abandoned Multics system.

Thus, Unix was born in the mind of Ken Thompson and continued evolving into its current form in response to its increasing use within Bell Labs. For example, the patent department's interest in Unix resulted in extensive word-processing capabilities being built into the system. As Unix grew, however, its lack of a high-level language became the limiting factor that spurred Thompson to write the language B just before the whole system was transported to one of the first DEC PDP-11/45s ever made. Several utilities were written in B, but it soon became evident that an interpretive language without structures or data typing would not be suitable for rewriting Unix.

Finally, the maintenance headaches became so splitting that Dennis Ritchie wrote C in order to shape Unix into a more manageable form. "One of my primary goals was to eradicate explicit machine dependencies like the Nuxi problem," comments Ritchie, inverting the two syllables of Unix in comic reference to the PDP-11 technique of storing the least significant byte of 16-bit words first.

C evolved along with the whole Unix project, making possible the addition of multiprocessing and the transportability of Unix to other machines. Now one of the most respected structured programming languages around, C is largely responsible for the widespread use of Unix in many multiple-user processing systems.

— R. Colin Johnson, "A Short History of Unix." Reprinted from *Electronics,* March 24, 1981. Copyright © 1985, McGraw-Hill Inc. All rights reserved.

---

can process separate, complete programs at the same time. This is referred to as *simultaneous* processing, and it is possible because of the operating systems software that controls the allocation of the arithmetic/logic circuits and the input/output devices. With multiprocessing techniques, systems of the same or different capacities can be connected, processing circuits can be shared, and workloads can be balanced as the processing requirements change. By way of analogy, think of the role of a bricklayer in the construction of a building. If the building must go up in a hurry, a second bricklayer can be assigned to work with the first; if there is no rush, only one bricklayer will be assigned to the building, and the second will go to a different job. Deciding whether there is a need and making the appropriate assignments is the role of the operating system.

VIRTUAL STORAGE

Excessive demands on the capacity of the CPU's primary memory, such as might be created by multiprogramming or by a single large program having an enormous number of instructions, can create problems in the computer system. A technique for handling such problems is to segment the programs and to execute one segment at a time. The most efficient way to accomplish this segmentation is to have the hardware and operating systems software work together automatically. Instead of calling the entire program from auxiliary storage, the operating system will call for program segments and move them into primary memory as they are required during the execution of a program. This continuous swapping of information between primary storage and auxiliary storage creates the illusion that primary memory is much larger than it actually is, and it is referred to as **virtual storage.**

When a computer is designed for virtual storage, programs are stored in a DASD, and they are organized either by segments or by pages. In the **segmentation** method, blocks of differing sizes related to different parts of the program logic are moved in and out of primary storage by the operating system. Typical segments might consist of all the statements within a loop or the statements found in a subroutine. Because memory is allocated according to the size of the segments, this procedure can take effective advantage of varying-sized blocks available in primary memory. However, memory can also be allocated to program segments on a first-come–first-served basis (see Figure 13.10).

When a **paging** system of program organization is used, the program is divided into units called pages. Each of the pages is the same size, just as each page in this book is the same size. As with book pages, there will be some wasted space if the pages are not completely filled. The primary storage unit is divided into page frames, and each page frame holds no more than a few thousand bytes (usually 2K or 4K bytes). With the paging system, the program logic does not influence the allocation of the program instructions into pages; the allocation is based solely on the capacity of each page and each page frame (see Figure 13.11).

During program execution, the operating system handles the swapping of the program segments or pages into and out of primary storage. One problem that the operating system can encounter when primary storage space is inadequate is called **thrashing.** Thrashing occurs when page segments are removed before they have been executed, and it puts a strain

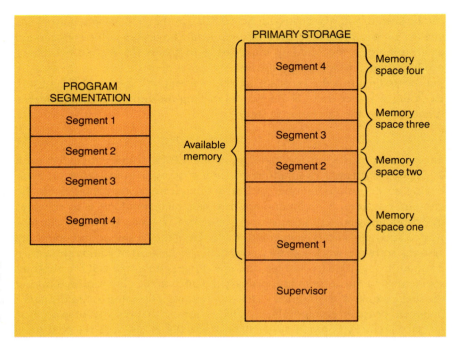

Figure 13.10

Virtual storage through program segmentation. Program segments are placed in available memory either by first-available space, as illustrated, or by best-fit space, which matches segment size to available memory size.

on the operating system, which has to swap the needed page back into primary memory. When swapping takes place needlessly — that is, when the segment has to be brought into primary memory several times before it is actually used — processing is slowed down and resources are wasted. These problems have put pressure on the developers of systems software to come up with a way of reducing thrashing. One technique that has been devised is to swap out of primary storage the least recently used page, rather than swapping a physical storage location regardless of its contents. This technique requires additional software to keep tabs on the

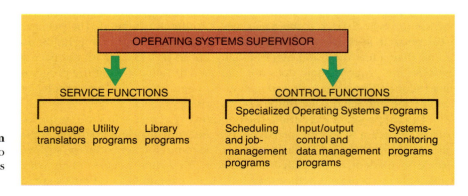

Figure 13.11

Virtual storage through program paging. The program is divided into pages that will fit into the page frames of the primary storage unit.

activity within the real memory; so, while helping to solve one problem, it creates another, since it complicates the systems software.

Regardless of the techniques used, virtual storage allows the programmer to prepare a program without being concerned about the size of the available real memory. Properly operated, software for virtual storage will remain *transparent* — that is, the programmer will not be aware of the swapping. Such software can act as the automatic transmission for memory allocation, and with smooth shifting taken care of, the programmer can concentrate on the applications problems rather than having to worry about the systems problems.

SUMMARY

Systems software consists of specialized programs that allow the computer to manage its own resources and operations, at its own speed, and without human intervention. These programs evolved out of a need created by the time lag between increased processing speeds and constant human operating speeds. The objective of this software is to see that the computer system runs as efficiently and effectively as possible.

Systems software is often machine-specific, and it is generally purchased from a computer manufacturer. Because purchased software is designed to meet general needs, systems software acquired in this way must be fine-tuned to meet the needs of a particular business. The person who does the fine-tuning and who maintains and adjusts the systems software is called a systems programmer.

The functions that systems software performs can be classified as control functions and service functions. The operating system's supervisor program oversees the performance of both kinds of functions. The supervisor is kept in primary storage; the other programs that comprise the systems software are kept in systems-residence devices, and the supervisor calls them into the CPU as needed. To communicate specific job instructions to the supervisor, the applications programmer uses job-control language (JCL). A job-control program, similar to a compiler, translates JCL into machine language.

The control functions performed by the operating system are carried out by scheduling and job-management programs, input/output control and data management programs, and systems-monitoring programs. Scheduling programs assess job priorities, and job-management programs initiate jobs, control errors caused by instructions and equipment, and deal with interruptions in program execution. Input/output control programs overcome the speed differences between input/output equipment and the CPU by making use of small, fast storage devices known as buffers. Buffers located in disk drives use spooling software to speed the transfer of data between the CPU, the disk, and the input and output devices. Data management programs provide polling and queuing routines for dealing with the traffic of data communications systems. They also keep track of the storage locations of the data. Systems-monitoring programs are aimed at preventing unauthorized access to data; they include such features as passwords and logs.

Service functions simplify the preparation of applications programs. They are carried out by language translators, utility programs, and library programs. Language translators include the various compilers and assemblers. Utility programs perform routine subprograms automatically, thus saving the applications programmer from having to repeat the instructions. The subprograms cataloged in the directory of a library program can be automatically added to an object program through a link/edit routine, and the operating system can then proceed with a load-and-go-operation.

Some operating systems are designed to enable the computer to concurrently process multiple programs. Such sharing of the computer's resources by a number of jobs at the same time is called multiprogramming, and it is the basis of modern timesharing systems, in which unrelated users have access to a single computer system. Operating systems also make multiprocessing possible—that is, the linking of two or more CPUs to form a coordinated system.

Virtual storage is a technique in which the operating system and the computer hardware work together automatically to create the illusion that primary storage is larger than it actually is. This technique is very useful when demands on primary storage are high. It involves the continuous swapping of information between primary and auxiliary storage, the storage of programs on a DASD, and the segmentation of programs into blocks or pages. Thrashing—the removal of pages of programs before they are executed—can be a problem when primary storage is inadequate.

KEY TERMS

BACKUP (379)
buffers (375)
control functions (369)
data management programs (375)
DITTO (379)
input/output control programs (374)
interrupt (374)
job (370)
job-control language (JCL) (370)

job-control program (370)
job-management programs (374)
library programs (379)
link/edit (379)
load-and-go (380)
log (377)
multiprocessing (383)
multiprogramming (381)
paging (385)
passwords (377)

polling routines (375)
queuing routine (376)
scheduling programs (372)
segmentation (385)
service functions (processing functions) (369)
spooling (375)
subprograms (378)
supervisor (executive, monitor) (370)
systems-monitoring programs (377)
systems programmer (369)
systems-residence device (370)
systems software (368)
thrashing (385)
throughput (382)
timesharing (382)
virtual storage (385)

DISCUSSION QUESTIONS

1. Explain why systems software evolved. What purpose does it serve?
2. Explain why systems software is usually supplied by the computer manufacturer rather than being written by the computer users. Describe the role of a systems programmer.
3. Describe the role of the operating system's supervisor program.
4. How does the operating system serve as the computer's traffic director? Identify and describe the more commonly used control programs found in an operating system.
5. How would a systems-monitoring program help in establishing a billing system for computer services?
6. What are job-management programs? How would job-management software be used in a mainframe computer environment? How do data management programs assist data communications systems?
7. Explain the ways in which systems software assists the applications programmer. Why is it often said that systems software distances the computer user from the computer hardware?
8. Explain the concept of multiprogramming and why it is essential to timesharing computer systems.
9. What is multiprocessing, and when should a business consider using it?
10. Discuss the value, the techniques, and the problems of virtual storage.

OUTLINE

IN-HOUSE SOFTWARE DEVELOPMENT: COSTS, CONSTRAINTS, AND THE NEED FOR PRODUCTIVITY

- The Economic Issues
- Constraints on In-House Software Development
  - Internal Constraints
  - External Constraints
- Techniques for Improving Programming Productivity

ALTERNATIVES TO IN-HOUSE SOFTWARE DEVELOPMENT

- Purchased or Leased Software
- Contract Programming
- User-Group Program Sharing

ARTIFICIAL INTELLIGENCE

- AI Techniques
  - Search Techniques
  - Heuristics
  - Pattern Recognition
  - Knowledge Representation
- AI Applications

SUMMARY

KEY TERMS

DISCUSSION QUESTIONS

OVERVIEW

Software developers face two major challenges for the remainder of this century. One is the effective and efficient use of resources, skills, and technology — the issue of improving programming productivity. In-house development of custom-designed software has become very expensive and faces many other constraints as well. These pressures are mandating that program development become more scientific, more structured, and more comprehensible to users and management alike. While that process is underway, a number of alternative routes to software development are becoming increasingly popular, among them commercial software packages and contract programming. The other major challenge facing software developers is the development of artificial intelligence, a phenomenon with far-reaching implications. These topics — the costs, constraints, and productivity of in-house programming; the alternatives to in-house programming; and the development of artificial intelligence — are the focus of this chapter. Our objectives here are to

- explain the economic issues involved in in-house software development.
- describe the constraints on in-house software development.
- discuss the techniques available for improving programming productivity.
- outline the alternatives to in-house software development.
- explain the role of software in the application of artificial intelligence to problem solving.

CHAPTER 14

THE STATE OF SOFTWARE TODAY

IN-HOUSE SOFTWARE DEVELOPMENT: COSTS, CONSTRAINTS, AND THE NEED FOR PRODUCTIVITY

The Economic Issues

Over the past twenty-five years, the cost of computer hardware has declined dramatically, while the cost of software — particularly software that a company develops in-house for its own specific purposes — has continued to increase. Figure 14.1 gives you some idea of the discrepancy in these costs. One reason for the decline in the cost of hardware is that the integrated electronic circuits are mass produced, which significantly cuts the cost of labor. In contrast, the development of software is highly labor-intensive, and the need for labor doesn't simply end with the completion of a program ready for computer execution. As we noted in Chapter 11, maintenance of the programs — keeping them responsive to users' needs, adjusting them when new hardware is acquired, and correcting errors that appear after the programs have been implemented — may occupy more than half of a programmer's time.

Another factor in the high cost of software is that programming has evolved into something of an art form, with all the inherent difficulties found in the imprecise world of the arts. Whereas electronic circuits and new hardware technology are tested, refined, and evaluated in a scientific laboratory before they are made available to the public, the laboratory for software is business itself. The testing that takes place during program development discovers only the most major developmental flaws, and the first software product is usually the final product. Because each project or job is unique, with many unknowns, there are few hard and fast rules for a programmer to follow when designing a solution to an information problem. Moreover, the programmer usually can devise a number of alternative

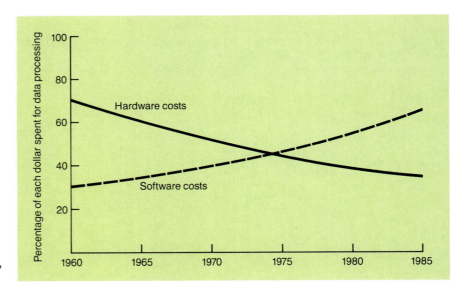

Figure 14.1
Costs of hardware and software, 1960–1985.

designs that would meet the users' needs. In short, the traditional approach to programming has been independent, freewheeling, and generally unstructured.

In view of the escalating costs of custom-designing and maintaining software, businesses have had to consider less expensive alternatives to developing their own programs in-house. Among these alternatives, which we'll discuss later in the chapter, are purchased or leased software, contract programming, and user-group program sharing. At times, however, no suitable alternative may exist; a firm may need special reports or a type of processing not usually done by other businesses, or it may have other unique requirements not met by a "generic" type of purchased software. For example, a jewelry manufacturer might need to track the wholesale prices of precious metals, or a school that has changed its status from junior college to university might need to redesign its registration system so that old course numbers coordinate with the requirements listed in the new catalog. The only way of solving such specific problems is to analyze the issues involved and to develop software that addresses them.

The expense of developing this kind of custom-designed software has given rise to a great deal of concern over improving programming productivity. One response to this concern has been the development of structured design and programming techniques. Another has been the development of specialized management techniques. Let's look first at the constraints that businesses face when they have no alternative but to develop their own programs in-house. We'll then look at the various techniques available to aid them in this process.

Constraints on In-House Software Development

Just because a firm needs or wants to develop its own software is not enough to make it happen. Forces both inside and outside the organization can have a constraining, or limiting, effect. Internal constraints include the size of the available staff and their individual skills, the availability of hardware, organizational issues, and cost. External constraints include legal requirements and the state of the hardware technology available to implement the software.

Internal Constraints. A data processing department has only a certain number of personnel available to meet requests for new software systems or systems enhancements. Very often, it's impossible to meet all these requests with the limited number of staff on hand. Allocating personnel to specific jobs is further complicated by the fact that most requests for systems change have some merit.

The skills of the available personnel can present yet another stumbling block to meeting requests for software development. The development of complex software, such as a program for simulating how the market will respond to a new product, requires technically trained staff with a wide range of skills, and such personnel are generally in short supply. This personnel shortage will probably continue throughout the century. Programming and systems analysis skills are not easily learned, and not everyone has the ability to master them. They usually require a college education or intense technical training. Companies that are in undesirable geographical locations or that don't pay competitive salaries are at a particular disadvantage in attracting experienced staff capable of developing and implementing new software systems.

Another internal constraint on software development can occur when a company lacks the hardware necessary to implement the program. A program for providing all managers with immediate access to information on inventory, finance, and production might sound like a wonderful idea until you realize that it would require the acquisition of a new terminal for each manager's desk and that the new terminals and supporting hardware would represent more equipment than all the hardware needed to maintain the company's accounting and payroll systems. The mechanics of supporting the system are another consideration. These include such factors as the wiring of terminals to user areas, signal distortions and telecommunications problems, available computer memory, contention for processing capabilities by other software systems, and the availability of necessary special equipment such as scanners and sensing devices. If the program is considered important enough, these mechanical details need not hold up development, but the trade-offs involved in implementing the program should always be given serious consideration. For example, if the new software system is installed and every manager has a terminal in use, will it bog down the computer system so that it responds to all users much more slowly? Is this slowdown acceptable? These are difficult questions, and the job of the data processing manager is to weigh the pros and cons of each system before deciding which ones to develop.

Organizational factors also play a role in software development. In most companies, resources are allocated within organizational divisions or functional areas. Because small divisions usually receive less funding for systems development than large divisions, they are limited in making major developmental efforts. Another organizational consideration is the issue of "turf." Certain components within the organization may see themselves as solely responsible for providing data processing and information-reporting services. When a new system is proposed to circumvent this established function, disputes over responsibility may arise.

The major issue underlying all other internal constraints on software development is usually one of cost. No business has unlimited resources, and the objective of effective resource management is to get the most from the resources expended. In deciding whether a proposed program is worth the allocation of scarce personnel and the expenditure of the other resources necessary to develop it, most companies rely on a

Table 14.1 A Cost/Benefit Analysis of a Project for Modifying an Order-Entry System

Project Costs

Programmer/analyst (15 days @ $200/day)	$3,000	
Machine time for testing	500	
Printed forms	200	
Training	600	
Total systems development costs		$4,300
Operational costs ($100/yr., system life = 5 yrs.)		500
Total estimated project costs		$4,800

Project Benefits

Clerical time savings (1 hr./wk., or 50 hr./yr. @ $10/hr. for 5 yrs.)	$2,500
Intangible benefits (improved competitive position and customer satisfaction, $500/yr. for 5 yrs.)	2,500
Total estimated projected benefits	$5,000
Net project return	$ 200

cost/benefit analysis. Costs can be classified as developmental and operational. **Developmental costs** are a one-time expense and occur as the system is being designed and the programs are being prepared. **Operational costs** are ongoing and reflect the expense of running the system after it is operational. Both kinds of costs must be considered if the cost/benefit analysis is to be accurate. The analysis also requires that the benefits of the proposed system be projected and that a monetary value be assigned to them. Table 14.1 shows a simplified cost/benefit analysis. As you can see from the figures in the table, this project would have to be considered marginal. Any miscalculation of the benefit estimates — and this process is subject to error — would cause the project to cost more than its estimated value. The company would probably have other proposals for projects that show a greater benefit for the resources expended, and it is unlikely that this project would be accepted on the basis of the cost/benefit analysis.

External Constraints. Legal requirements can be a very important external constraint on software development. In evaluating a proposed project, a company should first consider whether it has the legal right to collect the data necessary to feed the system; personal credit, for example, is a sensitive legal area, and the collection of certain data related to it is prohibited by law. The company should next consider whether it has the legal right to use the information after it has been compiled. For instance, one information system, which recorded the disposition of criminal cases and made this information available to subscribers, had to be scrapped because it overlooked the law that prohibits the disclosure of the identity of minors and the nature of the crimes in which they have been involved. All the court data had been entered into the system without regard for the ages of the individuals, and once the data base became operational, it was impossible to tell which data related to minors and which to adults.

The law also requires that protection be provided against unauthorized access to and manipulation of sensitive data, such as personal data and data relating to national security (e.g., contracts for military arms). Other legal constraints affect how data are kept and recorded. Tax agencies, for example, require compliance with standardized accounting and reporting procedures, and stringent legal requirements govern the tabulating and reporting of social security payments, the length of time that records must be kept, the manner in which the information may be used, and the persons to whom the information may be reported.

The state of the hardware technology available to implement the program can be another external constraint on software development. As we noted in Chapter 10, the merging of mainframes and microcomputers is an area fraught with frustration. Even when both computers are manufactured by the same firm, they are often incompatible, and programs calling for the linking of the two may be impossible to implement. Software systems involving the use of peripheral equipment that is still in a state of development may face similar problems. Optical scanners, audio systems, and hard-copy graphics are just a few of the areas in which technology is still developing at a rapid pace. Software systems that rely on proven technology obviously have a better chance of success than those involving experimental equipment.

Techniques for Improving Programming Productivity

A company that decides that the in-house development of custom-designed software is a cost-effective and necessary measure has at its disposal a number of tools that can improve the productivity of its programming efforts. These include the structured design and programming techniques that we described in Chapter 11: pseudocode, top-down design, HIPO charts, and modular programming. These techniques are aimed at simplifying the coding, testing, documentation, and maintenance of programs. An important thing to note, however, is that to improve programming productivity, a company should make a commitment to one programming method and should stick with that method. Standardizing the formats used in defining the programming tasks and in documenting the program will also help to improve programming productivity.

An exciting spin-off of the structured design and programming methods is the concept of **reusable code** — that is, semi-independent modules of programming code that can be used as building blocks in the development of various other systems (see Figure 14.2). The idea is quite similar to the concept of interchangeable parts, which fueled the Industrial Revolution,

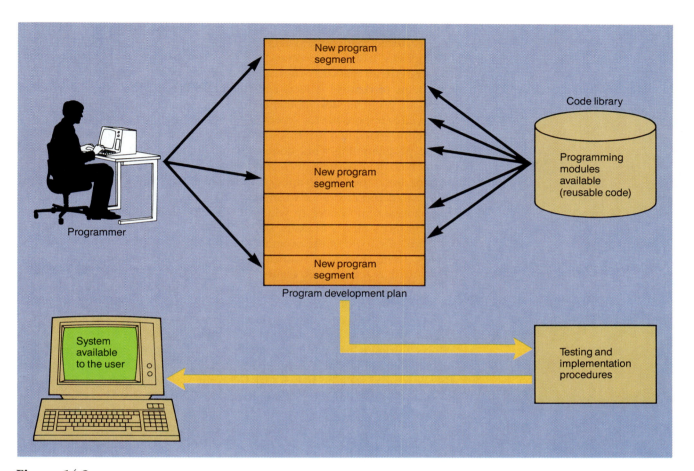

Figure 14.2
Reusable code.

and it is rapidly gaining in popularity. Some people believe that because of reusable code, the job of the programmer is changing and that in the not-too-distant future, programmers will be chiefly assemblers of programming modules. According to some estimates, by 1990 over 80 percent of the code in any program will be retrieved from a code library, and programmers will spend only 20 percent or less of their time on programming new systems. Reusable code can save both time and money, as the wheel doesn't have to be reinvented each time a program is developed. It therefore looks like a very promising approach to solving some of the programming problems that businesses and industry face. Properly managed, reusable code will increase the productivity of the programmer and at the same time allow businesses to create powerful systems in a quicker and less expensive way.

Because traditional business management techniques have not worked very well in the world of programming — where there are many unknowns, few established rules, and a prevailing spirit of independence — a number of specialized management techniques aimed at improving programming productivity have also evolved. The most popular of these techniques is the **structured walkthrough,** a formal review of design and programming that helps to remove defects and to clear up logic problems in the early stages of program development. The programmer whose work is to be reviewed is responsible for scheduling the structured walkthrough. Sometime before the scheduled meeting, the programmer distributes documentation of the programming work done to date to members of the **peer review team** who will participate in the session. This team usually consists of four or five other programmers or technical specialists. The role of the team is to detect errors and to improve design and coding in a nonthreatening, cooperative atmosphere in which there is no criticism of the individual programmer's merits or skills. During the session, the programmer "walks through" the logic of the program step by step, while the members of the review team, who have studied the program documentation in advance, voice their reactions (see Figure 14.3).

The structured walkthrough takes programmers out of the vacuum in which they have often labored. It requires that they formalize their thinking and that they make their programming efforts understandable not only to themselves but to their peers as well. This scrutiny of the programmer's efforts, during which flaws are uncovered and solutions are discussed, also creates a learning situation for less experienced staff. A primary benefit of the structured walkthrough is that as a result of the program's having been so clearly outlined, the program becomes much easier and cheaper to maintain. Because the person who develops the program is very rarely the same person who later maintains it, strict adherence to company standards

Figure 14.3
A structured walkthrough.
Stacy Pick/Stock, Boston.

on software development is very important; the structured walkthrough, properly executed, can help to implement such standards.

Another management technique that is finding favor in software development is the **chief programmer team.** Programs often have tens of thousands of lines of instructions. Because it would be impossible for a single individual to develop the entire program in a reasonable length of time, a team is often assigned to the project. Without leadership, team members may go their separate ways, and when it comes time to assemble the entire program, their efforts may not coincide with the efforts of the other team members. To avoid this situation, a senior technician is appointed chief programmer. The role of the chief programmer is to develop the general design and to oversee the work on the various components of the project, including the technical documentation. The chief programmer thus becomes the technical manager for the project.

The organization of the chief programmer team is in many ways like the organization of an apprentice system. Beginners are assigned the more straightforward and easily defined tasks such as designing forms, and if they need help, they can turn to the chief programmer. The experienced staff assume more challenging roles, learning from the experience and preparing ultimately to become chief programmers themselves. As with most apprentice systems, there can be problems; just because an individual is an experienced programmer does not mean he or she is an effective manager. Still, most would agree that the chief programmer team allows technicians with varying levels of skill to make significant contributions to a project and to learn and grow from the experience. It also allows the most experienced technicians to organize and control the development, coding, and testing activities, which is where the standards of the organization are most often applied. Management skills can be gained with experience, just as technical skills are. Figure 14.4 shows the organization of a typical chief programmer team.

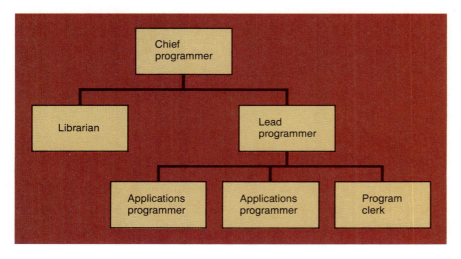

Figure 14.4

Organization of a chief programmer team.

ALTERNATIVES TO IN-HOUSE SOFTWARE DEVELOPMENT

Although in certain situations businesses may have no suitable alternative to developing their own specialized software in-house, there are many other situations in which an alternative source of software will provide the needed program in a more cost-effective way. As we noted earlier, these alternatives include purchased or leased software, contract programming, and user-group program sharing. Table 14.2 compares the costs of these alternative sources with the cost of in-house development of software; the figures shown in the table reflect the costs of an order-tracking system for a medium-sized business.

Purchased or Leased Software

Data processing requirements may seem unique to a particular business, but when viewed from the general world of commerce, they are often very similar to the information needs of many other businesses. Developing software from scratch to meet these needs is expensive and may not always be necessary. Both hardware manufacturers and software suppliers offer for sale or lease a number of software products designed to meet general business needs. Hardware manufacturers include such companies as IBM, Honeywell, and Digital Equipment Corporation. Software suppliers include computer stores such as Computerland and Entré, which carry a wide range of computer products, and companies that do nothing but develop and sell software, such as the Cullinet Company. Figure 14.5 gives you some idea of the tremendous variety of software packages commercially available today. Most of the products shown are registered trademarks.

A program for payroll processing is typical of the kind of software that

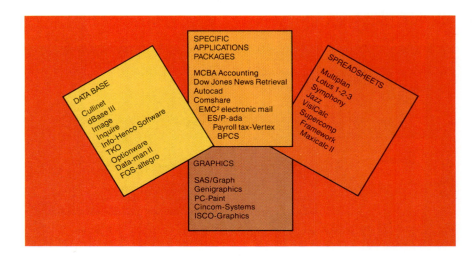

Figure 14.5
Commercially available software packages.

Table 14.2 Software Alternatives: Comparative Costs for an Order-Tracking Program Containing 7,000 Lines of COBOL Code

Source[a]	Costs					Meets Company Objectives
	Base	Testing	Training	Program Modification	Total	
In-house development	$11,660[b]	$3,000	$2,000	—	$16,660	100%
Lease	12,000[c]	500	1,000	$2,000	15,500	80%
Purchase	5,000	500	1,000	1,000	7,500	75%
Contract programming	10,000	3,000	2,000	—	15,000	95%
User-group sharing	1,000	500	1,000	3,000	5,500	65%

[a] Software from all sources has an estimated five-year life.
[b] 300 lines of programmer-produced code per week at a programmer cost of $500 per week.
[c] Based on a five-year rental at $200 per month.

can be easily adapted to the needs of different businesses, as the nature of an individual business has little to do with the way its payroll is processed. Even if the purchased or leased payroll program requires some modification to tailor it to a particular company's needs, it is often a wiser choice than developing the entire program from scratch. The company may have to compromise on a few points, such as report format or the way that files are structured, but the software that it buys or leases can meet its routine processing needs at a cost much less than that of an in-house-developed program.

Programs for financial analysis and word processing are also commercially available. Most individual businesses would not be able to afford the developmental efforts and expense that must go into producing this kind of software, but when the costs are spread over hundreds or thousands of users, the cost per user can be quite low. Similarly, data base systems, which require great developmental expertise and which are beyond the capability of most businesses to develop on their own, are a popular type of purchased or leased software.

Most programs for microcomputers fall under the umbrella of purchased or leased software. Microcomputer users seldom have the technical staff needed to develop new and complex software systems, and such systems might not be cost-effective even if they were available. Commercially developed microcomputer software is usually designed to function with a particular operating system. Several operating systems, among them CP/M and MS-DOS, which are also commercially available, are usable with a number of different brand-name microcomputers, and packages of applications software have been developed to conform to the specific characteristics of these operating systems.

In some types of portable microcomputers, the software is built into the unit as firmware (i.e., it is designed as a permanent part of a chip's circuitry). In other types of portable microcomputers, the software is loaded into bubble memory. Because bubble memory is nonvolatile, it can function very effectively as erasable programmable read-only memory, or EPROM: The internally loaded program will remain loaded even when the machine is turned off, just as if it were on a disk, and because it is stored in bubble memory rather than being designed as firmware, it can be quickly changed as processing needs change. For example, with one make of portable microcomputer, you can connect a telephone to a modem that is built into the microcomputer case, dial the manufacturer's toll-free number, and in a matter of seconds "order up" the software that you want loaded into your system's bubble memory via the telecommunications link (see Figure 14.6). As you go about your business and your processing needs change, you can erase the memory and enter a new program. This feature is

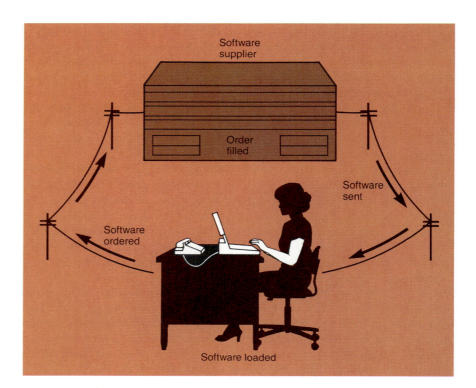

Figure 14.6
Loading software via a portable microcomputer with bubble memory.

particularly useful during on-site visits in which financial analysis or accounting work is done. At the end of the visit, you can load a word processing program into memory and delete the analytical software.

Malfunctions with microcomputer software can be very troublesome since there is generally no technical person available to figure out what has happened and, more importantly, what needs to be done to correct the problem. Advertisements imply that you plug the hardware in, load your software, and begin processing. What they don't mention is that the manual explaining how to use the software may weigh more than the microcomputer itself. The trend is toward more "user-friendly" systems, and as software entrepreneurs strive for new and better products, their goal will continue to be "plug-in-and-run" software, but, today, this kind of software is generally not available.

A chief drawback of all purchased or leased software is that it may be too general to meet specific needs, particularly needs relating to data collection, reporting, or interfaces with other programs. Businesses have come to expect a good match between software capabilities and users' needs, something that is not always achievable if the users' needs are not known at the time the software is being developed. The conflict between custom-designed software and commercially developed software is somewhat like the conflict you might experience if you went to an auto dealer with some very specific ideas in mind about the car you want to buy. Perhaps you want six doors, an extra trunk, three feet of ground clearance, and a number of other special features. The car dealer would no doubt look at you in wonder and suggest that you either inherit a million dollars and have your car custom-made or else settle for the model on the showroom floor that comes closest to what you want.

Contract Programming

A company that lacks the resources for in-house software development may at times need a highly specific program that is not commercially available. In such a case, the company may choose as its alternative contract programming. **Contract programming** is the hiring of outside technical personnel or specialty firms to develop and install programs to meet users' needs. Contract programmers can also take care of the overload of requests for new software systems that is associated with rapid growth, and they can provide technical support when there is a temporary need but no justification for a full-time position. Companies specializing in contract programming often concentrate their expertise in a particular business or application. For example, some firms develop software just for the banking industry. One well-known contract-programming firm is Boeing Computer

Services, a company that seeks out difficult problems and brings to bear a wealth of talent that could not normally be assembled by any single company doing its own in-house software development.

The hourly rate for contract programming can be quite high, but this method of program development has several compensatory features: It provides the versatility of in-house programming and immediate help without the need to recruit and hire permanent staff, to pay fringe benefits, or even to allocate office space, as the contract programmer may be a "telecommuter" who works from some other location through a terminal. These factors often outweigh the high costs involved.

Despite these advantages, contract programming does present certain risks. A company that hires a contract-programming firm it has never used before is dealing with an unknown, and once it turns a project over to a contact-programming firm, it relinquishes a certain amount of control over the way the program is developed. It is very hard to determine in advance if the firm will have the technical capabilities necessary to complete the project successfully, and because contract-programming firms generally bill on an hourly basis, a good deal of money can be expended before any incompetence is discovered. Moreover, these firms are plagued with the same problems that plague any company engaged in software development: Projects are hard to estimate and even harder to manage, and employee turnover and inexperience can add to these difficulties.

User-Group Program Sharing

A third, less common alternative to in-house software development is **user-group program sharing.** A *user group* is a group of firms that have the same hardware and similar processing and information needs. It is thus possible for these firms to share software that has been developed for certain routine applications, and, in most instances, the technical "fit" is quite good if not perfect. Usually, the computer manufacturer that has provided the hardware identifies the user group, and individual user firms either sell or lease the software they have developed to other members of the user group. Obviously, the more companies that share the same software, the larger the proportion of software development costs that a firm can recover.

A disadvantage of the user-group approach is that it reveals to the public any software that is made available to the user group, and most firms are not accustomed to dealing with software pirates or others who would use the software without compensating the developer. Typically, user-group software is not state-of-the-art or highly technical software that might weaken a firm's position if the competition were to get hold of it. For this reason, user-group program sharing is not as important an alternative to in-house software development as purchased or leased software and contract programming.

CORSAIRS OF THE TWENTIETH CENTURY

No, they do not sail in Viking ships, carry swords, or rampage through cities and towns striking fear into the hearts of all who cross their paths. They fly no skull and crossbones; in fact, they may not even have a boat, let alone a ship. Nonetheless, they qualify as pirates in every sense of the word. "They" are today's high-tech answer to Captain Kidd and Bluebeard: pirates who specialize in duplicating software without authorization. Instead of three years before the mast, most of them have two years of study at a graduate school of business.

Several reliable estimates suggest that between two and fifteen unauthorized copies are made for every software package that is purchased legally. Given that more than $3 billion worth of software was sold in 1985, it's easy to see why software vendors may get a bit exercised about today's Captain Kidds. However, not all these pirates make illegal copies for the purpose of reselling them, nor are they always aware that they are doing anything illegal. But, in the eyes of the law, making a copy of a program for a friend is just as illegal as copying a program from a diskette with the intent of reselling it.

Not all software piracy involves copying programs from floppy disks. It can also take the form of employees who leave their jobs with routines from large, sophisticated programs in hand for their new employers. A new software product amazingly like that of the former employer may shortly thereafter appear.

The ways in which companies attempt to protect their software range from carefully worked out software "locks" (software products themselves), which control and limit the duplication, to elaborate legal documents that the user must sign before the vendor will deliver the software. Some organizations, however, take a more casual approach to the copying of their software products. One organization, for example, has taken such a casual attitude that it even suggests you make copies of its word processing program for your friends. If your friends like the program, the company asks that they send $50, in return for which it will register them as users and put them on its mailing list. If your friends don't want to pay, that's all right, too; no hard feelings.

Most software vendors, however, attempt to protect their products from piracy, and in doing so they face something of a dilemma: If the protection schemes they devise are so complex they make the products hard to use, consumers will stop buying them. In the end, of course, vendors would lose more this way than they would from illegal copying. Some vendors believe the answer is to do more than just sell the user a disk with code. They advocate that software vendors become service organizations — that they not only initially sell the software but support the customer after the sale as well. Their reasoning is that if users feel an association with the vendor, they are more likely to adopt the vendors' view that software copying is on a moral par with shoplifting.

A number of practical problems arise in dealing with software pirates, not the least of which is the body of law relating to computers and software. In 1980, the copyright laws were amended to include software, but the actual scope of this protection is unclear. The Computer Software Copyright Act of 1980 does state that computer programs in the form of flowcharts, source code, and assembly code may be copyrighted. The protection afforded by the law when the software is in the form of machine code is, however, unclear. Also presenting something of a legal problem is software that is on a ROM chip; because a ROM chip is a thing rather than an idea, it is normally covered by a patent rather than a copyright. Recent court decisions have favored including all software under the copyright laws, a step that would help clarify matters. Of course, copyright laws address only the actual copying of software from disks; the problem of employees who take ideas to other organizations falls under trade secrets protection. Although the law has had to deal with this issue for years, it is still a gray area: It is often difficult to prove that the information that was taken is unique and unknown to the general public.

Although in the United States the software copyright laws are beginning to get some teeth, in other countries software copying is not only legal but also encouraged. This presents software vendors with a much more difficult problem, and to date they have no answers.

ARTIFICIAL INTELLIGENCE

The precise, carefully laid-out programs, or instructions, that enable the computer to process large volumes of data quickly and accurately also limit computer applications to tasks that are somewhat routine and relatively easy to describe. The objective of computer scientists working on the development of **artificial intelligence (AI)** is to enable the computer to solve *thinking* problems — that is, problems whose solutions require judgment, imagination, intuition, and other human characteristics, such as emotion and loyalty. To instill this kind of human intelligence in computers, to give them the ability to reason and to make value judgments, is the thrust and direction of AI research. Despite these rather awesome goals, AI involves no magic. What it does involve is a complex type of programming — much more complex than the familiar programming approaches that we discussed in previous chapters — to capture facts and to implement complicated algorithms.

AI has been a controversial area for many years, and at the heart of the controversy is the question, Can a machine think? In the introduction to this part of the book, we quoted Lady Lovelace's observation that a machine can do only what it is *programmed* to do, and we noted that that observation is as true today as it was in Lady Lovelace's day. This would seem to say that a machine *cannot* think for itself. However, if a machine can be programmed to program itself on the basis of its answers to past questions — or, to put it in human terms, to learn from experience to think for itself — is it then capable of thinking? Instilling this kind of capability in computers is, as we've said, the objective of AI research, and a machine capable of thought raises some unsettling questions. If computers were capable of intelligent behavior, would people become overly dependent on them? Is it possible that computers could become so complex that people would no longer be able to understand their decisions and actions, and so control of human destiny would rest with machines? While current applications of artificial intelligence indicate the many ways in which it may benefit us, none of us can afford to ignore these negative implications.

A number of years ago, Alan Turing, a British scientist, proposed a test to determine whether a machine can think. The **Turing test** involves an interrogator who uses a terminal to question two unseen respondents, one a human being and the other a machine. The goal of the machine is to fool the interrogator into thinking it is the human respondent. If the machine can do this, then, according to Turing's criterion, it must be exhibiting the human characteristics that we call intelligence; in other words, the machine can think. At present, the machine responds very well to many kinds of questions, but it fails the test when asked to respond to an emotional stimulus such as a poem. The amount of knowledge needed to respond to this kind of stimulus is beyond the capabilities of computers as we know them today, and whether it will ever be possible for computers to solve problems that require reasoning, learning, experience, and a reservoir of knowledge remains a hotly disputed question. Let's now take a look at the problem-solving methods that AI researchers have developed to bring

AI to its current state and at some of the ways in which AI is presently being used.

AI Techniques

Early experiments in AI included developing software for translating from one human language to another (e.g., a program for translating scientific papers from Russian into English) and programming the computer to play such games as checkers and chess (see Figure 14.7). From these early experiments, two facts became quickly obvious: (1) To be useful in solving difficult problems, an AI system must contain a great deal of knowledge, and (2) as the amount of knowledge increases, it becomes much more difficult to access the appropriate data. Capturing and storing this knowledge so that it is quickly accessible is as much a hardware problem as it is a software problem, and even today's powerful computer systems are severely limited in this regard. The emerging fifth generation of computers is attempting to solve the storage/access problem with dramatic increases in primary storage capacity and logic functions.

The early attempts to develop software for translating human languages — or **natural languages,** as they are called in the AI world — were a natural outgrowth of the success of the compiler programs, developed during the late 1950s and early 1960s, for translating high-level programming languages into machine language. Despite the success of their forerunners, the early

Figure 14.7
Belle, a chess-playing computer.
Courtesy of AT&T Bell Laboratories.

experiments in natural-language translations were largely a failure. It proved an extremely difficult, if not impossible, task to include in the programs all the alternative meanings that people attach to words and phrases and the contexts in which they assign those meanings. Consider, for example, how the computer might translate the word *nuts.* Is it lunch for the park squirrel, a mental condition, a request for spare parts, or the bravely defiant response that General A.C. McAuliffe gave to the German demand that he surrender during the Battle of the Bulge in December 1944? Even when translating the relatively precise terminology of scientific papers, the computer was seldom able to translate more than 80 percent of the material effectively. Success rates for translating political speeches or newspaper reports, where meanings are not so clear, were even lower, and the attempts of the 1960s to develop natural-language translation software were soon temporarily abandoned.

In programming computers to play games, researchers initially assumed that a large amount of knowledge stored in the computer's memory would not be needed, that the computer could decide each of its moves by computing the outcomes of all possible moves available at that time. This was a reasonable assumption since, with its enormous speed, the computer could be programmed to check a huge number of combinations — many more than a person could calculate — before selecting a move. However, as it turned out, the assumption was wrong. When viewed from an entire chess board, the possible responses each time a move is made approach 35 to the power of 50. This creates a tremendous number of computations and makes the program unmanageable. The fact that for a number of years computers have been beating expert chess players by following a strategy, learning from mistakes, anticipating future moves, and recognizing opponents' tactics is evidence that AI researchers found some techniques to lead them out of their difficulties. Foremost among the AI problem-solving techniques are search techniques, heuristics, pattern recognition, and knowledge representation. None of these techniques involves the algorithms used in traditional programming; instead, they attempt to exploit available knowledge.

Search Techniques. Human problem solving often involves a trial-and-error search of alternative solutions until an appropriate one is found. This is especially true for problems that have not been encountered before — situations in which a person has no clear idea of how to proceed. The difficulty with such **blind searching** — for both computers and people — is not just that it's time-consuming but also that every possible combination of problem elements must be evaluated, and with complex problems, the number of combinations can be overwhelming.

The inefficiencies of blind searching can be overcome by incorporating a control strategy that takes a systematic approach to examining the problem. The most common control strategy involves the use of a **search tree,** in which search paths branch out from a root (see Figure 14.8). By examining each of the nodes and choosing the appropriate branch, the search program

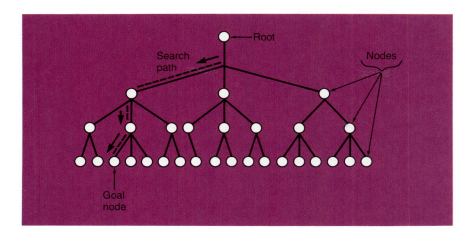

Figure 14.8
A search tree.

develops a path from the initial node to the goal node, bypassing nodes that are not relevant to the goal. Search trees work well when the reasons for selecting a path are clear, but that, of course, is not always the case.

Heuristics. It was by incorporating heuristics into their programs for game playing that AI researchers were able to reduce the tremendous number of computations that the computer had to perform to decide any one move. **Heuristic** means providing help or direction in solving a problem by indicating or pointing out a possible search path. When a traditional computer program is used, the computer is given a set of instructions to follow; these instructions are based on a logical solution developed by the programmer. When heuristics are used, the computer is supposed to respond to situations and conditions by developing a set of reasonable strategies and a solution. Based on the outcome of the solution, the computer evaluates the success of the course of action and modifies the logic as necessary. The next time the computer encounters a similar condition, it has "learned" from past experience, and the new solution it develops reflects this learning. This is why a computer can be used to play chess, and why it can get better at the game the more often it plays it.

Heuristic problem solving, then, relates to the process of discovery, and a heuristic problem-solving technique is one that offers a rule of thumb, a set of generalized guidelines that serves to narrow the possible combinations that must be evaluated. A heuristic applies to a specific situation and is worth trying when that situation arises. It is not, however, a hard and fast rule; it does not guarantee success because it does not work in every case. Obviously, this problem-solving technique differs radically from the controlled and precise algorithmic approach used in traditional programming.

A look out the window in the morning may serve as a heuristic, indicating a search path for the clothing you will wear that day. Although the rule of thumb will tell you that you don't need to wear a raincoat on a day that starts out clear and sunny, a sudden rainstorm during the day could cause you to get wet. Similarly, if you want to stay at high-quality motels during your vacation and choose a listing of AAA motels as your heuristic, you will surely overlook some excellent motels not associated with AAA, and you may also find an AAA motel that you do not consider high quality. On the whole, however, you'll probably be satisfied with your vacation arrangements. In most instances, the rule of thumb recommends appropriate actions; so when heuristics are incorporated into the AI program, they narrow the necessary searches and reduce the number of combinations that must be evaluated. They do, however, leave room for error; the rule of thumb always has exceptions.

Pattern Recognition. Selecting the appropriate heuristic requires an understanding of the problem being addressed. Pattern recognition looks for physical characteristics when evaluating discrete data, symbols, or other items, and for positions or patterns when evaluating complex problems. Industrial robots used in manufacturing facilities offer an example of pattern recognition in action. When a robot must pick up a part (a screw, nut, or other component), it has to be able to sense the shape and alignment of the part so that it can grasp it properly. Optical-sensing techniques give the robot this pattern-recognition ability. In a manufacturing setting, of course, parts can be somewhat standardized and controlled; with handwritten symbols or other less controllable items, the problems of pattern recognition become far more complex.

Think of the simple rule of thumb described earlier: "clear sky, no raincoat." What does a clear sky, a sunny sky, or a rainy sky mean? Obviously, you have developed the ability to judge the climate by sky color, clouds, and brightness. Providing a computer with this kind of pattern-recognition ability is a quantum leap from giving it the ability to recognize a manufacturing part. However, this is the kind of pattern recognition that needs to be programmed into the AI system if it is to choose the proper heuristics to help define the search.

Knowledge Representation. Knowledge must be stored in memory so that it is accessible to the AI programs in a convenient manner. Humans have the ability to recall knowledge without conscious thought. You don't think about what the sunny day means; you react automatically. Suppose there are a few clouds in the morning; how do you interpret that? You recall similar-looking days; some had rain, and some turned out fine. How does your brain assemble the knowledge, extracting it from the knowledge of thousands of other days on which you've looked out the window and noted the weather? Representing knowledge so that the computer can go through this same kind of automatic searching activity is beyond the present capability of primary storage and logic circuits. Advances in knowledge representation will be critical to the growth and success of AI research.

MAKING KNOWLEDGE USEFUL

The only way to get a computer to act intelligently is to give it plenty of knowledge about the task at hand, says Stanford's Bruce B. Buchanan.

The problem is that putting the knowledge in the computer is like cramming for an exam. First you teach it a long list of facts, then the special cases, then some rules of thumb, then examples from the real world, then some.... It goes on and on. "So one of the critical research problems in AI," says Buchanan, "is finding efficient means of building new knowledge bases."

For more than a decade, Buchanan has been a leader in developing expert systems — programs that distill the experience of a doctor, or a lawyer, or an accountant, so that a computer can give near-human advice. Today he is one of the senior principal investigators of Stanford's Heuristic Programming Project, in which some 70 faculty, researchers, and graduate students are investigating how computers can use and represent knowledge.

Buchanan himself is concentrating on three projects. One project is to teach computers how to learn in a medical setting — specifically how to extract a general rule about diagnosing jaundice by studying individual patients' case histories. A second is to write programs that can generate hypotheses and test them; the specific application is to determine the structure of proteins from data supplied by nuclear magnetic resonance and other techniques. And the third is to write programs that can evaluate the contents and quality of certain medical research articles, and then derive their own inferences.

"Medicine is a fairly strong focus of what I do," says Buchanan. In fact, much of Stanford's pioneering work in expert systems has been done in collaboration with the medical school. "It's a very good test bed," he says, "and nobody will allow us to cut corners."

"Bruce Buchanan: Making Knowledge Useful," *Science 85* (March 1985), p. 41. © 1985 by the American Association for the Advancement of Science (AAAS).

AI Applications

The area of AI research that has shown the most promise is called **expert systems.** These systems use the reasoning power of the computer to arrive at conclusions by combining a large number of factual data with the knowledge and understanding of experts in a particular field. Expert systems are designed to duplicate the problem-solving skills of these advanced practitioners. Medical diagnosis, circuit design, and chemical analysis require a great deal of specialized knowledge that few people possess, and they thus lend themselves to expert systems, or "knowledge engineering." These systems can be very useful tools in decision making; they do not, however, make the decisions. Like consultants, expert systems can give advice, but the decisions are up to the people who sought the advice. Table 14.3 describes some of the more popular expert systems in use today.

In an expert system, the data are stored in a computerized data base and are manipulated by **production rules.** When the production rules are applied, they return a set of probabilities that, when combined, identify the most likely solution or conclusion. The total number of production

Table 14.3 Expert Systems

System	Function
CADUCEUS	Used by internists in diagnosing medical problems.
DENDRAL	Aids chemists in determining the molecular structure of organic compounds by analyzing mass spectrograms.
DESI	Provides a natural-language link to an accounting system.
EL	Used in developing an understanding of electronic circuits.
Eliza	Provides natural-language processing for communications.
INTELLECT	Provides natural-language processing for general business and other problems.
LIFER	Answers questions about ships.
MYCIN	Used by physicians to aid in the diagnosis and treatment of bacterial infections.
Personal Consultant	Provides a systems development tool using the LISP programming language.
Prospector	Used to evaluate geologic data in mineral exploration.
R-1 (also called XCON)	Used by Digital Equipment Corporation to configure computer systems for customers.
The Negotiation Edge	Provides customized labor-relations negotiation advice.

rules is generally less than 1,000. Expert systems can therefore be developed to operate on microcomputers as well as on large computer systems, something not easily achieved with the more broadly based AI programs, such as systems for natural-language translation. To be effective, such broadly based AI systems require a much larger body of knowledge, which limits them to large-scale computers.

One experimental expert system being tested in medicine incorporates both the concepts of diagnostic medicine and the tremendous volume of facts associated with the diagnosis of disease. The physician enters vital signs, test results, observations, and other medical information into the system. After evaluating the data, the system suggests more testing or asks questions if the data are unclear; if the data are clear, it interprets them and suggests a possible diagnosis (see Figure 14.9). By incorporating the expertise of the best in the field of diagnostic medicine, the system can provide the physician with access to the most expert practitioners without requiring their physical presence. Prototypes of this expert system are in operation today, and it will be only a matter of time before it is refined and operating on a large scale.

Most military applications of expert systems are treated as classified

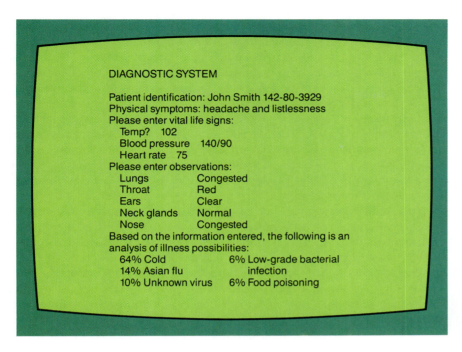

Figure 14.9
An expert system for medical diagnosis.

information. They include target-identification systems and combat-guidance systems. Aircraft flight tactics, based on the computer's evaluation of enemy maneuvers, give a "Star Wars" aura to military technology. Imagine having the world's best and most decorated fighter pilot as an AI copilot during times of conflict. By computerizing human knowledge and defining the production rules, the computer can provide the pilot with an expert system. This alone could be enough to provide a military advantage.

The implications of AI for business include expanding the capabilities of industrial robots so that they can evaluate sensory inputs, adjust the placement of materials, and modify manufacturing operations, just as a person would. Developing strategies, planning maintenance schedules, and evaluating financial data are just a few of the operational possibilities for AI in the business world of tomorrow.

SUMMARY

While hardware costs have been declining, software costs — particularly the costs of in-house software development — have continued to increase. A chief factor in the escalation of software costs is the labor-intensive nature of software development and maintenance.

When a company develops its own software in-house, it faces a number of internal and external constraints. Internal constraints include the size of the available staff and their individual skills, the availability of hardware, organizational issues, and cost. External constraints include legal requirements and the state of the hardware technology available to implement the software.

Several techniques are available to help a company improve the productivity of its programming efforts. These include structured design and programming methods, reusable code, and such specialized management techniques as the structured walkthrough and the chief programmer team.

Alternatives to in-house software development include purchased or leased software, contract programming, and user-group program sharing. Most microcomputer software is purchased or leased. Some of these microcomputer programs, such as those available for use with portable microcomputers, are very innovative. However, to date, the goal of "plug-in-and-run" software for microcomputers has eluded software developers. A chief drawback of all purchased or leased software is that it may be too general to meet specific processing needs. While contract programming can produce a custom-designed program to meet specific needs, it, too, has certain drawbacks, among them some loss of control over the way a program is developed. Because it can quite easily be pirated, the software available in user-group program sharing is generally not state of the art or highly technical.

Although it has been slow to develop, artificial intelligence offers great promise for future computing. The chief roadblocks in its development have been the structuring and storage of the vast amount of needed data, the development of appropriate software, and an understanding of the meaning of human intelligence. Foremost among AI problem-solving techniques are search techniques, heuristics, pattern recognition, and knowledge representation. AI is currently being used in medical and military applications of so-called expert systems. Future business uses include expanding the capabilities of industrial robots and using AI to develop business strategies and schedules and to evaluate financial data.

KEY TERMS

artificial intelligence (AI) (406)
blind searching (408)
chief programmer team (399)
contract programming (403)
cost/benefit analysis (395)
developmental costs (395)
expert systems (411)
heuristic (409)
natural languages (407)

operational costs (395)
peer review team (398)
production rules (411)
reusable code (396)
search tree (408)
structured walkthrough (398)
Turing test (406)
user-group program sharing (404)

DISCUSSION QUESTIONS

1. Why will programming productivity be such a major issue for the remainder of the century? Describe the techniques that businesses can use to improve programming productivity.

2. What is the most expensive source of programs? What software alternatives do businesses have?

3. Identify three internal constraints on software development and explain how they affect software development.

4. What are the external constraints on software development? How might a company best deal with these constraints?

5. Discuss the advantages and disadvantages of purchased software.

6. What is contract programming? Describe its advantages and disadvantages.

7. Explain why a firm might hesitate to engage in user-group program sharing.

8. Describe some of the early applications and some of the present applications of artificial intelligence. Why do you think AI has been slow to develop?

9. What future impact will artificial intelligence have in the manufacturing and factory setting? What are the problems of implementing AI in business?

10. Visit a computer store and make a list of the various categories of software available off-the-shelf for the microcomputer user.

PART · IV

Chapter 15 SYSTEMS DEVELOPMENT: AN OVERVIEW
Chapter 16 OUTPUT, INPUT, AND PROCESSING: SOME DESIGN CONSIDERATIONS
Chapter 17 USING COMPUTER INFORMATION SYSTEMS IN BUSINESS
Chapter 18 MANAGING A COMPUTER INFORMATION SYSTEM

SYSTEMS DEVELOPMENT, USE, AND MANAGEMENT

We have become a society dependent on information, and much of what we now call work involves the mental processes of an information worker rather than a physical laborer's brawn. Machines have taken much of the muscle out of earning a living, and information has become a commodity to be bought and sold, just as manufactured goods and farm products are. Like the steam engine of the Industrial Revolution, the computer has been a revolutionary force, creating a demand for more and better computer systems to produce more and better information.

In their rush to join the Information Revolution and to incorporate computing technology into their organizations, businesses have at times experienced frustration and even failure. Such problems are often attributable to the ways in which companies develop and use their computer information systems; management, too, can be a factor. The chapters in Part IV focus on what a business person needs to know about these important concerns. Our viewpoint here, as it has been throughout the book, will be that of the nontechnician, the information user who is concerned with effective systems development, use, and management.

Chapter 15 presents an overview of the systems development process, highlighting areas of special concern to the business person. Chapter 16 looks at some important considerations in output, input, and processing design. Chapter 17 focuses on the ways that businesses use computer information systems to assist in decision making and to improve productivity in the business office. Finally, Chapter 18 explores some of the various factors involved in managing a computer information system.

OUTLINE

INTRODUCING SYSTEMS CHANGE
- Volume of Data
- Internal and External Information Needs
- Cost Savings

CONSIDERATIONS IN THE SYSTEMS DEVELOPMENT CYCLE
- Evaluating Systems Proposals
  - Organizational Fit
  - Cost Effectiveness
  - Risk Assessment
- Planning for Systems Development
  - Personnel
  - Project Scheduling and Monitoring

PROJECT MANAGEMENT

SUMMARY

KEY TERMS

DISCUSSION QUESTIONS

OVERVIEW

No organization operates in a vacuum. Internal and external pressures to meet expanding information needs create the climate for change. Planning for this change, introducing it into the organization in a structured and systematic way, is the key to developing a successful information system. The formal series of steps known as the systems development cycle provides just such a structured approach, and, thanks to it, the days of systems development "by guess and by golly" are gone. No longer can programmers dismiss missed deadlines and overextended budgets with the blanket excuse that programming is an art, not a science; considerations of art or science aside, with careful planning, schedules and budgets can be controlled. This structured approach to systems development has also brought an end to the wandering and false starts that characterized many systems development projects of the past. Various management techniques, similar to those used in other segments of business, support the phases of the systems development cycle, adding a measure of control to the entire process.

In this chapter, we'll explore some of the reasons why changes in information systems are initiated. We'll then look at the major issues that must be addressed at various stages of the systems development cycle. Finally, we'll look at the management of systems development projects. Our objectives are to

- ◆ identify the reasons for introducing systems change.

- ◆ explain the issues involved in evaluating systems proposals.

- ◆ discuss the considerations that must go into planning for systems development.

- ◆ describe project management styles and the responsibilities of the project manager.

CHAPTER 15

SYSTEMS DEVELOPMENT: AN OVERVIEW

INTRODUCING SYSTEMS CHANGE

Most requests for development of new systems or changes to existing ones come from a company's information users. Since the functions of information users vary, the reasons for their requests vary also. The manager of an accounting department, for example, might request the development of a new system because of changes in the reporting requirements of a tax agency, while the vice-president in charge of product development might request a change in an existing system because of the introduction of a new product line. And any manager or other information user at any level might simply have an idea about how the information system could function more effectively. Generally, however, the reasons for introducing change can be grouped into three categories: to process an expanded volume of data, to meet internal and external information needs, and to achieve cost savings. At the basis of all these reasons for introducing change is the need to remain competitive. Technological innovation alone can be enough to make an existing information system obsolete, thus weakening a company's position in the marketplace.

Volume of Data

A hallmark of a company's success is expansion in the volume of its operations. When it expands, a company must collect and report additional data, and a manual accounting system may no longer meet its needs. A manual system that performed satisfactorily with a two-store operation would no doubt be severely strained by a twenty-store chain. Additional strain occurs when units of the business are distributed among different cities, states, and countries. An expanded volume of data to be processed and the need for distributed processing have been particularly important factors in influencing service organizations (such as stock markets, airlines, and government agencies) to convert to automated data processing systems. These factors have been especially evident in industries that provide financial services, such as the banking industry.

Checks are far more commonly used than cash in carrying on business transactions today; they account for more than half the payments that businesses receive. If the processing, sorting, and charging of these checks to the proper accounts had to be done by hand, it would be a gigantic task, and surely the fees for these services would be much higher than they are today. For a large bank that processes millions of checks daily, automation is the only way to handle the volume of data and still keep service charges at an acceptable level.

The volume of data to be processed, then, sometimes leaves a firm little choice but to develop a computer information system. If a firm is growing and wants to stay competitive, it has to consider automating its data processing system.

Internal and External Information Needs

The ability to capture, manipulate, and integrate data into useful information is critical to the success of any business. When businesses are small, owners can do these things in their heads, and there is little need for formal systems of collecting data and reporting information within the firm. When a business becomes larger and more complex, however, there may be too many details for a single individual to keep track of, and a need for more formal systems arises.

Outside reporting requirements may also be difficult to meet without clearly defined systems of collecting data and reporting information. Lending institutions and suppliers that extend credit, government tax and worker-protection agencies, and stockholders and other absentee owners are among the powers that influence the collection and processing of data. These powers expect information to be reported according to accepted procedures and formats, and they have established rules and standards for the timeliness and accuracy of business reports.

Cost Savings

The most obvious reason for introducing systems change is **cost savings** — that is, a reduction in labor, overhead, and investment, and an increase in productivity per unit. Cost savings can result, for example, from an automated inventory-management system that monitors sales and warehouse stock and reorders stock only when inventory is low. Because such a system keeps investment in inventory at a minimum, it reduces the need to borrow funds and the expense of paying interest on loans. An automated inventory-management system can also benefit a company in other ways: If orders are accepted only when stock is actually available, customer satisfaction is likely to be greater, and the company's volume of business is thereby likely to increase.

A system that can enhance a company's position by cutting costs or increasing its volume of business is, of course, desirable. But any systems development or change has its own costs. If the proposed system's benefits outweigh its costs, then a sound basis for developing the system exists. The difficulty lies in determining just what the specific costs and benefits will be. Table 15.1 shows some of the costs and benefits typically associated with implementing a computer-based business information system.

Costs are usually easier to pinpoint than benefits. Most new systems require expenditures for computer equipment; for the staff to design, program, and test the system; for training the system's users and operations personnel; and for maintaining the system after it has been installed. Except for the

Table 15.1 Typical Costs and Benefits of Implementing a Computer Information System

Costs	Benefits

Tangible Costs
  Hardware (including input, output, and storage devices, communications equipment, and processor upgrades or additions)
  Software (including systems analysis, programming, software purchases/leases, testing, and installation)
  Training for users, operators, and data entry personnel
  Maintenance for both hardware and software
  Operations costs associated with running the system, including forms and supplies
Intangible Costs
  Employee disruption and morale problems during systems changeover and installation
  Customer dissatisfaction during changeover and installation
	Tangible Benefits
	  Cost avoidance or reduction (e.g., reduced data processing costs, staffing needs, and investment requirements)
	  Increased revenues through improved operations, service, and product quality
	Intangible Benefits
	  Improved information through more timely reports, new information resources, and more flexibility in assembling information
	  Increased customer satisfaction and customer service
	  Improved employee morale because of better decision making and reduction of routine and dull tasks
	  Better market position because of faster and more effective response to competition

costs associated with designing and programming the system, these cost data can be estimated fairly accurately. The costs of systems analysis and programming depend largely on the length of time and the skills needed to develop the system, and estimating these factors is often a matter of judgment. The more like an existing system the proposed system is, the easier it will be to accurately predict the developmental costs associated with it.

Assigning dollar values to benefits is a more difficult matter. A system for producing outputs for customers could increase customer satisfaction, which could result in fewer lost accounts and a higher overall volume of business. But putting dollar values on such benefits is at best only a guess. Other benefits might be more timely reports, better quality of information, and more flexibility in assembling information for special needs. These benefits could, in turn, lead to a reduction in supervisory staff and administrative costs, as well as better control of funds and inventory. Once again, however, it's difficult to quantify these benefits and to assign a dollar value to them.

When computers were first appearing on the business scene and throughout the 1960s, one of their key selling points was that a firm using automation could reduce its staff. If the introduction of a computer system means that people can be reassigned or let go, dollar values can be assigned to the savings. Other savings might result from a reduced need for equipment (e.g., typewriters and calculators), for supplies and stationery, and for space for such things as file cabinets and desks. With the cost of office space quite high in most major metropolitan areas, replacing a file cabinet, desk, and typewriter with a terminal can be a cost-effective move.

CONSIDERATIONS IN THE SYSTEMS DEVELOPMENT CYCLE

A reasonable request for systems change usually sets the systems development cycle in motion. As you know from Chapter 3, this cycle has five steps, or phases: (1) *Identifying the need* involves determining the feasibility of proceeding with the project. (2) *Analyzing the system* involves scrutinizing the present system in order to produce a blueprint for the design of the new system. (3) *Developing design alternatives* involves drawing up several different designs, weighing the advantages and disadvantages of each, and developing specifications for the design alternative that is chosen. (4) *Developing the system* involves the technical work of programming and testing the system. (5) *Implementing and maintaining the system* involves changing over to the new system, conducting a postimplementation review, and keeping the system responsive to changing conditions once it is operational.

These steps serve as the basis of the careful planning that must go into developing an effective information system. Such careful planning is necessary because, depending on the complexity of the desired product, the systems development process can be very costly. Moreover, a carefully planned system will serve the user better, will produce benefits for the organization, and will be relatively easy to maintain. In contrast, a system that is developed "off the cuff" will cause operational headaches and maintenance problems, as well as frustration for the system's users. The phased approach to development that the systems development cycle provides also gives all team members a clear understanding of the steps to be taken in the overall process — an understanding that is essential to the development of an effective system. In addition, the phased approach helps to integrate and synchronize the team's developmental efforts.

Figure 15.1 provides a brief graphic review of the steps of the systems development cycle. Since we described all these steps in some detail in

Figure 15.1
Review of the systems development cycle.

STEPS	Identify the need	Analyze the system	Develop design alternatives	Develop the system	Implement and maintain the system
OUTPUTS	Feasibility study	Systems specifications	Design proposals	Program / Test data	Maintenance and documentation

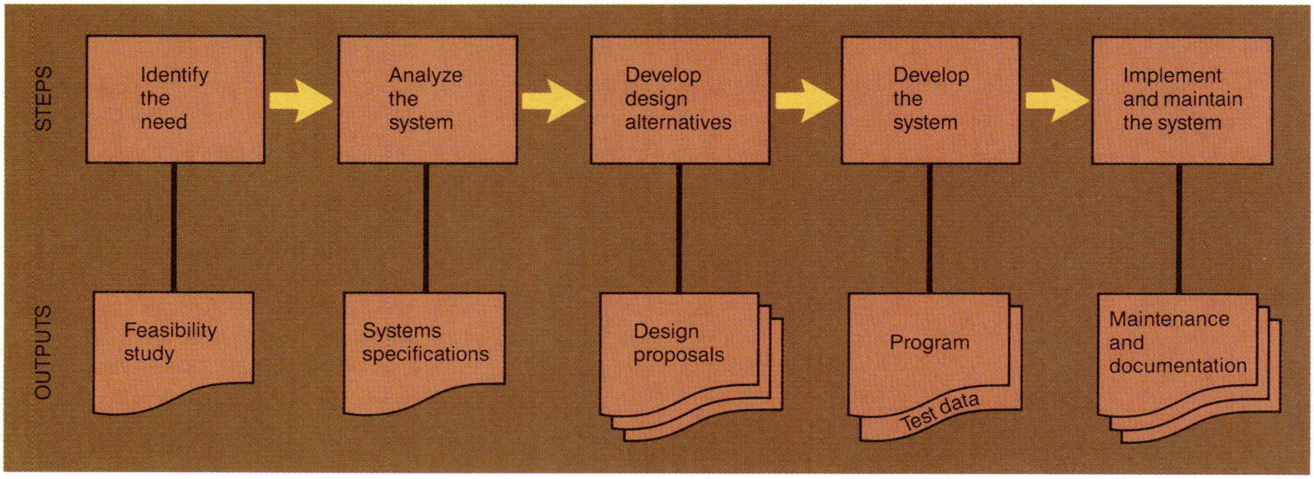

Chapter 3 and focused exclusively on the fourth step in Chapters 11 and 12, we will not repeat the discussion here. Instead, we will focus on some important concerns that are addressed at various stages of the systems development cycle and that must be kept in mind throughout the developmental process. In many ways, these concerns are not unlike the concerns that must be addressed in any other kind of business activity or project; a computer-related project does, however, have the additional concerns associated with rapidly developing technology and the introduction of change into the organization. An initial evaluation of the proposed system focuses on such issues as the system's organizational "fit," its cost effectiveness, and the degree of risk it involves; and a comprehensive plan for the system's implementation includes plans for personnel, work schedules, and a system for monitoring the progress of the project.

Evaluating Systems Proposals

As you know, the first step of the systems development cycle is to identify the need for the proposed system and to determine the feasibility of continuing with the project. Figure 15.2 shows how this step is carried out. Such an evaluation includes an assessment of the anticipated costs and benefits of the proposed system and its impact on the organization, and it therefore requires a thorough understanding of the organization's needs, goals, and resources.

No company has unlimited resources to expend on the development of an information system. No matter how worthy a proposed system's aims, the decision on whether to proceed with its development has to be made within the context of certain internal and external constraints. In Chapter 14, we described the constraints on software development; these constraints apply equally well to the development of the computer system as a whole. **External constraints** include legal requirements (e.g., the reporting requirements of the Internal Revenue Service leave a company little choice in the matter of how to develop an accounting system). They also include the state of the technology available to implement the proposed system (e.g., a proposal for a distributed data processing system would have to be abandoned if the communications/computing technology needed to implement it was not sufficiently developed). Important **internal constraints** include the size and skills of the staff available to work on the project, the availability of the hardware necessary to implement the system, and, of course, cost.

Since no firm has unlimited personnel, equipment, or funds to devote to systems development, some requests for new systems or systems changes will inevitably have to be delayed or denied. The problem of how to allocate scarce resources to specific projects can be a difficult one, as most

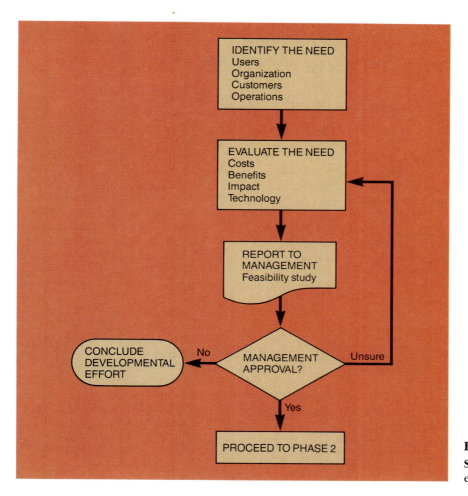

Figure 15.2
Step 1 in systems development: the evaluation process.

proposals are reasonable and offer the company some benefits. The problem is compounded in companies that have been using computers for some time: The confidence and trust that have usually been built up between the information system's users and its staff tend to promote an ever-increasing number of systems proposals. It doesn't take such companies long to see that they must find a way of ranking proposed projects, of assessing how much each project contributes to the overall objectives of the firm. The criteria used in making this assessment include the project's organizational "fit," its cost effectiveness, and the degree of risk that it involves. Evaluating these factors is a complex analytical task, and, unfortunately, the process is sometimes distorted by organizational politics. It is certainly not unheard of for a project to be approved simply because a particular individual or department has sponsored it rather than on the basis of its merits alone.

THE POLITICS OF SYSTEMS

Mr. Peters, vice president of information systems at XYZ Industries, had just finished telling a guest about the major systems in development for various departments in the firm. In particular, the marketing information system was a source of great pride because it was to be completed the next month both on time and within budget.

Just then, Peters received an interoffice memorandum from the marketing department announcing the formation of a Decision Support Systems group. Peters tried to disguise his surprise and confusion as he read the memo; then he escorted his visitor to the door and contemplated his next move. Surprise turned to anger as he thought about the "successful" system about to be installed in this user's department. This was the first time Peters had heard of the project. He wasn't even sure what the director of marketing meant by the term "decision support system."

This hypothetical case may seem extreme, but it's representative of the problems many dp [data processing] managers face as they struggle with the issues surrounding information systems. Peters had made sound purchases, was managing his people well, and was delivering the kind of MIS support XYZ seemed to want. Still, he was blind-sided by the DSS memo. The fact is that his failure was not technical or even managerial, at least in any traditional sense. It was a matter of politics.

The seeds were planted the day Peters joined the firm. The assurances of Johnson, senior vice president for administration, that Peters would really control information systems, and would have access to the right people, seemed adequate. But Peters allowed himself to be hired at the wrong level, by the wrong person. He went about his job without a clear-cut commitment from top management to an information systems plan, and thus was never entirely sure who his customers were or how they should be served. He didn't realize just how often systems and project decisions seemed to the other department heads to be pie-in-the-sky. It was a loss for XYZ as well as for Peters.

The very combination of the two words — politics and systems — may strike terror in the hearts of technically oriented computer professionals who just want to get the job done. Yet, politics is the means by which most important decisions are made. While corporations can't handle issues via a two-party system, corporate politics can nevertheless create an atmosphere for debate and consensus. Furthermore, harnessing political forces is the only sure way to succeed in establishing a systems organization. The dp manager's political manifesto is roughly this: system successes have relatively little to do with completing the documentation and handover phase of the project. Managing the organizational process to support information systems and technology is the single most important success factor.

Peter Keen nicely summed up the situation . . . when he wrote that "information systems development is an intensely political as well as technical process; organizational mechanisms are needed that provide MIS managers with authority and resources for negotiation. The traditional view of MIS as a staff function ignores the pluralism of organizational decision making and the link between information and power. Information systems increasingly alter relationships, patterns of communication, and perceived influence, authority, and control. A strategy for implementation must therefore recognize and deal with the politics of data and the likelihood, even legitimacy, of counterimplementation."

◆

—Samuel H. Solomon, "The Politics of Systems," *Datamation* (December 1983), p. 212. Reprinted with Permission of *Datamation*® magazine, © Copyright by Technical Publishing Company, A Dun & Bradstreet Company, 1983. All rights reserved.

Organizational Fit. Many proposed projects, while exciting to a small unit of the business, do not fit well within the overall organizational scheme and, if implemented, will cause disruption within the company. Projects involving microcomputer systems often illustrate this lack of **organizational fit**. Managers who request the implementation of microcomputer systems point out the benefits of having computing capabilities right on their desks: the ability to control strategic information; to work through planning and analytical models to search out the best course of action; and to have capabilities for accounting, inventory, and personnel recordkeeping that almost equal the capabilities of large computer systems. With all these benefits, how could a company possibly deny a manager the opportunity to use a microcomputer system?

As you might have guessed, that question was a purely rhetorical one. The manager of the accounting department will point out that a microcomputer system is virtually unauditable, that there is no way to control the system and its use or to capture the transaction data the auditor needs to verify that the operation is in accordance with established accounting standards. The manager of the data processing department will address the issue of interfacing with the main computer system and will point out that the microcomputer and the main computer will have a difficult time "talking" to each other. Thus, the microcomputer system may be isolated and unable to access data contained in the main system, and its data may have to be rekeyed before being transferred to the main system.

This is not to say that the microcomputer system is not good for business; only that there must be an understanding of the total organizational picture and a determination of how the microcomputer system, or any other system, will fit into it — *before* the system is acquired or developed, not afterward. A comprehensive organizational plan for the information system — a plan of action that takes into consideration the strategy of the firm, its objectives, and the resources available for systems development — goes a long way toward minimizing the risks and disruptions associated with introducing new systems and hardware.

Cost Effectiveness. Cost savings, while an excellent reason for proposing a systems change, are only part of the cost-effectiveness issue that must be considered in evaluating a systems proposal. **Cost effectiveness** is, in other words, a broader concept than cost savings. It is concerned with the allocation of the firm's resources to obtain the greatest overall return on the investment, and it addresses such issues as the utility, financing, return, and long-term implications of the proposed system. An evaluation of cost effectiveness thus presents a picture of a system's *total* costs and benefits. The total costs would, of course, include the costs of acquiring the hardware; of developing, operating, and maintaining the system; and of data collection.

An analysis of cost effectiveness also involves a comparison of the proposed system with other projects competing for the same resources. Can the present technical staff be used to develop and maintain the system, or will the firm have to hire new personnel? Will the project contribute to the achievement of overall organizational goals, or is it limited to solving an information problem in a single department? These are the kinds of questions that need to be answered before an assessment of cost effectiveness can be made.

Table 15.2 A Cost-Effectiveness Analysis

	Cost Summary	
	Proposal 1	Proposal 2
Costs		
Analysis and design cycle	$40,000	$12,000
Development	100,000	25,000
Hardware	50,000	10,000
Total	$190,000	$47,000

	Benefit Summary					
	Year 1	Year 2	Year 3	Year 1	Year 2	Year 3
Tangible Benefits						
Reduced employee costs	$10,000	$11,000	$12,000	$1,000	$1,100	$1,200
Reduced inventory costs	5,000	5,000	5,000	—	—	—
Increased profits	20,000	25,000	30,000	5,000	5,000	10,000
Intangible Benefits						
Customer service and satisfaction	10,000	12,500	12,500	5,000	5,000	5,000
Better decisions	10,000	15,000	15,000	5,000	5,000	5,000
Better market position	10,000	15,000	15,000	5,000	5,000	5,000
Total	$65,000	$83,500	$89,500	$21,000	$21,100	$26,200
3-year total		$238,000			$68,300	

Table 15.2 shows some of the factors involved in analyzing the cost effectiveness of two proposals. At first glance, proposal 1 looks good because of the large potential savings associated with it. Note, however, that almost half the benefits are intangible and are therefore difficult to predict accurately. Proposal 2 shows a better return in terms of the initial investment, as it ties up less capital; however, it, too, has high intangible benefits. Other considerations not shown in the table but that should be studied before a decision is made include the resources available to implement the project (borrowed funds, for example, will add to a project's cost) and the system's long-term implications (the analysis in the table takes only three years into account; the life of a system may be considerably longer).

If a proposed system can be acquired in different ways, the cost-effectiveness analysis must also include cost data for each option. For example, an expanding auto-parts wholesale firm that wants to automate its bookkeeping system may have several choices: It can purchase a complete system specifically designed for the auto-parts business; it can purchase a computer and commercial software from different vendors; or it can purchase a computer and develop its own software. Each option has different acquisition and operating costs, and to determine which is the most cost-effective option, the total costs of each must be assessed. If all three options meet the firm's other evaluative criteria, then the most cost-effective system will be the best choice. During the first phase of the systems development cycle, the cost data that are developed will be rough — just detailed enough to give management a "ballpark" estimate of what is involved. During the third phase, as design alternatives are developed, detailed cost data will be prepared.

Risk Assessment. **Risk** may be defined as the potential for project failure. Project failure may be partial, such as exceeding a budget, or it may be complete, such as not delivering any part of the desired system. Not all projects pose the same degree of risk, and assessing just how much risk a new system does involve is an important part of evaluating systems proposals. A number of factors contribute to risk, and each factor must be carefully analyzed if a proposed system's potential for failure is to be accurately assessed.

Risk is associated with project size. Because large projects are more complex than small ones, they are also riskier. They require more staff, longer schedules, and more interaction with information users. The number of users involved in a project is another indicator of risk. The more users and the more varied their viewpoints and objectives, the more difficult it is to satisfy them. Projects that involve users from more than three of a company's departments or branches are generally considered to have a very high degree of risk.

Large sums of money associated with a single project also indicate increased risk. Failure of a project budgeted for 10 percent of the annual resources available for systems development is less critical than failure of a project that consumes 75 percent of those resources. As with any investment, diversification provides protection against risk by spreading resources rather than concentrating them.

Projects that break new ground are riskier than those that update existing systems. The least risky project is one that modifies a computer system to improve performance and to add new features; the most risky is one that implements an entirely new system to address a new information problem. Developing a new system to synchronize all the traffic lights in Chicago, for example, would be much riskier than developing enhancements for the city's existing payroll system.

Finally, projects that require a high level of specialized technical skill involve considerable risk. A system that uses an econometric model and high-level mathematics to simulate the real economic world has a great deal of risk associated with it. Developing the formulas, relating the real world to the formulas, and validating the outputs are complicated tasks. Compared with an inventory system, in which the processing operations and the outputs are clearly defined and easily understood, systems involving models and simulations present a much higher degree of risk. Figure 15.3 shows one project that incorporates some of the high-risk factors we have mentioned and another in which risk is low.

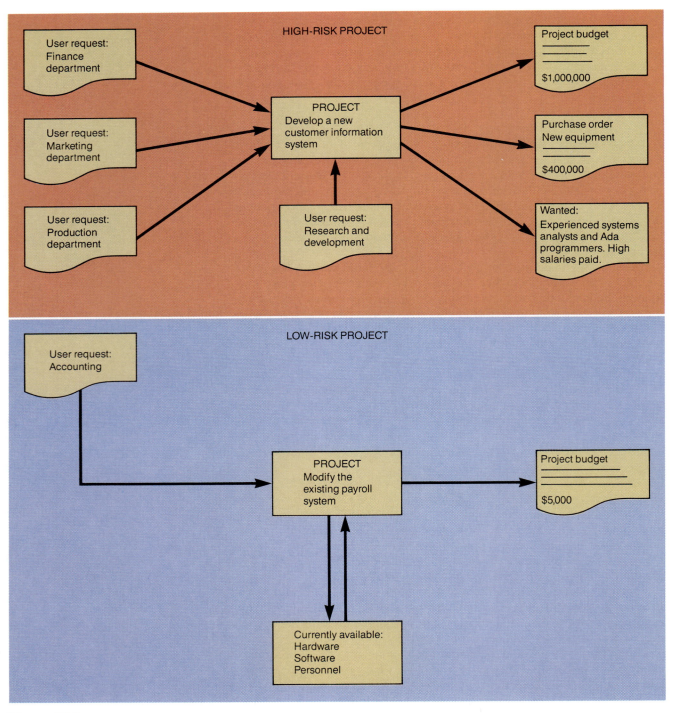

Figure 15.3
Risk factors in systems development.

Planning for Systems Development

Plans are an integral part of all phases of the systems development cycle. Even in the first phase, it's necessary to have a rough plan to guide the objectives of the study team that evaluates the systems proposal, a schedule for completion of the feasibility study, and a budget to control the study's costs. In the next phase, a chief objective is the development of a broad plan that will guide the design activities that follow. In the third phase, a plan of specifications for the chosen design alternative must be developed; this plan specifies the output, input, and processing requirements of the new system, as well as the procedures to be used in testing and implementing it. The fourth phase requires detailed technical plans for programming the system. As noted, plans for implementing the system are made well in advance of actual implementation, and ease of maintenance is a constant concern throughout the developmental process.

As Figure 15.4 shows, project planning is a bit like decomposition in

Figure 15.4
Planning scope.

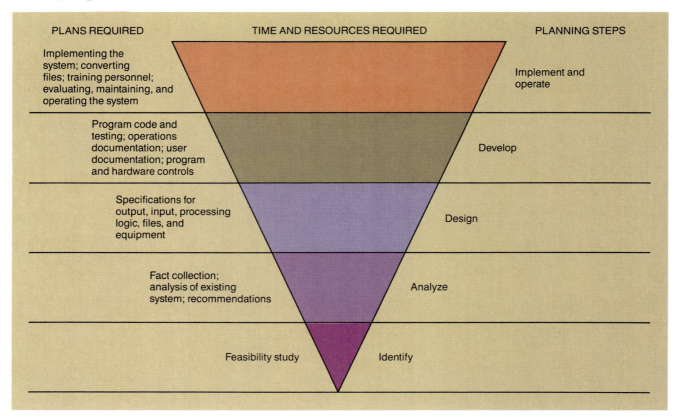

reverse. The systems development cycle begins with a rough plan that is very limited in scope. As the project progresses, the plan expands to include a number of more elaborate and refined operational plans relating to specific components of the project.

A comprehensive **implementation plan** is used to coordinate the project's various operational plans, and it describes the project in terms of personnel requirements, work assignments, time requirements for project components, schedules, and budgets (see Figure 15.5). The implementation plan establishes a priority schedule and a monitoring system to be used in managing the project. The **project priority schedule** details the various tasks, or project modules, to be accomplished and sequences them in building-block fashion; just as you wouldn't attempt to put a roof on a building before the walls are built, neither would you attempt to perform

Figure 15.5
The comprehensive implementation plan.

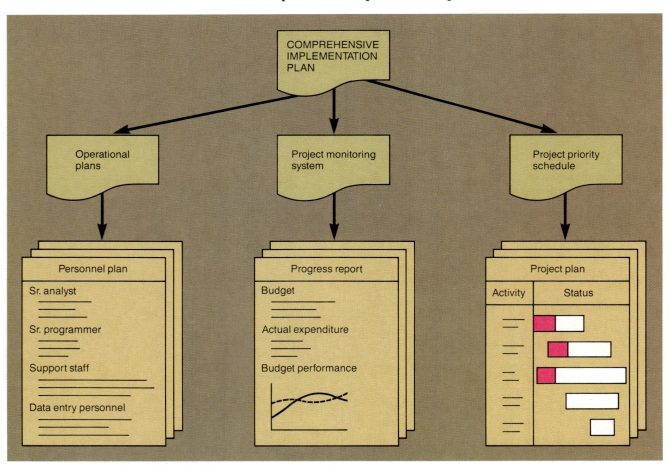

certain project tasks before performing others that create the foundation for the project. The **project monitoring system** defines the means by which progress in the various tasks will be measured and reported to management.

Personnel, scheduling, and monitoring are particularly important concerns in project planning. Let's take a look at some of the reasons for their importance.

Personnel. The approval of a systems proposal is the signal that change in the organization is going to occur. And resistance to change — particularly change caused by the introduction of a new technology — is a very common human reaction. The word *sabotage,* as you may remember if you read the boxed anecdote in Chapter 2, is derived from *saboter,* a French word meaning to clatter one's *sabots,* or wooden shoes. *Saboter* began to take on another meaning — to botch — when European textile workers in the nineteenth century, afraid that a new technology would cost them their jobs, reacted by throwing their *sabots* into Jacquard's loom.

While personnel today are unlikely to start tossing their sandals and sneakers into the computer hardware, their resistance to systems change can take other forms. And these other forms can do just as good a job of botching the works as the *sabots* once did; they can also be much less obvious and more difficult to detect. For example, the design of a new system depends on data gathered during the analysis of the current system. And these data come from people, who, if they feel that their jobs are threatened, may quite easily and quietly withhold or distort essential data about present operations. Incomplete and inaccurate data, can, of course, have disastrous effects on the system that is developed, but these effects won't become obvious until much later, not until after a great deal of effort and many resources may have been expended on developing the system. Moreover, if the people most affected by a system don't want it to succeed, it probably won't. A sloppy work effort and an apathetic attitude can be just as effective a form of sabotage as withholding or distorting data. Not all people will react to systems change in this way, of course, but the possibility that some of them will certainly exists.

Resistance to change, then, is a psychological factor that must be recognized and addressed at the earliest stages of systems development. Because it's generally a quiet and insidious kind of resistance, it can be easily ignored, but ignoring it isn't going to make it go away; a plan for dealing with it is necessary. An effective method of dealing with such resistance is to keep all affected personnel as fully informed about the new system as possible and to solicit their reactions and suggestions — in other words, to establish a dialogue. By "all affected personnel," we mean people at all levels — clerical and operations staff, information users, and managers — anyone who will be involved in the system. People are likely to be much less resistant to change if they know how the change will affect them, why it is being undertaken, and what its benefits will be. And they are likely to be even supportive of the new system if they feel that by offering their suggestions, they are helping to shape it. Briefings by project managers, newsletters and memos, and working sessions involving both managers and other employees can create a climate conducive to open communication and a spirit of cooperation and participation. The creation of such a climate will go a long way toward reducing confusion and fear within the workforce.

In addition to reducing resistance to change, this kind of participation and dialogue can have other benefits as well. In fact, as you may recall from Chapter 3, an essential ingredient in the success of any computer information system is the involvement of users in the total developmental effort. Obviously, information users will not do the technical work of coding and testing the programs, but their inputs into the development of design alternatives, systems specifications, and project plans can be invaluable. Moreover, the more involved they are with the systems study team, the harder they will work for the success of the system. Without the involvement of information users, the system that is developed will in all likelihood be isolated from the reality of the organization's operations.

An ongoing dialogue about the new system is also a way of gaining management support, and without such support, most new systems are doomed to failure. It's difficult to support what you don't understand, and ever since computers were introduced into the business world, understanding between management and computer specialists has been lacking. The natural hesitancy to avoid something you don't completely comprehend has resulted in the development of systems that don't meet managers' needs — systems designed by technical staff more knowledgeable about the computer than about the organization. Such avoidance on the part of managers may be the single biggest problem that businesses have faced in automating their information systems.

Much of the lack of understanding between management and technical staff has had to do with poor communication. The technical specialists, the scientists and mathematicians responsible for the computing, have not always found it easy to convey their ideas to managers. As a result, managers have often come away without a clear understanding of how computers work, or even how to make them work; they have also often seemed unaware that a computer system is not developed overnight. Unreasonable requests, last-minute changes that upset schedules, and requests for systems with a complexity or magnitude beyond the capabilities of the organization have led to frustration on both sides and a feeling of working at cross-purposes. The way out of this unproductive situation, and to gain management support for systems development, is to give management enough information to understand what's going on. However, the communication of this information can't be left to chance; it must be built into the project plans. Besides the methods of communication mentioned earlier, periodic progress reports and formal reports for managers are ways of ensuring that this communication will take place.

Personnel planning must also provide detailed plans for the people involved in data collection and data entry. These individuals are the ones most directly affected by the systems change; they will have to learn new procedures as well as work with unfamiliar data collection and data entry forms. Plans for these employees are very important for two reasons:

1. The data that enter the system become part of the business's data base; if these data are inaccurate or incomplete, the data base will be too. Thus, data collection and data entry are the functions that have the single most important impact on the entire processing operation.

2. Whenever data are processed by computer, the procedures for collecting and entering the data must be clearly defined and correctly implemented. Computers can't make judgments to compensate for inaccurate data, and you can't count on them as you could on a clerk to know what you should have put on a form but didn't have time to complete. It's therefore necessary to anticipate and plan for all possible data collection and data entry situations and to delineate a carefully structured set of rules for the personnel involved in these operations.

Plans for data collection and data entry personnel should also take into account the training and motivation of these employees. Most data collection is done by people who complete source documents or enter transaction data onto forms as a routine part of their jobs. Included in this group are assembly-line workers and sales personnel. These individuals seldom see the end product of the data collection effort — the business report — and usually don't consider the collection of data a very important part of their work. The training that these people receive in data collection is often nonexistent; "read the instructions and fill out the form" characterizes the thinking in many firms.

Similarly, the training of data entry operators, who are responsible for converting data from source documents into machine-readable form, is brief; it usually takes only a few months to learn the required keyboarding skills. Data entry is a low-paid job characterized by high turnover and low prestige. Given the lack of importance that most companies attach to it, it's not surprising that lack of motivation among data entry personnel is as much a problem as it is among those who don't consider data collection an important part of their work.

The less well trained and motivated data collection and data entry personnel are, the more direction and structure they will need in performing their very important functions. Of course, motivation and training could — and should — be improved by other methods, such as educating these people in the importance of their jobs, giving them a more professional status, and rewarding work on the basis of quality rather than quantity. The last method would be much easier than trying to build elaborate controls on accuracy into the computer system.

Data collection forms, as we noted in Chapter 6, are a useful way of providing direction and structure for data collection personnel; they can also make the job of the data entry operator easier. However, systems change means that both data collection forms and data entry procedures change. Remembering to use the new forms, putting the data in the right spaces, following the new instructions for collecting and entering the data — all these are data collection and entry problems associated with the introduction of new systems. Systems change also means that the appearance of outputs may change. Reports may have new headings and may put the information in different places. Training sessions describing the anticipated changes and outlining new procedures for the data collection and data entry personnel as well as the users of the output are a great help in minimizing these difficulties, especially if the sessions take place before the new system is installed and operational.

New systems often require new support staff, and this, too, requires planning. To fill these new positions with the best possible candidates, the personnel department needs adequate information on the education and experience that the job demands, as well as an outline of expected duties and responsibilities. The recruiting, interviewing, and hiring of new staff often take place before the system is developed, which necessitates careful advance planning for the training of these new staff members.

Project Scheduling and Monitoring. We mentioned earlier that the comprehensive implementation plan establishes a project priority schedule and a monitoring system. The former outlines the sequence in which the various project tasks are to be performed, and the latter specifies how progress in various project activities will be measured and reported to management. The point of creating a priority schedule and a monitoring system is to establish **project control,** a means by which actual performance can be measured against the plan for performance. By comparing actual progress with the schedule for progress, managers have a sound basis for determining when changes — either in the schedule or in the project itself — are necessary.

A schedule also gives managers a means of controlling the financial aspects of a project. Because a systems development budget is drawn up with the overall objectives of the project in mind, it does not specify the time frames in which particular monies are to be spent. For example, a project budget might allocate funds for programmers' salaries in one lump sum. A schedule gives managers a way of later comparing the programming work done within a certain period with the funds expended; without a schedule, it would be impossible to identify the work done in each time frame.

Work packaging — that is, the breaking down of the project into small and manageable units to be assigned to the technical staff — is an important part of project scheduling and monitoring. If individual work units are carefully defined in the early stages of systems development, all the pieces of the project should fall into place as the project nears completion. Work packaging also helps to ensure overall management control of the project, and it provides flexibility if rescheduling or reassignment of staff becomes necessary. The alternative to work packaging, which is to give a programmer/analyst a systems request and then to sit back and wait for the system to be completed, does not give management any options if the project encounters delays or problems. Giving one programmer/analyst the responsibility for developing the whole system may also limit the involvement of users in the development of the system, since the programmer/analyst may choose not to consult them; and, as we've already noted, without such involvement, the success of the system is dubious.

Establishing a schedule depends on the identification of measurable goals, or milestones. **Milestones** are key activities that can be monitored to determine the progress of the project, and they usually involve the delivery of a program, a format design, or a report or other document. Milestones often initiate interaction between users and technical staff, and such interaction serves as a review to assure management that the project is proceeding according to plan. By reporting on scheduled milestones, the project monitoring system keeps managers informed of the status of the project and allows them to make informed decisions throughout the systems development cycle. For example, if the programming is scheduled to be 50 percent completed by July 1, and the July 1 report indicates that only 30 percent is completed, the project manager reviews the options. These might include adding more staff to speed up the programming, accepting the delay and altering the schedule accordingly, or modifying the other components of the project to allow for the programming slowdown. The decision would be based on a number of variables, and it is the responsibility of management to be aware of them. Figure 15.6 shows a typical, though somewhat simplified, report submitted by a monitoring system.

Various kinds of tools make project scheduling an easier chore. One popular scheduling tool is called a **Gantt chart.** As illustrated in Figure 15.7, the length of each horizontal bar of a Gantt chart corresponds to the time required to complete an activity. When the Gantt chart is initially prepared, each bar is open, indicating that none of the activities for that project has been completed. As work progresses, the bars are filled in to show how much of the work has been done. At the end of each reporting period, copies of the chart can be easily distributed to managers, giving them a quick but meaningful overview of how the project is progressing. For large projects, an overall schedule and chart would be prepared, and a number of detailed charts would be used to report the progress of each project component.

Another popular scheduling tool uses **critical path networks** to illustrate the relationships between tasks and schedules. Like Gantt charts, critical

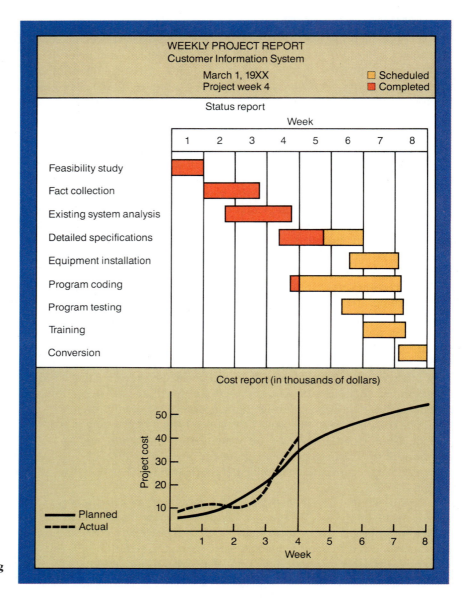

Figure 15.6
A report from a project monitoring system.

path networks record events and time relationships, but they differ from Gantt charts in that they also show how each event relates to other events and they identify those events critical to maintaining the schedule. When used for project reporting, a critical path network helps point out delays that will affect project completion time. Managers thus have the opportunity to divert resources to critical areas to maintain the overall schedule. Figure

Activity	Week						
	1	2	3	4	5	6	7
Initial activity	▬	▬					
Intermediate activity		▬	▬				
Completion activity				▬	▬	▬	
Preparation of report							▬

Figure 15.7
A Gantt chart at the start of a project.

15.8 shows a simplified critical path network in which the critical path from start to event 2 to finish takes a total of seven weeks. Delays related to events 1, 3, and 4 would not affect the completion date of the project unless they exceeded the seven-week period.

Some of the specific concerns to be addressed in project scheduling include schedules for hardware to be used in program debugging and testing and installation schedules for new equipment, if required. Another specific and important concern is a schedule and cutover plan for implementing the new system. Implementation may take place in various ways. A switchover to the new system with no backup system in operation is called a **plunge** or **cold-turkey systems conversion.** This kind of conversion poses potential problems, including the inability to check the performance of the new system against what is known to be correct (i.e., the outputs of the old system).

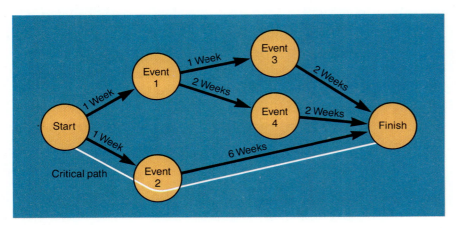

Figure 15.8
A critical path network.

A **parallel systems conversion** runs both the old and the new systems at the same time. This type of conversion allows the performance of the new system to be checked against that of the old and at the same time provides a backup operation. For example, in a parallel conversion of a manual card-oriented inventory system, the cards would continue to be posted by hand while the new computer system was checked. At the end of the test period, the inventory would be checked for discrepancies. This kind of operation is expensive, as the work is being done twice, once by the old system and once by the new. It does provide a high degree of safety, however, and it is generally used when new financial systems are being implemented.

Parallel operations are sometimes not feasible, usually because they are too expensive or because no old system is in place. In these cases, a **pilot systems conversion** may be used. In this implementation process, one particular unit or segment of the new system is carefully monitored and evaluated. In the meantime, implementation of the rest of the system is delayed. Once all the bugs have been worked out of the part of the system tested in the pilot installation, the remainder of the system is installed throughout the organization. A failure during the pilot installation will not cause disaster throughout the organization, as it will affect only one component of the firm. For example, in a pilot conversion, a firm might install a new accounting system only in its Boston office. When all the bugs have been worked out of the system, it would install the system in all its other offices. Plans for systems conversion are important because a balance between cost effectiveness and systems safety needs to be maintained. Figure 15.9 illustrates the various methods of systems conversion and the degree of risk associated with each.

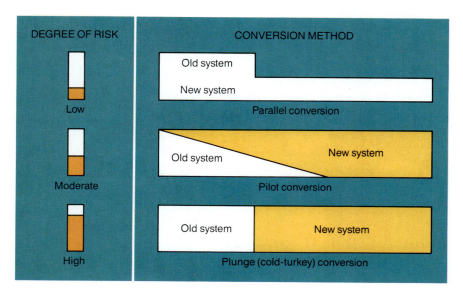

Figure 15.9
Methods of systems conversion and related risk.

PROJECT MANAGEMENT

Project management takes two distinct forms: matrix management and line management. **Matrix management** is so called because several project managers are involved in the planning (see Figure 15.10). The project management team is composed of individuals from a number of departments; the technical staff are assigned according to the nature and complexity of the project. Each manager has a specific function and responsibility in the project, and each also becomes a project leader for the resources within his or her department. For example, if matrix management was being used in a project devoted to developing a system for reporting on sales calls, the management team would include a member from the marketing department, a member from central administration, and a member from the information systems department. The marketing representative's function would be to ensure that the outputs met the needs of management and that the data collection forms were appropriately designed. Central administration's representative would be responsible for seeing that the goals of the organization were understood and that the project design met those goals. The function of the representative from the information systems department would be to manage the day-to-day programming activities of the project staff. As the project progressed, leadership would pass from one manager to another, depending on the activities underway at the time. Matrix management, then, involves shared responsibility for the successful completion of the project.

The more traditional style of project management is **line management,** in which there is one project manager (see Figure 15.11). Workers are assigned to the project staff and remain on the staff until the project is completed. All project participants report to the project manager, who is solely responsible for the success of the project.

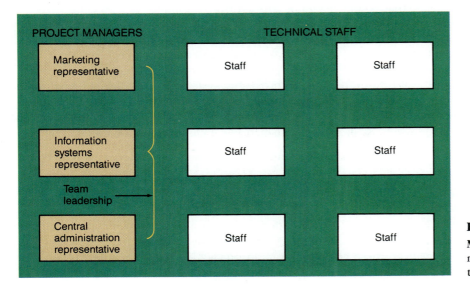

Figure 15.10

Matrix management. Team leadership moves among the project managers as the project progresses.

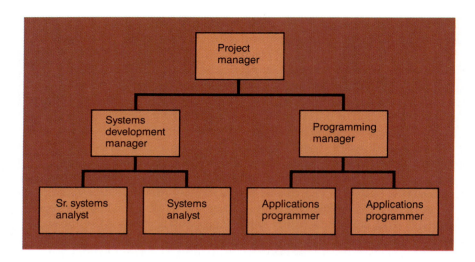

Figure 15.11
Line management.

There is no best way to manage a systems development project. The selection of a management style is often a function of the style of management used throughout the organization, of the staff resources available, and of the complexity of the system that is being developed. The advantage of matrix management is that management of the project rests in the hands of the team member most familiar with the situation or technology currently at issue. With line management, in which a single individual is in charge and stays in charge, the lines of authority are clear and unchanging, but project motivation may be reduced, especially in areas with which the assigned project manager is unfamiliar or in which he or she has no interest.

Regardless of management style, project managers are responsible for seeing that sound planning and control techniques are used throughout the systems development cycle. One of their important specific responsibilities is to define project objectives and tasks. Tasks common to most projects include evaluating alternative solutions, reviewing technical considerations, reporting to and reviewing progress with users and technical managers, and evaluating interfaces with existing systems. To simplify program documentation—and hence maintenance—project managers should, whenever possible, use the same format for describing these tasks. Other specific responsibilities of the project manager include the following:

1. Developing work schedules based on the tasks that have been defined.
2. Estimating project costs and preparing appropriate budgets.
3. Preparing a staffing plan for the project.

Project managers thus function as directors of the work and planning activities involved in the project, but they have a larger overall responsibility to manage these activities from an organizational perspective as well.

CASE STUDY: RITCHCO AUTO PARTS
Part I

Art Richardson is the owner and president of Ritchco, a small auto parts business. He took a chance when he bought the business from his father four years ago, and he's been battling ever since with the pressures of competition, change, and technology. Realizing it would take every bit of knowledge and skill he could acquire to make a success of the business, Art even took the time to get an MBA. Although he is proud of what he has accomplished in these past four years, he still cannot afford to be complacent; the auto parts business is fiercely competitive, and he's constantly on the alert for anything that will give him a competitive edge.

Art's father started Ritchco in his garage as a sideline — something to do after a day of work as a postal employee. The business had prospered in a small way, mainly because of the personal attention Art's father gave his customers. Most of his sales were to small repair shops and garages; he had made no real effort to develop a retail business.

Art was teaching business administration at a small, private college at the time he bought his father out, and he was eager to see if he could translate theory into action and profits. Believing that the primary source of growth is name recognition — something he couldn't attain without a retail operation — Art's first goal was to move the business out of the backyard garage. He wanted a facility that would serve both as a retail center and a warehouse. The building he selected was on a busy highway near an interstate, only two miles from the center of town. Art thought the location ideal for scheduling deliveries to commercial accounts as well as for developing a walk-in retail business. He proceeded to remodel the facility into an attractive salesroom and warehouse.

As the business expanded, there was no way Art could run it by himself as his father had done. He hired and trained two sales representatives to call on commercial accounts and several sales clerks to answer the phones, take orders, and wait on customers. He also hired two delivery drivers and bought two vans. He was on his way.

Three years after buying the business, Art was the picture of success. He had just opened his third store, had twenty-two employees, and was meeting his profit objectives. But despite his success, Art was uneasy. He talked over his concerns with a friend:

Art: "I don't know what's happening, John. I just can't seem to keep up with the work. The stores are doing well but the paper work is killing me. And to top it off, I think one of my employees is cheating me. Either that, or someone's just plain careless. Even working seven days a week, I can't seem to catch up. We're constantly taking orders for merchandise that checks out on our inventory cards, but then we can't find it in the warehouse, so we're always having to juggle parts between stores. And what's more, the clerks are always making math errors on customer invoices. I have to check everything. There must be a better way to go about this — I just wish I knew what it was."

John: "Maybe a computer would help. I was just reading in the newspaper about a firm that found a lot of relief from paper work once it had a computer system up and running. It might be worth thinking about."

Art: "I wouldn't know where to begin. A computer seems like a pretty big step for a small company like mine, and I don't know much about computers. I've seen some ads, but I don't know if the problems they talk about are the same ones I have in my business. But maybe I should look into it."

1. Why do you think Art was having trouble keeping up with the paper work?

2. Identify four problems that are evident from the description of the business operations at Ritchco Auto Parts.

3. If Art decides to investigate the use of a computer in his business, what steps should he take? What questions should he ask?

SUMMARY

The reasons for introducing systems change include a need to process an expanded volume of data, a need to meet internal and external information needs, and a desire to achieve cost savings. At the basis of all these reasons for introducing systems change is the need to remain competitive.

A reasonable request for systems change usually sets the systems development cycle in motion. The five steps of this cycle serve as the basis for the careful planning that an effective information system requires. Certain important concerns, which are addressed at various stages of the systems development cycle, must be kept in mind throughout the developmental process. These include the issues involved in evaluating systems proposals and in planning for systems development.

An initial evaluation of a proposed system assesses the contributions that the system can make to overall organizational goals. The criteria used in making this assessment include the project's organizational fit, its cost effectiveness, and the degree of risk it involves. Such evaluation provides a way of ranking projects, which is necessary because decisions about systems development must be made within the context of certain constraints. Chief among these constraints are the limitations of the resources that a company has available for systems development.

Plans are an integral part of all phases of the systems development cycle. Planning for personnel and scheduling and monitoring the project to ensure project control are particularly important concerns in systems planning. Planning for personnel requires a consideration of how to deal with resistance to change, how to involve users in the developmental effort, and how to gain management support; it also requires consideration of the data collection and data entry personnel, the system's users, and new staff. Among the factors involved in project scheduling and monitoring are the division of the project into work packages and the identification of measurable milestones. Gantt charts and critical path networks can be very useful tools in project scheduling. An important specific concern in project scheduling is a cutover plan for implementing the new system.

Project management takes two distinct forms: matrix management and line management. In matrix management, leadership shifts from one team member to another as the project progresses through various stages. Line management follows the more traditional approach of assigning one individual to be the manager of the project from start to finish. Project managers are responsible for the work and planning activities involved in the project, but they also have a broader responsibility to manage these activities from an organizational perspective.

KEY TERMS

cost effectiveness (427)
cost savings (421)
critical path networks (437)
external constraints (424)
Gantt chart (437)
implementation plan (432)
internal constraints (424)
line management (441)
matrix management (441)
milestones (437)

organizational fit (426)
parallel systems conversion (440)
pilot systems conversion (440)
plunge (cold-turkey) systems conversion (439)
project control (436)
project monitoring system (433)
project priority schedule (432)
risk (429)
work packaging (436)

DISCUSSION QUESTIONS

1. Identify the most common reasons for introducing systems change within an organization. What do all these reasons have in common?

2. Describe the steps of the systems development cycle and explain the usefulness of this approach.

3. Identify the internal and external constraints on systems development.

4. Discuss three criteria by which systems proposals are evaluated. Apply these criteria to the purchase of a used car.

5. Why is it important to consider resistance to systems change in project planning? What is an effective method of dealing with such resistance? What other effects might this method have?

6. Why is planning for data collection and data entry personnel important? What considerations should go into these plans?

7. What is project control, and how is it established? What do milestones and work packaging have to do with project control? Describe how you would establish project control in the preparation of a term paper.

8. Describe two tools used in project scheduling.

9. Discuss the various ways in which systems conversions may be implemented.

10. Identify the two main forms of project management and explain how they differ. Describe the responsibilities of project managers.

OUTLINE

OUTPUT

Organizational Factors
- Size
- Management Style
- Nature of the Business
- Goals of the Business

Output Formats, Schedules, and Distribution Lists
- Formatting
- Scheduling
- Distribution

INPUT

Kinds of Information
Data Complexity
Information Use

PROCESSING

Sequential File Organization
Direct File Organization
Indexed-Sequential File Organization

SUMMARY
KEY TERMS
DISCUSSION QUESTIONS

OVERVIEW

Think for a minute about the last time you took a vacation. Before you could make any other plans, you had to decide where you wanted to go. Only then could you decide how you were going to get there and what you would take with you. To be sure you had an enjoyable vacation, you probably found out enough about the climate to select appropriate clothing. Naturally, in making all these plans, you also had to decide whether you could afford the vacation.

Developing a computer information system is not altogether unlike planning a vacation. The first thing you have to decide is your destination — in this case, the desired outputs of the system. Once you've identified those, you can begin to develop the inputs and processing activities needed to produce the outputs. This order of activity may seem a bit awkward at first glance, but it's really just a matter of common sense: To get what you want, you usually first have to decide what you want; you then work backward to determine what you need in order to get what you want. Along the way, if you're a realist and if you really want to achieve your goal, you'll take into account whatever factors have an important bearing on that goal (in the case of vacation planning, ski clothes in Puerto Rico aren't going to make for an enjoyable vacation, and bankrupting yourself would no doubt not be worth the holiday).

In developing a computer information system, the end product — the output — and the means of achieving it — the input and processing activities — are equally important design considerations: Without a clear idea of the output needed, you won't collect the appropriate input data or use the appropriate processing procedures; and unless you do collect the appropriate data and use the appropriate processing procedures, you won't produce the desired output. Doing all these things correctly depends on an awareness of various factors involved in output, input, and processing design. Our focus in this chapter is on some of the critical factors that must be considered if an effective computer information system is to emerge from the systems development effort. Our objectives are to

◆ describe the organizational factors that affect the design of an information system's outputs.

◆ discuss the formatting, scheduling, and distribution of outputs.

◆ explain the considerations that must go into designing the inputs for the system.

◆ describe the considerations involved in effective processing design and the design alternatives available for structuring data files.

CHAPTER 16

OUTPUT, INPUT, AND PROCESSING: SOME DESIGN CONSIDERATIONS

OUTPUT

Although a clear understanding of the desired output is critical to the development of a successful computer information system, designing the output entails more than just knowing what you want. You also have to know the resources required to get what you want, understand what you are capable of doing, and keep within the budgeted costs for the project. For example, it would make little sense to try to develop a complex and sophisticated data base system that requires a high level of technical expertise and a considerable expenditure of resources when none of the technical staff has more than two years of computing experience, none of it with data base systems, and the information systems department works within a very limited budget.

In addition to understanding the desired outputs and the resources available to produce them, anyone involved in systems development should also have an awareness of certain other factors that influence output design, among them various organizational characteristics and requirements relating to output formats, schedules, and distribution lists. (**Output formats** refer to the way the output is displayed — the organization or style of columns, headings, spacing, and character placement, and whether the output is in hard-copy or soft-copy form.)

Organizational Factors

Businesses have different demands for information, and they use their information in different ways. These differences are related to differences in organizational characteristics. Size, management style, the nature of the business, and the goals of the business — all have a bearing on the information, or output, that a company needs.

Size. Usually, the larger a firm, the greater its need for output and the more output it can afford. As Figure 16.1 indicates, small businesses are less likely than large businesses to need formal reporting systems, since personal contacts between owners and employees and first-hand observations can take their place. Small businesses are also less likely to be able to afford complex information systems and the staff necessary to develop and maintain them. In fact, until the introduction of the microcomputer and the subsequent development of commercial software, most small companies that wanted to automate their data processing or information systems had to rely on commercial timesharing services or other firms offering computer services. The output formats of these small companies were thus limited to what the commercial services had available, regardless of whether the formats effectively met the businesses' information needs. Today, microcomputers and versatile commercial software give small businesses the opportunity to develop a variety of outputs and to meet most of their information-reporting needs at a low overall cost.

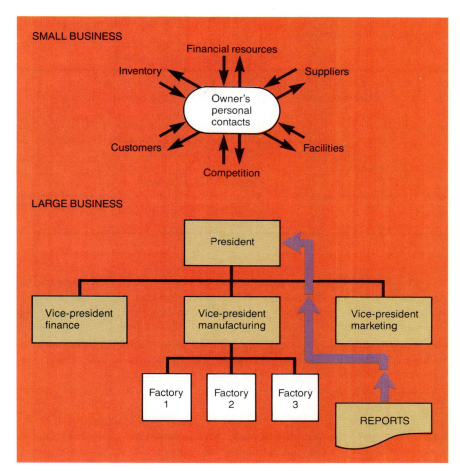

Figure 16.1

Business size and the need for output. In small businesses, personal contacts and first-hand observations reduce the need for formal information-reporting systems. In large businesses, top-level managers must rely on formal reports to stay informed about the business's operations.

Management Style. Management styles can be grouped into four categories: traditional, scientific, behavioral, and quantitative. Table 16.1 summarizes the distinguishing characteristics of each of these management styles.

The underlying assumption in **traditional management** (also called **process management**) is that if you understand the functional aspects of the business (administration, production, marketing, and finance), you can learn to manage. Traditional management puts great emphasis on generating information about the business's operations and transactions. Its belief is that by reviewing this information, managers can get a picture of what the business is doing and what needs to be done or what decisions need to be made. All organizations have some traditional managers, and all business information systems therefore need to generate outputs relating to the operations of each functional area. Many organizations, however, combine traditional management with other management styles in an effort to be more effective.

Table 16.1 Characteristics of Various Management Styles

Management Style	Emphasis	Typical Information Needs
Traditional	Functional aspects of an organization (administration, production, marketing, and finance)	Regularly scheduled reports describing production, sales, and financial transactions
Scientific	Work measurement and analysis	Highly analytical information: time-and-motion studies and reports on quality control and individual productivity
Behavioral	Individuals rather than procedures or functions	Skills inventories, performance reports, and personal characteristics
Quantitative	Models that simulate the real environment and test decisions	Projections, especially as they relate to profits, production, and distribution

An assembly line is **scientific management** in action. This management style measures the work to be done, trains workers in precise activities such as machine operation and assembly, and in effect considers the worker as an extension of a machine. Work is broken down into very small units, and work assignments are quite specific. The information-reporting system focuses on generating outputs that allow precise control of the operations. Reports on production, scheduling, error, waste, and quality control are very detailed and point to work units rather than describing the operation as a whole. Managers use this analytical information to refine the system, to reduce opportunity for error, and to adjust work schedules for the highest productivity. Scientific management is rarely the only management style used to run an organization, as some business activities that are part of any operation don't lend themselves to this kind of precise analysis. However, when combined with traditional management, scientific management has proven to be a powerful force in modern industry.

Behavioral management is based on the belief that individuals are at least as important to an organization as procedures and work activities. Because the focus of this management style is on people, its information needs are less clearly defined than those of other styles, and outputs are therefore more difficult to develop. Unlike procedures or machines, people are unpredictable, and behavioral managers have to deal with situations that can't always be planned in advance. Information needs are thus often undefined until the need for a decision arises. The job of the systems developer is to anticipate the information that will be needed and to provide at least a framework from which the behavioral manager can work.

Records relating to individual performance, skills inventories, and personal information are the sorts of outputs that behavioral management uses. In a small firm, most of this information is probably developed without anyone's being aware of it. The manager knows each of the employees personally and in time develops an understanding of their personal characteristics. Management decisions will no doubt reflect this special knowledge, whether the manager consciously thinks about it or not. In a larger organization, such extensive personal contact is usually not possible, and a formal information system is needed to replace the personal associations. Developing such a system is not an easy matter, for, as we've noted, the information needs of behavioral management are not very clearly defined.

The information needs of **quantitative management** are quite different from those of the other management styles. Quantitative management relies heavily on models, or simulations, of real situations to provide input for the decision-making process. Data are analyzed critically, usually according to a set of formal decision rules, and decisions are based on the results of the analyses. Mathematical computations play a major role in the information system and require technical personnel with special skills in high-level mathematics. Although data pertaining to the business's operations must, of course, still be kept and processed, the reporting requirements for operational data change because these data become inputs for the model rather than information for the manager. Many of these data (often called *feedback*) are processed directly, and the results of the processing generate a decision. For instance, instead of a manager's deciding to change a machine setting because many of the outputs are not passing inspection, the quantitative system would process the quality-control data, determine the production process that needed adjustment, and automatically make the necessary change. The outputs are electronic signals, never seen by human beings.

As you can see, management style clearly affects the design of the outputs needed by an organization. This factor must therefore be considered carefully if the information system is to meet the needs of its users.

Nature of the Business. The nature of a business also affects its information needs. In general, the information needs of a business that produces traditional products or services are more easily defined and met than those of a business that develops entirely new products or that deals with state-of-the-art technology. For example, a firm that has been manufacturing washing machines for fifty years will no doubt have a pretty good idea of the manufacturing activities and markets for washing machines, and its information system will be well developed and refined to be of the greatest possible benefit in the decision-making process. In contrast, the information needs of a company that produces pollution-control equipment, using a technology so new no one else has it and very few understand it, are very unclear. Such a company needs ways of projecting manufacturing requirements, potential sales, and any other information needed to compete successfully, all of it unique information since the technology is so new. Because information needs vary according to the nature of individual businesses, it's difficult to set standards for the design of outputs. What will serve the needs of the washing machine company will probably not serve the needs of the high-technology company.

Goals of the Business. What a business plans for its future can make a great deal of difference in its information needs. Growth generally requires aggressive decision making and often entails risk. An elaborate information system can help to minimize risk by providing management with a rich base of information on which to make decisions. A mature firm — one whose growth is slow or nonexistent — needs information more for the purpose of protecting its position than to capture new business. Such a firm might be satisfied to make decisions on the basis of less complete information than an aggressive, expanding business would. It might opt for a fairly elaborate customer-information system, a more concise inventory system, or a more modest system altogether. The output design, then, must take into consideration the goals of the firm if the information system is to meet users' needs effectively.

Output Formats, Schedules, and Distribution Lists

Considerations in output formatting include the physical design of the outputs and the selection of the media that will be used to display or produce them. Scheduling the outputs — arranging the processing activities to produce the outputs when needed — and preparing distribution lists for the outputs are also important concerns in output design, for if the output isn't delivered to the right person at the right time, it's not going to influence the decision process.

Formatting. The graphic capabilities of today's computer systems have created a major upheaval in the design of business outputs, particularly business reports. Although alphabetical listings and columns of numbers may still be the most effective way of providing the shop supervisor with detailed information on production schedules, available personnel, and raw materials, they are no longer the only way of providing computerized information (see Figure 16.2). Upper-level plant managers, who need to compare planned production with actual production, find it far easier to assimilate the information they need if it is in the form of bar graphs rather than in alphabetical or numerical form. In just a few seconds, with no need to hunt for specific data or to sift through columns of numbers, the manager can see how well the plant is functioning. Thus, systems developers must understand the information needs of individual users of the system before they begin the physical design of the outputs. It would be unusual to find the same kind of graphic outputs serving both operational and administrative decision makers.

Among the seemingly obvious but often overlooked details of output design are the following (see Figure 16.3):

1. *Durability of the document.* Will it withstand repeated handling?

2. *Size of the type.* Is it large enough for people to read easily?

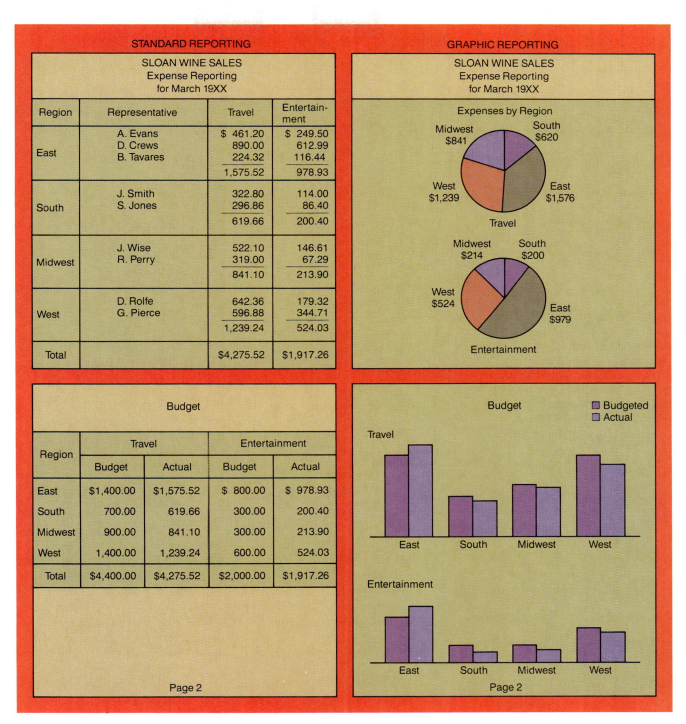

Figure 16.2
Graphic outputs: the old and the new.

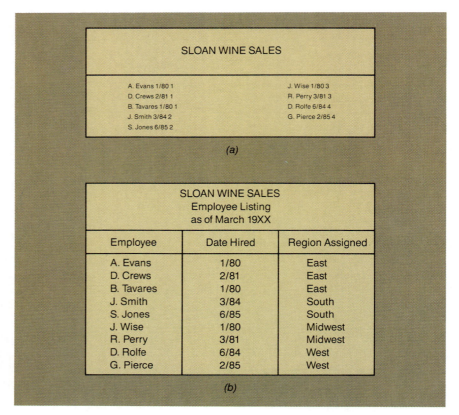

Figure 16.3
Details of output design. A poorly designed report (*a*) is confusing and hard to read and handle; it lacks headings, is not dated, has very small type, and is printed on nonstandard-sized paper. A well-designed report (*b*) is printed legibly on standard-sized paper and includes appropriate dates and headings.

3. *Distinction of the headings and labels.* When an information system generates a large number of reports, many of them looking very much alike, it's important that adequate identification be built into the design format.

4. *Size of the output.* Because computer printers can print up to 132 characters per line, oversized printouts, which are quite a bit larger than a standard 8½-by-11-inch document, can be very efficient, especially when the output consists of large volumes of historical data to be stored in archives. Oversized printouts present all-too-obvious difficulties, however, when you have to stuff them into a standard file cabinet. The varying sizes of checks, invoices, and mailing items are also a consideration in output design, as these items must fit into envelopes, be processed through check scanners, or be attached to correspondence. While the stock (paper) for any of these items can be custom-cut, it's much cheaper to use a standard-sized output stock.

The medium of the output — soft copy or hard copy in preprinted or non-preprinted form — is another issue to be considered in output design,

GRAPHICALLY SPEAKING WITH DR. EDWARD R. TUFTE

There's something wrong with computer graphics, says Edward R. Tufte, noted statistician and information designer: "Too much chartjunk. No sense of visual craft." And it's largely because of the current machinery's almost complete lack of wysiwyg, he says.

Lack of what?

What you see is what you get. Tufte, author, designer, and publisher of a widely acclaimed book, *The Visual Display of Quantitative Information,* says that for all the computer's convenience and speed, it too often seems to get in the way of making good graphics. In fact, in many cases applying the computer to graphics seems to have been a step backward, for in the change from monotype to microcode much of the graphical wisdom accumulated since Gutenberg began printing books 500 years ago has been lost. The computer's dazzling power to crunch numbers has blinded its users, almost literally, to the crude and often confusing nature of its graphical output.

The visual craft of master cartographers, typographers, and other graphic artists traditionally has been enhanced by the transparency of their tools — what they saw was what they got — and, in Tufte's view, the computerization of graphics production has worked to undo much that was gained over the centuries.

"Too often we're asked to admire the computer, not the information," says Tufte. "What good are 4,028 colors without [the user having] any sense of color? What good are 22 type fonts if they all have jaggies? Computer graphics has tremendous potential, but for several reasons it's largely unexploited."

This isn't to say that computers haven't done some wonderful things for statistical graphics, he emphasizes. The computer has enabled an increase of some 5,000-fold in the density of information portrayed in a graphic. He points to a remarkable computer-generated map, created at Princeton University by P. James E. Peebles and colleagues, showing the distribution of the 1.3 million galaxies in the northern galactic hemisphere. It contains more than 2.2 million tiny rectangles, each of which is shaded according to a 10-tone gray scale. The darker the rectangle, the greater the density of galaxies in that portion of the sky. This map is instantly readable because the gray scale is a naturally understood hierarchy. The many false color maps drawn with the aid of computers often require the observer to constantly refer to a legend so that the entirely artificial color scheme can be interpreted properly. The galaxy map yields a data density of 110,000 numbers per square inch — a record, says Tufte....

But he is quick to point out that the computer has led to a "tremendous number of awful things with no sense of visual craft. We see too much chartjunk, noninformation squiggles, ... lousy type, bizarre color combinations, and so forth."

Too often, Tufte says, those who use computers to produce statistical graphics have not learned the three basics, think, see, and count. None of these elements are completely gone from the computer, he says, but there's been a damaging segregation of the technical means from the substance and the visual craft....

"The glory will be when [graphics machines] reach the status of people with real visual craft," he concludes, "when the traditional standards of excellence are met by modern technology. Just because you have high technology shouldn't mean low quality."

— John W. Verity, "Graphically Speaking with Dr. Edward R. Tufte," *Datamation* (April 1, 1985), pp. 88–92. Reprinted with Permission of *Datamation®* magazine, © Copyright by Technical Publishing Company, A Dun & Bradstreet Company, 1985. All rights reserved.

---

and the choice generally depends on the application. As indicated in Figure 16.4, for certain applications, soft copy is the better choice.

Preprinted forms can be expensive, costing several times as much as non-preprinted forms. The latter are forms generated on blank, unlined

SOFT COPY	HARD COPY

• More secure than hard copy because it can be erased from CRT screen after use, but terminals may not be available to all users
• Faster and more convenient than hard copy for inquiry or occasional use
• Provides graphics that may not be available in hard-copy form
• Inexpensive because no supplies required
	• Provides permanent record and is admissible in court
	• Allows for multiple copies
	• Easy to distribute
	• Can utilize preprinted or non-preprinted forms
	• Preprinted form
	  —will not smear or smudge when handled, but printing expense may not be justified by use of the output
	  —saves printing time
	  —provides special graphics, type sizes and styles
	• Non-preprinted form
	  —saves on inventory and updating of forms and on paper changing because entire output is computer-generated
	  —no alignment problems

Figure 16.4
Choices of media for output.

paper by a computer program; the computer program can direct the printing of all headings, instructions, and information, which for most internal business reporting is very cost-effective. Preprinted forms also have the disadvantage of needing to be precisely aligned while the computer output device prints the processed information. However, in certain situations, the preprinted form can more than make up for these deficiencies, especially when only a small amount of computer-generated output is needed to complete the form. Using a preprinted form for a paycheck, for example, is cost-effective since most of the information remains the same from check to check, and only a small amount of computer-generated output needs to be added. Preprinted forms can also provide graphics and type sizes and styles that may not be available from the computer output device. Both preprinted and non-preprinted forms can be on colored paper, which is useful for indicating the distribution routing of reports.

Scheduling. To ensure that the system operates at peak efficiency and that the outputs reach the users at exactly the right time, output design must consider the scheduling of the outputs. Most business outputs are produced as scheduled reports, exception reports, or inquiry reports. (For a discussion of how businesses use these traditional kinds of reports, see Chapter 7.)

Scheduled reports are the most economical kind of report to produce, since they can be planned in advance and can be run any time, day or night, making efficient use of the computer resources. Scheduled reports may be needed as often as every business day, as might be the case for a listing of transactions or inventory, or as seldom as once a year. The timing, or cycling, of the report is important, because the more often the report must be generated, the more costly the reporting process. A report that must be run every day not only eats up considerable computer time and paper; it also makes demands on data collection personnel, who must provide a constant supply of current data.

Exception reports, which contain information only on significant deviations from planned results, may be issued at regular intervals or at the time the deviation occurs. The latter procedure is usually used only to report on deviations in critical areas, such as an overdraft in a checking account. The more usual procedure is to compare operational data with the operational plan at regular intervals (daily, weekly, or monthly, depending on the nature of the data) and to issue a management report at these intervals when the data deviate significantly from the plan.

Because the whole point of an inquiry report is to give the users the information they request whenever they request it, there is no way of preplanning or scheduling such a report. Inquiry reporting is costly since computing resources must be standing by and available to search the data files whenever an inquiry is made. However, without it, airline reservations systems couldn't run, nor could automatic bank-teller machines. Inquiry reporting is also a powerful managerial tool when combined with data base software. This combination allows managers either to search through the data with specific goals in mind or to browse through, combining the data in ways that may provide new insights into the business.

Distribution. A schedule should ensure that the outputs are delivered at the right time; a distribution list should ensure that they are delivered to the right person. Very often, however, distribution lists expand almost uncontrollably, and, as a result, reports go to people who don't need them. Mystified though these people may be by reports for which they have no earthly use, they get them anyway, simply because no one has bothered to change the distribution list to reflect changes in the positions and responsibilities of personnel. Because each copy of a report costs money to produce, the distribution list should be checked periodically to see if any names should be deleted. When the report being distributed contains important or confidential information, deleting names of recipients can be a sticky job. Some people attach status to receiving this kind of report and may feel strongly about being removed from the distribution list, even though the report contains no information pertinent to their jobs.

The information user, rather than the systems analyst, is usually responsible for preparing the distribution list for the outputs of a new system. This task requires an awareness that sensitive information — such as information on the company's financial condition, marketing strategies, or manufacturing procedures — could be used to the company's detriment if it should fall into the wrong hands. It also requires a concern for the security of such outputs as paychecks.

INPUT

The data that go into the processing system have to be the right data to produce the desired output, and they have to be accurate and complete. At the same time, the entire processing system needs to be cost-effective if the data processing effort is to be justified from the organization's point of view. When collecting and processing data, the concepts of accuracy and completeness take on shades of gray; they are not absolutes as you might at first think. Accuracy can be as simple as keeping dollars and cents in order, or, in manufacturing microprocessor chips, it can mean precise machine alignments of millionths of an inch. The use of the outputs determines the degree of accuracy needed. The completeness of the data presents similar difficulties in definition, as more data can always be collected if you are willing to wait another day, spend a little more, or search a little harder. Whether the additional data will contribute to the usefulness of the information produced by the system is the question that must be addressed.

The systems analyst has to make decisions about the degree of data accuracy and completeness needed to produce the desired output, but these decisions must be made within the framework of the budgets for the system — the cost-effectiveness constraints that every business faces when it allocates its resources. On the one hand, the data must be accurate and complete enough so that the system is not processing and producing "garbage." On the other hand, the data should not be any more accurate and complete than needed to produce the desired output, since, as a rule, the more accurate and complete they are, the more expensive it is to collect them.

Careful analysis and design of the inputs can do quite a bit to avoid the possibility of winding up with a lot of expensive nonsense and to ensure that the information the system produces will be worth the costs of collecting and processing the data. Among the questions that input design should address are the following:

1. What kind of information is the system being designed to produce?
2. How complex are the data needed to produce the information?
3. Does the ultimate value of the information offset the costs of collecting the data?

Kinds of Information

The information that a computer system is designed to produce generally falls into one of two categories: information the firm is required to produce, or information the firm will use in managing the organization and its operations. The required information is needed to satisfy the demands of government agencies, owners, and other interested parties, such as lending institutions and suppliers who are extending credit. The second category of information is needed to enhance the company's position by giving it a sound basis on which to make decisions. We'll call this kind of information "desired" information, although it, too, is often really "required" if a company is to survive in today's competitive business environment.

The data needed to produce the required information are often well defined and easy to collect from records of operations, transactions, and other daily activities. The definitions of the data may be already established by the government agencies or laws that require the information (e.g., the Banking Commission or the Occupational Safety and Health Act); by the accepted data reporting standards of professional groups (e.g., the generally accepted auditing standards of certified public accountants); or by policies and procedures set by the company itself.

To demonstrate the usual ease of defining and collecting data to meet required information needs, let's look at a fairly typical business situation: The federal government notifies the personnel director of a manufacturing company that, for the safety of the employees, one out of every twenty-five employees must be trained in first aid (see Figure 16.5). The personnel director asks that a system be developed to report on first-aid coverage for each workday. It would not be difficult to check which employees have current first-aid cards and to add that information to the personnel file.

Figure 16.5
Using a computer system to meet required information needs.

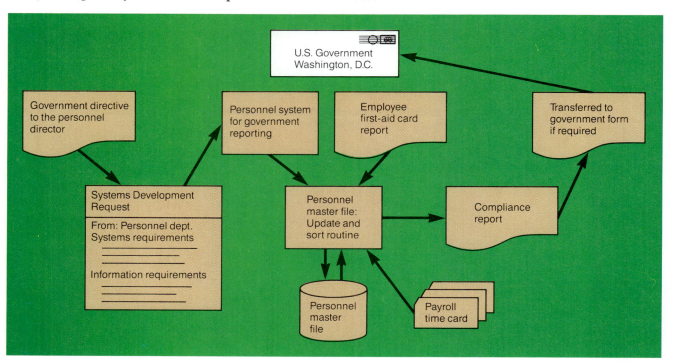

When it is time to generate a compliance report, all that is required is a sorting of the personnel records to identify all employees with first-aid cards and a linking of these data with the payroll time-card data to see who was on duty each day and who had a first-aid card.

In contrast to required information, desired information is not regulated by laws, standards, or policies. No rules govern what its content should be, what format it should be in, or even if it should be. The problems arising from this lack of definition can be illustrated by looking at the question of how information pertaining to budgets should be reported. Such information is a very common kind of "desired" information. Managers need budget information to determine whether their departments are operating within acceptable limits or whether they need to make adjustments. Budget information requires the collection of current financial data (e.g., data on payments for wages, raw materials, heat, lights, and administrative overhead) that can be compared with the financial plan — that is, the budget. Because no rules govern how budget information should be reported, it is often left to the manager to determine the most effective means. A printed exception report consisting mainly of text may satisfy one manager, whereas another may prefer a scheduled report in tabular form. Graphic representation is gaining popularity in budget reporting, especially when comparisons with previous years' data are useful. The processing cycle for budget information is usually monthly, although managers may find it worthwhile to increase reporting to a weekly or even a daily basis. The variety of possibilities and the lack of hard and fast rules mean that determining the inputs for desired information can be complicated; the choice has to depend on the data collection and processing resources available to the firm and on the importance of the information in day-to-day decision making.

Data Complexity

Data complexity refers to the precision of the data needed to produce the desired output; it also refers to the degree of difficulty involved in obtaining the data. Estimated data are less complex than data calculated to approach 100 percent accuracy and completeness. Internal data (i.e., data that a company itself generates in the course of doing business) and data collected from a single source are easier to collect — and therefore less complex — than external data or data collected from multiple sources.

The more complex the data needed to produce the output, the more resources required to collect the data; and the more resources diverted to collect data, the fewer available for some other activity. Logic dictates that businesses, which never have infinite resources to expend on information systems, set restrictions on the complexity of the needed data. These restrictions will be guided by the nature of the business. For example, an automobile manufacturer has to collect precisely calculated data relating to the safety of its product; engineers use prototypes to run all kinds of tests on brakes, steering, handling, and other critical components. In contrast, a carpet manufacturer, while concerned with quality control of color, dye, yarns, and backing, will not be nearly so thorough in collecting data as the automobile manufacturer; since human life is not at stake, estimated data will suffice. However, even the automobile manufacturer can't collect data on every operation performed during the day. Most decision making can rely on almost-complete data processed into almost-complete information; waiting for the last shred of data will probably not improve the ultimate decision, but it will certainly add to the costs of data collection.

The reason that data collected from a single source are easier to collect and therefore less complex than data collected from multiple sources is fairly obvious: It's usually easier to deal with one problem than with two. It's also fairly obvious why internal data are easier to collect and less complex than data that come from sources outside the company: With internally generated data, the company can control the data collection activities and maintain standards to ensure the necessary degree of data accuracy and completeness.

Data on activities not under the control of the firm — for example, data on the products and manufacturing procedures of competitors — may be difficult, if not impossible, to collect. Moreover, these data, which are usually based on the reports of sales staff, are more likely to be rough estimates than anything approaching completely accurate fact. Data from other sources outside the company, such as trade publications and trade associations, may be easy enough to collect but not so easy to process by computer. They can, however, contribute greatly to the company's information base and should be taken into consideration in planning the information system.

Information Use

To design a cost-effective information system, it's necessary to look carefully at how the information that is generated will ultimately be used. If the value of the information obtained does not offset the costs of collecting the data needed to produce it, then the system is not cost-effective. For example, if an industrial engineer can estimate that the cost of producing a widget will be $1.26, it would hardly be cost-effective to collect elaborate and complex data to show that the actual per unit cost is $1.25674. The estimated cost is close enough to be usable in the decision process. In some cases, such as in estimating the trajectory of a space vehicle, greater precision would, of course, be both necessary and cost-effective, despite the greater costs of data collection. The point is that the cost effectiveness of an information system hinges not upon the absolute costs of obtaining and processing the data, but upon the use to which the processed data will be put. More precise information requires more detailed and more complete data; and more timely information often requires online, interactive data collection procedures. It's important to strike a balance between the greater costs involved in producing information and the ultimate use of the information.

PROCESSING

Processing design focuses on such matters as the logic and arithmetic operations needed to process the data into the desired output, the sequencing of the operations, and controls to ensure and safeguard the integrity of the data (e.g., the editing routines discussed in Chapter 6 are part of the routine processing operations). Processing design also includes structuring the data files and devising routines for accessing the data base if a data base is being used.

As indicated in Figure 16.6, a number of factors help identify the best processing procedures for a particular application. These include the considerations that we discussed in the preceding sections — the kinds of

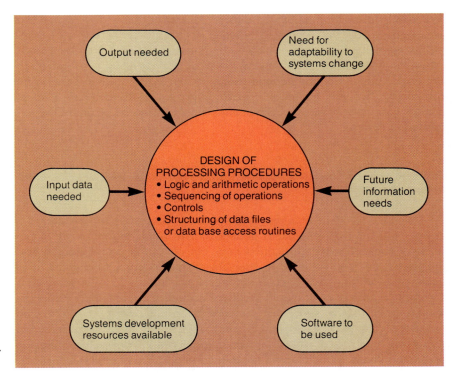

Figure 16.6
Influences on the design of processing procedures.

output needed, the nature and source of the data to be processed, and the issues of cost effectiveness and the resources (hardware, staff, and funds) available to implement the system. Another determining factor in the design of processing procedures is the software the system will use. Unless the software is custom-designed in-house, the processing design may have to be adjusted to meet the needs of the program logic. The use of any other software — that is, purchased or leased software or software acquired through contract programming or a user group — may also dictate the way data files are structured and the kind of programming language, operating system, and processing equipment used.

While systems analysts must focus on these specific concerns during the design phases of the systems development cycle, they must at the same time keep some broader concerns in mind. The processing system should not only meet the company's current information needs but also anticipate its future needs. To design such a system, analysts have to be aware of the company's overall strategy and goals. Businesses in general are applying computers to an ever-widening variety of problems. The growth of office automation has created a whole new set of pressures on the computer hardware, as well as on the rest of the information system; electronic message systems require quick-response systems with large storage capacities. Add to this the trend toward networking and the problems it presents in terms of data access, data security, and incompatible equipment, and you can clearly see why effective processing design must look beyond the needs of the moment to the needs of the future.

Another factor to be considered in terms of meeting future information needs is the rapid pace of change in computer hardware and the need for compatibility between the hardware and the software. Processing systems should be designed to be easily adaptable to any anticipated changes. Unless the new hardware acquired for a system is what vendors call "upward-compatible," meaning that very little needs to be done to transfer programs to the new system, then the new hardware may require significant — and costly — changes to the software. It will never be possible to develop programs that are completely independent of the hardware, but the more independent the programs are, the easier it is to adapt them to any kind of hardware.

Among the important specific concerns that processing design must address is the matter of file structuring. The question to be asked here is, How can files best be organized to meet the needs of a particular processing application? The files that businesses keep contain data on a variety of subjects — sales, customers, inventory, and so on — and they are organized and processed in different ways to meet the information requirements of specific applications. Sequential file organization, direct file organization, and indexed-sequential file organization are the three most common ways of structuring data files. (A data base is, of course, another way of organizing data, and we will discuss it in detail in the next chapter.)

Sequential File Organization

The simplest way to store records within a file is in physical sequence; that is, the "next" record is the one that physically comes after the present one (see Figure 16.7). In this kind of sequentially organized file, a key field may be used to indicate the beginning of the record, and a key is often used to indicate the end of the record as well. The key, a field of data that the computer is told to look for, is much like a house number: It identifies a location, but it doesn't indicate what resides at that location.

When files are organized sequentially, the computer processes successive physical records, each one in turn, until all the data are processed and accounted for. Sequential file organization is thus a natural for magnetic tape because access on tape must be to one record after the other with no skipping around. If you wanted only the last record in the file, you would have to check all the records along the tape before you found it. However, if you were processing a payroll, and every employee was to get a check, you would need to access every record in the file; so, in this instance, the sequential organization would be advantageous. Sequential organization is also efficient in certain applications in which data collection is sequential or the data can be sequentially sorted. An example of the latter kind of application is the updating of customer purchases and charge accounts, in which the computer first sorts the charge items into the same sequence as the master file sequence (probably ascending account number) and then processes the transactions.

With sequential file organization, record length does not have to be limited, and the system can be designed to accept inputs without restrictions on the size of a field or record. Because a key can be used to indicate the start of each record, the records can be easily distinguished. In processing applications in which the length of data varies greatly, this flexibility in record length is a useful feature.

A problem with sequential file organization, besides the inability to access a specific record without passing through all the preceding records,

Figure 16.7
Sequential file organization. In this file, a key field (employee number) indicates the start of each record.

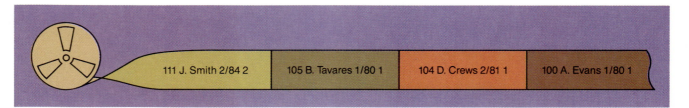

is that a certain amount of logical organization is lost. For example, if your key was an employee number based on date of hire, you would have difficulty searching for an employee by name; you would have to go through the cumbersome process of looking at one record after another until you found the right name.

Direct File Organization

With direct file organization, records are stored in no apparent physical order; the record key provides the means of accessing the data (see Figure 16.8). The simplest form of direct organization would be to have the record key become the storage address of the data, although this is not usually possible with anything but the simplest applications. As we noted in Chapter 13, the operating system's data management program can provide addresses for directly organized files by generating them mathematically. This method of creating data addresses is known as **hashing,** or **randomizing,** and it uses mathematical formulas to translate the record key or key field, such as a stock number, directly into a disk address. This transformation allows the computer to access each of the records quickly and directly, without having to go through the entire file, as it must when files are sequentially organized.

Directly organized files are stored in a direct access storage device (DASD). The storage addresses for the DASD that the hashing techniques create often look somewhat like a phone number, with the area code representing the cylinder number, the prefix representing the disk surface number, and the last digits representing the track number. The values of these address numbers would probably be smaller than a phone number, but they do the same thing—that is, they narrow the location from the entire system to a specific spot within the system.

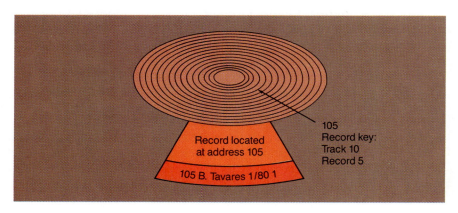

Figure 16.8
Direct file organization.

Hashing can be accomplished in a number of ways. A simple way to convert the record key to a storage address would include the following three steps:

1. Estimate the file storage requirements and determine the number of tracks on the DASD needed to hold the file. If you had a file of 1,000 records, each containing 100 bytes, you would need to store 100,000 bytes (1,000 × 100 = 100,000). If each track of the DASD held 10,000 bytes, you would need 10 tracks to hold the file (100,000 ÷ 10,000 = 10).

2. Choose the prime number — that is, a number that can be evenly divided only by itself or by 1 — that is closest to, but not greater than, the required number of tracks. In this case, since the required number of tracks is 10, the prime number would be 7. (Examples of other prime numbers are 5, 11, and 13.)

3. Divide the record key by the prime number, and use the remainder for the track address. If the record key is 2,000, the remainder — and the track address — would be 5 (2,000 ÷ 7 = 285 plus a remainder of 5).

A problem in using hashing to generate the storage address is that different keys can randomize to the same number. When that happens, a record already exists at the storage address identified by that number, and a **collision,** or **synonym,** occurs. By increasing the complexity of the hashing formula and providing overflow storage areas, you can minimize the possibility of collisions.

Indexed-Sequential File Organization

In **indexed-sequential file organization** (also called **indexed-sequential access method,** or **ISAM**), records are stored in the file in a sequence as determined by their record keys. At the same time, the operating system maintains a directory, or index, to the specific location of each record. This method thus combines the processing advantages of both sequential and direct file structures: It allows for the efficient batch processing of transactions and for the direct retrieval of information through the index. For example, a utility company could use indexed-sequential file organization to process its monthly bills in a batch and to allow direct access to records when customers have questions about their accounts. Because magnetic tape cannot provide direct access, indexed-sequential file organization requires disk storage.

The key fields of the records are used to establish the address information

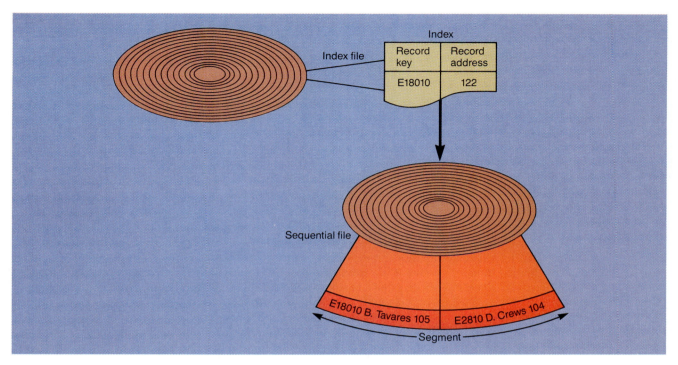

Figure 16.9
Indexed-sequential file organization. The computer can process the records on the sequential file in a batch or, using the index, it can go directly to the segment of the file on which the record is stored.

for the index, and the index divides the sequential file into segments (see Figure 16.9). The index allows the computer to go to the segment of the file on which the record is stored without having to search through each record along the way. This is rather like arranging to meet a friend under a clock in a crowded room; rather than searching throughout the room, you narrow the search considerably.

When directly processing a record stored on an indexed-sequential file, the computer first goes to the index, reads it sequentially until it finds the record reference, and then goes to the segment of the disk where the record is stored. It then reads through the records in the segment until it finds the appropriate record. As you can see, the access provided by this method of file organization is bound to be slower than that provided by the direct method, since the computer must read the index sequentially before it locates the segment, and it must then read the segment sequentially until it finds the record. Usually, the computer must perform several hundred read operations before it retrieves the desired record. However, when

CASE STUDY: RITCHCO AUTO PARTS
Part II

You will recall from the case study in the last chapter that Art Richardson was troubled by the increasing amount of paper work involved in running Ritchco. He was also having problems with customer orders. Often, an item listed in inventory could not be located, and his clerks were making lots of billing errors. After talking to a friend, Art started to think about buying a computer system for Ritchco, and he decided he had better do some research to find out whether a computer could help him. He was encouraged to find out that computers have become less expensive and that they are useful in solving business problems similar to the ones he was experiencing. He also learned that computers have enormous storage capacities — certainly more than enough to take care of his inventory needs — and that they allow instant access to records. He was particularly impressed by the fact that a single computer can service several terminals.

What Art learned about computers spurred him on to launch an informal feasibility study. He began the study by analyzing the kinds of data that Ritchco processes — lots of long and complicated part numbers, price discounts that vary according to whether the account is retail or wholesale, and special promotional items for short-term price discounts. He also thought about the way Ritchco was handling the data: The sales clerks and representatives were carrying much of the information around in their heads. He had known for a long time that he needed more accurate and up-to-date inventory records. His accountant kept him advised on overall profits, but he now realized that with a computer he could analyze profits by various merchandise groupings to help decide on inventory levels and store layout. Even before he had finished the feasibility study, Art was "hooked" on the idea of computerizing Ritchco.

As enthusiastic as he was, however, Art knew he had to carefully examine his procedures and organization before jumping into something as revolutionary as a computer information system. Knowing that a computer would be right for him wasn't enough. He had to think about the impact it would have on his business, his customers, and his employees and about the kinds of problems he would encounter as he converted his manual system to a computerized one.

1. What kind of organization do you think Ritchco Auto Parts is? What management style would you expect from Art? Why?

2. List at least four categories of outputs that Art might reasonably expect from a computer system. Describe how each would be used, when it should be generated, what kind of format it should have, and what should be done with the original and any copies that might be made.

3. Describe the file organization that would be most appropriate for Ritchco and explain why it would be the best choice.

4. Do you think Art would have difficulty in collecting accurate data to process with a computer system? Explain your answer.

◆

---

compared with the access provided by sequential file organization, this method is much faster, since the computer does not have to read the entire file sequentially. As you might expect, adding the index does make for a more complicated accessing scheme within the operating system. Table 16.2 shows the advantages and disadvantages of the three methods of file organization.

Table 16.2 Comparison of File-Organization Methods

Method of File Organization	Advantages	Disadvantages
Sequential	Efficient for processing high-activity files (e.g., payroll), in which almost every record is processed each time the program is run	Access delays because records must be read in the order in which they appear in the file
Direct	Allows any record to be accessed at random and provides the shortest access time; most efficient for use with a large file that has low processing activity	Requires more expensive hardware and media than sequential organization; not as efficient for processing high-activity files
Indexed-sequential	Allows both sequential and direct processing, thus providing flexibility	Delays in processing because the index adds one more step to the data retrieval process

SUMMARY

The first consideration in designing a computer information system is the output the system is meant to produce. In designing the outputs, system analysts must work within the constraints of the resources available to implement the system. Factors affecting output design include the size of the firm, its management style, and the nature and goals of the business. Other considerations include output formatting (the physical design of the output and the media used to display them) and the scheduling and distribution of the outputs to ensure that they reach the right people at the right time.

Input data should be accurate and complete enough to produce the desired output, but no more accurate and complete than necessary, since the more accurate and complete the data are, the more expensive it is to collect them. With required information, the kind of data needed are often predetermined by laws, by the standards of professional groups, or by policies and procedures set by the company itself. Standards for desired information are usually ill defined, if they are defined at all, and this lack of definition creates problems for the systems analyst. Data complexity refers to the degree of data accuracy and completeness needed to produce the desired output and to the degree of difficulty involved in obtaining the needed data; companies must set limits on the level of complexity of needed data. A determining factor in input design is the ultimate use of the information; the use must justify the costs of data collection and processing.

The design of processing procedures depends on the desired output, the data to be processed, the resources available, and the software being used. In designing systems to meet current information needs, the systems analyst should also keep in mind the future information needs of the company. Among the specific processing concerns that the systems analyst must address is the matter of file structuring. Three design options are available — sequential, direct, and indexed-sequential file organization — and each has certain advantages in certain applications.

KEY TERMS

behavioral management (450)
collision (synonym) (466)
hashing (randomizing) (465)
indexed-sequential file organization (indexed-sequential access method, ISAM) (466)

output formats (448)
quantitative management (451)
scientific management (450)
traditional management (process management) (449)

DISCUSSION QUESTIONS

1. Explain why the desired outputs of the system should be the first consideration in designing a computer information system.

2. What organizational factors influence the design of the outputs? Give an example of how each would influence the systems analyst.

3. Describe four often overlooked details of output design. Why do you think systems developers often forget about these details?

4. What is a distribution list? Explain why it is important that the distribution list be carefully maintained.

5. Discuss the considerations that go into collecting accurate and complete data for entry into a computer information system. Can an accurate system be cost-effective?

6. Describe the main issues that input design should address.

7. Explain the differences between desired and required information. How do these differences affect the design of the system? Why are complex data more difficult to collect than simple data?

8. Discuss the factors that affect the design of processing procedures. What do these procedures include?

9. Describe the three main forms of file organization. Give an example of how each would be effectively used to process business data.

10. Visit a local business and interview a systems analyst. What does this analyst think are the most important design considerations? Why?

OUTLINE

USING THE COMPUTER AS A MANAGERIAL TOOL

 Managerial Functions and Information Needs
 Management Information Systems
 Data Base Management Systems
 Decision Support Systems

USING THE COMPUTER TO IMPROVE PRODUCTIVITY: OFFICE AUTOMATION

 Word Processing
 Electronic Messages
 Electronic Filing

SUMMARY

KEY TERMS

DISCUSSION QUESTIONS

OVERVIEW

The pace and the pressures of business today are far greater than they were even just a decade ago. Managers have less and less time to react to a situation before they must make a decision. At the same time, the stakes riding on the decision are likely to be higher, since the size of many businesses has increased. Stiff competition from both foreign and domestic competitors puts pressure on managers not only to make rapid-fire, critical decisions but also to increase the productivity of their operations and personnel.

The computer, of course, has been a driving force in creating this fast-paced, sometimes frantic business environment. In many instances, it is also a company's lifeline — an indispensable aid to survival in this age of the Information Revolution. The computer can be used to produce information that will give managers a sound basis for decision making and planning, and in this role, it may serve as the engine of a management information system, tying together the flow of information within a business and letting it move from one functional area to another. The computer can also be a powerful tool for improving productivity within the business office. In this chapter, we'll take a look at each of these important uses of computer systems. Our objectives are to

- describe the functions that different levels of managers perform and the kinds of information they need.

- explain how a computer-based management information system serves as a managerial tool.

- discuss the role of a data base in a management information system.

- explain how data base management systems and decision support systems contribute to a management information system.

- identify the ways in which computers are used in office automation to improve productivity.

CHAPTER 17

USING COMPUTER INFORMATION SYSTEMS IN BUSINESS

USING THE COMPUTER AS A MANAGERIAL TOOL

As we noted in Chapter 3, all companies have some type of management information system (MIS). The basic function of an MIS is to provide managers with information they can use in making decisions. The MIS may or may not include a computer system; the means by which information is reported may be as informal as a street-corner conversation with a competitor. However, in view of the pace and complexity of today's business world, an increasing number of companies are finding computers a very valuable way of increasing the efficiency of their information systems and hence the effectiveness of their decision making.

Improvements in hardware, particularly improvements in primary storage, have enabled designers to develop data base management systems (DBMSs) and decision support systems (DSSs). DBMSs and DSSs are sophisticated software systems that greatly enhance the ability of an MIS to provide managers with useful decision-making information. With this software, the MIS can integrate the data generated by the various functional areas of a business into a common data pool and make the data available to managers throughout the firm. These systems thus not only help to reduce data redundancy but also allow planners to use information from the entire business rather than from just a single functional unit. Before we look at an MIS and the software that supports it, let's review the functions that managers perform and the kinds of information they need to perform these functions effectively.

Managerial Functions and Information Needs

The basic responsibility of management is to make decisions that will effectively and efficiently transform the firm's labor, capital, and other resources into outputs of goods and services — in other words, to direct actions and produce results. The tasks, or functions, that managers perform in fulfilling this basic responsibility include planning, organizing, controlling, and communicating. As you can see in Figure 17.1, managers at all levels perform these tasks, but the amount of time they spend on each varies according to the level of management.

Because top-level managers — presidents and vice-presidents — are concerned with making **strategic decisions** about the future of the company, they spend much of their time in *planning*. Planning involves establishing organizational goals, such as profit targets and production quotas, and developing policies and strategies for achieving these goals. Implementing such strategies might require decisions about introducing new products, acquiring manufacturing space and the technology needed to meet planned quotas, and generating new sources of financing.

Any decision contains an element of uncertainty, but at top levels of

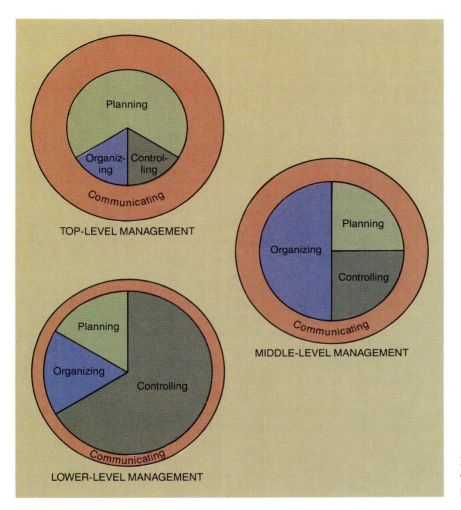

Figure 17.1
Time spent on managerial functions, by managerial level.

management, the amount of uncertainty surrounding a planning decision is likely to be considerable. For example, a decision to enter a foreign market can be risky as there are likely to be many unknowns. To establish manufacturing and distribution facilities in another country, top-level managers would need information on the regulatory and political situation of the country, as well as on the labor force, construction costs, operating costs, and potential profitability of the new market. Information can help top-level managers evaluate the risks and reduce uncertainty in their decision making, giving the company a better chance of developing a profitable operation.

The problems top-level managers encounter are often unique, occurring only once, so precedents for dealing with them may not exist. Judgment has to play a large role in this kind of "nonprogrammed" decision making. Managers at this level must rely on summarized information from both internal and external sources to keep them informed on how the business and the general economy are doing. Internally generated information consists of historical and operational data and is presented in the form of financial and production summary reports. External sources — for example, trade publications (magazines, newsletters, and newspapers), government sources, and market surveys — provide information on larger issues, such as the competition, the general business climate, and the economy. Because it's usually difficult to anticipate or define the kind of information that top-level decision makers will need, it's difficult to develop an information system to meet their needs. The emergence of specialized software in the form of decision support systems, which allow managers to easily access and combine business data in unique ways for one-time reports and analyses, is helping to bridge the gap between the traditional information system and the top-level manager.

Middle-level managers are responsible for making **tactical decisions** about how to effectively allocate production resources in order to implement the strategic plans made by top-level managers. They must therefore be familiar with the strategic plans as well as with the resources available to implement them. In meeting their responsibility for allocating resources, middle-level managers spend a considerable portion of their time in *organizing* — that is, in grouping activities and establishing procedures for performing the activities. Responsibilities of middle-level managers would include scheduling production so that workloads are evenly distributed, preparing budgets, and recruiting and training personnel. The information middle-level managers need to perform this organizing function would include budgeted funds, market demand, production capacity, inventory, workforce availability, and so on. Such information is more detailed than the information required by top-level managers, and it relies to a greater extent on internally generated operational data.

In contrast to the future-oriented planning done by top-level managers, the planning done by middle-level managers is of a more immediate nature. For example, a production manager responsible for maintaining adequate raw materials to allow for uninterrupted factory operations would need to plan for suppliers, warehouse space, transportation, and financing. In this area, too, the information that middle-level managers need is more detailed than that used by top management, but it's of the same nature. For instance, both a top-level manager and a middle-level manager would need to be aware of a general shortage of the petroleum products used in the manufacture of plastics, but the middle-level manager would also have to know sources of supply, prices, currency exchange rates, and transportation options.

In addition, middle-level managers are concerned with *control* — that is, with measuring performance against the plan for performance. They are therefore consumers of exception reports. For example, when labor costs exceed budgeted amounts, it is the middle-level manager's job to be aware of the situation, to find out why it occurred, and to take corrective action. Exception reports alert middle managers to such deviations from plans and also save them from having to read descriptions of operations that are proceeding according to plan.

Lower-level managers, such as shop supervisors, make **operational decisions** to implement the activities and procedures outlined by middle-level managers. They order materials, assign personnel to specific tasks, schedule jobs, hire replacement personnel, and in a variety of other ways keep the operations of the company moving. A major focus of their work is on *controlling* the day-by-day operations — comparing the results of operations with established goals and making adjustments when necessary. The information that lower-level managers need is therefore detailed and consists of internally generated operational data. Time is generally a critical factor in collecting this information, as adjustments must be made quickly if they are to be effective.

Much of the decision making that takes place at lower levels of management is routine and repetitive. The same kind of decision occurs with some degree of regularity, and procedures for dealing with the decision in the same way each time it occurs can be developed. For instance, when the supply of wire in an electronics firm is running low on the assembly line, the shop supervisor must make a decision to reorder. A computerized inventory system can keep track of how much wire is located in the warehouse, how long it will take to get the wire to the assembly area, and even how much wire will be needed to fill production orders for the day.

Each time a plan at any level is formulated, it needs to be *communicated* to the other levels of management. Although the strategic plan is typically general and subject to constant revision, it is usually formally conveyed in writing. Middle-level managers communicate their tactical plans to lower-level managers through budgets and formal operational plans, which are usually developed with the assistance of lower-level managers. At the lower levels of management, communication of plans is often informal and one-on-one; such communication may consist of a telephone call or a face-to-face conversation to convey information on a work assignment or a temporary production adjustment. Because operational decisions require a quick response, businesses often have a general "framework" plan, which gives lower levels of management a good deal of discretion in making changes as necessary.

Table 17.1 summarizes the information needs of different levels of management. Regardless of the managerial level of the decision maker, information on which decisions are based needs to be accurate, complete, concise, relevant, and timely.

Table 17.1 Information Needs of Various Levels of Managers

Information Characteristics	Top-Level Managers/ Strategic Planners	Middle-Level Managers/ Tactical Planners	Lower-Level Managers/ Operational Planners
Amount of detail	Information is generally very summarized, often graphic, to illustrate trends rather than specific activities.	Details are summarized so they can be compared with a plan to measure performance.	Information is detailed, relating to daily activities, work schedules, and general operations.
Source	Heavy reliance on externally generated information.	Internal sources are summarized; some external sources (customers, the competition, the marketplace) are used.	Most data are internally generated from production operations and sales transactions.
Timing	Because strategic planning is long-term, reporting is often done monthly or even quarterly; often timed to the profit-reporting cycle.	Reports are generally cycled on a periodic basis, often timed to planning- and budget-reporting periods.	Reports are often needed daily and are usually scheduled and distributed according to a routine plan.
Amount of structure	Because strategic planning often requires investigation of a wide range of ideas and issues, reporting is quite unstructured.	Reporting is generally structured to coordinate with the planning data; unstructured reporting may be necessary when such tactical decisions as the selection of alternative suppliers are necessary.	Because of the detail required, reporting is very structured.
Degree of complexity	Data are reduced to a concise summary or graphic to provide information about trends rather than details.	Reporting is often complex, comparing actual activities with plans and showing deviations and past experiences.	Reporting is uncomplicated and straightforward, containing a great deal of detail.
Types of reports	Forecasted growth for several years; major moves by competition; company performance, especially profits; financial markets, interest rates, and projected trends; one-time inquiries.	Marketing reports, projected sales, regional performance, budget reports, competitive activities, currency exchange rates, purchasing reports.	Production schedules, employee assignments, materials on hand, inventory on hand, past-due accounts, shipping schedules.

Management Information Systems

When computers were first introduced into the business world, and for several years thereafter, they were thought of solely as "number crunchers" and were used mainly for the processing of routine operational data, such as payrolls and sales transactions. In time, managers came to recognize the potential contributions of the computer to decision making. It became apparent that the data being collected and processed for routine accounting and recordkeeping could be compiled in new and different ways to provide useful decision-making information.

Out of this observation grew the concept of a **computer-based management information system.** Such a system may be defined in many ways. For our purposes, it is a system or a set of systems that uses a computer to collect, condense, filter, and manipulate data so that it meets not only a company's routine data processing and reporting needs but also the information needs of the company's managers. A computer-based MIS thus processes transaction data, updates files, and generates a variety of reports, including scheduled, exception, and inquiry reports. In contrast to a traditional data processing system, which is designed solely to increase operational efficiency, an MIS is also aimed at improving the productivity and effectiveness of decision makers.

As so often happens when a new idea is introduced, initial enthusiasm about a computer-based MIS created some unrealistic expectations. Managers and systems designers alike visualized an overnight wonder — a total information system that would gather and process internal and external data relating to past, present, and projected events, storing them in a single data base to which all managers in all functional areas would have instant access. Such a system would also be *fully integrated* in the sense that it would combine all the information needed for the managerial functions of planning, organizing, and controlling. It quickly became obvious that developing such a fully integrated, total system would be an enormous undertaking, and, in fact, it continues to challenge systems designers today. Instead of attempting to develop such a system all at once, most firms drew up long-term plans for gradually integrating their existing information systems into the MIS.

If you consider the differences in the information needs of decision makers at various managerial levels and the fact that the different functional areas of a business create their own flows of information and have their own information needs, you'll begin to see the difficulty involved in developing an integrated information system that can simultaneously meet such diverse needs. The problems of defining or anticipating the information needs of top-level managers, as well as the needs of these managers for information on the external world — which may be hard to incorporate into a computer system — add to the difficulty of developing a fully integrated MIS.

Figure 17.2 illustrates the concepts involved in developing an MIS. As you can see in the figure, the data base is the foundation of the MIS. It is the means by which the information systems of each of a business's functional areas are linked. A *data base,* as you may remember, is a way of organizing data files so that the data can be accessed and used for multiple purposes. Such a method of organizing and storing data is essential to the intent of an MIS to allow individual managers to use the same data for different purposes.

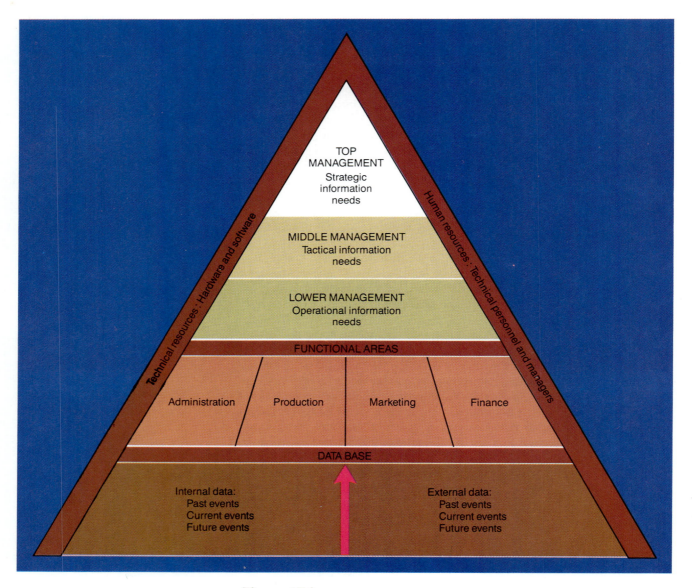

Figure 17.2

Concepts involved in developing an MIS. Different levels of managers need different kinds of information, and different functional areas create their own flows of information and have their own information needs. The data base integrates this information, making it accessible to everyone throughout the organization.

Before the concept of a computer-based MIS was introduced, all the functional areas of a business created their own data files and maintained their own information systems. This led to a great deal of **data redundancy**—

that is, the same data were often contained in the files of different departments. Multiple data files and information systems also created added expense and the possibility of other problems: Each time an item of data had to be changed in one file, the same change had to be made in all the other files. Such updating of files can be expensive, but if files aren't consistent, the data will lack integrity, and a lack of **data integrity** can lead to some fairly serious problems. For instance, let's assume that a customer of the Hometown Bank changes the address on a checking account but fails to mention that the address change should also be made for a safe deposit box. If the notice of the rental due on the safe deposit box fails to reach the customer through the mail, the account may become delinquent, and the bank will ultimately have to force open the box to clear the account. A data base will take care of such problems, since with this method of data organization, the processing of a single transaction causes all related files to be updated at the same time. A data base thus not only helps ensure data integrity but also increases processing efficiency.

Another problem arising from the creation of data files by individual departments was that the data were organized to meet the needs of particular applications programs. Thus, it was generally quite difficult to access and use the data for any other purpose. With a data base, the data are independent — that is, they are organized according to their own characteristics and are not dependent on the needs of a particular program. **Data independence** means that different programs can share the same data base; it also means that managers from different functional areas can share the same data. For example, if the marketing department is planning a major sales promotion, it will need information from the production department on production capacity and inventory, and the marketing vice-president will need general information to make the decision to proceed with the promotion. The MIS provides a summary of stock available and of production capacity, along with the information the vice-president requires. Once the decision is made to proceed, it's necessary to prepare operating plans to increase production, to distribute the inventory, and to control manufacturing requirements and materials. The same data may be accessed several times to generate these different plans, with the applications programs processing the data to meet the specific requirements of the user. Once the sale begins, the MIS collects data from orders received and summarizes the data for the vice-president. Meanwhile, because the firm still needs to conduct other business and to take care of existing customers, the MIS also processes the daily transaction and production data. An MIS's use of a data base thus serves a dual purpose: It enhances decision making for the entire organization while fulfilling basic data processing needs.

Although we've been referring to "the" data base, we should point out that most MISs do, in fact, have several data bases. In developing an MIS, a systems designer may decide that rather than attempting to create a single data base for all the functional areas of a business, the better and safer approach would be to create individual data bases for each area (see Figure 17.3). Thus, the data base for production would incorporate into

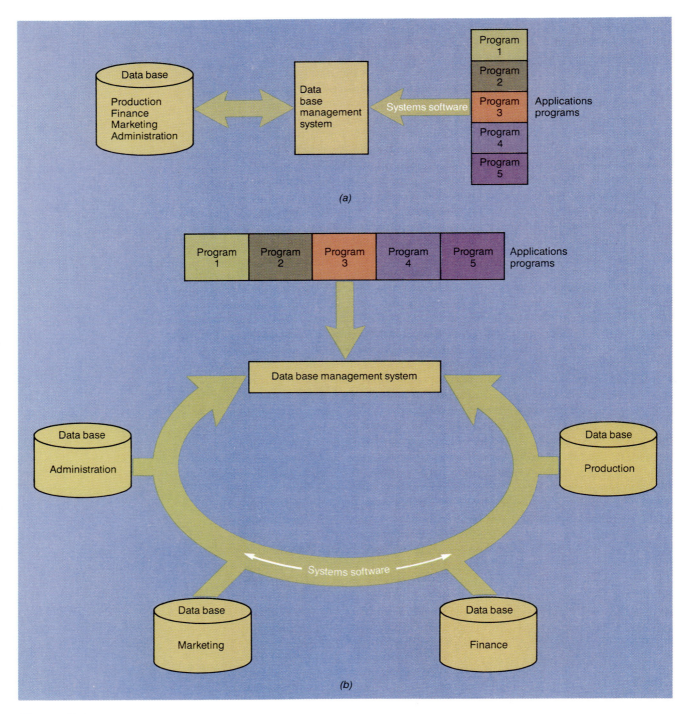

Figure 17.3
Data bases: (*a*) a single data base; (*b*) individual data bases.

related files all the files formerly used in the individual systems for raw materials, finished goods inventory, and cost accounting, and it might even include the data for equipment maintenance. Whether a single data base or individual bases are used, applications programs provide users with access to the data.

While a data base has many advantages, it also has some drawbacks. An error in one record in the data base can have reverberations throughout the system. For instance, an error in the dollar amount of reported sales will cause an error in the monthly profit and loss calculations, will affect the reporting system for accounting, and may even become the printed word as a part of the annual report sent to stockholders. Correcting such errors can be difficult, since it may require that the entire reporting cycle be rerun. Moreover, a data base is complex and expensive to develop, implement, and operate, and it requires a considerable investment in hardware to support its needs for extensive memory and processing capabilities. Because all the data are stored in a centralized spot and are accessible to many users, a data base also raises concern for the security of the data.

Ensuring the security of the data base system — protecting the data from access by unauthorized users — is among the responsibilities of a **data base administrator (DBA)** (see Figure 17.4). This person is also responsible for seeing that the structure and use of the data are defined consistently throughout the organization. Data definitions are maintained in a **data dictionary,** and the DBA disseminates information pertaining to data standardization to users of the data base and sees that the standards are enforced. The DBA also organizes the data for efficient storage so that users can access them through their applications programs. Because the DBA must respond to information needs throughout the organization, the data base is generally organized so that it can take advantage of a data base management system.

Figure 17.4
A data base administrator.
Courtesy of Aetna Life & Casualty.

Data Base Management Systems

A *data base management system (DBMS)* is a series of integrated programs designed to simplify the tasks of creating, accessing, and managing a data base. Since the data base itself may be quite complex, with many linkages and relationships among the data, the programs that manage the data base are also likely to be complex, as well as expensive to develop. For this reason, most companies don't design their own DBMSs. Instead, they purchase such systems from hardware vendors or software suppliers. Commercially developed DBMSs have been available for mainframes since the early 1970s, and minicomputers have been using these systems since the mid-1970s. Today, DBMS packages are available even for microcomputers. Of course, these systems are not as powerful as the large-scale DBMSs, but they do offer similar advantages for under $1,000. It is not unusual for DBMS software for a mainframe to cost more than $100,000.

DATABASE TO THE ROCK STARS

When Rick Springfield's band began a three-month national tour last fall, the members packed six trucks with 35 people, 75 tons of stage and sound equipment, and a Compaq Plus portable computer running Rbase 4000.

Even rock stars aren't immune to the computerization of the business world. And running a nationwide tour is a complex business. Springfield's "roadies" keep track of everything from complex lighting requirements to night-by-night ticket sales to detailed information about radio stations in every city on the tour.

Springfield is a handsome Australian singer who became well-known with a hit record, "Jessie's Girl," and in the role of Dr. Noah Drake on ABC's "General Hospital" soap opera. When he and his group arranged the tour last year, they decided they needed a central database system to keep track of ticket prices and sales, information about past and present performances, and information about local radio stations, stage capacities, costs, and backstage specifications. Lacking computer expertise and the time to set up a system, the group hired Ted Wrablik, owner of Baseline Consulting of Westwood, California, to design a flexible database for easy access to tour information. The system had to transmit the information back to the headquarters of the group's talent management company, Major Way Management, while the group was on the road.

Wrablik set up a system with a Compaq Plus portable for use on the road, an IBM PC XT in the office in Encino, California, and two Hayes 1,200-baud modems to connect them. Wrablik says he selected the $495 Rbase 4000 database program because it is menu-driven, allows a large number of variable fields, and is easy to use for those who aren't computer experts.

The consultant set up two databases with a detailed, menu-driven program to use them. The main database handles tour costs — promotion, advertising, talent, travel. The second database includes information about the radio stations in every city Springfield visited to help plan the publicity and the tour.

Four members of Springfield's 35-person entourage used the computer while on the tour bus. (Springfield himself is not a computer user.) Information was sent by modem to the home office, where Springfield's agency made a printout to determine whether a particular show made a profit.

On the next tour, Wrablik says, Springfield wants to get more regional information on local radio stations to improve the promotion effort. Wrablik says setting up the system went smoother than he expected, although he had some file management problems.

The group's biggest problem, says Jeb Baird, Springfield's manager, was getting through on the home office's single telephone line. After a second line was installed, Baird says, the "transition [to a computerized operation] was relatively smooth."

Although most musicians still run their tours by paper, a growing number are, like Springfield, starting to use portable computers on the road. Todd Rundgren and Styx both have computers, according to Dulcy Israel, a writer at *Rolling Stone*, the music magazine. Jefferson Starship, Journey, Tina Turner, and George Thorogood and the Destroyers use personal computers, too. Thorogood has about $6,000 worth of computer equipment, including a Compaq, in the back of his tour bus.

Steve Kahn, production road manager for the rock group Santana, took a NEC PC 8201 on the Santana-Bob Dylan tour in 1984 to keep track of accounting data. Using the built-in modem, Kahn sent the data back to the Bill Graham Presents home office. Kahn also carried a battery-powered printer to generate hard copy. "Almost any group of any size these days uses portable computers on the road," Kahn says.

Even lesser-known bands are starting to buy portable computers. Mitch Jacobs of the Keystone Family Group agency, which manages the California group Eddie and the Tide, says he is in the process of getting a Macintosh or Compaq computer for the group's tour this summer. Jacobs says he plans to put "everything" in the database — financial settlements, tour budgeting, advance paperwork, color charts for lighting, travel plans, and stage charts.

Computers will probably be an increasingly common sight on rock band buses, along with the guitars, amplifiers, and other tour paraphernalia.

—Karen Springen, "Database to the Rock Stars," *InfoWorld* (March 25, 1985), p. 16. Reprinted by permission.

In a computer information system in which data are organized in files rather than in data bases, managers and other nontechnical users who need special information not available through regular computer channels or reports must ask a programmer to extract this information for them. To do this, the programmer will have to write a program when time allows. Needless to say, this method of gathering information is usually not very swift. Moreover, if the information need isn't adequately defined, the programmer may not be able to write a program at all.

A chief advantage of a DBMS is that it allows the nontechnical person to use **query** (or **inquiry**) **languages** to bypass the programmer and to directly access the data base (see Figure 17.5). Query languages may be *formal,* meaning that the user must follow specific guidelines when giving the computer instructions, or they may be *natural,* in which case the user

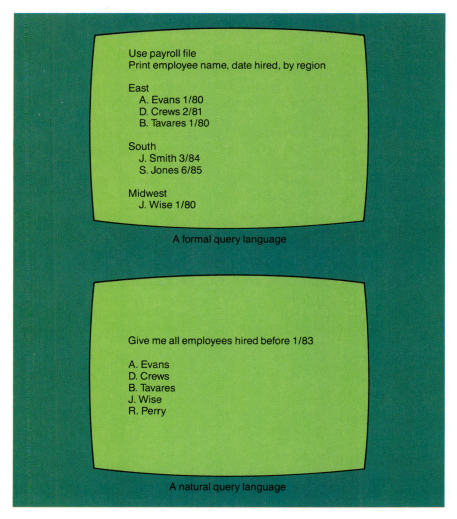

Figure 17.5
Query languages.

has a great deal of flexibility in communicating with the computer. Whether formal or natural, query languages are very similar to everyday language and are easy to learn. Using query language, a manager can "browse" through the data base, examining and combining the data in unique ways. In response to the simplified query-language commands, the DBMS will retrieve, present, and process the data stored in the data base.

Obviously, because of the flexibility that query languages provide, the response time of a DBMS is bound to be much faster than that of a traditionally organized file-processing system, in which a programmer must write special programs to extract information not available through existing programs. In addition, the flexibility of DBMS software allows the programmer to develop a program "on the fly," often in a matter of days, by first roughly designing the inputs and outputs and then refining them with the user. This technique is known as **prototyping** (see Figure 17.6).

In addition to allowing access through query languages, the DBMS allows access to the data through the programming languages used in applications programs; the organization must, of course, still do the routine processing, which is best accomplished through the traditional applications programs. This multiple-language capability of a DBMS allows scheduled, routine reports, as well as inquiry reports that provide decision-making information, to be generated from the same data pool. A DBMS may also be used to provide access to external data made available at a certain price by other organizations. For example, most businesses wouldn't find it economical to maintain a large data base on patents, but when this information is made available for a small fee, it can provide managers with useful data in a cost-effective way. Table 17.2 shows some of the data bases to which a company today may purchase access.

Table 17.2 Some Commercially Available Data Bases

Data Base	Supplier	Contents
National Crime Information Center	U.S. government	More than 5 million records of criminals and stolen property available for use by law enforcement agencies
Inquire	National Library of Medicine	Medical research and related data available to physicians and medical researchers
Bests	A. M. Best Co.	Performance data on over 3,000 firms in the insurance industry
Dow Jones News Retrieval	Dow Jones Co.	Business, financial, and general news
Compuserve	Compuserve, Inc.	A collection of many data bases, from gourmet recipes to online gift shopping
Electronic Yellow Pages	Market Data Retrieval, Inc.	Records of 10 million businesses and professionals for direct-mail marketing
The Source	Source Telecomputing Corp.	A collection of many data bases, from news reporting to airline schedules

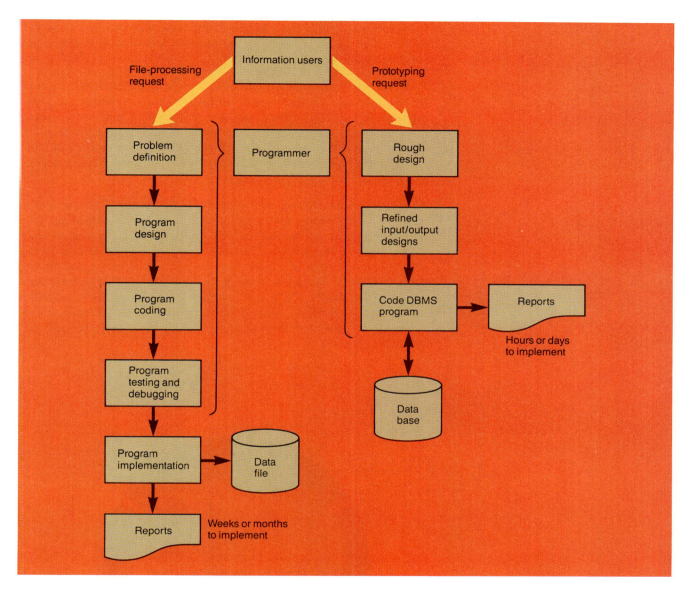

Figure 17.6
Response times to a file-processing request and a prototyping request.

Other features of a DBMS include the following:

1. *Security controls.* A DBMS normally contains a number of security controls to protect the data from access by unauthorized users, as well as from accidental or deliberate alteration or destruction. These controls

include passwords to limit access to the data, edit checks to test the accuracy of the data entering the system, and backup routines for copying entire files.

2. *Routines for ensuring that the data can be simultaneously shared by multiple users.* A data base is designed to serve a number of users, often more than one at the same time. While data contained in a data base are being updated, users may want to access the same data for an inquiry report. The routines that the DBMS provides control concurrent access and allow a number of different users inquiry access at the same time.

3. *Flexibility in identifying and selecting data.* Because the users of a data base have different information needs that follow no preset pattern, the system must be flexible enough to allow them to identify and select data in different ways. A DBMS allows individual records to be selected on the basis of the keys used for direct access; it also allows users to identify and select data on the basis of the value of each data element (see Figure 17.7). For example, if a bank wanted to identify its major accounts, the data would be searched for all balances in excess of $10,000, and any balances equal to or less than that amount would be ignored.

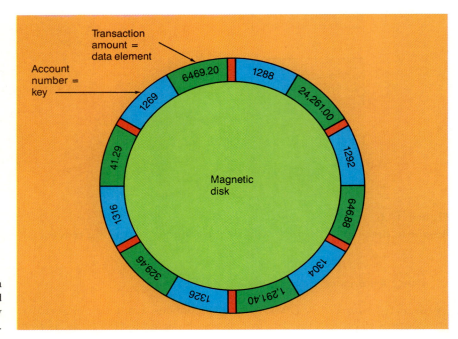

Figure 17.7

Two methods of accessing data with a DBMS. Data may be identified and selected by searching for a key or by comparing the values of data elements.

Decision Support Systems

A *decision support system (DSS)* is a set of software tools that provides managers with direct access to a data base as well as with the ability to simulate, or model, the real world. Such a system can be a valuable addition to an MIS. Whereas the focus of a large part of an MIS is on structured decision making, the focus of a DSS is on solving relatively unstructured, nonroutine problems that require the manager's judgment. A DSS is thus particularly useful to managers when they are engaged in planning. As Figure 17.8 shows, the inputs to a DSS include both historical and current operational data, as well as data gathered from external sources; the output

Figure 17.8
Inputs and outputs in a DSS.

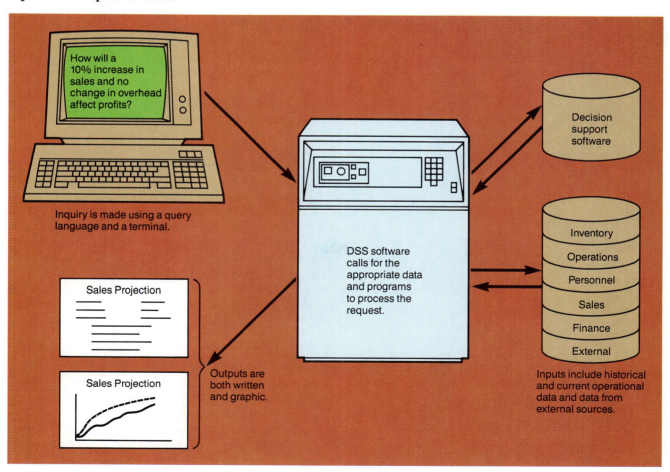

is projected information that reduces the uncertainty about the outcome of a decision.

The key feature of a DSS is its ability to simulate the real world. Sitting at a terminal, a manager can pose a series of "what-if" questions to the computer. The DSS then mathematically manipulates the historical and current data and shows the projected outcomes. When the manager changes the data — for example, the occupancy rate of a hotel — the DSS quickly shows how the change would affect all the other variables.

A DSS may be integrated and coupled with a firm's data base, or it may be decoupled so that it operates as an independent system. The electronic spreadsheets used with microcomputers are examples of *decoupled systems:* The data must be prepared and formatted before they can be entered into the computer. When a DSS *is* coupled to the data base, the computer can continuously monitor the data entering the data base and the reports being generated. The computer will constantly search for unusual conditions that require management intervention, and the DSS will report these conditions as they occur by issuing exception reports. For example, with a coupled DSS, the computer can monitor a budget, and the system will report any expenditures that exceed budgeted amounts. The manager will then determine whether the increased expenditures are appropriate or whether corrective action should be taken.

VisiCalc is a microcomputer spreadsheet program that operates as an independent DSS tool. Using VisiCalc, the manager enters selected financial data and manipulates one or more variables to determine the effect of the changes on the rest of the financial statement. By reflecting the impact of the decision on the real world, the simulation model allows the manager to test ideas and possible decisions. A manager might enter the financial data for operations for the year and test several decisions by changing one or more variables to determine their impact on the firm's profits. What would happen to profits if advertising expenses were increased by 50 percent and sales increased by 10 percent as a result of the expanded advertising? Although the results could be calculated by hand, it would be a time-consuming and tedious process. The computer makes fast work of it. Another advantage of using simulation is that no company resources except computer time are involved as decisions are tested.

USING THE COMPUTER TO IMPROVE PRODUCTIVITY: OFFICE AUTOMATION

In Part I, we pointed out the usefulness of computer systems in improving productivity. Because of this usefulness, computers have become a standard fixture in many factories. Interestingly enough, however, in the business office, where productivity is a major concern, the full effect of computing technology has yet to be felt. In fact, it is only in the last decade that we have seen a serious effort to apply computer systems to meeting the needs of the business office.

One reason that automation has been slow to reach the business office is the difficulty involved in linking computers with communications technology. Another reason is the nature of the work done in an office. As we pointed out in Chapter 4, most of the routine office tasks — bookkeeping, inventory control, and other kinds of repetitive recordkeeping — were automated some time ago, and what is left in the office are for the most part complex, nonrepetitive activities that require some human judgment and are therefore not easy to computerize. Nevertheless, three common business functions have been very successfully automated: Systems for word processing, electronic messages, and electronic filing have been helping to improve productivity in an increasing number of business offices.

Word Processing

Business seems to run on paperwork, much of which consists of correspondence and operational and managerial reports. The typewriter helped standardize the size and shape of the characters used in preparing these documents, but it did little to assist in the preparation of the text material itself. A word processing system uses computing technology to capture and manipulate letters and numbers and combines this feature with printing capabilities (see Figure 17.9). Such a system can generate memos, letters, and reports; edit them and make corrections or adjustments; and print them. All this is done without having to retype or rekey the unrevised part of the text. The power of a word processing system becomes evident when you compare it with the traditional means of typing a letter to be sent to a number of customers. Once the text is keyed into the word processing system, all that needs to be changed is the customer's name and address; the rest of the letter can be reproduced from the stored text. Using word processing equipment and techniques, typists can produce more output of better quality, thus improving office productivity.

Word processing systems also include automated text-editing features that can make a document appear as if it had been specially prepared for the person who will receive it, even though it was produced in bulk. With a mailing list coded to reflect certain characteristics of individual recipients, and with a pool of special terms to be used as indicated by the codes, a firm can use its word processing system to generate sales letters that appeal directly to individual customers, and it can produce them on a letter-quality printer. Since it's often hard to tell that such a letter was not individually prepared, this technique can be an effective sales tool.

It's difficult to type or keyboard a complex report containing many columns of numbers without making some errors. The beauty of a word processing system is that you can edit the text on the terminal's screen and correct the errors before printing the final report. Not only do you not have to retype all pages containing errors; your final output is also more likely to be error-free. It's generally accepted that a word processing system improves both the quality and the quantity of the text produced in a business office.

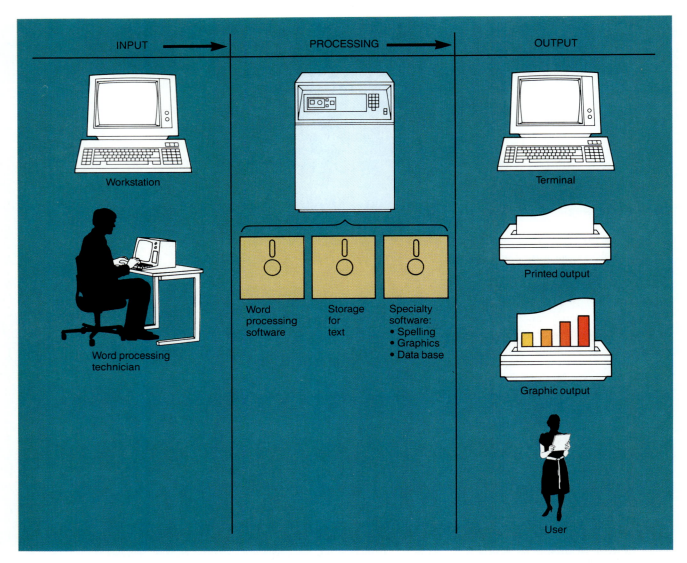

Figure 17.9
A word-processing system.

Electronic Messages

It has often been said that as communications technology improves, the world shrinks. In colonial America, messages to England went on the next available ship, and it could take months for them to reach their destination. Today, with computing/communications technology, you can make a tele-

CASE STUDY: RITCHCO AUTO PARTS
Part III

The time has finally come. After months of deliberation, Art has decided to proceed with buying a computer system for his business. He has yet to look at hardware, realizing that he must first identify the outputs he wants to get from the system. Let's look at some of the ideas he has written down:

1. Strategic decision-making information: useful in opening new stores and in targeting new markets.
2. Tactical decision-making information: useful in selecting suppliers and pricing products.
3. Operational decision-making information: useful in determining whether inventory is available for an order and in establishing discounts.

Rough as it is, this list does provide a starting point for Art to investigate how he can best utilize a computer in his business. Although he learned about word processing in the course of his research, he isn't sure he has enough correspondence to justify using it. Electronic messages seem more suitable for organizations that are larger than Ritchco; electronic filing seems to have some use, but he doesn't really understand it. What interests him particularly are the features of decision support systems, a topic he read about in a trade journal. He certainly needs all the help he can get when it comes to making profitable decisions and staying ahead of his competitors.

1. Add to Art's list at least five other ways in which Ritchco might use strategic, tactical, and operational information.
2. Describe how Art might use the computer to improve his personal productivity and the productivity of his office staff.
3. Describe how decision support systems might help Art run his business more effectively. Would any particular tools be more appropriate than others? Why or why not?

phone call or a computer terminal communication to England in a few seconds. This technology has led to the development of electronic message systems, which are being used in businesses for interoffice, as well as local and long-distance, communications.

Using telephone lines to transmit the electronic signals generated by a computer, electronic message systems allow you to receive messages from, as well as to leave messages in, computer storage, to be accessed as desired (see Figure 17.10). All individuals who are part of the message system have personal accounts with access to the storage device. Any message routed to you is left in your account (i.e., placed in storage for you), and you can read it when convenient. A message you send to someone else is delivered to that individual's account, or if you send a "mass mailing," the message can be routed to everyone's account. An audio signal can be used instead of a written message; the computer stores and forwards the voice message, lending a more personal feel to the communication. An electronic message system can help eliminate the inefficiency that often characterizes the taking and delivery of messages in a business office. It can save hours wasted in listening to busy signals and can also do away with the problems of misfiled, misrouted, or lost correspondence.

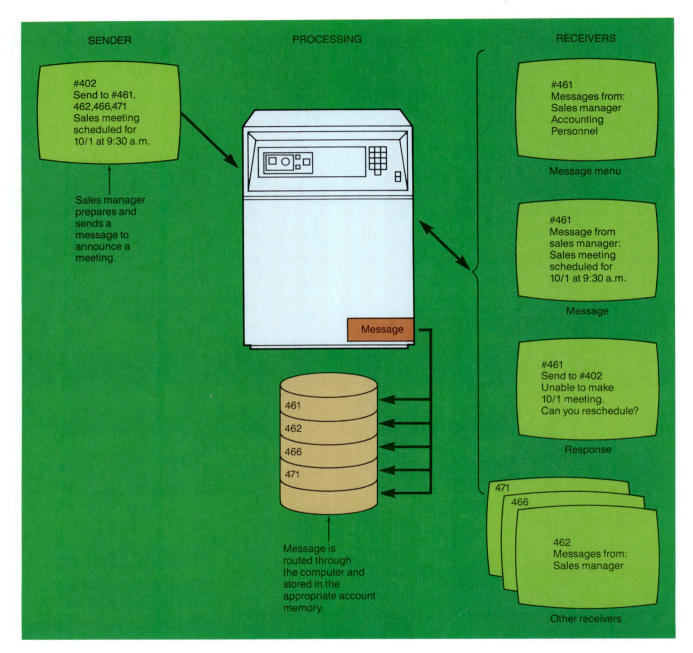

Figure 17.10

An electronic message system. Each individual who is part of the message system has an account number that corresponds to a location in the storage device. The user can access the messages when convenient.

An expansion of the electronic message system is the **computerized appointments calendar.** Using a computer to schedule all appointments makes it much easier to set up a meeting at a time convenient for everyone involved. The computer can search for a time when all individuals who are to attend the meeting are free and can schedule the meeting without wasting time in making a lot of phone calls. It can also reschedule the meeting if necessary, again without having to make phone calls and check alternative days and times. Also, since all appointments are listed in the system, the computer can locate people when they are not in their offices.

Electronic Filing

Filing is perhaps the most error-prone operation in any office. Many people find it boring and tedious work, and when that's the case, they're likely to get a bit careless about which folder they grab when they're inserting a letter or memo. Once the folder is replaced in the file cabinet, the misfiled document may never find its way to the proper folder. With an electronic filing system, the document is generated for a computer account that corresponds to a file label. When it is time to file the message, the computer files it magnetically; no paper is involved, just electronic signals. The filing is done automatically, and an index, or record, by date and document title is kept to describe where each document in the system is filed.

Once the document is electronically filed, finding it again is a simple matter. Once you've given the computer the preparation date and document title, it can search the item out and retrieve it very quickly. The computer then copies the document and transmits it to a display screen or printer. Note that the document is *copied,* not extracted; because it is not removed from the file, it will be continuously available to whoever needs it. In a traditional filing system, removal of a document from the file means that no one else can have access to it until it is returned.

SUMMARY

To fulfill their basic responsibility of directing actions and producing results, managers at all levels perform the same functions: planning, organizing, controlling, and communicating. However, the amount of time they spend on each function varies according to managerial level, as does the type of information that managers require.

A computer-based management information system (MIS) serves two purposes: It meets a company's routine data processing needs, as well as the information needs of the company's managers. A fully integrated MIS would provide all the information needed to perform all managerial functions. Such a system remains a largely unrealized goal. The difficulties involved in developing a fully integrated MIS stem from the differences in the information needs of different levels of managers and from the different flows of information and the different needs for information within each of a business's functional areas.

A data base is the foundation of an MIS. It links all available data and allows managers to use the same data for different purposes. It also reduces data redundancy, helps to ensure data integrity, increases processing efficiency, and creates data independence. The drawbacks of a data base are that errors in it can be carried throughout the system; it is complex and expensive to develop, implement, and operate; and it creates security problems. A data base administrator (DBA) is responsible for managing the operation of the data base.

Supporting an MIS are two important software tools: data base management systems (DBMSs) and decision support systems (DSSs). A DBMS is a series of integrated programs designed to simplify the tasks of creating, accessing, and managing a data base. Because DBMSs are usually complex and expensive to develop, most such systems are purchased. Features of a DBMS include query languages, which allow nontechnical users to access the data base without the help of a programmer; data access for routine processing and reporting applications; security controls; routines for ensuring that the data can be simultaneously shared by multiple users; and data access by keys as well as by the values of data elements.

A DSS is a set of software tools that gives managers the ability to simulate, or model, the real world so that they can test the impact of various decisions without committing company resources. A DSS is particularly useful in planning. Such a system may be integrated with a company's data base, or it may operate as an independent system. With a DSS that is coupled to a data base, the computer can continuously monitor the data, and the system can be used to produce exception reports. With a decoupled DSS, such as VisiCalc, the data must be prepared and formatted before being entered into the computer system.

Although computer systems can improve a business's productivity, automation has been slow to reach the business office, where productivity is a major concern. Among the reasons for this delay are the difficulties involved in linking computers with communications technology and the fact that most of the work now done in offices is nonrepetitive and requires some judgment. Despite these problems, three automated office systems have been quite successful in improving productivity in the business office: word processing systems, electronic message systems, and electronic filing systems.

KEY TERMS

computer-based management information system (479)
computerized appointments calendar (495)
data base administrator (DBA) (483)
data dictionary (483)
data independence (481)
data integrity (481)
data redundancy (480)
operational decisions (477)
prototyping (486)
query (inquiry) languages (485)
strategic decisions (474)
tactical decisions (476)

DISCUSSION QUESTIONS

1. Define the basic responsibility of management. What functions do all managers perform to fulfill this responsibility?
2. Describe the involvement of managers at various levels in each managerial function and the kinds of information they need to perform these functions effectively.
3. What purposes does a management information system serve? Give an example of how an MIS can support each managerial function.
4. Discuss the difficulties involved in developing an integrated MIS.
5. Describe the role of a data base in an MIS. What are its advantages and disadvantages?
6. Explain how a data base management system supports an MIS. What are the main features of a DBMS?
7. How does a decision support system differ from a DBMS? How does it support an MIS?
8. Describe some of the problems you might encounter if you were trying to automate an office in which the technology in use consists of typewriters and mechanical adding machines.
9. Describe the three automated office systems that have been implemented with considerable success. How does each improve the productivity of a business office?
10. Visit a local business that has a computer system and one that does not. Describe how each processes data and how the MIS of each operates.

OUTLINE

THE INFORMATION SYSTEMS MANAGER

MANAGING HARDWARE

    Developing Requests for Hardware Proposals

    Evaluating Hardware Proposals
- Performance
- Vendor Support
- Financing Alternatives

MANAGING SOFTWARE

    The "Make or Buy" Decision

    Evaluating Software

MANAGING ORGANIZATIONAL ISSUES

    Organizational Changes

    Managing Technical Personnel

SUMMARY

KEY TERMS

DISCUSSION QUESTIONS

OVERVIEW

When a building-materials supply firm decided to automate its accounts-receivable records, it purchased a "ready-to-use" hardware and software package. After a month of operation, the system malfunctioned, and the bugs could not be found. Because the records for the accounts receivable had been created to meet the special requirements of the hardware and software package, they couldn't be easily transferred to another system. It took more than three weeks to work the bugs out of the system, and in the meantime, the firm was unable to bill customers for more than a million dollars' worth of purchases. At the same time, its bills from suppliers came due, and it had to borrow heavily to keep its credit rating intact. The interest turned out to be more than the cost of the computer system.

When another company decided to expand its computing capabilities, it invested more than a million dollars in new hardware. By the time this equipment was completely installed, it was technologically obsolete, as a different computer manufacturer had come forth with far superior equipment. Since its competitors were able to take advantage of this new equipment, the company found itself at a decided disadvantage.

In yet another company, the managers of individual departments were given the go-ahead to purchase microcomputers for their own use. Of the twenty microcomputers that were purchased, only two were able to communicate with the company's mainframe system.

In all these instances, the management of the information system could be described as "reactive"—that is, no one gave a great deal of thought to potential problems or future information needs until a crisis occurred. With information being so vital a commodity in today's business world, and with computer information systems representing substantial investments of scarce resources, to follow such a reactive approach is to court disaster. A company's success with its computer information system depends heavily on effective, farsighted management. In this chapter, we'll take a look at the role of the manager of an information system and at the issues involved in information systems management. Our objectives are to

- define the responsibilities and job qualifications of an information systems manager.

- explain the issues involved in acquiring computer hardware and in evaluating and comparing different computer systems.

- discuss the "make or buy" decision that the information systems manager must make in regard to software and examine the issues involved in evaluating software.

CHAPTER 18

- describe the changes that occur within an organization when it introduces computers.
- discuss the problems involved in managing technical personnel.

MANAGING A COMPUTER INFORMATION SYSTEM

THE INFORMATION SYSTEMS MANAGER

Whereas a project manager is usually concerned with overseeing the development of one specific software system, an **information systems manager (ISM)** is responsible for planning, organizing, controlling, and integrating the overall information resources of the firm. An ISM should therefore possess all the skills normally associated with managing a complex organization, including the ability to lead and motivate highly trained personnel. In addition, an ISM should have a technical knowledge of computing, a clear understanding of the firm's goals, and a knowledge of the special characteristics of computer personnel.

Finding the right mix of technical expertise and managerial skills in the same person can be a difficult task for a company that is searching for an information systems manager. Individuals who make excellent technical employees often don't succeed as managers. This may be because their training has been concentrated in technical areas, or it may simply be that the kind of person who succeeds as a technical specialist is not the same kind of person who succeeds as a manager. Persons with managerial skills, on the other hand, often lack the necessary technical knowledge. They may also be unfamiliar with specialized techniques for managing data processing personnel. Part of the reason for the difficulty is that the field of information systems management is in its infancy; it has not had hundreds of years to mature as has manufacturing and sales management.

The need for both technical knowledge and managerial skill is evident in what is perhaps the biggest single task of an ISM — that is, determining which requests for new or revised systems should be acted upon and given resources, and which should be delayed or denied. As you know, in any business, computing resources are scarce resources, and no firm has the capacity to satisfy all the requests for systems development that it receives. A business's justification for capturing and processing data into information is that the whole process costs less than its contribution to profits or to reduction of costs. In deciding which projects merit the allocation of scarce resources, the ISM reviews estimates submitted by the individual or department making the systems proposal. These estimates summarize the technical specifications for the new system and compare the projected benefits of the new system — time savings, increased customer satisfaction, and so on — with its expected costs. At this point, the cost data are probably far more reliable than the benefit data, but the analysis does give the ISM some basis for comparing systems requests. Those proposals that appear to offer the most benefit to the organization at the least cost are generally the ones selected for implementation.

While using cost/benefit analyses to assess which projects will have the greatest payoff is certainly not new to business, it is somewhat new to computing, and it promises to make the job of the ISM a bit easier in that it imposes a more businesslike structure on project selection. Because a cost/benefit analysis submits a project to close financial scrutiny and provides a basis for comparison, it tends to rule out the possibility that a project will be selected merely because it is technically challenging, interesting, or submitted by a friend or an influential member of the firm.

Effective information systems management means not only allocating a firm's computing resources in a judicious and cost-effective way that will further the company's goals; it also means providing a plan that assesses the present and future information needs of the company (see Figure 18.1). Such a plan is based on a study of the organization's entire information system and overall information needs. This study is very similar to the feasibility study of the systems development cycle. The difference is that the overall study focuses not just on a single project or information need but on the total information system. It determines what information improvements are needed, what alternatives are available to meet these needs, what vendors provide appropriate hardware and software, and what methods of evaluating, acquiring, and implementing new systems will be used.

Figure 18.1
Overall plan for a company's information needs.

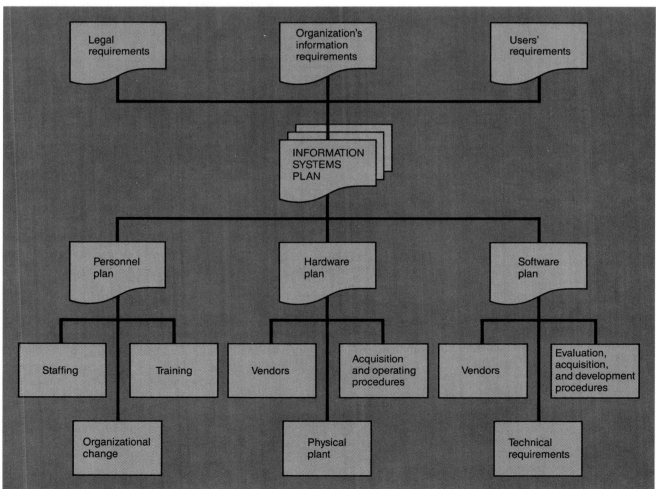

When a decision is made to meet the firm's information needs by acquiring new or additional hardware, the focus of the ISM's planning shifts to the required software and the physical environment needed to house the equipment. (Responsibility for preparing the physical environment usually rests with building engineers or plant specialists.) Another concern of the ISM at this point is the preparation of a plan for dealing with organizational changes and new staffing needs.

With the possible exception of the plan for organizational changes, planning for computers is not much different from planning for the installation of a new piece of manufacturing equipment. Firms that have standardized procedures for preparing the various plans generally have the fewest problems in implementing new computer systems. In large-scale information systems, the planning process is often a continuous one, with the ISM responsible for constantly assessing the firm's information needs, available hardware, software requirements, and new ways of meeting the company's information needs. Planning for computers can be complicated by the fact that installation of a new system may take the better part of a year, and in the meantime, the firm's information needs may have changed or new technology may have made the system obsolete.

The issues involved in managing an information system can be grouped into three categories: hardware, software, and organizational issues. An ISM should be knowledgeable in all these areas and should consider appropriate alternatives before making a decision that will affect the organization for many years to come. Because the many dollars expended to acquire hardware are so visible, hardware is the most obvious of the issues facing the ISM. Obsolescence of equipment is always a concern, as are integration of and coordination and communication among different systems. Although somewhat less obvious and tangible than hardware, software is an equally important issue, for without good software, the best hardware in the world will be of little value. The organizational issues that an ISM must deal with include the changes in the organization that take place whenever a company introduces computers and the unique problems involved in managing data processing personnel.

MANAGING HARDWARE

Deciding what kind of hardware the company should acquire involves knowing what kind of equipment is available, what the company does, how it does it, and what it plans to do in the future. Transaction volume, the size and number of the company's records, the kind of data collected, and the type of access to stored data are important considerations in any computer-acquisition decision. For instance, if customers have always been able to telephone the company to find out their account balances, then it is important that the new system maintain this kind of direct access. In other words, the hardware specifications that are developed for a proposed computer system should be based on a careful analysis of the company's present operations as well as its projected information needs. Developing these specifications is the ISM's first step in acquiring computer hardware.

MANAGING HARDWARE 503

Developing Requests for Hardware Proposals

Selecting a hardware vendor can be as difficult as a firm wants to make it. The easiest solution is to pick the largest computer company and let it design the system. There is safety in this approach, since even if the system doesn't perform well, the ISM can always try to defuse criticism by pointing out that the company that built the system was the biggest and, according to the reasoning of some people, therefore the "best." (In actuality, of course, the biggest is not necessarily the best; many of today's highly successful microcomputer manufacturers started out as very small firms producing excellent products in the 1970s and early 1980s.) A far better approach to acquiring computer hardware is to develop specifications and to ask computer companies to propose a system to meet the specifications. The descriptions of the specifications that are presented to computer vendors are called **requests for proposals (RFPs).**

An RFP may be equipment-based, performance-based, or vendor-based. As shown in Figure 18.2, in an **equipment-based RFP,** the firm spells out the specific hardware capacities and operational characteristics that it wants — for example, the CPU's memory capacity and operating speed and the

Figure 18.2

An equipment-based RFP. Specifications for an actual system would be much more detailed than those shown here.

Invitation to Bid
   Sealed proposals marked "COMPUTERIZED TAX SYSTEM" will be received until 10:00 A.M., Thursday, October 20, 1985, at the office of City Hall, Anytown, USA.

Qualifications of Bidders
   The city may make such investigations as it deems necessary to determine the ability of the bidders to perform work.

General Conditions
   It is the intent of the RFP to fully describe the parameters of an automated tax system utilizing state-of-the-art technology to be implemented for the Assessor's and Collector's Departments. The resulting contract will include hardware, software, and system implementation. The system shall include:
   1. Specific data collection and reporting systems as described.
   2. Printing and CRT capability for the Assessor's and Tax Collector's Office.
   3. Hardware, systems software, and all related installation costs.

Method of Award
   The city reserves the right to reject any or all bids and to select a bidder who is not the low bidder as it deems in the best interest of the city.

Current System
   None currently exists.

New Tax System Specifications
   1. Fully compatible with the IBM-XT Personal Computer and the Compaq portable computer.
   2. CPU memory of at least 6 million bytes.
   3. CPU operating speeds of at least 1 million instructions per second.
   4. Disk memory of at least 500 million bytes per disk drive unit.
   5. Data transfer rates of at least 1 million bytes per second to or from disk memory devices.

Invitation to Bid
   Sealed proposals marked "COMPUTERIZED TAX SYSTEM" will be received until 10:00 A.M., Thursday, October 20, 1985, at the office of City Hall, Anytown, USA.

Qualifications of Bidders
   The city may make such investigations as it deems necessary to determine the ability of the bidders to perform work.

General Conditions
   It is the intent of the RFP to fully describe the parameters of an automated tax system utilizing state-of-the-art technology to be implemented for the Assessor's and Collector's Departments. The resulting contract will include hardware, software, and system implementation. The system shall include:
   1. Specific data collection and reporting systems as described.
   2. Printing and CRT capability for the Assessor's and Tax Collector's Office.
   3. Hardware, systems software, and all related installation costs.

Method of Award
   The city reserves the right to reject any or all bids and to select a bidder who is not the low bidder as it deems in the best interest of the city.

Current System
   None currently exists.

New Tax System Specifications
   The desired COMPUTERIZED TAX SYSTEM for the city will consist of two distinct modules: tax role administration for the Assessor's Office and tax collection for the Collector's Office. The following summarizes the required functions:
   1. Maintain real property records.
   2. Provide online inquiry/maintenance functions.
   3. Provide various reports such as property class summary, exemption summary, etc., as detailed.
   4. Tax billing and collection systems including tax review/levy for all property types, quarterly billing, and others detailed.
   5. Daily payment listings.
   6. Delinquent account listings.

Figure 18.3

A performance-based RFP. The performance-based RFP does not decribe any hardware; all specifications are described in terms of functional requirements. Those shown here are abbreviated; a real RFP would go into much greater detail.

capacities and characteristics of peripherals. If the firm has a good knowledge of currently available equipment and doesn't restrict itself by defining the specifications too narrowly, this approach can work quite well, providing cost and performance data that allow the ISM to compare the proposals of different vendors. However, an equipment-based RFP usually rules out the acquisition of leading-edge technology, since the specifications contained in the RFP are based on existing hardware.

A **performance-based RFP** avoids the difficulty presented by an equipment-based RFP by defining the specifications in terms of performance requirements, such as the volume of data to be processed and the associated need for speed, rather than in terms of hardware characteristics (see Figure 18.3). The hardware configuration into which the computer vendor translates these performance requirements may therefore include the latest equipment;

> Invitation to Bid
> A proposal marked "COMPUTERIZED TAX SYSTEM" is requested by 10:00 A.M., Thursday, October 20, 1985, at the office of City Hall, Anytown, USA.
>
> Qualifications of Bidders
> The city may make such investigations as it deems necessary to determine the ability of the bidders to perform work. Only IBM equipment will be considered, and all installation and maintenance must be performed by IBM technicians.
>
> General Conditions
> It is the intent of the RFP to fully describe the parameters of an automated tax system utilizing state-of-the-art technology to be implemented for the Assessor's and Collector's Departments. The resulting contract will include hardware, software, and system implementation. The system shall include:
> 1. IBM 4341 mainframe with 4 megabytes of primary memory and six 2614 printing terminals.
> 2. A minimum of two 3344 IBM disk drives with a minimum of 500 megabytes of storage each.
> 3. Systems software including DOS/VS Release 34, COBOL compiler, Vollie, ISAM.
> 4. Software for name and address file, tax roll master, property location, tax collection master, exemption, and payment history.
> 5. Installation, testing, and maintenance of both hardware and software.
>
> Method of Award
> The city reserves the right to reject or accept the bid as it deems in the best interest of the city.

Figure 18.4
A vendor-based RFP. The specifications given here could be much more detailed; often, however, organizations leave the detail to the vendor, giving only general parameters and performance guidelines in the RFP.

it is not limited by the technical knowledge of the purchaser. A problem with this approach is that developing the projected volume of data and other performance requirements can be a time-consuming task for the firm, and translating the data into a hardware configuration can be equally time-consuming for the vendor. Unless they think they have a good chance of making a sale, many hardware vendors won't respond to a performance-based RFP.

A **vendor-based RFP** is directed to a single vendor that the firm has selected to assemble alternative systems for meeting a specific set of processing requirements (see Figure 18.4). A firm may choose this approach because it wants to ensure that all its hardware is compatible, because it has confidence in the vendor, or because it doesn't feel comfortable in evaluating the proposals of multiple vendors. The obvious risk in this approach is the lack of competition and the firm's need to rely on the integrity of the vendor to deliver a satisfactory system at a fair price.

In some ways, acquiring a computer is like buying life insurance: Just as it's difficult to compare insurance policies because they all have different features — cash values, dividends, premiums, and so on — it can be difficult to compare proposals for different computer systems. The challenge lies in establishing the ground rules by developing the specifications so that the features of different systems can be compared.

Evaluating Hardware Proposals

Once the hardware vendors have submitted their proposals, the ISM's next step is to ascertain whether the proposals meet the minimum requirements set out in the RFP specifications. Those that do are then evaluated and compared using vendor-supplied hardware and data. Cost, of course, is an obvious issue in evaluating computer systems, but it should never be the first concern. In fact, cost shouldn't even be considered until after the various systems have been tested for performance. The best system may cost the least, or it may cost the most; it is the best not because of what it costs, but because it does the required job in the most appropriate fashion. The final hardware selection should be based on a combination of factors, including performance, vendor support, and financing alternatives. It would be unusual for a proposal to place first in all categories; selection thus generally involves weighing trade-offs and picking the system that most closely meets requirements.

Performance. To evaluate the performance of each of the proposed systems, the firm develops test data representative of the kind of data the system will actually have to process and runs these data through some typical programs (see Figure 18.5). The main concerns in this testing process are to determine how each proposed system manipulates data and files and handles auxiliary storage, and to measure each system's storage and processing capacities as well as its operational speed and efficiency. Among the hardware characteristics examined are the cycle time of the CPU, which determines the number of instructions that can be processed in a second; the maximum storage capacity of the CPU and the auxiliary storage units; the transfer rate of data from auxiliary storage to the CPU; and the speed of the various input and output devices. While speed is important, too much emphasis on it can cause a firm to lose sight of the reason it needs the system. If the processing of the firm's data will take only four hours a day, speed is not as important as it would be if the firm planned to process data twenty-four hours a day. Producing the desired output in a timely manner and ensuring that the system can grow with the firm are more important considerations than blazing speed alone.

Ease of operation is another important criterion in evaluating the performance of the proposed systems. Ease of operation includes the actual running of the computer equipment, the development of programs for the new system, and the conversion of existing programs for use with the new system. The systems software provided by the computer vendor — the operating system, compilers, utility programs, and other features that govern the efficiency of the computer system — also need to be evaluated. Once each system has been tested in terms of all these performance characteristics, the test data can be compared.

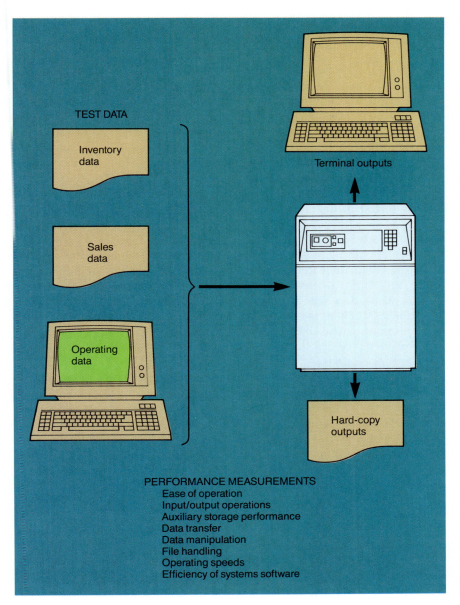

Figure 18.5
Evaluating the performance of a proposed system with test data developed by the firm.

Vendor Support. **Vendor support** refers to the computer manufacturer's ability to provide maintenance for the equipment, to assist in installing the new system by helping to test it and to train personnel in its use, to modify the hardware and software as the technology evolves, and to provide effective systems software. (As we have already noted, systems software is also one of the criterion used to evaluate the system's performance.)

The importance of vendor support in the computer-acquisition decision depends largely on the location and size of the organization that is acquiring the equipment and on the nature of the data it is processing. For example, for a company located in a metropolitan area where many maintenance alternatives are available, vendor support won't be as large an issue as it will be for a company in a rural area where few, if any, maintenance alternatives exist. Similarly, a large company with a sizable technical staff of its own needn't be as concerned with vendor support as a small company with a limited technical staff. For an organization that processes critical data, vendor support is always a prime concern. Air traffic controllers are not interested in hearing the woes of the maintenance department and being told that the radar-control computer will be fixed "in a week or so when the tech rep from Atlanta is in town"; quick response is essential to this operation. In the business world, companies that use automated systems for dispatching delivery vehicles, scheduling production, and managing funds can't afford to have these systems out of operation for any length of time while they wait for a part or a maintenance technician. In other applications, such as an automated system for running a small retail store, the computer hardware may be less critical to daily operations. In such a case, maintenance can be delayed a few days without seriously disrupting the firm's operations.

With hundreds of computer vendors to choose from, it's often difficult to tell the "good" vendors from the "not-so-good" ones. Several major companies have tried to compete in the computer business and have failed. In the late 1960s and early 1970s, companies like Xerox, General Electric, and RCA withdrew from manufacturing and selling computers after incurring substantial losses. Since the introduction of microcomputers, the number of computer vendors has multiplied. Many of the more than two hundred firms now manufacturing and selling microcomputers will undoubtedly fail, leaving customers with no maintenance or support for their computing equipment.

Another maintenance problem presented by microcomputer systems is that they are not usually sold by the manufacturer. Computer stores, department stores, and even toy stores are the most common vendors of these systems. Although some of these vendors have their own maintenance facilities, most of them have to send the equipment elsewhere for repair. The low initial cost of the equipment allows little margin for profit in providing customers with the level or quality of service available with large computer systems.

In evaluating vendor support, the ISM should consider the following factors:

1. *Vendor performance over time.* What is the vendor's history in meeting its promises? Is the vendor financially strong and an active force in the market?

2. *Experience and reliability of equipment.* How long has the vendor been developing and marketing the type of equipment being evaluated? How reliable is the equipment?

3. *Staff.* Is the vendor's staff well trained and experienced? Does the vendor have a large staff turnover?

4. *Provision of training.* Does the vendor offer adequate training in the use of its products?

5. *Maintenance contracts.* Does the vendor advise all users when updates are available or when modifications are necessary to meet changing conditions?

6. *Documentation.* Are the necessary manuals and systems documentation available? Are they of satisfactory quality?

7. *Availability of emergency service.* Does the vendor provide a hotline to knowledgeable support staff? How quickly can the vendor be reached, and how quickly does the vendor respond?

Financing Alternatives. The alternatives available for financing the purchase of computer hardware are another important consideration in the acquisition decision. Computer hardware can be purchased outright, just as you would purchase a building or a piece of manufacturing equipment, or it can be leased from a computer vendor or from a third party. Each alternative has advantages. The choice depends on the firm's requirements and available cash. The decision to purchase or to lease should be based on a consideration not only of the firm's present computing objectives but also of its future information needs.

The arguments against purchasing a computer include the following:

1. Computing technology is evolving so rapidly that the economic lifespan of a computer system may be only a few years.

2. Most businesses are not knowledgeable about the latest technological innovations, the markets for used equipment, and the procedures for removing or installing computer equipment. This lack of knowledge may deter a company from making desirable equipment changes once it has purchased a computer system.

3. Purchasing computer hardware may not be the best use of a company's funds, as the capital might earn the firm a greater return if invested in inventory or raw materials.

Technological obsolescence of computer hardware is not as large a concern for a mature and established firm as it is for a growing firm. If the specifications for the hardware have been properly developed, a purchased computer system should meet the needs of a mature firm for a number of years. A growing firm, on the other hand, has to cope with continual expansion and ever-increasing processing requirements, and it may need state-of-the-art computer hardware to keep up with an increasing number of applications and a growing volume of business. Without the latest equipment, it could lose its competitive edge. If such a company purchases its computer hardware, it may encounter serious problems when it wants to upgrade the system or to make significant changes to it.

Leasing a computer can provide a hedge against technological obsolescence: Many leases offer customers the opportunity to upgrade their equipment as improvements become available, and some also have cancellation clauses that allow the lessee to cancel the contract before maturity. Although a firm may have to pay a penalty for cancellation, paying it may be well worth the chance it provides to get out of the contract. The lease is usually for one to five years, and at the end of this period, the lessee is not obligated to purchase the equipment. Another advantage of leasing is that no large initial expense is involved, so a firm doesn't have to tie up its capital or drain its credit reserves. The lease is a pay-as-you-go contract, and accountants usually consider it an expense, just like rent. Because no depreciation schedules, tax concerns, or liabilities are reported on the financial statements of the firm, recordkeeping for leased equipment is much easier than for purchased equipment.

A disadvantage of leasing is that it may ultimately cost a firm more than if it had purchased the system outright. More and more ISMs are convinced, however, that paying such a premium is worth the flexibility and the lessening of technological and financial risk that leasing provides. Leasing has been a particularly popular way of acquiring large computer systems. It has also recently become a common way of acquiring microcomputers to meet peak computing needs and to try out new systems. Microcomputers, which require no environmental controls and are easy to truck about, can be leased for a few hundred dollars a month.

Leasing from a third party — that is, a firm other than the manufacturer of the equipment — is usually less expensive than leasing from the manufacturer, but it may offer less systems flexibility if the third party doesn't have a full product line available. Leases with third parties usually include the same upgrading options and cancellation privileges as leases with manufacturers. An important consideration in third-party leasing is the financial stability of the third party. Most third-party lessors purchase their equipment on credit, and the collateral for the credit is the equipment they lease out. If the third party should default on its payments, its creditors could repossess the equipment, creating a major problem for the lessees.

MANAGING SOFTWARE

The "Make or Buy" Decision

One of the most pressing decisions facing an ISM of the 1980s is whether to "make" the applications software that a computer system requires — that is, to custom-design it either through in-house development or through contract programming — or to "buy" it — that is, to purchase or lease it

Table 18.1 Advantages and Disadvantages of Alternative Sources of Software

Software Source	Advantages	Disadvantages
In-house development	Designed to meet the needs of a specific application or user. Developers know the organization and are more sensitive to its goals and objectives.	Expensive to develop and maintain; can be difficult to manage during development; may require a highly skilled staff. Projects often take a year or more to complete.
Contract programming	Skilled technical staff can be added as needed, with no long-term employment obligations. Software is custom-designed to meet specific needs. Teamwork and extra staff may shorten the time needed to develop a system.	Expensive; involves the risk that the contractor may not perform up to specifications. Project control is difficult because the systems designer is not an employee of the organization, and security may be a concern.
Purchase or lease	Fully developed and ready to install. Common processing requirements can be met at a low cost, and the software may have features (especially security and control features) not available with custom-designed software.	May not meet the specific needs of the organization; may require extensive modification to be usable.

ready-made from a hardware manufacturer or a software supplier. As shown in Table 18.1, each of these options has certain strengths and weaknesses, and the ISM has to make the decision on the basis of which option best meets the strategic objectives of the firm and the needs of the functional area for which the system is being designed.

The rising cost of software, which we discussed in Chapter 14, is one reason for the pressure surrounding the "make or buy" decision. The proportion of the data processing budget devoted to software acquisition and support has been increasing annually since the beginning of the 1980s — partly because the cost of hardware has been declining, with improved technology providing greater processing capabilities per dollar expended, and partly because of the highly labor-intensive nature of software development. Another reason for increased expenditures for software development is the ever-larger base of systems users, who put pressure on information systems departments to provide programs to meet their particular needs.

In deciding how to meet these needs, the ISM is faced with the choice of make or buy. If the decision is to make the software through in-house development, the firm must hire, maintain, and manage a large technical staff. As we noted in Chapter 14, in-house software development is very expensive; it can cost ten times as much as buying a commercially available software package. It can also be difficult to manage: Since each project is somewhat different from any other project, it's often hard to judge the time and resources that a project will require. Moreover, most data centers have some sort of crisis with glaring regularity, drawing technical staff away from their assignments for hours, days, or even weeks. Once a project is approved and assigned, monitoring the work of the technical staff can be tricky, since the kind of work they do doesn't tend to generate many measurable outputs. Moving quickly to bring a program that is not fully tested online may get a programmer in on schedule and under budget, but the cost in maintenance and breakdowns may far outweigh the initial savings. Because software is so critical to the success of any data processing effort, management has generally hesitated to exercise the kind of control exhibited in production and marketing.

The great advantage of in-house-developed software is that it is custom-designed to meet the needs of a particular application. If an application has very unusual features or is highly sensitive, in-house development may be the only feasible way of acquiring the necessary software. While a contract programmer can also custom-design a software system, the advantage of in-house development over contract programming is that the programmers and systems analysts involved in the project are part of the permanent staff and they therefore have a firsthand knowledge of the business, its computing resources, and its information needs. Another, less obvious advantage of in-house software development is the programming skills that it adds to the pool of employee skills.

Despite the attractiveness of in-house-developed software, an increasing number of firms are finding that many of their systems needs can be met by commercially developed software that is available for sale or lease. Routine functions such as payroll and accounting were the original candidates for commercially developed software, but today a wide range of these programs is covering a growing number of specialized needs. Some of this software is part of a **bundled** (or **turnkey**) **system** — that is, it is tied to a hardware product — but many other software packages can be configured to fit most of the popular computer systems. A bundled system simply requires plugging the hardware in and loading the software; processing can then begin. With software that is not part of a bundled system, some adjustment is usually required before the system can become operational.

Taking advantage of ready-made software available for sale or lease is undoubtedly the easiest way for an ISM to get full value from a computer system. Such software is the obvious choice when the application for which the program is needed is a common one and doesn't justify the expense of custom design. The lower cost of purchased or leased software results from the supplier's ability to spread the developmental costs over a number of different users. Moreover, because software suppliers usually specialize in a limited number of applications, the programs they develop may be of a higher quality than those developed in-house. For example, a commercially developed program may offer stronger security and control features than a program developed within the firm.

Because commercially developed software is immediately available, it may present an attractive option to a company that is in urgent need of a system and that doesn't want to wait the year or two that it could take

DECISION SUPPORT SYSTEMS:
Integration or Chaos?

The proliferation of microcomputers and the usefulness of decision support systems have created a schism in many organizations — and one more problem that the information systems manager must face. Traditionally, data processing departments have controlled the production and flow of information within their firms. Programs were developed in a systematic and structured way, with careful attention being paid to organizational standards. Much of the information produced was operational in nature, the goal being to support the firm's production cycle with accurate and complete information. Technology was as yet unable to meet decision makers' needs for strategic, analytical information.

With the appearance of DSS software, all that has changed. Today, users often assume direct responsibility for meeting their own information needs. With numerous, separate information systems operating outside the data processing fold, chaos and dissension often result. DSS users and data processing professionals line up in two camps — to the detriment of the organization. DSS users, disgruntled at the inability of their micros to access data from the company's mainframe and euphoric about the quick response of their personal systems, express their irritation at the logjam of systems development projects in the data processing department. They decry the slow, deliberate snail-like pace at which projects are evaluated. Data processing professionals, on the other hand, express their dismay and alarm at the disintegration of standards, the threats to data integrity, the incompatibility of hardware, and the DSS demands on computing resources that degrade the other data processing activities of the firm.

The solution to this Mexican standoff is the challenge that today's ISMs face. Most agree that the only way out of the impasse is integration and a centralized policy that capitalizes on the strengths of both camps. Such a centralized policy would establish standards to ensure compatibility of hardware, compatibility of DSS software with the hardware, centralization of data so that all users have access to the data, and security of the data. Achieving these goals and integrating the data processing and DSS functions will require flexibility and compromise on both sides. The data processing department will have to be willing to see itself as more an information utility than a developer and dispenser of programs and information. DSS users, on the other hand, will have to be willing to give up a certain amount of autonomy in the interests of conforming to company-wide standards.

Some firms are already giving integration top priority. One commercial bank has established a resource center that allows users to try out approved microcomputer systems before they choose a system for their own departments. Allowing users to choose their own systems fosters a spirit of cooperation between users and data processing staff. At the same time, restricting the choices to systems that meet organizational standards reduces problems of incompatibility and maintenance.

A manufacturer of construction equipment has chosen as its approach to integration intelligent workstations in which all the DSS software is mainframe-based. Because the company operates in several countries, its ISM decided that the only way to ensure that users receive consistent services was central control of the entire system. Although this approach does make control easier, it also limits DSS applications. However, a benefit not originally perceived is that because hardware and software are consistent throughout the worldwide facilities, a transfer to another facility doesn't disrupt a user's ability to effectively use the DSS.

While achieving integration will not be easy, the benefits will be great: reduction in the logjam of systems development projects as DSS users take advantage of prototyping to create their own programs; a rich pool of data available to all users; and coordination in meeting the needs of decision makers at all levels throughout the firm for strategic, tactical, and operational information.

to custom-design a program. Commercially developed software is also an attractive option when a company has a backlog of programming or when its technical staff is too small or lacks the experience or expertise to provide the needed services. However, in such cases, contract programming may be an even more attractive alternative. Because contract-programming firms can draw their staff from a wide geographical area and are not confined to a rigid salary scale, they may be able to provide a company with more technical talent on a temporary basis than the company itself could attract on a permanent basis. This is particularly true when a company is not in a metropolitan area or a desirable location such as the Sun Belt, when its hardware is not state of the art, or when it has a reputation for dull and uninteresting projects.

The company that decides to "buy" its software should be aware of certain disadvantages: To meet its particular needs with purchased or leased software, the company may not only have to adjust the software but also alter its hardware or acquire new equipment. Many companies believe that purchased or leased systems are too general to be useful and that by the time they get through fine-tuning the software to meet their specific needs, the cost is often more than if they had developed the system from scratch. Larger firms with very specific data processing requirements are particularly apt to feel this way. The company that decides instead to use a contract programmer to "make" its software must be aware that it gives up a certain amount of control over the systems development process. In addition, the company becomes dependent on another firm or individual; if the system being developed is a highly sensitive or critical one, this dependence can pose serious problems.

Evaluating Software

Whether the software is made or bought, it should fit into the overall plan for the company's information needs established by the ISM (see Figure 18.1). The procedures for software evaluation outlined in such a plan took on added importance in the early 1970s, when a court order required major computer manufacturers to "unbundle" their hardware and software packages — that is, to price and sell their hardware and software products separately. Before this court order, most manufacturers provided bundled systems of hardware and commonly used software under a single pricing structure. Because software was included in the price of the system, there was no need to evaluate it beyond deciding whether or not to use it. With hardware and software now sold separately, firms must judge the effectiveness of the individual software products available in the marketplace.

With the large number of software packages now available, evaluating and comparing software systems can be a complicated task. Directories that offer independent evaluations of software packages are available to assist the ISM in this process. Since the introduction of the microcomputer and the subsequent proliferation of software titles competing for attention, the number of software directories has been rapidly multiplying. Such directories are usually aimed at a specific market or function, and they evaluate the product in terms of performance, cost, reliability, compatibility, support, and operational characteristics. Software directories come in the form of hardbound books and looseleaf folders; they are also available online. The online directories are usually the most current as they can be updated much more easily than the printed directories.

As Figure 18.6 shows, the ISM's assessment of commercially available software generally includes a technical evaluation of the system's specifications and its documentation; an evaluation of the firm supplying the software,

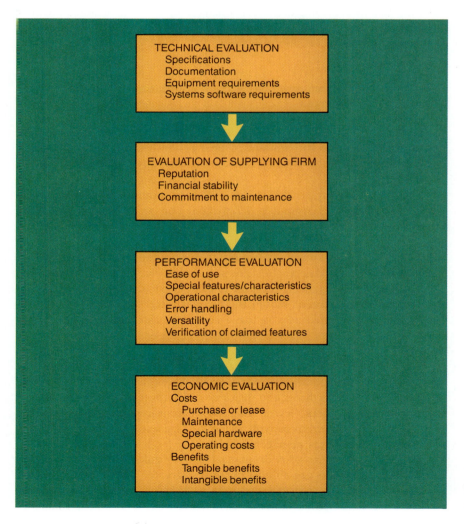

Figure 18.6
Evaluating purchased or leased software.

including its commitment to maintaining the software once it is installed and operational; a performance evaluation, which tests the software's operational characteristics, ease of use (including the ease of learning the new system and getting it operational), error-handling capabilities, and versatility; and an economic evaluation, which analyzes the costs and benefits of the software system. The performance evaluation also includes a verification of claimed features, either through careful testing or through contact with other firms that have used the same system. The profile that results from all these evaluations is indicative of the value for the money that the software provides.

MANAGING ORGANIZATIONAL ISSUES

As we noted earlier, the organizational issues that an ISM must deal with fall into two broad categories: the changes in the organization brought about by the introduction of computers, and the unique problems involved in managing data processing personnel.

Organizational Changes

As surely as night follows day, change follows the introduction of computers into an organization. The amount of change that occurs depends on the existing structure of the organization and on how fully it uses its computing resources.

One of the first questions to arise when computers are introduced is where to locate the computer department (or, as it is called in some companies, the data processing or information systems department) within the organization. The first, and very successful, applications of computers in the business world were in accounting. Computers were seen as logical extensions of the bookkeeping machines and other electromechanical devices used to keep the accounting records. It was quite natural, then, to organize the computer department within the financial area. Although information has become recognized as a valuable corporate asset that crosses all departmental boundaries, in over half of U.S. businesses today, the computer department still reports to the chief financial officer. This reporting tradition has probably handicapped managerial applications of computers, since financially oriented applications have generally been given first consideration. In Japan, on the other hand, the majority of computer departments report to general management; fewer than 20 percent report to finance. This reporting structure is credited with giving the Japanese a broader perspective on information systems management.

Because computers provide managers with quick and easy access to information, managers are able to exercise a greater degree of centralized control. The introduction of computers is therefore likely to change the structure of the organization itself (see Figure 18.7). The very nature of

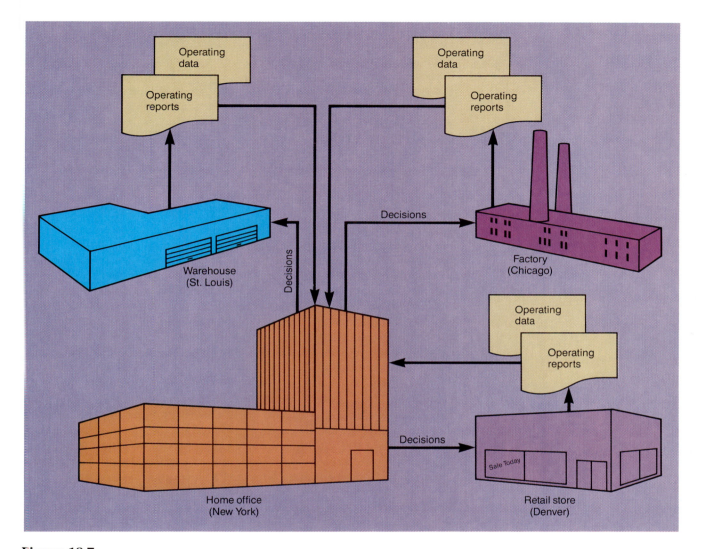

Figure 18.7

Changes in organizational structure caused by computers. With computers, information can be quickly and easily assembled and sent to the home office, thus reducing the need for decision making at branch offices and creating a more centralized structure.

the computer requires that a firm objectively understand its operations, and it leaves little room for subjectivity or discretion. Thus, operations such as data collection and information reporting become more formalized and rigid. Similarly, more quantification becomes evident in the decision-making process. Because computers deal very effectively with numerical data, as many decision criteria as possible are reduced to numerical form. Decision areas are consolidated, and decision making moves to higher levels within the organization so that fewer decision makers operate in a more centralized fashion.

An interesting result of the greater structure surrounding decision making is that employees have fewer opportunities to learn managerial skills through making small, actual decisions. Mistakes made in such minor decisions have traditionally provided junior employees with a valuable learning experience at small cost to the firm. Thus, the centralization of control and the consolidation of decision making brought about by computer systems means that a valuable training ground for managers is lost. On the other hand, of course, decision support systems can provide effective simulated training grounds.

Another phenomenon that arises when computers are introduced is the competition for computing resources. This competition is quite unlike contention for the typical business resource; obtaining adequate raw materials to complete a manufacturing run is simply not comparable to obtaining the year-long services of a programmer to develop a new manufacturing-control system. Although cost benefit analyses have given the ISM a new tool for dealing with this competition, many managers are unfamiliar with the procedures needed to develop acceptable cost benefit studies and are unwilling to learn them. Unfortunately, when that's the case, many worthwhile projects may be overlooked.

Job displacement and employee unrest are among the other important changes that management must be prepared to deal with when a company introduces new computer systems. Job displacement means that the company will either have to lay off employees or retrain them, and retraining the reluctant employee can be a troublesome task. As we noted in Chapter 15, employee resistance to change is the rule rather than the exception, and making plans for dealing with it is an important part of the systems development process. The ISM must be ready and able to cope with the human problems that arise when a new computer system calls for the reorganization of working groups and the subsequent breaking up of personal relationships.

Managing Technical Personnel

The personnel whom an ISM must manage include systems analysts, programmers, computer operators, data entry operators, clerical workers, secretaries, and maintenance personnel. While all these people are essential to the operation of a computer system, systems analysts and programmers play particularly crucial roles.

The role of a systems analyst is to design and modify computer systems to meet particular information needs. To do this, a systems analyst must not only understand the business and the information needs of the system's

CASE STUDY: RITCHCO AUTO PARTS
Part IV

Art's enthusiasm continues to build as he moves closer to acquiring a computer system for his business. After talking with several business acquaintances and the staff at the chamber of commerce, he is confident that he understands something about the steps he should take before buying a computer. His first decision is a tough one: Should he look at software and hardware produced by different vendors, or should he explore only bundled, or turnkey, systems? Art decides that he does not have the time or technical expertise to evaluate software from various sources. The risk of making a mistake seems to be much less if he limits his investigation to turnkey systems.

Art has seen ads in trade journals for several packages that are designed exclusively for auto parts businesses. Deciding that this is a good place to start, he calls three vendors and makes appointments with their sales representatives. Two of the vendors have demonstration sites in nearby towns. The third will have to bring a demo system to Art's office. As might be expected, all three systems seem to perform beautifully, and, except for a few small differences in things like report layouts, they seem very similar. Art realizes that the selection process is going to be more complicated than he had anticipated.

The selection plan that Art maps out includes four steps:

1. Check the background of each vendor. Art wants to be sure that the vendor he chooses has a record of satisfactory service after the sale as well as the financial strength to remain in business.

2. Determine the responsiveness of the support personnel after the sale. Art wants to meet the people who will be the direct link to the vendor; the success of the system will depend on the relationship he establishes with them.

3. Talk to others who have purchased the package. Art wants the opinion of users in small businesses like Ritchco on the performance, reliability, and versatility of the package.

4. Arrange for vendors who pass the criteria laid out in the first three steps to give a field demonstration using Ritchco data. Art wants to simulate a real transaction and reporting situation.

Art is confident that these four steps will help him identify the system that is best suited for his data processing needs. He assigns weights to the features of the various systems according to how important each feature is to him. Using a check sheet to keep track of the pluses and minuses of each system, he finally decides on the system he is going to buy. Now he must decide whether to purchase or lease the system and how to arrange financing. His final step is to develop an implementation plan that will ensure a smooth transition from the manual system to an automated one. After all these months of searching for the right system, Art doesn't want to see the system fail simply because his employees don't understand what is going on.

1. How could Art find out about the financial condition and responsiveness of the vendor?

2. List the questions Art should ask other users of the turnkey systems.

3. Why did Art develop a weighted scale of the features of each system? Where did the various weightings come from?

4. What questions should Art ask as he explores the various financing alternatives?

5. Has Art overlooked anything in his search for the best computer information system? Are there any resources that he did not take advantage of?

Postscript: Art Richardson is a real person who actually went through the trials and tribulations of automating his own business. He found it a trying experience for several reasons, not least of which was not knowing the right questions to ask. He knows the auto parts business but felt at a loss when sales representatives started their dazzling and often-confusing sales pitches. His ultimate choice of a turnkey system that was also the choice of several local and satisfied users seems to have been a good one. The transition was smooth and the problems few.

users but also be able to communicate with a wide range of people and to solve information problems logically. Programming has often been a stepping stone to the job of systems analyst. Lately, however, more systems analysts are entering their positions with a background in one of the functional areas of the business, such as finance or production, or with college training or training received in a company program.

One problem in promoting programmers to systems analysts is that some programmers are technically oriented and would rather deal with machines than with people; and, as we've just noted, systems analysis does require considerable interaction with people. Of course, the first step in program development — analyzing the problem — also requires the ability to communicate well with people, but as we noted in Chapter 11, this step is often done by a systems analyst rather than a programmer. The bulk of a programmer's work requires an ability to handle a large amount of intricate detail and to work closely with the machines, rather than the people, of the computer system. Many programmers thus face something of a dilemma when they are offered a promotion to systems analyst: If they reject the promotion, they limit their growth within the firm; if they accept it, they must be willing to accept a radical change in the kind of work they do.

Computer operators are responsible for running the computer equipment and for overseeing the input and output media, documents, and forms. They do not schedule the jobs to be run or get involved with the design or programming of systems or with the applications within the firm. As noted in Chapter 15, despite the importance of data entry, the training that data entry operators receive is brief. The work itself is repetitive, and many people would find it boring. However, because data entry requires a minimal amount of training — usually less than six months — there is a continual supply of newly trained and eager recruits, many of whom are not planning to make the job a lifelong career.

In short, the personnel who make up a computer department are a rather varied lot, and the ISM whose job it is to manage them must not only have considerable skill in communicating and dealing with people but also have enough technical knowledge to be able to understand their job concerns. In addition, of course, an ISM should have a thorough understanding of the business and its information needs. Many ISMs today have been promoted from jobs as systems analysts or programmers, and they have little, if any, formal training or experience in management. Some people believe that ISMs who move up from jobs as systems analysts are better able to cope with managerial responsibility than those who move up from programming.

To be an effective manager, the ISM must be aware of certain occupational characteristics of systems analysts and programmers. The first of these characteristics is high turnover, a problem that has plagued the computing field from the very beginning. One cause of turnover is a chronic shortage of technically trained people; almost every computer facility operates with fewer staff than it is authorized to hire, simply because it can't find the additional trained people that it needs. Another cause is the spark of interest that a new challenge creates in many systems analysts and programmers. These people are puzzle solvers; they are usually quite bright and need continuous intellectual stimulation. After working on a system for a year or two, most of them begin to get bored. A new firm with a new project is often enough to spark their interest.

The high salaries paid to systems analysts and programmers may also present problems for the ISM. Generally, these salaries are considerably higher than what other employees with similar training and years of experience might expect to get. Unequal pay scales can create staff problems, especially between functional groups.

Many programmers and systems analysts are also characterized by an inclination to identify more closely with a programming language or a vendor's hardware products than with the organization itself. Because they seldom get involved with what the firm does on a daily basis, they are not "bankers," "retailers," or "manufacturers" in the sense that accountants or engineers might be. They are first and foremost programmers and analysts, often with little attachment to the company that employs them. Providing them with what they see as a challenge is an important part of information systems management. Experiments have shown that challenging or interesting work is likely to be a greater motivation for these individuals than increases in salary.

A need for continual and extensive training throughout their careers is another occupational characteristic of programmers and systems analysts that an ISM should be aware of. Although some things in computing technology may stay the same, they are few and far between. For example, while the COBOL language itself might not change, new routines and commands are constantly being added to it, and the ways that particular computer systems handle it also change on a fairly regular basis. To keep up with the dynamic state of computing technology, a technical staff person may need from two to four weeks of specialized training a year. This training is of a purely technical nature, focusing on such things as how to use new design tools and techniques and new data base management systems and other software products.

SUMMARY

To plan, organize, control, and integrate the overall information resources of the firm, an information systems manager (ISM) needs managerial skills, a technical knowledge of computing, a clear understanding of the firm's goals, and an awareness of the special characteristics of computer personnel.

One of an ISM's biggest tasks is to decide which requests for new or revised systems should be acted upon. Cost/benefit analyses can be a useful tool in this process. Another important function of the ISM is to conduct a study of the firm's entire information system and, on the basis of this study, to develop a plan for meeting the firm's present and future information needs. The issues involved in planning and managing an information system include hardware, software, and organizational issues.

The first step in acquiring computer hardware is to develop specifications for the new system; these specifications should reflect a careful analysis of the firm's current and projected information needs. Once developed, the specifications are presented to selected computer manufacturers, which then assemble and propose computer systems that they believe meet the specifications. The firm's requests for proposals (RFPs) to computer manufacturers may be equipment-based, performance-based, or vendor-based. Once the computer vendors have submitted their proposals, the ISM evaluates them. Although cost is an obvious concern in evaluating hardware proposals, it should never be the first concern. Hardware selection should be based on a combination of factors, including performance, vendor support, and financing alternatives.

Because of the increasing proportion of the data processing budget devoted to software acquisition and support, the ISM's decision on whether to "make or buy" the required applications programs is surrounded by a good deal of pressure. Software can be made — that is, custom-designed — through either in-house development or contract programming, or it can be acquired from a hardware manufacturer or a software supplier. Each option has certain strengths and weaknesses. Whether made or bought, software should fit into the ISM's overall plan for the firm's information needs, and commercially available software should be evaluated according to the procedures outlined in that plan. Software directories that offer independent evaluations of commercially developed software can be a useful tool to the ISM in the evaluation process.

The organizational issues an ISM must handle include the changes brought about by the introduction of computers and the unique problems involved in managing computer personnel. Organizational changes include the new presence of the computer department within the organization and the need to assign it a place in the organizational structure; the centralization of control, as well as the quantification and consolidation of decision making at higher levels of management; contention for computing resources; and job displacement and employee unrest and resistance. The variety of personnel who staff a computer department can be a challenge to the ISM's managerial skills. Certain occupational characteristics of systems analysts and programmers present the ISM with some unique problems. These characteristics include high turnover, above-average pay scales, a lack of identification with the organization, a need for stimulation and challenge, and special training requirements.

KEY TERMS

bundled (turnkey) system (512)
equipment-based RFP (503)
information systems manager (500)
performance-based RFP (504)
requests for proposals (RFPs) (503)
vendor-based RFP (505)
vendor support (507)

DISCUSSION QUESTIONS

1. Identify the responsibilities and qualifications of an ISM. If you were hiring an ISM for a large firm, would you consider certain qualifications more important than others? Explain your answer.

2. Describe two specific tasks of an ISM. How does an ISM go about performing these tasks?

3. Why is the development of systems specifications such an important part of hardware acquisition? What considerations should go into this development? Explain how RFPs differ.

4. In evaluating hardware proposals, why should cost not be considered until the performance of the proposed systems has been tested? How does a firm go about testing performance? What criteria does it evaluate?

5. If you were evaluating hardware proposals for an automated teller system for a small bank in a rural area, what questions would you ask about vendor support? If you were buying a microcomputer for your own use, what would you want to know about the vendor?

6. Discuss the advantages and disadvantages of the various financing alternatives available for acquiring computer hardware.

7. Discuss the advantages and disadvantages of the different methods of acquiring software.

8. List the contents of the various evaluations that an ISM makes when assessing commercially developed software.

9. What organizational changes occur when a company introduces computers? How would you, as an ISM, deal with these changes?

10. What challenges does the management of computer personnel present? Describe the occupational characteristics of systems analysts and programmers that can pose unique problems for an ISM.

PART · V

Chapter 19 COMPUTERS AND SOCIAL ISSUES
Chapter 20 CONTROLLING THE SOCIAL COSTS OF COMPUTERS: SOLVING THE ETHICAL DILEMMA

COMPUTERS AND SOCIETY

Today, computer systems make it technically and economically feasible to collect, store, and retrieve information quickly and easily. While this power to store and retrieve information has had positive effects, it has had some negative effects as well. Not everyone who uses computer information systems is concerned with the rights of individuals or with the negative social effects that the misuse of computers can create. So, a technology that presents a tremendous opportunity for improving the lives of all who come in contact with it also has a dark side, a side that we cannot afford to overlook.

The computer is, in short, a two-edged tool. It can be a boon to society, helping to solve all kinds of human problems, or it can be a bane, undermining personal rights and eroding individual dignity. Which edge the computer or any other tool cuts on depends not on the tool itself but on the individual who is wielding it.

In Chapter 19, we'll discuss some of the positive effects of computers and summarize some of the problematic social and ethical issues that they raise. In Chapter 20, we'll discuss some of the ways in which computer abuses and misuses may be controlled.

OUTLINE

IMPROVED SERVICES AND PRODUCTS

PRIVACY

EMPLOYMENT

COMPUTER DEPENDENCE

COMPUTER CRIME

SUMMARY

KEY TERMS

DISCUSSION QUESTIONS

OVERVIEW

The improved services and products that computers provide have their costs, costs that are difficult to measure in terms of dollars and cents. How do you calculate the value of personal privacy, for example? Work plays a major role in the lives of most people; how do you measure the social impact when automation of work eliminates jobs and displaces workers? What are the long-term implications of our dependence on computers — will we allow them to rule our lives, or will we make them our servants? Will malfunctions of large computer installations cause business and industry to grind to a halt? Stories of the ease with which people have gained unauthorized access to data and have manipulated those data for their own profit — or even just for fun — abound. What are the implications of these acts for businesses, for national security, for ethical standards? Because it seems so easy, clean, and nonviolent, will computer crime inspire a new breed of criminal?

There are no certain answers to these and similar questions that continue to arise as computing technology plays an ever-increasing role in our everyday lives. The questions arise in the first place because of the ways that people use computers, and only people can provide the answers. In this chapter, we'll review some of the benefits that computers bring us and examine some of the social and ethical issues that the uses of computers raise. Our objectives are to

- review some of the ways in which computers have improved services and products.

- explain how misuse of computers can pose a threat to personal privacy.

- discuss the positive and negative effects of computers on employment and on the environment of the workplace.

- define the meaning of computer dependence and discuss its possible effects.

- compare computer crime with other kinds of crime and identify its social implications.

CHAPTER 19

COMPUTERS AND SOCIAL ISSUES

IMPROVED SERVICES AND PRODUCTS

As society becomes more and more service-oriented, businesses, too, are shifting their emphasis from manufacturing and production to the delivery of goods and services. Service industries have far less lead time in planning than manufacturing has; decision making and responses to customer requests usually must be very rapid. Because they build up an inventory, manufacturers have a certain amount of flexibility if they encounter shortages of raw materials or difficulties with manufacturing procedures. Toy manufacturers, for example, take orders for Christmas toys almost a year before the holiday season, and they begin production many months before the toys will be shipped to the stores. The retail store, on the other hand, has a customer at the counter who wants the product *now*. A few days' delay in obtaining inventory for sale may cause a customer to trade elsewhere or may even start a riot, such as the customer uprising that occurred over the shortage of Cabbage Patch dolls during the 1983 Christmas season. Computers can help to meet the needs of service-oriented businesses by monitoring inventory, expediting orders and shipments, projecting demand, and maintaining customer accounts.

Banking is a widely used service that has grown and prospered with the use of computers and data communications. The introduction of automated teller machines has allowed banks to provide customer services on a twenty-four-hour-a-day basis, with no increased cost to the customer. These machines are an extension of **electronic funds transfer (EFT)** systems, which the banking industry is currently using to move funds throughout the world. EFT involves both computing and communications technology. It uses an electronic signal instead of a paper document (such as a check or voucher) to represent the financial transaction. Communications systems quickly transmit the transaction signal from one bank or organization to another. Whereas paper documents may take days to process, the EFT signal can be processed in a matter of minutes or even seconds. EFT systems may eventually create a totally checkless and cashless society. You can already use EFT to have your paycheck automatically deposited in your bank account and to automatically pay preprogrammed bills. Banks also offer plastic credit cards that take advantage of electronic credit approval and accounting when you charge goods and services, as well as integrated bank statements that include data on checking, savings, retirement, investment, and loan accounts. Figure 19.1 shows a few of the ways in which computers have helped banks improve their services.

With low-cost, computer-controlled switching and long-distance systems, computers have improved telephone services (see Figure 19.2), and, for the first time in the history of telephone communications, have led to serious competition in that industry. Before the introduction of computers, such services and such competition would not have been possible.

Power companies use computers to manage the electrical load being distributed through their lines and to monitor substations, transformers, and switching stations. Maintaining an even flow of power to customers requires more than just starting a generator; power must be available for peak loads in the morning and evening and for air conditioning during a

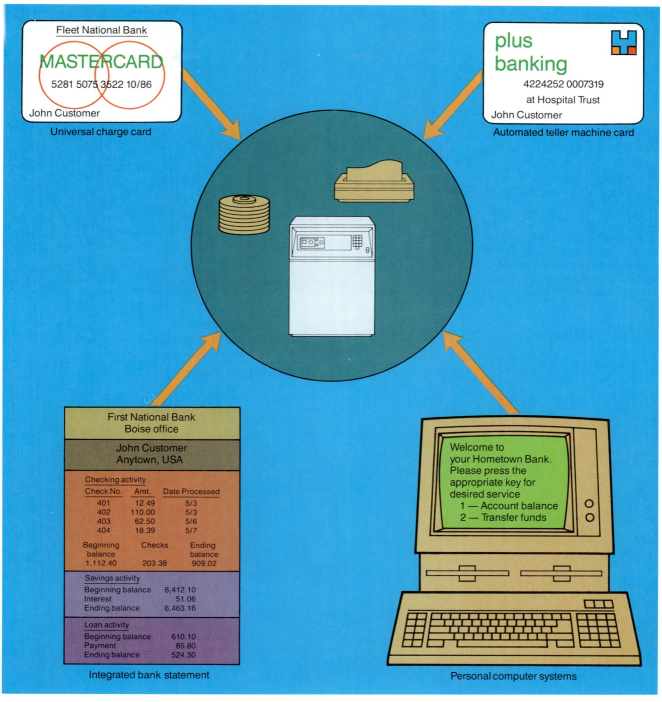

Figure 19.1
Banking by computer.

Figure 19.2
A telephone "robot customer" being checked by a technician. The robot takes extensive network measurements by automatically telephoning other robots around the country. The resulting information helps systems planners specify telephone network performance.
Courtesy of AT&T Bell Laboratories.

heat wave. And all this power must be delivered at a cost affordable to the average consumer. Computers enable power companies to meet these various requirements in an effective and efficient way. Figure 19.3 shows the control panel of a modern power plant.

Figure 19.3
The control panel of a computerized power plant.
Copyright by John Zoiner/Peter Arnold, Inc.

FISCAL AWARENESS FOR FARM SURVIVAL

These are among the worst of times on American farmsteads. A combination of high interest rates, declining land values and overproduction is driving farmers off the land.

To help combat the plight of the individual farmer, one group of cooperative lending agencies, the Western Illinois Production Credit Associations, have turned to DEC Rainbow computers with the aim of instilling a new fiscal awareness in their farm-owning borrowers.

Kent McCullough, the PCA branch manager in Macomb, Ill., explains the objective: Western Illinois PCAs have $42 million in outstanding loans to 700 borrowers and will loan upward of $100 million this year. Less than one percent of the loans are in critical circumstances. One-quarter to one-third have weaknesses, some major, most minor. These farmers will survive, but they'll have to change the way they do business.

For the most part, farmers are production oriented — neither interested in nor cognizant of the many economic factors that can weigh on their very survival. In bygone booming agricultural times it made little difference. Today's hard times, however, call for a new attitude on the farm.

"The relationship between the farmer and his PCA has changed," McCullough says. "It used to be a once a year visit with an exchange of pleasantries, a brief discussion of market conditions and a cursory look at the balance sheet. Now when a loan officer underwrites farm expenses he asks a lot more questions and uses some sophisticated management tools to check the answers."...

McCullough explains how the computers come into play: "Whenever a farmer comes in for a new loan, or renewal, we give him a balance sheet and cash flow form to fill out along with his regular loan application. When he returns the information, it's keyed into the Rainbow.... At the next meeting we look at the analysis of the information together. If there's a question, or if the applicant wants to explore some what-ifs, we work together on the computer. Sometimes we run through as many as two or three cash flow options — an impossible task without the Rainbow."

The computer is particularly helpful as the PCA office enters the crunch of each loan cycle. Loan applications and renewals for operating expenses start around the first of November, increase in intensity through December, and get really hectic by March.

McCullough emphasizes the importance of the computer in saving time. "By linking our Balance Sheet to the Balance Sheet Loan Trends we save a third in entry time; when we compare actual to projections, we save 50 percent over manual entry; and in complex update operations, where errors are bound to happen, the computer takes 15 minutes to do what it might take two hours."

"With the computer we spend 15 minutes entering data and doing calculations and an hour with the farmer looking at his earnings statements — helping him plan," McCullough says. "It used to be just the opposite. Now we're more useful, as well as more efficient."

— Dick Landis, "Fiscal Awareness for Farm Survival." Reprinted with permission from *Personal Computing*, February 1985, p. 18. Copyright 1985, Hayden Publishing Company.

Computers are even being used to improve farm management. Instead of feeding their livestock only grains grown on their own farms, farmers today can use computers to monitor the prices of all grains on the market and to blend the most cost-effective feed to get the protein and mineral levels they want. Thus, computers can help farmers get the most nutritious feeds, which translate into better livestock growth, for the dollars they spend.

Figure 19.4
Computers and improved health care.
Copyright 1984 Bill Gallery/Stock, Boston.

Figure 19.5
Computers and services for the handicapped.
Courtesy of Sperry Corporation.

Computers have also contributed to improved health care and services for the handicapped (see Figures 19.4 and 19.5). Educational institutions have successfully applied computers to teaching everything from electronics to mathematics (see Figure 19.6). Government agencies have used computers

Figure 19.6
Computers and education.
Courtesy of Commodore Electronics Ltd.

Figure 19.7
Military applications of computers: flight simulation.
Courtesy of Perkin-Elmer Corporation.

to improve the delivery of services and to cut waste and inefficiency; they are used in everything from military flight simulation (see Figure 19.7), law enforcement, and firefighting to the delivery of social services and the processing of payrolls for government employees. Millions of social security payments are made each month, many through EFT arrangements with banks; imagine the paper snarls that would occur if the computers used in making these payments suddenly disappeared. In short, we've come to expect a level of service delivery that would not be possible without the computer's ability to organize, store, and quickly retrieve vast amounts of data.

Computers have also given us better, safer, and less expensive products. Computer-aided design techniques can translate concepts into computer graphics and computer-generated design specifications. Before an item is manufactured, the computer can be used to test physical properties, manufacturing techniques, and anticipated stresses. Once the design is satisfactory, models or prototypes can be made and actual manufacturing can begin. Because computer-aided design allows the industrial engineer to bypass much of the expense and delay associated with the traditional approach of building and testing models, the costs of product development are often much less. These savings can be passed along to consumers in the form of lower prices.

The ways in which computers are used to improve goods and services continue to multiply. These applications seem to be limited only by the imagination of the people using the computers and the available software. Computer-related improvements in services and products are not without social costs, however. The issues most often cited in the context of the social costs of computers are a loss of privacy, unemployment or job displacement, computer dependence, and the creation of a new category of crime known as computer crime.

PRIVACY

Personal privacy implies that data and information will be used only for the purpose for which they were collected and only with the consent of the individual involved. Permission to collect and disseminate personal data is frequently given voluntarily, if unknowingly. For example, when you apply for a credit card, a life insurance policy, or a home mortgage, you may, without even thinking about it, be authorizing a firm to investigate your personal life — your credit history, your bank account balances, and even your image in your neighborhood. Do these data then belong to the owners of the data base to do with as they see fit? Or do they belong to them only when the data are used for the explicit purpose for which they were collected?

Before the proliferation of computer systems, invasion of privacy was not a very common problem. The inefficiencies that are part of any manual data processing system make it too difficult or too expensive to coordinate and maintain large banks of data pertaining to any subject, whether it's of a personal or a business nature. With computers, however, a large **data bank** can be fairly easily established, and the dissemination of information is much more efficient. Figure 19.8 conveys a sense of the vast size of today's data banks.

Has your privacy been invaded when you receive a "junk mail" advertisement or an intrusive and annoying sales phone call? The usual "culprit" behind these nuisances is a data bank. The company doing the sales promotion

Figure 19.8
A modern data bank.
Copyright Liane Enkelis/Stock, Boston.

most likely got your name and address as part of a data bank that it bought from another company with which you have done business in the past. Such a data bank most often consists of a mailing list of people with specific characteristics, and it is usually gleaned from such sources as magazine subscription lists, purchase warranties, or contest or giveaway signups. However, the source may even be a public agency; in many states, when you register a new car, the motor vehicle registry sells your name and address to firms that would like to sell you a product that would be attractive to new-car owners — for example, seat covers or floor mats. The data are not being used for the purpose for which they were collected, and they are being used without your consent. Cases have been brought to court to determine whether such situations constitute an invasion of privacy, but to date no nationwide policy has been established.

The data banks maintained by government agencies have the potential for invading personal privacy in quite a different way. Figure 19.9 gives you some idea of the amount and kinds of personal data stored in the files of federal, state, and local governments. Add to this vast store of personal data the ability to correlate files by social security number, and you can see that the possibility of a nationwide surveillance of individual citizens certainly does exist; and it, in turn, raises unpleasant questions about a potential for totalitarian government. EFT systems could also lend themselves to surveillance and invasions of privacy. For example, the IRS might decide to use the EFT system to monitor your financial transactions. If you spent more than you showed for earnings, the IRS would have cause to dig deeper into your personal affairs. EFT systems could also be used to restrict the kinds of purchases you could make.

Surveillance on a national scale aside, individual employees in both the public and private sectors have easy access every day to vast amounts of data on the personal lives of thousands of their fellow citizens. Very often, there is nothing more than their own code of ethics to keep these employees from snooping through the files to see what they can find out about people they know. Depending once again on their own ethics, they may use this information for a variety of purposes other than the purpose for which the data were collected. The case of a representative from Idaho who was running in a tight race for reelection to Congress illustrates this point. A member of the opposition party happened to be also a member of a local credit-reporting agency, and through this agency it was learned that the representative did not do a very good job of paying his bills. This information was leaked to the press, and front-page stories soon appeared. Regardless of the outcome of the lawsuit that ensued (which, incidentally, the representative won), and regardless of the outcome of the election (which he also won), the harm had been done. The representative's privacy had been violated.

Computers, as you know, have long and unerring memories. Unlike people, they don't forgive and forget. Is it fair that someone should be denied an educational loan in 1986 because that person defaulted on a

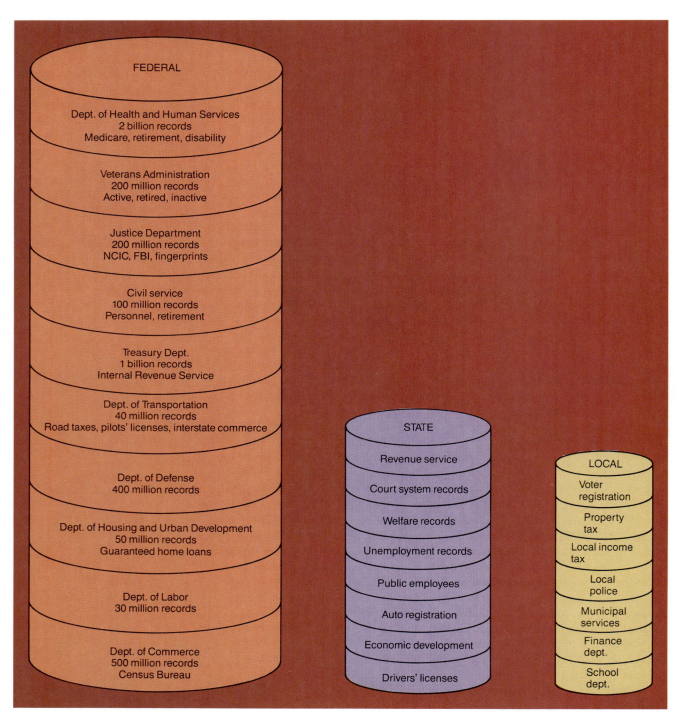

Figure 19.9
The data banks of federal, state, and local governments.

car loan in 1978? People change; data in magnetic form do not. The other side of the coin, of course, is that the data banks responsible for these potential infringements of personal rights also allow businesses to make informed decisions about issuing credit, thus decreasing the risk to the firm; data banks are responsible, too, for more efficient operation of government and businesses and for improved consumer services.

Data errors pose another threat to personal rights. How would you like to be refused employment because of inaccurate data entered somewhere in a computer record, or even because of accurate data but in a record belonging to someone else having the same name as yours? Errors are unavoidable in any data collection system. People are involved in the operations, and people make mistakes. Most of the time, these mistakes are insignificant. A misspelled name or an incorrect street address, for example, doesn't usually have serious consequences. As we've just indicated, however, inaccurate data can at other times cause individuals serious harm. And detecting or correcting inaccurate data after they have been stored in a computer system can be very difficult. If you were turned down for a job on the basis of inaccurate data in a computer record, how could you know that was the reason for rejection? If you did somehow discover the inaccuracy, it would no doubt take a while to get the data corrected, with the burden of proof on you to support your claim, and in the meantime, you would suffer the unjust consequences.

In a credit bureau, a data error might occur because someone placed a bad credit rating in the wrong file, misfiled a court action, or failed to record the resolution of a disputed account. In a bank, someone might credit your deposit to the wrong account. A law enforcement file could have you incorrectly listed as a dangerous (or even a nondangerous) criminal; either way, you would encounter all sorts of problems if you were stopped for a traffic violation.

Despite their potentially serious consequences, most data errors are the results of honest mistakes. Others, however, have less honest origins. Suppose, for example, that the insurance investigator who has been assigned to investigate your application for a life insurance policy has twenty other applications to investigate in the same day. It's impossible to do them all properly in this amount of time; so as five o'clock rolls around, the investigator hurriedly fills in all the unfinished forms with whatever data come to mind. The data on your form might show you to be a fine, upstanding citizen; on the other hand, they might not. If your insurance application is turned down on the basis of such fictitious data, your personal rights will have been infringed, but you'll probably never know it.

EMPLOYMENT

As we said in the introduction to this part of the book, the computer is a two-edged tool. And there seem to be at least two ways of looking at every social issue that the uses of computers raise. Data banks, as we've noted, increase efficiency; depending again on how people use them, data banks can also threaten personal privacy. Similarly, computers have eliminated

Figure 19.10
A few jobs created by computers.
Photos (clockwise from top left) courtesy of Aetna Life & Casualty; Perkin-Elmer Corporation; Cray Research, Inc.

jobs; but, on the other hand, they've also created a number of new jobs (see Figure 19.10).

The effects of automation on job loss have probably been most pronounced in the factory, where robots have for some years been replacing people on assembly lines. Before the end of the century, robots may reduce the industrial workforce to 10 percent of the total working population (see Figure 19.11). However, as office automation spreads, clerical workers will increasingly feel the effects of computerization. Other areas in which computers have done away with human labor include oil refining, where computer control has replaced the work of engineers; accounting, where posting and balancing of accounts is done by computers rather than by bookkeepers; and long-distance telephone systems, in which computerized direct-dial systems have replaced human operators.

What has happened to all the people whose jobs have been eliminated by automation? Some have found new jobs within the same company; others have found jobs similar to their old ones with noncomputerized companies. Still others have acquired the skills needed to perform the new jobs created by computers. And still others are unemployed and may even have given up trying to find work of any kind.

The people best able to cope with the effects of job elimination are young employees who don't have long-standing careers to protect. When they have to change jobs, they can usually learn a new type of job and move into a new career with relative ease. The transition is much more difficult for employees who have invested years in their jobs — people like clerical supervisors, senior bookkeepers, and department managers. When these people must change jobs, they are not giving up just a year or two

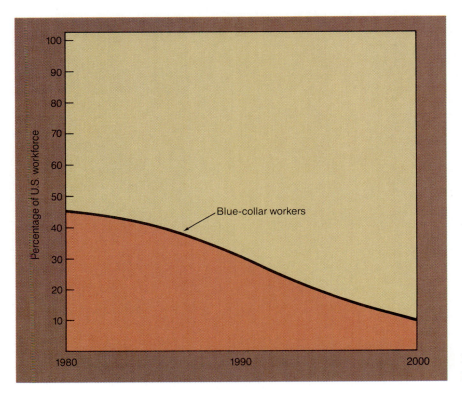

Figure 19.11
Blue-collar employment, 1980–2000.

of work experience and a few months of training; they are often giving up twenty or thirty years, and they must think about being on the bottom of the ladder instead of the top. Most of them have little hope of ever making it to the top again. Individual trauma and despair are thus one of the heaviest costs of computerization.

In addition to eliminating jobs, computers have changed the environment of the workplace. Some people say this change is for the better, that by relieving the tedium of work, computers allow more opportunity for creative thought and thereby increase people's satisfaction with their jobs. Others say that the pressures of increased automation compound the possibility of information overload for employees; if that is the case, technical, managerial, and administrative workers face more headaches in the years to come (see Figure 19.12). Critics also claim that by its very nature, the computer stifles creativity, imagination, and curiosity. They point to the kind of formalized thinking that the computer's precise on-off states require as a deterrent to the skills needed to produce literature and art. And it is indeed true that the human capacity for ambiguity that literature and art reflect is at present simply not part of the computer's make-up. Nonetheless, as Figure 19.13 shows, the computer can be a useful tool in creative endeavors.

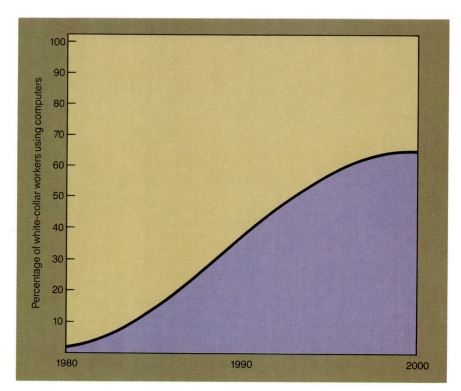

Figure 19.12

Computer use by technical, managerial, and administrative workers, 1980–2000.

Figure 19.13
Computer-aided art restoration. A digital image processing system, capable of displaying more than 32,000 hues, has been used to analyze damaged portions of a sixteenth-century painting being restored in Rome. The analysis helps experts select restoration colors that will minimize the damage yet retain the integrity of the original painting.
Courtesy of IBM Corporation.

Networking, data communications, and electronic message systems are also changing the environment of the workplace. Some people believe that the result of telecommuters working out of their "electronic cottages" is increased productivity. Others believe it is isolation and an unquantifiable loss in terms of personal relationships among employers and employees. Critics point to the growing impersonality of business in general — to a tendency to treat people as numbers — as one of the costs of computerization. In fact, inflexible, standardized procedures can create an environment in which both employees and customers feel like helpless nonentities. But it's not the computer that creates this environment; it's the people who run the shop.

Social unrest over changes brought about by new technology is not a new phenomenon; it's been going on ever since the Industrial Revolution shifted society from an agricultural base and people left the farms for factory work in the city. We are now witnessing another revolution, the Information Revolution, and the way work is done is bound to change. Employment opportunities in the computing field will expand, and new jobs will continually open up as others are eliminated. Unfortunately, many of the people whose jobs will be eliminated won't have the skills needed to perform the new jobs. High unemployment among unskilled workers could therefore coexist with a shortage of, or even a critical demand for, skilled and technically trained workers. The educational system will have to change to cope with the problem, as it did to meet the need for factory workers who could read and write. Some people will never be able to learn the necessary skills, and society's challenge for the remainder of the century will be to find ways of providing these people with meaningful opportunities for work.

COMPUTER DEPENDENCE

Whether we're always aware of it or not, and whether we like it or not, we live in a world that has become in large measure "computer-dependent." Commercial airlines, for example, couldn't operate without the computers that run their reservations systems. The world of finance would no doubt grind to a halt without the computerized systems on which the banking industry relies. Communications would be in a fairly hopeless snarl if the computers that control telephone systems failed. These are just a few of the areas in which we have come to rely on computers; there are many others. The reason for our **computer dependence** is, of course, the improvement in goods and services that computers have brought us; we've become happily accustomed to an improved standard of living. That is the positive side of the coin. Let's consider the negative.

The more we depend on computers, the more vulnerable we are to the effects of computer breakdowns. Think for a moment what would happen if the computers that control major transportation and communications systems suffered a simultaneous breakdown. Potential for disaster would be great, and many people would suffer enormous anxiety as, stranded in various places around the world, they would be unable to contact family or friends. A crippling breakdown of major systems is, of course, unlikely — but only because of the total commitment and support these systems receive. Without such commitment and support, any system of any size can fail and cause hardships proportionate in severity to the extent of people's dependence on it.

Reduced competition is another possible effect of computer dependence.

For example, in a checkless or cashless society created by an EFT system, it is possible that only a few very large "superbanks" would emerge. The reduction in competition that would result could reduce bank services and increase service charges to the customer. The pressures that would create just a few superbanks are not unlike the pressures that caused only a few automobile manufacturers to emerge out of the more than fifty such manufacturers that existed at the turn of the century. Distribution of their products, economies of scale, tremendous capital investment, and the assembly line forced these manufacturers to become very large (as Ford did), to join forces with others (as General Motors did), or to fade very quickly (as the Stanley Steamer did).

Credit reporting is an industry in which computer dependence has already reduced competition and created a few large credit bureaus, whose fees often reflect the monopoly they enjoy. Because these large organizations maintain comprehensive data banks on consumers throughout the country, they can pass information back and forth quickly and accurately. Small, individual credit associations or credit-reporting agencies, whose facilities are more limited, often find it very hard to compete, especially in areas where people move around a great deal.

Computer dependence also raises many questions about the quality of our lives. Will such dependence mean that members of the next generation won't be able to balance a checkbook because they do all their buying with plastic cards and have never even seen a check? Will mathematical skills become a thing of the past, replaced by personal pocket computers capable of doing any calculations needed in our everyday lives? Will our tendency to regard anything printed on green-striped computer paper as gospel increase our vulnerability to deception, manipulation, and invasions of our privacy and freedom? Will we abdicate personal responsibility in exchange for the "good life" the computer can provide? Some people see evidence of the inroads that computers can make on our democratic processes in the voting apathy that computerized predictions of election outcomes can induce. If you already know your candidate is going to win (or lose), why get out and vote?

Looming behind all these questions that computer dependence raises is the shadow of an Orwellian "Big Brother" regime in which personal rights and freedom simply don't exist. At the moment, the creation of such a regime seems unlikely. But at the moment, research into artificial intelligence has not yet perfected a machine that can think. The prospect of a machine capable of thought is unsettling for most of us. Why? For one thing, it touches on an area that has always been regarded as uniquely human: intelligence. For another, it raises the specter of complete human dependence on machines. If machines can make better decisions than we can, write better poetry and music, paint better pictures, what is our role in the world to be? If computers, with their great speeds and memories, can be made to program themselves on the basis of their past "experiences," will they eventually be able to outthink us? Will they become so complex that we'll no longer be able to follow the logic by which they reach decisions and, what's more, take actions? In short, will human fate ultimately rest with machines? The answer, of course, is that it will only if we let it.

COMPUTER CRIME

Judging from the coverage it gets in newspapers and magazines, **computer crime** is a very popular topic. Its appeal seems to lie in its apparent differences from other kinds of crimes: It is "clean" and nonviolent; it requires a certain amount of cleverness; it is usually perpetrated by a seemingly upstanding white-collar employee; and it sometimes has about it a "Robin Hood" aura of taking from the rich to give to the poor. Basically, however, computer crime is little different from other kinds of crime. Embezzlement, whether done with computer, pencil and paper, or quill pen, is embezzlement nonetheless. A bank teller who manipulates customers' accounts and thereby cheats an old lady out of her life's savings might be classified as a "computer criminal" because he or she uses the bank's computer to do the manipulation. But, in fact, the computer has nothing to do with the crime itself. Moreover, much of what passes for computer crime doesn't require any technical expertise beyond a knowledge of the data collection and information-reporting features of the computer system. Table 19.1 describes some typical computer crimes; while some of these crimes were rather clever, none of them were very "clean," and all of them ultimately hurt a good many people.

Although crime with a computer is crime nonetheless, in certain respects, computer crime *does* differ significantly from other kinds of crime. The ease of committing a computer crime is today fairly great, and the risk of getting caught is fairly low. In the early days of computing, when all data were processed in a batch, it was easy to institute physical controls that protected the system from casual manipulation. This is not to say that security problems did not exist during the 1950s and 1960s—just that they were fewer, and control was easier. The introduction of interactive processing, in which terminals can be located in an insecure environment such as a secretary's desk, created new and much more difficult problems of control. As data communications technology improved and interactive systems became more popular, the security problems magnified.

The ease with which a computer system's security may be breached has recently been demonstrated by a rather alarming number of **hackers,** who, with no criminal intent, have gained access to large-scale interactive systems, such as the NASA (National Aeronautics and Space Administration) system. To do this, all the hacker needs is the telephone number for the main computer system, a personal computer that can randomly generate thousands or even millions of passwords, and patience. Once a password match is made, the system is exposed to manipulation by the hacker, and the damage can be great. For instance, using personal computers and a

Table 19.1 Typical Computer Crimes

Crime	Amount of Loss	Description
Data manipulation in the Federal Food Stamp Program	$150,000	Data entry clerks accessed data through terminals and entered and deleted transactions to obtain food stamps for their own benefit.
Embezzlement at the Security Pacific National Bank	$10,000,000	A bank employee transmitted money to Switzerland by manipulating the computer system and later used a New York account to pick up the money.
Illegal requisitions at Pacific Telephone and Telegraph	$1,000,000	A college student used the telephone system's ordering and inventory codes to illegally requisition telephone equipment and later sold the equipment for a profit.
Fraud in federal-assistance claims processing	$100,000	Processing clerks added fictitious claimants to the claims files and sent the benefits checks to themselves.
EFT abuse at the Dime Savings Bank	$1,500,000	Personnel used electronic funds transfer to move funds from low-activity accounts to fraudulent accounts.
Fraud in the Equity Funding Life Insurance Company	$100,000,000	Executives used the computer to falsify sales and insurance policies, to inflate financial statements, and to manipulate stock prices by reporting false profits.
Data manipulation by a federal caseworker	$100,000	A caseworker reinstated benefits for deceased clients and other closed accounts, and collected the benefits for personal use.

telephone, several high school students gained access to the statistical and patient data contained in the computer system of a major research and teaching hospital. Although their intent was to have fun in seeing if they could breach the security of the system, the result of their "fun" was that they erased several major files and did incalculable damage to medical research.

The proliferation of microcomputers in business offices has compounded the problems of computer security. Microcomputers are often complete, stand-alone systems containing company data and programs. Since they are located in the business office, the data and programs are exposed in one location. Also, microcomputer systems, which are designed for ease of operation, are easy to manipulate. Add to these circumstances the fact that many firms using microcomputers have no staff technically trained in computers, and you have the opportunity for easy system manipulation with small risk of detection.

A lack of technical knowledge of computers among executives and other personnel is not the only reason computer crime is hard to detect. The crime itself might consist of stealing data or programs simply by copying the originals. Since the originals are not missing, who could know a crime has been committed? When an employee leaves one company for a job with another and takes along a magnetic tape containing a complete

THE REVENGE OF THE HACKERS

In the mischievous fraternity of computer hackers, few things are prized more than the veil of secrecy. As Newsweek *San Francisco correspondent Richard Sandza found out after writing a story on the electronic underground, ... a skilled hacker's ability to exact revenge can be unnerving. Sandza's [follow-up] report:*

"Conference!" someone yelled as I put the phone to my ear. Then came a mind-piercing "beep," and suddenly my kitchen seemed full of hyperactive 15-year-olds. "You the guy who wrote the article in *Newsweek*?" someone shouted from the depths of static, chatter and giggles. "We're gonna disconnect your phone," one shrieked. "We're going to blow up your house," called another. I hung up.

Some irate readers write letters to the editor. A few call their lawyers. Hackers, however, use the computer and the telephone, and for more than simple comment. Within days, computer "bulletin boards" around the country were lit up with attacks on *Newsweek's* "Montana Wildhack" (a name I took from a Kurt Vonnegut character), questioning everything from my manhood to my prose style. "Until we get real good revenge," said one message from Unknown Warrior, "I would like to suggest that everyone with an autodial modem call Montana Butthack then hang up when he answers." Since then the hackers of America have called my home at least 200 times. My harshest critics communicate on Dragonfire, a Gainesville, Texas, bulletin board where I am on teletrial, a video-game lynching in which a computer user with a grievance dials the board and presses charges against an offending party. Other hackers — including the defendant — post concurrences or rebuttals. Despite the mealtime interruptions, all this was at most a minor nuisance; some was amusing, even fun.

The fun stopped with a call from a man who identified himself only as Joe. "I'm calling to warn you," he said. When I barked back, he said, "Wait, I'm on your side. Someone has broken into TRW and obtained a list of all your credit-card numbers, your home address, social-security number and wife's name and is posting it on bulletin boards around the country." He named the charge cards in my wallet.

Credit-card numbers are a very hot commodity among some hackers. To get one from a computer system and post it is the hacker equivalent of making the team. After hearing from Joe I visited the local office of the TRW credit bureau and got a copy of my credit record. Sure enough, it showed a Nov. 13 inquiry by the Lenox (Mass.) Savings Bank, an institution with no reason whatever to ask about me. Clearly some hacker had used Lenox's password to the TRW computers to get to my files (the bank has since changed the password).

It wasn't long before I found out

customer list, the company will probably not feel the effects of the theft until the other firm uses the list to solicit new business. By then, the damage will have been done — and, in any case, it would probably be impossible to prove the list was ever taken. Similarly, when a programmer takes programs or parts of programs from one job to another, in all likelihood no one will ever know that the software developed and paid for by one firm was pirated by another. The simplest computer crime of all is to purchase a software package for a microcomputer and to duplicate it for multiple users. How could the software developer ever know that its product was being used by five managers instead of solely by the one who purchased it?

what was being done with my credit-card numbers, thanks to another friendly hacker who tipped me to Pirate 80, a bulletin board in Charleston, W. Va., where I found this: "I'm sure you guys have heard about Richard Standza [sic] or Montana Wildhack. He's the guy who wrote the obscene story about phreaking in NewsWeek [sic]. Well, my friend did a credit card check on TRW . . . try this number, it's a VISA . . . Please nail this guy bad . . . Captain Quieg [sic]."

Captain Quieg may himself be nailed. He has violated the Credit Card Fraud Act of 1984, signed by President Reagan on Oct. 12. The law provides a $10,000 fine and up to a 15-year prison term for "trafficking" in illegally obtained credit-card account numbers. His "friend" has committed a felony violation of the California computer-crime law. TRW spokeswoman Delia Fernandez said that TRW would "be more than happy to prosecute" both of them.

TRW has good reason for concern. Its computers contain the credit histories of 120 million people. Last year TRW sold 50 million credit reports to agencies seeking information on their customers. But these highly confidential personal records are so poorly guarded that computerized teenagers can ransack the files and depart undetected. TRW passwords — unlike many others — often print out when entered by TRW's customers. Hackers then look for discarded printouts. A good source: the trash of banks and automobile dealerships, which routinely do credit checks. "Everybody hacks TRW," says Cleveland hacker King Blotto, whose bulletin board has a security system the Pentagon would envy. "It's the easiest." For her part, Fernandez insists that TRW "does everything it can to keep the system secure."

In my case, however, that was not enough. My credit limits would hardly support big-time fraud, but victimization takes many forms. Another hacker said it was likely that merchandise would be ordered in my name and shipped to me — just to harass me. "I used to use [credit-card numbers] against someone I didn't like," the hacker said. "I'd call Sears and have a dozen toilets shipped to his house."

Meanwhile, back on Dragonfire, my teletrial was going strong. The charges, as pressed by Unknown Warrior, include "endangering all phreaks and hacks." The judge in this case is a hacker with the apt name of Ax Murderer. Possible sentences range from "life exile from the entire planet" to "kill the dude." King Blotto has taken up my defense, using hacker power to make his first pleading: he dialed up Dragonfire, broke into its operating system and "crashed" the bulletin board, destroying all of its messages damning me. The board is back up now, with a retrial in full swing. But then, exile from the electronic underground looks better all the time.

— Richard Sandza, "The Revenge of the Hackers," *Newsweek* (December 10, 1984), p. 81. Copyright 1984, by Newsweek, Inc. All rights reserved. Reprinted by permission.

Other types of computer crime include stealing computer time, changing computer programs, and manipulating input data. These, too, are not easy to detect. Most computer crimes are, in fact, discovered accidentally. In one case, for example, the president of a modest-sized engineering firm, who prided himself on knowing all his employees by name, was reconciling his payroll account one day and happened to see several names he didn't recognize. When a quick search of the premises failed to turn up the mysterious new employees, he used the computer to check their addresses and found that all the unknown individuals had the same address as one other employee. As it turned out, this employee had manipulated the computer system to send paychecks for the fictitious employees to his address. He had also opened bank accounts under the fictitious names and so cashed the checks with little difficulty. Such chance reviews, rather than planned audit or control procedures, are the usual erratic means by which computer crimes come to light.

Even when a computer crime is detected and the identity of the criminal established, the crime may go unprosecuted because of the company's reluctance to report illegal manipulations of its computer system. Company executives may simply be unwilling to admit that they were duped by a computer-oriented scam. Another reason for this reluctance to prosecute is that prosecuting advertises the fact that the company's computer system is vulnerable, and it may give potential criminals ideas about how to breach it. Prosecuting the crime may also create an adverse company image that will scare off potential customers and stockholders. In addition, a company may be reluctant to prosecute because of the potential liability of managers to stockholders for any losses incurred as a result of the crime. No one knows for sure how many computer crimes go unreported, but the figure may be as high as 85 percent. One can only speculate about the costs of these losses to business and industry and about the ways in which the costs may be passed on to consumers.

The cases that are prosecuted may not result in conviction simply because police officers, prosecutors, judges, and juries may be mystified or bamboozled by the technology involved in the crime. They may also be swayed by the nature of the crime, which in all likelihood does not pose any violent threat to society, and by the appearance of the accused, who probably wears a suit and tie to work and has a college education. For the same reasons, the convictions that do occur usually result in sentences so lenient that they're not likely to be much of a deterrent to other computer criminals. With so many violent criminals running loose, judges and juries apparently find it hard to sentence computer criminals to long jail terms. One of the longest sentences ever handed out for a computer crime was ten years, of which five and a half years were served. The accused was an accountant indicted on charges of grand theft and forgery, and the theft involved the embezzlement of more than a million dollars.

The crime just cited indicates another way in which computer crime differs from other kinds of crime, and that is in the magnitude of the amount stolen. As Table 19.2 shows, the average larceny is for $2,000, while the average computer manipulation involves $400,000; and the total amount stolen by computer manipulation may be as high as $2 billion per year. Given that so many computer crimes go unreported, these figures could be much higher.

The social implications of computer crime are of a rather high magnitude, too. If the security of NASA's computer system can be breached by a hacker, what other inroads might a determined computer professional make on national security? If computer criminals can breach a bank's security

Table 19.2 Amounts Stolen in Various Kinds of Crime

Type of Crime	Average Amount Stolen per Crime	Estimated Total Amount Stolen per Year
Larceny	$2,000	$600,000,000
Computer manipulation	$400,000	$200,000,000–$2,000,000,000
Software copying	$500	$800,000,000

and manipulate the funds in a savings account, why can't they also breach other computer systems to gain access to personal data? Given the relative ease of committing computer crime, the low risk of detection, and society's general unwillingness to report such crimes and to mete out appropriate punishments, computer blackmail could well become the garden-variety crime of the future, as common an occurrence as car thefts in major metropolitan areas — and a potentially far more costly one, too.

SUMMARY

Computers offer us a wide range of improved services and products. But they also raise some thorny social issues that none of us can afford to ignore. While large data banks help organizations to make informed decisions, to increase the efficiency of their operations, and to improve their services and products, they also pose a threat to personal privacy. Data errors, too, can infringe on personal rights.

Computers have created a whole new industry of jobs, but they have left a number of people unemployed. When computers are used to design, assemble, and paint automobiles, the sticker price of new cars may be lower than when people did these jobs, and the cars themselves may be safer. But what do such benefits mean to someone who has spent twenty years in the automobile factory and who is now unemployed and has no hope of finding work again? The changes computers have wrought in the environment of the workplace are subject to dispute; some people claim that computers have increased creativity and productivity, while others say that computers stifle creativity and promote depersonalization.

Computer dependence has some serious social implications, in terms both of the effects of computer breakdowns and of the quality of life. Computer dependence also has the potential to reduce competition among businesses. The issue of complete human dependence on machines is the specter raised by artificial intelligence.

In that the nature of the crime is the same whether a computer is used or not, computer crime is little different from other kinds of crime. In certain respects, however, it does differ significantly from other kinds of crime. Computer crime is relatively easy to commit and difficult to detect; and even when detected, it often goes unreported. Many of the cases that are prosecuted do not result in conviction, and the punishments meted out to those criminals who are convicted are unusually lenient. The amounts stolen are generally much greater than those stolen in other kinds of crimes. Computer crime not only poses a serious threat to businesses; it also has implications for national security and personal privacy.

KEY TERMS

computer crime (544)
computer dependence (542)
data bank (534)
data errors (537)

electronic funds transfer (EFT) (528)
hackers (544)
personal privacy (534)

DISCUSSION QUESTIONS

1. Give three examples of the ways computers have improved services in your community. Are there any ways that computers have reduced services?

2. Describe how computers are used to improve products.

3. What do you consider the most serious social issue raised by computers? Explain your reasoning.

4. How do data banks threaten personal privacy? List the requirements that you think should be necessary before a data bank is allowed to release personal data.

5. Explain how data errors can affect personal rights. How do such errors arise?

6. Discuss the positive and negative effects of computers on employment. What might be done to diminish the negative effects?

7. Discuss the controversy that exists over the ways in which computers are changing the environment of the workplace.

8. What is computer dependence? Discuss its possible effects.

9. How is computer crime similar to other kinds of crime? How is it dissimilar? Explain why the various types of computer crime are difficult to detect and why computer crime often goes unreported.

10. Discuss the social implications of computer crime.

OUTLINE

COMPUTERS AND THE ETHICAL DILEMMA

LEGISLATION

COMPUTER SECURITY AND CONTROL

Threats to Computer Security
- System Manipulation by Outsiders
- System Manipulation by Insiders
- Physical Threats

Computer Controls
- Systems Controls
- Machine Controls
- Physical Controls
- People-Oriented Controls

Computer Auditing

SUMMARY

KEY TERMS

DISCUSSION QUESTIONS

OVERVIEW

In the last chapter, we talked about the costs of computerization. We pointed out there that computer crime costs businesses an untold amount of money. Even less quantifiable, but certainly no less real and vital, are the costs of invasions of privacy, infringements of personal rights, and erosion of democratic processes. These are costs no free society can afford to pay, and most sprout from the same root: a desire to further one's own ends and a willingness to overlook the impact of those ends on the lives of other people. The choice between personal gain and the common good has always constituted an ethical dilemma, but never more so than today, when computers place an unusual kind of power in the hands of an unprecedented number of people.

The ethical dilemma itself will never be completely solved, as selfishness is part of human nature. There are partial solutions to it, however, and they are also the only ways we presently know to control the social cost of computers. One way is legislation. As Aristotle observed over two thousand years ago, "The generality of men are naturally apt to be swayed by fear rather than by reverence, and to refrain from evil rather because of the punishment that it brings, than because of its own foulness." In other words, if people won't legislate their own behavior, society must do it for them. The other way of controlling the social costs of computers is to build internal and external controls into the computer system.

In this chapter, we'll examine the ways in which computers have compounded the ethical dilemma and the ways in which the social costs of computers can be controlled. Our objectives are to

- explain how computers tend to create ethical dilemmas for people and how these dilemmas relate to some of the social costs of computers.

- describe the laws that have been enacted to control these social costs.

- identify the various kinds of threats to computer security and explain how they relate to the social costs of computers.

- discuss the controls that can be instituted to combat threats to computer security.

- explain how computer auditors attempt to control the social costs of computers.

CHAPTER 20

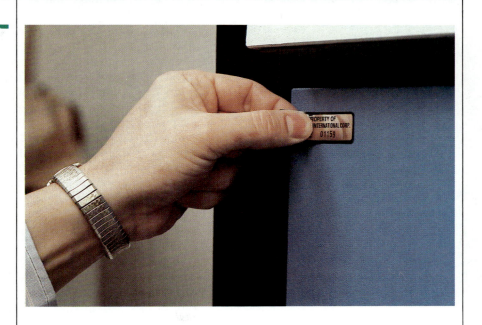

CONTROLLING THE SOCIAL COSTS OF COMPUTERS: SOLVING THE ETHICAL DILEMMA

COMPUTERS AND THE ETHICAL DILEMMA

In business as elsewhere in our society, the proposition "If I win, you lose" creates an ethical dilemma. One of the basic ethical tenets of our society is "Do unto others as you would have them do unto you." If I win and thereby cause you to lose, I have transgressed this tenet. In other words, our ethics charge each of us with balancing a desire for our own personal gain against a consideration of the common good. This is not an easy charge, and it is the basis of the ethical dilemma. In most cases, I no doubt would prefer to win. When my company gets new customers, where do they come from? Probably from another company that has until now been quite adequately meeting their needs. As a society, we applaud free enterprise; we therefore often regard the acquisition of new customers as a sign of success, without questioning how those new customers were obtained.

For quite some time, the message "Do unto others as you would have them do unto you" has not seemed to translate well into the corporate business community, or the government sector either. When you add to this ethical gap the sense of autonomy and power that a microcomputer gives even the casual user, you compound the ethical dilemma. The power of computing can be easily used for the common good, or it can be manipulated for personal gain without thought of its impact on others. The issues that most commonly create ethical dilemmas for business computer users include the following:

1. *The unauthorized use of computer time.* Is it ethical for an employee to use the firm's computer to play games or to keep the scores for the local bowling team?

2. *The penetration of the computer system as an intellectual exercise.* Is it ethical to get past the security system for the fun of it, to access and review confidential information if there is no intent of misusing or manipulating it?

3. *The property rights to computer programs and data.* What can employees use, take with them, or distribute to others outside the business where the data and programs were developed? Do data, programs, and program logic belong to the firms that paid for developing them, or do they belong to the programmers and other employees who created them? Ownership of personal data presents special problems. Who owns these data? Who may have access to them? For what purposes may they be used?

4. *The use of computers for influencing public opinion.* The tendency of many people to regard any computer-generated document as accurate gives computer users the opportunity to influence or deceive by manipulating data on computerized lists, financial information, bills, and so on.

5. *The issue of personal ethics and morality versus organizational loyalty.* What should an employee do if he or she discovers that the firm's billing system is being manipulated to overcharge customers, but that this same manipulation is enabling the firm to avoid bankruptcy?

To get a better understanding of the kinds of ethical dilemmas that arise in the context of business and computing, let's look at a few typical scenarios. There's no universal agreement about what constitutes ethical behavior in these situations; you have to be the judge:

1. To fulfill the requirements of an advanced class in computer science, the students are expected to solve a significant technological challenge. The instructor has found that if students are assigned the task of penetrating the college's computerized administrative system or the computer systems of local businesses, they learn a great deal about the operations of computer systems and about computer security. Is giving this assignment to students ethical behavior on the part of the instructor? If students perform the assignment, is their behavior ethical?

2. A firm has purchased computer timesharing services for some of its data processing needs. This same firm maintains a technical staff of programmers. While working with the timesharing system, one of the programmers discovers how to gain access to all the programs and data stored in the system. Thus, the software and data of all the timesharing system's users are now open and available to the firm upon request. Knowledge of competing businesses' sales data, which are stored on the timesharing system, would give the firm a competitive advantage, and the competing businesses would never know their systems had been disturbed. Should management take advantage of this "technological break" and use the information?

3. A programmer has unintentionally made an error in developing the billing program for a medical laboratory associated with a general hospital. Because of the error, some patients have been billed for a full range of diagnostic tests, even though some of the tests were not ordered or performed. Because almost all the bills were sent directly to insurers such as Blue Cross, the hospital has received no customer complaints. While making a minor adjustment to the program, the programmer discovers the error. Correcting it would mean that many thousands of dollars would have to be returned to the insurance companies, since the error has been in existence for more than a year. Ignoring the error would maintain the status quo and would not cause anyone to complain. The programmer reports the error, but the business office does nothing about it and tells the programmer to ignore it. What should the programmer do?

4. XYZ Company sells products on credit and has access to data on the credit histories of most people in the community. Ms. Figworthy, a prominent citizen in the community, has been writing letters to the editor of the local newspaper complaining about products she's purchased from XYZ. As a result of these letters, XYZ's sales have dropped off. Ms. Figworthy's credit file shows that she has many past-due accounts and a poor credit rating. Making this information public would surely reduce her credibility. Should XYZ Company release this information?

FIGHTING COMMON SENSE

Ethics is like medicine, to be taken only when needed.
— From the *Wreckage of Agathon,* by John Gardner

We believe [copy protection] impedes the use of [Wordstar 2000] enough to warrant . . . suspension [of copy protection].
— Glen Haney, president of Micropro

Copying software is like prostitution: it's been around since the beginning and outlawing it won't make it go away.

Still somebody has to try, if for no other reason than people's refusal to accept the inevitable. So we see the software industry struggling with ever-more-arcane copy-protection methods. The latest involves persuading hardware manufacturers to put special encrypted, integrated circuit "keys" into personal computers. These would figuratively stamp an ID number into software when it was initialized, preventing the software from being used on another machine. . . .

Even if this method is implemented, like all others, it will fail.

The basic problem is that you can't legislate morality. If a majority of people believe something is all right, then it is impractical to try to stop them. Certainly, the public does not believe that whole-scale piracy is ethical or justifiable. When a company buys one copy of a program and makes dozens or even hundreds of copies for professional use throughout the firm, that's clearly illegal and unethical. But the public at large sees limited copying for personal use as not only justifiable but also natural. . . .

Recently, Future Computing did a study that claims one "unauthorized" copy is made for every "authorized" copy. I wonder what Future Computing would find if it did a survey of people in the software industry and asked: Have you ever taped a television program? Have you ever violated copyright laws by photocopying articles from magazines or books and distributing them to others? . . . Have you ever made a tape of someone else's record album? . . .

Let's compare software licensing with reality. Licensing: Only one person can use a program and on only one machine. Reality: The general public perceives no ethical difference between carrying a calculator home to do the department budget over the weekend and carrying a spreadsheet program home to do that same budget on a home computer. The general public also sees nothing wrong with giving a copy of a word processor, purchased to do correspondence, to a sibling to acquaint him with using computers. . . .

The only viable solution to software piracy is peer pressure, reinforced by lawsuits against major offenders. . . . Education and realistic licensing, either developing copy-protection methods that don't encumber the consumer or eliminating them altogether, are the keys. The user and the industry don't need more high-tech stumbling blocks to using personal computers, nor do they need continued hypocrisy.

—James E. Fawcette, "Fighting Common Sense," *InfoWorld* (March 4, 1985), p. 5. Reprinted by permission.

As you can see from these scenarios, the course of action taken when an ethical dilemma arises often depends solely on an individual's own code of ethics. Unfortunately, personal ethics don't always adequately govern the collection and use of data, the use of technology, and encroachments on personal privacy. The drive for personal gain often overrides a consideration of the common good, and when individuals are placed in the position of having to choose, the choice they make will not always be the most moral or ethical one.

LEGISLATION

Since personal ethics are not by themselves enough to control the social costs of computers, several laws have been enacted for this purpose. Most of these laws have to do with protection of privacy and access to personal data. However, computer crime was specifically addressed in a piece of legislation introduced in Congress in 1977. Known as the **Federal Computer System Protection Act,** this law would have provided stiffer sentences for computer criminals and would have clarified issues of unauthorized access to computer systems and manipulation of programs and data. Although the bill was never enacted into law, several states have since passed their own computer crime laws.

Federal laws focusing on personal privacy include the following:

1. **Fair Credit Reporting Act** of 1970. This act regulates how private organizations, particularly credit-reporting firms, manage their information about individuals. Individuals must be told if they are denied credit because of a credit report; they also have a right to learn the contents of their credit records and to challenge and correct erroneous data. The act is designed to prevent organizations from unfairly denying credit to individuals.

2. **Freedom of Information Act** of 1970. The key element of this law is that it makes operational details of the data collection activities of federal agencies available for public scrutiny. It also gives individuals the right to inspect certain personal data collected and stored by the federal government.

3. **Privacy Act** of 1974. This act gives individuals the right to review and challenge the accuracy of records about themselves that are maintained by federal agencies. The act substantially augments the Freedom of Information Act. It provides for the following: (a) The federal agency that collects and maintains files containing personal data must take precautions to ensure reliability of the information and to prevent its abuse. (b) Individuals must be informed of what personal data are being collected, how the data will be used, and how erroneous data can be corrected. (c) When information is used for purposes other than the purpose for which it was collected, the consent of the individual must be obtained.

4. **Education Privacy Act** of 1974. When a public or a private school receives federal funding, this act protects the individual's right to privacy in terms of evaluations and course grades. Included under this protection would be such things as transcripts of academic work, examination scores, and final grades for individual classes.

Although the Privacy Act of 1974 pertains only to the federal government and its contractors, it had a wider impact because several states enacted **fair information practices laws** modeled after it. The Privacy Act also required that the federal government set up the **Privacy Protection Study**

COMPUTER LAW

Not too long ago, "computer law" existed mostly in legal journals. The vendors, of course, had their counsels ... but that was about it. "It was all theoretical," recalls John C. Lautsch, chairman of the computer law division of the American Bar Association's Section of Science and Technology. "You would read about it and say to yourself, 'Well, that's interesting,' and then return to your divorce cases."

It's not theoretical anymore. The reason is simple: the tremendous growth of the computer industry. This $140 billion business now includes thousands of computer companies.... At the same time, there are hundreds of thousands of businesses buying computers and becoming absolutely dependent on them. All of this gives urgency to formerly theoretical questions: what liability do vendors have? What kinds of protections can users negotiate? How can employees be prevented from stealing trade secrets? What rights do employees have to programs they develop on their own time? When is it permissible to copy software? How do you stop a company from selling a program that's a rip-off of yours? ...

Although computer law has burgeoned only recently, legal questions were raised almost from the moment computers appeared on the scene.... The first computer case involved the admissibility of computer-generated traffic statistics at a 1951 hearing before the Interstate Commerce Commission. Other cases around that time dealt with the impact of computers on employee rights, such as ... how dismissals and tranfers resulting from the introduction of computers should be handled.

The first lawsuits by unhappy users of computers appeared in the late 1950s.... The Industrial Supply Corp. of Florida sued Sperry Rand to recover $75,000 it had paid for a Univac 60 [and] emerged victorious.

The first reported case of computer crime occurred in 1966 in Texas, when a programmer for Texas Instruments tried to sell some programs to Texaco. In a landmark ruling, a Texas judge held that a software program, though invisible and intangible, should be considered "property" under the definition of the state's larceny statute.

As the industry picked up steam in the late 1960s and early '70s, there was an increase in the number of cases involving dp employees

---

Commission. Among the recommendations of this commission were the following:

1. Individuals should be able to inspect any personal data that are being gathered.
2. Limits should be placed on the kinds of data collected and stored in data banks.
3. Procedures should be established to ensure that data are accurate and secure.
4. Organizations that collect data should bear the responsibility for how the data are used.

Legislation is being developed to address these issues, but it is a slow process.

While the laws that have been enacted have helped to control the misuse and abuse of computer systems, they are far from being the complete answer to the ethical dilemma. No piece of legislation could, of course, ever cover the myriad situations that arise in everyday living. Moreover, jumping ship to join competing firms or start their own....

Privacy issues also came to the fore around this time. The 1965 attempt to establish a federal Data Center was dropped after extensive criticism. Courts, however, upheld the use of computers to cross-check the earnings of recipients of government benefits, a tactic that the Reagan administration has lately reinvoked....

Damage awards for disgruntled computer users ... wrangling over software protection ... privacy ... antitrust ... trade secrets ... computer crime. These are the hot topics in computer law today. But they may be only a prelude to the major issue that many attorneys see looming on the horizon — liability. Consider these cases:

A computer-controlled hospital life support system suddenly goes haywire. The system used by an architecture firm incorrectly calculates the stress requirements of a new, large public building. The computer-controlled fuel-measuring system on an aircraft fails and the plane runs out of fuel in midflight....

"The growing array of liability-laden situations is so unbelievable," says Daniel Brooks [a Washington, D.C., attorney], "that those who discuss them openly risk sounding like Chicken Little constantly screaming that the sky is falling."...

If computers lead to a rethinking of liability laws, it won't be an event without precedent. Lawrence M. Friedman explains in his *History of American Law* that it was the industrial revolution, particularly the railroad, that dramatically changed American law in this area. "From about 1840 on, one specific machine, the railroad locomotive, generated on its own steam (so to speak) more tort law than any other in the 19th century. The railroad engine swept like a roaring bull through the countryside, carrying out an economic and social revolution; but it exacted a toll of thousands, injured and dead."

So far, computers haven't been accused of mayhem on this scale. As the ABA's John Lautsch puts it, "Computers are really pretty reliable. Their main use is in areas that don't cause severe harm to people. They don't blow up in your face. They've just been used to manipulate information."

In the long run, though, that makes them, for good or ill, the most powerful machines of all.

—Joseph Kelly, "Computer Law," *Datamation* (June 15, 1985), pp. 116–126. Reprinted with Permission of *Datamation*® magazine, © Copyright by Technical Publishing Company, A Dun & Bradstreet Company, 1985. All rights reserved.

---

none of these laws addresses the issues of ownership of data in the private sector, disclosure of the information contained in the data banks of organizations not receiving federal or state aid, unauthorized use of information and the associated responsibility, and responsibility for errors and corrections when errors are discovered. To date, there is no clear responsibility for the operation and maintenance of privately controlled data banks, and individuals who are harmed by the use of such a data bank have little or no recourse.

Effective lobbying by special-interest groups, which so often takes the bite out of the laws that are ultimately enacted, makes it unlikely that legislation will ever provide a foolproof safeguard against invasions of personal privacy. Access to personal data means commercial gain for certain groups, such as direct-mail advertisers and firms that grant credit, and the people who stand to gain are not going to give up their ability to collect and use personal information without a struggle. Furthermore, the people who lobby for reduced controls over personal information usually have greater resources to promote their cause than those who champion a more restrictive policy.

COMPUTER SECURITY AND CONTROL

Another universally accepted means of controlling some of the social costs of computers is to build internal and external controls into the computer system. Of course, any security measures designed by human beings can be broken by human beings; so, like legislation and personal ethics, these safeguards do not provide absolute protection against computer crime and infringements of personal rights. Let's look first at the variety of threats to security that businesses with computer systems face. We'll then consider the controls they can institute to combat these threats. Finally, we'll consider the tools available to help the **computer auditor,** the person charged with being sure the controls are adequate, in place, and functioning.

Threats to Computer Security

Any business must, of course, be concerned about unauthorized access to its computer system. Such access literally opens the door to a variety of computer crimes and to illegitimate use of sensitive and valuable data. Sensitive and valuable data include not only personal data but also information that would give competing firms an advantage if it were to fall into their hands — for example, mailing lists with the names and addresses of prospective customers; data on marketing, sales, and production; data on product design or formulas; or data containing the results of customer surveys.

Unauthorized access is not, however, the only threat to the security of a computer system. *Authorized* access can result in the same manipulations and improper uses of data; the only difference is that authorized access is obviously easier and the manipulations are done by insiders to the firm rather than by outsiders. Insiders also have a greater opportunity than outsiders to destroy the integrity of data before the data enter the computer system. Such destruction may be deliberate or accidental, but in either case, the net effect is to undermine the whole purpose of the computer system — that is, the production of accurate, complete, useful outputs.

Other threats to the security of a computer system are physical in nature. They include fire, natural disasters, environmental problems, and physical damage by people.

System Manipulation by Outsiders. Outsiders who want to gain unauthorized access to a company's computer system have a growing number of opportunities to do so. Terminals and stand-alone microcomputers located in insecure environments and personal computers used in conjunction with telecommunications links to the main computer are potential soft spots in the security of the computer system. By tapping a telephone line or coaxial cable, interrupting a microwave signal, or manipulating a local area network, outsiders can penetrate a data communications system and manipulate the signals in a variety of ways (see Figure 20.1). With today's emphasis on telecommunications and distributed data processing networks, penetration has become a major issue for designers of computer systems.

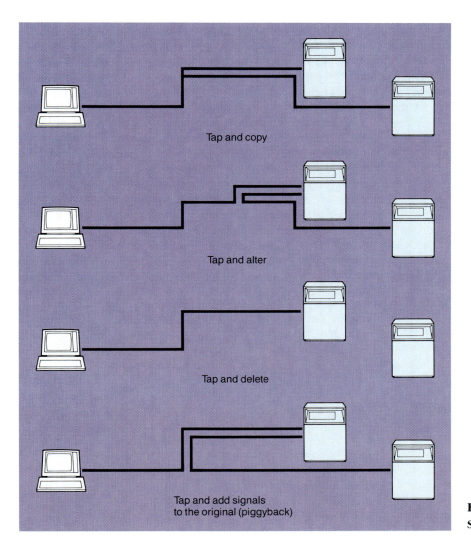

Figure 20.1
Signal manipulation by outsiders.

Generally, when an outsider penetrates a computer system, it is a deliberate penetration, not an accidental or chance one. Most outside penetrators fall into one of three categories:

1. Disgruntled ex-employees who are seeking revenge on the company.
2. Puzzle solvers who are more interested in seeing if they can break into the system than in causing harm.
3. Individuals who want to profit from the penetration.

Each category of penetrators presents special problems. The disgruntled ex-employee knows how the company operates, often has friends still working there, and can appear innocent while creating problems in the computer system. A casual walk through the computer room to pick up a friend for lunch can be the opportunity to run a small magnet over an exposed magnetic tape; the action would be undetected and yet would cause havoc when the tape was run.

Although puzzle solvers may not intend to cause any harm, they often do. While fishing for passwords to penetrate the system, these hackers try thousands of combinations, with no idea of what the results of any of them might be. Consequently, they may change files, destroy data, or even completely shut the computer system down for a period of time.

People seeking a profit are the most sophisticated of the outside penetrators. Because they stand to gain financially, they are often willing to spend money on bribing insiders to help them break into the system. Gaining access to passwords and codes for EFT systems so that they can steal funds, duplicating customer lists so that they can steal customers, and changing college grades for payment are just a few of the ways that this group of outside penetrators manipulates computer systems for profit.

System Manipulation by Insiders. Two groups of employees have considerable opportunity to manipulate the system: those who work with the computer (programmers, data entry clerks, and operations personnel), and those who have access to a terminal or to the computer (usually the system's users). Manipulation can be either intentional or unintentional, and it is often hard to tell the difference. For example, in most cases, it would probably be impossible to tell whether a data entry clerk was making keyboard errors deliberately or accidentally, or whether a member of the operations staff had mounted the wrong tape of data with malice in his heart or not. Because computer systems depend on people, such errors will always occur. Although they can be costly, there's no way to completely eliminate them. The best that can be done is to reduce their impact by training staff, by monitoring operations at critical stages, and by instituting some of the various controls that we will discuss later in the chapter.

The potential for manipulation of the system by a technical employee, especially a programmer, is perhaps the greatest hazard a computerized business faces. Programmers communicate directly with the computer on a daily basis, and they know the software better then anyone else in the firm. It's almost impossible for a computer auditor, who spends a few days reviewing documentation and operations, to be as knowledgeable about the system as the programmer; this fact adds to the other difficulties associated with detecting computer crime, which we discussed in the last chapter.

The problem of larcenous employees — whether technical specialists or not — is not a new one for business. Embezzlers and industrial spies have been around for years. What is new are the computerized aids for altering data, adjusting files, and obtaining sensitive information. The speed of accessing and changing data, the concentration of a firm's information resources in a single location, and the occasional need to remove employees from data processing activities call for new methods and procedures.

COMPUTER SECURITY AND THE VULNERABILITY OF DATA

When a squad of espionage agents stationed itself near the Denver plant of a major defense contractor, no one paid any attention. In fact, no one noticed them until [they] marched into the plant and reported, "Gentlemen, we have a security problem."

Startled executives in the plant gasped when they saw exact transcripts of their every personal computer keystroke and word-by-word replays of their most confidential telecommunications laid before them. Nearly every electronic activity in the plant had been duly recorded, in many cases by merely tuning sensitive radio receivers into the emissions generated by the plant's computer gear.

"They came in and just destroyed us," one executive told a security consultant....

Fortunately, the agents were on our side. The National Security Agency's goal in the experiment was to determine the state of electronic security in the defense industry, and, according to the computer security consultant hired to help straighten things out in the aftermath, it was in a sorry state, indeed.

The darkest side of the story was not simply the loss of important strategic information but that no one at the targeted plant had been aware that its security had been breached....

Since then, new security measures taken at the plant have become an example that the rest of the defense industry is following....

In nondefense industries, not required by the government to take strict security measures, computer security is lax. Few PC [personal computer] users give security a second thought, perhaps thinking that spy stories are mere products of paranoia, an overactive imagination, or an overdose of James Bond. But the consultant working with the Denver plant believes the evidence is otherwise.

"Why do some companies lose bids to competitors who undercut them only by a dollar or two?" he asks. "Such very narrow margins probably illustrate intelligence gathering on the competitor's part."...

According to a survey conducted by the American Bar Association, computer security problems are already immense. About 40 percent of the organizations responding to the ABA questionnaire indicated that they had detected and verified the occurrence of "incidents of computer crime" within the year immediately before the survey. The survey pegged those single-year losses between $145 million and $730 million.

Even the ABA's multimillion-dollar figures hardly hint at the true cost of losses attributable to computer security failures because most victims never even know a crime has taken place.

According to Robert Wise, corporate communications manager of Sentry Software, "Between 90 and 95 percent of all computer security breaches go undetected." Potentially, then, the cost of inadequate computer security may be over $15 billion.

Experts agree that the fastest-growing problem area in computer security is now the personal computer. Although elaborate security measures are routinely employed on mainframe computers, PCs afford almost unlimited opportunity for intrusion. The current trend to integrate PCs into networks and mainframe systems now makes once secure data more vulnerable....

In fact, when it comes to security, the PC is a box of woes that even Pandora wouldn't touch. Confidential information can leak out in countless ways.

With the exception of the few portable PCs that use bubble memory, all PCs rely on some form of magnetic medium for mass storage....

The information that magnetic media contains is readily copied. Personal computer media are readily transportable and therefore easy to conceal and steal. A whole hard disk of data can be loaded onto a tape cartridge that slides discreetly into a jacket pocket.

Moreover, the personal computer can change a minor annoyance, theft of office equipment, into a major disaster when the equipment stolen is a computer containing all of a company's records....

When a PC is connected to any kind of communications system — telephone line, network, or micro-to-mainframe line — security problems are bound to multiply.

— Winn L. Rosch, "PC Data Is Vulnerable to Attack." Reprinted from *PC Magazine*, July 23, 1985 (pp. 33–34). Copyright © 1985 Ziff-Davis Publishing Company.

Physical Threats. Businesses have always had to be concerned about threats to their security arising from physical causes such as fire, floods, and earthquakes. Sabotage, too, is not a new concern. But computers put a few new twists on some of these old problems and require some special solutions. For example, the combination of electrical equipment and a lot of combustible material (computer printouts, punched cards, etc.) under the same roof increases the risk of fire; moreover, if water or other liquids are used to extinguish a fire in the computer center, they will damage both the magnetic and paper media and the computer hardware (e.g., water will oxidize the CPU's electronic circuits). Water damage is, of course, also the threat posed by floods and by the high winds that arise during a cyclone or a hurricane, which knock out windows and allow rain to pour in.

The volatility of primary storage in today's computer systems creates another new kind of physical threat to security. Power failures or sudden spikes or drops in the supply of power can permanently erase data or create data errors. Also, magnetic fields created by electric motors operating near the computer center can disturb the integrity of the data stored on magnetic media.

Sabotage of computer systems — intentional physical damage done by people — is a far more common occurrence than you may think. People who blame computers for many of the world's social and economic ills have often, in fits of passion, attempted to take their frustrations out on a computer system. Computer systems have been bombed, run into by autos, shot up, knifed, attacked with sledge hammers, and damaged in a number of other ways. In the next section, we'll consider the controls that can be instituted to protect the computer system from these and other kinds of threats.

Computer Controls

As we mentioned in Chapter 19, safeguarding the security of the computer system is a far more difficult task today than it was in the past, when all data were processed in a batch. The introduction of interactive processing, the recent proliferation of microcomputers, and improvements in data communications systems have compounded both the number and the complexity of threats to computer security. However, a number of controls can be used throughout the data processing cycle to protect both the computer and the data. These include systems controls, machine controls, physical controls, and people-oriented controls.

Systems Controls. Systems controls are so called because they are a part of the routine processing operations; they may be included in a series of control programs, or they may be built into the hardware. Such controls are generally developed by the systems study team during the analysis and design phases of the systems development cycle. Systems controls are concerned with ensuring the integrity of the data and with controlling access to the data.

Checks on data integrity include batch controls, editing, and parity checks. Batch controls, as you may remember from Chapter 6, total the transactions going into the computer and then total the processed results. If the two totals don't match, an error has occurred and must be checked out. Batch controls are used when data are processed in a group or when master files are updated at the end of a business day or other business cycle. They are one of the simplest data control techniques but also one of the most useful and important. Since no paper documentation describes what has taken place within the computer during processing, batch controls help ensure that the transactions are in balance. They are also useful to auditors, who must verify transactions.

Editing includes checks on the reasonableness and range of the data as they enter the computer, as well as simple tests of the fields' alphabetical and numerical characters. As we noted in Chapter 6, editing procedures help maintain a high level of accuracy during data entry. Testing the characters of the fields, for example, can ensure that all the data to be used in the calculations are numerical. And correcting errors before the data are processed saves having to change the processed, updated records. Editing checks, as well as batch controls, can be considered both systems controls and people-oriented controls, since they check on errors created by people.

Parity checks, discussed in Chapter 5, are another means of ensuring the accuracy of the data. The addition of a parity bit to each binary-coded character to make up odd or even parity makes it possible to detect errors in transmitted data.

Systems controls used to restrict access to data to authorized individuals include encryption and passwords. With encryption, data are scrambled during transmission from one computer site to another (see Chapter 9). Encryption thus prevents outsiders from capturing or manipulating the data signals. The scrambling is done with special codes known only to the sending and receiving systems. Because the codes can be designed for telephone distribution, the normal telecommunications system can still be used.

Passwords are used with interactive systems to control both entry into the system and access to specific information (see discussion of systems-monitoring programs in Chapter 13). In nonsensitive systems, a general password may be used. However, in sensitive systems, individuals may have their own passwords, which the system uses to identify their authority to enter the system and to access particular data and programs. The password is easily changed, requires no special hardware, and functions much like a key to a lock; you can have a key to an individual room, a key to a building, or a master key that fits all locks in an entire complex of buildings.

As we've already noted, passwords are not foolproof. Using personal computers, telecommunications links, and a good deal of patience, an increasing number of hackers have recently been demonstrating this fact. One way to deter hackers is to disconnect any entry attempt that does not use the correct password on the first two tries. A printed log of all attempts to use the computer system can also act as a deterrent to unauthorized entry.

Machine Controls. Like any machinery, computer equipment can malfunction. It can also be misused — for example, a computer operator might inadvertently allow a tape unit to write new data over a mounted spool of tape, thus destroying the data encoded on the tape. To ensure that such occurrences won't affect the ongoing operations of the business, certain precautions should be taken.

One precaution found in any business data processing operation is the creation of backup files — that is, second copies of data files and programs that can be stored away for future reference. Backup files should be stored in locations completely separate from the main computer system. Thus, if data and programs are destroyed because of head crashes, problems with humidity or temperature, power failures or fluctuations, fire, natural disasters, or any other reason, the firm can recover the data and programs from the backup library. Transaction data, as well as the data on master files, are copied; so the business can, if necessary, reprocess all the data and reconstruct the complete files.

Write-protect rings for tape drives are useful in preventing the misuse of this equipment and the consequent destruction of data. The tape unit is usually set up so that it can either read or write data on a mounted spool of tape; when a write-protect ring is used, the unit can't write data unless the write-protect ring is installed in the center of the tape (see Figure 20.2). Because installing the write-protect ring requires a conscious effort on the part of the computer operator, the chance of erasing data by accidental writing is reduced.

Some new computer systems have **self-checking mechanisms** that test the circuits each time operations begin. The simultaneous running of a diagnostic program and monitoring of the electronics reduces the odds that an equipment failure or malfunction will occur during actual processing. Some of these systems have built-in redundant circuits that are automatically activated when a problem in the main circuits is identified.

Physical Controls. Physical controls involve designing computer centers to minimize threats from fire, natural disasters, and various environmental factors, and controlling access to areas where the computer, data, and outputs are stored.

To minimize the risk of fire, the area for output activities should be physically separate from the central processing unit (Figure 20.3). Output activities usually involve a lot of paper and other combustible materials. Keeping such materials near the processing equipment increases the risk

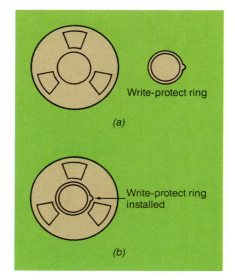

Figure 20.2
The functioning of a write-protect ring. When the write-protect ring is removed (*a*), the tape can only be read. When the write-protect ring is in place (*b*), the tape can be both read and written to.

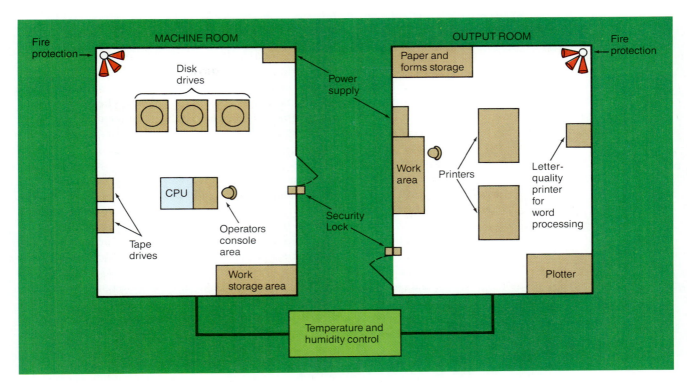

Figure 20.3
Suggested physical design for a computer center.

of fire since a spark caused by a malfunction in one of the CPU's electrical cables, connections, or other components could easily ignite them. If a fire should break out in the CPU area, it can be extinguished more easily if the bulk of flammable materials is located elsewhere; by the same token, a fire in the input/output area won't damage the processing equipment. Another important consideration in controlling computer fires is the development of a firefighting plan that ensures that both personnel and firefighters know where materials are stored and that they use appropriate chemicals and techniques (e.g., if Halon gas is used in fire extinguishers instead of water or other liquids, damage to sensitive components, such as the electronic circuits and magnetic media, can be avoided).

The design of the computer center should also take into consideration the threats to security posed by natural disasters. Floods can be caused not only by the overflowing of nearby bodies of water but also by drainage backups in a sewer system. It's therefore advisable to locate the computer center on floors not likely to be reached by any water level. Limiting the number of windows in a new building or blocking windows in an existing building reduces the chances of water damage from high winds that can shatter the glass, allowing rain or snow to pour in. In areas prone to earthquakes, special building designs are required.

If the computer is being housed in an old building, existing water and steam pipes can create serious environmental problems, since if the pipes were to burst, they could cause a lot of damage. Thus, in an old building, the computer room and the floors above it should be checked for such possibilities. The area around a computer room, whether in a new or an old building, should also be checked for electric motors or other elements that, by creating magnetic fields, can alter or destroy the data stored on magnetic media. As a safeguard against power failures, independent or uninterruptible power supplies should be available.

Problems related to temperature and humidity can be controlled by special air-conditioning units or by an **environmental control system.** Such a system will prevent the buildup of static electricity; static electricity, by creating shorts or sparks, can alter the data stored on magnetic media. An environmental control system will also give longer life to electronic components and help prevent the erratic errors, unaccounted for by programs or data entered, that sometimes occur in computer systems. Usually, an environmental control system is not shared by other units in a building; it is devoted solely to the computer center. Also, it is often designed to have excess capacity so that it will be able to maintain the desired environment regardless of external conditions.

Controlling access to the areas where the computer, data, and outputs are stored is probably the easiest physical control to implement. Given the ways in which people — intentionally or otherwise — have done physical damage to computer systems, it is also an important control. Obviously, the best way of preventing such damage is to make it difficult for people to locate and gain access to the computer. For this reason, the computer is no longer the "million-dollar bowling trophy" that companies were once so proud to display in a glass case located on the main floor of corporate headquarters. Many computer facilities these days are located away from headquarters in isolated buildings with no identifying signs, a limited number of entries and exits, and few, if any, windows. Security guards are posted, and identifying badges or electronically sensitized plastic are often required for entry. Instead of badges or cards, some facilities use devices that can identify individuals by voice patterns or fingerprints (see Figure 20.4).

The extent of the security measures taken to control physical access depends on the sensitivity of the system and the data. Access to a bank's computer system may be carefully controlled because of the nature of the data and the importance of keeping the system in full operation. In the headquarters of one bank, for example, the elevator does not even stop on the floor that houses the computer system; to get there, you must go to a special elevator manned by a security guard and show your identification. In contrast, a computer system that processes and stores the business records of a music store would be much less sensitive and would not require such stringent measures of access control.

Figure 20.4
Fingerprint identification in a computer center. A navy officer presents a finger for scanning to gain access to a sensitive computer facility.
Courtesy of Command Productions, Inc.

People-Oriented Controls. People play an essential role in the operation of the computer system; quite literally, they can make or break it. Because all members of a computer center's staff have some access to the system, they also have the opportunity to damage the system and to manipulate programs or data. Businesses have reduced such problems by carefully screening applicants. The screening process includes checking applicants' references and making sure they are under no undue pressures, such as serious financial problems; employing only those who have good personal records; and *bonding* employees. (Bonding means that an outside agency investigates an individual — his or her habits, credit history, and so on — and guarantees to reimburse the firm up to a specific amount if the individual misappropriates the firm's funds or resources.) A good personal record doesn't mean an employee will not try to manipulate the system; it only means that the chances are reduced.

Once hired, not every employee needs physical access to all the sensitive areas of the computer system. By determining which employees need access to which areas and by restricting them to those areas, chances for manipulation are reduced. Similarly, not every employee needs access to all the soft- and hard-copy outputs of the system. A procedure for determining who may have access to sensitive data, who should receive reports, and how reports should be distributed needs to be established. Distribution is an important consideration since an employee could gain unauthorized access to sensitive data while a report is in transit. Mail-room procedures, sealed envelopes, and courier services can be used to control the distribution of outputs. A procedure is also needed to govern program modification, since it too presents an opportunity for system manipulation.

Figure 20.5 summarizes the variety of controls that can be used to combat exposures in a computer center. Working together, these controls can form a protective envelope for the information system.

Figure 20.5
Controls for safeguarding a computer center: a protective envelope.

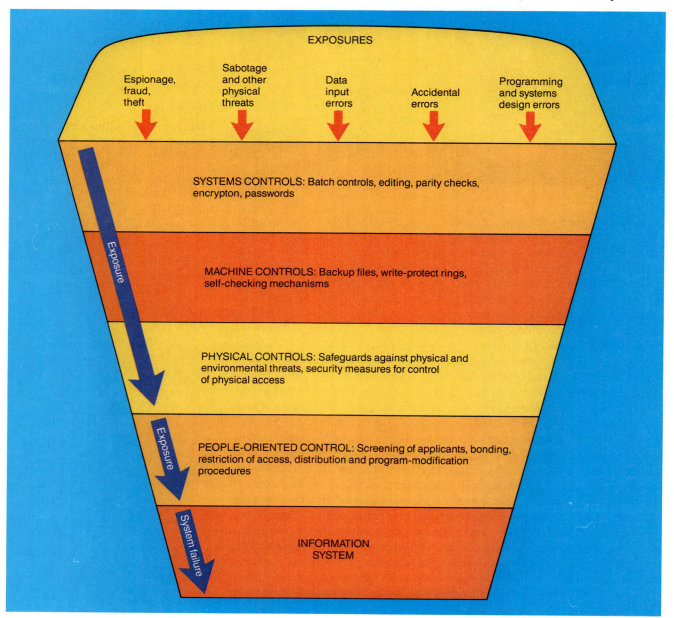

Computer Auditing

Auditors have been verifying the activities of businesses for hundreds of years using written records and paper documents and have thereby uncovered an untold number of unethical business flimflams. Because very few written records and paper documents are available for checking and review in a computer system, auditing a computer system is a far more difficult task than auditing a traditional paper-oriented business system. It is made even more challenging by the fact that many computer programs and file structures are unique and locally developed, and it is therefore difficult for the auditor to fully understand them in the short time usually available for the audit. In addition, many auditors have a limited understanding of computing technology since their training has been in accounting, not in computer systems. A number of tools have been developed to make the task of the computer auditor somewhat easier. They include the test-data method, the snapshot technique, log evaluation, and specialized audit software.

The **test-data method** verifies the accuracy of the processing by using input data that are designed to produce a particular set of results. These known data are entered in the system, unknown processing activities take place, and the auditor compares the actual output with the output that the input data should have produced. If a discrepancy shows up, it indicates either a problem with the processing activities or a program designed to manipulate the accounting system. This method gives auditors with limited computer training a method for verifying programs and applications.

The **snapshot technique** is used to get a picture of the data elements in the computer's memory at the time processing is going on. The results are not a visual photographic snapshot such as a camera would produce; rather, they are printed on a report that the auditor can use to reconstruct the processing activity that was occurring when the snapshot was taken (see Figure 20.6). Auditors use this technique mainly to determine why some computer systems produce questionable results.

Many computer systems maintain ongoing logs, or records, of all data entries, all programs run and the run times, and all terminals that have had access to the computer. By sampling this log, the auditor can get a picture of the data processing activity that has been going on (see Figure 20.7). For example, if the sampling showed that the payroll system had been accessed at an unusual time, the auditor would be alerted to look for a problem. Sampling is necessary because in most cases, the number of transactions would make it difficult, if not impossible, for the auditor to check and evaluate each transaction individually. Auditors rely on a careful evaluation of the samples taken; if the samples check out, they assume that the system is performing the other processing activities properly. **Log evaluation** is particularly useful in auditing large computer systems in which many jobs are run in the course of a day and in which many data entry devices and terminals are connected to the computer.

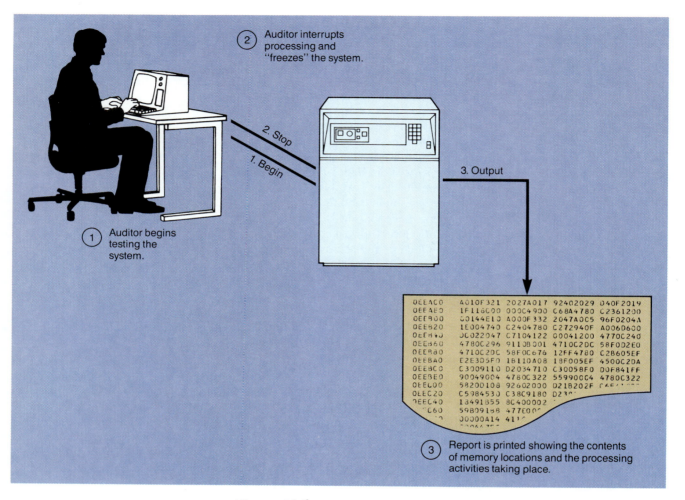

Figure 20.6
The auditor's snapshot technique.

One of the problems with auditing actual data and programs is the possibility that the auditor will accidentally destroy a file or make an error that will permanently change the program or data in some way. Auditors have often done this without being aware of it. And, at times, test data will not do the job. **Specialized audit software,** such as a Touche-Ross product called STRATA, has been developed to fill this void. Such software replicates the actual files, takes a sampling, and executes the firm's programs. With these routines, the auditor, using real data, can get an excellent picture of the actual operating characteristics of the system but can avoid the

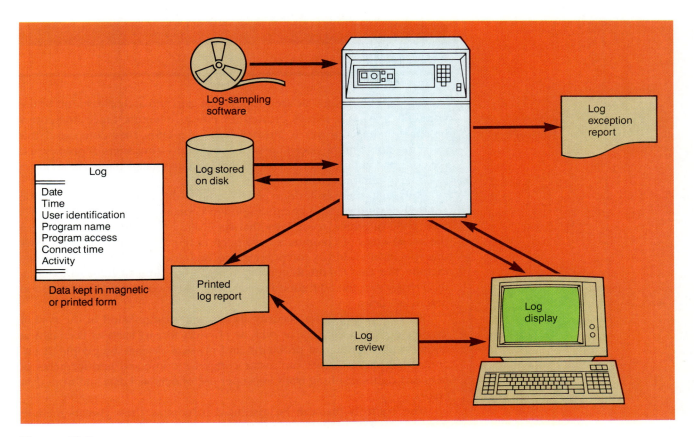

Figure 20.7
Log evaluation by an auditor. With a printed log, the auditor can review entries at random, looking for unusual activity or inappropriate access. With a disk log, software is used to extract a sample, which the auditor reviews and codes for an exception report when irregularities are found.

problems inherent in auditing actual processing runs and using the actual data files.

In any organization, the auditor is charged with testing the systems to assure management and owners that the systems are operating according to accepted standards and plans. In a sense, the auditor is the first line of defense for each individual who comes into contact with computer systems. By ensuring that the systems are operating properly, computer auditors protect individuals from manipulation, harassment, and financial loss. What started out as a sound business activity has become a useful social activity as well.

SUMMARY

The conflict between a desire for personal gain and a consideration of the common good has always created an ethical dilemma. Since computers increase people's power to further their own ends, they compound this dilemma. Some of the social costs of computers — invasions of privacy and the costs of computer crime — are rooted in an unprincipled use of computers to achieve personal gain.

Although the resolutions of the ethical dilemmas that arise in the context of business and computing often depend solely on an individual's own code of ethics, some laws that spell out a few guidelines relating to the social costs of computers have been enacted. Several states have laws that specifically address computer crime. Laws focusing on personal privacy include the Fair Credit Reporting Act, the Freedom of Information Act, the Privacy Act, the Education Privacy Act, and various state "fair information practices" laws.

Threats to computer security include the manipulation of the system by outsiders and insiders, as well as physical threats such as fire, natural disasters, environmental problems, and physical damage by people. If uncontrolled, these threats can foster computer crime and infringements of personal rights resulting from improper use of personal data and from data errors.

The controls that can be instituted to combat these threats include systems controls, machine controls, physical controls, and people-oriented controls. Systems controls are concerned with ensuring the integrity of the data and with controlling access to the data. They include batch controls, editing, parity checks, encryption, and passwords. Machine controls are aimed at reducing machine failure or misuse and the impact of such occurrences on the ongoing operations of the firm. They include the creation of backup files, the use of write-protect rings with tape drives, and the use of self-checking mechanisms in computer systems. Physical controls are aimed at minimizing threats from fire, natural disasters, and environmental problems, and at controlling access to areas where the computer, data, and outputs are stored. Controls relating to people are concerned with the hiring process, with restricting access to sensitive outputs only to those employees who actually need such access, and with procedures for program modification.

The computer auditor is the person charged with being sure the controls are in place, adequate, and functioning. Computer auditing is a far more difficult task than traditional auditing. Several tools are available to make the job of the computer auditor somewhat easier. They include the test-data method, the snapshot technique, log evaluation, and specialized audit software.

KEY TERMS

computer auditor (560)
Education Privacy Act (557)
environmental control systems (568)
Fair Credit Reporting Act (557)
fair information practices laws (557)
Federal Computer System Protection Act (557)
Freedom of Information Act (557)
log evaluation (571)
Privacy Act (557)
Privacy Protection Study Commission (557)
self-checking mechanisms (566)
snapshot technique (571)
specialized audit software (572)
test-data method (571)
write-protect rings (566)

DISCUSSION QUESTIONS

1. What is the ethical dilemma created by the proposition "If I win, you lose"? How do computers contribute to this dilemma?

2. Describe the issues that can create ethical dilemmas for business computer users. How do they relate to the social costs of computers?

3. What do you think is the most effective way of controlling computer crime and computer-related invasions of privacy?

4. Discuss three laws that have been enacted to safeguard personal privacy.

5. What are the chief threats to the security of a computer system? How do these threats relate to computer crime and to infringements of personal rights?

6. What is the purpose of systems controls? Describe the specific methods used to implement these controls.

7. Explain the purposes served by backup files, write-protect rings, and self-checking mechanisms.

8. If you were responsible for remodeling a building to house a computer center, what factors would you consider in your design?

9. Why is the hiring process in a computer center a matter of great concern? For which jobs do you think applicants should be screened most carefully? How would you go about screening them?

10. Describe the role of the computer auditor and the tools used in computer auditing.

OUTLINE

SYNTAX AND LOGIC
DATA
Numeric and String Data
Constants and Variables

ARITHMETIC EXPRESSIONS
THE INSTRUCTION SET

The PRINT, PRINTTAB, and PRINT USING Statements
The LET Statement
The READ, DATA, and RESTORE Statements
The INPUT Statement
The REM Statement and Other Documentation
The END Statement
The GOTO Statement
The IF/THEN Statement
The FOR/NEXT Statement
The DIM Statement: One-Dimensional Arrays
The DIM Statement: Two-Dimensional Arrays
The GOSUB Statement
Functions

CREATING AND ACCESSING FILES

IBM-PC, Microsoft BASIC, and TRS-80 Files
Apple Files
Commodore Files

PROBLEMS
GLOSSARY

OVERVIEW

Computers are works of engineering art. By themselves, however, they are of little value — nothing more than expensive lumps of metal, silicon, and plastic. To be useful, electronic computers must be told precisely what to do, how to do it, and the sequence in which to do it. Such detailed computer instructions are called program statements, and taken together they form a computer program. A programming language with precise rules of statement construction and punctuation provides us with a means of communicating these instructions to the computer.

Since the advent of the Computer Age, many computer languages have been written for many different purposes. Because most of these languages were developed to meet specific needs and special applications, only a few have gained widespread acceptance. One programming language that continues to be widely used is Beginner's All-Purpose Symbolic Instruction Code, or BASIC. Developed in the mid-1960s at Dartmouth College by John G. Kemeny and Thomas E. Kurtz, BASIC is today the most popular programming language for use with microcomputers. One reason for its popularity is that owing to it simple structure and relatively small number of instructions, BASIC can be easily learned.

BASIC was originally designed for use by students who had access to a large, interactive, timesharing computer system. Using BASIC and terminals connected to the computer by cables or telephone wire, numerous students could simultaneously communicate with a central computer. With the introduction of the microcomputer, BASIC broke out of the confines of the academic setting. Recognizing that microcomputers required a simple programming language if they were to realize their commercial potential, microcomputer manufacturers marketed their machines with a BASIC language interpreter (or translation program) as part of the package. Because there are so many manufacturers of computers, many versions of BASIC have evolved over the past few years. Although all versions retain certain fundamental rules, each manufacturer has added enhancements or extensions to suit its own particular hardware. The different versions of BASIC are sometimes called *dialects* of the language.

The fundamental rules of BASIC have been standardized in what is known as **ANSI** (American National Standards Institute) **BASIC.** The rules of the language and the examples and programs presented in this appendix conform to the accepted standard; they should therefore work on any system. Once you've mastered the fundamentals of the language, you can consult the proper systems manuals for any enhancements that may be present in a particular system.

APPENDIX

PROGRAMMING IN BASIC

SYNTAX AND LOGIC

The BASIC language, like any computer language, has its own **syntax** — that is, a special vocabulary and rules of grammar, spelling, and punctuation. Certain **key,** or **reserved, words** — that is, words that have a specified, unique meaning to the interpreter or translation program — must be incorporated into a program to elicit certain responses from the computer system. For example, in BASIC, the key word INPUT is used to bring data from an external device (such as a keyboard) into the computer's memory; the key word PRINT is used to take processed data out of the computer's memory and record it on an output device; the key word GOTO executes a branching instruction within the program. (As we noted in Chapter 11, **branching** means that control is transferred from one point in a program to another.)

The rules of syntax are inflexible in BASIC; the programmer must learn the rules and incorporate them into the program in their proper place. Should the programmer misspell any key words or use them inappropriately, the interpreter detects the rule violation as an error in the program and informs the user. Only when all such **syntax errors** have been removed can the computer successfully execute the program.

In addition to making syntax errors, programmers sometimes make another type of error, called a **logic error.** Logic errors arise when, even though the program is syntactically correct, the instructions are illogical and produce erroneous results. For example, if a programmer intended to add two pieces of data and print the result, but instead coded the instruction to multiply the two values and print the result, the computer would go ahead and perform the multiplication operation, even though that is not what the programmer intended. The instruction's syntax was correct (assuming that the multiplication symbol was acceptable), but the programmer was guilty of a logic error.

Because the computer is a machine, and a machine cannot possibly determine what the programmer intended, the computer will execute an illogical instruction. In other words, the computer will process instructions in the order that the programmer writes them and without regard for the logic involved. Beginning programmers find that removing syntax errors from computer programs is relatively easy since the translation program flags, or notes, the bad instruction. Finding the cause of a logic error, however, is not so simple since the computer cannot provide help in locating it.

DATA

Computer instructions in BASIC or in any other computer language manipulate data. Data are the facts and figures being computed or evaluated — for example, grades of students, telephone numbers of employees, and balances owed by customers. The data are organized in **fields** (one or more consecutive characters that together represent specific data), **records** (collections of fields), and **files** (groups of related records).

All programming languages contain instructions for the input and output of the data. For example, if the programmer wants to issue an instruction in BASIC to bring some data into memory so that they can be worked upon, the programmer writes a READ instruction. But the word READ all by itself is not complete enough. Similarly, if data are to be printed, the key word PRINT by itself is not enough. The programmer must follow the word READ with the exact data that are to be read and the word PRINT with the exact data that are to be printed.

Numeric and String Data

BASIC contains two major classifications of data: numeric data and string data. **Numeric data** refer to values that will typically be used in arithmetic operations. As the term implies, a numeric field may contain only numbers. It may also contain a decimal point and the plus or minus sign. No other characters are permitted in a numeric field. If a programmer tries to assign the name of a city or anything else that contains nonnumeric characters to a numeric field, the computer will detect this as an error and cease processing. **String data** may contain any and all characters. The word *string* implies that the contents will simply be a series (or string) of **alphanumeric data**—that is, characters made up of letters, numbers, special symbols, and/or spaces. Obviously, the computer cannot perform arithmetic operations with string data.

One of the first rules of the language has already been given: The programmer must use certain key, or reserved, words when the situation calls for them. The programmer cannot use these words indiscriminately since they have specified, unique meanings for the translation program. Because the list of key words in BASIC is quite limited as compared with lists in other languages, a beginning programmer should have little difficulty understanding how to use them and when to incorporate them into a program.

Constants and Variables

A second rule the programmer must learn is that in BASIC (or any other language, for that matter) certain fields of data will remain constant for the entire run of the program. For example, 5 percent might be taken out of each employee's pay for retirement; such an unchanging figure is called a **constant,** since it remains the same for each employee. Because in this case the constant consists of numeric data, it would be more specifically called a *numeric constant.* A *string constant,* on the other hand, consists of unchanging alphanumeric data.

In contrast to constants, certain fields change their contents or values as the program progresses; such fields are called **variables.** Most fields that computer programmers deal with consist of variable data. For example, people's names in payroll programs are *string variables;* employees' rates of pay and students' grades on examinations are *numeric variables.* Because the values of variables change, an instruction to read in a variable like rate of pay would not contain an actual value such as $12.25. What the instruction would contain is a **variable name** — a programmer-supplied label that refers to an address in the computer's main memory that contains the data. Since the value of the rates of pay may differ for each employee, the value of this variable place in memory would change repeatedly during the run of the program.

In BASIC, the rules for composing names for variables vary slightly from system to system. The examples used here follow the general ANSI rule. For numeric variables, the name may be only a single letter or a letter followed by a single number. For example, all the following names are valid for numeric variables in BASIC:

  A H9
  G1 K
  B2 R3

By the same token, the following are illegal names and would be flagged as syntax errors during program translation:

  BB (two letters)
  5C (first character is numeric)
  R-1 (contains a special character)
  T15 (contains three characters)

Note that these names are valid for numeric data only. If we attempted to assign nonnumeric, or string, characters to any of these fields, the computer would not be able to continue processing. The ANSI rule for composing a string variable name is that it must contain a single letter followed by a dollar sign (the string character) or a single letter followed by a number followed by a dollar sign. The following are examples of acceptable string variable names:

  A$ H$
  B1$ C2$
  G4$ T9$

As with numeric variable names, the use of any other characters in string variable names would result in a syntax error.

It is important to understand that when the programmer gives a variable a name such as A or A$, it means that there is a location in memory called

A or A$, and in this location are the data to be processed. The main memory of any computer has many thousands of locations to which the programmer can assign variable names. However, the computer does not "think" in the terms of the variable name contained in the program instruction but rather of the location in memory addressed by that name. The computer then manipulates the contents of the location according to what the instruction says.

For a computer to execute an instruction, a translation process in which the instruction in BASIC is converted to machine language must take place. The variable name the programmer calls A becomes a binary address in memory that will hold some value. The translation program (the compiler or the interpreter) assigns the variable name to a particular binary address; exactly which address it is assigned to is not material to the programmer. Each time a new value of A is introduced into memory either by being read in or by being computed, the old contents are erased. Because the contents of A therefore continually change, this location in memory is called a variable.

One more point should be made about the rules for composing the names of variables in BASIC. Because the newer microcomputers have much larger memories than their predecessors, the various dialects of BASIC have expanded the number of characters that are legal within a variable name. Although all names still must begin with a letter and all still use the dollar sign as the string character, some dialects now allow six, eight, or as many as thirty characters in a variable name. Some even allow a period to separate words in the name, such as in PAY.RATE. These enhancements allow the programmer to compose more meaningful names. Since one of the important aims of programming is to write code that is easy to read and understand, users of the newer micros are encouraged to take advantage of expanded names. For the sake of continuity, however, all the examples used here will conform to the ANSI standard.

Review Questions

1. What does the term *key word* mean?
2. What two types of data are used in BASIC?
3. What is the term for a field of data that changes often during a program run?
4. What are the ANSI standards for composing the names of numeric variables and string variables in BASIC?
5. What happens to the contents of a location in memory when a new field with the same variable name is read in?

ARITHMETIC EXPRESSIONS

Numeric data may be manipulated within the computer by adding, subtracting, multiplying, dividing, and raising a number to a power by exponentiation. BASIC allows the following symbols for these standard arithmetic operations:

    +   Addition
    −   Subtraction
    *   Multiplication
    /   Division
    **   Exponentiation

The first four symbols are common to all systems. However, the double asterisks, which raise a number to another power, are valid only on certain systems; other systems use an up arrow or a small caret symbol in their place. You should check the proper systems manual to determine which symbol a particular computer uses.

Unless an instruction is properly coded, the computer will never "understand" that a particular operation should take place. In BASIC, for example, the asterisk is needed for multiplication. If the intent is to multiply the contents of the variable location X by the contents of the variable location Y, the **expression** — that is, the valid mathematical formula — would be X * Y. Arithmetic expressions may contain numeric variable names, such as A, B1, and C2, and/or numeric constants, such as 25, 3.5, and 100.

In BASIC, a predetermined order governs the performance of arithmetic operations. This order is called the **hierarchy of operations.** The computer always performs arithmetic operations from left to right, but certain operations take precedence over others. In general, addition and subtraction have equal priority and are done last; multiplication and division have equal priority and are done next to last; exponentiation has the highest priority and is done first. If the programmer wants to override this natural hierarchy, the part of the expression to be done first would be placed in parentheses. The following examples illustrate the hierarchy of operations:

1. A + B − C: Causes the computer to add the values of A and B and then subtract the value of C from this sum, since addition and subtraction have equal priority.

2. A − B * C: Causes the computer to multiply the value of B by the value of C and then subtract this product from the value of A, since multiplication has priority over subtraction.

3. A/B **2: Causes the computer to square the value of B and then divide the value of A by this result, since exponentiation has first priority.

4. (A + B) * C: Causes the computer to add the values of A and B (since they are enclosed in parentheses) and multiply this sum by the value of C.

At times, the programmer may want to place parentheses around part of an expression for the sake of clarity. Using parentheses in this way will make the expression easier to read and does not violate any rule of the language. For example, D + A * 2 would be the same as D + (A * 2). In both cases, the multiplication is done first.

> **Review Questions**
>
> 1. What five arithmetic operations may be performed in BASIC?
> 2. What elements may arithmetic expressions in BASIC contain?
> 3. What does *hierarchy of operations* mean when the computer is doing arithmetic?
> 4. In the following expression, which operation would be done first? A + B/C
> 5. In the following expression, which operation would be done first? A * (B − 10)

THE INSTRUCTION SET

BASIC, like any other language, has what is known as an **instruction set,** which is the format, or the structure, of the instructions in the language. In BASIC, each instruction begins with a **line number,** any positive integer between 1 and some maximum number specified by the particular system. A systems manual must be consulted for the maximum line number for any particular system, but this number is always so high that a programmer would probably never use an illegally high number. The TRS-80 system, for example, specifies 65529 as the upper limit, and the Apple II system specifies 63999 as the upper limit.

The lowest line number does not have to be 1, nor does the increment have to be 1 each time. What is important is that each successive line number be greater than the one before it, because the computer will execute the program in line-number sequence, starting with the lowest-numbered line. Most programmers begin the first line with 10 and use 10 as the usual increment after that. This procedure allows the programmer to insert one or more new lines between existing lines. Thus, if the programmer determines that a new line has to be inserted between line 110 and line 120, the line can be given any number between 111 and 119.

When the new line or lines are entered, they are listed on the screen after the last line of the program. They therefore appear to be out of sequence, but, in fact, they are not. When the computer starts to run the program, its first step is not to execute the first line of the program, but to sort the program into sequence by line number. Thus, when the program runs, a new line will occupy an address in memory between the two existing lines. A new line 115, for example, would be inserted between lines 110 and 120, and a new instruction numbered between 210 and 220 would likewise be sorted into order. Once the sorting is complete, the computer begins executing the program, starting with the lowest-numbered line.

The line number is followed by the **statement,** the instruction that tells the computer what to do. Computers are able to execute input and output operations, arithmetic operations, and branching operations as specified by the programmer. Obviously, the commands that will tell the computer to perform these operations must be coded according to the rules of the syntax of the language. This is where the concept of the key word, or reserved word, comes in. Remember that the translation program has a repertoire of instructions it can understand. If the programmer specifies that data should be read into memory, the proper key word must be used. That is, the programmer cannot invent a key word just because it sounds reasonable. The number of key words a programmer has to learn to begin writing programs is not very large; once the most common words are understood, picking up advanced features is quite easy. The most common statements in BASIC are PRINT, LET, READ, DATA, INPUT, REM, END, GOTO, IF/THEN, and FOR/NEXT.

One more point should be made before we look at the first of the BASIC statements. After a statement is entered, a signal must be given to the computer system to show that the statement has been completed and that a new statement will begin. The signal is given by pressing the key marked ENTER or RETURN on the keyboard. This key is similar in principle to the carriage-control button on an electric typewriter. With a computer program, the key enters the instruction into memory and returns the *cursor* (the symbol on the CRT screen showing where the next character will appear) to the next line in the leftmost position of the screen. The programmer can then begin to enter the next sequential statement.

The PRINT, PRINTTAB, and PRINT USING Statements

The **PRINT** instruction directs the computer to perform an output operation — or, put another way, to route to an output device, such as a CRT screen, a printer, or a disk drive, the values specified in the statement. In the absence of an instruction to the contrary, the PRINT statement will route all output to the usual systems output device: the CRT screen attached to the computer. This is known as a *default option.*

The values displayed in response to the PRINT statement may be the variable names representing the values stored in main memory, or they may be numeric or string constants. A string constant used in a PRINT statement is referred to as a **literal** and is always enclosed in quotation marks; the computer then literally displays the data enclosed within the quotes.

The form of the PRINT statement in BASIC is as follows:

(line number) PRINT (variables and/or literals)

For example, if the programmer asks in line 100 that the values of the numeric variables A, B, and C and the string variable D$ be displayed on an output device, the command would be

100 PRINT A, B, C, D$

Note that after the key word PRINT, the names of the variables appear. Remember that when variables appear in any type of statement, the programmer is not referring to a literal A but rather to the contents of the address in memory referred to as A. Note also that spacing follows the conventions of good English composition and that the variable names are separated by commas. Commas are the usual way to separate variable names, although they may also be separated by semicolons.

By using commas, the programmer is specifying that print zones are to be used when printing (or displaying) this information. A **print zone** is a specified number of positions set aside as the length of one output field. Print zones proceed from left to right, and the number of positions varies from system to system. The size of a print zone is partly determined by the number of available positions on the output device, usually a CRT screen. For example, the TRS-80 Model III is capable of displaying 64 characters, and therefore the screen is divided into 4 print zones of 16 characters each. The Commodore has a 40-column screen that uses 4 print zones of 10 characters each. The Apple II also has a 40-column screen but uses 2 print zones of 16 characters each and 1 zone of 8 characters.

In the previous example, the value of A would be displayed in the leftmost positions of the first print zone, the value of B in the leftmost positions of the second zone, the value of C in the leftmost positions of the third zone, and the value of D$ in the leftmost positions of the fourth zone. If there are not enough print zones to display all the data requested by the print statement, the extra values start on the next line in zone 1. For example, the Apple II, which has only 3 zones, would display the values of A, B, and C on the first line and then display the contents of D$ in print zone 1 of the next line.

Literals can also be displayed by means of the PRINT statement. For example, in response to the instruction

100 PRINT "THIS IS A BASIC PROGRAM"

the computer will literally display the words that appear between the quotes. This is the rule for printing literals. The programmer may put anything between quotes, including key words. Because there is only one literal in this example, it would be printed beginning in column 1 of the output device and would continue until the entire literal is printed. It is also possible to print more than one literal:

```
100 PRINT "STUDENT NAME", "AVERAGE", "GRADE"
```

In this example, three literals are going to print. The use of commas has the same significance as in the printing of values of variables; that is, because commas separate the literals, the literals will be printed or displayed in print zones. If the value of a literal extends past the end of the print zone, the value of the next literal begins in the first position of the zone following the one partially used. For example, the literal STUDENT NAME is 12 characters long. If a Commodore with its 10-character print zone is used, the literal takes up 2 complete zones. The literal AVERAGE would be displayed beginning in print zone 3.

Any combination of literals and variables can be used on the same line. For example,

```
100 PRINT "THE AVERAGE SCORE IS", A
```

would print the literal beginning in zone 1 and the value of the variable A in the leftmost position of the zone after the end of the literal.

An arithmetic expression may also be specified in a PRINT statement, as in the following example:

```
100 PRINT "THE AVERAGE SCORE IS", A/100
```

In this case, the value printed would be the result of the arithmetic operation of dividing the value of the numeric variable A by the numeric constant 100. If, for example, the value of A is 8,500, the computer would display THE AVERAGE SCORE IS 85. Again, because the comma is used, the information would be displayed in print zones.

It is also possible to specify that the print zones be overridden and the values displayed in a more compact manner. This is accomplished by using semicolons rather than commas to separate the variables and or literals. For example,

```
100 PRINT A; B; C
```

would display the value of A in the leftmost position of the screen and then leave one space between the end of the value of A and the beginning of the value of B. Likewise, there would be one space between the end of the value of B and the beginning of the value of C. If we wanted the value of A to be printed right after a literal, we might code as follows:

```
100 PRINT "THE VALUE IS"; A
```

This code would put the value of A right after the literal instead of putting it in the next print zone.

With most systems, one additional space is left on the extreme left of the value of a numeric field for the negative sign. In other words, if the value of A is positive or zero, the value will be displayed starting in output position 2; position 1 will be left blank. If the value of A is negative, the negative sign will be placed in column 1 and the value started in column 2. This procedure would carry over to all other fields as well.

It is perfectly legal and logical to mix commas and semicolons in the same statement. For example,

    100 PRINT "A = "; A, "B = "; B

would display the characters between the quotes and immediately follow them with the value of the variable A. Since a comma follows the variable name, the characters between the second set of quotes would start in a new print zone. The value of the variable called B would then be printed after this second literal.

A limitation of the PRINT statement is that it is somewhat cumbersome to format data in columns for ease of reading. Most systems have a TAB option that overcomes this limitation. It performs much like the tabulator key on a typewriter, which moves the print mechanism over to a particular column. The general format of the **PRINTTAB** statement is as follows:

    (line number) PRINTTAB(column)(variable or literal)

When PRINT is used alone, such as in PRINT K, the value of K is placed in the leftmost position of zone 1. With TAB, one may place the value of K starting in any column. If the value of K is to be printed starting in column 10, the value of L printed starting in column 20, and the value of M printed starting in column 30, and one-letter literals were to appear over the three values, coding would be as follows:

    80 PRINTTAB(10)"K"; TAB(20)"L"; TAB(30)"M"
    90 PRINTTAB(10)K; TAB(20)L; TAB(30)M

This format should be generally acceptable, although some systems may require a space (or no space) between PRINT and TAB. Some systems also require semicolons to separate values, some require commas, and some allow either. Note that the word PRINT need appear only once on the line.

Using the option of PRINTTAB, the programmer may easily arrange general headings, column headings, and the data under these headings in ways that are more meaningful to the user of the output. If a number used in TAB is not beyond the end of the previous value, such as TAB(20)A; TAB(10)B, the value of B will be printed just to the right of the end of the value of A since it cannot possibly be printed beginning in column

10, as requested. Also, if TAB(10)"PROGRAM"; TAB(14)"ONE" were coded, the word *one* would be printed starting in column 17 since the word *program* would occupy columns 10 through 16.

The **PRINT USING** statement is a very convenient feature for formatting columns of data. With this feature, the programmer can override the restrictions of the other forms of PRINT and make the output appear much more attractive and meaningful. Unfortunately, PRINT USING is not part of the ANSI standard. Its syntax varies between systems even when it is allowed; you should consult a systems manual for the exact syntax for any particular system.

In general, the format of PRINT USING is that an "image" of the output is coded along with the command to print it. The following example would print four pieces of numeric data. (The format should be appropriate for many systems, among them the IBM/Microsoft and the Apple MacIntosh.)

```
170 PRINT USING 300, I, H, R, G
...
300: #######       ##.#       $##.##       $$##.##
```

Line 170 says to use the image found in line 300 when printing the four variables named. The first variable, called I, is seven integers long and should be printed starting in print column 1. This will be followed by seven blank spaces. The value of the next variable, H, will then be printed with a decimal point and one number to the right of the decimal point. This will be followed with seven blank spaces. The value of R will be printed with a dollar sign in a fixed position, two integers, a decimal point, and two decimal positions. This will be followed by seven blank spaces. The value of G will be printed with a dollar sign that will "float" to the first significant digit, as many as three integers, a decimal point, and two decimals. If one or more leading zeros appear in a field, spaces will be printed instead of zeros. The colon after line number 300 indicates that it is not a command to the system but a line referred to by another line.

The printing of string data differs from the printing of numeric data. The IBM Microsoft and the Apple MacIntosh have different codes for leading and trailing blanks and for centering the field. The following example asks that the value of a left-justified string field be printed in positions 1 through 20 and that a second string field be centered in positions 30 through 40:

```
170 PRINT USING 300, A$, B$
300: 'LLLLLLLLLLLLLLLLLLLL        'CCCCCCCCCC
```

The apostrophe followed by twenty Ls means that a twenty-character string field is to be printed and that the field should be left-justified. The entering of the apostrophe followed by ten Cs means that a ten-character string field should be centered in this field. Other options are available with PRINT USING and are explained in the systems manuals.

Review Questions

1. What may appear after the word PRINT?
2. What happens when the value of a variable or a literal extends over the end of a print zone?
3. Write PRINT statements to do the following: (a) print the values of F and G in zones 1 and 2; (b) print the literal ACCOUNTING REPORT starting in zone 1; (c) print the literal TOTAL SALES and variable T beginning in print zone 1 and separated by a single space.
4. Prepare the following BASIC statements: (a) a PRINTTAB statement to print variable C starting at print position 26 and a literal "CLASS LIST" starting at print position 40; (b) a PRINT USING statement to print a floating dollar sign, six integers, a decimal point, and two decimals starting at print position 1.
5. What are the advantages of the PRINT USING statement?

The LET Statement

The command **LET** assigns a value to a variable — either a numeric variable or a string variable. The general format of the LET statement is as follows:

(line number) LET (variable name) = (value or expression)

The LET statement actually puts the value in a storage location in memory. Because only a variable can represent a storage location, the entry between the key word LET and the equal sign must be a legal variable name. On the right side of the equal sign will appear the name of a variable, the name of a constant, or an arithmetic expression. All the following statements are legal within the language:

```
150 LET X = Y
160 LET Z = 8.8
170 LET A = B * C
180 LET D$ = E$
190 LET Z$ = "THE END"
```

Line 150 assigns the value of Y to the variable X. In other words, if the value of Y happens to be 175, once the statement is executed, both fields will contain 175. This instruction simply causes the computer to copy the value of one field into another. It does not erase the contents of Y from memory after the statement is executed, but it does erase all the previous contents of X. For example, if X contained 1,000 before execution, the new value of 175 replaces the old value, and the old value is lost. This would be so under all circumstances.

Line 160 says to replace the contents of the variable called Z with the numeric constant value 8.8. After execution, then, the value of Z would be 8.8, regardless of its contents before the statement was executed. Line 170 says to replace the previous contents of the variable A with the results of the arithmetic expression on the right side of the equal sign. After execution, variable A holds the new value, and the values of B and C remain unchanged.

Lines 180 and 190 are examples of LET using string data. In line 180, the value of the string variable D$ is replaced with the value of the string variable E$, with the value of E$ remaining unchanged after execution. Line 190 replaces the previous contents of Z$ with the literal, or string constant, THE END.

The following examples are illegal within the language and would cause the computer to issue syntax error messages:

```
200 LET Z  = C$
210 LET Z$ = A
220 LET Z$ = X/Y
230 LET K  = "WELCOME"
```

These statements are illegal for the following reasons: Line 200 attempts to assign the value of a string variable to a numeric variable; line 210 attempts to assign the value of a numeric variable to a string variable; line 220 attempts to assign the results of an arithmetic expression to a string variable; and line 230 attempts to assign the literal, or string constant, between the quotes to a numeric variable. The computer stops executing the program when it comes across illegal instructions such as these and issues a message to the programmer — for example, SYNTAX ERROR, followed by the line number that caused the error. The programmer must then examine this line and take corrective action.

Almost all, if not all, systems today allow the programmer to omit the word LET. In other words, LET has become a *noise word* — an optional word that may make a statement more descriptive but may or may not be used, depending on the programmer's preference. For example, these two statements would produce exactly the same results:

```
100 LET X = Y * Z
110 X = Y * Z
```

Although the word LET is no longer mandatory, beginning programmers should probably use it because of its descriptive nature. Look at this expression, for example:

100 X = X + 1

Literally, this statement says that X is equal to X + 1. But how can X be equal to more than itself? When the word LET is used in the statement, the meaning is clearer: Assign to X the value of itself plus 1. In this appendix, we will use the optional word LET whenever we assign a value to a variable, even though use of the word may not be necessary.

As an example of putting the PRINT statement and the LET statement together in a small program, suppose that the value of A is to be 150 and the value of B is to be 225, and these values are to be added and placed in a field called C; then the values in all three fields are to be printed. We might code such a program as follows:

```
10 LET A = 150
20 LET B = 225
30 LET C = A + B
40 PRINT "VALUE OF A", "VALUE OF B", "VALUE OF C"
50 PRINT A, B, C
```

Although this is an extremely short program (only five lines long), it is a valid example of how BASIC statements are set up. Line 40 would print the three literals in the first three print zones, and line 50 would print the three values right under each literal. One thing, however, is missing. If we typed only these five lines, we would wait forever for the computer to execute the instructions and print the output as described. The computer would not respond because all that has been coded are five expressions in BASIC — that is, five statements, each with a line number as its first entry. To get the computer to respond, the programmer must tell the computer that the last statement has been coded and the program should now be executed. Because there is no statement within the BASIC language that can communicate this message, the programmer must issue a systems command.

A **systems command** (which does not get a line number) is a command to the operating system to perform some function. For example, the systems command **RUN** tells the system to start executing the program. In response, the system will first sort the lines by line number and then start executing the statement that has the lowest line number. Another useful systems command is **LIST**, which tells the system to display the entire program on the screen in line-number order. If, for example, a three-line program was coded consecutively with line numbers 30, 20, and 10 and the programmer typed LIST, the lines would be sorted and listed in ascending order. When the programmer spots an error in a program that has been displayed by using the LIST command, several ways of correcting it exist. The most obvious way to correct an error is to type in a whole new line, but the line may also be edited instead of completely retyped. Different systems use different methods for line editing; these methods are explained in the appropriate systems manuals.

Review Questions

1. What is the purpose of the LET statement?
2. What may appear to the left of the equal sign?
3. What may appear to the right of the equal sign?
4. What would happen if you tried to assign the answer to an arithmetic operation to a string variable?
5. Prepare LET statements to do the following: (a) assign the value 12 to D; (b) add 1 to the variable A.

The READ, DATA, and RESTORE Statements

Before the computer can assign values to variables in response to the key word LET and before it can display data on an output device in response to the key word PRINT, the data have to be brought into main memory from an input device. Actually, there are two ways of bringing data into memory: by using the key word READ and by using the key word INPUT. **READ** is used when the data are included in the program itself. The **INPUT** statement, which we will discuss in the next section, stops the program during execution and allows data to be entered at that point from a keyboard. Which word is used depends on when the programmer plans to enter the data — before the program is run, or during program execution.

As we noted earlier, without instructions to the contrary, the PRINT statement causes the output to be printed on the CRT screen; similarly, the word READ causes the keyboard to be used as the input device. The general format of the READ statement is as follows:

(line number) READ (variable names)

The minimum number of variable names that may appear in a READ statement is one, and there is no limit to the number of variable names that may appear on one line. That is, if the programmer wants to bring in an employee's identification number and hours worked, the programmer could code a single READ statement containing both variable names:

10 READ N, H

The programmer could also code two separate statements:

    10 READ N
    20 READ H

Since statement 20 is the next statement following the first READ, these two instructions would produce the same results as the instruction in the first example. Good style dictates that both variables be entered in one READ, but the computer would not issue an error message if the variables were coded as separate statements.

The variable names in a READ statement must be separated from each other by commas. No comma may appear after the last variable. For example, if the programmer wanted to issue a READ statement to bring into memory the values of a student number, a student name, and the student's scores on three exams, the READ statement might look like this:

    10 READ S, N$, E1, E2, E3

To compute the average of the three exams and then to print out the number, name, and average, the programmer might code the following:

    20 LET A = (E1 + E2 + E3)/3
    30 PRINT S, N$, A

In the three statements just given, something is missing. When the computer is asked to execute a READ statement, somehow and somewhere the values of the variables that it is being asked to read have to be specified. With no allowance for the values of the variables given in this program, the computer would stop executing it because it would be illogical to continue without knowing the value of S or of any of the other four variables.

The syntax of BASIC demands that when READ is used, an additional line must be coded to assign values to all the variables named in READ. Values are assigned to the variable names in READ by the **DATA** statement. The DATA statement for the small program just described would contain an actual student number, an actual name, and actual scores for the three exams. In contrast to the READ, LET, and PRINT statements, the DATA statement does not contain an operation code. For this reason, it makes no difference what line number is assigned to a DATA statement. Although the DATA statement may be coded anywhere in the program, programmers usually code DATA statements at the very bottom of the program. Putting DATA statements in the middle of the program clutters up the flow of logic, but putting them at the bottom does not interfere with the other statements, which, because they contain operation codes, must be coded in the order in which they are to be executed.

Our three-line program, coded with the additional DATA statement, would look like this:

```
10 READ S, N$, E1, E2, E3
20 LET A = (E1 + E2 + E3)/3
30 PRINT S, N$, A
40 DATA 1234, FRANK SMITH, 93, 87, 75
```

Note that there are five values in the DATA statement, and each value is separated from the next by a comma. When the computer comes across READ for the first time, it finds the first DATA statement and assigns the first value (1234) to the variable named S; the next value (FRANK SMITH) to the variable named N$; and the values 93, 87, and 75 to E1, E2, and E3, respectively. Although it is not important to the computer where the DATA statement is coded (it could even be coded as the first statement in the program), it is very important that the values in the DATA statement be entered in correct sequence to match the purpose of the variables named in the READ statement. For example, if a DATA statement was coded as

```
40 DATA FRANK SMITH, 1234, 93, 87, 75
```

the programmer would be asking that a string value (Frank Smith) be assigned to a numeric variable. Under these conditions, the computer would stop and issue the programmer an error message indicating that the value in the DATA statement does not agree with the mode of the variable name. It is also very important that there be enough data in the DATA statement to fill all of the variables in the READ statement; that is, if there are five variables in the READ statement, the DATA statement must contain five data elements.

The number of DATA statements, like the number of READ statements, is not important to the computer. For example, coding the values as follows would produce the same results as the other example did:

```
40 DATA 1234
50 DATA FRANK SMITH
60 DATA 93
70 DATA 87
80 DATA 75
```

Although this syntax is perfectly legal within the language, it would obviously be a waste of time to code statements in this way; it would also invite all sorts of clerical errors.

One more point about the syntax of the DATA statement should be made. Originally, the syntax of BASIC demanded that the value of a string variable like FRANK SMITH in a DATA statement be enclosed in double quotes — for example:

```
40 DATA 1234, "FRANK SMITH", 93, 87, 75
```

Some systems may still demand that double quotes be used, although most systems now allow the value to be coded in the DATA statement without quotes. Even without the quotes, the computer knows where the value of the string variable ends since it reads all the characters until it comes to a comma, which it recognizes as the end of the string value. Leaving a space after each comma is merely a matter of style; it does not affect the legality of the DATA statement in any way.

The programming example in Figure A.1 brings in all the statements considered thus far, including PRINT, LET, READ, and DATA. Line 10 of the program instructs the computer to print literal column headings in the first five print zones. Line 20 instructs it to read in four variables: the employee's identification number, name, rate of pay, and hours worked. Line 30 sets the value of the variable G equal to the value of R multiplied by the value of H. Line 40 sets the value of the variable D equal to the value of G multiplied by the numeric constant .25 (25 percent). Line 50 sets the value of the variable N equal to the value of G minus the value of D. Line 60 prints the five values. Because the commas are used to separate the variable names, the computer will print the values under the proper headings. Line 70 is the statement that assigns the values to the variable names found in line 20.

One point should be made about the variable name chosen for the employee identification number (I, in this example). Since this field is not to be used to do arithmetic, the programmer has the choice of calling the field either numeric or string. It is important to be consistent in the type of name assigned to such fields. That is, they should always be called numeric or always be called string. Consistency in naming would minimize, and probably eliminate, chances for clerical error when entering data. In the examples that follow, fields such as identification numbers will always be assigned numeric variable names.

Occasionally, values entered through DATA statements need to be used more than once. The **RESTORE** statement allows the *data pointer* — the means by which the computer keeps track of which data have been used and where it left off in the DATA statements — to be positioned at the

```
10  PRINT "NUMBER","NAME","GROSS","DEDUCTIONS","NET"
20  READ I,N$,R,H
30  LET G = R * H
40  LET D = G * .25
50  LET N = G - D
60  PRINT I,N$,G,D,N
70  DATA 3456, MARY BROWN, 10.00, 40
```

Figure A.1
BASIC program containing the PRINT, LET, READ, and DATA statements.

Figure A.2
Use of the RESTORE statement.

```
10  PRINT "NUMBER","NAME","GROSS","DEDUCTIONS","NET"
20  READ I,N$,R,H
30  LET G = R * H
40  LET D = G * .25
50  LET N = G - D
60  PRINT I,N$,G,D,N
70  DATA 3456, MARY BROWN, 10.00, 40
80  RESTORE
90  READ I,N$,R,H
```

lowest numbered line that contains a DATA statement; thus, data read previously can be reread. The syntax of this command is simply the word RESTORE.

If, for example, the program shown in Figure A.1 required additional processing activities using the data a second time, the instructions might look like those shown in Figure A.2. Line 80 instructs the computer to position the data pointer at the first data element found in line 70, even though the data have already been used for previous computation and printing. Using line 90, the computer can now read the data into main memory for additional processing.

Review Questions

1. What character is used to separate values in DATA statements?
2. What would happen if the computer found a string value in the DATA statement when the READ statement called for a numeric value?
3. What would happen if the computer came across a READ statement and no DATA statement could be found?
4. What is the function of the RESTORE statement?
5. Prepare a READ statement to do the following: (a) read a string variable called N$ and a numeric variable called P; (b) read a series of four numeric variables called I1, I2, I3, I4; (c) read the name and employee number for six different employees (you select the appropriate variable names).

The INPUT Statement

As mentioned in the previous section, the key word INPUT can be used to bring into main memory data values from the keyboard and to assign the values to variable locations in memory. INPUT works very much like the key word READ. However, INPUT has no accompanying statement like the DATA line always used with READ. The syntax of the INPUT statement is as follows:

   (line number) INPUT (variable names)

A READ command would be coded in this way:

   10 READ A, B, C

With INPUT, the syntax for the same command would be as follows:

   10 INPUT A, B, C

The syntax, then, is almost identical. As in READ, the variables must be separated by commas, and the minimum number of variable names on a line is one. The big difference is that the INPUT statement does not have the equivalent of a DATA statement. Remember that when the computer encounters READ, it looks for (and should find) a DATA statement somewhere in the program. With INPUT, the computer stops execution when it comes across the INPUT command and, by displaying a question mark on the screen, asks the programmer to enter the values from the keyboard.

When the INPUT statement is used, the programming is *interactive*; that is, the programmer and the computer are in a conversational mode, communicating in a question-and-answer environment. When it encounters INPUT, the computer stops and displays a question mark. The programmer then enters the values of the variables asked for. Once the values are successfully entered, the computer picks up the program with the next statement and executes all statements until it comes across another INPUT statement. The computer then asks the programmer for more values, and the process is repeated until the program is finished.

Like the values in READ statements, the values called for by INPUT may be included in multiple statements or in a single statement. For example, the computer would interpret three lines coded as

   10 INPUT A
   20 INPUT B
   30 INPUT C

just as it would if the three variable names were included in a single statement. Again, as with READ, good style dictates how many variables should be included in a single INPUT statement.

If all three variable names are included in one statement, the programmer has two options. The first option is to enter the values, separated by commas, on one line; the second option is to press the ⟨RETURN⟩ or ⟨ENTER⟩ key after each value. Suppose, for example, that the values to be assigned to A, B, and C are 100, 200, and 300, and that the computer comes across this statement:

    10 INPUT A, B, C

The programmer may enter the values as follows:

    100, 200, 300 ⟨ENTER⟩

The programmer may also enter the values in this way:

    100 ⟨ENTER⟩
    200 ⟨ENTER⟩
    300 ⟨ENTER⟩

As might be expected, if the value entered by the programmer is string and the variable name in the INPUT statement is numeric, the computer stops and issues an error message. For example, if the statement looks like this:

    10 INPUT A

and, responding to the question mark, the programmer types HELLO, an error message will result because the value of a numeric variable can be only valid numeric characters.

Another point about entering values with INPUT is that a string value must be enclosed in quotes. Remember that in most systems, the value of the string variable found in the DATA statement does not have to be enclosed in quotes; but it may be if the programmer so desires. Quotes are not optional with INPUT. If the variable in the INPUT statement is N$, and the programmer types JOHN without quotes, the system responds with REDO or something similar.

When entering numeric values, the programmer must make sure that the only characters entered are the legal numeric characters: 0 through 9, a decimal point, the plus sign, and the minus sign. String values must be enclosed in quotes. The following examples illustrate these rules:

    10 INPUT I, N$, H, R
    20 LET G = R * H
    30 PRINT I, N$, G

Assume that this program is asking that an identification number, a name, the hours worked, and the rate of pay be entered. Since the first statement is an INPUT statement, the computer would display a question mark on the screen. The programmer would respond in this way:

1234, "FRANK SMITH", 40, 12.55

The computer would then assign the first value (1234) to I, the second value (FRANK SMITH) to N$, and the values 40 and 12.55 to H and R. The computer would then proceed to statement 20, perform the arithmetic, and execute statement 30 to print out the results. If, however, the programmer entered FRANK SMITH first, the computer would issue an error message, just as it would if FRANK SMITH was not enclosed in quotes.

A feature of INPUT not found in READ is the ability to code **prompts** into the INPUT statement. Prompts help the person interacting with the program to understand what data are required. They are especially useful when many INPUT statements are interspersed throughout the program, since the programmer must know exactly what types of values the computer expects. Using the example just given, we might extend the input statement to read as follows:

10 INPUT "ENTER ID, NAME, HOURS, RATE"; I, N$, H, R

When the program is run, this instruction causes the computer to print the message within the quotes on the screen. Note the syntax of the statement. After the completion of the prompt (the close quote), a semicolon must be entered to separate the prompt from the variable names. The variable names, as always, must be separated by commas. When the program is running and the computer executes this statement, the computer will display the prompt and put the question mark right after the prompt instead of on a separate line. The following would appear on the screen:

ENTER ID, NAME, HOURS, RATE ?

The user responds by keying in the desired values (separated by commas) and pressing ⟨ENTER⟩. The computer assigns the four values to the four variable names, and the program then goes on to the next statement. As happens with INPUT without the prompts, if the programmer enters only three values, the system will respond with another question mark.

Some systems, like Apple II, will not display the question mark after the prompt, while others, like the TRS-80, will. This should not cause a problem, but it is something to be aware of. For example, if the programmer wanted to enter a prompt in the form of a question, the prompt might look something like this:

10 INPUT "WHAT IS THE CUSTOMER'S ID NUMBER"; I

If the system being used (such as the TRS-80) included the question mark automatically, this statement would suffice. If, on the other hand, the question mark was not displayed automatically, the programmer could alter this statement by putting a question mark within the quotes:

10 INPUT "WHAT IS THE CUSTOMER'S ID NUMBER ?"; I

Putting the question mark within the prompt makes the message generated by the INPUT statement a little clearer when the program is being executed.

Prompts are not part of ANSI BASIC but are available on most systems. If this feature is not available, the programmer can provide prompts by coding the statement with two lines, the first being a PRINT statement. For example,

10 PRINT "ENTER ID, NAME, HOURS, RATE"
20 INPUT I, N$, H, R

will provide the same type of prompt as we saw in our earlier example. Because the PRINT statement contains a literal message in quotes, the literal will be displayed on the screen just as the prompt is. By entering a semicolon as the last character of a PRINT statement, the programmer is asking the computer not to issue a carriage control. In other words, if the semicolon is used, the question mark generated by the INPUT statement in line 20 would be displayed on the same line as the PRINT statement. If the semicolon is not coded as the last character of the PRINT statement, the question mark would be displayed on the line following the printed line. In any event, whether or not the semicolon is used, the computer would proceed to statement 20 and see that the INPUT statement asks that four values be entered.

Review Questions

1. What is the general format of the INPUT statement?
2. What does the computer do when it encounters an INPUT statement?
3. How many variable names can appear with a single INPUT statement?
4. What is a prompt?
5. Give an example of an INPUT statement with a prompt asking the programmer to enter the current date.

The REM Statement and Other Documentation

At times, the programmer may want to enter into the program certain notes or comments to describe certain functions that are taking place. All programming languages have built into their instruction sets a feature for entering this kind of documentation into the program. The key word used to make a descriptive comment within a BASIC program is **REM** (an abbreviation for the word *remark*). REM can be very useful. For example, the variable names in older versions of BASIC are often restricted to one letter or a letter and a number; a programmer working with an older version of BASIC can use a REM statement to better describe the meaning of the variable names and the logic of the program.

A REM statement may be incorporated into a program whenever the programmer believes that a remark is warranted. A program may have dozens of remarks or no remarks at all; it is entirely up to the programmer. The general format of the REM statement is as follows:

(line number) REM (followed by the note or comment)

For example, if the programmer wants to code a remark that lists the name of the program as the first entry in the program, it may be entered like this:

10 REM ***** STUDENT GRADE PROGRAM *****

Any character may follow a REM statement. The asterisks that we've just used are purely optional; they merely make the message stand out. REM statements may also include key words. The computer will ignore the REM statement during the execution of the program. REM is not a command to the computer to do anything; it simply makes a descriptive comment. Programmers in BASIC or in any other language often make comments about what the program is doing during certain phases so that errors become easier to locate.

A programmer using a version of BASIC that restricts a variable name to one letter or a letter and a number might code REM statements at the beginning of the program to explain what the variable names mean. For example:

10 REM **** I = STUDENT ID NUMBER ****
20 REM **** N$ = STUDENT NAME ****
30 REM **** E1, E2, E3 = EXAM GRADES ****

Like REM statements, *program flowcharts*, which show the processing steps needed to solve a problem, also serve to document the program. As

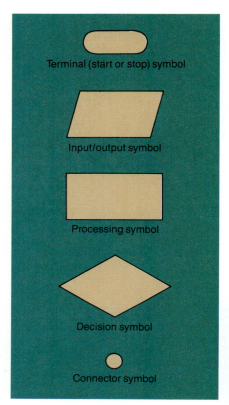

Figure A.3
Program flowchart symbols.

we noted in Chapter 11, these charts provide a road map for tracing the program logic from the first step to the last. Figure A.3 reviews the symbols recommended by the American National Standards Institute for use in program flowcharting. As we also noted in Chapter 11, *pseudocode* is another tool that can be used to document the logic of the program. It uses a combination of programming syntax and English words to describe what the program is to accomplish. Figure A.4 shows how both a flowchart and pseudocode would document the logic of a program for reading in some inventory data, computing the total cost, and printing the output.

For a very small problem, the construction of a flowchart might not seem worth the time it takes to prepare it. Although this may be true for a program with only a few instructions, beginning programmers all too often carry this thinking over to larger problems and consequently fail to plan sufficiently for the writing of more complex programs. Any experienced programmer will agree that time spent in the design phase of the program will pay dividends when you have to locate and correct logic errors later

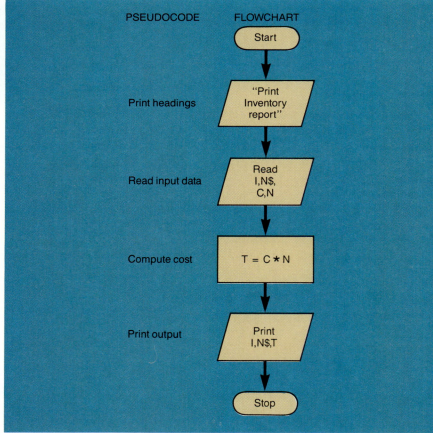

Figure A.4
Problem solution in pseudocode and flowchart form.

on. If the programmer has done a thorough job in the planning phase, logic errors should not occur. If one does appear, the careful programmer will know exactly what part of the program caused the problem and will be able to correct the error with a minimum of effort.

> **Review Questions**
>
> 1. How are comments or notes inserted into a program?
> 2. What is the purpose of REM?
> 3. Can REM be coded on the same line as another statement within the language? Why or why not?
> 4. What other program documentation is used besides the REM statement?
> 5. Prepare a REM statement to (a) identify a program name; (b) identify a programmer's name; (c) describe several variables that will be used in the program.

The END Statement

Many systems no longer require the END statement in a BASIC program. Originally, END had to be present within the program, and it had to be assigned the highest line number. The **END** statement served two purposes: It told the computer the program was over (no more executable statements), and it was a reference point that programmers used to signal that they had come to the logical termination of the program. Although the END statement is usually not required today, many programmers still prefer to use it since it does serve as a reference point signaling the termination of the program. Often the programmer uses a line number such as 999 for the END statement regardless of the line number of the previous statement. The general syntax of the END statement is as follows:

(line number) END

The GOTO Statement

Figure A.5 contains the REM, INPUT, PRINT, READ, DATA, LET, and END statements. It is an example of a *single-pass program* — that is, a program that has no provision for branching or looping; the instructions are executed

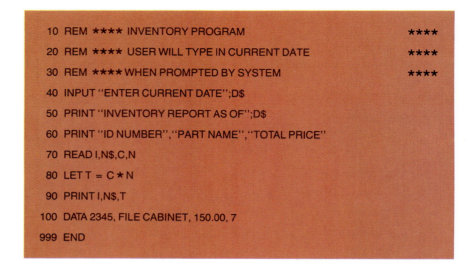

Figure A.5
A single-pass program.

one time only. A single-pass program would be sufficient for processing only one unit of inventory. If a company had a thousand different items in its inventory, it would have two choices — to write the READ, LET, and PRINT statements a thousand times, or to return, or branch back, to the READ statement (line 70) after each line was printed in response to the PRINT statement in line 90. Branching back would allow the READ, LET, and PRINT instructions to be executed again and again. Repetitive branching within the program is called a **loop.**

In BASIC, the command that directs the computer to branch unconditionally from one place in the program to another is the key word **GOTO.** The GOTO statement allows the computer to branch back and execute a loop repeatedly. However, in the absence of an instruction to stop the loop, an **infinite loop** will occur; the computer has no way to break the cycle and will execute the loop an infinite number of times. In other words, something has to be present to inform the computer that it has looped as many times as the programmer wants, and now another action should take place.

The loop can be terminated in one of two ways. One way is for the computer to count the number of times it executes the loop and to take an alternative action when it has executed the loop the desired number of times. The second way is for the computer to continually search the READ statement for a signal that the last desired record has been processed. When it encounters this signal, the computer stops executing the loop and takes alternative action. With either option, the program must contain an instruction that asks, each time the loop is executed, whether the condition that terminates the loop has arisen. The progammer would include such an instruction by incorporating an **IF/THEN** statement in the program.

The IF/THEN statement is a **conditional branch** — that is, the branch, or transfer of control from one point in the program to another, takes place only if a certain condition is met. In contrast, the GOTO instruction is an **unconditional branch** — that is, it causes control to be transferred every time the statement is executed.

The general format of the GOTO instruction is as follows:

(line number) GOTO (another line number)

For example, if at line number 250 the programmer coded a GOTO instruction to branch to instruction 30, the instruction would look like this:

250 GOTO 30

Obviously, unless a line in the program is numbered 30, an error will result. The GOTO statement provides one reason for numbering lines in the program (another reason for numbering is that the program is executed in line-number sequence from low to high). The GOTO command does not say GOTO READ or GOTO LET; it says GOTO a specific place in the program that is identified by a line number.

Referring back to the inventory program in Figure A.5, if a GOTO was inserted after the PRINT statement on line 90, the flowchart and the resulting program would look like those shown in Figure A.6. Even a cursory examination of the logic of this program reveals that something is radically wrong. What is the sense of branching back if all data have been processed? Suppose, however, that ten more DATA statements numbered 110 through 200 are inserted. This would be a start in the right direction; if there is another DATA statement, the computer will take the values in this statement and assign them to the variables named in READ. For example, if the program contained a line numbered 110, which looked like this:

110 DATA 2567, WORK BENCH, 250.00, 10

the computer would assign these four values to the four variables named in the READ statement, just as it did when it executed the READ statement for the first time. These new values would replace the old values in the four variable locations in memory. Remember that these locations in memory are called variables because the values change often during the run of the program. If there were other DATA statements after statement 110, the same pattern would apply: The computer would continually assign the four values in each DATA statement to the locations in memory referenced by the READ statement.

Although adding DATA statements gives the computer something to process, it does not solve the problem of how to tell the computer to get out of the loop and stop the program after it has processed all the data. For example, look at the END statement on line 999 in Figure A.6. Even

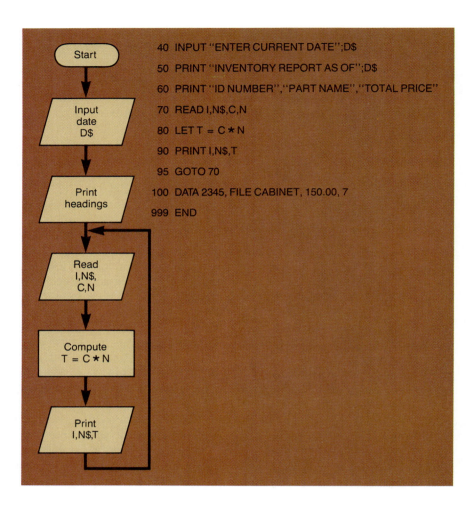

Figure A.6
Use of the GOTO statement.

if more data were inserted after line 100, the END statement would never be executed in this program because the GOTO after the PRINT always sends the program back to the READ statement. The program needs an instruction telling the computer that when it has processed the last piece of data, it should execute an alternative instruction.

To provide such an instruction, the programmer codes into the program as a DATA statement a **dummy,** or **trailer, record.** The purpose of this record is to signal the end of valid data. The programmer codes the dummy record as the highest-numbered DATA statement; the computer will therefore go to the dummy record last. The programmer also assigns dummy values to the trailer record's fields. Any values will do, as long as they cannot possibly arise in an actual record. Let us assume that the dummy values the programmer uses are all 0's. By placing an IF/THEN statement right after the READ statement, the programmer can instruct the computer to test each value to see if it is equal to 0. If the value is other than 0 (meaning that it is a good, or valid, record), the IF/THEN statement instructs the computer to continue processing. If the value is 0, the IF/THEN statement tells the computer to take an alternate path. If processing is complete, the logical alternate path would be a branch to the END statement.

Review Questions

1. What statement tells the computer to execute an unconditional branch?
2. How can infinite looping be prevented?
3. What follows the word GOTO?
4. What would happen if the GOTO statement contained a line number that did not exist in the program?
5. What is the purpose of a dummy, or trailer, record?

The IF/THEN Statement

The IF/THEN statement probably causes more logic errors in computer programs than any other statement. All languages have a statement similar to this instruction built into their instruction set. The IF/THEN statement instructs the computer to compare or test data and, when a test condition is met, to proceed with an action. When the test condition is not met, the program proceeds to the next sequential statement.

The computer's ability to compare data and take alternate paths when a certain condition or combination of conditions is present (or not present) is the heart of programming logic. If the programmer does a poor job of defining exactly what alternate paths should be taken when certain conditions are present, all sorts of logic errors will arise. As we've already noted, the solution to the problem should be clearly defined in minute detail before the first instruction is coded.

The format of the IF/THEN statement is as follows:

(line number) IF (condition) THEN (action)

If the condition specified is present, then the action stated will be executed. The action could be a branching instruction — for example, THEN (go to line number) — or it could be any other legal statement in the language, such as a LET statement. Here are examples of both types:

70 IF I = 0 THEN 999
90 IF A = B THEN LET T = T + 1

The first example asks the computer to examine the value of the variable called I to see if it is equal to 0. If it is equal to 0, then a branch to the statement on line 999 will take place. If the value of I is not equal to 0, then the branch will not take place; rather, the program will proceed to the next statement in the program. The second example says that the computer should evaluate the values of the variables called A and B. If their values are equal, then the variable called T should be incremented by 1. The difference between the two examples is that the first contains a branching instruction; in the second example, the statement immediately following the IF statement is always executed regardless of whether the IF is true.

Figure A.7 shows our sample inventory program rewritten with a trailer record on line 150, and on line 75 the condition that the program branch to the END statement when the trailer record has been read. As you can see, this program differs from the previous examples. Each time it executes the READ statement, the computer takes the four values found in the next sequential DATA statement and assigns these values to the four named variables. As long as the value of the variable called I is not equal to 0, then the branch to statement 999 does not take place; the program goes on to the LET statement in line number 80. When the computer brings the four dummy values from the highest-numbered DATA statement into memory and the IF statement is finally true, it then executes the branch to statement 999 and the program is terminated. This example contains only five valid records, but the program would work in exactly the same way with any number of records.

A word of caution about coding the dummy DATA statement: Looking at the program in Figure A.7, you might at first think that the trailer record doesn't need to contain more than a single 0, since it is only this first field that the computer evaluates in response to the IF statement on line 75. However, the syntax of READ and DATA statements demands that there be enough data to fill all the variables named in the READ statement. Remember that the READ is executed before the IF. The computer doesn't even "know" a statement 75 exists until it successfully executes statement 70. Therefore, the computer will stop and issue an OUT OF DATA error message if all four fields are not given data values when the computer executes statement 70.

In a large program requiring many comparisons of data, the IF/THEN statement takes on great importance. It can be used to make simple comparisons by asking (1) if the values are equal, (2) if one value is greater than another, (3) if one value is less than another, (4) if the values are not equal, (5) if one value is greater than or equal to another, and (6) if one value is less than or equal to another. In addition, multiple comparisons can be made by asking if one condition is true *and* another condition is true. It is also legal to ask if one condition is true *or* another condition

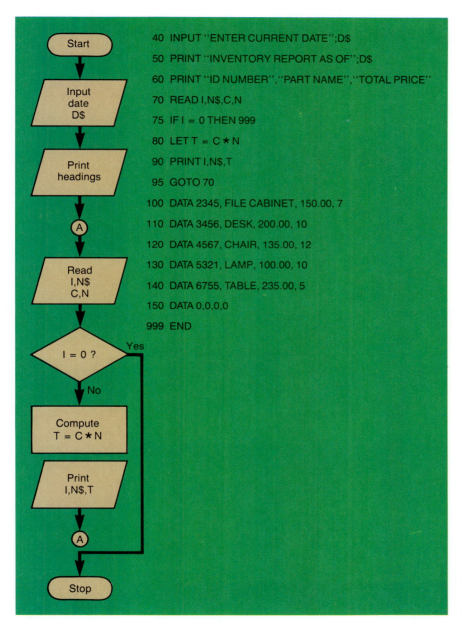

Figure A.7
Use of a trailer record and a branching statement.

is true. The IF/THEN statement can also be extended by the key word ELSE, which says to take one action if the comparison is true and another action if the comparison is not true.

The following examples, which show the relational symbols used to indicate the comparisons taking place (=, >, <, <>, >=, <=), are simple comparisons:

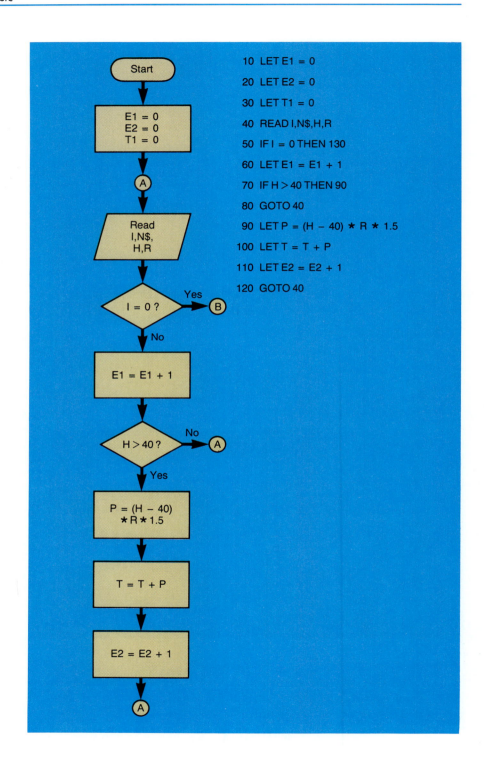

Figure A.8
Use of the IF/THEN statement.

EQUAL TO	90 IF X = Y THEN 200
GREATER THAN	90 IF X > Y THEN 200
LESS THAN	90 IF X < Y THEN 200
NOT EQUAL TO	90 IF X <> Y THEN 200
GREATER THAN OR EQUAL TO	90 IF X >= Y THEN 200
LESS THAN OR EQUAL TO	90 IF X <= Y THEN 200

In each of these examples, the computer will extract the values of the variables called X and Y and evaluate them according to the requested comparison. If the condition is true, the computer will branch to line 200. If the comparison shows that the condition is not true, the branch will not take place; rather, the computer will examine and execute the next sequential statement after statement 90.

Although spacing along the line from left to right is up to the programmer, it is generally best to follow the rules of English composition. In the examples just given, a space is left before and after each variable name because the spaces make it easier to read the names. Spacing between relational symbols, however, depends on the system. Some allow it; others don't.

Figure A.8 shows a program containing IF comparisons. Assume that the input data are employees' numbers, names, hours worked, and rates of pay. The output will be a count of (1) the total number of employees, (2) the number of employees who worked more than 40 hours during

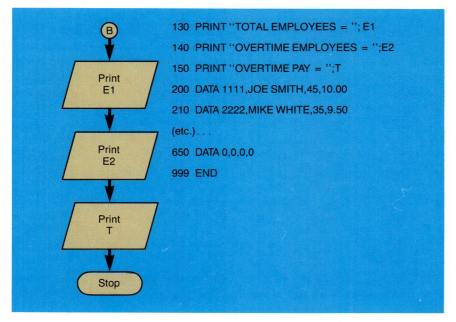

Figure A.8 (continued)

the period, and (3) the total amount of overtime paid out during the period (overtime is paid at the rate of time-and-one-half for hours over 40). In other words, the total output from the program will be three lines. On each line of output will be a message and the figures generated during the program.

The program shown in Figure A.8 illustrates not only the use of the IF/THEN statement but also two other principles often used in computer programs: the idea of counting within a program (i.e., adding 1 to a variable, inside or outside an IF statement), and the idea of accumulating a running total within a program. The two variables that will be used for counting (E1 and E2) and the variable that will be used for accumulating (T1) are set at a value of 0 before the main part of the program is executed. This is not absolutely necessary since BASIC, unlike other languages, will assume a value of 0 for a numeric variable the first time the variable is used. The variables are coded here merely as a matter of style; the program would work just as well without them. If they are coded in this way, however, it can do no harm and could lead to more efficient programming later on.

Note the logic of the flowchart and the coding that results from this logic. First, the values of the variables used in counting (E1 and E2) and accumulating (T1) are established as 0. Data are read in, and the check is made for the trailer value. If a record other than the trailer is read in, then the number of employees is increased by 1. Then comes a question about the number of hours that this employee worked. If the hours total 40 or less, the program proceeds to the next instruction (line 80), which sends it back to read the next record. If the number of hours is more than 40, then the program proceeds to compute the overtime pay, accumulate the total overtime pay in the variable called T, increase the number of overtime employees by 1, and then branch back to read another record. Finally, when the trailer has been read, and I is equal to 0, the program branches to line 130 and prints the three lines required. Note that each line to be printed will contain a literal message and the value of the variables that were used either to count or accumulate.

Certain statements can be written in different ways, especially when they involve the logic of an IF condition. For example, the statements beginning on line 70 in Figure A.8, which asks the value of hours, could be coded as follows and produce the very same results:

```
70 IF H <= 40 THEN 40
80 LET P = (H - 40) * R * 1.5
90 LET T = T + P
100 GOTO 40
```

Line 70 asks if the value of the hours worked is less than or equal to 40. If it is, a branch takes the program back to read the next record. If the condition is not true, the program proceeds to line 80 and computes the overtime pay for this employee. Another way to code this statement would be to incorporate the ELSE option (a second alternative) into the IF/THEN statement:

70 IF H > 40 THEN GOTO 80 ELSE GOTO 40

The computation of the overtime pay and the accumulation of the total overtime pay really could have been done in one instruction. For example, the following line would accomplish the same thing as lines 80 and 90 together:

80 LET T = T + (H − 40) * R * 1.5

In this one statement, the value of T is set to its current value plus the answer generated by the computation of the overtime pay. However, saving one statement here and there is not crucial; what is crucial is that the logic be correct and the program easy to read. It is sometimes better to code extra statements since they make the program easier to read and easier to debug should a logic error occur.

The program shown in Figure A.9 has the same input as the program in Figure A.8 (number, name, hours, and rate of pay) and prints out the numbers, names, gross pay, deductions (computed as 20 percent of gross pay), and net pay for all employees. The three totals to be calculated are total gross pay, total deductions, and total net pay; these values will be printed after the trailer record has been detected. This time a blank line will be printed (line 170) before the total line is printed. The printing of the totals in line 180 incorporates a comma as the first character after the word PRINT. The comma tells the computer to skip the first print zone — that is, to leave it blank. The literal "TOTALS" will be printed in the second print zone, and the three accumulated values will be printed in zones, 3, 4, and 5 under the three columns containing gross pay, deductions, and net pay.

The program in Figure A.10 shows how multiple IF/THEN statements are used to process student grades. Input consists of student names and scores for three exams. Output will be student names, averages, and grades received. If the average is 90 or better, the grade will be an A; if the grade is at least 80 but less than 90, the grade will be a B; if the average is at least 70 but less than 80, the grade will be a C; if the average is at least 60 but less than 70, the grade will be a D; if the average is less than 60, the grade will be an F.

In this program, headings are printed over the three columns, and then a blank line is printed to separate the headings from the detail lines. The trailer record contains dummy data (in this case "XXX") in the name field. After the average is computed, a series of IF/THEN statements inquires about the value of the variable reserved for the average, called A. Each

614 APPENDIX/PROGRAMMING IN BASIC

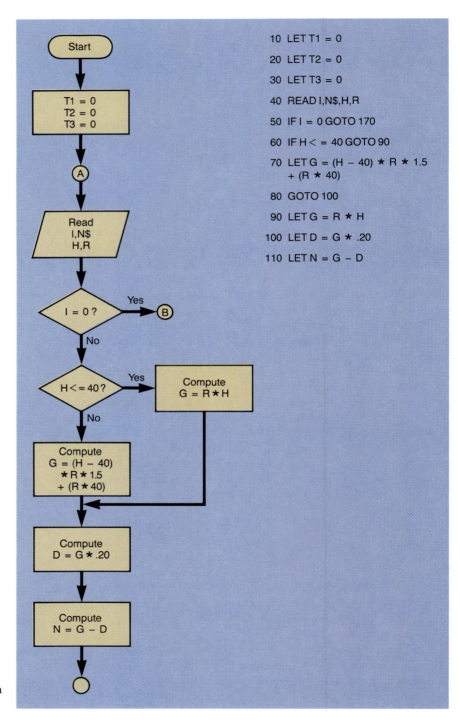

Figure A.9
Processing employee records with the IF/THEN statement.

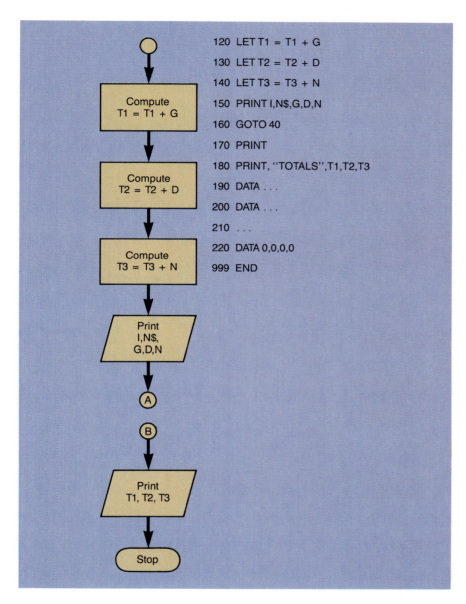

Figure A.9 (continued)

IF/THEN statement except the first and last are compound statements, which means that both conditions must be met before the action can be taken after the THEN. It's easy to code a logic error into a program such as this. For example, coding it as follows is syntactically correct, but the logic will result in wrong grades for almost every student:

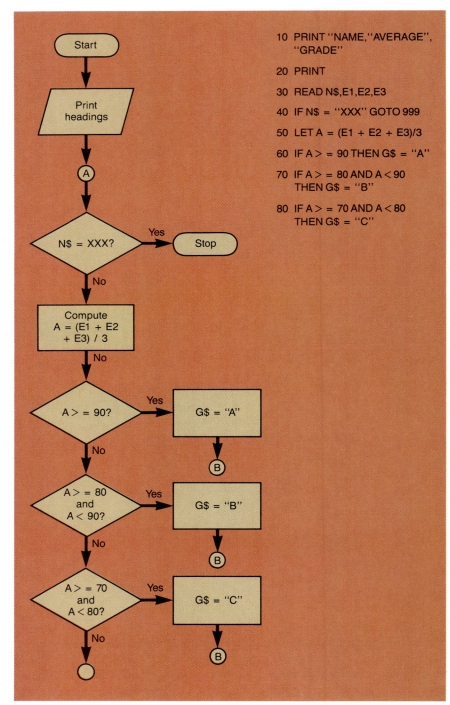

Figure A.10
Processing student grades with multiple IF/THEN statements.

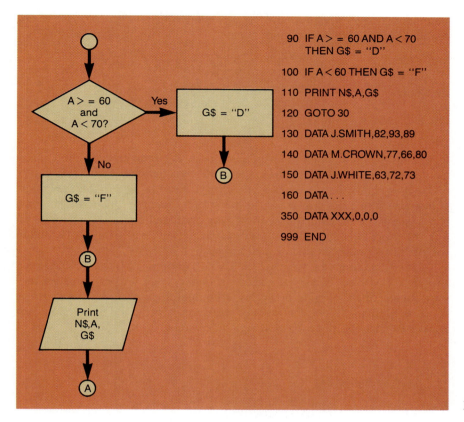

Figure A.10 (continued)

```
60  IF A >= 90 THEN G$ = "A"
70  IF A >= 80 THEN G$ = "B"
80  IF A >= 70 THEN G$ = "C"
90  IF A >= 60 THEN G$ = "D"
100 IF A < 60 THEN G$ = "F"
```

This coding may at first seem logical, but closer examination will reveal that all students with a grade of 60 or better will receive a D. Even if a student's average is 95 and the grade of A is assigned, the computer will then see that the average is also greater than 80 and so will assign a B; the average is also greater than 70 and greater than 60. Thus, even though the average was 95, the student will end up with a D because the answers to the questions in lines 70, 80, and 90 are also found to be true.

The logic of this program could be coded in a different way. For example, after assigning the grade to G$, the program could branch to the PRINT statement. In other words, if the condition is true, two operations should take place: (1) assign the grade, and (2) branch to the PRINT statement. These operations are accomplished by inserting a colon between the first action and the second:

```
60 IF A >= 90 THEN G$ = "A": GOTO 110
70 IF A >= 80 THEN G$ = "B": GOTO 110
80 IF A >= 70 THEN G$ = "C": GOTO 110
90 IF A >= 60 THEN G$ = "D": GOTO 110
100 IF A <= 60 THEN G$ = "F"
110 PRINT N$, A, G$
```

Rewriting the statements this way eliminates the logic error in the earlier example, since if a student's average is 95, two things happen: The grade of A is assigned, and the program branches to line 110, where the computer is instructed to print the grade. In the earlier example, this same student was assigned a B since the average was evaluated for a second time in line 70. Note that in line 100 there is no need to say GOTO 110, since the program proceeds to line 110 anyway.

Clearly, although the syntax of the IF/THEN statement is not troublesome, the logic involved can cause major problems. Logic errors point up the importance of thoroughly analyzing a computer program before starting to code it. The absence of syntax errors in a program is certainly no guarantee that the program will run successfully.

Review Questions

1. Give an example of branching to line 50 if the condition that A is less than B is found to be true.
2. How are data compared with an IF/THEN statement?
3. Give an example of branching to line 50 if the conditions that both A and B are equal to 100 are true.
4. What does the computer do when it finds that a conditional statement is not true?
5. How can an alternate action be coded into an IF/THEN statement if the condition asked is found to be not true?

The FOR/NEXT Statement

The **FOR/NEXT** statement, which takes advantage of the computer's counting ability, is a convenient way of coding a loop into a program. The key word FOR is coded to begin the loop and to tell the computer how many times to execute the loop; the key word NEXT is the termination point of the loop. Between these two lines, any number of statements may be coded. The FOR/NEXT statement is used when the number of times the loop is to be executed is known in advance — for example, when a company has twenty different pay classifications to process. In contrast, the IF/THEN statement is used when the number of loop executions needed is not known in advance; the loop will terminate when the test condition is met.

The general format of the FOR statement is as follows:

(line number) FOR (variable) = (value) TO (value)

Here is an example of such a statement:

190 FOR K = 1 TO 100

In this example, K is the variable that will be used to count the number of times the loop is executed. This variable (also called the *index*) is followed by an equal sign and then a value that gives an initial value to the variable. In this case, the variable K is set to an initial value of 1. This initial value is followed by the key word TO, which is followed by another value. This second value is the value the computer will use as a reference to determine if the loop has been executed the number of times asked for. The number 100 in this case is the terminal value of K. In other words, this statement asks that K be set to the value of 1 and increased every time the loop is executed until the terminal value of K is reached. Any number of statements may follow the FOR statement, but the terminal statement of the loop has to be the key word NEXT, followed by the variable name found in the FOR statement (K, in this case). For example, if we wanted to code a loop that simply prints the value of a variable from 1 to 100, we might do it this way:

10 FOR K = 1 TO 100
20 PRINT "THE VALUE OF K IS"; K
30 NEXT K

These statements tell the computer to loop through the three statements 100 times. The computer will set K to an initial value of 1. It will then execute all statements until it comes across NEXT K. When it reaches this NEXT statement, it will increase K by 1 and check to see if the value of the variable is greater than the terminal value found in the FOR statement. If the value of the variable is not greater than the terminal value, the computer will execute the statements within the loop again and continue this procedure until the specified condition is met. When the condition is met (K is greater than 100), the computer will stop executing the loop and proceed to the statement following NEXT K.

Note that although the loop is executed exactly 100 times, the value of K will be 101 when the loop is terminated because the computer gives K a value of 1 to begin with, and after executing the loop one time, it increases K and makes it 2. The way the statement works, then, is that the computer asks if the value of the variable (index) is greater than the terminal value and not equal to it. In most systems, use of the variable name in the NEXT statement is optional; that is, the word NEXT need not be followed by the variable name if the programmer decides to leave it off. Most programmers do include the variable name, however, because it is a good form of documentation.

All programs will loop somewhere in the course of the logic, and, under usual looping circumstances, the FOR/NEXT statement is preferred to the IF/THEN statement. Suppose, for example, that we wanted to know how much $1,000 would be worth at 12 percent interest compounded annually for 10 years. The program shown in Figure A.11 uses the IF

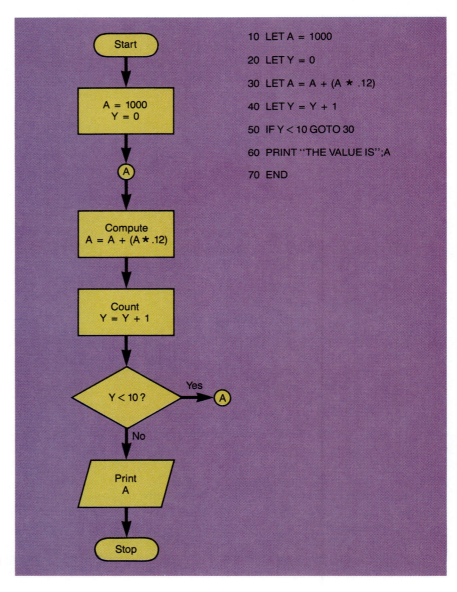

Figure A.11
Computing annual interest with the IF/THEN statement.

statement to solve the problem. This program sets the amount to $1,000 and the number of years to 0. It then computes the worth after the first year, adds 1 to Y, and asks if Y is less than 10. If Y is less than 10, the program branches back to compute the value again, and this process continues until Y is equal to 10. In Figure A.12, the same logic is coded using the FOR/NEXT statement. This little program does not seem to have a great advantage over the previous one, but when the logic involved becomes more complex, the simplicity of FOR/NEXT beomes more evident.

Suppose, for example, this same program was recoded to put the compounding of the amount on a quarterly instead of a yearly basis, and the value was to be printed out at the end of each year. This change would involve an outer loop to count the years and an inner loop to count the quarters. (This kind of configuration — one loop inside another loop — is called a **nested loop.**) Figure A.13 shows this logic coded using the IF statement. As can be seen, the inner loop is set up to count the quarters, and the outer loop is set up to count the years. This time, after each year

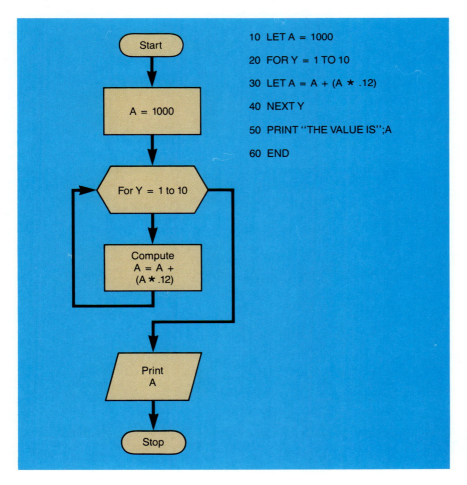

Figure A.12

Computing annual interest with the FOR/NEXT statement.

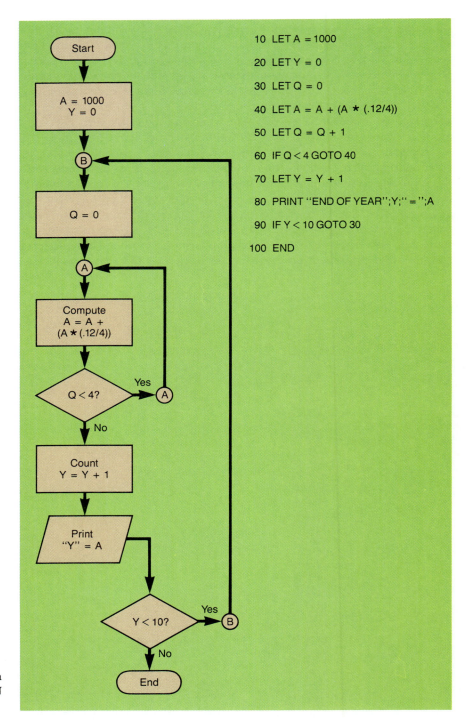

Figure A.13
Computing quarterly interest with nested loops and the IF/THEN statement.

is printed in line 80, Q must be reset to 0 so that the inner loop can start all over again. Note that the interest rate (12 percent) must be divided by 4 so that the correct quarterly rate can be computed.

Figure A.14 is an example of the same logic coded with a FOR/NEXT statement within a FOR/NEXT statement. As you can see, it is not just fewer statements that make FOR/NEXT preferred; it is the simplicity of

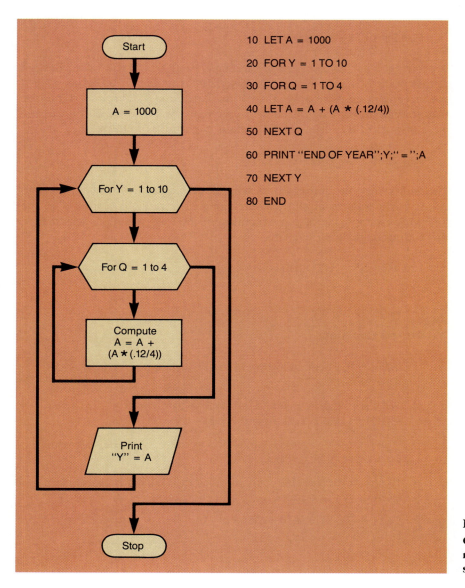

Figure A.14
Computing quarterly interest with nested loops and the FOR/NEXT statement.

the flow of the logic that blends so well with the principle of executing a loop a known number of times. Because of the simplicity of the statements, making a clerical error with nested FOR/NEXT loops is much less likely than with the IF/THEN method.

Some extensions and options of the FOR/NEXT statement should be mentioned. In the FOR statement, the initial value and the terminal value may be variable names as well as integers. For example, a statement such as

```
100 FOR C = X TO Y
```

is perfectly legal. As long as the variables X and Y hold the values desired at this point in the program, the statement is perfectly logical as well. If the increment must be other than 1, the extension STEP is coded into the FOR statement. For example, if the programmer wants to increase a variable by 2 instead of the usual 1, the coding might be as follows:

```
100 FOR A = 1 TO Z STEP 2
```

The index may be decreased as well as increased. If the need arises to count backwards from the present value of a variable (called S in the following example) and stop execution of the loop when S is less than 1, the coding might look like this:

```
100 FOR K = S TO 1 STEP −1
```

Review Questions

1. What is the general syntax of the FOR statement? Of the NEXT statement?
2. Why use the FOR/NEXT statement to go into a loop when IF/THEN can accomplish the same thing?
3. How can the variable name used as the counter be increased by a number other than 1?
4. How can the variable name used as the counter be subtracted from as well as added to?
5. Can a FOR/NEXT statement be coded within another FOR/NEXT?

The DIM Statement: One-Dimensional Arrays

All the examples used thus far have dealt with variable names that represented only a single value at a time. If R was used as a variable name for the rate of pay, there could be only one place in memory called R because each time a new value was read in or computed, the value previously stored in the location referred to by the variable name R was replaced with the new value. But suppose that you had a payroll requiring 50 or 100 rates of pay to be read in. You could read these data into memory by using as many different variable names as there are rates, but this process would be tremendously cumbersome.

Fortunately, there is an easier way to read in and store multiple items of data. BASIC, like all other languages, permits the programmer to deal with groups of related data items by means of an **array**, also called a **matrix**. An array that stores a single list of data is called a **one-dimensional array**, or **list**. With an array, the programmer can reserve as many locations in memory as are needed and refer to all of them by the same variable name. To do this, the programmer must first tell the computer how many locations in memory are to be reserved for the array. These locations are called **elements**, or **cells**. The **DIM** (an abbreviation for dimension) statement is the means by which the locations in memory are established; it tells the computer how many locations are needed. BASIC will allow an array to be used with a maximum of ten cells without using DIM, but it is a good idea to use DIM in each case since if affords good documentation.

The general format of the DIM statement is as follows:

(line number) DIM (array name) (number of cells)

For example, if an array called R was going to be created, and R needed 25 cells, the code would be as follows:

10 DIM R(25)

Arrays may be set up to hold either numeric or string variable data. The syntax in each case would be exactly the same except that the string variable name would have a dollar sign after it. An array to hold the names of the fifty states might be set up like this:

20 DIM S$(50)

If more than one array was going to be used, the programmer could either code separate DIM statements or code them all with one DIM statement like this:

10 DIM R(25); S$(50)

Obviously, you must first establish the array before you can load data into it; the DIM statement therefore must be coded with a line number less than any line number that refers to it. DIM statements are typically coded at the very top of the program, even though one of the arrays may not be referred to until much later in the program.

An array, then, is a group of storage locations, or cells, in which data are stored. These data can be referred to later by means of any legal statement in the program. The entire array is given a name, such as R or S$. However, to call for the contents of any individual cell in the array, the programmer must have some sort of reference that indicates which cell is needed. A subscript provides this reference. A **subscript** is either a positive integer or a variable name that has a positive integer as its value. It is coded in parentheses immediately after the array name. For example, if the first cell of array R is being examined with an IF statement to see if the value is 0, it might be coded as follows:

50 IF R(1) = 0 THEN (any legal statement)

As noted, a variable name that has a positive integer as its value may also be used as a subscript. If the variable K contained a 1, then the following statement would produce the same results as the previous statement:

50 IF R(K) = 0 THEN (any legal statement)

The use of a variable name as a subscript is much more common than the use of an integer since the value of the integer can never change, while the value of the variable can change as many times as the programmer wants it to change. Thus, the variable name affords greater flexibility. We should note, however, that the range of the variable name is limited to the number of elements reserved in the DIM statement. If reference is made to the array name with a subscript that is in excess of the number of elements in the array, a run-time error will result to show that the subscript is out of range.

BASIC will also allow an arithmetic expression to be used as a subscript. For example, if the value of X + Y was the value needed as a subscript, you could code the following:

50 IF R(X + Y) = 0 THEN (any legal statement)

To illustrate how an array is created, let's assume that a company has different rates of pay for various job classifications. Rather than the rate of pay being in each employee's pay record, the rates will be stored in an array before the individual pay records are read. Once the array is created, the appropriate pay rate can be extracted from the array according to the job classification code that would be in each employee's pay record.

The number of elements must first be reserved in memory with the DIM statement (see Figure A.15). Assume that the company has twenty different job classifications, each with a different pay rate. Since the number of elements is known in advance, the FOR/NEXT statement is used; it will cause the program to loop twenty times. Because of the FOR/NEXT, the subscript (called K, in this case) will be automatically increased by 1 each time the loop is executed. The READ/DATA statements will be used to bring in the rates of pay.

As Figure A.15 shows, once the DIM statement has reserved the twenty-element array, statement 30 will read in the variable named in the array (R). Since R is the name of an array, a subscript must be used whenever R is referred to. Thus, line 30 refers to R(K); K is the subscript, which identifies the individual cell within the array. Just as with a READ statement without an array, the value of the variable is found in the DATA statement. Because the FOR/NEXT statement is used, each time the READ is executed, the value of K is 1 more than it was the previous time through the loop.

The first time that the computer executes line 30, it reads the first value found in the first DATA statement. Since K is at that point equal to 1, the value of the first cell in the array would be 5.55. The second time through the loop, K is equal to 2, and therefore the second element in the array would be assigned the second value from the first DATA statement (5.93). This pattern is followed until the loop is executed twenty times, after which all twenty cells in the array would have been filled with data.

As mentioned earlier, an array can be string as well as numeric. Assume that the same program that processes the rates of pay will also process the job title of the employee for that pay period. The programmer will therefore have to reserve memory for a twenty-element string array and compose a name for the array in a DIM statement. Statements very similar

```
10  DIM R(20)
20  FOR K = 1 TO 20
30  READ R(K)
40  NEXT K
50  DATA 5.55, 5.93, 6.05, 6.34, 6.88
60  DATA 7.26, 7.67, 8.11, 8.22, 8.51
70  DATA 8.96, 9.23, 9.78, 9.95, 10.45
80  DATA 10.88, 11.23, 11.67, 12.33, 12.89
```

Figure A.15
Creating a one-dimensional array.

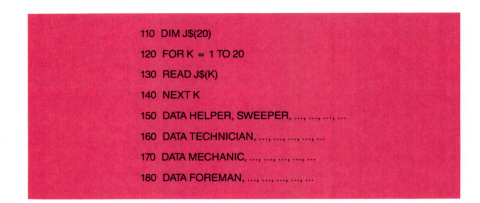

Figure A.16
Creating a job-title array.

to those in Figure A.15 would be used to read twenty different job titles and store them in the twenty-element array reserved with the DIM statement. The coding shown in Figure A.16 picks up at line 110 the program shown in Figure A.15 and creates the job-title array, using the same logic as was used to create the rate array.

Each time the loop is executed, K is increased by 1, and the next title is read from the proper DATA statement and stored in the next highest element of the array. The subscript K is used again since it was not important to save the value of K after the R array was created. Remember that the value of K was 21 after the first array was created. When statement 120 is executed for the first time, the computer resets K at 1, so its previous value is not material to the program.

The best way to picture either of these arrays is to think of twenty empty boxes (numbered 1 to 20), which are reserved with the DIM statement. Each time the FOR/NEXT statement is executed, a value is brought in and stored in the next higher-numbered box. In computer terms, these boxes are actually addresses in memory. The values in the R array, which contains numeric data, are automatically set to 0 before the loop is executed, and the values in the J$ array, which contains string data, are set to blanks before the loop is executed. When the loop is satisfied (executed twenty times), the cells are filled with data, and the next phase of the program can begin.

It would be perfectly legal and logical to create both arrays together. Of course, the sequence in which the DATA statements would be constructed would be very important, since the rates and titles have to be set up with one following the other. For example, if the first value for the rate array was 5.55 and the first title was HELPER, then the first DATA statement must show this. The following statements show both arrays constructed together:

```
10 DIM R(20), J$(20)
20 FOR K = 1 TO 20
```

```
30 READ R(K), J$(K)
40 PRINT R(K), J$(K)
50 NEXT K
60 DATA 5.55, HELPER, 5.93, SWEEPER, ..., ... (remaining data)
```

The values in the arrays are to be printed just after they are read so that the values can be examined for clerical errors.

Once the array is filled with data, the values can be accessed with any legal BASIC statements. For example, to add the twenty values and secure an average of the twenty elements, the code would be as follows:

```
210 LET T = 0
220 FOR K = 1 TO 20
230 LET T = T + R(K)
240 NEXT K
250 LET A = T/20
260 PRINT "THE AVERAGE IS"; A
```

In this exercise, the accumulator variable T was set to zero, and then the loop added the twenty different values to T. When the loop was over, T was divided by 20 and the answer was put into A. Then A was printed along with an explanatory message.

If we wanted to search this array for the first cell that holds a value over 10.00, our search could begin in the first element and continue until the value of one of the cells is found to be over 10.00. For example:

```
310 FOR K = 1 TO 20
320 IF R(K) > 10.00 GOTO 340
330 NEXT K
340 PRINT "VALUE"; R(K); "WAS FOUND IN CELL"; K
```

This routine starts the search in the first cell and asks if its value is greater than 10.00. If it is, then a branch takes place to line 340, where the message is printed. If it is not, K is increased by 1, and the search continues until the IF statement is found to be true. This routine does not allow for the possibility that no value greater than 10.00 will be found; the following is another way to write the same routine and allow for this possibility:

```
410 FOR K = 1 TO 20
420 IF R(K) > 10.00 THEN PRINT "VALUE"; R(K);
    "WAS FOUND IN CELL"; K: K = 21
430 NEXT K
440 IF K = 21 PRINT "NO VALUE WAS GREATER THAN 10.00"
```

In this case, when the IF statement is true, some sort of signal or indicator must be set up so that one message will be printed and the other (not found) message will not. The indicator used was the setting of K equal to

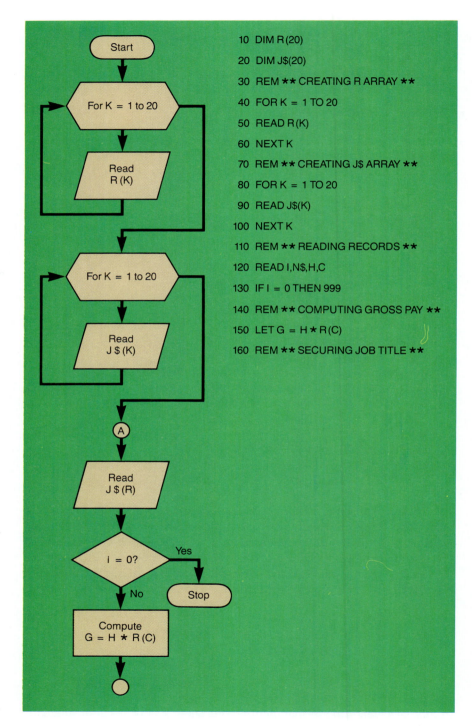

Figure A.17
A multiple-array payroll program.

21. When the IF statement was found to be true, the message was printed and K was set to 21. When the next line in the program said NEXT K, this increased K and made it 22. The computer then checked to see if the value of K was greater than the terminal value of 20. Since it was found to be so, the loop was terminated, and the computer proceeded to statement 440. Statement 440 asked if K was equal to 21. Since it was not (it was equal to 22), the IF statement found on line 440 was not printed. If the condition that a value was greater than 10.00 was never true, then when the loop was terminated, the value of K would be 21. Under these circumstances, the message found in line 440 would be printed. There are a variety of ways of setting such a signal in a program. Any check can be used as long as it is clear and easy to read.

Figure A.17 shows a complete program that creates the two arrays for the rates and job titles and reads in the individual pay records. These pay records contain the employee's identification number, name, hours worked, and work code. The work code (C) is crucial. Each time a new employee's record is read, the code is used as a subscript to extract the rate of pay from the array so that the rate can be multiplied by the hours worked (line 150); that is, if the code is 9, the ninth element in the array is accessed and its contents multiplied by the hours worked. The code is also used to extract the proper job title from the J$ array (line 170). Again, if the code is a 9, then the ninth element in the J$ array is accessed.

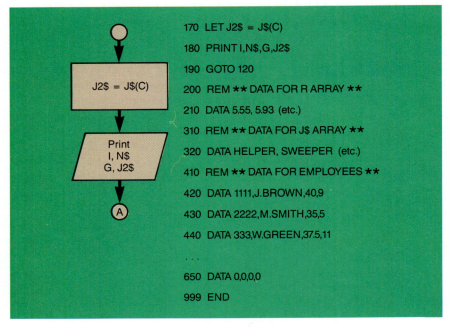

Figure A.17 (continued)

The output will be individual lines with the employee's identification number, name, gross pay, and job title.

Note the location of the DATA statements. Since the R array is created first, all twenty rates must appear as the first twenty values in the DATA statements. Since the J$ array is created second, the next twenty values must be the twenty job titles. After this, the DATA lines containing the regular pay data are coded with the trailer record containing all zeros, which is the signal that all the other "good" records have been processed.

The point was made previously that if a subscript was a zero or a number in excess of the number of elements in the array (over 20), a run-time error would result. One method of preventing such an error is to check the range of the code before computing the gross pay. This could be done by putting before line 150 a line like the following:

```
145 IF C = 0 OR C > 20 GOTO 195
```

These lines would then be added:

```
195 PRINT "EMPLOYEE"; I; "CODE ="; C
196 GOTO 120
```

These additions would eliminate the records with a bad code before the gross pay was computed. If the condition asked in the IF statement was true, the program would branch to line 195, print an error message, and branch back to read the next record. Although this procedure may be logical for this particular example, a business report would not look very attractive with error messages interspersed every so often between regular lines of meaningful data. It certainly would be preferable to "save" these error records and print them all together at the bottom of the report or on a separate report. One way of doing this would be to put them into another array. To do so, the programmer must reserve memory for these errors using a DIM statement. The number of array elements chosen needs to be greater than the highest possible number of errors that could occur.

In the following example, when an error occurs, the ID number and the bad code will be saved so that the reason for the error can be investigated when the program is finished. Since both the ID number and the code are to be saved, two different arrays need to be set up. Assume that the programmer knows that a maximum of ten errors will exist.

```
25 DIM E1(10); E2(10)
145 IF C = 0 OR C > 20 GOTO 195
195 LET K = K + 1
196 LET E1(K) = I: LET E2(K) = C
197 GOTO 120
```

Line 25 is a DIM statement that sets up two different arrays. E1 array will hold the ID numbers, and E2 array will hold the codes when errors occur.

Line 145 makes the check for the bad code. Line 195 makes the provision to step up one element in the array. K was 0 to begin with, so the first time that an error occurs, K becomes 1. Line 196 places the ID number into the first cell of E1, and then the code is entered into the first cell of E2. The program then branches back to read the next record. Each time an error occurs, the program branches to line 195, increases the subscript K, and puts the data into the next two elements of the two arrays.

Data stored in an array can be manipulated by any legal statements within the language in the same way that nonsubscripted data can be manipulated. They can be sorted by a variety of methods and compared to see if a certain condition exists (such as a value in the array matching a value read in or computed elsewhere in the program) or compared to find the highest or lowest value.

In the next example, an array called V will be searched to find the highest value. The output will be a line printed with the value itself. Assume that the array has been previously created with 100 different values, which are in random order. The following routine will search the array for the highest value:

```
310 LET H = -9999
320 FOR K = 1 to 100
330 IF V(K) > H THEN H = V(K)
340 NEXT K
350 PRINT "THE HIGHEST VALUE IS"; H
```

The first step is to set an independent variable equal to an artificially low value (-9999, in this case). The reason for setting up this variable is that it will hold the successively higher values as the loop continues. The first time the IF statement is executed, the condition has to be true. Therefore, whatever value is in the first cell will now be stored in H. Then each successive value is compared against H. Note that the IF statement does not compare data items in the array against each other but compares items in the array against H. When the last value has been examined, the loop is terminated, and statement 350 causes a line to be printed showing what the highest value was.

Review Questions

1. What is an array?
2. What kinds of data may be coded in arrays?
3. How are the cells in the array referred to after the array is created?

> 4. What will happen if the variable name used as the subscript holds a value beyond the number of cells in the array?
>
> 5. Prepare the necessary program statements to establish the following: (a) an array B1 with twenty cells; (b) two arrays, D and D1, each with fifty cells; (c) two arrays, D1 with twenty cells, and F with fifteen cells. Include the necessary READ statement(s) to enter the data.

The DIM Statement: Two-Dimensional Arrays

An array does not have to be one-dimensional — that is, a single list of data; it can also be two-dimensional. A **two-dimensional array,** also called a **table,** is useful when certain data have to be arranged in rows and columns. In BASIC, if an array has two dimensions, it is referred to with two subscripts. When the two-dimensional array is declared with the DIM statement, the number of elements is set by row and column. For example, for an array of data that shows the sales of six salespersons for five days of a week, the DIM statement would be as follows:

10 DIM S(6,5)

Such an array would have six rows and five columns. The use of the terms *rows* and *columns* is purely a matter of convenience; to the computer, the data are arranged in thirty consecutive locations, not in rows and columns. The two terms, however, are useful for programmers since it is easy to picture six horizontal rows and five vertical columns.

When creating a two-dimensional array, the programmer uses logic almost identical to the logic used in constructing a one-dimensional array. With the two-dimensional array, each salesperson has five sales figures, so each time the computer comes across a new salesperson, one subscript (for the salesperson) is held steady, and the other subscript (for the days) is varied from 1 to 5. The obvious way to proceed is to use the nested FOR/NEXT loop, where the outside subscript (the row) is varied from 1 to 6 and the inside subscript (the column) is varied from 1 to 5. Figure A.18 illustrates this concept. The outside loop, using subscript R, counts the rows 1 to 6. The inside loop, using subscript C, counts the columns 1 to 5. The first time the READ statement is executed, the computer will take the first value in the first DATA statement and assign it to the cell referenced by row 1, column 1. Then, holding the subscript R steady, it will read in the four remaining values from the first DATA statement and assign them to row 1, columns 2, 3, 4, and 5. Then R is increased to 2, C is reset to 1, and the process continues with the data from the second

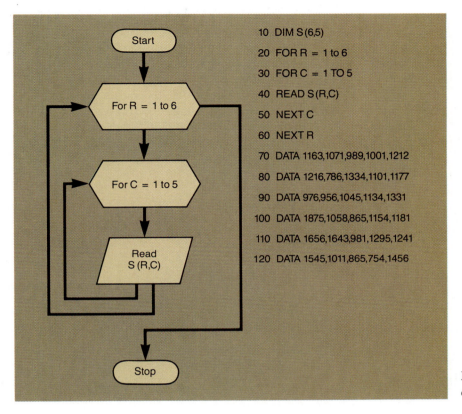

Figure A.18
Creating a two-dimensional array.

DATA statement. This continues until R becomes 6 and C is varied from 1 to 5 for the last time.

The thirty-element array is now filled with sales data, but it is arranged so that individual statistics for the salespersons can easily be compared and manipulated. Although this array is not configured by actual rows and columns in memory, the programmer can visualize the data as arranged like the data in Figure A.19.

	1	2	3	4	5
1	1163	1071	989	1001	1212
2	1216	786	1334	1101	1177
3	976	956	1045	1134	1331
4	1875	1058	865	1154	1181
5	1656	1643	981	1295	1241
6	1545	1011	865	754	1456

Figure A.19
Table illustrating a two-dimensional array.

Figure A.20 shows how a routine picks up the program after the array is created and finds the highest sales in each of the five days. Each time the sales for one of the days for all six salespersons have been examined, a line is printed with the high sales for the day. This logic is only a small extension of the logic involved in the processing of a one-dimensional array. This time C (the column subscript that represents the day of the week) is held steady, and the subscript R (the row representing each of the six salespersons) is varied from 1 to 6. The IF/THEN statement continually compares each of the six values against the previous high in the variable called H. Note again that H is first set to an artificially low value of −9999 so that with the first comparison, the value in the first cell in the array

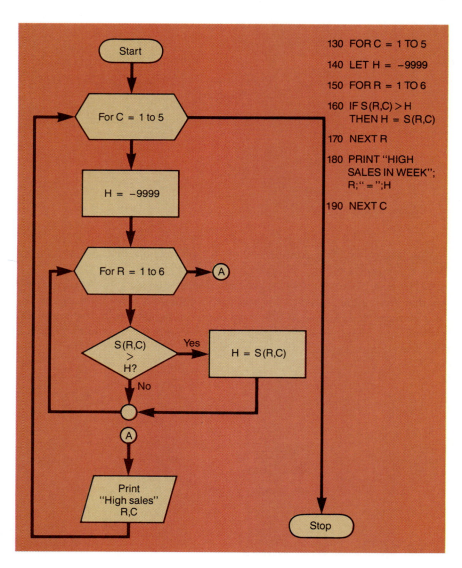

Figure A.20
Program illustrating a two-dimensional array.

must replace the initial value of H. Once the comparison is made six times, a line containing the sales figure and also the day (1 through 5) is printed. Since the outside loop is not satisfied, the logic flows back, resets H to −9999, and makes the comparison with C equal to 2. This process is continued five times, and when the fifth day is printed, the outside loop is satisfied (C is greater than 5), and this part of the program is over.

These same data can be used to secure all sorts of other statistics. For example, it may be valuable to find the total sales for all salespersons and the total sales for each of the six salespersons and to compute each person's percentage of total sales. If the programmer continually thinks in terms of rows and columns, this logic becomes easier to follow. First, to secure the total sales for all salespersons, the programmer may code a simple nested loop with a FOR/NEXT within another FOR/NEXT and continually add to a total sales figure. To secure the sales for each person, the five sales figures for each person have to be added. This is done within the inner loop. When this inner loop is done five times, the percentage is computed and a line is printed. The outer loop, which counts the rows, is done a total of six times since there are six salespersons. Figure A.21 contains some coding that will generate the total of all sales and then compute the sales and the percentage of sales for each person.

Suppose that when the sales array is read in, another array is created to hold the names of the salespersons. When the computer prints individual statistics, the person's name can then be used rather than a designation like salesperson 1. Since the names will go into a one-dimensional array, only one subscript is required, and it will be R. Although the creation of the name array could be accomplished within the outer loop when the sales array is created, assume that it is created as follows:

```
182 DIM N$(6)
184 FOR R = 1 TO 6
186 READ N$(R)
188 NEXT R
190 DATA J. JONES, F. SMITH, B. BLACK
192 DATA D. MILLER, P. GREEN, T. BROWN
```

Figure A.22 shows the two arrays set up next to each other. This figure represents a one-dimensional array with the names of the salespersons and a two-dimensional array with the sales figures. The task now is to manipulate the sales figures, and when a line is to be printed, to print the name of the salesperson as well as the sales figures. Going back to Figure A.21, when line 390 was executed and the sales percentage figure printed six times, it was the row subscript (subscript R) that held values 1 through 6. Looking at the name array, the programmer could easily extract the salesperson's name using the subscript R:

390 N$(R); "SOLD"; P; "PERCENTAGE OF TOTAL SALES"

If the "Salesperson of the Week" had to be found, one simple statement after 390 could do so. The variable P held the percentage of sales for each

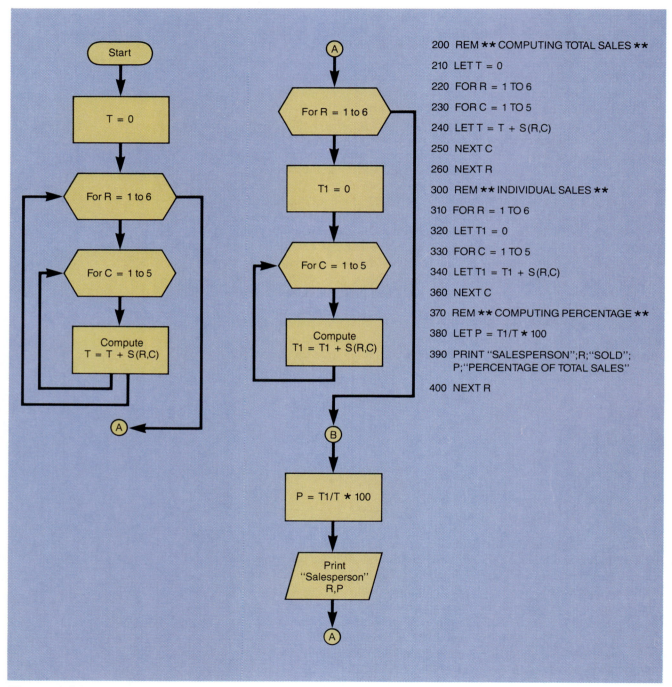

Figure A.21
Coding a two-dimensional array with nested loops.

		1	2	3	4	5
1	J.JONES	1163	1071	989	1001	1212
2	F.SMITH	1216	786	1334	1101	1177
3	B.BLACK	976	956	1045	1134	1331
4	D.MILLER	1875	1058	865	1154	1181
5	P.GREEN	1656	1643	981	1295	1241
6	T.BROWN	1545	1011	865	754	1456

Figure A.22

Combining one-dimensional and two-dimensional arrays.

individual. Now it must be determined whether the present value of P is greater than the previous high percentage. A line number like 205 could be used to initially set H1 to a low value. At line 395, the present value of P will be compared to H1. If P is greater than H1 (it has to be, the first time the comparison is made), H1 is reset. But now, in addition to resetting H1, a variable called N2$ will be used to hold the name of the person whose sales percentage caused the comparison to be true. When the outer loop is over and the program proceeds to line 410, the name of the top salesperson can be printed:

```
205 LET H1 = -9999
395 IF P > H1 THEN H1 = P: N2$ = N$(R)
405 PRINT "SALESPERSON OF THE WEEK IS"; N2$
```

Review Questions

1. How is a two-dimensional array different from a one-dimensional array?

2. When would you use a two-dimensional array?

3. How is a nested loop used to enter data into a two-dimensional array?

4. Prepare program statements to establish the following arrays and to enter the data using a READ statement(s): (a) array F3 having three rows and six columns; (b) array H$ having ten rows and ten columns; (c) array Z$ having five rows and five columns and array A having ten rows and two columns.

5. Prepare a program segment that adds the rows and columns of a five-row, six-column array B.

The GOSUB Statement

Logic errors often occur because of branching operations within computer programs. *Modular,* or *structured, programming* can help to reduce such errors. In this kind of programming, the entire program is divided into parts called modules, each of which performs only a single task. For example, some modules perform input/output operations; others may perform certain calculations. Each module is given a title, or name. In BASIC, naming can be accomplished with the REM statement. Programmers often highlight a new module by outlining REM statements with rows of asterisks at the beginning and end of the module. REM can also be used to describe the functions of a particular module.

Control in modular programming flows from top to bottom. This is true both for the overall program and for each individual module. When planning the logic of one module, the programmer usually is not concerned with other modules since each module is separate and unique within the program. Certain computer languages, such as COBOL and Pascal, lend themselves to modular programming. Unfortunately, BASIC does not. A programmer working in BASIC can, however, attempt to attain a form of modular programming by breaking the different parts of a program into smaller, more manageable portions.

In coding program modules, the use of the GOSUB statement is recommended. The **GOSUB** statement is used to transfer the flow of control from the main logic of a program to another module, often called a **subroutine.** The general format of this statement is as follows:

(line number) GOSUB (line number)

Like the GOTO statement, the GOSUB statement results in a branch to the line number following the statement. Unlike a GOTO, however, a GOSUB indicates that the program should return to the next line in the program following GOSUB. Programmers often choose a line number far down in the program for the location of the subroutine—for example, 2600 or 3500. Because the subroutine is located quite a way down in the program, a lot of room is left for coding other statements. Coding a GOSUB statement as follows would violate any good programming practice:

150 GOSUB 230

In this case, after the computer executes the statements in the subroutine and control returns to the statement following line 150, the program will very soon proceed to the subroutine beginning on line 230. Thus, a GOTO will probably have to be coded to jump over the statements that make up the subroutine.

The first statement in a subroutine can be any legal statement within the language, including a REM statement. To let the computer know that it has come to the end of the routine and that control should return to the statement following GOSUB, the programmer uses the key word **RETURN**. The general format of the RETURN statement is as follows:

(line number) RETURN

No line number follows the word RETURN because BASIC itself has set a condition to automatically go back to the line immediately following GOSUB. For example:

340 GOSUB 2100
350
. . .
2100 REM ** OVERTIME PAY ROUTINE **
. . .
2170 RETURN

Upon the command found in line 340, the computer will execute an unconditional branch to line 2100. It will execute all the statements coded until it comes to RETURN. It then automatically branches back to the line following the GOSUB statement. The GOSUB can also be incorporated into a conditional statement, as follows:

340 IF H > 40 THEN GOSUB 2100

This statement would cause a branch to the subroutine only if the value of H was greater than 40.

In Figure A.23, the program that created the two arrays (the rate array and the job title array) is rewritten using GOSUB. The program statements code the creation of the two arrays in two separate modules, both far enough down in the program that they do not interfere with the general flow of logic. They are coded this way because they really are separate and distinct from the main flow of logic, and they therefore belong by themselves, away from the main flow. As you can see in the figure, all the statements relating to the creation of the array, including the DATA statements, are coded within the module. The part of the program that isolates the error records (those with a code out of the range 1 through 20) could also be isolated within its own module to help maintain the flow of logic. Picking up the program at statement 50, after the creation of the two arrays, the coding for the error module might look like that shown in Figure A.24.

Any program can be written without using GOSUB, but the incorporation of this command makes for a better flow of logic by isolating the statements that make up the different modules, or subroutines, of the program. Subroutines can be coded together with a logical beginning and ending, resulting in a program that is easier to write, easier to read, and less likely to cause a logic error. Programs that make extensive use of GOSUB develop the

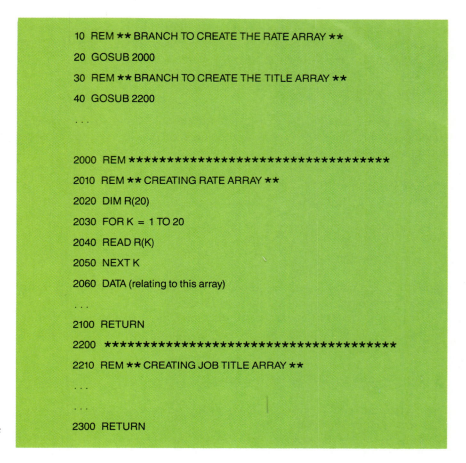

Figure A.23
Modular programming using the GOSUB statement.

"mainline" portion of the program as the lowest numbered part of the program. This *mainline* (sometimes called the *driver*) calls in the different modules one at a time, providing the programmer with more control over the flow of the logic and ease of debugging should a logic error occur.

Figure A.25 shows a comprehensive program that makes extensive use of the GOSUB statement. The program involves processing the records of company salespersons to report their sales performance. The company has twenty-five branches and fifteen different classifications of salespersons. Each employee's record contains the employee's identification number, name, the code for the branch in which the employee works (values 1 through 25), a code for the month that the employee was hired (values 1 through 12), the year that the employee was hired (4 digits), a code for the classification of salesperson (values 1 through 15), and the sales that the employee generated this month.

In the first phase of the program, three separate modules are used to

```
50   READ I,N$,H,C
60   IF I = 0 GOTO 9000
70   REM ** CHECKING FOR BAD CODE **
80   IF C = 0 OR C > 20 THEN GOSUB 2400
     . . .
     . . .
     . . .
2400 REM *****************************
2410 REM ** CREATING THE ERROR ARRAY **
2420 LET K = K + 1
2450 LET E1(K) = I; LET E2(K) = C
2460 RETURN
```

Figure A.24
Creating an error array.

create three arrays. The first is a fifteen-cell array that holds the sales quotas for the fifteen different types of salespersons; the second is a twenty-five-cell array that holds the names of the different cities where the branches are located; and the third holds the names of the twelve months of the year.

Once these arrays are created, the program instructs the computer to read the employee records and to create lines of output for the body of the report. Lines of output will be printed only for those salespersons who met or exceeded their quota. The branch at which the salesperson works and the month in which the salesperson was hired will be secured from the proper arrays in a separate module. Output (for those who met or exceeded their quota) will be the salesperson's identification number, the salesperson's name, the branch where the salesperson works, the month and year that the salesperson was hired, and the amount by which the sales quota was exceeded.

A count will be kept of those who did and did not meet their sales quotas. The salesperson with the highest sales and the salesperson with the lowest sales will also be computed in a separate module. After the last employee's record has been processed, the count of those who did meet and those who did not meet their quotas will be printed, along with the names and sales figures of the salesperson with the highest sales and the salesperson with the lowest sales.

The DATA lines have been omitted in the figure, but they would be included at the end of the program beginning with line 1000. The sales quota figures would be entered first, then the names of the branches, then the names of the months, since this is the order in which the three arrays

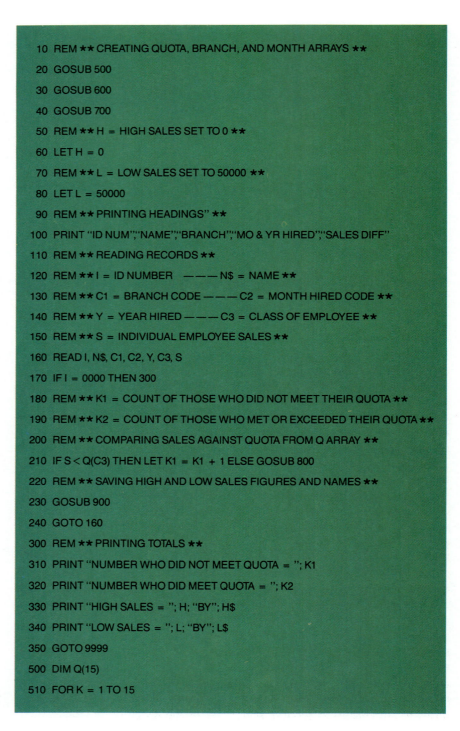

Figure A.25
A comprehensive program illustrating modular programming.

```
10  REM ** CREATING QUOTA, BRANCH, AND MONTH ARRAYS **
20  GOSUB 500
30  GOSUB 600
40  GOSUB 700
50  REM ** H = HIGH SALES SET TO 0 **
60  LET H = 0
70  REM ** L = LOW SALES SET TO 50000 **
80  LET L = 50000
90  REM ** PRINTING HEADINGS" **
100 PRINT "ID NUM";"NAME";"BRANCH";"MO & YR HIRED";"SALES DIFF"
110 REM ** READING RECORDS **
120 REM ** I = ID NUMBER  ——— N$ = NAME **
130 REM ** C1 = BRANCH CODE ——— C2 = MONTH HIRED CODE **
140 REM ** Y = YEAR HIRED ——— C3 = CLASS OF EMPLOYEE **
150 REM ** S = INDIVIDUAL EMPLOYEE SALES **
160 READ I, N$, C1, C2, Y, C3, S
170 IF I = 0000 THEN 300
180 REM ** K1 = COUNT OF THOSE WHO DID NOT MEET THEIR QUOTA **
190 REM ** K2 = COUNT OF THOSE WHO MET OR EXCEEDED THEIR QUOTA **
200 REM ** COMPARING SALES AGAINST QUOTA FROM Q ARRAY **
210 IF S < Q(C3) THEN LET K1 = K1 + 1 ELSE GOSUB 800
220 REM ** SAVING HIGH AND LOW SALES FIGURES AND NAMES **
230 GOSUB 900
240 GOTO 160
300 REM ** PRINTING TOTALS **
310 PRINT "NUMBER WHO DID NOT MEET QUOTA = "; K1
320 PRINT "NUMBER WHO DID MEET QUOTA = "; K2
330 PRINT "HIGH SALES = "; H; "BY"; H$
340 PRINT "LOW SALES = "; L; "BY"; L$
350 GOTO 9999
500 DIM Q(15)
510 FOR K = 1 TO 15
```

```
520  READ Q(K)
530  NEXT K
540  RETURN
600  DIM B$(25)
610  FOR K = 1 TO 25
620  READ B$(K)
630  NEXT K
640  RETURN
700  DIM M$(K)
710  FOR K = 1 TO 12
720  READ M$(K)
730  NEXT K
740  RETURN
800  REM ** PUTTING BRANCH NAME FROM B$ ARRAY INTO B1$ **
810  LET B1$ = B$(C1)
820  REM ** PUTTING NAME OF MONTH FROM M$ ARRAY INTO M1$ **
830  LET M1$ = M$(C2)
840  REM ** COMPUTING DIFFERENCE BETWEEN SALES AND QUOTA **
850  LET D = S − Q(C3)
860  LET K2 = K2 + 1
870  PRINT I, N$, B1$, M1$, Y, D
880  RETURN
900  IF S < L THEN LET L = S: LET L$ = N$
910  IF S > H THEN LET H = S: LET H$ = N$
920  RETURN
1000 DATA . . . .
9999 END
```

Figure A.25 (continued)

are created. Following these lines of data would come the individual employee data lines with the dummy, or trailer, value being 0000. An alternate way to code the DATA statements would be to include the data for the arrays within the modules that create the arrays themselves and then code the data for the employee records at the end of the program.

Functions

BASIC has numerous built-in **library functions,** also called **predefined functions,** that perform mathematical operations, such as generating a random number or finding the square root of a number. These built-in functions free the programmer from writing the mathematical routines to generate such values. Several ANSI library functions are common to all computer systems. Certain systems also include other functions that are not part of the ANSI standard. The general format for invoking a library function is as follows:

(line number) Name of Function (argument)

The functions include those shown in Figure A.26; the argument is a numeric constant or variable. In each example given in Figure A.26, the variable name X is used as the argument. The first four functions are trigonometric functions that are useful in mathematical, engineering, and scientific applications. The next three, LOG, EXP, and SQR, deal with raising a number to a particular power. The last four are mathematical functions that would be useful in business as well as in scientific applications.

The integer, or INT(X) function, is used to generate the integer less than or equal to the value of the argument. This function does not round to the nearest integer; the decimal portion of the number is truncated instead. For example, the following statement will return the integer part of X to Y:

100 LET Y = INT(X)

If the value of X is 10.7, the value of Y becomes 10. If the value of X is 13, the value of Y becomes 13. INT(X) can also be used to round a number to its nearest integer, tenth, hundredth, or to any degree of accuracy desired. To round a number to its nearest integer, you might write:

150 LET Y = INT(X + .5)

This statement would take the value of X, add 0.5 to it, and put the integer portion of X into Y. If the value of X is 7.7 and 0.5 is added to this value, the integer placed into the variable Y is 8. To round to two decimal places (dollars and cents, for example), a similar statement would be used; this time the amount to add would be 0.005:

250 LET Y = INT(X + .005)

The algebraic sign, or SGN(X) function, yields one of three possible values. If X is positive, then SGN(X) would yield +1. If X is negative, then SGN(X) would yield −1. If X is 0, then SGN(X) yields 0.

The absolute value, or ABS(X) function, returns the absolute value of the argument. The absolute value is always positive, even if the argument is negative. For example, if the value of X is −13.25, then the statement

FUNCTION	MEANING
SIN(X)	Trigonometric sine function, X in radians
COS(X)	Trigonometric cosine function, X in radians
TAN(X)	Trigonometric tangent function, X in radians
ATN(X)	Trigonometric arc tangent function, X in radians
LOG(X)	Natural logarithm function
EXP(X)	e raised to the X power
SQR(X)	Square root of X
INT(X)	Greatest integer less than X
SGN(X)	Sign of X
ABS(X)	Absolute value of X
RND	Random number between 0 and 1

Figure A.26
ANSI library functions.

    300 LET Y = ABS(X)

would generate the value of 13.25 in variable Y.

    The randomize, or RND, function is used to generate a random number between 0 and 1 or between any other two numbers; that is, any value between these two numbers may occur. Some systems either require or suggest two statements for this function. Others, such as the Apple II, require only one statement — for example:

    70 LET Y = RND(0)

This statement will generate a random number between 0 and 1. Other systems may use this same format, but it is suggested that a second statement be used in addition to the first. The TRS-80, for example, may use the statement just given, but an additional line with only the word RANDOM on it would ensure that a completely unpredictable sequence of random numbers is generated each time the computer is turned on. For example, the following three lines would be used with the TRS-80:

    10 RANDOM
    20 LET X = RND(0)
    30 LET Y = RND(100)

Line 20 generates a random number between 0 and 1. Line 30 generates a whole number greater than 0 and less than 101. The Pet Commodore also recommends the use of an additional statement preceding the RND statement, although the one statement can be used by itself also. The systems manuals for each system explain this function further.

CREATING AND ACCESSING FILES

Files may be either sequential or random. Sequential files are generally easier for the programmer to understand and code. When the computer creates a **sequential file,** it simply writes each succeeding record onto the next available space on the disk or tape without regard to the contents of the record. **Random files** consist of records placed in order by a record number assigned within the program. When records from a random file are read back into memory, they are accessed in order by this code rather than by their physical sequence. Because the majority of BASIC programming involves sequential disk files, our discussion will focus on the procedures and commands necessary for using these files.

Each computer system has its own unique commands within BASIC for creating and retrieving sequential files. Once you understand the basic format, you can consult the systems manual for the syntax that a particular system requires. The following discussion covers four popular systems — IBM-PC, TRS-80, Apple, and Commodore — as well as the generally accepted Microsoft BASIC.

IBM-PC, Microsoft BASIC, and TRS-80 Files

The principal statements in BASIC for dealing with sequential disk files are OPEN, CLOSE, PRINT # (sometimes called WRITE #), and INPUT #.

Before a file can be written to or read from, the computer must be told that the file exists; the command that does this is the word **OPEN.** The number of characters allowed in the file name depends on the system; file names are generally limited to eight characters or less. A sequential file may be opened as an *output* file — that is, created — by using an "O", or opened as an *input* file — that is, read from an already created file — by using an "I." The "O" and "I" must be enclosed in quotation marks and followed with a comma. In addition, the file must be given a sequence number, such as 1, 2, or 3, to identify it. The following statements would open an output file called INVFILE and an input file called CUSTFILE:

```
100 OPEN "O", 1, "INVFILE"
110 OPEN "I", 2, "CUSTFILE"
```

The first statement tells the computer that the program will create a new file called INVFILE and that that file is assigned sequence number 1. The second statement says that an existing file called CUSTFILE will be accessed during the program, and it is assigned sequence number 2. You should consult the manual for the particular system you are using for the syntax to assign a file to a particular disk drive; without a drive designator, the output file is automatically assigned to the first unprotected diskette. You should also consult the systems manual for the correct syntax if you wish to put a password on the file name.

When the file is opened as input, the system checks the disk directory to make sure the file exists. If the file does not exist, an error message is displayed; otherwise, the file is opened. When the file is opened as output, the system creates the file name in the disk directory. The first record written will be on the first available space on the disk surface.

To indicate that access to an open file is no longer needed, the programmer uses the key word **CLOSE**. When no file numbers accompany CLOSE, the computer closes all open files. To close only a specific file, the programmer must include the sequence number used when the file was opened. For example:

100 CLOSE
110 CLOSE #1

The first statement tells the computer to close all open files; the second closes only the file with sequence number 1.

Data values are written into the file by the **PRINT #** statement. The PRINT # statement is followed by the variable names, which are usually separated by semicolons; commas are not normally used with PRINT # since they bring the print zone principle into play and waste a great deal of disk space. The following statement would write the values of four numeric variables into the file opened as file 1:

200 PRINT #1, A; B; C; D

The file designator (#1) means that this file will have a record written to it. When the data are being accessed later on, the system will know when a particular numeric field ends since it uses the space created by the semicolon to separate the data.

Because a space is a valid string character, a comma within quotes is placed after each string field to indicate the end of the field. When the computer reads the record back in, it uses the comma (and not a space) as the signal that the string field has ended. To create the numeric fields A and B, the string fields C$ and D$, and the numeric field E, you would code:

200 PRINT #1, A; B; C$; ","; D$; ","; E

Microsoft BASIC and IBM-PC allow the **WRITE #** statement to be substituted for PRINT #. When WRITE # is used, the system automatically puts a comma after each data value, so there is no need to put the literal comma after a string field as must be done with PRINT #. The following example uses the WRITE # statement to create a record with two string variables followed by two numeric variables:

150 WRITE #1, A$, B$, X, Y

The **INPUT #** statement will retrieve data values from a record on disk. The total number of variables used in this statement must equal the number of variables used when the file was created. For example, assuming that a file was opened as file number 1 and each record contains a numeric variable followed by three string variables, the following statement would retrieve the data:

    300 INPUT #1, A, B$, C$, D$

Note that a comma is used to separate the variable names. If the mode (string or numeric) of any of these four fields is not as described in the statement, then a run-time error would result and the program would terminate. This would happen, for example, when string data are read when the variable name used was numeric.

The **EOF** (end of file) function is a built-in feature of the language that tests for the end of the file; that is, when the computer encounters a CLOSE statement, it writes an EOF indicator after the last record in the file so that when the file is reopened and the records are being read back in, the computer will know when it has no more records to read. As noted earlier, the dummy, or trailer, data contained in the highest numbered DATA statement do the same thing—that is, they signal the end of "good" data. Although a dummy record can be written as the last record in a file, it is more convenient for the programmer to ask if the EOF has been encountered than to ask if the dummy record has been brought into memory. To do so, the programmer codes an IF/THEN statement containing the EOF test condition immediately before the INPUT # statement. The following is an example of reading an existing file with ID numbers, names, and account balances:

```
10 OPEN "O", 1, "CUSTFILE"
20 PRINT "ID NUMBER", "NAME", "BALANCE"
30 IF EOF(1) GOTO 80
40 INPUT #1, I, N$, B
50 PRINT I, N$, B
60 LET T = T + B
70 GOTO 30
80 PRINT "TOTAL OF ALL BALANCES = "; T
90 CLOSE
100 END
```

Apple Files

An Apple computer has special commands for gaining access to a file. The programmer must first tell the system that a file is to be used. This is done by simultaneously pressing the CTRL (control) key and the D key. For convenience and to make the commands more easily recognizable, Apple programmers usually give a string variable name, typically D$ (D being the first character of "disk"), to CTRL-D by coding this statement:

10 D$ = CHR$(4)

This command assigns the ASCII character D to the string name D$. Any time that the PRINT D$ command appears, the computer will know that it refers to a file. This command must immediately precede any OPEN statement. For example, to open a file called INVFILE, you would code:

10 PRINT D$; "OPEN INVFILE"

An Apple file is not specifically opened as input or output. The system will look up the name in the disk directory. If the file exists, you may access the records with INPUT statements, but writing to it will destroy the previous contents. If the file does not exist, the system will create the name in the directory. This file may now be created through the usual BASIC statements.

The file is closed by again using the PRINT D$ command immediately before the CLOSE statement:

200 PRINT D$; "CLOSE INVFILE"

The WRITE command, which is also preceded with PRINT D$, prepares the file to receive data. Following this command, any PRINT commands will route data values to the file rather than to the CRT or the printer. The following is an example of an Apple file prepared to accept data through the WRITE and OPEN statements, the creation of four names and phone numbers in the file through the PRINT statement, and then termination of the file through the CLOSE statement:

```
10 REM ** CREATION OF A FILE WITH APPLE **
20 LET D$ = CHR$(4)
30 PRINT D$; "OPEN EMPFILE"
40 PRINT D$; "WRITE EMPFILE"
50 FOR K = 1 TO 4
60 READ N$, P$
70 PRINT N$; ","; P$
80 NEXT K
90 J. BROWN, 235-7979, W. WHITE, 245-3788
100 P. BLACK, 244-7656, R. GREEN, 434-9708
110 PRINT D$; "CLOSE EMPFILE"
999 END
```

To access an existing file, Apple uses the command INPUT, but the command READ must precede the INPUT statement since READ will prepare the file as input in a similar way that WRITE was used to prepare the file as output. As always, CHR$(4) is assigned to D$ before any reference to the disk file can be made. This program will read back the four records created in the above program. Line 70 of the program will print the values on the screen:

```
10 REM ** ACCESS OF AN APPLE FILE **
20 LET D$ = CHR$(4)
30 PRINT D$; "OPEN EMPFILE"
40 PRINT D$; "READ EMPFILE"
50 FOR K = 1 TO 4
60 INPUT N$, P$
70 PRINT N$, P$
80 NEXT K
90 PRINT D$; "CLOSE EMPFILE"
100 END
```

Commodore Files

The general format for creating or accessing a file with a Commodore computer is OPEN with a device code. This device code is always 8 for a single-disk system. The command also contains a file sequence number, which may be any number from 2 to 127, and a channel number from 2 through 14. For convenience, the channel number should be the same number as the file number. OPEN would also contain the letters SEQ meaning sequential file. It may be abbreviated by the single letter S. The last entry when writing to the file is the letter W and when reading the file the letter R. The following is an example of an OPEN statement on a Commodore system:

```
10 OPEN 3, 8, 3, "EMPFILE, S, W"
```

The number 3 after the word OPEN is the file number. The 8 is the device code. The next number is the channel number. The name EMPFILE is the file name. The S means that it is a sequential file, and the W means that the file will be written to or created. After the file is opened, the PRINT # command will put data into the file. The following shows how the file created with an Apple computer would be created with a Commodore:

```
10 OPEN 3, 8, 3, "EMPFILE, S, W"
20 FOR K = 1 TO 4
30 READ N$, T$
40 PRINT #3, N$; T$
50 NEXT K
60 CLOSE #3
```

70 DATA J. BROWN, 235-7979, W. WHITE, 245-3788
80 DATA P. BLACK, 244-7656, R. BROWN, 434-9708
90 END

Note that a PRINT # statement (line 40 in this example) must contain the sequential file number, as is the case with other systems. Once this file has been created, it can be read back in by changing the W to R in the OPEN statement. To access the same file, the INPUT # command (followed by the file number) is used. The following code would open the file, read the four records, and print the contents on the screen:

10 OPEN 3, 8, 3, "EMPFILE, S, R"
20 FOR K = 1 TO 4
30 INPUT #3, N$, T$
40 PRINT N$, T$
50 NEXT K
60 CLOSE #3
70 END

Review Questions

1. What statement must precede any reference to a disk file in BASIC?
2. How may a file be opened in BASIC?
3. What statement is used to terminate the use of a disk file?
4. What does EOF mean?
5. What command is used to put data onto a disk? To bring data from a disk?

PROBLEMS

1. Write LET statements for these tasks:
   (a) Assign the value of 99.99 to Y.
   (b) Assign the value of "HELLO" to H$.
   (c) Assign the value of the expression of A + B to C.
   (d) Increase the value of A by 1.
   (e) Double the value of K.

2. Write a program that will assign two numeric variables to two different variable names and then print four lines: the value of the first minus the second, the value of the first plus the second, the value of the first multiplied by the second, and the value of the first divided by the second.

3. What will be printed when this program is executed?
   100 LET X = 100
   200 LET Y = 200
   300 LET Z = X − Y
   400 PRINT X, Y, Z, Y, X

4. Using READ and DATA, write a program that will read in two numeric variables and one string variable and that will then print these three values.

5. Using READ and DATA, write a program that will read in a customer's ID number, name, old balance, and amount of purchases. The program should also print out four of the fields plus the new balance (old balance plus purchases).

6. Using INPUT, write a program that will prompt a student to enter his or her name and grade point average. Output is to be a blank line followed by a line with the two values that were entered.

7. A car travels M miles and uses N number of gallons of gasoline to travel this distance. What is the cost of the trip if the gasoline costs $1.22 per gallon, highway tolls cost $4.50, and the overhead costs are computed as being $.15 per mile traveled? Using the INPUT statement, write a program to bring in the miles traveled and gallons of gasoline used and to print out the total cost along with a self-explanatory message.

8. What will happen when this program is executed?
   100 READ A, B, C
   110 LET D = A + B + C
   120 PRINT D
   130 GOTO 100
   140 DATA 12, 24, 36
   150 DATA 20, 40, 60
   160 DATA 15, 10, 25.25
   999 END

9. Using the INPUT statement, write a program that will bring in the unit cost and number of units sold for three products. The program should print out the unit cost, the number of units sold, and the total selling price of each of the three products. Use a variable name to count the number of times that a line is printed.

10. Using the INPUT statement, write a program that will bring in salespersons' names and the sales for three of the products they sell. Output

is to be each salesperson's name and total sales. Print some column headings over the two columns of output and accumulate the final total value of all items sold. Print out this final total under the second column before terminating the program. Use XXX as the terminal value.

11. Write a program that will carry on a conversation with the computer. A prompt will ask WHAT IS YOUR NAME? After the user responds, the computer will say HELLO (name) HOW ARE YOU? The user will respond FINE or NOT SO GOOD. If the response is FINE, the computer will answer THAT'S GOOD (name). If the response is NOT SO GOOD, the computer will respond THAT'S TOO BAD (name). In either case, the computer will print HAVE A NICE DAY (name).

12. Using the READ and DATA statements, write a program that will bring in employees' names, hours worked, and work code. The possible values of the work code will be a 1, 2, or 3. Within the program (using IF statements), assign the value of 10.00 to the rate of pay if the work code is 1, 12.50 if the code is 2, and 15.00 if the code is 3. Print out the name, hours worked, the rate of pay (secured through the IF statement), and the gross pay for each employee. Include at least one employee with each of the different work codes.

13. As an extension of the program in problem 12, write a program to include the possibility that the code is not within the range 1, 2, or 3. If an out-of-range code is read in, print it along with an error message and continue processing with the next employee.

14. As an extension of the program in problem 13, write a program to include an additional variable: a code for the shift that the employee worked. A code of 1 will result in no additional compensation, a code of 2 will result in a shift differential of 5 percent of gross pay, and a code of 3 will result in a shift differential of 10 percent of gross pay. Allow for the possibility that a code not within the range of 1 or 2 or 3 may appear. If a code is within the acceptable range, compute the employee's gross pay to include the additional shift differential. Print out the employee's name, gross pay without differential, the dollar amount of the shift differential, and the final gross pay.

15. Write a program to bring in five variables: the customer's number, the customer's name, the customer's old balance, the amount of payment, and the amount of purchases. Output will be the same five fields, the amount of interest the customer owes (which could be zero), and the new balance. If the amount of the old balance is greater than the amount of payment, then the customer will pay 1.5 percent interest on the difference. The new balance will be the old balance minus the payment, plus the purchases, plus the amount of interest. Be sure to include enough data for all contingencies.

16. Using the INPUT statement, write a program that will compute the worth of a savings account at the end of a specified period given a

specified rate of interest. Four variables should be brought in: the amount of the initial deposit, the number of years that the fund will remain in the account, the annual rate of interest, and the number of times per year that the rate is compounded (quarterly, daily, etc.). Print out the balance at the end of the time period. After a line is printed, prompt the user to answer "yes" or "no" to a question asking if more input data exist.

17. Using the same approach as in problem 16, include a PRINT statement to see what the accumulated balance will be at the end of each year. The printed line should include a message such as "AMOUNT END OF (year)" and the actual amount.

18. Write a program that will create a fifteen-cell array of rates of pay. Then write a routine that will print out the values in the array on fifteen separate lines.

19. Using the array created in problem 18, write coding that will examine the data to find the largest value and the smallest value of the fifteen cells. Print out these two values with self-explanatory messages. Hint: Compare each value in the array against a variable that holds the previous high (or low) value—not one value in the array against another value in the array.

20. Write a program that will create a five-by-ten array (table) of numeric data, add up all the values, and compute an average of the values.

21. Write a program that will create a sequential disk file to include students' numbers, names, accumulated credits, and grade point averages. Write coding to access this file and accumulate (a) the total number of students in the file; (b) the total number of students who have less than 10 credits; and (c) the total number of students who have a grade point average of less than 1.00. After the last record has been read, print out these three values with self-explanatory messages.

GLOSSARY

Alphanumeric data Any one character or a series of characters made up of letters, numbers, special characters, and spaces.

ANSI BASIC The accepted standards of the BASIC language as defined by the American National Standards Institute.

Array (matrix) A group of storage locations that are given a single variable name. Individual elements in the array can be referenced by the variable name followed by one or more subscripts.

Branching The transfer of control from one point in a program to another.

CLOSE A key word that tells the computer that access to a file is no longer needed.

Conditional branch The transfer of control from one point in a program to another based on the results of a comparison of data.

Constant A numeric or string value that does not change for the run of the program.

DATA A key word used in conjunction with the READ statement to supply values for variables.

DIM A key word that reserves data elements for an array.

Dummy (trailer) record A record coded as the highest-numbered DATA statement whose data signal the end of real data.

Elements (cells) Storage locations that are a part of an array.

END A key word that signals the logical and physical ending of a program.

EOF A key word used with a sequential disk file to detect the end of a file.

Expression A valid literal, variable, or mathematical formula.

Field One or more consecutive characters that together represent specific data.

File A group of related records.

FOR/NEXT Key words that allow the program to loop until a specified condition arises.

GOSUB A key word that tells the computer to leave the present point in the program and execute a subroutine; used in conjunction with RETURN.

GOTO A key word that tells the computer to execute an unconditional branch to another statement elsewhere in the program.

Hierarchy of operations The priority given to the performance of multiple arithmetic operations in a single formula.

IF/THEN A statement that instructs the computer to evaluate fields of data and to execute a certain operation if the condition evaluated is true.

Infinite loop A programmer's error that causes the same series of statements to be repeated endlessly.

INPUT A key word that tells the computer that data values are to be entered into memory from the keyboard in an interactive mode.

INPUT # A key word used to access data from a file.

Instruction set The number, or repertoire, of commands that are available in a programming language.

Key (reserved) words Words that have a specified, unique meaning to the translation program. Such words cannot be used as variable names.

LET A key word that assigns a value to a variable.

Library functions (predefined functions) Preprogrammed, built-in routines that programmers can use without having to recode the required logic.

Line number The number that must precede each statement so that the computer will know the order in which to execute the statements.

LIST A command to the operating system to display the program on the CRT screen in line-number order.

Literal A string constant used in a PRINT statement.

Logic error A programming error created by using illogical instructions rather than improper syntax.

Loop A series of instructions that are executed repeatedly until a specific condition arises that tells the computer to stop executing the statements.

Nested loop A loop programmed within another loop; generally used to manipulate two-dimensional arrays.

Numeric data Data that contain the digits 0 through 9 and that can be used to perform arithmetic calculations.

One-dimensional array (list) An array with a single list of values referred to by a single subscript.

OPEN A key word signifying that a file is to be created or accessed.

PRINT A key word that tells the computer to perform an output operation.

PRINT # A key word that tells the computer that output values should be placed in a file.

PRINTTAB A key word that adds a tabular spacing function to printing output.

PRINT USING A key word that allows the formatting of output.

Print zone A specified number of positions set aside as the length of one output field.

Prompt A message printed on a CRT screen to explain to the user what input should be entered; usually used in conjunction with the INPUT statement.

Random file A disk file that is created and accessed in order by a key field rather than on a physical, sequential basis.

READ A key word that tells the computer to bring into memory the values of the variables found in a DATA statement.

Record A collection of data fields that make up a unit of a file.

REM A key word used when coding a note or comment into a program.

RESTORE A key word that tells the computer that values in a DATA statement previously brought into memory by READ statements should be reread when the next READ command is executed.

RETURN A key word that must be used as the terminal line of a subroutine branched to by a GOSUB statement.

RUN A systems command that tells the computer to begin executing the program.

Sequential file A file in which the data items are physically recorded in the order in which they are entered.

Statement One instruction or one line of a program. Each statement in BASIC must include a line number and a command.

String data Data that contain the alphabetic, numeric, and special characters that the computer can recognize. Such data cannot be used to perform arithmetic operations.

Subroutine A sequence of statements coded together away from the mainline of the program; used primarily to increase readability of the program or to avoid the rewriting of program segments that are referred to more than once.

Subscript A variable that is coded with a DIM statement to indicate how many elements, or cells, there are in an array.

Syntax The basic rules of a computer language that must be adhered to by the programmer when coding the program.

Syntax error A programming error caused by the incorrect construction of program statements.

Systems command An instruction that tells the computer's operating system that a specific function should be performed.

Two-dimensional array (table) The arrangement of data in a table so that the data are referred to by two subscripts.

Unconditional branch A branch that occurs in response to a program statement each time the statement is executed.

Variable A numeric or string value that changes repeatedly during the execution of a program.

Variable name The programmer-supplied label for a variable as composed by the programmer.

WRITE # A key word used by some systems to perform an output operation to a file.

GLOSSARY

Access arms Arms that support the read/write heads on a magnetic-disk drive.
Access management software Software designed to limit access and to control the level of access to an information system.
Access speed The time required to locate and retrieve data from storage.
Accumulator A temporary storage place in the CPU that holds the accumulated results of computations.
Acoustic coupler A special type of modem that is used with a portable terminal and that has a telephone handset for transmitting data.
Ada A programming language developed by the Department of Defense to provide a single, powerful, standardized language for both business and scientific applications.
Address A number that identifies a location in primary storage; a number that identifies a storage area on a magnetic disk.
Address register A temporary storage area in the CPU used to hold the operand just before the instruction is due for processing.
Administration A functional area of business whose purpose is to coordinate all the activities of the business to meet a common objective.
Algorithm A logical sequence of steps that lead to the solution of a problem.
Analog A form of transmission in which data are sent in a continuous variable wave pattern.
Analog computer A computer that processes variable and ever-changing data.
Annotation symbol A program flowchart symbol used for descriptive comments that are written directly on the flowchart.
APL Abbreviation for A Programming Language; a language with powerful interactive features that is well suited to processing unstructured problems.
Applications programs Instructions that direct the computer to perform specific tasks.
Archive reports Files of detailed historical data.
Archives Long-term recordkeeping facilities for storing historical data and records of past transactions.
Arithmetic/logic unit The section of the CPU that processes computations and performs logic operations.
Artificial intelligence (AI) The human ability to learn, reason, and solve problems simulated by a machine.
ASCII The American Standard Code for Information Interchange; a popular computer coding system.
Assembler Systems software that translates assembly language into machine language.
Assembly language A programming language that uses letter codes (called mneumonics) to communicate with the computer.
Assembly listing A printed reproduction of the program instructions that were entered into the computer.
Asynchronous transmission The sending of a character of data as an isolated unit. Special signal bits identify the beginning and end of each character.
Audio-input (voice-recognition) device A device that accepts spoken words as input data and enters them into the CPU as electronic signals.
Audio-output device A device that converts electronic signals from the computer into spoken messages.
Audit review Verification that the system is performing according to specifications.
Auxiliary storage (secondary storage, external storage) Storage that supplements the computer's primary storage unit.
BACKUP A microcomputer utility program that reproduces a file or entire floppy disk as a protective measure.
Backup file A copy of a file that is generally stored away from the computer area to allow the reconstruction of the records should the originals be destroyed.
Band The range of frequencies of a transmission channel.
Bar code Vertical bars coded to represent specific data to a computer system.
Bar-code reader A device that optically scans bar codes, converts them into electronic signals, and enters them into the computer system.
BASIC Abbreviation for Beginners All-purpose Symbolic Instruction Code; an easily learned programming language that is used extensively with microcomputers.
Batch A kind of processing in which data are held to be processed as a group some time after the transaction that created them.
Batch control A procedure that compares a manual tally of the transactions going into the computer system with the total produced by the computer.
Baud A unit for measuring the speed of data transmission by describing the number of times per second that a line changes condition.
Behavioral management A management style based on the belief that individuals are at least as important to an organization as procedures and work activities.
Binary numbering system A numbering system that uses only two digits, 0 and 1.
Bit Abbreviation for binary digit; a 0 or 1.
Bits per second (bps) A measure of speed in data communications.
Blind searching Trial-and-error testing of alternative solutions to a problem.
Block Two or more logical records grouped together and read as a unit.
Bottom-up programming A programming technique that tends to concentrate on the detail of the prob-

lem solution without regard for the overall solution.

Branch pattern A logic pattern that causes the computer to break the normal sequence of instructions by bypassing or skipping a number of instructions.

Broad bandwidth A band capable of transmitting data at very high speed — up to 500,000 bps.

Bubble memory A storage device that uses chip technology and a thin film of magnetic material to represent and store data in nonvolatile form.

Buffers Small, fast storage elements used to compensate for differing speeds of input, processing, and output equipment.

Bundled (turnkey) system A combination of hardware and software sold as a package.

Byte A number of bits, often eight, that form a storage unit capable of holding one character of data.

Card reader A device that scans the patterns of holes in punched cards and transmits them as electronic impulses into the computer system.

Cassette A device used to hold magnetic tape.

Cathode ray tube (CRT) The component of a display screen that receives signals from the computer and translates them into images on the screen.

Central processing unit (CPU, processor) The heart of the computer; composed of the primary storage unit, the arithmetic/logic unit, and the control unit.

Chain printer A line-at-a-time printer whose character set is assembled on a chain that passes in front of a series of print hammers. The hammers strike the characters and transfer the images through a ribbon onto the paper.

Channels Communications lines for transmitting signals to and from the computer system.

Character-at-a-time printer (serial printer) A computer output device that prints one character at a time.

Character A number, letter, special symbol, or blank.

Chief programmer team A project team headed by an experienced programmer who is responsible for developing the general design and overseeing the work on the various components of the project.

C language A programming language developed by Bell Labs as a part of the UNIX operating system. It has many of the characteristics of assembly language and a great deal of portability.

Coaxial cable A communications channel consisting of a conductive cylinder of copper and an inner wire insulated from the conductive cylinder.

COBOL Abbreviation for COmmon Business-Oriented Language; the most popular programming language for business applications.

Coding The process of converting the logic of a problem solution into detailed instructions written in a programming language.

Coding forms Preprinted forms that contain the requirements of a specific programming language for positioning and sequencing program instructions and identifying their function.

Collision (synonym) A problem that occurs when different keys hash, or randomize, to the same storage address.

Communicating A managerial function involving the transfer of information both inside and outside the organization.

Communications satellite A device that orbits the earth and that can accept, store, and transmit signals sent from one earth station to another.

Compiler A set of instructions that tells the computer how to translate instructions written in a high-level language into machine language; part of the systems software.

Complex (distributed) network A network with cross-communications links between all computers in the network.

Compression The removal of blanks and recoding of numerical data in a more concise form for data transmission.

Computer A programmable electronic device that can accept input data; process, store, and retrieve those data; and produce output.

Computer-aided design and computer-aided manufacturing (CAD/CAM) The use of the computer to draft and analyze an engineering design and to control manufacturing equipment.

Computer-assisted instruction (CAI) The use of the computer to assist in drill and routine learning exercises.

Computer auditor The person charged with being sure that the controls on the computer system are adequate, in place, and functioning.

Computer-based management information system A system or set of systems that uses a computer to collect, condense, filter, and manipulate data so that it meets not only a company's routine data-processing and reporting needs but also the information needs of managers.

Computer crime A crime that involves the manipulation of the data, programs, or outputs of a computer system.

Computer dependence Reliance on computers for the production of necessary goods and services.

Computerized appointments calendar The use of an electronic message system to schedule and confirm appointments with others who use the same message system.

Computer-managed instruction The use of the computer to tailor educational programs to meet the specific needs of individual students.

Computer operators Personnel who control and coordinate the computer hardware.

Computer output microform (COM) Computer output on film in greatly reduced form.

Concentrator A device that evaluates data signals and combines and routes them through specific channels.

Connector symbol A program flowchart symbol used to illustrate the program flow when flowlines would be hard to follow.

Contention A process used by multiplexors and concentrators to continually check a terminal line and send a signal when the line becomes free.

Contract programming The hiring of outside technical personnel or specialty firms to develop and implement programs.

Control clerks Personnel who catalog, monitor, record, and control the flow of data and programs to and from the computer.

Control functions Functions carried out by specialized operating systems programs that control the operation of the system and the performance of various tasks.

Controlling A managerial function that involves measuring actual performance against established goals.

Control structures The four basic logic patterns that the computer can execute.

Control unit The part of the CPU that directs the sequence of all input and output activities, the arithmetic and logic operations, and the transfer of data to and from primary storage.

Cost/benefit analysis An analysis of the developmental and operational costs and tangible and intangible benefits of a proposed system.

Cost effectiveness Economy produced by allocating a firm's resources to obtain the greatest overall return on investment.

Cost savings A reduction in labor, overhead, and investment and an increase in productivity per unit.

Critical path network A graphic technique for illustrating scheduled events and time relationships.

Cursor A symbol on a CRT screen showing where the next character will appear.

Cylinder The organization of like-numbered tracks on each of the surfaces of a disk pack so that the read/write heads can access a number of records with one movement of the access arms.

Daisy wheel A rimless plastic or metal wheel with a character embossed on the end of each of its spokes that is used in a character-at-a-time impact printer. A hammer strikes the character against a ribbon, causing the character to be printed onto the paper.

Data The unevaluated facts and figures that form the raw materials for processing.

Data bank A large group of data that can be accessed by computer.

Data base A method of organizing and storing data in which files are independent of applications programs and are available to satisfy a number of different processing needs.

Data base administrator (DBA) The person responsible for seeing that the data used in a data base are defined consistently throughout the organization and that the standards and security procedures for accessing and using the data are enforced.

Data base management system (DBMS) A series of integrated programs designed to simplify the tasks of creating, accessing, and managing a data base.

Data base software Software designed to serve as an interface between the data base and the users and to limit data redundancy.

Data bus A holding area for storing signals routed from a keyboard to the control unit of the CPU.

Data collection personnel Personnel who collect input data.

Data communications system A rapid means of transmitting data in the form of electronic signals from one location to another.

Data complexity The precision of the input data needed to produce the desired output.

Data cycle The logical data processing sequence of input, processing, and output.

Data density The capacity of auxiliary storage media.

Data dictionary Data definitions as used in a particular data base.

Data entry personnel Personnel who prepare and enter data into the computer system.

Data errors Inaccuracies in input data.

Data independence A condition that occurs when data are organized according to their own characteristics and not according to the needs of a particular applications program. It allows different programs to share the same data base.

Data integrity Consistency among and accuracy within data files.

Data management programs Systems software that deals with the flow of data during program execution.

Data redundancy Repetition of the same data in different files.

Data transfer rate The speed at which data can be read from or written to a storage medium.

Debugging and testing The process of correcting syntax and logic errors in a program.

Decision support system (DSS) A set of software tools that allows users to directly access a data base and to simulate, or model, the real world.

Decision symbol A program flowchart symbol used to represent the comparison called for in a logic operation.

Decision table A program design tool that shows in table form the actions that should be taken if certain conditions exist.

Default option A standard, predetermined way of handling input, processing, or output that the systems software will follow unless a program instruction tells it to do otherwise.

Demodulation The process of converting a signal from analog to digital form.

Desk checking An inspection of program instructions by the programmer to see if the logic and syntax are correct.

Destructive write Descriptive of the erasure of data from a storage location that occurs when new data are recorded in that location.

Detailed report A report that contains information on a business's day-to-day activities.

Developmental costs One-time expenses that occur as a system is being

designed and the programs are being prepared.
Diagnostic messages Messages produced by the compiler describing the syntax errors it has detected during program translation.
Digital A form of transmission in which data are sent as binary, or on-off, pulses.
Digital computer A computer that processes discrete data — that is, data that are individually distinct and that can be counted.
Digitizing tablet A touch-sensitive input device.
Direct access The ability to go directly to a record without having to read all the preceding records in the file.
Direct access storage device (DASD) A type of storage unit that allows the computer to skip over unwanted data and go directly to the needed data.
Direct file organization A method of organizing and storing data so they can be retrieved in any order or at random.
Direct processing A method of processing data in which a key field is used to indicate the exact location of each record.
Disk pack A stack of magnetic disks mounted on a hub and spindle.
Distributed data processing (DDP) Processing done by using communications channels to link a number of computers.
DITTO A utility program that makes a copy of a file.
Documentation The process of compiling information on a program that will be of use to the system's users, programmers, and operations personnel.
Dot matrix printer A printer that uses a grid of wire pins to form characters and strikes the pins against a ribbon to create an image on paper.
DO-UNTIL structure A variation of the loop logic pattern in which the computer will repeat a series of program steps until a certain condition occurs.
DO-WHILE stucture A variation of the loop logic pattern in which the computer will repeat a series of program steps while a certain condition is being met.
Drum plotter An output device that uses computer-controlled pens and a continuous roll of paper moving over a drum to produce graphic output.
Drum printer A printer whose characters are embossed on a drum. As the drum turns, the characters are positioned in front of hammers, which strike and create an image on the paper.
Dumb terminal A terminal that can perform only as an input and output device.

EBCDIC Extended Binary-Coded Decimal Interchange Code; a popular computer coding system.
Editing A control procedure for checking the accuracy of data as they enter the computer system.
Education Privacy Act A federal act of 1974 that protects a student's right to privacy in terms of evaluations and course grades.
80-column punched card (Hollerith card) A card capable of holding 80 bytes of data that is used for data entry and storage.
Electronic filing Filing done with electronic signals rather than paper.
Electronic funds transfer (EFT) The transfer of funds via electronic signals rather than paper documents.
Electronic message system (electronic mail) A system that uses telephones and computers to receive and send messages.
Electronic spreadsheet A microcomputer program for manipulating financial data.
Electrostatic printer A printer that creates a charged field on a drum, which then picks up ink particles and transfers the image to paper.
Electrothermal printer A printer whose print-head elements are electrically heated to produce an image on specially treated, heat-sensitive paper.
Encryption The coding of data for security purposes.
Engineering simulation The computer-aided development of an environment for testing engineering designs.
Environmental control system A special unit that controls the temperature and humidity in a computer room.
EPROM Abbreviation for erasable programmable read-only memory; a special type of erasable memory chip used in the CPU.
Equipment-based RFP A request for a systems proposal that specifies the desired hardware capacities and operational characteristics of the system.
Error management software Software designed to prevent errors in data transmission and to initiate correction procedures when errors are detected.
Even parity A parity check that requires that the total of the 1 bits for each character be an even number.
Exception report A report that contains information only on results that differ substantially from those that were planned or projected.
Execution time (E-time) The time during which data are retrieved from primary storage and the arithmetic/logic unit performs the specific operation called for in a program instruction.
Expert system A system that uses the reasoning power of the computer to arrive at conclusions by combining a large number of factual data with the knowledge and understanding of experts in a particular field.
External constraints Limitations stemming from forces outside the organization that affect systems development.

Fair Credit Reporting Act A federal act of 1970 that regulates how private organizations manage their information about individuals.
Fair information practices laws State laws based on issues covered in the Privacy Act of 1974, which gives individuals the right to review federal records pertaining to themselves.
Feasibility study A document that

spells out the findings of the first step in the systems development cycle.

Federal Computer System Protection Act Legislation introduced in 1977 that specifically addressed computer crime. Although it was never passed, it induced several states to enact similar legislation.

Fiber optics Very thin, light-conducting threads of glass or plastic that are used to transmit data signals at the speed of light.

Field A collection of related characters.

File A group of data composed of one or more records that are stored and processed as a unit.

Filtering The process of removing certain data from the data that are captured and/or processed.

Finance A functional area of business whose purpose is to manage the company's funds and to report how those funds have been applied.

Firmware Programs that are permanently built into the computer circuits and are therefore fixed and unchangeable.

Fixed record A record with a limited size, such as an 80-column punched card.

Fixed word-length A term describing a computer that holds a consistent number of characters in each address in primary storage and that moves the data a word at a time.

Flatbed plotter An output device that functions like a drawing table and that produces graphic output on a flat sheet of paper.

Floppy disk (floppy, diskette) A low-cost storage medium for microcomputers.

Flowline A program flowchart symbol used to connect the other symbols of the flowchart.

Formed-character printer A printer whose characters are embossed on a ball, cylinder, thimble, ribbon, or daisy wheel. The characters are either struck by a hammer or are part of the hammer mechanism itself.

FORTRAN Abbreviation for FORmula TRANslator; a popular programming language for scientific applications.

Freedom of Information Act A 1970 law that makes the operational details of federal data collection activities available for public scrutiny.

Front-end processor A minicomputer that relieves a host computer of many of the data communications chores by checking and routing signals, polling terminals, and compensating for different transmission speeds.

Full-duplex A mode of data transmission in which signals can go both ways at the same time.

Function keys Keyboard keys that can be programmed to execute certain routines.

Function management software Data communications software for processing input/output requests, maintaining logs, determining message priority, and managing the temporary storage of signals

Gantt chart A chart that uses bars representing various project tasks to show the status of a project.

General-purpose computer A computer that can perform a variety of processing tasks.

General-purpose register A temporary storage area in the CPU used for both addressing and computational purposes.

GIGO Abbreviation for garbage in, garbage out; descriptive of what happens when the computer receives bad data or faulty instructions.

Graphic plotter A device specially designed for producing hard-copy graphics.

Graphics software Programs that can convert numerical and character data to pictorial form.

Grid (core plane) A latticelike structure used to hold magnetic cores for primary storage.

Hackers People who use personal computers to gain access to computer systems and who may cause harm by damaging programs or data even if they did not intend to do so.

Half-duplex A mode of data transmission in which signals can go in either direction but in only one direction at a time.

Hard copy A permanent record of computer output, usually on paper or in microform.

Hard disk A magnetic storage medium consisting of a machined-metal platter coated with a material that can be easily magnetized.

Hardware The computer machinery used for input, processing, storage, and output.

Hashing (randomizing) A mathematical procedure that translates a record key directly into a disk address.

Head crash The crash of a read/write head on the surface of a magnetic disk, which destroys some of the recording surface.

Hertz (Hz) A unit of frequency equal to one cycle per second.

Heuristic An AI technique that indicates a possible search path in the solution of a problem.

High-level languages Programming languages that resemble everyday human language.

HIPO (hierarchy plus input-output-processing) charts A program design tool that uses three levels of diagrams to depict the problem solution.

Historical data Records of past transactions.

Host computer A central computer connected to remote computers in a network configuration.

IF-THEN-ELSE structure A structure occurring in the selection logic pattern, which uses a logical comparison to select an appropriate program path.

Impact printer A printing device in which a mechanical motion creates physical contact between character, ribbon, and paper.

Implementation plan A plan that coordinates a project's various operational plans and that describes the project in terms of personnel needs, work assignments, time requirements, schedules, and budgets.

Indexed-sequential file organization (indexed-sequential access method, ISAM) A method of file organization that allows both sequential and direct access.

Indexing system A system for determining the addresses of data called for in a program.

Information Raw facts and figures that have been processed so that they are meaningful and useful.

Information-oriented flowchart A flowchart that shows the flow of information within a system or organization.

Information Revolution A term used to describe the social changes brought about by computing and communications technology.

Information systems manager The person responsible for planning, organizing, controlling, and integrating a firm's overall information resources.

Inkjet printer A printer that forms characters by spraying electrically charged ink particles onto paper or some other surface.

Input devices Equipment used to enter data into the computer system.

Input interface circuit A circuit that decodes a signal created by the depression of a key on a microcomputer keyboard and routes it to the microprocessor unit.

Input/output control programs Systems software that coordinates input, processing, and output to make the most effective use of the computer hardware.

Input/output symbol A program flowchart symbol used to represent either input or output on all types of media.

Inquiry report A report made in response to an information request whose timing cannot be predicted or scheduled.

Instruction register A temporary storage place in the CPU used to hold the op code just before the instruction is due for processing.

Instruction time (I-time) The time during which the control unit fetches an instruction from storage, decodes it, and puts it in the CPU's registers.

Integrated circuit A circuit created by etching the design of the electronic circuits on a small silicon chip.

Integrated software Software that combines a number of microcomputer applications — word processing, graphics, spreadsheet, and data communications — and that allows the user to merge data from separate programs.

Intelligent terminal A terminal that has the processing capabilities of a microcomputer.

Interactive A kind of processing in which data are processed immediately after they are entered into the computer system.

Interactive language A programming language that allows the user to communicate directly with the computer while preparing or using programs and to receive immediate response from the computer.

Interblock gap (IBG) The blank space between two blocks of logical records.

Interfaces Communications or sharing of data or outputs between two components of a system or between two systems.

Internal constraints Limitations within an organization that affect systems development.

Interpreter A translation program that translates each source-program statement one at a time and that does not create object programs.

Interrecord gap (IRG) The blank space maintained between logical records.

Interrupt The cessation of program execution because of a program, data, or equipment error.

Job A unit of work to be performed by the computer.

Job-control language (JCL) The language that the programmer uses to converse with the systems software.

Job-control program Systems software that translates instructions in job-control language into machine language.

Job displacement A change in employment brought about by technological change.

Job-management programs Systems software that controls the computer resources used during program execution.

Key (key field) A field chosen as the basis for the sequencing of records.

Keypunch machine A keyboard device that prepares data for computer processing by punching holes in cards.

Key-to-disk device A machine with a keyboard for transferring data from a source document to a magnetic disk.

Key-to-tape device A machine with a keyboard for transferring data from a source document to a magnetic tape.

Kilobyte (K) A unit of storage containing 1,024 bytes.

Knowledge workers (information workers) People whose work involves information.

Large-scale integration (LSI) A circuit-manufacturing technology of the 1970s that allowed as many as 64,000 electronic circuits to be placed on a single silicon chip.

Laser Abbreviation for light amplification by stimulated emission of radiation; a very strong and concentrated light beam used in reading and writing data on optical disks, in data communications, and in laser printers.

Laser printer A printer that uses a laser beam to project an image onto a photosensitive surface.

Letter quality Quality of printed output suitable for business correspondence.

Librarians Personnel who catalog, monitor, record, and control the flow of data and programs to and from the computer.

Library programs Systems software that catalogs and maintains a directory of frequently used subprograms.

Light pen An input device that contains a light-sensitive photocell, which, when touched against a CRT screen, creates signals that are picked up by the computer.

Line-at-a-time printer An output device that prints an entire line at one time.

Line management A style of project management in which one manager is in charge during the entire project and the project staff reports to that manager.

Line of sight A kind of transmission in which the signal goes in a straight line from the sending unit to the receiving unit without following the curvature of the earth.

Link/edit A systems software routine that links subprograms with the object program for program execution.

Load-and-go The operating system routine that executes a program.

Local area network (LAN) A communications network that is privately owned by the organization using it.

Log An ongoing record of all data entries, all programs run and the run times, and all terminals that have had access to the computer.

Log evaluation An audit technique that samples the computer log for unauthorized access and program runs.

Logic The organization, sense, and sequence of program instructions.

Logical record A record pertaining to a single transaction or activity.

Loop pattern A logic pattern in which the computer repeats a series of program steps while a certain condition is being met or until a certain condition occurs.

Machine cycle The cycle during which a program instruction is executed; consists of instruction time and execution time.

Machine language A computer language that uses the 0's and 1's of the binary numbering system, which correspond directly to the on-off states of a digital computer.

Macrocode A code used in high-level languages in which a single program instruction conveys a number of machine-language instructions.

Magnetic core A small, donutlike metallic core strung on a wire grid and used in primary storage.

Magnetic disk A storage medium consisting of a metal or plastic platter coated with a material that can be magnetized to represent data.

Magnetic-disk drive A device used to read and write data on magnetic disks.

Magnetic-ink character recognition (MICR) A system that records data as stylized symbols printed with a high-carbon ink that can be scanned by automated equipment.

Magnetic tape A storage medium composed of mylar and coated with a material that can be magnetized to represent data.

Magnetic-tape drive A device used to read and write data on magnetic tape.

Main board (mother board) A board within a microcomputer that contains the microprocessor chip.

Mainframe A large-scale computer.

Management information system (MIS) The means by which managers get the information they need to make decisions.

Management science Mathematical techniques used to simulate the real business environment.

Marketing A functional area of business whose purpose is to distribute goods and services.

Mark-sense reader An electronic scanner used for optical-mark recognition.

Mass storage unit A device that combines features of tape and disk technology with a mechanical retrieving arm to provide online storage for billions of characters of data.

Master file A file that contains relatively permanent information.

Matrix management A style of project management in which team leadership shifts among several project managers as the nature of the work underway changes.

Megabyte (M) A unit of storage containing a thousand kilobytes, or approximately 1 million bytes.

Membrane keys Keys depicted on a flat plastic surface with no physical separation between them.

Menu A listing of available programs.

MICR inscriber A device that reproduces the amount of a transaction in magnetic-ink characters.

Microcomputer A small, powerful, low-cost computer.

Microfiche A miniature photographic copy of computer output on a sheet of film approximately 4 by 6 inches.

Microfilm A miniature photographic copy of computer output on a continuous roll of film.

Microprocessor A silicon chip, smaller than a postage stamp, that contains all the circuitry for the arithmetic/logic and control units.

Microwaves Super-high-frequency radio waves that can transmit data signals through the atmosphere.

MICR reader/sorter A device used to translate MICR symbols into electronic signals and to sort the collected data.

Milestones Key activities that can be monitored to determine the progress of a project.

Minicomputer A computer with the components of a mainframe but often having a lower cost, smaller physical size and primary storage capacity, and slower processing speeds.

Mneumonics Letter codes used in assembly language to communicate with the computer.

Modem A device used to convert signals from digital form to analog and from analog to digital.

Modular programming A programming technique that divides the problem solution into work packages, each of which is a self-contained module, or unit, of processing.

Modulation The process of converting a signal from digital to analog form.

Monitor The video display unit of a microcomputer.

Mouse A handheld device used to control the movement of a cursor or other symbol on a CRT screen.

Multiplexor A device that combines data signals from a number of terminals into one input flow that can be sent over a single channel.

Multiprocessing Simultaneous processing done by two or more computers that are linked to form a coordinated system.

Multiprogramming The processing that occurs when several programs are in primary storage at the same time and the CPU gives each of the programs its undivided attention for a short period of time.

Narrow bandwidth A band capable of transmitting data at speeds from 1,800 to 9,600 bps.

Natural languages Human languages, which require very complex translation programs if they are to be intelligible to a computer.

Network A system of computers and terminals connected by a communications link that provides rapid transfer of data.

96-column punched card A card that can hold 96 bytes of data and that is used for data entry and storage.

Nondestructive read The ability of the computer to read stored instructions and data over and over again without destroying them.

Nonimpact printer A printing device that forms characters by ink spray, heat on chemically treated paper, laser beams, or electrostatic processes similar to photocopying.

Nonprocedural language A programming language with built-in logic around which programs are designed.

Nonvolatile Descriptive of storage in which the retention of data does not depend on a constant source of power.

Object program A source program translated into machine code, ready for processing.

Odd parity A parity check that requires that the total of the 1 bits for each character be an odd number.

Office automation The use of computer systems and communications technology to perform office tasks.

Offline Not in direct communication with a computer.

Offline data collection methods Methods whereby data are recorded on a storage medium and are held for later entry into the computer for processing as a batch.

Online In direct communication with a computer via a plug, cable, telephone, or other communications line.

Operand The part of a program instruction that specifies the primary storage address of the item of data to be processed; also, the item of data to be processed that is held at that address.

Operating system A major component of systems software consisting of a supervisor program and a set of specialized programs that carry out various control functions.

Operational costs The ongoing costs of running a system.

Operational data Data derived from the current operations of a business.

Operational decisions Decisions having to do with controlling a business's day-to-day operations.

Operation code (op code) The part of a program instruction that specifies the type of processing to be performed.

Optical-character recognition (OCR) The ability of a device with an electronic scanner to convert images of numbers, letters, and other characters into electronic signals.

Optical disk (laser disk) An auxiliary storage medium on which data are recorded and read by laser beams.

Optical-mark recognition (OMR) The ability of a device with an electronic scanner to convert marks on a source document into electronic signals.

Organizational fit The congruence of a system with the overall scheme of an organization.

Organizing A managerial function that involves grouping activities and establishing procedures to implement them.

Output devices Devices that decode electronic signals from machine-readable form to a form that people can understand.

Output formats The ways that computer output is displayed, including the organization and style of columns, headings, spacing, and character placement.

Output interface circuit A circuit that coordinates the output signals with the indicated output device.

Page-at-a-time printer A printer that uses nonimpact technology to produce an entire page of output at one time.

Paging A technique used with virtual storage to divide a program into units of the same size that correspond to the sizes of units within primary storage.

Paper tape Tape punched with holes representing data; used for data entry and storage.

Paper-tape reader A device used to sense holes in paper tape and to convert them into electronic signals to be sent to the CPU.

Parallel systems conversion The implementation of a new system while the old system continues to run.

Parity bit An extra bit added to a byte to check the accuracy of data transmission.

Pascal A programming language designed for structured programming applications.

Password A unique code used to control access to a computer system.

Peer review team Individuals who participate in a structured walkthrough.

Performance-based RFP A request for a systems proposal that defines equipment specifications in terms of performance requirements.

Peripheral devices Hardware used for input, output, and storage.

Personal computer Any computer used for personal purposes; generally a microcomputer.

Personal privacy The concept that data and information will be used only for the purpose for which they were collected and only with the consent of the individual involved.

Pilot systems conversion The implementation and testing of a segment of a new system before the entire system is installed.

Pixels Picture elements that form the grid of a CRT screen.

Planning A managerial function that involves formulating goals and developing policies and programs to achieve them.

PL/1 Abbreviation for Programming

Language/1; a programming language that operates effectively as a batch or interactive language.

Plunge (cold-turkey) systems conversion The implementation of a new system with no backup system in operation.

Point-of-sale terminal A device that functions both as a cash register and as a means of collecting data at their source and transmitting them as electronic signals directly into the computer system.

Police intelligence system A computer information system that maintains and integrates police data derived from a number of sources.

Polling A technique used by multiplexors and concentrators to continually check terminals to see if there is a message to be sent.

Polling routine A data management routine for monitoring terminals on a continuous basis and for accepting signals when the terminal is active.

Ports Outlets in the back of a microcomputer where cables for peripheral equipment can be attached.

Postimplementation review An evaluation of a system's impact on the organization, the users, and the budget.

Predefined-process symbol A program flowchart symbol that represents operations and procedures that have been specified elsewhere.

Primary storage unit (internal storage, main memory) The section of a computer that temporarily stores program instructions, data, and the intermediate and final results of processing.

Privacy Act A federal act of 1974 that gives individuals the right to review and challenge the accuracy of records about themselves that are maintained by federal agencies.

Privacy Protection Study Commission A commission mandated by the Privacy Act of 1974 that issued a number of recommendations relating to the control of data banks.

Procedural language A programming language that allows the programmer to develop the logic and to code the procedures needed to solve the problem.

Processing symbol A program flowchart symbol that represents the required processing operations.

Processor unit The physical "box" that houses the CPU.

Production A functional area of business whose purpose is to manufacture and deliver a company's products.

Production rules The rules by which data are manipulated in an expert system.

Productivity The rate at which workers produce goods and services.

Program The step-by-step instructions the computer must have to perform any task.

Program-development approach The structured approach of analyzing the problem, designing a solution, coding the program, debugging and testing it, and documenting it.

Program dump A printout of the entire contents of a computer's memory at any point during program execution.

Program flowchart A graphic, detailed illustration of a program's logic.

Programmer A specialist who designs, writes, and tests computer programs.

Programming The process of converting systems specifications into step-by-step instructions that the computer can understand.

Programming language A system of communicating with a computer.

Program modules Self-contained units that can be coded and tested independently of the rest of the program.

Program statement A program instruction.

Project control Control over a project achieved by comparing actual performance with the plan for performance.

Projected data Data used in forecasting that are created by mathematically manipulating historical and current operational data.

Project monitoring system A system for measuring and reporting progress in various project tasks.

Project priority schedule A plan that details the various tasks to be accomplished and sequences them in building-block fashion.

PROM Abbreviation for programmable read-only memory; a memory chip contained in the CPU that allows the user to write a program on it. Once written, the program cannot be changed.

Protocols Procedures that synchronize the activities of network components.

Prototyping A technique used in conjunction with a DBMS that allows a programmer to develop a program in a matter of days.

Pseudocode A design tool that uses ordinary human language to describe the logic of a program.

Quantitative management A management style that relies heavily on simulations of real situations to provide input for the decision-making process.

Query (inquiry) languages Languages very like ordinary language that are used to access a data base and to produce inquiry reports.

Queuing routine A data management routine that establishes and manages a waiting line for incoming and outgoing computer signals.

RAM Abbreviation for random access memory; the type of memory used in the primary storage unit.

Range of the data A bracket into which input data should fall.

Read/write head The component of a drive unit that magnetizes or reads small spots representing data on the surface of the tape or disk.

Reasonableness of the data A term referring to data expectations derived from previous data.

Record A collection of data pertaining to a particular person, transaction, or event.

Reel A device for holding magnetic tape.

Registers Temporary storage places in the CPU used to hold instructions and data and to speed the transfer of those items and the performance of arithmetic/logic operations.

Remote terminal A terminal located at the source of the data that uses a telecommunications link to send and receive signals.

Requests for proposals (RFPs) Descriptions of systems specifications presented to vendors when hardware is to be acquired.

Reusable code Semi-independent modules of programming code that can be used as building blocks in systems development.

Ring network A network in which each computer is connected to two other computers.

Risk The potential for project failure.

Robotics The study of the construction, maintenance, and use of robots.

Robots Computer-controlled machines.

ROM Abbreviation for read-only memory; a chip used in the CPU that has a program etched into its circuitry. ROM can only be read, not written to.

Routine A sequence of program instructions.

RPG Abbreviation for Report Program Generator; a nonprocedural programming language used to prepare business reports.

Scanner A device that senses marks or characters and converts them to electronic signals.

Scheduled report A report generated at regular intervals.

Scheduling programs Systems software that assesses priorities and selects jobs for processing as computer resources become available.

Scientific management A management style that measures the work to be done, trains workers in precise activities, and in effect considers workers as an extension of a machine.

Search tree A problem-solving strategy in which search paths branch out from a root.

Sectors The pie-shaped divisions of a magnetic disk that provide addressable memory locations.

Segmentation A technique used with virtual storage to divide a program into parts related to the program logic.

Selection pattern A logic pattern in which the computer must choose between alternative paths.

Self-checking mechanism A mechanism that allows a computer to test its circuits each time operations begin.

Semiconductor An element that allows electricity to pass through it only when the voltage exceeds a certain level.

Semiconductor storage Storage that consists of tiny integrated circuits etched on silicon chips.

Sequential access Access to records characterized by the need to read the records one after the other until the desired data are found.

Sequential file organization A method of arranging records in a file in some kind of sequence.

Sequential processing The processing of records in sequence, one after another.

Serial transmission The transmission of data signals one after another.

Service functions (processing functions) Functions carried out by systems software that simplify the preparation of applications programs.

Silicon An element abundant in the earth's surface that can act as a semiconductor of electricity.

Simple-sequence pattern A logic pattern in which the computer executes a series of steps that follow one after another without opportunity for a decision or transfer.

Simplex A mode of data transmission in which signals can go in one direction only.

Smart terminal A terminal that has a limited amount of primary storage and that can perform some processing instructions.

Snapshot technique An audit technique used to get a picture of the data in the computer's memory at the time of processing.

Soft copy Output in temporary form.

Software Programs for operating and running the computer, as well as the instructions and procedures that people need to get the computer to solve specific processing problems.

Software package Mass-marketed software designed to meet a common need.

Source-data automation The recording of data in machine-readable form at the time and place the data are generated.

Source document A transaction record that provides a business with an internal source of data.

Source listing A printed reproduction of the program instructions that were entered into the computer.

Source program The program as written by the programmer.

Special-purpose computer (dedicated computer) A computer with built-in processing instructions that is designed to perform one task only.

Specialized audit software Software that replicates actual files, takes a sampling, and executes programs, allowing the auditor to get a picture of the operation of the system without having to audit actual programs or use actual files.

Spooling The transfer of data to or from a disk done in conjunction with buffers and accomplished by systems software.

Standardized programming language A programming language that will run on different computers without significant modification.

Star network A network in which a central host computer supports a number of computers that are connected to it but not to each other.

Storage medium A physical substance capable of storing data in encoded form.

Storage register A temporary storage place in the CPU for holding the data to be used in processing.

Stored program A program stored in the memory of a computer and coded the same way as the data.

Strategic decisions Decisions having to do with a firm's organizational goals and future.

Structure chart A chart used with top-down design that shows the de-

composition of a problem into more detailed program modules.
Structured programming and design A programming approach that limits the use of branching and emphasizes top-down design and modular programming.
Structured walkthrough A formal peer review of design and programming that helps remove defects and clear up logic problems in the early stages of program development.
Subprogram A set of instructions on a routine part of an applications program.
Summary report A report that condenses information.
Supercomputer A very large computer capable of processing hundreds of millions of instructions per second.
Supervisor (executive, monitor) The master program that has control over all the programs that comprise the systems software.
Synchronous transmission The transmission of blocks of characters, rather than a character at a time, by synchronizing the sending and receiving units.
Syntax The rules of language construction.
Syntax error A programming error due to incorrect construction of program statements.
System A group of interrelated elements working to accomplish a specific goal.
Systems analyst A specialist who designs a computer system and provides the communications link between user and programmer.
Systems development cycle The steps involved in developing a system: identifying the need, analyzing the system, developing design alternatives, developing the system, and implementing and maintaining the system.
Systems flowcharts Flowcharts that provide a broad graphic overview of the processing activities of a computer system.
Systems maintenance The modifications made to a system to accommodate changes in hardware, software, users' needs, and company policies.

Systems-monitoring programs Systems software for preventing unauthorized access to a computer system.
Systems programmer A person who installs and maintains systems software.
Systems-residence device An online storage device, usually a magnetic-disk drive, used to store the programs that comprise the systems software.
Systems software A set of programs that direct the operations of the computer hardware.

Tactical decisions Decisions about how to effectively allocate production resources in order to implement strategic plans.
Telecommunications link A telephone line connecting a remote terminal with the main computer system.
Telephone line A commonly used data communications channel.
Terminal symbol A program flowchart symbol that represents the beginning or end of a routine or of an entire program.
Test-data method An audit technique that uses input data designed to produce a particular set of results to verify the accuracy of processing.
Text editing The process of making revisions to a written document; a feature of word processing software.
Thrashing A problem that occurs with virtual storage when a segment or page of program instructions is swapped in and out of primary storage before the instructions have been processed.
Throughput The time that elapses between the placement of a processing request and the delivery of the output.
Timesharing system A system in which a number of terminals operated by unrelated users are connected to a central computer by a communications link.
Time slice A procedure that provides a segment of time for each terminal whether active or not.
Top-down design Structured program design that begins with a broad problem definition and breaks that definition down into successively smaller and more detailed program modules.
Touch-sensitive and light-sensitive devices Input devices that allow the user to enter data by touching a screen or tablet with a finger, light pen, or stylus.
Tracks The concentric circles of a magnetic disk and the channels of a magnetic tape on which data are recorded.
Traditional management (process management) A management style based on the belief that a person who understands the functional aspects of a business can learn to manage.
Transaction file A file containing relatively temporary data used to update a master file.
Transistor An abbreviation for transfer resistor: an electronic component that relies on silicon to control the flow of electricity.
Transmission density The number of signals transmitted over a channel at the same time.
Transmission management software Software that coordinates computing and communications devices, transmission channels, and speeds, and that assigns and maintains communications routes.
Turing test A test designed to determine whether a machine can think.

Unit record A complete record contained on one punched card.
Universal Product Code (UPC) A bar-code system used to represent product data.
User-group program sharing The sharing of software for routine applications by firms that have the same hardware and similar processing and information needs.
User-programmable terminal A terminal that has the processing capabilities of a microcomputer.
Users People who use computers to obtain information.
Utility programs Programs that perform routine tasks and that are part of the systems software.

Vacuum tubes Electronic components, capable of representing one item of data, that were used in the first generation of computers.
Variable word-length A term describing a computer that holds one character in each address in primary storage and that moves the data a character at a time.
Vendor-based RFP A request for a systems proposal directed to a single vendor.
Vendor support A computer manufacturer's ability to maintain equipment; to assist in installing a system; to modify hardware and software as the technology evolves; and to provide effective systems software.
Verification The process of repeating the keyboarding to identify errors in data entry.
Verifier A machine used to rekey data to check for errors in data entry.

Very large scale integration (VLSI) A circuit-manufacturing technology that allows hundreds of thousands of circuits to be placed on a single silicon chip.
Very narrow bandwidth A band capable of transmitting data at the relatively slow speed of 45 to 150 bps.
Video display terminal A device that can simultaneously code data and enter the data into the system. It has a keyboard for entering data and a screen for viewing both input and output.
Virtual storage A continuous swapping of data between primary storage and auxiliary storage, which creates the illusion that the capacity of primary storage is much larger than it actually is.
Volatile Descriptive of semiconductor storage in which the retention of data depends on a constant supply of power.

Wand reader An input device used to scan optical characters.
Waveguides Metal tubes that act as pathways for very-high-frequency radio waves.
Winchester disks Disk platters packaged together with read/write heads in a sealed container.
Word A number of bytes that can be given a uniquely numbered address and placed in one storage location.
Word processing A computer-based system for preparing, editing, storing, and printing text.
Word processing software Software designed to format and edit text.
Work packaging The breaking down of a project into small and manageable units to be assigned to technical staff.
Write-protect ring A protective device that must be manually installed on a magnetic-tape reel before the tape can be written on.

INDEX

Access arms, 230
Access speed, 220
Access to computers:
  methods for controlling, 262, 568
  unauthorized, see Computer crime; Security of computer systems
Accumulator, 129
Accuracy of computers, 7
Acoustic coupler, 256–57
Ada, 353–55
Ada, Countess of Lovelace, 37–39
Address, 126–28, 134–35, 228–30, 376, 465
Address register, 129
Aiken, Howard, 42–43
Algorithm, 310–11
American National Standards Institute (ANSI), 314
American Standard Code for Information Interchange (ASCII), 139
Analog computer, 8, 9
Analog transmission, 256
Analytical Engine, 37–39, 41
APL (A Programming Language), 356–57
Apple I, development of, 54
Applications programs:
  definition of, 26
  development of, see Program development
  for microcomputers, 288–94
Appointments calendar, computerized, 495
Archive reports, 192
Arithmetic/logic unit, 21, 124, 132
Artificial intelligence (AI), 54–55, 176, 406–13, 543–44
ASCII, 139
Assembler program, 48, 339, 377
Assembly language, 47, 337–38
Assembly listings, 339
Asynchronous transmission, 254
Atanasoff, John, 44
Audio input, 179, 285
Audio output, 22, 195, 209–10, 285
Auditing of computer systems, 82, 571–73
Automated teller machines, 25
Auxiliary storage, 22–26, 220–38
  direct access, 221, 228–38
  for microcomputers, 282

  selection criteria for, 238–39
  sequential access, 221, 223–28

Babbage, Charles, 35–39, 56, 133
Backup files, 224, 566
BACKUP utility program, 379
Bandwidths of transmission channels, 246–47
Banking:
  benefits of computers to, 528
  data entry systems used in, 170
  use of direct access storage devices in, 25
Bar codes, 174–75
Bardeen, John, 48
BASIC (Beginner's All-purpose Symbolic Instruction Code), 334–35
Batch controls, 157, 565
Batch processing, 17, 52
Baud, 247
Berry, Clifford, 44
Binary digit, 132
Binary numbering system, 27, 45, 137–38
Bit, 132
  parity, 140
Bits per second (bps), 247
Blind searching, 408
Blocks, record, 227
Bottom-up programming, 323
Branch pattern, 313, 315, 316
Brattain, Walter H., 48
Bubble memory, 237–38, 402
Buffers, 375
Bundled system, 512
Business(es):
  applications for artificial intelligence in, 413
  applications for computer output in, 188–94
  information needs of, 67–68, 448–52
  organizational changes in, caused by computers, 516–18
  service-oriented, benefits of computers to, 528
Business data, sources of, 68–69, 154
Byte, 132–36

Card reader, 18, 23, 165
Carriers, common and private, 246

Cassettes for magnetic tape, 167, 282
Cathode ray tube (CRT), 16, 156, 207–09
Central processing unit (CPU), 20–22, 124–49
  arithmetic/logic unit of, 21, 124, 132
  control unit of, 21–22, 124, 132
  primary storage unit of, 20–21, 124–28, 132, 134–36
    components used in, 141–43
    registers in, 128–29
    selection criteria for, 148
Chain printer, 200
Channels for data transmission, 246–47
Character-at-a-time printers, 196–99
Characters, definition of, 13
Chief programmer team, 399
Chips for computers:
  design and manufacture of, 144
  integrated circuit, 50
  memory, types of, 146–47
  microprocessor, 52–54, 278–82
Circuit board, 48
Circuit design, 144
C language, 355–56
Coaxial cables, 247, 249
COBOL (COmmon Business-Oriented Language), 49, 340, 345–47, 354
Coding forms, 335–36
Coding of data, 136–41. See also Program coding
Color spectography, 208
Colossus computer, 42
Common carriers, 246
Communications satellites, 247, 250
Communications systems. See Data communications systems
Compiler, 49, 339–40, 377
Complex network, 266–67
Compression of data, 259
Computer, definition of, 4
Computer-aided design (CAD), 102–04
  of computer chips, 144
  graphic plotters used in, 205–07
Computer-aided manufacturing (CAM), 102, 104–06
Computer-assisted instruction (CAI), 113–15, 117
Computer auditing, 571–73
Computer categories, 56–61

673

Computer crime, 544–49
Computer dependence, 542–44
Computer evolution, 34–55
Computer generations, 46–55
Computer graphics, 208, 290, 452–56
Computer hardware. *See* Hardware
Computer job, definition of, 370
Computer laws, 405, 557–59
Computer-managed instruction (CMI), 113
Computer operators, 28, 518, 520
Computer output:
 business need for, 188–89
 cost-effective use of, 461–62
 designing format for, 452–56
 distribution of, 457
 factors determining need for, 448–52
 hard-copy, 196–207
 for management science, 192–93
 by robots, 210–13
 scheduling of, 456–57
 selection criteria for devices for, 213–14
 soft-copy, 207–10
 traditional forms of, 190–92
 used as input in other processing activities, 193–95.
  See also Output devices; Output formats
Computer output microform (COM), 22, 202–05
Computer personnel. *See* Personnel
Computer security. *See* Security of computer systems
Computer software. *See* Software
Computer Software Copyright Act of 1980, 405
Concentrator, 259
Contention, technique of, for data communication, 259
Contract programming, 403–04, 510–12, 514
Control clerks, 28
Control structures, 312–13
Control unit, 21–22, 124, 132
Copyright for computer software, 405
Core plane, 142
Cost-benefit analyses:
 benefits of using, 395, 500
 of implementing a computer system, 421–22
Cost effectiveness of systems change, analysis of, 427–29

Cray supercomputers, 56–57, 133
Creativity, effect of computers on, 540
Credit Card Fraud Act of 1984, 547
Credit rating, effect of computer errors on, 72, 537
Crime, computer, 544–49
Crime control, use of computers for, 110–11
Critical path networks, use of, as scheduling tool, 437–39
CRT. *See* Cathode ray tube
Cylinder method for magnetic-disk storage, 231–32

Daisy wheel print mechanism, 196
DASD. *See* Direct access storage device
Data:
 coding of, 136–39
 compression of, 259
 controls to ensure accuracy of, 155–59
 definition of, 10
 sources for business-related, 68–69
Data banks, threat of, to personal privacy, 534–37
Data base, function of, 15, 479–83
Data base administrator (DBA), responsibilities of, 483
Data base management system (DBMS), 90–91, 474, 483–88
Data base software, 289–90
Data bus, 280
Data collection:
 consequences of errors in, 102
 degree of complexity involved in, 460–61
 offline methods of, 159–60, 163–70
 procedures for, 155–57
 source-data automation as method of, 160, 170–81
Data collection forms, 155–56, 436
Data collection personnel, 28, 155–56, 435–36
Data communications systems, 12
 development of, 244–46
 input/output control in, 374–76
 selection criteria for equipment in, 269–70
 specialized hardware for, 255–61
 specialized software for, 261–63
 transmission channels in, 246–53
 See also Data transmission
Data cycle, 10–12
Data density, 226–27

Data Encryption Standard, 262
Data entry, 16–17, 159–81
 error detection in, 157–59
Data entry personnel, 28, 155–56, 435–36
Data errors:
 causes of, 140, 154–55
 correction of
  on magnetic media, 169–70
  on punched cards, 164–66
 in data base, consequences of, 483
 impact of, on personal rights, 537
 made to manipulate computer system, 562
 procedures to eliminate, 140–41, 155–59, 374, 565, 570
  See also Error management
Data filtering, 69–70
Data integrity, 481
 systems controls for, 565
Data management programs, 375–76
Data processing:
 batch, 17
 design considerations for, 462–69
 direct, 14–15, 221, 228–229
 early methods of, 34–40
 early systems for, 42–48, 244
 interactive, 17
 manual, 10, 12
 multiprogram, 381–82
 sequential, 14, 221, 223–24
 simultaneous (multiprocessing), 383–85
 timesharing, 382–83
  See also Distributed data processing
Data security, access management software for, 262. *See also* Security of computer systems
Data transfer rate, 222
Data transmission:
 analog, 256
 channels for, 246–53
 digital, 256
 measuring speed of, 247
 range of frequencies for, 246–47
  See also Data communications systems
Debugging of programs, 307, 357–62
Decimal numbering system, 136, 137–38
Decision making:
 computerized information for, 68, 474
 effects of electronic mail on, 99

INDEX

management information systems as resource for, 90, 478–83
as a managerial function, 89, 474–77
Decision support system (DSS):
features of, 91, 474, 476, 489–90
integration of, with organizational standards, 513
management science as component of, 192–93
use of microcomputers for, 278
Decision table, 319–22
Dedicated computer, 7
Default option, 344, 372
Demodulation, 256
Depersonalization and computers, 100, 115, 117, 541–42
Design, computer-aided (CAD), 102–04
of computer chips, 144
graphic plotters used in, 205–07
Design considerations for information systems, 448–69
Design tools, 314–22
for structured programming, 322–28
Desk-checking, 359
Destructive write, 128
Diagnostic messages, 339
Difference Engine, 35, 37, 38
Digital computer, 8
Digital transmission, 256
Digitizing tablets, 181
Direct access auxiliary storage, 25–26, 221–22, 228–38
Direct access storage device (DASD), 14, 15, 25, 221, 465
Direct data entry, source-data automation as form of, 160, 170–81
Direct file organization, 14, 221, 465–66
Direct processing, 14–15, 221, 228–29
Disk drives, 18, 19, 22, 23, 167, 230–34
Disk pack, 230
Disks, magnetic, 18, 22, 26, 159, 166, 167, 169–70, 221, 228–34
floppy, 18, 166, 169, 234, 282
hard, 18, 166, 232, 282
Winchester, 234
See also Optical disks
Distributed data processing (DDP), 245
networks for, 263–69
Distributed network, 266–67

Distribution of computer output, 13, 452, 457
DITTO utility program, 379
Documentation of programs, 80, 82, 307, 362–63
Dot matrix printer, 197, 284
DO-UNTIL structure, 312
DO-WHILE structure, 312–13
Drum plotter, 205–06
Drum printer, 200
Dumb terminal, 176

EBCDIC, 139
Eckert, J. Presper, 44, 46
Editing check of data, 157–59, 565
EDRAW (erasable-direct-read-after-write) disks, 235
EDSAC (Electronic Delay Storage Automatic Computer), 46
Education and computer use, 113–15
Education Privacy Act of 1974, 557
EDVAC (Electronic Discrete Variable Automatic Computer), 46
Elections, use of computers in, 107–08
Electronic filing system, 84, 495
Electronic funds transfer, 528
Electronic mail. See Electronic message system
Electronic message system, 84, 492–95
effects of, 99
example of, 88
Electronic spreadsheet, 61, 91, 146–47, 291–92, 490
Electrostatic printer, 200
Electrothermal printer, 199
Employment, effects of computers on, 101–02, 104–06, 538–40
Encryption, 262, 565
Engineering design, computer-aided, 102–04
ENIAC (Electronic Numerical Integrator and Calculator), 44–45
Environmental control system for computer protection, 568
EPROM (erasable programmable read-only memory), 147
Error management, specialized software for, 263, 374
Errors. See Data errors; Logic errors; Program errors; Syntax errors
Ethics and computer use, 535, 554–56
Exception reports, 190, 457, 477
Execution time (E-time), 130
Exit poll, 108

Expert systems, 411–13
Extended Binary-Coded Decimal Interchange Code (EBCDIC), 139
External storage. See Auxiliary storage

Fair Credit Reporting Act of 1970, 557
Farm management, benefits of computer use in, 531
Feasibility study, 74, 431
Federal Communications Commission (FCC), 246
Federal Computer System Protection Act, 557
Fiber optics, 251
Fields, definition of, 13
File organization, methods of, 13–15, 25, 223–24, 463–69
Files:
backup, 224, 566
definition of, 13
master, 223–24
transaction, 223–24
Financial analysis, use of electronic spreadsheets for, 291–92
Firmware, 146–47, 402
Fixed record, 163
Fixed word-length storage, 134–35
Flatbed plotter, 206
Floppy disks, 18, 166, 169, 234, 282
Flowchart:
information-oriented, 77
program, 80, 314–19
symbols for, 314, 316
systems, 77, 314
Formatting of computer output, 448, 452–56
Formed-character printer, 196
Forms:
data collection, 155–56
preprinted, for computer output, 455–56
FORTRAN (FORmula TRANslator), 49, 348–49
Fourth-generation languages, 354
Freedom of Information Act of 1970, 557
Front-end processor, 260–61
Full-duplex transmission mode, 254
Function management, specialized software for, 262

Gantt chart, 437, 439
General-purpose computer, 7
General-purpose register, 129

Gigabyte, 235
"Gigascale" integration, 144
GIGO (garbage in, garbage out), 7
Goldstine, Herman, 45
Government uses of computers, 106–12, 532–33, 535, 536
Graphic output, 22, 208–09, 290
   design considerations for, 452–56
Graphic plotters, 194–95, 205–07
Grids for magnetic-core storage, 142

Half-duplex transmission mode, 254
Handicapped persons:
   input devices for, 161, 179, 181
   instructional benefits of computers to, 113
   output aids for, 180, 195, 210
Hard copy, 194–95, 196–207
Hard disks, 18, 166, 232, 282
Hardware:
   compatibility of, 270, 463
   criteria for evaluating, 506–09
   definition of, 4
   financing alternatives for, 509–10
   microcomputer, 278–86
   miniaturization of components for, 52
   selecting a vendor for, 503–05
   specialized, for data communications systems, 255–61
   types of, 17–26
   See also specific devices
Hashing, 465–66
Head crash, 232
Health, hazards of computer use to, 98–100
Health care, use of computers in, 115–17, 411–12
Heuristics, 409–10
Hexadecimal coding system, 137
High-level languages, 49, 338
   translation programs for, 340–41, 377
   types of, 342–57
HIPO (hierarchy plus input-processing-output) charts, 325–26
Historical data, business use of, 68
Hoff, Ted, 52, 54
Hollerith, Herman, 40, 41, 163
Hollerith card, 163
Hollerith code, 163–64, 224
Hopper, Grace, 47, 49, 360
Host computer, 245, 263
Human language, software for translation of, 407–08

IF-THEN-ELSE structure, 312
Impact printers, 196–97, 200
Indexed-sequential file organization, 466–68
Indexing systems, 128
Industrial robots, 104–06, 210–13
Information, 10
   communication of, 12
   computerized, uses and sources of, 68–71
Information needs:
   categories of, 458–60
   factors determining, 448–52
   of managers, 474–78
Information-oriented flowchart, 77
Information Revolution, impact of, 66–68
Information systems manager (ISM), 500–22
Inkjet printer, 199
Input control procedures, 157–59
Input data:
   accuracy and completeness of, 458
   complexity of, 460–61
   definition of, 4
   determining cost-effective use of, 461–62
   kinds of information used as, 458–60
   output used as, 193–95
Input devices, 16–18, 159–81, 282–83, 285
   selection criteria for, 182
Input/output control programs, 374–75
Input stage of data cycle, 10
Inquiry reports, 190, 195, 457
Instruction register, 129
Instruction time (I-time), 130
Integrated circuits, 50
   design and manufacture of, 144
Integrated software for microcomputers, 292–94
Intelligent (user-programmable) terminals, 176–78
Interactive language, 342
Interactive processing, 17, 52
Interblock gap (IBG), 227
Interface circuits, microcomputer, 280–82
Internal storage. See Primary storage unit
International Business Machines Corporation (IBM), development of, 40–42
Interpreter, 341

Interrecord gap (IRG), 227
Interrupt, 374
Iverson, Kenneth, 356

Jacquard, Joseph, 37
Japan, robotics technology in, 106, 213
Job, computer, definition of, 370
Job-control language (JCL), 370
Job-control program, 370
Job displacement, technology-related, 101, 538–40
Job-management program, 374
Job opportunities, computer-created, 101, 538
Job security, impact of computers on, 101–02, 106
Jobs, Steve, 54

Kapor, Mitch, 293
Kemeny, John, 6, 7, 342
Keyboards, microcomputer, 282–83
Key field, 14, 464
   conversion of, to storage address, 465–66
Keypunch machines, 18, 164
Key-to-disk device, 167
Key-to-tape device, 167
Kilobyte (K), 136
Knowledge representation, need for, in artificial intelligence, 55, 406, 410, 411
Kurtz, Thomas, 342

Language. See Programming languages
Language translators, 26–27, 339–41, 370, 377
Large-scale integration (LSI), 52
Laser disks. See Optical disks
Laser printer, 200, 202
Lasers, 234, 251–52
Law enforcement, use of computers for, 110–11
Legislation, computer-related, 405, 557–59
Librarians, 28
Library programs, 379–80
Light pen, 181, 285
Light-sensitive devices, 181, 208–09
Line-at-a-time printers, 200
Line management, 441–42
Line-of-sight transmission signal, 250
Link/edit routine, 379
Local area network (LAN), 267–69
Log, 377
Log evaluation, 571

INDEX

Logical records, 227
Logic errors, 340, 357–59
Logic patterns, 312–13
Loop pattern, 312
Lotus Development Corporation, 293

Machine cycle, 130
Machine language, 27, 47, 125, 126–27, 336–37, 339–41
Macrocode, 338
Magnetic bubble memory, 237–38, 402
Magnetic-core storage, 141, 142
Magnetic disk drives. *See* Disk drives
Magnetic disks. *See* Disks, magnetic
Magnetic drums, 141
Magnetic ink character recognition (MICR), 170–72
Magnetic tape, 18, 25, 159, 166–67, 169–70, 221, 225–28
Magnetic-tape drives, 18, 19, 22, 23, 167, 225–26
Main memory. *See* Primary storage unit
Mainframe computers, 52, 59
    interfacing of, with microcomputers, 294–96
Management:
    functions of, 89, 474–77
    of an information system, 500–21
    styles of, 449–51
    types of, for systems development projects, 441–42
Management information system (MIS), 89–90, 474
    computer-based, 478–83
    software tools for support of, 90–91, 483–90
Management science, computer output for, 192–93
Manager(s):
    functions and responsibilities of, 89, 474–77
    information needs of, 70–71, 474–78
    information systems, responsibilities of, 500–22
    project, responsibilities of, 442
    use of computers by, 89–91, 474–90
Manufacturing, computer-aided (CAM), 102, 104–06
Mark I, 43, 360
Mark-sense reader, 173
Mass storage unit, 236–37
Master file, 223

Matrix management, 441
Mauchly, John, 44, 46
Medical care. *See* Health care
Medical training, use of computers for, 117
Megabyte (M), 136
Memory chips, types of, 146–47
MICR, 170–72
Microcomputer(s):
    applications of, 60–61, 276–78
    BACKUP program for, 379
    commercially developed programs for, 401–03
    development of, 53, 54
    hardware for, 278–86
    interfacing of, with mainframe computers, 294–96
    output devices used with, 196, 197, 202
    as part of distributed data processing network, 245
    security problems with, 545, 563
    selection criteria for, 296–300
    software for, 286–94
    stand-alone, 169
Microfiche, 202–03, 204
Microfilm, 22, 202
Microprocessor chips, 52–54, 278–82
Microwaves, 247, 250
Military use of computers, 112, 412–13
Minicomputers, 51–52, 59–60
Mneumonic codes, 47
Modems, 256–57, 285
Modular programming, 326–28
Modulation, 256
Monitor, microcomputer, 283–84
Mouse, microcomputer, 285
Multiplexor, 257–59
Multiprocessing, 383–85
Multiprogramming, 381–82

Napier, John, 36
National Crime Information Center (NCIC), 110
National Institute for Occupational Safety and Health, 98
Natural language, software for translation of, 407–08
Networks, data communications, 245–46, 263–69
Nondestructive read, 128
Nonimpact printers, 199, 200–02
Nonprocedural language, 350, 354
Nonvolatile storage, 142, 237–38

Object program, 339, 377, 379
OCR, 173–76
Octal coding system, 137
Office automation, 84–91, 490–95
    problems of, 97–102
Offline data collection, 17–18, 159–60, 163–70
Offline operations, definition of, 16
OMR, 173
Online operations, definition of, 16
Operand, 125, 126
Operating system, 26, 287, 368, 370, 372–77
Operational data, business use of, 69
Operation code (op code), 125, 126
Optical-character recognition (OCR), 173–76
Optical disks, 22, 234–36
Optical-mark recognition (OMR), 173
Optical-recognition devices, 172–76
Oughtred, William, 36
Output. *See* Computer output
Output devices, 22, 196–213, 282–86
    selection criteria for, 213–14
Output formats, 448, 452–56
Output stage of data cycle, 12

Page-at-a-time printers, 200–02
Paging, use of, in virtual storage, 385
Paper tape. *See* Punched paper tape
Paper tape reader, 225
Parallel processing, 133, 180
Parity bit, 140
Parity checking, 140–41, 157, 565
Pascal, 350–53
Pascal, Blaise, 36
Passwords, 377, 565–66
Pattern recognition in development of artificial intelligence, 410
Peer review team, 398
Peripheral devices, 20
    for microcomputers, 282, 284–85
Personal computers. *See* Microcomputers
Personnel:
    computer, roles of, 28
    consideration of, in project planning, 433–36
    effects of automation on, 98–101
    screening of, for computer access, 569
    technical, management issues concerned with, 518–21
Photomask, 144
Pixels, 208

Plasma screen technology, 283–84
PL/1 (Programming Language 1), 357
Plotters, graphic, 194–95, 205–07
Point-of-sale terminals, 178
Police intelligence system, 111
Politics, use of computers in, 107–08
Polling routines, 259, 375–76
Power companies, benefits of computers to, 528–30
Power failure, as threat to computer security, 564
Power surges, as source of data communications errors, 263
Preprinted forms, use of, for computer output, 455–56
Primary storage unit, 20–21
   addresses in, 126–28
   areas of, 125–28
   capacity of, 132–36, 148
   compared with auxiliary storage, 220–21
   components for, 141–47
Printed output, design considerations for, 452–56
Printers, 22, 196–202
   for microcomputers, 284
Privacy:
   federal laws concerned with, 557–59
   impact of computers on, 102, 107, 111–12, 534–37
Privacy Act of 1974, 557
Privacy Protection Study Commission, 557–58
Private carriers, 246
Procedural languages, 350
Processing. *See* Data processing
Processor. *See* Central processing unit; Front-end processor
Productivity and office automation, 84–85, 96–97, 490–95
Program, definition of, 4
Program algorithms, 310–11
Program coding, 307, 334–36
Program debugging, 307, 357–60
Program development, 306–12, 334–36, 357–63
   design tools for, 314–22
   high-level languages used in, 341–57
   logic patterns used in, 312–13
   structured design tools for, 322–26
Program documentation, 307, 362–63
Program dump, 361–62
Program errors, 339–40, 357–60
Program flowchart, 80, 314–19

Program instructions, 125
Program interrupt, 374
Programmer(s), 26
   chief, 399
   managerial issues involving, 518–21
   potential for manipulation of computer system by, 562
   systems, 369
Programming, 307
   contract, 403–04
   modular, 326–28
   reusable code used in, 396–97
   structured, 313, 322
   techniques for improving productivity of, 396–99
   See also Program development
Programming languages, 334–38
   assembly, 47, 337–38
   fourth-generation, 354
   high-level, 49, 341–57
   interactive, 342
   job-control, 370
   machine, 27, 47, 125, 126–27, 336–37, 339–41
   nonprocedural, 350
   procedural, 350
   query, 485–86
   standardized, 50
   translation programs for, 26–27, 339–41, 370, 377
Programming teams, 307, 398–99
Program modules, 314
Program sharing, user-group, 404
Program statement, 334
Program testing, 307, 357–62
Projections, business, use of computerized data for, 69
Project management, types of, 441–42
Project managers, responsibilities of, 442
Project monitoring system, 436–40
Project scheduling, 432, 436–40
PROM (programmable read-only memory), 147
Protocols in transmission management software, 262
Prototyping, 79, 486
Pseudocode, 80, 322–23
Punched cards, 18, 163–66, 224–25
Punched paper tape, 224–25

Questionnaires, use of, in systems analysis, 76–77
Queuing routine, 376

Random access memory (RAM), 146, 278–79
Randomizing, 465–66
Read-only memory (ROM), 146–47, 278–79
Read/write heads, 226, 230–34
Record blocks, 227
Record key, 14, 221, 224, 228, 229, 464
   conversion of, to storage address, 465–66
Records:
   definition of, 13
   methods of organizing, 14–15, 221, 223–24, 228, 464–69, 479–83
Reels for magnetic tape, 167
Registers, 128–29
Remote terminals, 176
Reports, business:
   scheduling of, 456–57
   types of, 190–92
Requests for proposals (RFPs), 503–05
Reusable code, 396–97
Ring network, 266
Risk assessment in systems development, 429
Robots, 104–06, 210–13
   pattern recognition in, 410
RPG (Report Program Generator), 350

Sabotage, derivation of, 41
Sabotage, as threat to computer security, 564
Scanners, 16, 160, 172
Schedules, project priority, 432
Scheduling of computer output, 456–57
Scheduling programs, 372–74
Schreyer, Helmut, 42
Search tree, 408–09
Secondary storage. *See* Auxiliary storage
Sectors on magnetic disks, 228–29
Security of computer systems:
   controls used for, 564–70
   with data bases, 487–88
   problem of, with interfacing, 295
   systems monitoring programs for, 376–77
   threats to, 560–64
   See also Computer crime
Security of data communications systems, 262
Segmentation, use of, in virtual storage, 385

Selection pattern, 312
Semiconductor, 48
Semiconductor storage, 141, 142–43
Sequential access auxiliary storage, 25–26, 221, 223–28
Sequential file organization, 14, 221, 464–65
Sequential processing, 14, 221, 223–24
Serial printers, 196
Serial transmission, 254
Shockley, William, 48
Signal transmission, types of, 253–55
Silicon, 48, 50, 143, 144
Simple-sequence pattern, 312
Simplex transmission mode, 253
Simulation:
   engineering, use of, for testing designs, 103–04
   medical, use of, for physician training, 117
Social services, use of computers in, 107
Soft copy, 194, 195, 207–10
Software, 4, 26–27
   consideration of, in processing design, 463
   contract programming as source of, 403–04
   custom-designed versus commercially developed, 510–14
   directories for assessment of, 514–16
   duplication of, as form of computer crime, 405, 546
   in-house development of, 392–99
     alternatives to, 400–04
   laws pertaining to, 405, 556, 558–59
   microcomputer, 286–94
   purchased or leased, 400–03
   specialized
     for auditing, 572–73
     for data communications, 261–63
   user-group sharing of, 404
   See also Systems software
Software piracy, 405, 546
Source-data automation, 160, 170–81
Source documents, 154
Source listings, 339
Source program, 339, 377
Special-purpose computer, 7–8
Spectography, color, 208
Speed of computers, 4–6
Spooling, 375
Spreadsheets. *See* Electronic spreadsheet

Star network, 265
Storage media, 17–18. *See also* Disks, magnetic; Magnetic tape; Optical disks; Punched cards; Punched paper tape
Storage register, 129
Storage. *See* Auxiliary storage; Primary storage unit; Virtual storage
Stored-program concept, 45, 46, 124
Structure chart, 323
Structured programming, 313, 322, 326–28
Structured walkthrough, 398
Subprograms, 378
Summary reports, 192
Supercomputers, 56–58
Supervisor program, 370
Synchronous transmission, 254–55
Syntax errors, 339–40, 358–59
Syntax of programming language, 323
Systems analysis, process for, 74–78
Systems analysts, 28
   managerial issues involving, 518–21
Systems change, reasons for introducing, 420–22
Systems controls, 564–66
Systems conversion, methods of, 439–40
Systems development, 71–82, 423–40
   communication between management and technical staff in, 434
   constraints on, 424
   dealing with personnel resistance to, 433–36
   evaluating proposals for, 424–430
   involvement of information users in, 74, 434
   management methods for, 441–42
   organizational considerations in, 448–52
   organizational politics and, 425, 426
   planning for, 431–40
Systems flowchart, 77, 308, 314
Systems maintenance, 82, 307, 362
Systems-monitoring programs, 376–77
Systems programmer, 369
Systems-residence device, 370
Systems software, 26, 286–87, 368–88
   control functions of, 372–77
   service functions of, 377–80

Tape. *See* Magnetic tape; Punched paper tape
Tape drives. *See* Magnetic-tape drives

Telecommunications, 176, 244, 256, 402
Telecommuting, 258, 404
Telegraph lines, transmission rate of, 247
Telephone lines:
   data communication using, 244, 247–49
   signal distortion and transmission errors in, 263
Telephone service, benefits of computers to, 528
Terabyte, 235
Terminals:
   dumb, 176
   point-of-sale, 178
   remote, 176
   smart, 176
   user-programmable (intelligent), 176–78
   video display, 16, 22, 156, 207–09, 283–84
Text editing, use of video display terminals for, 208
Thrashing, 385–86
Throughput time, 382
Timesharing systems, 244, 382–83
Time slice, 258
Top-down design, 323–24
Touch-sensitive devices, 181, 208–09, 285
Tracks:
   disk, 228
   tape, 226
Transaction file, 223–24
Transistors, development of, 48
Translation programs, 26–27, 339–41, 370, 377
Transmission channels, 246–53
Transmission density, 247
Transmission management, specialized software for, 262
Turing, Alan, 406
Turing test, 406
Turnkey system, 512
Typewriter, voice-activated, 180

Ultra large scale integration (ULSI), 144
Unemployment, computer-related, 106, 538–39
Unit record, 163
UNIVAC (Universal Automatic Computer), 46–47

Universal Product Code (UPC), 174–75
Unix operating system, 369, 384
User-group program sharing, 404
User-programmable terminal, 176–78
Utility programs, 287, 378–79

Vacuum tubes, 47
Variable word-length storage, 135
Verification procedure, 157
Verifier, 165
Very large scale integration (VLSI), 52, 143, 144
Video display terminal (VDT), 16–17, 22, 156, 207–09, 283–84

Videotext services, 268
Virtual storage, 385–87
Visual table of contents (VTOC), 325
Voice-recognition devices. *See* Audio input
Volatile storage, 142–43
von Leibniz, Gottfreid Wilhelm, 36
von Neumann, John, 45, 46, 133

Walkthrough, structured, 398
Wand reader, 16, 174
Watson, Thomas J., Sr., 43
Waveguides, data communication using, 252–53
Weizenbaum, Joseph, 27, 41

Winchester disks, 234
Wirth, Niklaus, 350
Word processing, 84–85, 491, 492
   software for, 288–89
   criteria for selection of, 297
   uses of, 107–08, 208, 276
   voice-activated, development of, 180
Work packaging, 436–37
Workplace environment, computer-generated changes in, 540–42
Wozniak, Steve, 54
Write-protect ring, 566

Zuse, Konrad, 42